Economic Perspective

P.239

EYC

Economic Perspective

David M. Streifford
Department of Business Administration
St. Louis Community College—Forest Park

IRWIN

Homewood, IL 60430
Boston, MA 02116

Executive editor: John R. Black
Developmental editor: Melanie Murphy
Project editor: Gladys True
Production manager: Carma W. Fazio
Designer: Jeanne Wolfgeher
Cover Art: Forcade and Associates
Compositor: Weimer Typesetting Company, Inc.
Typeface: 10/12 Times Roman
Printer: R. R. Donnelley & Sons Company

Library of Congress Cataloging-in-Publication Data

Streifford, David M.
    Economic perspective.

    1. Economics.   I. Title.
    HB1715.S923   1990   330   89–19834
    ISBN 0-256-07950-1

Printed in the United States of America
1 2 3 4 5 6 7 8 9 0   D O   7 6 5 4 3 2 1 0

■ *This book is dedicated to my wife, Gayle, and my daughters, Debbie and Kim. I am deeply grateful for their support and understanding during this seemingly endless project.*

Preface

This book is for you. It is designed to interest you in economics, to provide fundamental economic concepts and principles, and to equip you with the skills and knowledge to analyze current economic problems and issues.

At least three types of students will take this one semester introductory economics course: liberal arts majors who have selected economics as a social science elective (or requirement), students in career or vocational programs such as data processing/computer science or journalism, and students preparing for further coursework in economics. Regardless of your reason for enrollment, however, the course should be one of the most important fields of study you undertake.

A Few Suggestions

As you read this book, pay close attention to graphs. (Most economics teachers like to use graphs to illustrate relationships.) The first chapter has a section devoted to graphical analysis (Your Economics Survival Kit) in order to help you review how to read, understand, and construct graphs.

Because much of the material in the course will be new, it is also important to be aggressive: Ask questions to the text (and your instructor), take notes, and never, ever let a question go unanswered into the exam. Murphy's Law always operates here: If you are not sure about some idea, it will be on the test!

The Economic Perspective is organized to make your first venture into economics as interesting as possible. To that end, and to enable you to learn economic principles and apply them to economic issues, the book is organized to maximize your participation in your learning. Each chapter opens with a Chapter Preview, a light overview of the chapter's contents; Chapter Objectives, a list of the things you should know after reading the chapter; and a FOCUS, a brief but poignant vignette that discusses some of the chapter's key ideas in relationship to important issues and events. THINKING IT THROUGH questions appear throughout each chapter in order to review material and to motivate you to think about what you have read. These THINKING IT THROUGH sections are useful devices to check your understanding of the material.

Each chapter also has two CASES-IN-POINT. These are integrated into the text and contain several Questions to Consider. They are designed as applications of economic theory and concepts to specific issues and economic policies. At the end of each chapter, there is a list of IMPORTANT TERMS TO REMEMBER (with page references), a CHAPTER SUMMARY, DISCUSSION AND REVIEW QUESTIONS, and A BRIEF LOOK AHEAD (describing what the next chapter contains).

Although exactly twenty-five years ago, I remember very well my first course in economics. Like most colleges courses, I got plenty of warnings from friends—what a tough course economics is, that it's nothing but graphs and math, and how dreadfully boring it is. Of course, from other classes I also knew that boredom often meant lack of interest and/or understanding. Knowing I had to take the course, I decided to give it my best shot. If I went into the course predisposed to dislike it, I knew it would be tough and slow-going. So, I made a little pact with myself to keep an open mind. What proved most important, however, was to get involved: Do the reading assignments, answer the end-of-chapter questions and problems, and participate in class discussions. Commitment to learning economics enabled me to successfully conquer the so-called *boredom factor*. After the first month in the course, I began to enjoy the readings, class lectures, and discussions.

A WORD TO TEACHERS

This book is designed for a one-term survey of economics. It is a balanced treatment of microeconomics and macroeconomics, blending analytical, descriptive, and policy economics. Not an issues book, economic problems and issues nonetheless are woven throughout the text in order to illustrate and apply economic principles and concepts. The challenge was to write a book that was comprehensive in scope without being too long to cover in one term.

Organization

The book is organized into three parts. Part I is an introduction to the fundamentals of markets, scarcity, choice, opportunity cost, production possibilities, comparative advantage, alternative economic systems, and supply and demand. Part II covers microeconomics and Part III covers macroeconomics. International economics (trade, finance, and the balance of payments) is covered in the last chapter (19), although international topics are integrated into each chapter.

Treating microeconomics first was a difficult decision, especially because many teachers prefer a macro-first organization. For purposes of conceptual unity and transition from the introductory material, however, microeconomics seems to be a more natural beginning. Presenting macroeconomics first with *Economic Perspective* is quite easy, however, and there will be no loss of continuity. The organization would be: Chapters 1–3, 11–19, and 4–10. And, if there appears to be too much material to cover, several chapters may be deleted without disrupting the intellectual order. I sometimes omit Chapter 8 (Industrial Organization and Antitrust), or assign pages within the chapter, Chapter 10 (Public Choice and Benefit-Cost Analysis), and Chapter 18 (Economic Stabilization: Prospects and Problems).

Important Features

Three principles guided me as I wrote: Keep the reader in mind, use a lively conversational style, and wherever possible, introduce new economic concepts and principles by first describing an issue or policy problem in nontechnical language. Special features of *Economic Perspective* include:

- a conversational or informal style that is appealing to the student
- balanced micro and macro sections
- international topics integrated throughout the book
- a complete chapter devoted to economic stabilization issues (covering differences among Keynesian, Monetarist, Supply-Side, Rational Expectations, and New Classical economists, as well as the important policy implications)
- a complete chapter on public choice and benefit-cost analysis
- the basic supply and demand model or derivatives are featured in 12 chapters
- the Aggregate Supply–Aggregate Demand model, relating the price level to real GNP is fully developed
- a simple two-person game theory is used to illustrate the behavioral assumptions of self-interest and rationality
- a complete discussion of the job search model is presented
- examples are used which relate to a diverse population of students
- frequent use of THINKING IT THROUGH questions imbedded in the text to check the reader's understanding
- large, easy-to-read graphs with scales done on graph paper (very few abstract graphs)
- the most current data available for all tables, charts, and graphs

- use of small businesses and service sector businesses to illustrate economic decision making, such as hair salons, ice cream parlors, and small food stores (instead of focusing exclusively on Fortune 500 manufacturers)
- CASES-IN-POINT (two per chapter) that highlight the application of economic principles to a current issue or policy problem
- a FOCUS that opens each chapter, in a nontechnical way relating an issue to the subject of the chapter
- a list of important terms at the end of each chapter, with page references
- an end-of-chapter summary
- discussion and review questions at the end of each chapter
- A Brief Look Ahead closes each chapter, tying the current chapter to the next one
- concepts presented are cited and discussed in subsequent chapters wherever appropriate for learning reinforcement and maintaining conceptual unity
- definitions of all terms are provided in three places—in the text itself, in the margin, and in a glossary (with page references)
- step-wise explanations and solutions are presented for topics such as the graphical approach to profit maximization and the expenditures multiplier

Ancillary Materials

Several useful supplementary materials accompany *Economic Perspective*.

A *Study Guide and Workbook* provides the lists of important terms, chapter outlines, and summaries, true–false, multiple choice, and essay questions, Hands-on exercises (generally graphical in nature), study hints, and answers to all of the questions.

An *Instructor's Manual* contains five primary sections: how *Economic Perspective* differs from other introductory books (for instructors changing books), a chapter outline, suggested answers to all of the THINKING IT THROUGH, CASE-IN-POINT, and DISCUSSION AND REVIEW questions, teaching hints, and suggested resources.

Two test banks are available: a printed version and one on disk (IBM-compatible). The *Test Bank* offers 2,000 items. Each chapter contains 60 multiple choice questions (each with five choices), 10 true-false, 10 fill-in-the-blank, 20 essay, and several problems (hands-on exercises). Answers are provided for the multiple choice, true-false, fill-in-the-blank, and problems.

An *Economics Tutorial* is available to all adopters as well. This ancillary is a set of interactive computer tutorials covering the more difficult concepts of the course, such as supply and demand, elasticity, cost theory, the multiplier, fiscal policy, and the multiple creation of deposits and monetary policy. These have been used in various versions over several years and have proven to be an entertaining way to reinforce important concepts.

ACKNOWLEDGMENTS

For the many people who contributed to this project, I owe a debt of gratitude. First, a hearty thanks is given to the individuals who reviewed the first and second drafts. They are:

James Q. Aylsworth	Lakeland Community College
Edwin M. Cobb	Elgin Community College
George M. Eastham	California State Polytechnic University
Gail A. Hawks	Miami-Dade Community College
Jerry J. Knarr	Hillsborough Community College
Daniel R. Knighton	Moorhead State University
Catherine M. Null	University of Kentucky
Robert Payne	Portland Community College
Barbara Reagan	Southern Methodist University
Joseph A. Renzy	St. Louis Community College, Florissant Valley
Terry L. Riddle	Central Virginia Community College
Ted Scheinman	Mount Hood Community College
H. R. Swaine	Northern Michigan University
Roger C. VanTassel	Clark University
Howard M. Wilhelm	James Madison University

The staff at Irwin also deserve a special thanks for their commitment, creativity, innovation, and professional work throughout this project. The project team included John Black, Publisher, Melanie Murphy, Developmental Editor, Randy Haubner, Marketing Manager, and Gladys True, Project Editor.

A special word of thanks goes to Russell Boersma. Although not with Irwin, Russ provided many hours of encouragement and advice. Thank you.

David M. Streifford

Brief Contents

Contents

PART II   Microeconomics   89

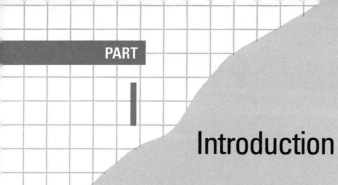

Introduction

1

Economics and You

Andrew Sacks, TSW-Click/Chicago

There are three main elements in this first chapter: to define and explain economics, to present an overview of economic problems and issues, and to provide "Your Economics Survival Kit." Because this is probably your first venture into a regular course in economics, it is important that you develop a feel for what you will learn in this course. Moreover, economics is more interesting and definitely more fun if you learn to work effectively with graphs.

After completion of this chapter, you should be able to do the following:

1. Define economics and explain the scarcity-choice dilemma.
2. Define, describe, and give an example of an economic problem.
3. Distinguish between and provide examples of normative and positive economics.
4. Define and explain the relationships among the goals of economic freedom, economic equity, and economic efficiency.
5. Explain what is meant by the term *deindustrialization*.
6. Draw a graph illustrating a relationship between two variables; label the graph; describe the relationship.
7. Identify direct and inverse relationships on graphs.

Burden of College Is Pushing More into Debt

"Middle- and lower-income families are going deeper into debt to send their children to college, a congressional report says. This data makes it clear that paying for a college education has become a much heavier burden for most families than it was a decade ago, [the authors] said in a joint statement.

"The report says that in the past 10 years, college costs have risen about 10 percent at public colleges and more than 25 percent at private institutions, while family income has remained stagnant. The report says that America's college students depend increasingly on borrowing to finance their education,·. . . [and] it raises the possibility that college debts can affect students' career choices and postpone home-buying, marriage, and even the decision to have children. And it points out that as borrowing increases, students have less certainty about their ultimate ability to repay.

"Undergraduates, in particular, face uncertainty about what kinds of jobs they will get and how much they will earn and what levels of inflation and salary increases they will have upon graduation.

"[B]orrowing by students has tripled over the past decade and now amounts to $10 billion. . . . At least one-third, and perhaps as many as half, of all students now leave school in debt. At the same time, federal aid has been dramatically cut back. . . .

"Middle- and upper-income American families have lost much, and in many cases, all of their eligibility to get federally subsidized student loans, and families in the lower and lower-middle income categories are receiving far less in grant and scholarship assistance than they did 10 years ago, making it necessary for them to borrow far more heavily."

"[The authors] estimated that 14 million students were attending college. Of that number, they said, about one-third participate in federal, state, or institutional loan programs. The study shows that borrowing under such programs was $9.8 billion in [the spring term of 1986] compared with $3.5 billion for the 1975–76 school year." (All figures are adjusted for inflation, expressed in 1986 dollars.)[1]

---

[1] Excerpted from "Burden of College Is Pushing More into Debt, Study Finds," *St. Louis Post-Dispatch,* December 29, 1986.

Inflation is defined as a rise in the general level of prices. For example, if the rate of inflation for a given year is 5 percent, then the price level is 105 percent of the prior year's level of prices. Thus, if the government budgets the same dollars for all forms of student aid in 1990 as in 1989 and the price level is 5 percent higher, then 1990 spending

The high and rising cost of a college education is an economic problem for a growing number of students. Many families simply do not have the resources to pay the rising college tuitions, and the problem is compounded by diminishing federal support. Although U.S. society claims to place a high premium on education, more and more families have been priced out of the market. Moreover, governments find that tax receipts are insufficient to support the level of services people want (and not just in education). Something has to give. The upshot is that millions of young people are forced to take out loans to go to college, and millions more are forced to forgo college until they build a nest egg.

ECONOMICS: THE SCARCITY–CHOICE DILEMMA

Economics *studies how society allocates scarce resources to satisfy competing and unlimited wants.*

Scarcity *means an insufficient amount of resources to satisfy our unlimited wants.*

Economics studies how society allocates scarce resources to satisfy competing and unlimited wants. As a social science, its focus is human behavior. But unlike sociology, psychology, and other social sciences, a central idea of economics is **scarcity;** that is, there is an insufficient amount of resources to satisfy our seemingly unlimited wants. Indeed, one definition of economics is the study of how society tries to overcome scarcity, or, more specifically, how families, businesses, and governments allocate scarce resources among competing and unlimited wants.

As our FOCUS illustrates, the high and rising cost of college qualifies as an economic problem because families and governments simply do not have enough resources to satisfy the wants of millions of college-bound students. Because resources are scarce, relative to our wants, we have an economic problem.

If you think that economic problems involve money, you're right. It was F. Scott Fitzgerald who said, "The rich are different from us." To this, Ernest Hemingway responded, "Yes, they have more money."[2] However, it is more than money (or the lack of money) that defines an economic problem. The following CASE-IN-POINT demonstrates how political rhetoric raised expectations about the elimination of poverty and greatly exacerbated an already serious economic problem.

---

will buy 5 percent less. This is what is meant by *real* dollars; the figures have been adjusted for inflation by dividing the actual dollars spent by the price level, 105, in our example. Thus, when you see a statement such as "expressed in 1986 dollars," it means that the actual dollars spent have been deflated for the amount of inflation. We will devote much more attention to this important idea in Chapters 11 and 12.

[2] Quoted in a footnote in *The Crack-Up,* edited by Edmund Wilson (1945).

What Is an Economic Problem?

Fifteen years ago, Neil Jacoby wrote an article for *Center Magazine.*[3] Entitled "What Is a Social Problem?" the article dealt with the root cause of the Detroit and Los Angeles race riots in the late 1960s. Jacoby argued that President Johnson's Great Society programs raised expectations among the nation's dispossessed—blacks, Hispanics, and other minority groups—who, for a variety of complex reasons, did not participate fully in U.S. riches. When it became apparent that the Food Stamp Program, the Manpower Development and Training Program, and other types of federal assistance did not live up to the expectations created, a huge expectations-reality gap was created. Major promises had been made by President Johnson, like conducting the War on Poverty. When it became clear that poverty was the victor, people rose in revolt. The promises had raised expectations far beyond the ability of the administration to deliver. As the expectations-reality gap increased, people expressed their discontent in the form of protests, social revolt, and finally riots. For example, the Watts section of Los Angeles still bears testimony of the firebombing, destruction, and looting that occurred in 1965.

Economic problems are much like social problems. People have wants to be satisfied. If the economy's resources are insufficient to satisfy these wants, then we have an economic problem. Unknowingly, President Johnson aggravated an already serious economic problem by stimulating the wants of selected groups of Americans. By promising to end poverty, Johnson placed himself in an impossible situation. How could he keep his promises to end poverty at home while he was committed to fighting a war in Vietnam? There just weren't enough resources to accomplish both.

Questions to Consider

1. *Explain what is meant by the* expectations-reality gap.
2. *The idea that unfulfilled expectations create social and economic problems implies that politicians and others should be careful not to create artificially high expectations. If promises are so difficult to keep, why do politicians make so many promises? Would politicians be better off if they tried a reverse psychology, that is, promise less than they know they can deliver?*
3. *Can you think of other examples of the expectations-reality gap, perhaps in your school, family, or place of business?*

[3] *Center Magazine* is a publication of the Grantsmanship Center. Neil Jacoby was professor of business administation at the University of California at Los Angeles during a time of social ferment: protests, marches, moratoriums, and riots.

President Johnson and the Congress faced a serious problem of resource allocation in the mid-1960s. How could they finance the Vietnam War and reduce or end poverty at home without running headlong into budget problems? If they had decided that the number one priority was the eradication of poverty, perhaps they could have allocated sufficient resources to do so. However, Johnson was unwilling to raise taxes or to cut other programs to help finance either the war or the new domestic programs. To coin a phrase, Johnson wanted "guns and butter."[4]

The economic problems facing the Johnson administration were not unique. Hard choices had to be made. Moreover, choosing what to do and how much to spend are difficult decisions because no nation has an unlimited pool of resources at its disposal. For example, if the United States requires an educated labor force, we must decide whether federal and state governments should support higher education through loans, grants, and scholarships. If you think that government should be involved, then ask yourself how much? Should all deserving students be supported? How would you define *deserving?* More difficult still, what other areas deserve government support: aid to troubled industries, medical research, fixing the nation's broken-down bridges, building dams, preserving wilderness areas, or providing for the nation's defense? Whether you answered Yes or No to any of these questions, you can probably think of another area not mentioned which is deserving of support. There is a lot of work to be done.

The point is that our *wants are unlimited.* If our resources were also unlimited, we would not have an economic problem. Unfortunately, scarcity prevails. We do not have enough resources to satisfy our insatiable appetites. Hence, we are confronted constantly with the need to make choices.

If we want more than there is available, we need to choose what to do. And choice involves making decisions among alternatives based upon certain criteria. For example, the Congress and the president must decide what is more important: fixing roads and bridges or helping one million students get through college; building Star Wars, or finding a cure for Acquired Immune Deficiency Syndrome (AIDS); cleaning up toxic waste, or providing assistance to U.S. exporters. It would be wonderful if we could do it all, but scarcity persists as a cruel economic fact of life.

As you have just seen, because there is so much we want to accomplish with our limited resources, we are forced to make tough choices. The decision-making process, however, whether it be in government,

---

[4] Politicians, civic leaders, and others often refer to the combination of military and all nonmilitary governmental expenditures as guns and butter. Curious as it may seem, the label does capture the preferences and priorities of federal budgets, especially if there is a marked shift from one category to another or if more of each is pursued.

business, or in the household, involves more than gathering information to make informed choices. When local government holds a public forum to discuss rezoning a section of the community from residential to commercial use, people will express widely different opinions about what to do. Our values also play a central role in making decisions. Even if we agree on the facts, it is far more difficult to develop agreement when individual values differ.

Normative versus Positive Economic Statements

Positive economics *refers to statements of fact, relationships among facts, and projections based upon facts.*

Can you easily separate statements of fact and opinion? This seemingly simple task is easier said than done. Economic statements may be divided into two main groups: positive and normative. **Positive economics** refers to statements of fact, relationships among facts, and projections based upon facts. For example, the statement "Unemployment in 1985 was 7.2 percent" is a fact. It is free of interpretation and individual values.[5] Another example is "If the price of compact discs (CDs) decreases, consumers will buy more CDs (assuming other things do not change)." Because this is a projection based upon historically consistent relationships and a statement which can be easily verified, it is a positive economic statement.

Normative economics *refers to statements which include value judgments.*

Normative economics refers to statements which include value judgments. For example, to say that "We should eliminate poverty in our lifetime" is a judgment. However noble and important it may be, many people would disagree with such a statement. Another example is the statement "Because many families cannot afford to pay for their children's college educations, the federal government ought to provide more assistance in the form of grants." Although the first part of the statement *may* be accepted as an undisputed fact, it does not follow logically that the federal government should become involved in any way. You may think so, but others certainly disagree.

It is important to distinguish between positive and normative economics because they are often used together, resulting in confusion for the reader or listener. It is easy for the skilled orator to couch an emotionally charged allegation (normative) in a fabric of undisputed facts. However, if we are able to sort values from facts and projections, then we will be more able to analyze what is really at issue. Is it the facts which are in dispute, or is it the opinion which is in question?

---

[5] Unemployment, as officially measured by the federal government, includes all people currently not employed but who are looking for work. Dividing the total unemployed by the civilian labor force, defined as the employed plus the unemployed, yields the unemployment rate. We will devote much more space to this important subject in later chapters.

> ### THINKING IT THROUGH
>
> Would society's resources be better utilized if more tax dollars were spent on job training and summer youth programs? Would we be able to reduce the high costs of law enforcement? Are these normative or positive economic questions?

Normative Economics and Economic Goals

As we have seen, normative economics generally prescribes a course of action to realize a goal (often unstated), and both the action and goal often are subject to disagreement and debate. But there are goals with which a clear majority of Americans readily agree.

Economic Freedom. The right to own resources and to use them in order to satisfy our wants is **economic freedom.** Included are the freedoms of occupational choice, property rights, and the freedom to purchase goods and services, subject, of course, to one's income. Freedom also implies that there will be differences among individuals. Some of us have more education, more income, fancier and more expensive cars and homes, higher-income jobs, and so forth. As long as freedom remains more important than security or equality, such differences will persist.

Economic freedom *is the right to own resources and to use them in order to satisfy our wants.*

Economic Equity. Like economic freedom, **economic equity** is a relative term. It deals with the broad and nebulous issue of fairness. Is the distribution of income in the economy equitable (fair)? Would you prefer to redistribute income from the wealthy to the poor? Should income be distributed equally? Although these are obviously normative economic questions, it is probably true that most Americans believe that *equality of opportunity* is better than *equality of results;* that is, people should have equal opportunities to pursue their goal of the good life, however that may be defined. This may mean that enough of us will tax ourselves to provide better housing and job training for the poor. But it also means that we probably would oppose guaranteeing $10,000 income for every man, woman, and child in the United States. Every nation must deal with the issue of equity in the distribution of goods and services.

Economic equity *refers to the issue of the fairness of resource, income, and product distribution.*

Economic Efficiency. Much less controversial is the goal of **economic efficiency.** This means that the economy's resources are allocated in such a way that it is impossible to improve the well-being of any one person without harming another. Also referred to as *allocative efficiency,* it means that no other mixture of resources and goods and ser-

Economic efficiency *means that the economy's resources are allocated in such a way that it is impossible to improve the well-being of any person without harming another.*

vices will increase society's total satisfaction. If society somehow determines that having fewer cars and cleaner air is a desirable change in resource allocation and the country moves in that direction, then economic efficiency will increase. In other words, what and how much a nation produces determines its progress in achieving economic efficiency.

How to produce is another important question faced by businesses, and, as you may suspect, the choice generally will be the least costly method of production. Closely related to the goal of economic efficiency is this idea of *technical efficiency*—producing a given amount of output at the lowest cost. Of course, businesses may produce their products using many different combinations of resources, but they have a strong interest in minimizing their costs of production. For example, it may be possible for General Motors to produce the same number of cars at a lower cost by introducing more robotics technology. However, such a change creates a conflict between equity and efficiency (economic and technical). Because the new technology probably means that jobs will be eliminated, workers and their unions may oppose such changes. To them, the issue is one of equity: they see themselves as victims of efficiency.

Such decisions about what, how, and for whom to produce are important microeconomic questions, answered in different ways by the nations of the world. These questions will be addressed further in the next chapter.

We turn now to a look at some important economic issues and problems during the 1980s. Each of the subjects presented is discussed in greater detail later in the book. For now, we will review the past decade's economic record and think about the future.

THE ECONOMY IN TRANSITION: A PROLOGUE

A major theme of this book is "The Economy in Transition." In order to understand more about our changing economy and the forces responsible for the changes, it is essential to gather pertinent economic data. Statistical facts and trends from the past, along with some assumptions, will enable you to make more reasoned projections and decisions about the future. In the next few pages, you will take a brief tour of the economy in the past decade. On the way, you will examine many of our nation's most difficult economic problems as well as some of the more promising economic prospects for the 1990s. These are the topics found in magazines and newspapers that you will learn to understand when you finish this course.

"These Are the Best of Times; These Are the Worst of Times."

The 1980s represent some of the best and the worst of economic conditions. We started the decade with inflation at 13.5 percent and an unemployment rate of 7 percent. The prime rate (a bank's baseline interest rate charged for loans to businesses) was 15.5 percent, and 18 months later it stood at 19 percent. The nation's output, measured by the real gross national product (1980's total output adjusted for inflation), was $5.3 billion less than 1979's real gross national product (GNP). Economic conditions were so dismal that some economic observers added the unemployment and inflation rates for a year to estimate a misery index. In 1980, the misery index was 20.5 percent, the highest since the Great Depression.

The Reagan administration resolutely attacked the inflation problem and produced the economy's worst recession since the Great Depression of the 1930s.[6] A combination of budget cuts and very high interest rates ultimately broke the back of inflation, but only at a very dear price. The number of jobless people increased by more than 3 million between 1980 and 1982, and the unemployment rate stood at 9.6 percent in 1983. (In fact, the jobless rate exceeded 10 percent for several months.) The austere economic policies did bring down the rate of inflation, however; it was less than 4 percent by 1983.

During a slow economy when production is stagnant or declining, unemployment is increasing, and the rate of inflation is winding down, workers are unable to win wage gains equal to or greater than inflation. The result is less real income. Figured in 1984 dollars, the median family income in 1984 was $67 lower than in 1980.

Economic conditions did improve as the economy came out of the recession. The prime rate decreased to 7.5 percent by late 1986, inflation edged downward to 1 percent, and the economy generated nearly 10 million new jobs between 1980 and 1986. (One important factor explaining lower inflation was the decline in oil prices caused by the breakdown of the Organization of Petroleum Exporting Countries [OPEC] cartel. In early 1987, however, the cartel successfully restricted oil production and drove oil prices up again.)

Perhaps the most perplexing problem of the 1980s was the unemployment situation. Over 8 million people were out of work at the same time that the economy experienced rapid job creation. The jobless rate remained far above its post–World War II average as the labor force expanded faster than the economy created jobs. Although the rate of unemployment edged below 6 percent by 1988, this official measure re-

---

[6] A recession is defined as two quarters of declining economic activity, measured by the real gross national product.

ported by the Bureau of Labor Statistics fails to account for discouraged workers—those who have given up hope of finding work. Discouraged workers generally account for about 15 percent of the unemployed, or approximately 950,000 in late 1988.

Deficits in the federal budget and in international trade became serious problems in the 1980s as well.[7] The federal budget deficit grew in excess of $200 billion by 1985. The interest charges on the debt became still more burdensome, further aggravating the government's job of budget cutting to reduce the deficit.

A political impasse rapidly took shape in the efforts to reduce the deficit as Reagan insisted upon budget cuts while many congressmen preferred higher taxes. The Reagan administration also supported a balanced budget amendment to the Constitution, requiring the Congress to balance the budget every year. Although very controversial, the idea gained increasing favor among the states, and by early 1985 nearly two thirds of the states had approved the idea. Afraid that such action was too extreme, Congress made a temporizing move. In 1985, it enacted the Gramm-Rudman bill. This legislation mandated a balanced budget by 1991 through a schedule of annual deficit reduction targets.

The U.S. trade imbalance was also of growing concern. A trade deficit arises when a nation's imports exceed its exports, and many economists agree that the problem is aggravated by the federal deficit. Because interest rates in the United States were relatively higher than in other countries, other nations wanted to buy American securities. Since foreign purchases of U.S. bonds and other securities must be made in U.S. dollars, the value of the dollar increased relative to foreign currencies. By 1983, it was evident that the dollar was already overvalued (too expensive) for many countries, as U.S. exports leveled off and imports increased substantially. Americans went on an import buying binge because our dollar could buy more Japanese yen, French francs, and German marks. Oddly enough, even after the dollar's value declined against the yen and other currencies, Americans increased their consumption of Japanese automobiles, French wine, and German cutlery. Americans evidently had acquired an import addiction. Unlike what occurred in the 1960s, "Made in Japan" took on positive connotations in the 1970s and 1980s.

The trade deficit is a problem for the United States because a trade imbalance may translate directly into a loss of jobs and a lower standard of living. Why? If imported goods exceed exports, then more dollars leave the U.S. economy than flow in. This drain can lead to a slower rate of economic growth. In response to this increasing imbalance of

---

[7] A budget deficit occurs when expenditures exceed tax receipts; a trade deficit occurs when a country buys more from other countries (imports) than it sells to other countries (exports).

trade, labor groups and members of Congress have called for protection-ist legislation. The proponents assert that we need to protect our jobs at home by imposing tariffs (taxes) and quotas on imported autos, wine, and cutlery, to name a few. Opponents of trade barriers argue that tariffs and quotas will lead to higher prices on imported goods and services and a corresponding decrease in the quantity of goods imported.

THINKING IT THROUGH

Will American workers benefit from import restrictions? How might our trading partners react?

There is also much concern about the poor productivity record of ser-vices.[8] Indeed, for the 1979 to 1986 period, the American Enterprise Institute reports that productivity was increasing at less than 1 percent per year and projects negative figures for several years. Compounding the productivity problem is a lack of academic and expert attention to services. Nearly all college and university business programs are preoc-cupied with solving problems faced by manufacturers. (If you don't think so, just look into any accounting, marketing, or management text-book. This is the material that college students are studying in prepa-ration for careers concentrated overwhelmingly in the service sector.)

Deindustrialization refers to the long-term decline in domestic manufacturing.

What does this mean for goods-producing industries? Perhaps two of the most descriptive labels used in the 1980s were **deindustrialization** and *the hollow corporation*. Each term refers to the long-term decline in domestic manufacturing, most notably in the areas of automobile pro-duction, textiles, and, more recently, even in the catchall category re-ferred to as *high tech*. The term *hollow corporation* refers to the loss of the manufacturing component in the firm's overall organization. And, as you have already seen, this loss means that we must import the product for sale or for final assembly in the United States. Deindustrialization is a more general term which is used to label the decline in goods-producing industries.

How bad is it? Is the United States losing its industrial base? Will this apparent trend precipitate hard-line government trade policies? An-swers to these and related questions are extremely difficult to deter-mine. However, there is solid evidence that the major change is a *relative* shift from goods-producing to service-producing industries. Manufactur-ing, agriculture, mining, and construction all reached new peak levels of output in 1985, 1986, and 1987 after recovering from the very deep 1982

---

[8] Productivity is the output per worker per hour.

recession. Although a shift away from goods production to service production has occurred, the shift is a relative one; that is, using production as the criterion, the service economy is growing faster than the goods-producing sectors. Measured in absolute terms, however, the goods-producing industries are experiencing increases in production. *What do you think?* Is this evidence of the deindustrialization of America?

Looking ahead, the service economy will be a big winner in the 1990s. Projections from private and public sources estimate that nine of every ten new jobs will be in services. The combination of corporate restructuring, rapid internationalization of U.S. businesses, and government deregulation suggests fast growth of service enterprises.

Corporations have undergone major reorganization in recent years. Entire layers of the corporate bureaucracy have been removed, and whole divisions have been cut out. This restructuring will create a demand for a wide range of services from landscaping to public relations, operations formerly handled internally by companies.

A second factor is a growing commitment on the part of U.S. businesses to enter the global marketplace. As this trend matures, the internationalization of U.S. business will trigger increased demand for communications and data processing, services in which the United States has had a historic advantage. Government deregulation, the third factor, will present the private sector with service business abandoned by the federal government.

Assuming that these projections come true, what service industries are most likely to expand the fastest in the 1990s? Four industries appear to have the greatest potential. First, communications: areas like fiber optics and cellular mobile phones promise the greatest growth. Second, business services: computer repair technicians, temporary employment services (like Temps and Kelly Services), and child care are likely to produce the greatest growth. Third, health care: this includes new specialty medical centers (e.g., Alzheimer's disease clinics and surgery centers); HMOs are expected to increase membership from 21 million in 1985 to over 35 million by the mid-1990s; and the pharmaceutical industry is expected to experience a boom as the population ages. (The Bureau of Labor Statistics forecasts a 7.5 percent annual growth rate for phamaceuticals to 1995.) Fourth, travel and recreation: from pool halls, dance lessons, and aerobics to Pacific cruises, the amusement industry will experience rapid growth.

One of the most interesting aspects of life is change. The periodic ups and downs of the economy, shifting consumer tastes, and the emergence of whole new industries and new jobs are but a few of the fascinating transitions through which we all live. The U.S. economy is forever undergoing transition. Before leaving the dynamics of change, read the following case about the service economy, education, jobs, and competition.

America's Work Force: The Key to U.S. Competitiveness

According to many analysts, the quality of the U.S. work force is declining, as evidenced by sagging productivity and international competitiveness. At the same time, ironically enough, the United States's new service economy has generated millions of jobs. Of course, most of these new jobs are part-time or temporary, and they are concentrated in relatively low-wage, low-skill growth sectors such as clerical work, retail sales, and fast-food operations.

A statistical profile of this booming work force helps to shed light on the problem.

- Twenty percent of all jobs today are part-time, compared with 15 percent in 1954
- According to a study by the National Association of Working Women, part-time workers earned an average of $4.50 an hour, compared with $7.80 for full-time workers
- Fifty-eight percent of female "temporary" workers are unable to find permanent full-time employment, stuck working for temporary help agencies
- Twenty-eight percent of part-time workers earn the minimum wage.

Another related dimension of this competitiveness and productivity problem is the quality of the work force. Recent evidence indicates that the U.S. work force is not keeping up with world-class standards of education and skill-levels. For example, 8 percent of America's youth (14–21 years of age) are unable to read and write at the fifth-grade level. And this degree of functional illiteracy increases to as much as 20 percent if slightly higher standards are used. By contrast, less than 1 percent of Japanese youth is functionally illiterate.

If the United States is to remain a major player in the global economy, nearly everyone agrees that the key is a high-quality labor force. But how can service-sector work be turned into decent, breadwinner jobs that offer career ladders to a middle-class future and help create a more productive economy? Private businesses do provide on-the-job training, but such job upgrading programs pose a risk for the firms, because there is no assurance that the workers won't sell their skills to a competitor. Labor force upgrading is thus what economists call an *externality*, a cost or benefit that affects society but not the individual firm. Moreover, the problem is compounded by the lack of a national training system for the millions of young people who will not go to college. Unlike Germany, which has a publicly financed and privately operated apprenticeship training system, or Japan, whose private corporations provide extensive training and skills upgrade programs, there is no national publicly financed training for the noncollege bound in the United States.

If job upgrading is truly an externality, one solution is to adopt a national training policy and have the government subsidize the cost. This is already being done in California on a small scale, financed in part by a 0.1 percent payroll tax. Managers submit a skills-upgrading plan, and the state pays part of the training cost. And other countries spend much more than the United States does. France and Sweden for example, spend about 3 percent of their gross national product on a variety of labor market subsidies, much of which is earmarked for life-long learning.

Another approach would encourage employers to pay more attention to providing opportunities for advancement within the company for their low-level workers. Some union contracts allow a nurse's aide, for example, to take part-time courses and become a licensed nurse. And Massachusetts offers college tuition as part of a career-advancement program in order to reduce turnover among aides in mental hospitals.

Job upgrading and lifetime learning are new concepts for the American economy. But in a competitive global market, they are not merely quality-of-life issues but questions of economic survival.[9]

Questions to Consider

1. *This CASE-IN-POINT argues that the service sector is generating "millions of relatively low-wage, low-skill jobs." It also suggests that much of this work is temporary, while the workers want and need full-time employment. Is this an accurate picture of the service economy? What about the millions of accountants, engineers, lawyers, physicians, nurses, computer programmers and systems analysts, etc.?*
2. *Many nations spend a greater percentage of their national budgets on education and training than the United States. Do you support the idea of providing federal subsidies for job upgrading and life-long learning and education? Why or why not?*

IMPORTANT TERMS TO REMEMBER

deindustrialization, p. 13
direct relationship, p. 25
economic efficiency, p. 9
economic equity, p. 9
economic freedom, p. 9
economics, p. 5
graph, p. 20

inverse relationship, p. 25
normative economics, p. 8
origin, p. 22
positive economics, p. 8
scarcity, p. 5
X-axis, p. 21
Y-axis, p. 22

CHAPTER SUMMARY

You have covered a lot of material in this chapter. The purpose was twofold: to acquaint you with contemporary economic issues and trends, and to provide you with Your Economics Survival Kit. The theme of the book is "The Economy in Transition." Is there any doubt that the U.S. economy is in the midst of important changes—changes which will affect you?

---

[9] Council of Economic Advisors, *Economic Report of the President, 1985*, pp. 234 and 278; Lester Thurow, "Creating a World-Class Team," in *The Changing American Economy*, edited by David Obey and Paul Sarbannes (New York: Basil Blackwell, Inc., 1986), pp. 169–79; Robert Kuttner, "Economic Watch," *Business Week*, February 16, 1987; Barbara Lerner, "American Education," *Public Interest*, 69, Fall 1982.

The important concepts covered included the following:

1. Scarcity means that there are not enough resources to go around to satisfy everyone's wants; that is, resources are limited (scarce), because our wants are unlimited.

2. Economics is a branch of the social sciences which studies how society allocates scarce resources among competing and unlimited wants. Because of scarcity, we must choose which resources to satisfy which wants. These choices constitute a major subject of economics.

3. Positive economics refers to statements of fact and economic forecasts; for example, if the price of microcomputers declines, consumers and businesses will buy more microcomputers, other things being equal.

4. Normative economics refers to statements of opinion; for example, because the nation's highways and bridges need repair, we should increase taxes to finance the work.

5. Several goals relating to economic activity are widely accepted. Economic freedom is the right to own resources and to use them in order to satisfy wants. Economic equity refers to the fairness of resource distribution. And economic efficiency means that the economy's resources are allocated in such a way that it is impossible to improve the well-being of any one person without harming another. No other mixture of resources and goods and services will increase society's total satisfaction.

6. Many economists think that the U.S. economy is going through deindustrialization, defined as the decline of our goods-producing industries. Attributing this mainly to the maturation and growth of European, Canadian, and Japanese industries, observers perceive the evolution of the U.S. hollow corporation. The hollowing phenomenon is the loss of a firm's manufacturing component, substituted by a need to import the finished product or the intermediate component for assembly. Other analysts do not deny the fact of a hollowing of corporations, but ask if the decline of production is relative or absolute. Indeed, they point to statistics which show that production has actually increased.

DISCUSSION AND REVIEW QUESTIONS

1. The definition of scarcity states that our wants are insatiable. Think of the characteristics of the goods you buy. What products and services actually have additional want-creating properties? Which products and services have necessary or desirable complementary products and services?

2. Evaluate the following statement: "We could eliminate scarcity if there were no advertising."

3. Classify the following statements as positive or normative:
   a. If the price of orange juice increases, consumers will buy less orange juice, other things being equal.
   b. Orange and orange juice prices are too high.
   c. Because rents have increased 35 percent faster than the cost of living, we need to place a ceiling on rents to protect tenants from further rent hikes.

4. To what extent is the U.S. economy experiencing deindustrialization? How would you measure such changes?

5. Are the goals of economic freedom, equity, and efficiency compatible? As they are defined, can we achieve all three? Are there inherent conflicts? Will the pursuit of a more equitable distribution of income result in less freedom and efficiency?

6. In a treatise on freedom and other economic goals, a British socialist once said that "Freedom for the pike is death for the minnow." Since pikes and minnows are fish, and assuming that he was referring to the U.S. economy, what did he mean?

7. Given the following data, make a graph illustrating the relationship. Be sure to design a scale, label each axis, connect the points (in annual order), and label the years along the curve.

Inflation and Unemployment, 1975–1986

Year	Inflation (percent)	Unemployment (percent)
1975	9.1	8.5
1976	5.8	7.7
1977	6.5	7.1
1978	7.7	6.1
1979	11.3	5.8
1980	13.5	7.1
1981	10.4	7.6
1982	6.1	9.7
1983	3.2	9.6
1984	4.3	7.5
1985	3.6	7.2
1986	2.6	7.0

(SOURCE: *Survey of Current Business; Federal Reserve Bulletin*)

8. What is the percentage decrease in inflation between 1982 and 1983? What is the percentage increase in unemployment from 1980 to 1982?

A BRIEF LOOK AHEAD

The next chapter begins where this one began—with scarcity and the economizing problem. Because all nations face the reality of scarcity, they must answer the same fundamental economic questions. To understand the problem of scarcity and choices, a model of production possibilities is presented. And because assumptions are important to all economic models and theories, you will be engaged in a test of your economic behavior. Important economic trends also are presented in the FOCUS and CASES-IN-POINT. Remember: Read critically; underline only really important things; take notes; write in the margins of the book; ask questions as you read; and raise questions in class and in conference with your instructor. Find answers to your questions before the test.

YOUR ECONOMICS SURVIVAL KIT

Have you heard that economics is all about graphs and math? Although there is some truth to this, it is more accurate to say that economists use math and graphs to represent important information. Graphs, for instance, are useful because they capture a great deal of complex information and present it in a relatively simple form.

Although graphs are not so crucial as to make or break you, they are always important. When you encounter one in the text, you should devote time to fully understand it. To understand a graph, you should be able to describe the relationship illustrated in the graph. And, conversely, you should be able to draw the graph given the description. With this introduction, let's begin building your economics survival kit.

HOW TO READ AND UNDERSTAND GRAPHS

Remember:

A graph is always an illustration picturing how two sets of figures are related to one another.

Example 1: Study Hours and Leisure Hours

Situation: You are 18 years old and a full-time student.

Suppose you decide to plan your working day. A considerable part of each 24 hours must be allocated to sleep, meals, and class attendance. Suppose these matters take up 14 hours per day. This leaves the remaining 10 hours to divide between study on the one hand, and leisure and recreation on the other.

That 10 hours could be divided in an infinite number of ways. At one extreme would be 10 hours of leisure and 0 hours of study time. This particular time allocation must be considered unsatisfactory in the sense that its pursuit tends to lead to unpleasant interviews with the dean of students or similar people of limited imagination.

At the other extreme would be 10 hours for study and 0 for leisure and recreation, or the week-before-examinations allocation. Among the possible choices are these:

	A	B	C	D	E	F	G
Leisure hours	10	8	7	6	4.5	2.5	0
Study hours	0	2	3	4	5.5	7.5	10

What we have are two sets, or lists, of figures. One set gives possible study hours; the other gives possible leisure hours. More important, *these figures are tied to one another. Each study-hour figure is paired off with a leisure-hour figure.* If we start with the assumption of only 10 available hours, then the figure of 6 leisure hours must be linked with 4 study hours, and with no other figure; 5.5 study hours is linked with 4.5 leisure hours, and so on. Here, the linking rule is simple: The two members of each pair must together add up to 10.

Review.   The illustration above is a simple one, but confirm your grasp of it by completing the following blanks before you go on.

1.   The example involves leisure time and _____ time. Total daily time to be allocated between these two is _____ hours, so that 4 hours of leisure time must be linked with _____ hours of _____ time.
2.   If hours are divided into half hours, quarters, and so on, we can have as many pairs of numbers as we please, but each pair must satisfy the rule that _____ .

Graphical Illustration

A graph illustrates a series of numbers, all linked together by some rule.

This example reveals precisely the kind of situation a **graph** always illustrates: a series of numbers, all linked together by some rule.

Figure 1–1 on page 22 is a graph illustrating the study-leisure situation. Go over it carefully, but, before starting, remember that all unfamiliar things appear complicated. You cannot tell whether they are really complicated or not until you have spent at least a little time in growing familiar with them. It may help your familiarizing process if you know that the whole system of graphical illustration began with a bored man lying in bed, gazing at a crack in the ceiling.

The man was René Descartes, the French philosopher and mathematician. Descartes had been confined to bed with an illness. As he lay on his back, going through the tedium of recovery, this thought struck him: To locate the position of any point or small spot on the ceiling, you need two measurements—a pair. You must have two—one is insufficient—but two is all you need. Thus, a particular point might be exactly eight feet from that edge of the ceiling toward your feet and two feet from the left-hand edge ceiling edge.

Doesn't this sound simple? You start by agreeing to take these two edges of the ceiling as base lines or zero lines. Every point on the ceiling has associated with it two figures (each of the figures being a measurement from one of the two edges or base lines). From a point, you can obtain a pair of figures which locate that point.

But Descartes was more interested in the fact that you can turn things around and start with the pair of figures rather than the point. Given any pair of figures, you can illustrate them as a particular and unique point on a two-dimensional surface, whether that surface happens to be a ceiling or a sheet of paper. Even more interesting, if you have a *series* of pairs somehow linked together, as in the study-leisure example, you can illustrate them as a *line*. (A line, for our purpose here, is just a particular accumulation of points.) And the way that line runs—whether up or down, whether curved or straight, and so on—is an illustration of the kind of linking rule which those pairs of points must satisfy.

Economics is filled with topics in which this linking together of two sets of numbers is important, and graphs are useful just because they illustrate so readily and easily the nature of the relationship involved. They are useful, that is, once you have spent sufficient time to grasp the mechanics of their construction.

In Figure 1–1, the vertical line at left and the horizontal line at bottom correspond to the two edges of Descartes' ceiling. Each is divided off with a number scale, and the meaning of these numbers is indicated by the labels: "Hours of study" (horizontally) and "Hours of leisure" (vertically).

The slanting line carrying points labeled *A* through *G* is the actual graph illustrating the study-leisure relation. But you should concentrate first on the horizontal and vertical measuring line.

X-axis *is a convenient line for measuring distances in the horizontal or west-and-east dimension.*

The horizontal line is the horizontal axis or the **X-axis.** This horizontal axis is just a convenient line for measuring distances in the horizontal or west-and-east dimension. In the study-leisure example, one member in each pair must stand for a certain number of study hours. In Figure 1–1, study time has been given the west-and-east dimension, and the space in this dimension has been divided into numbers from 0 to 10, with 0 at the extreme left, 10 at the right.

This horizontal or *X*-axis goes at the bottom of the diagram as a matter of convenience and custom, not because it must sit there. Think of this horizontal axis as a kind of sliding line which could be moved up or down the diagram as you would move a ruler—always keeping it exactly horizontal. For example, look at the two mark on the *X*-axis. Above it is a grid line extending up to point *B*. Any point on this grid line stands for two study hours, because it is two measuring units away from the left-hand edge. If you moved the horizontal axis upward, the two mark thereon would touch all points on this grid line up to *B* (and beyond), and only points on this line.

FIGURE 1–1
Study versus Leisure

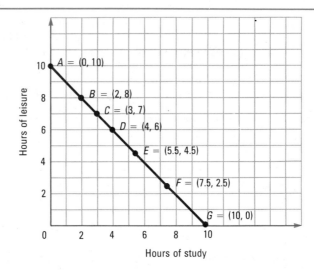

This graph illustrates all of the possible combinations of allocating 10 hours of free time between study and leisure. Seven points are shown, points A–G, but there are an infinite number of possibilities. Each point must satisfy the linking rule that study hours plus leisure hours equals ten.

Y-axis *is the vertical line used to measure distances in the vertical or north-and-south dimension.*

Similarly, the vertical line at the left is the vertical axis or **Y-axis.** It should be regarded as a measuring line which could be swept from left to right across the diagram in order to measure off amounts of leisure time. Thus, any point on the horizontal grid line running through *B* stands for eight hours of leisure time.

It is convenient to give the two axis lines their positions at the bottom and at the left because each of them can then perform a service for the other. In Figure 1–1, the vertical axis is primarily the measuring line for leisure time. But because of its position, it is also the zero line for study time. Any point on this vertical axis stands for zero study hours. Similarly, any point on the horizontal study-time axis records zero leisure hours.

Origin *is the lower left-hand corner point at which the two axis lines meet.*

The lower left-hand corner at which the two axis lines meet is the **origin.** It signifies zero study hours and zero leisure hours.

Review.   Add the correct word in each blank below, or circle the correct alternative among those given.

3. A graph has _____ dimensions, horizontal or east and west, and _____ or south and north. Hence any pair of numbers, such as a combination of study and leisure hours, can appear on the graph as a single _____ .

4. In the horizontal or west-east dimension, a figure of zero would be recorded on the line at
    a. extreme left   **b.** extreme right
    c. very bottom   **d.** very top

5. In the vertical dimension, 0 would be recorded on the line at
    a. extreme left   **b.** extreme right
    c. very bottom   **d.** very top

6. The measuring line used to place numbers shown in the west-east dimension is called the _____ _____ or the _____ _____ . The south-north measuring line is the _____ _____ or the _____ _____ .

7. In Figure 1–1 point *B* stands for the combination of two _____ hours and eight _____ hours. In Figure 1–1, leisure hours are measured _____ .

8. Point *D* stands for _____ leisure hours and _____ study hours; nine study hours and one leisure hour would be a pair indicated by a point between points _____ and _____ .

Drawing a Graph

Since you have to learn about graphs, you should draw graphs. On a piece of graph paper, redraw Figure 1–1 yourself. First, draw and label your axis lines. What are you measuring in the vertical (south-north) direction? Write this at the top of the vertical axis. Pick a scale for each of the axes; that is, choose how much distance you are going to use to represent one hour. Record as many pairs of numbers as you please: ten leisure hours and zero study hours; nine and one; five and five; and so on. They should all lie along a line comparable to *AG*. After you have satisfied yourself about this fact, you may draw the entire line. It sums up all the possible points you could mark if you had sufficient time and patience.

This last idea bears repeating. You cannot possibly find any add-up-to-10 combination that does not appear somewhere on *AG*. *AG* includes every possible pair that satisfies this linking rule. Moreover, *AG* can be trusted in another respect. It has no point that does *not* meet the linking rule. In other words, *AG* is an exact graphical representation of the add-up-to-10 rule in the sense that (1) it includes *all* points that satisfy this rule and (2) it includes *only* points that satisfy this rule.

Review.   Answer the following question by circling the correct alternative among the three offered.

9. Take any point inside the triangle formed by the three lines of Figure 1–1 (below and to the left of *AG*). The pair or measurements for any such point
    a.   must together total more than 10
    b.   must together total less than 10
    c.   must together total 10

Problem

Use graph paper and a ruler. Suppose you have $20 which was given to you for your 21st birthday with the stipulation that you spend it only for liquid refreshments (and you must spend it all). The price of champagne is $5 per bottle and the price of beer is 50 cents per bottle. How can we show your alternatives graphically?

Draw your axes (plural of axis) and label one "Bottles of champagne" and the other "Bottles of beer." Now, if you spend all your money on champagne, how many bottles can you buy? _____ If you spend all of it on beer? _____

You now have these points (fill in the missing values):

	A	B
Champagne	—	0
Beer	0	—

Put these points on your graph. Now draw a straight line connecting them (use a ruler). This line represents all the combinations of beer and champagne that you can buy if you spend all of the $20. Fill in the following table by referring to your graph; then label these points (*C*, *D*, and *E*) on your graph as well.

	C	D	E
Champagne	3	—	1
Beer	—	20	—

Example 2: Demand for Pizza at Margie's Pizzeria

Now that you are an expert in the linking rule, take a look at the following table. Each row of data, Price per pizza ($) and Quantity of pizzas per month sold, is linked; that is, a price is paired off with its corresponding quantity. True, you can't add price and quantity any more than you can add apples and oranges. But the two figures are still linked as a quantity-price pair.

	Pizza Sales, Margie's Pizzeria July 1989	
	Price	**Quantity**
A	$7.50	250
B	6.00	350
C	4.50	450
D	3.00	600

Point *A* illustrates the first pair: a price of $7.50 and a quantity of 250; point *B* indicates another pair: a price of $6 and a quantity of 350, and so on. The interesting feature about Margie's pizza sales is that the lower her price, the greater the number of pizzas sold. This is known as an **inverse relationship:** as price decreases, the quantity demanded (or sold) increases, and vice versa. (*Indirect* and *negative* are two other terms which mean the same as inverse.)

Inverse relationship *exists when two variable move in opposite directions.*

This data is plotted on graph paper in the same way that study time and leisure time were graphed in the previous example. First, a scale must be designed. You need to determine a measurement for price (each dollar and/or cents) for the vertical (or *Y*) axis, and another scale for the quantity along the horizontal (or *X*) axis. Once this is done, take a ruler and mark off the scale along each axis. Next, label all known data along both axes. In other words, print the $3.00 next to the mark representing this price, $4.50 next to the mark signifying a price of $4.50, and so on. Then, do the same thing along the quantity axis, labeling the quantities at each respective location. Once this is done, you are ready to begin plotting the pairs of data.

Figure 1–2 on the next page illustrates the completed demand curve for Margie's pizza during the month of July. Point *A* is plotted in two stages: First, locate the vertical line which represents a quantity of 250. Second, locate the horizontal line which represents the price of $7.50. The intersection of these two lines determines the unique point *A*: 250 pizzas at a price of $7.50 per pizza. Points *B, C,*

FIGURE 1–2

Pizza Sales, Margie's Pizzeria

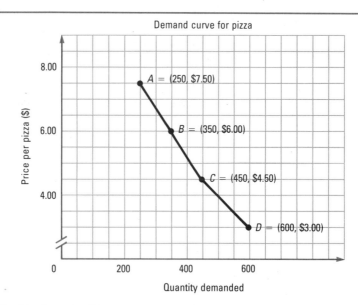

Demand curve for pizza

Margie's pizza sales illustrate an inverse relationship: As price decreases, she sells more pizzas (the quantity demanded increases). Each point on the demand curve is plotted as a quantity, price pair (e.g., point A has an X-axis value of 250 and a Y-axis value of $7.50).

and D are located in precisely the same way. Once all points are labeled, connect them with a single line. What is the result? A demand curve.

Now it's your turn. The table below illustrates the relationship between attendance at a community pool and the temperature. This relationship is different from the previous example in one important respect. Here both variables move in the same direction. In other words, this is a **direct** (or *positive*) **relationship.** As the temperature increases, attendance at the pool also increases, and vice versa.

Direct relationship *occurs when both variables move in the same direction.*

	Temperature	Attendance
A	60	10
B	70	30
C	80	60
D	90	120
E	100	180

Take a piece of graph paper and a ruler, and make a graph of the temperature-attendance relationship. Be sure to create a scale, label each axis, plot the pairs of data, and connect the points.

Example 3: Abstract Graphs

Once you know how to plot data on a graph, and you begin to feel more comfortable about interpreting graphical relationships, drawing graphs to capture the essence of a relationship is easy. And expressing even complex ideas in a simple graph is often very helpful in analyzing the relationship. Figure 1–3 illustrates a number of abstract graphs—graphs without scales.

Each of the examples on page 28 illustrates commonplace relationships in everyday life. A company's cost per unit of production is shown in Figure 1–3a. Note that the curve is U-shaped, indicating that at both low and high output levels cost per unit is high. Of course, many businesses have an objective of minimizing their average costs of production.

Figure 1–3b illustrates the relationship between fuel consumption, measured as miles per gallon (MPG), and the vehicle speed, measured in miles per hour (MPH). This says that MPG increases up to 55 MPH, after which MPG decreases (up to 85 MPH). A moving violation issued by a police officer isn't the only cost connected with speeding.

It's your turn to interpret Figure 1–3c. As illustrated in this graph, what is the relationship between income and age? (Note: Be careful about making unwarranted cause-and-effect statements.)

FIGURE 1–3 a-c   Abstract Graphs

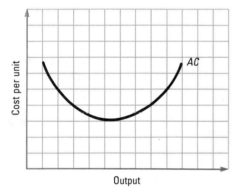

a

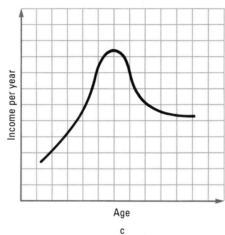

c

b

a. Typical U-shaped average cost (AC) curve, illustrating decreasing and then increasing cost per unit of output over a firm's short-run production range.

b. City driving at low MPH and highway driving at high speed (illegal MPH) each produce a lower MPG than highway driving at legal MPH.

c. What is the relationship between income and age as depicted in this diagram? Based upon this graph, can we say that increasing age causes increased income? Can we say that having a lot of money only ages you? Is there a cause-and-effect relationship here?

Economic Systems and the Economizing Problem

Julius Fekete, The Stock Market

In this chapter, you will investigate the nature of economic systems—what exactly an economic system is, how one system differs from another, and the underlying economic problem common to all people regardless of the system in which they live.

Chapter 1 introduced you to a number of important economic concepts and problems. The two elements found in each of the issues raised are scarcity and choice. Because there aren't enough resources to go around, we are forced to make choices about how to use our time, resources, and money in order to satisfy our wants. We now return to the concept of scarcity in this chapter, describe in greater detail the basic economic resources available, and relate the problem of scarce resources to how choices are made in each of the economic systems.

One of the ways economists reveal the implications and consequences of choice is with the concept of opportunity cost and the use of a production-possibilities model. With the aid of this model, we will be able to analyze a number of economic problems faced by nations with different economic systems. The production-possibilities model also enables us to discuss the importance of assumptions in the development of economic theory.

Finally, this chapter explores the foundation for all economic exchange—the theory of comparative advantage and the concepts of specialization and division of labor.

After completion of this chapter, you should be able to do the following:

1. Compare and contrast free market economies (pure capitalism) and command economies (socialism and communism).
2. Diagram and use the production-possibilities curve to explain the concept of opportunity cost.
3. Define the assumptions of self-interest and rationality and explain how they are used in the development of economic theory.
4. Use the theory of comparative advantage to describe and explain why a person or nation benefits from trade (exchange).

Are There Economic Problems in Liechtenstein?

Liechtenstein is a very small nation, a mere 61 square miles tucked in between the borders of Austria and Switzerland. Because of its feudal past and a royal family headed by Crown Prince Hans Adam, one might think that Liechtenstein has little economic vitality. Indeed, at the end of World War II, Liechtenstein had high unemployment and more than a third of the population earned its living from farming.

Today, Liechtenstein boasts an average income of $15,000, nearly double that of the United Kingdom, and only a dozen or so of its 26,400 citizens are unemployed. Moreover, with 54 percent of its labor force employed in manufacturing, Liechtenstein is more industrialized than Switzerland or West Germany. What accounts for this economic miracle?

When Prince Hans Adam's father, Prince Franz Josef II, became the ruler in 1938, he adopted what is now called supply-side economics in an effort to promote prosperity. According to Prince Hans Adam, the formula is simple: a combination of low tax rates, little or no governmental interference, and tight banking secrecy laws. For example, the personal income tax rate begins at 4.2 percent and reaches a maximum of 17.85 percent at an income of $64,000. Corporate taxes are also low. And, despite a dependence upon immigrant labor to supplement its tiny internal labor market, Liechtenstein has never experienced a strike or major labor unrest. State aid is nonexistent, and the government runs a balanced or surplus budget.[1]

Liechtenstein sounds like a utopia when compared to the economic problems faced by its neighbors and trading partners. As you probably gathered from the brief FOCUS above, the economic system in Liechtenstein is strongly capitalistic. Although it has a feudal past and still has a royal family, this tiny little nation boasts one of the world's most successful economic records. Its record is based, in part, upon an endowment of natural resources and a form of economic organization highly conducive to economic growth. What makes it so successful? How does it solve its economic problems? In order to answer these and other questions, it is important to gain a perspective about economic systems in general and the basic economic questions facing all nations.

[1] Adapted from *The Wall Street Journal*, July 10, 1985, p. 29.

THE ECONOMIZING PROBLEM

Economizing problem *is how to allocate scarce resources among competing and unlimited wants.*

Small and large nations alike face a common all-pervasive **economizing problem**—how to allocate scarce resources among competing and unlimited wants. Although remarkably successful, Liechtenstein still must address this problem. Faced with a limited domestic market for its goods and services, Liechtenstein has turned its attention to international markets. Businesses export well over 50 percent of their industrial and agricultural goods, and over 80 percent of their financial services are rendered to companies in other countries. Productivity (output per person per hour) also remains the highest of any nation in the northern hemisphere, largely because of, according to many economists, low tax rates and minimal governmental regulation of business.

Whether rich or poor, whether fully developed or developing, all nations must solve the economizing problem in their own ways. Moreover, all nations attempt to reduce scarcity by striving to maximize their production potential. These production possibilities, in turn, depend upon economic resources, technology, and efficiency of economic organization. It is important to examine each of these ingredients.

Economic Resources

Economic resources *are an economy's land, labor, capital, and entrepreneurship.*

Land *refers to all natural resources, such as air, water, and forests.*

Labor *represents all forms of human exertion, physical and mental, applied to economic activity.*

Capital *refers to physical assets used in production.*

A nation's **economic resources** (or factors of production) may be divided into four general categories: land, labor, capital, and entrepreneurship. First, **land** refers to all natural resources. Examples include air, water, forests, minerals, and air. Second, **labor** represents all forms of human exertion, physical and mental, applied to economic activity. (Economic activity is defined as any work which gets counted in the GNP.) Day laborers, bus drivers, plumbers, nurses, engineers, and civil servants are all a part of the labor force. Third, **capital** refers to physical assets used in production—machinery, equipment, buildings, inventory, and goods in various stages of completion. Examples of capital include things like computers, drill presses, copying machines, and company cars, but *not money*. Money is not considered capital because it is not, by itself, productive. It is merely a paper asset. (Because accounting principles count money as capital, it is helpful to distinguish between *financial capital* [cash, stocks, bonds, and other paper assets] and *physical capital* [ma-

---

THINKING IT THROUGH

Is your instructor's pen a piece of capital? What about a taxicab off duty? Is motor oil land or capital? What about a Federal Reserve Note (dollar bill)?

chinery, buildings and equipment]. Accountants count both financial and physical assets as capital; economists only consider physical assets as capital.)

Entrepreneurship *is risk-taking, decision-making ventures that bring land, labor, and capital together.*

Entrepreneurship is the fourth factor of production—risk-taking, decision-making ventures that bring land, labor, and capital together in order to provide a good or service. Bill Gates, the president of Microsoft, Inc., and Steven Jobs, the founder and developer of Apple, are such entrepreneurs, as are such famous historical figures as Thomas Edison, Alexander Graham Bell, and Eli Whitney.

Each of the inventors and entrepreneurs mentioned here broke new ground. Their contributions created new ways of organizing work, producing goods and services, thereby materially changing people's lives. The Apple personal computer, the electric light, the telephone, and the cotton gin each represent a new *technology*—contributions to our knowledge about production and how we organize work. Technological change is largely responsible for increased productivity and a higher standard of living.[2]

Economizing is accomplished by combining resources in the most efficient mixture to provide those goods and services deemed most desirable by society. It is an allocation problem. But how are the preferences of individuals communicated? How does a business (or nation) know whether to produce more or fewer cars? And what is the most efficient combination of resources to render a service or produce a good? These questions and others flow naturally from the economizing problem, and they are answered by a nation's system of economic organization.

ECONOMIC SYSTEMS

Economic system *is the organization of households, business firms, and government(s) to answer the questions of what, how, and for whom to produce.*

An **economic system** is the organization of households, business firms, and government(s) to answer the basic questions of *what to produce, how to produce,* and *for whom to produce.* Remember the discussion in Chapter 1 about what the federal government should produce? Fixing roads *or* providing education? Now take that question one step further. Should government produce education at all? How should education be produced? By local public school districts, by businesses, by religious organizations? By whom? And perhaps a more important issue for some

---

[2] Technological change may be broken down into two different, but related developments. First, an invention is a new or improved capital resource. A good example is the IBM personal computer. An invention may also be a new method of production (i.e., reorganizing the production assembly line so that each worker is responsible for producing the entire product). Second, an innovation is the commercial application of the invention. Many new ideas actually become inventions, but are not applied commercially for many years. Frances Howe's sewing machine is such an invention. It was invented in 1836, but not applied in factory production for decades.

people—for whom? Should everyone be entitled to a college education? Should education be treated just like other personal services, like buying a vacation cruise? Or is it more like national defense which, if it is worthwhile, should be provided to all? (We will discuss the topic of public goods in greater detail in Chapter 10.)

Free market economy *is an economic system in which most decisions are made by private businesses and households.*

Command economy *has highly centralized decision making, limited economic freedoms, and greatly restricted consumer choice.*

There are two basic types of economic systems—**free market economy** and **command** (or planned) **economy**. In pure form, they are easy to understand. As applied to real world nations, however, it is more difficult to classify a particular nation as free market or command because most nations are hybrids. For this reason, it is helpful to think of economic systems on a continuum according to major characteristics. Moreover, a third economic system is added, the mixed economy, in order to represent better the diversity of economic organization. Please refer occasionally to Figure 2–1 as you read.

Central to the continuum in Figure 2–1 are two basic questions: First, how much freedom does the individual have to pursue self-interest? And second, what is the private-public mixture of decisions about the use of economic resources? As you can tell from the model, economic freedom, occupational choice, private property rights, the profit motive, and individual decision making are all extensive under free market systems. Moreover, each of these characteristics diminishes in importance as you move across the continuum from mixed to command economies. How does this help us in understanding the ways in which nations confront the economizing problem and the basic economic questions of what to produce, how to produce, and for whom to produce?

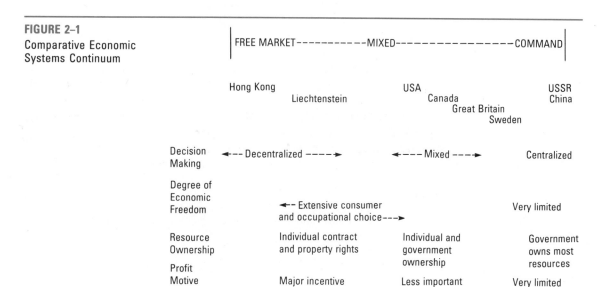

FIGURE 2–1
Comparative Economic Systems Continuum

Under free market economies, most decisions are made by private businesses and households. The questions of what, how, and for whom are left to the market to answer. This means that the forces of supply and demand largely determine what gets produced, how production is organized, and for whom the product is made. For example, following the OPEC oil embargo, U.S. automobile companies made a decision to produce more fuel-efficient compact cars. What role did U.S. consumers play in the decisions made by General Motors Corporation (GM), Ford, and Chrysler to produce smaller cars? Do you think that the Big Three would have made this choice if their sales and profits had not taken a nosedive?[3]

The question about how to produce refers to the resource mixture and organization of production. One clear long-term trend is the substitution of capital for labor in virtually all goods-producing industries. In the automobile industry, for example, firms have substituted robotics, computer-controlled assembly lines, and other capital resources for labor in an effort to increase productivity. A similar pattern of capital substitution has occurred in agriculture as farmers and agribusinesses strive to increase the yield per acre. Those unable to afford the expensive machinery and the cheaper costs of production which come with new technology become the victims of the marketplace. The result is all too familiar: farm foreclosures and bankruptcies. Hundreds of thousands of farmers left the farm for the city in the late 1970s and 1980s.

In the preceding paragraphs, the questions of what and how were addressed. But what about the third important question—for whom to produce? How is this answered in the free market system? Perhaps the best way to explain this is to paraphrase a very well-known maxim from Karl Marx, the famous 19th-century philosopher and architect of *communism*. In summarizing the communist creed, Marx said that the communistic (command type) economic system should be organized on the principle "from each according to his ability, to each according to his need." Adapting this to a capitalistic or free market economic system, one could say that *capitalism* is organized on the principle "from each according to his ability, to each according to his ability." This means that under pure capitalism, society owes little if anything to the individual. The individual is entitled to nothing. One gets only that which one can buy in the marketplace. This is the essence of pure capitalism.

Under the pure form of communism conceived by Karl Marx, every person would work to advance the interests of the nation. Everyone

---

[3] The U.S. government was also extensively involved. Rather than permitting the market to determine gasoline prices following OPEC's oil embargo, the government set price ceilings on gas at the pump. The upshot was long lines of customers at most gas stations—a sure sign of shortage.

would apply their labor for the betterment of society, not for the opportunity of acquiring more things for themselves. In a communistic state, self-interest would cease to exist, for self-interest is destructive of community. In return, individuals would receive life's essentials—food, shelter, medical care, education, and so forth.

In the purely capitalistic free market economy, self-interest occupies center stage. According to Adam Smith, a late 18th-century Scottish philosopher and political economist, the pursuit of self-interest by each individual would ensure the promotion of the welfare of the entire society. People would be led by an "invisible hand" of competition, and the free market would determine the most efficient and equitable outcome.

The nations of the world do not conform exactly to the free market (pure capitalism) or command (pure communism) models. Perhaps the best example of the free market economy is Hong Kong—often considered a capitalistic utopia. With virtually no government regulations, firms are free to engage in unrestrained competition. At the other extreme of the continuum are Soviet Russia, China, and Cuba. In these command economies, the great majority of decisions are made by the government. Long-range plans are made by planning agencies, and these plans determine what, how, and for whom goods and services are produced. In Hong Kong, buyers and sellers meet in the market, each negotiating furiously to obtain the best possible deal on price. In Russia, the market is substantially replaced by planning. All prices are established by the central planning board. There is very little negotiation.[4]

Mixed capitalism *is an economic system in which private decision making is often regulated by government.*

Mixed Capitalism. Under a system of **mixed capitalism,** some of the decisions about what, how, and for whom to produce are made by government. The United States is perhaps the best example, although Canada and Australia qualify as well. Although the profit motive reigns supreme, and individuals have considerable freedom of occupational choice and opportunity to venture into new businesses, government plays a major role in regulating the affairs of private business.

Examples of government regulation are virtually everywhere. If you think of the so-called alphabetic agencies created over the last 100 years, you get a good feel for the scope of such regulations. Consider

---

[4] Markets do exist in Soviet Russia and China, but they play a very small role in the overall economy. Prices are still established by planning boards. Markets serve mainly to allocate available supplies among buyers according to a first-come, first-served queue. Markets in the United States perform this allocation function, but they also provide the important information function by sending signals to buyers and sellers. In Hong Kong, the United States, and Canada, most markets are relatively free of government control. This means that markets transmit information which may be acted upon by buyers and sellers.

the Occupational Safety and Health Administration (OSHA). It inspects and sets standards of health and sanitation across U.S. industry. The Food and Drug Administration (FDA) is responsible for testing all new drugs before they may be prescribed or sold over the counter. It also inspects food-processing plants, such as meat-packing operations, to ensure that the process and the products meet federal standards. And the Environmental Protection Agency (EPA) enforces air, water, and land (solid waste) pollution standards established by federal statute. These and many other agencies and commissions restrict the free market by regulating the manufacture, mining, and processing of goods in the name of the public interest.

In the United States, governmental regulation of business is preferred to governmental ownership, an option that other nations have embraced. Great Britain, for example, has nationalized (and denationalized and renationalized) the coal, steel, gas, and electric industries. (Nationalization is the process by which the government seizes ownership and/or control of the industry.) Such governmental ownership and control of the means of production, if widespread, is often called *socialism*. England, Denmark, and Sweden are three examples of countries in various stages of socialism.

Capitalistic Communism. Although central planning is still paramount, a new wave of economic reforms has been under way for several years in the Soviet Union. Plagued by sluggish economic performance, Premier Gorbachev ushered in sweeping reforms called *perestroika* (restructuring). Concentrating initially on the agricultural sector, Gorbachev aims to boost farm productivity and workers' earnings by permitting the market instead of the Soviet planners to set prices. The plan is to set aside 30 percent or more of total farm output for sale by collective farms, where farmers share in the profits and thus have an incentive to work harder. Similar market-based reforms are planned for manufacturing as well, especially efforts to apply modern technology in the production of civilian and nondefense capital goods. Of course, the success of such reforms largely depends upon the willingness to forgo Soviet preoccupation with military supremacy.

Under Deng Xioping, China has launched even more radical capitalistic reforms of its highly traditional command economy. Like the Soviet Union, China has concentrated its reforms in the agricultural sector. Eschewing the term *free market,* the Chinese describe their efforts as a move toward unregulated markets within a socialist context. Free-market or unregulated, as much as 30 percent of the Chinese economy has been removed from the centralized planning process.

More recently, Vietnam shows signs of rejecting highly centralized planning in favor of greater reliance upon individual decision making and other tenets of free-market capitalism. In 1986, 12 years after the northern and southern parts of Vietnam were unified, the Vietnamese Sixth Party Congress adopted *doi moi,* the Vietnamese word for "renovation" or "change of direction." And the direction is changing in favor of the profit motive.

It is ironic that thirty years after Nikita Khrushchev's famous "We will bury you" speech, several communist nations are looking to the virtues of capitalism and the free market. It is also noteworthy that many in the United States, at the same time, are disgusted by what they see as a lust for profits. The corporate take-over frenzy of the 1980s, highlighted by the $25 billion buyout of RJR-Nabisco, underscores the critics' charge that unbridled greed has replaced a healthy search for efficiency and profits.

Will these reforms succeed? Will China, the Soviet Union, and Vietnam create a capitalistic communism? Will they be able to withstand internal political resistance to these changes? Or are these programs just a flirtation with capitalism? If Yugoslavia is any gauge, they just might succeed.[5]

PRODUCTION POSSIBILITIES AND OPPORTUNITY COST

As you know by now, all nations—regardless of economic system—must answer the fundamental questions of what, how, and for whom to produce. Moreover, all nations must solve the economizing problem. Because economizing involves making choices, and because choices require decisions about alternatives, the concept of opportunity cost becomes important.

Opportunity Cost

You probably did not realize it, but Your Economics Survival Kit has already dealt extensively with opportunity cost. Remember the graph about study time and leisure time? Take a look at the graph on page 22. In this example, for each hour of leisure time chosen, one hour of study time is sacrificed. This is the concept of **opportunity cost:** *sacrifice of*

Opportunity cost *is the sacrifice of the best alternative.*

---

[5] Yugoslavia has blended a totalitarian government and a market-oriented economy. Yugoslavia is a socialist state under Yugoslavian Communist Party control. However, Yugoslavia also has an economic system in which agriculture and most industry are managed by worker cooperatives. Resources are leased by the state to these labor-managed firms which, in turn, make decisions regarding employment, production, pricing, and related matters. After-tax profits are distributed as worker bonuses (so-called *socialist dividends*), loaned to other firms, or used for public improvement projects.

the best alternative. Each hour of study time is measured in terms of leisure time given up (and vice versa). Thus, the opportunity cost of one hour of leisure is one hour of study time. Expressed in more colorful terms, the opportunity cost of more fun is a lower grade point average (GPA) or failing. No wonder economics is called the "dismal science"!

The concept of opportunity cost is very real to the United States Air Force. It costs about $7.5 million to train a pilot for the huge C-5 Galaxy transport plane, yet more than 80 percent of these pilots leave the Air Force after completing their first enlistment (from six to eleven years, depending upon their training). From 1985 to 1988, the Military Airlift Command alone lost over 500 pilots, and very few retired. Where did they go? To find much better-paying jobs with private commercial airlines doing essentially the same work. Although the Air Force plans to offer bonuses up to $12,000 for those who remain in the service through their 14th year, the pilots can still make twice as much with the private airlines. How can the Air Force compete with those kinds of numbers?

Opportunity cost is a concept central to all of economics. Because consumers, businesses, and government agencies are each dealing with the all-pervasive economizing problem, every choice has its opportunity cost.

THINKING IT THROUGH

As you are reading this book, what is your opportunity cost? Leisure? Work? Whatever it is that you can do with your time and money instead of the current activity is your opportunity cost—the best forgone alternative.

Production Possibilities

Opportunity cost is a useful concept because it forces us to evaluate alternatives in the decision-making process. The alternative to more cars (and highways) may be mass transit. Looked at another way, the choice is between private goods (cars) and public goods (mass transit)— goods provided mainly by government.[6] Another way to view this is the

---

[6] Most public goods are provided by governments. National defense, highways, police and fire protection, national parks, and public education are examples of such public goods. They are different from private goods, like chewing gum, in two ways: First, once the public good is provided, it cannot be withheld from anyone. Second, once the good is provided, it may be provided to others at no additional cost.

choice between more automobiles and a cleaner environment. A nation's production possibilities will further illuminate the importance of choice and opportunity cost.

How much can a nation produce? As we have already seen, the productive potential of a nation depends upon its factors of production, its technology, and its method and organization of production—how efficiently the goods are produced. If we begin with the assumption that all of the nation's resources are fully and efficiently employed, and if we limit our analysis to the extreme short run, then the nation's resource base and technology are fixed. This means that if we want more missiles for national defense, we must give up cars, mass transit, or some other item. As the old cliche goes, "There's no such thing as a free lunch."

Production-possibilities curve *illustrates a nation's capabilities to produce.*

Figure 2–2 below depicts a typical **production-possibilities curve.** It should look very similar to the ESSK diagram in Chapter 1.

What's different? First, instead of depicting the inputs—study time and leisure time—the graph illustrates GPA and FUN, the alternative outcomes of your economizing problem. Second, after sleeping, eating,

FIGURE 2–2

Production Possibilities:
GPA versus Fun,
Version 1

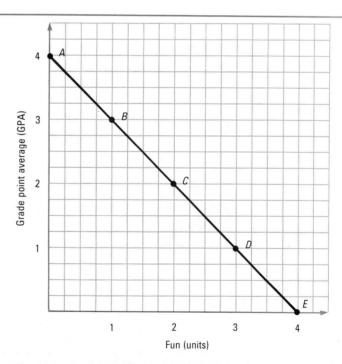

The straight-line *P-P* curve shows all of the possible combinations of GPA and fun. Because Herman is equally efficient in the production of both goods, the *P-P* curve is a straight line (i.e., it has a constant slope). For example, if Herman's current position is at point *C*, he has allocated 4 hours to study and 4 hours to leisure, producing a 2.0 GPA and 2 units of fun. What is Herman's opportunity cost of one additional unit of fun?

and working, you now have only eight hours in the day to devote to the pursuit of FUN or your GPA. The linking rule is now eight (8) hours: the total of FUN time and GPA time must equal eight hours. Your problem is to decide how to allocate the eight hours between these two activities.

According to our assumptions, the entire resource base is fixed. This means that you cannot claim to find more efficient means of studying and thus devote more time to fun. What are your alternatives? At the extreme, you can study eight hours per day and provide no time for fun. At the other extreme, you can party every night and allocate no time to improving your GPA. These extremes, when joined by a straight line, determine your production possibilities. We all know people who have opted for one extreme or the other, and it seems that they are not very happy—at least in the long run.

The opportunity cost of fun is expressed in terms of your GPA: less fun, higher GPA; more fun, lower GPA. For example, assume that you are now at point *B,* allocating six hours per day to studying and two hours per day to fun. The outcomes are a 3.0 GPA and 1 unit of fun. What is your opportunity cost of one more unit of fun? According to the model we have constructed, the opportunity cost of one more unit of fun is a lower GPA (2.0 instead of 3.0).

The production-possibilities curve as drawn shows a constant trade-off between GPA and fun. (Another way of saying this is that the slope of the production-possibilities curve is constant.) This means that the trade-off between fun and GPA is constant all along the frontier. Anywhere along this line, to get one unit of fun, you must give up one point on your GPA.

THINKING IT THROUGH

Is this a realistic assumption? Are you equally efficient in study time and leisure time? Will each extra hour of your study time produce the same increase in GPA?

An alternative to the straight-line production-possibilities curve is illustrated in Figure 2–3. This graph is based on the same economizing problem: how to allocate eight hours between GPA production and fun. What is different is the slope of the frontier. Instead of a straight line, the production-possibilities frontier is bowed out. This means that the opportunity cost of fun in terms of GPA (and GPA in terms of fun) will change all along the curve.

FIGURE 2–3

Production Possibilities:
GPA versus Fun,
Version 2

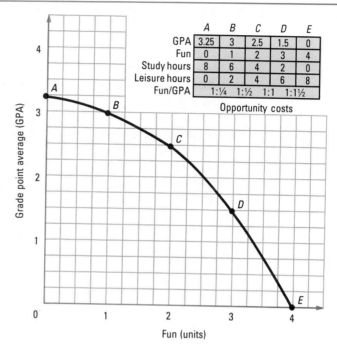

	A	B	C	D	E
GPA	3.25	3	2.5	1.5	0
Fun	0	1	2	3	4
Study hours	8	6	4	2	0
Leisure hours	0	2	4	6	8
Fun/GPA		1:¼	1:½	1:1	1:1½

Opportunity costs

Grade point average (GPA)

Fun (units)

What's different in Version 2? Because the *P-P* curve is bowed out, the slope changes all along the curve. This means that Herman is no longer equally efficient in the production of fun and GPA. As shown in the table, Herman must give up increasing amounts of fun to add an additional point to his GPA.

Version 2 of the GPA-FUN production-possibilities curve may be more realistic for most of us. Although some of us can earn a perfect 4.0 GPA, it is unlikely. In this model, the possibilities at the extreme are 3.25 GPA and 0 fun, and 0 GPA and 4 units of fun. Moreover, the curve is drawn to reflect a new assumption: each extra hour of time devoted to studying will produce increased GPA, but at a decreasing rate. Another way of saying the same thing is that one must give up increasingly greater GPA points in order to get an additional unit of fun. This is known as the *law of increasing opportunity cost*. Let's see how this works.

First, assume that we begin again at point *B*, this time with a 3.0 GPA and 1 unit of fun. To have one more unit of fun, the opportunity cost is only a one-half point reduction in GPA (movement from *B* to *C*). Not bad! But what if you decide to really party tonight, increasing fun to three units? As you can see from the graph, your GPA will fall to 1.5. What's going on? Instead of a constant opportunity cost, the trade-off is getting worse. If you look at this relationship going in the other direction—moving up the curve instead of down the curve—you still experience increasing opportunity cost. As you forgo each unit of fun, your GPA increases, but by smaller and smaller increments. Starting at point E, with a 0 GPA and 4 units of fun, you decide to sacrifice 1 unit of fun for a higher GPA. The opportunity cost of the increased GPA (1.5) is 1 unit of fun (from E to D). Elated at the improved GPA, you decide to give up an additional unit of fun. This time, the sacrifice of 1 fun unit also increases your GPA. However, this time the GPA rises by only a single point, from 1.5 to 2.5. What GPA improvement can you make in moving from C to B? Why does the GPA increase, but at a decreasing rate?

Moving from E to D, from D to C, and from C to B resulted in an increased GPA, but each increase was smaller than the previous one. Why? In answering this question, we need to go back to the original assumptions of the production-possibilities model, that is, the shape of the curve. In other words, why is there a curve instead of a straight line? Devoting less time to fun and more time to study is very efficient and productive when the combination is eight hours of leisure time and zero hours of study time. You can still relax enough with four hours of time devoted to leisure. However, the more time given up from leisure for study, the less efficient you become in your studying. The old adage "All work and no play makes Jack a dull boy" may have some truth to it! What balance between study time and leisure time, between GPA production and fun works best for you?

The following case further illustrates the concept of increasing opportunity cost. As you read this case, think of how and why some resources allocated to environmental quality (pollution reduction) may be unsuitable for the production of other goods.

CASE
• IN •
POINT

Environmental Quality versus GNP

Situation: A Public Issues Forum

Issue: Should We Formulate a National Policy on Environmental Quality?

Forum Participants: Reginald Ashby, Public Relations Officer for American Steel Corporation; Joan Menendez, Director of Consumer Affairs, Americans United Against Pollution; and William Washington, News Correspondent, "America Today."

William Washington, News Correspondent for "America Today," opened the forum with two questions to the participants: "Just how serious is the U.S. pollution problem? What should be done?"

"Sure we have pollution. To live is to pollute," responded Reginald Ashby, the spokesperson for American Steel Corporation. "Everyone knows that we cannot have absolutely pure air and water. The cost would be horrendous! We must live with the reality that production and consumption necessarily entail a degree of pollution. Further reduce pollution and we will only reduce production, consumption, and our standard of living."

"I couldn't disagree more," replied Joan Menendez, the Director of Consumer Affairs with Americans United Against Pollution. "To say that living is polluting is nothing but a cop-out. Of course we all pollute, but this begs the question. The real issue is what can be done to improve our quality of life. We're not talking about a soda can thrown from a car window or a cigarette butt smashed on the sidewalk. We are talking about the air we breathe and the water we drink. The nation's corporations seem to think that they can dump poisonous wastes from industrial plants at will. Even cities, which are responsible for enforcing pollution abatement laws, are guilty of dumping raw sewage into our lakes and rivers."

Questions to Consider

1. *Draw a production-possibilities graph illustrating the alternatives of GNP (all other goods) on the vertical axis and environmental quality (pollution prevention) on the horizontal axis. Should the production-possibilities curve be a straight line or curvilinear? Why?*

2. *Mr. Ashby argues that we must sacrifice consumer goods and live with a reduced standard of living if we take steps to clean up our environment. Ms. Menendez suggests that no such trade-off is necessary. Even if a decline in living standards will occur, she seems to be saying that it is a necessary price to pay for clean air and water. Must society choose between more production and consumption on the one hand and increased environmental quality on the other? Why or why not?*

The production-possibilities model is useful because it enables us to examine alternatives and the opportunity costs associated with choices. However, like all models, it suffers from basic limitations imposed by the assumptions—in this case, the assumptions regarding a fixed resource base, which is fully and efficiently employed and fixed technology. If we relax these assumptions, however, we can show the gains from population growth, improved and new technology, and more efficient methods of organizing production. Figure 2–4 below illustrates production possibilities over time.

Figure 2–4 illustrates economic growth, shown as a shift of the production-possibilities frontier from PP_1 to PP_2 (from 1982 to 1990). Because of an increasing population and labor force, a higher percentage of people working, and improved technology, the United States is capable of producing more of both private and public goods. In other words, in the long run (if we relax the assumptions of the model), we are free of the onerous implications of opportunity cost. Of course, we still must choose whether we want to be at point C, point D, or point E. What determines where society lands (at which combination of private and public goods)?

The PP_1 curve illustrates the combination of public and private goods which the United States was capable of producing in 1982. However, 1982 was a recession year: the 9.7 percent unemployment rate far exceeded the U.S. average jobless rate of about 6 percent. As a result, the United States was actually located at point A (or some similar point)

FIGURE 2–4

Production Possibilities: Public versus Private Goods

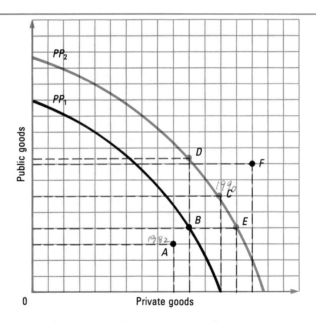

In 1982, PP₁ shows the alternative combinations of public and private goods, assuming full employment of the factors of production. 1982 was a recession year, however, and the U.S. operated inside its *P-P* curve at point *A*, instead of realizing its potential at point *B*. By 1990, with a larger labor force and advanced technology, the United States was capable of producing at point *C* on PP₂. What does point *D* represent? Can the United States reach point *D* today, assuming that the year is not yet 1990?

inside the production-possibilities curve. Point *A* represents inefficient use of resources; the United States was not able to reach its production possibilities. What about point *F*? If the year is 1990 and we are operating at point *C*, can the United States produce at point *F*? Why or why not?

Figure 2–5 illustrates a fundamental choice every society must make in resource allocation. Production of consumer goods, such as household appliances and video games, takes resources away from the production of capital goods, machinery, and equipment which promise to make both capital and consumer goods production more efficient and to increase economic growth.

In order to demonstrate this, we show two different starting points: *A* and *C* on *PP*₁. If society is located at point *A*, it has chosen to devote the great majority of its resources to consumer goods production and only a minimal amount to capital formation. As its resource base expands over time, it experiences modest economic growth, winding up at point *B* on *PP*₂. By comparison, if society forgoes more current consumption in favor of increased capital goods production, shown as point *C* on *PP*₂, it will experience greater economic growth. In this case, it

FIGURE 2–5
Capital and Consumer
Goods and Economic
Growth

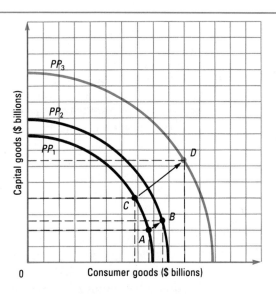

Economic growth is represented by movements from *A* to *B* and from *C* to *D*. If society devotes more resources to capital goods today (point *C* on *PP*₁, rather than point *A*), then greater economic growth will result. (Compare point *D* on *PP*₃ and point *B* on *PP*₂.) The arrows show the growth paths.

will land at some point such as *D* on PP_3. Thus, if more consumer goods and fewer capital goods are produced, then society will realize more of each good in the future. In response to the challenge presented by the Soviet Union's space program in the late 1950s (Sputnik), the United States launched a major space initiative. The investment of such resources paid off handsomely in the form of new technologies, not to mention joining the Soviets in manned space exploration.

Of course, choosing which combination of capital and consumer goods involves a delicate balance of private and public decision making. Just what the appropriate mixture of capital and consumer goods should be is also very difficult to determine. We know that more investment in capital goods today will pay off in the years ahead. However, such a decision requires people to live with fewer consumer goods today. Conversely, shifting resources away from capital formation will result in more consumer goods. Consumers in the Soviet Union, for example, have complained bitterly that too few resources are allocated to consumer goods, resulting in terrible shortages and long lines for such staples as shoes and bread. Indeed, widespread consumer dissatisfaction is partly responsible for the reforms undertaken in recent years.

MICROECONOMICS AND MACROECONOMICS

Microeconomics *is the study of the individual units that make up the economy.*

Macroeconomics *is the study of the performance of the total economy.*

The production-possibilities model is also useful in understanding the differences between macroeconomics and microeconomics. The study of economics is broken down into two distinct branches—micro and macro. **Microeconomics** is the study of the individual units that make up the economy—business firms, labor unions, households, and so forth. **Macroeconomics** is the study of the big picture—the performance of the total economy. The analogy to a jigsaw puzzle is often helpful. The individual pieces of the puzzle are to microeconomics as the completed puzzle is to macroeconomics. Please do not think for a moment, however, that any jigsaw puzzle is as complicated as the macro- or microeconomy. After all, there is a finite number of pieces to every jigsaw puzzle.

Figure 2–4 may be used to understand the differences between micro and macro. At point *A* in 1982, the U.S. economy was operating inside its production-possibilities curve. A macroeconomic question is how to move the economy to its potential or how to stimulate the economy to reach its production possibilities. Once at point *B*, however, the United States is operating on its frontier. It cannot do more. However, it can produce a different mixture of public and private goods, and this is a microeconomic decision.

Fallacy of composition *error is assuming that what is true for the part is also true for the whole.*

Understanding the difference between macroeconomics and microeconomics is often a matter of logic. Policymakers sometimes make an error in logical reasoning known as a **fallacy of composition** error—assuming that what is true for the part (the individual firm, for example) is also true for the whole (the entire economy). Let's use a simple example to see how this fallacy works. Imagine that you are at a football game. It is the fourth quarter and the game is tied. It is "fourth and ten" and your team is on the opponent's 20-yard line. The ball is snapped, the quarterback fades back, and you stand up to see better. Therefore, if everyone stands up, everyone will see better. Right? If you've been to ball games, you know this is wrong. What is true for the individual (the micro part) is not necessarily true for the group (the macro).

Economics is full of such fallacies, and many are the result of not understanding the difference between micro and macro. One additional example more apropos to this course involves farming. Agriculture is a very competitive industry despite extensive governmental involvement in the form of subsidies and other aid. Farmers are interested in making profits in their operations, but how do farmers increase their incomes? Generally, they plant more crops and try to sell more. Thus, if Farmer Brown increases production in order to make more money, all farmers will make more money by increasing production. This is a common example of the fallacy of composition.[7]

Post hoc fallacy *is the faulty assumption that if event A precedes event B, then event A is the cause of event B.*

Another logical error is called the **post hoc fallacy:** if event A precedes event B, then event A is the cause of event B. A simple example illustrates this common fallacy. If an employer gives a bonus to an employee in recognition of superior work, and the employee's productivity subsequently declines, the employer reasons that the bonus has caused complacency, a loss of interest in work, and a decrease in output. Although this is possible, there are many other variables that could explain the change in performance. Another example: in an effort to escalate the coming of spring, each March or April you journey to the mountaintop with friends and hold a spring ritual. It has never failed; springtime arrives within weeks. Obviously, your ritual has caused spring to arrive!

The post hoc fallacy basically illustrates sloppy thinking. Merely because one event or action precedes another, there is no solid basis for

---

[7] What is true for Farmer Brown is not true for all farmers. If most or all farmers increase their output, then supply will increase. Assuming that demand remains unchanged, the increased supply will create a surplus of the good and depress prices and incomes for all farmers. This is the dilemma faced by farmers and one of the main reasons for government assistance in the form of subsidies, acreage retirement plans, and other aid.

arguing that one causes the other. However, the tendency of people to find simple, albeit incorrect, causes of particular outcomes, requires economists to develop theories which may be tested. In this way, we can ascertain the difference between cause-and-effect relationships and mere correlations.

ECONOMIC MODELS AND THEORIES

Theory and **model** are terms referring to sets of propositions based upon assumptions.

The production-possibilities graphs with which you have been working are examples of economic models (sometimes called theories). What are models? Theories? **Theory** and **model** are terms referring to sets of propositions based upon assumptions. Propositions are statements which define and describe relationships between the variables involved.

The production-possibilities model, like all models, has a number of propositions. First, if a nation is operating on its production-possibilities frontier, any decision to produce more of one good will result in a decrease in the production of other goods. In other words, the nation cannot have more of each. This is the essence of scarcity. Second, again operating on the production-possibilities frontier, each decision to produce more of one good will involve an increasingly greater sacrifice of other goods. This is known as the law of increasing cost. These two propositions are valid to the extent that a set of assumptions remains true. First, all resources are fixed in supply. (Another way of saying the same thing is that the time period under consideration is so short that resources may not be varied.) Second, all resources are fully and efficiently employed. This means that the nation is operating on the production-possibilities frontier. Third, technology and the method and organization of production are fixed; thus, there can be no changes made in production.

All theories and models have two major characteristics: they are abstractions and generalizations. An *abstraction* is a statement which is removed from reality—the real world in which we live. The production-possibilities model is abstract because it simplifies reality by assuming that resources and technology are fixed. The real world is just too complex to describe and explain with a single theory. A *generalization* is a statement which is so broad that it may be applied to a great number of and types of situations. If the production-possibilities model is sufficiently general, the model has the capability of describing and explaining a wide range of cases. Moreover, the more general the model, the more abstract it is. For example, the production-possibilities model would be less abstract if it could be applied only to one country, but it cannot be both country specific and general.

Economists often use the words *model, theory, law,* and *principle* interchangeably. *Whenever you see one of these words, it means a set of abstract and general propositions based upon assumptions.* As you read this book, you will encounter many more economic theories (laws, principles, and models). Because many of these employ a common set of assumptions regarding economic behavior, it is useful to examine what they are and what they mean.

Assumptions

Self-interest *is the idea that we make decisions which benefit ourselves.*

Two fundamental assumptions common to nearly all economic theories and principles are self-interest and rationality. First, individual behavior is guided by **self-interest**—the idea that we make decisions which benefit ourselves (or, alternatively, that the benefits of some action exceed the costs). This is not to suggest that all people are greedy and do not consider others. On the contrary, self-interest means only that each person seeks to satisfy his or her wants, whatever they may be.

Rational *behavior means that people seek the greatest expected return from each decision.*

Second, economic behavior is rational. In economics, **rational** behavior means that people seek the greatest expected return from each decision. This means that we prefer more to less, and thus we try to maximize satisfaction, however measured.

The following case addresses each of these assumptions.

CASE
▪ IN ▪
POINT

Your Economic Behavior

Are you self-interested and rational? Economists think so! The table shown below illustrates the dollar payoffs in a game. You are Player X and you are playing the game with or against Player Y. Columns A and B contain the payoffs from the two times when the game is played. Rows I through V are the alternative strategies in playing the game. Each cell contains a pair of numbers in parentheses. The first number in the parentheses is your payoff; the second number is Player Y's payoff. This is all you know about the game.

Two-Person Game
Player Y

	A	B
I	(6,5)	(5,4)
II	(5,5)	(4,4)
III	(4,-1)	(4,-2)
IV	(3,6)	(4,5)
V	(1,1)	(3,4)

Questions to Consider

1. Review the various strategies, I through V. Which one do you select in playing both games, A and B? (Choose only one strategy for both games.)

2. What does your strategy suggest about your economic behavior? Which strategy is the self-interested, rational strategy? Which strategy implies a preference for equality? What does strategy III mean?[8]

What is really interesting about this game is *why* you chose a particular strategy (and rejected the others), not which strategy you selected. In making your decision, you examined the alternatives, evaluated the payoffs, and acted on limited information. We make such decisions nearly every day.

THE LAW OF COMPARATIVE ADVANTAGE

Nowhere is choice more important than in deciding what kind of job to take. Because we are not endowed with the talent and skills to do all things equally well, we must choose in which economic activity (occupation) to specialize. And, much like the GPA versus FUN example, in which the decision to have more fun involved an increasingly lower GPA, the choice of one kind of work over another also involves important cost conditions. Let's look at an example.

---

[8] Which strategy you select is governed chiefly by your values. Also important is how you play the game. For example, as Player X, you were told to play the game with or against Y. Did you think of making an agreement with Y to share the payoffs? Or did you automatically assume that cooperation was not part of the game? These assumptions about how to play the game, as well as the particular strategy to adopt, are guided by ingrained values; thus there is no correct strategy to the game. With these comments in mind, let's analyze the various strategies.

Strategy I is regarded as the self-interested and rational strategy. Why? The combination of payoffs maximizes your total return. Even though Player Y does relatively well, to be truly self-interested and rational means that you do not consider the returns to Y. Selecting strategy II implies that you are more interested in equality of payoffs than in choosing that which provides the most for you. Choosing strategy III suggests that you are more interested in receiving more than Y receives than you are in what you get. Unlike strategy I, strategy III maximizes the difference between X and Y. The implication is a revealed preference for inequality. Finally, selecting either strategy IV or V probably means that you do not fully understand the rules of the game. One interpretation of strategy IV is that you are more altruistic than self-interested and rational. Strategy V implies that you are minimizing your payoffs, and this suggests that you are neither self-interested nor rational.

TABLE 2–1
Production Possibilities and Comparative Advantage

Daily Output	MUTT		JEFF	
	A	**B**	**C**	**D**
Photographs	18	0	20	0
Trees trimmed	0	3	0	4

Table 2–1 illustrates the daily production of photographs and trees trimmed for Mutt and Jeff.

In a full day's work, Mutt can produce 18 photographs and do no tree trimming, or he can trim three trees and produce no photographs. Jeff, on the other hand, can trim four trees or produce 20 photographs. Because Jeff's daily output is greater than Mutt's for each service, Jeff has an *absolute advantage*. Does this mean that Jeff should produce both photos and tree trimming services? In order to answer this question, we need to examine the cost conditions for each producer.

Let's begin with Mutt producing combination A, 18 photos and zero trees. Mutt then decides to cut trees instead. What is Mutt's cost of trimming each tree? For each tree trimmed, Mutt must give up six photographs. What about Jeff? If Jeff stopped photography in favor of tree trimming, his cost would be five photographs per tree trimmed. Because Jeff's cost per tree is lower than Mutt's cost (5:1 versus 6:1), Jeff has a *comparative advantage* in tree trimming.

What about photography? Since Mutt's cost of each photograph is one-sixth of a tree, and Jeff's cost per photograph is one-fifth of a tree, Mutt's cost is lower and thus he has a comparative advantage in photography.

The **law of comparative advantage** says that a person (business or nation) should *produce that good or service for which the costs of production are least, measured in terms of opportunity cost.* In Mutt's case, the opportunity cost of producing photographs is expressed in trimmed trees, a ratio of one photo gained for one-sixth of a tree lost. Jeff's cost is slightly higher: he gains one photo for each one-fifth of a tree trimming sacrificed. Even though Jeff is able to produce more of both goods on an absolute basis, Mutt is comparatively more productive in photography.

*The **law of comparative advantage** says that a person (business or nation) should produce that good or service for which the production costs are least, in terms of opportunity cost.*

THINKING IT THROUGH

Does the theory of comparative advantage conform to the characteristics of theories (or models) discussed earlier? Is is abstract? Is it general? What assumptions are evident?

IMPORTANT
TERMS TO
REMEMBER

capital, p. 33
command economy, p. 35
economic resources, p. 33
economic system, p. 34
economizing problem, p. 33
entrepreneurship, p. 34
fallacy of composition, p. 49
free market economy, p. 35
labor, p. 33
land, p. 33
law of comparative advantage,
    p. 53

macroeconomics, p.48
microeconomics, p. 48
mixed capitalism, p. 37
model, p. 50
opportunity cost, p. 39
post hoc fallacy, p. 49
production-possibilities curve,
    p. 41
rational, p. 51
self-interest, p. 51
theory, p. 50

CHAPTER
SUMMARY

1. All nations face the same economizing problem: how to allocate scarce resources among competing and unlimited wants.

2. Economic resources (also called factors of production) are divided into three categories: land, labor, and capital. Land refers to all non-man-made resources, such as timber in forests, bodies of water, and minerals in the earth. Labor is all mental and physical effort, ranging from un-skilled and semi-skilled labor to corporate management. Capital is every-thing else, specifically productive assets (machinery, equipment, and buildings), such as drill presses, trucks, computers, and unfinished and finished goods inventory. Entrepreneurship is the fourth economic re-source—the risk-taking role played by owners and employers of resources.

3. Economic systems refer to the specific ways that nations organized re-sources to answer three fundamental economic questions: what to pro-duce, how to produce, and for whom to produce.

4. Economic systems range from command economies (like Russia and China) to market economies (like Hong Kong and Liechtenstein). Mixed economies, like the United States, Australia, and Canada, lie somewhere in between the extremes of market and command.

5. Command economies are characterized by highly centralized decision making, limited economic freedoms, and greatly restricted consumer choice. Government answers the what, how, and for whom questions. In free market economies, the government plays a limited role. Decisions about what, how, and for whom to produce are made in the marketplace where supply and demand rule. Mixed economies are hybrids. They com-bine the features of command and free market economies, and they are marked by extensive government regulation of business.

6. The production-possibilities curve illustrates a nation's capabilities to produce, assuming full employment of resources and fixed technology. Excessive unemployment and/or inefficient use of resources is shown as a point inside the production-possibilities curve.

7. The opportunity cost of producing more of one good is expressed in terms of other goods given up. Moreover, the opportunity cost increases as more and more of a good is produced. For example, as society shifts more and more resources into defense goods, it must give up increasingly greater amounts of nondefense goods.

8. Production possibilities for individuals and nations also reveal the law of comparative advantage. This important principle tells us that people will produce those goods and services which cost least, measured in terms of opportunity cost. Even if you can produce more of everything compared to someone else, the law of comparative advantage shows how someone else can produce one of the goods cheaper in relative terms.

DISCUSSION AND REVIEW QUESTIONS

1. Gerald Ford served as president of the United States from 1974 to 1976 following the Watergate scandal and the resignation of President Nixon. Struggling with the severe wheat shortage, OPEC's oil embargo, and an inflationary recession, Ford initiated a campaign to make the United States self-sufficient. He decreed that the United States should do everything in its power to free itself of dependency on imported resources. In light of the theory of comparative advantage, was Gerald Ford "barking up the wrong tree"? Can any nation become self-sufficient in all production? Why or why not? Explain.

2. "Capitalism unleashes huge pressures for change: the profit motive and the threat of bankruptcy. Can a line be drawn between unworthy lust and a worthy incentive?"[9] Do you think it is possible to separate the virtues and vices of capitalism, any more than we can with socialism and communism?

3. Shown below is BETA's production-possibilities table illustrating six of the possible combinations of educational services and defense production (measured in billion of dollars). Using this data, draw a production-possibilities graph with defense on the horizontal axis and education on the vertical axis. Label each point, *A* (0,80), *B* (20,75), etc.

Beta's Production Possibilities Table

	A	B	C	D	E	F
Education	0	20	50	65	75	80
Defense	80	75	60	40	20	0

4. Assume that this production-possibilities curve represents BETA's capacity to produce education and defense in 1990. BETA is currently operating at point *B* ($75 billion of defense and $20 billion of education).

---

[9] Robert Samuelson, "The Irony of Capitalism," *Newsweek*, January 9, 1989, p. 44.

    a. What is BETA's opportunity cost of providing an additional $30 bil-
lion of educational services—moving from point *B* to point *C*? From
point *C* to point *D*? From *D* to *E*?

    b. Explain why BETA must sacrifice an increasingly greater amount of
defense for each additional unit of education.

    c. Locate a new combination of $50 billion of defense and $40 billion of
education. Label this point *G*. What does position imply about
BETA's utilization of its resources?

    d. The year is 2000. BETA's labor force has increased by 25 percent,
and several new technological changes have made its production of
defense and education much more efficient. Draw a new production-
possibilities curve representing BETA in the year 2000.

5. Explain in what way the following statements are fallacies of
composition.

    a. "What's good for GM is good for the country!"

    b. "Chronic long-term unemployment is impossible. If more people are
looking for work than businesses want to hire, wages will fall. Ultimately, lower wages will induce businesses to hire more workers, thus
restoring full employment."

6. Table 2–1 shows that Jeff outproduces Mutt in both goods, tree trimming
and photography. How can Mutt have a comparative advantage in
photography?

A BRIEF LOOK AHEAD	

A BRIEF LOOK AHEAD

Having established the nature of economic systems and how they work
in general terms, the next chapter delves into the finer points of market
behavior. Chapter 3 is devoted to an examination of how a market
works. Supply and demand are explored in detail.

    The next chapter is pivotal. Because so much of the U.S. economy
(and other relatively free market economies) is rooted in the marketplace and the interaction between buyers and sellers, this material is
extremely important to all other chapters. If you were to decide what
single chapter is most important in your introductory course in economics, this is it!

The Market Economy:
A Micro View

Bob Daemmrich/ Stock, Boston

The purpose of this chapter is to present the basics of supply and demand. The emphasis is on graphical analysis, so pay close attention to the graphs. Many examples will be used so that you will be able to apply the principles to any market situation.

In addition to the supply and demand graphs, terminology is very important. Be on the lookout for the difference between a *change in quantity demanded* and a *change in demand* (and a *change in quantity supplied* versus a *change in supply*). These are often confused.

After completion of this chapter, you should be able to do the following:

1. Draw a general supply and demand graph, label the axes, and create a scale for each axis.
2. Distinguish between a movement along a demand curve or a supply curve and a shift of the curve(s).
3. Describe and explain why free market prices tend to gravitate toward equilibrium.
4. Use supply and demand graphs to analyze market conditions such as rent controls and minimum wages.

Markets Everywhere!

John Edwards arrived home late one night after a hard day's work. John is 66 years young and a retired union plumber. That's right, retired—so to speak! When he discovered that his social security benefits and pension guaranteed a lifestyle slightly above the poverty level, he decided to launch his own business.

"Why not offer bargain plumbing repair services to retired people like ourselves?" John asked his wife Susan a few years ago. And so the business began—and thrived! Within a few months, John had more business than he could handle. Never a workaholic, however, John managed to control how many jobs he took on. "Just enough to supplement the retirement benefits," Susan reminded him.

The Internal Revenue Service (IRS) doesn't know of John's work, and they never will if John has anything to say about it. Why? "I was hopping mad when I discovered that my social security benefits would be reduced by 50 cents for every dollar I earned in retirement in excess of $8,150." Scrupulous in reporting every dime of income—even in the moonlighting days when his kids were in college—John decided that this was too much to bear.

John is a participant in a common but illegal market transaction. Ironically, his problem and solution may even be understood and supported by some of you. However, for John and the thousands like him, the IRS does not empathize! Not reporting earned income is classified as fraud. Illegal or not, risky or perfectly safe, John's underground activity is an example of a market transaction in which something of value (one's income) is given up to gain something of value (e.g., a toilet that works).

MARKETS AND COMPETITION

A market is a place where buyers and sellers meet for exchange.

A **market** is a place where buyers and sellers meet for the purpose of exchange. When John sells his plumbing services in the underground economy, he receives an income—an expenditure to the householder paying in cash. When you run to the local store for a gallon of milk, you are a consumer (or buyer). Economists often say that grocery shoppers and people in need of plumbing services are on the demand side of the transaction. The grocers and plumbers are the sellers and are on the supply side of the transaction.

Gallons of milk, loaves of bread, and liters of soda are usually bought at a premium at the neighborhood market. You may be willing to pay more, mainly because it is convenient (it saves time). However, ask yourself what you would do if there were two or three stores located close to your home. Would you shop (look for the lowest price) at two or more stores? Or would you even want to shop for the best buy? Probably not.

Competition *exists when two or more sellers share the same market.*

The presence of more than one local store introduces the important role of competition. **Competition** exists when two or more sellers share the same market (prospective buyers), each vying for consumers' dollars. With two or more competitors so close, it is likely that each is very aware of his or her competitors' prices. Accordingly, prices among the stores probably will be very close, if not identical. Another example of price competition occurs among two or more gas stations located at the same intersection.

Competition also exists on the demand side—two or more consumers vying for the available products. Generally speaking, the more sellers facing a given number of buyers, the lower the product price. Conversely, the more buyers facing a given number of sellers, the higher the product price. If there is only one local grocery store, prices are likely to be higher. Perhaps you have experienced the sinking feeling when, pulling into the only gas station in town to "fill-er-up," you discover that the price per gallon is fifty cents higher than you usually pay.

We have looked briefly at two different markets—groceries and underground plumbing services—one legal and one illegal. Before we examine the mechanics of the marketplace with the tools of supply and demand, consider the following CASE-IN-POINT about a really hot market.

CASE
• IN •
POINT

One Hundred Dollar Sneakers?

Brightly colored sneakers in hundreds of different designs and youths wearing unmatched or unlaced sneakers—have you seen these fashions lately? They started in the inner-city neighborhoods of New York City. Remember the "boom box" portable stereos that spread from inner-city neighborhoods all across the United States? Well, we're in the middle of another trendy and contagious fad: high-fashion sneakers.

No longer are athletic shoes just for athletics. Inner-city youths across the United States are buying high-priced sneakers at a record-setting pace. Why the sales explosion? Brian Washington, an 18-year-old Harlem youth, explains his collection of 150 pairs: "A man's got to have style, or he's half a man. The fact is, in the inner city you are what you wear—on your feet." And Reebok, Nike, Converse, Avia, and other athletic footwear firms are cashing in on the style-conscious youths. Retail sales of athletic shoes reached nearly $10 billion in 1988, double 1982's sales.

Gone are the days of the drab and conventional $25 black or white athletic shoe. While the plain high-top or low-top shoe is still produced, it's the $100-a-pair Nike Airwalkers, Evolvo 830s, Air Jordans, Alphas, and Revolutions that are getting all the attention. They've got style. How long the fashion will last and what new designs and colors the sneaker will take is anyone's guess. But for now, the colorful and pricey sneaker is as popular as Nintendo's "Two Mario Brothers."[1]

Questions to Consider

1.   The tennis shoe companies have gone to great lengths to identify exactly the type of shoes teenagers want. Extensive market surveys, product prototypes, and paying teenagers to attend week-long seminars and conferences to discuss and evaluate the latest trends and products are commonplace in this lucrative market.

Does all this market strategy mean that the consumer is not sovereign? Has business replaced the market with planning? Or are businesses merely responding to consumer tastes and preferences?

2.   Companies hope that the fashion spreads to the much larger and potentially even more lucrative white teenage market. But if this happens, will black and Hispanic teenagers still buy the product? If white youths begin to emulate black and Hispanic youths, will the latter just move on to another trend which they regard as uniquely theirs?

If the foregoing case seems to be too far removed from reality, consider the meteoric success of the IBM personal computer (PC) and the subsequent growth of the PC clone market.

The first IBM personal computer with a 10 megabyte (MB) hard disk sold for $3,500 in 1983. It was targeted to the business market, and businesses bought IBMs like there was no tomorrow. IBM produced a machine with what is known as *open architecture*—internal parts (microprocessor chip and circuitry) which could easily be copied without violation of copyright. You've heard of the old saying—"Give 'em an inch and they'll take a mile." Well, that is a mild understatement of the microcomputer revolution which ensued.

The innovation-imitation cycle had begun. Compaq, AT&T, ITT, Epson, PC's Limited (now Dell), Leading Edge, to name a few, not only produced compatible machines (machines that would run the same software produced for the IBM), but they also sold them at half to two

---

[1] "The Well-Heeled: Pricey-Sneakers Worn In Inner City Help Set Nation's Fashion Trend," *The Wall Street Journal,* December 1, 1988, pp. A1, A6.

thirds the IBM price. The scale of production had been expanded, enabling firms to cut prices dramatically and still realize a healthy profit. By 1987, prices of the original IBM 10 MB machine had fallen to $1,750. And other manufacturers were still undercutting IBM by 25 percent.

IBM had nearly 50 percent of the personal computer market in 1983. That market share fell to 30 percent by 1988. A revolution had occurred.

THE LAW OF DEMAND

Millions of people bought personal computers because the price had fallen within their idea of what was reasonable. And prices could fall because firms were producing a product whose costs of production declined as the firms increased output.[2]

*The **law of demand** states that there is an inverse relationship between quantity demanded and price.*

The **law of demand** states that there is an inverse relationship between quantity demanded and price, other things being equal; that is, as the price of personal computers declined, the quantity demanded of PCs increased, other things being equal. The converse is also true: as price increases, the quantity demanded will decrease, other things being equal.

The law of demand holds true for all markets, for goods and services, and for economic resources. Consider the market for legal services. In many cities, there is a surplus of lawyers. Increased competition has motivated many enterprising lawyers to advertise their services at cut-rate prices, much to the dismay of established law firms. People who have never before considered legal services for wills, divorces, and real estate transactions have begun to hire these lawyers. Prices are lower, and more legal services are rendered.

Consider the market for lumber. Forest fires caused by one of the worst droughts in history destroyed a substantial portion of timber resources in the summer of 1988. The result was much higher lumber prices and a corresponding decrease in the amount of lumber demanded (for home repair and new construction).

Consider the market for dental care. As more U.S. employers offered dental insurance as part of standard fringe benefits, people visited their dentists more frequently. Why? Insurance made dental care accessible on a more regular basis by effectively reducing the direct price of dental care to those covered. Or consider the automobile market. Dealer incentives in the form of rebates, reduced financing charges, and special add-on no-cost features greatly increase sales. Such incentives probably

---

[2] Prices of memory chips, like the 256 RAM chip, fell by over 50 percent within a few months in 1986, only to be followed by further rounds of price cutting as the Japanese came to dominate the industry.

caused people to buy new cars sooner than they otherwise would have elected to do.

In order to examine this price-quantity relationship more closely, let's look at the market for diet soda. The following table lists the quantity of six-packs of diet soda bought at various prices during the month of July 1989. The relationship illustrates the law of demand: at higher prices, the store sold fewer six-packs; at lower prices, people bought more six-packs. For example, at a price of $2.50 consumers purchased 25 six-packs; at a price of $2.00, consumers bought 100 six-packs. The quantity demanded thus varies inversely with price, other things being equal.

Beware treacherous terminology! The entire table or schedule of quantities bought at corresponding prices is called **demand.** The word demand refers to total market sales—quantities sold at all prices, not just what is bought at a specific price. **Quantity demanded** (Qd) is the term used to refer to a specific amount bought at a specific price (e.g., 100 six-packs at a price of $2 per six-pack). This distinction may seem trivial, but it is all important. Remember the difference.

The same information may be illustrated on a graph, where the relationship between price and quantity demanded is even more clear. Note that price is always measured on the vertical axis and quantity on the horizontal axis.

The data from the table are plotted in pairs: 250 and $1.25 (point *F*); 200 and $1.50 (point *E*); 150 and $1.75 (point *D*); 100 and $2.00 (point *C*); 50 and $2.25 (point *B*); and 25 and $2.50 (point *A*). Once the coordinates are plotted, the points are connected to get the demand curve. Note also how the axes are labeled: Price per six-pack and six-packs per month.

Demand refers to the entire table or schedule of quantities bought at corresponding prices.

Quantity demanded is the term used to refer to a specific amount bought at a specific price.

Movement along the Demand Curve

If the price is reduced from $2.50 to $2.25, what happens to the number of six-packs sold? Because this is a relationship between only two variables, if one changes, then the other must change. Therefore, if the price

---

TABLE 3–1

Demand Schedule for
Diet Soda (six-packs per
Month, July 1989)

Price	Quantity Demanded
$2.50	25
2.25	50
2.00	100
1.75	150
1.50	200
1.25	250

The table (demand schedule) shows the relationship between price and quantity demanded. The law of demand states that quantity demanded varies inversely with price, other things being equal. In other words, as price decreases, quantity demanded increases, and vice versa.

FIGURE 3–1

Demand for Diet Soda
(six-packs per Month,
July 1989)

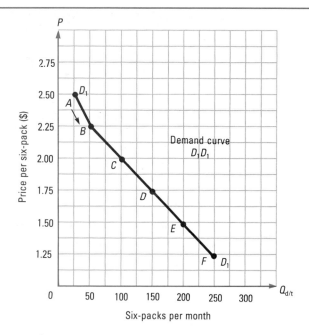

This figure shows the inverse relationship between price (P) and quantity demanded (Q_d). As P ↓ from \$2.50 to \$2.25 (point A to point B), the Q_d ↑ from 25 to 50 six-packs. The movement along the demand curve from A to B is called an increase in quantity demanded.

falls from \$2.50 to \$2.25, then the quantity demanded increases from 25 to 50. Because quantity demanded is the dependent variable (it depends upon price), the causation always goes from price to quantity, and not vice versa. This **change in quantity demanded** is shown as a *movement along* the existing demand curve from point A to point B. Now let's look at the difference between a movement along the demand curve (a change in the quantity demanded) and a shift of the demand curve (a change in demand).

Change in quantity demanded *is shown as a movement along the existing demanded curve, from point to point.*

Shift of the Demand Curve

Determinants of demand *include income, tastes and preferences, prices and availability of related goods or services, expectations about prices and income, and number of consumers.*

Remember that the law of demand is qualified with the phrase "other things being equal." Those other things, or **determinants of demand,** are important aspects of market conditions. These determinants are grouped into five categories.

The Determinants of Demand

1. Income
2. Tastes and preferences

3. Prices and availability of related goods or services
   a. Substitutes (coffee and tea; butter and margarine)
   b. Complements (coffee and doughnuts; bread and butter)
4. Expectations about prices and income
5. Number of consumers

Each demand curve is a reflection of these market conditions. Naturally, if market conditions change, you would expect demand to change as well. For example, if your income increases, you will buy more goods and services. Conversely, if your income declines, you will buy less.[3] Since nothing has been said about price, the entire demand curve shifts rightward or leftward. Please see Figure 3–2 on the next page. Graph A illustrates a rightward shift (increase) of demand; Graph B shows a leftward shift (decrease) of demand.

Tastes and preferences are known to be influenced by effective advertising. Remember the "Pepsi Generation" ads? They were very instrumental in increasing Pepsi sales. Remember the Ultrabrite toothpaste ad which strongly suggested that using Ultrabrite would improve your sex appeal? Sales soared following those ads. Indeed, the purpose of most advertising is to increase demand (illustrated as a rightward shift of the curve: please refer to Graph A).

The prices and availability of related goods also have a bearing on demand for a good or service. Take for example, racket sports: If the price of tennis rackets increases, the demand for tennis balls will decrease, other things being equal. Consider the relationship between wine and cheese. If the price of wine increases, the demand for cheese will decrease, other things being equal. (See Graph B.) In this latter example, an increase in the price of wine will decrease wine consumption; that is, fewer bottles of wine will be sold. And, since cheese is a complementary good (consumed with wine), the demand for cheese will decrease. It is important to note that less cheese is sold because of a higher price of wine (a complementary product), not because of a higher price of cheese.

The relationship between the price of one item and the demand for its substitute is also very important. For example, if the price of butter decreases, the demand for margarine also will decrease, other things being equal. Based upon this brief discussion on complements and sub-

---

[3] The term *normal goods* is used to refer to the direct relationship between increased income and increased consumption. Examples are steak, automobiles, and dining out. However, there are some products and services, called *inferior goods*, for which consumers will decrease consumption when their incomes increase (and vice versa). An example is shoe repair services. Instead of buying new shoes during a period of declining income, people will have their shoes repaired. And, conversely, when their incomes are rising, people will purchase new shoes instead of having the old shoes resoled.

FIGURE 3–2 Shifting Demand

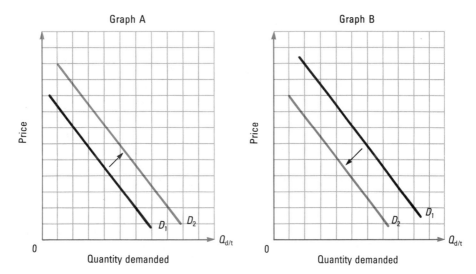

Graph A: Demand shifts to the right, from D_1 to D_2. Also referred to as an increase in demand, the entire curve shifts as a result of a change in one or more determinants of demand (e.g., income, tastes and preferences, etc.).

Graph B: Demand shifts to the left from D_1 to D_2. Also referred to as a decrease in demand, the entire curve shifts as a result of a change in one or more determinants of demand (e.g., prices of related goods, expectations, number of consumers, etc.).

stitutes, we can develop a rule of thumb about changes in the price of a product and the demand for its related good. Other things being equal, if the price of X increases (decreases), the demand for its complement Y will decrease (increase). How about changes in the price of A and the demand for its substitute B? If the price of A increases (decreases), the demand for its substitute B will increase (decrease).

THINKING IT THROUGH

If the price of compact discs decreases, what will happen to the demand for pre-recorded audio tapes? LPs? If the price of peanut butter increases, what will happen to the demand for jelly?

Expectations about your income and prices are also very important. Situation: It's mid-December and your boss has just rewarded you with a year-end bonus. You will get it sometime in January. Would you buy that new car you've been thinking about or take a fun vacation that you've been postponing? Economic research and consumer surveys clearly show that people will increase spending now, based upon expected future income. This is shown as a rightward shift of the demand curve for the product in question.

Situation: Presidents have the discretionary power to impose tariffs (taxes) on a wide variety of imported goods. Assuming that the president has just threatened to add a 200 percent tax on selected gourmet goods imported from Europe (French wine, Danish cheese, British gin, etc.), and assuming that you are a consumer of such items, what would you do? How would you illustrate this market phenomenon on a graph?

The final determinant of demand is market size or the number of consumers. Population growth, birth and death rates, and migration patterns affect the size of the consumer market. But these factors also often interact with changes in tastes and preferences. For example, when Pope Paul IV issued his famous decree in 1966, lifting the ban on meat consumption among Roman Catholics, the demand for fish declined and fish prices fell by an average of 12.5 percent.[4] Thus, even changes ostensibly outside the realm of commerce have a strong economic impact.

Looking to the future, the composition of the general consumer market has been changing in rather predictable ways. For example, by the year 2000 nearly 25 percent of the U.S. population will be over 65 years of age. This demographic change has sweeping implications for the health-care industry. Another demographic change that appears to be happening is a mini-baby boom. This will have a major effect on the demand for infant wear, baby food, toys, and related products.

All of these determinants of demand (or *other things being equal*) were assumed to be constant for the time period involved in our diet soda market. For example, consumer income was assumed to be constant, as were prices of substitutes and complements. Although you may think that such assumptions are unrealistic, the important point is that we would not be able to isolate any meaningful relationship between prices and quantities demanded if we did not make such assumptions.

Change in demand *refers to a shift of the demand curve caused by a change in one or more of the determinants of demand.*

What happens if consumer income changes or if the price of regular soda (a substitute for diet soda) changes? *When one or more of the determinants changes, the entire demand curve shifts to a new position.* This shift is also known simply as a **change in demand.** For example, what if consumer income increased? Because people are now able to buy more diet soda at every price (the market conditions have changed), we illustrate this on the graph as a rightward and upward shift of the curve. This is shown in Figure 3–3. (It may be helpful to think of an increase in demand as a shift of the curve away from the origin and a decrease in demand as a shift toward the origin.)

---

[4] Frederick W. Bell, "The Pope and the Price of Fish," *American Economic Review* (December 1968), pp. 1346–1350.

FIGURE 3–3

Change in Demand (Increase)

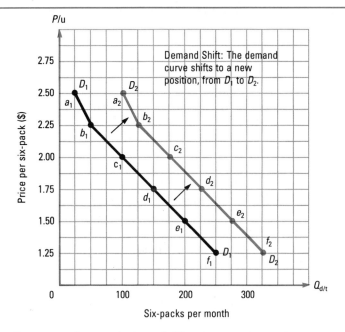

This figure illustrates an increase in demand. When consumer income increases, consumers are able to buy more six-packs of diet soda at every price. Other determinants will also have a similar effect, e.g., a decrease in the price of a complementary product such as potato chips, or a change in consumers' preferences for sugar-free or low-sugar beverages.

The new demand curve is labeled D_2. It is drawn to the right of D_1, indicating that at every old price, consumers will buy more diet soda. For example, at a price of $2 consumers buy 75 additional six-packs (175 instead of 100). (Note that this change is referred to as an increase in demand, *not* an increase in quantity demanded.) What is the difference between a change in demand and a change in quantity demanded?

Question: True or False—If the price of diet soda increases, the demand for diet soda will decrease, other things being equal.

If you said false, you are correct. It is false because a change in price will cause only the quantity demanded to change. Demand will change if, and only if, one of the determinants changes. Now, let's look at the supply side of the market.

SUPPLY

The supply of goods and services and economic resources is the other side of the market. Unlike demand, however, supply has no simple law. Cost conditions vary dramatically from industry to industry and from firm to firm. It is much more difficult to generalize about the relationship between price and quantity supplied.

Businesses may face one of three types of cost conditions. First, firms may incur *increasing costs* as they increase production. Accordingly, they are willing to increase production only if they think that they can pass on these cost increases to customers. A second case deals with *constant costs*. Many firms can increase production with no change in the cost of each unit produced. This implies an ability to hold the line on prices. The final case is *decreasing costs*. Businesses often find that as production increases, the unit cost of production decreases. This situation enables the firm to reduce prices if it wants to increase its market share (its sales as a percent of industry sales).

We will deal more extensively with these different cost cases in Chapter 5, "Costs of Production." For now, we will discuss the increasing cost case.

The term **supply** refers to all of the quantities supplied at all of the market prices in some time period, other things being equal. Many firms face increasing costs as they increase output. For this reason, the supply curve is upward sloping. Businesses will increase production only if they can raise prices to cover increased costs. Illustrated below is a table and corresponding graph of the quantity supplied of diet soda at various prices during the month of July 1988. **Quantity supplied** is the term used to refer to a specific amount offered for sale at a specific price (e.g., 100 six-packs at $2).

The table and graph illustrate the willingness of firms to increase the quantities supplied as the price increases (and vice versa). This is known as a direct relationship: both variables move in the same direction. In the language of economists, quantity supplied varies directly with price, other things being equal.

Unlike the demand curve, the supply curve slopes upward and to the right. Assuming that the current price is $2 per six-pack, how many six-

Supply *refers to all of the quantities supplied at all of the market prices in some time period.*

Quantity supplied *refers to a specific amount offered for sale at a specific price.*

TABLE 3–2
Supply Schedule for Diet
Soda (six-packs per
Month, July 1989)

Price	Quantity Supplied
$2.50	250
2.25	150
2.00	100
1.75	75
1.50	50
1.25	25

The table (supply schedule) shows the relationship between price and quantity supplied. As price increases, quantity supplied increases, and vice versa. Quantity supplied thus varies directly with price, other things being equal.

FIGURE 3–4

Supply of Diet Soda

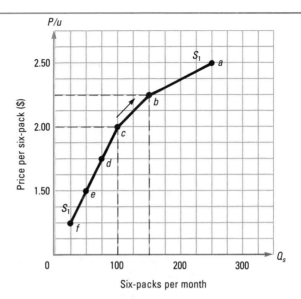

The supply schedule shows the direct relationship between price (*P*) and quantity supplied (*Qs*) An increase in price from $2.00 to $2.25 will cause firms to increase quantity supplied from 100 to 150 (from point *C* to point *B*), other things being equal. Note: Be careful not to confuse supply with quantity supplied. Changes in product price cause changes in quantity supplied, illustrated as a movement along the same supply curve. A change in supply (or a shift of the curve to a new position) will occur only if one or more of the determinants of supply changes, such as expectations of higher prices, improved technology, and so forth.

packs are firms willing to supply? Read the graph to find the answer. Go up to $2 on the vertical axis. Follow the $2 price line over to the supply curve. From the point where the $2 price line intersects the supply curve at point *C*, follow the output line down to the horizontal axis. Read the quantity supplied at that point where the output line intersects the horizontal axis (at 100 six-packs).

Movement along the Supply Curve: A Change in Quantity Supplied

As we noted with the demand curve, changes in price cause a movement along the curve. The same holds true with the supply curve. As price increases, perhaps as a result of an increase in consumer demand, the existing supply curve indicates the new quantity firms will offer. For example, if price increases from $2.00 to $2.25, the number of six-packs supplied increases from 100 to 150 (from point *C* to point *B*). This is known as a **change in quantity supplied** and is represented as a *movement along* the existing supply curve.

A change in quantity supplied *is represented as a* movement along *the existing supply curve.*

SHIFT OF THE SUPPLY CURVE

Determinants of supply
*include costs of production,
technology, expectations
(about prices, sales, and
output), prices of related
goods, and the number of
suppliers.*

Change in supply *occurs
when one of the determi-
nants changes and the
entire supply curve shifts
leftward or rightward.*

The supply curve of diet soda, like the demand curve, is constructed
with a set of other-things-equal assumptions. Also known as **determinants of supply,** these determinants define the slope and location of the
supply curve. When one of the determinants changes, the entire supply
curve changes position, shifting leftward or rightward. This is known as
a **change in supply.** (As with the demand curve, it is helpful to think of
an increase or rightward shift of the supply curve as a shift away from
the origin and a decrease or leftward shift of the supply curve as a shift
toward the origin.) The determinants that cause the changes in supply
are grouped into five categories.

Determinants of Supply

1. Costs of production (wages, interest, rent, etc.)
2. Technology
3. Expectations (about prices, sales, and profits)
4. Prices of related goods
    a. substitutes
    b. complements
5. Number of suppliers

Whenever one or more of a firm's costs of production increases, the
supply curve will shift to the left (decrease). The standard costs to a
firm are its wages and salaries, materials, rent, supplies, and interest
expenses, to name a few. However, external costs may also be borne by
the firm. For example, if a sales tax is levied on the sale of a product or
service, this is considered a cost of goods sold. The effect of a sales tax
is to shift the supply curve to the left. Please see Graph A in Figure
3–5.

Technological factors, including the scale and organization of the
firm, are very important as well. Perhaps the most well-known technological effect is the introduction of mass production. When specialization and division of labor are introduced into a business, the average
cost of production generally declines dramatically. This is illustrated as
a rightward shift of the supply curve. A recent case in point is the min-
iaturization of circuitry and microchips in virtually all electronic goods.
The result was a dramatic decline in unit costs and a rightward shift of
the supply curve. This is illustrated in Graph B, Figure 3–5.

Prices of substitutes and complements in production also are important determinants of supply. Farmers decide what to plant in the spring
based in part upon the prices received for their crops in the previous
harvest season. If wheat prices are down, then many farmers may elect

FIGURE 3–5 Shifting Supply

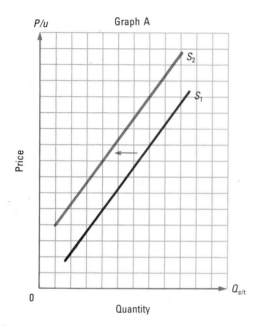
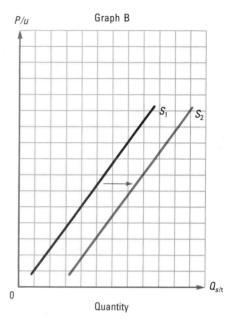

Graph A: Supply shifts to the left, from S_1 to S_2. Also referred to as **a decrease in supply**, the entire curve shifts as one or more of the determinants changes.
Graph B: Supply shifts to the right, from S_1 to S_2. Also referred to as **an increase in supply**, the entire curve shifts as a result of a change in one or more of the determinants.

to plant soybeans or some alternative crop. Therefore, a decline in the price of wheat will result in an increase in the supply of soybeans, illustrated as a rightward shift of the soybean supply curve and a leftward shift of the wheat supply curve.

Like consumer expectations about prices and income, **expectations about costs, prices, profits, and sales** play a vital role in production decisions. If a firm's expectations about future sales and profits are grim, it will cut production. Conversely, if a firm thinks prices and profits will be higher in the next year, the supply will increase.

Finally, the supply curve will be affected by the **number of suppliers** in the market. Situation: reported sales and profits of microcomputers increased 145 percent from 1984 to 1985. Result: Many new firms produced and marketed a microcomputer in order to capture a share of the profits. The supply curve of personal computers shifted to the right. (See Graph B, Figure 3–5.)

EQUILIBRIUM AND DISEQUILIBRIUM

Equilibrium *is the intersection of the supply and demand curves.*

Now let's put supply and demand together. The intersection of the supply and demand curves determines the **equilibrium**—a market condition in which quantity supplied and quantity demanded are exactly equal at a unique price. Figure 3–6 illustrates equilibrium at a price of $2 and a quantity of 100 six-packs.

Equilibrium is a temporary condition because markets are nearly always in transition. If we start from an equilibrium, as the determinants of supply and demand change in response to changing economic conditions, the market experiences **disequilibrium,** a state in which there is either a shortage or surplus. Let's take each of these in turn.

Disequilibrium *is a state in which there is either a shortage or surplus.*

A shortage *occurs when the quantity demanded exceeds the quantity supplied at the current price.*

A **shortage** occurs when the quantity demanded exceeds the quantity supplied at the current market price. It may also be defined as *excess quantity demanded.* Look at Figure 3–6. If the market price per six-pack is $1.75, there is a shortage of 75 six-packs: suppliers offer 75 at this price, but consumers want to buy 150. Note that the shortage is measured as the horizontal distance between the supply and demand curves at the prevailing price of $1.75.

FIGURE 3–6
Supply and Demand and Equilibrium

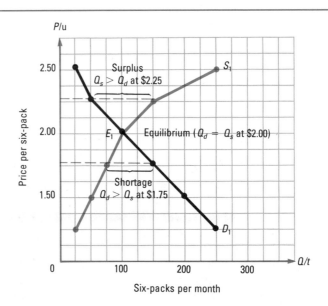

The intersection of supply and demand determine market equilibrium. This location is unique because it is the only price at which the quantity demanded is equal to the quantity supplied. At prices above equilibrium, such as $2.25, there is a surplus (or excess supply) of 100 six-packs. At prices below equilibrium, such as $1.75, there is a shortage (or excess demand) of 75 six-packs. For both cases of disequilibrium, however, there is tendency for price to move back toward the equilibrium.

When you head to the local supermarket to pick up a six-pack, this may be your customary (if not predictable) purchase. However, you might also be throwing a party. For this event, you might buy a case or more. Other customers may do likewise. The result is that there is a temporary shortage of diet soda. Because the manager of the store has no way of estimating precisely the demand for six-packs from week to week, the best that the manager can do is make a calculated guess based upon sales history and assumptions about market conditions.

A **surplus** *occurs when the quantity supplied exceeds the quantity demanded at the current price.*

A **surplus** occurs when the quantity supplied exceeds the quantity demanded at the current price. It is also called the *excess quantity supplied*. If the market price for diet soda is $2.25, then suppliers are offering 100 more six-packs than consumers want to buy at the prevailing price. (Quantity supplied is 150 and quantity demanded is 50.) As with a shortage, a surplus also is measured as the horizontal distance between the supply and demand curves.

Like a shortage, a surplus may develop just as unpredictably. Unbeknown to the store owner, a number of customers may decide to switch to regular soda. Why? Perhaps because of a change in tastes. Regardless of the reason prompting less sales of diet soda, the point is that the store will have more diet soda in inventory than customers want to buy.

Surpluses and shortages are situations in which the market is in disequilibrium. Both logic and intuition tell us that with each situation the tendency is for the market to move toward equilibrium. For example, if stores have an excess supply of diet soda, managers will run a sale in order to reduce inventory. At temporarily lower prices, consumers will buy more six-packs, and the surplus will diminish. Indeed, the surplus may easily turn into a shortage if consumers decide to really stock up at these bargain prices. It is next to impossible for the soft drink companies to establish prices which will mesh exactly the quantity supplied for thousands of stores with the quantity demanded for millions of consumers.

The principles of supply and demand are everywhere. As we have seen already, if demand increases and supply remains unchanged, then you would expect the price to rise. Why? Let's look at the actors involved in still another marketplace to understand the dynamics of the process.

Shellfish of all kinds are growing in popularity. If more people decide to try shrimp, and if suppliers are unaware of this change in consumers' tastes and preferences, then what will happen? The first signal of this change in market conditions is a shortage. At the prevailing market price, people want to buy more shrimp than sellers have to offer. Suppliers will note that their supplies are being bought in a shorter time period. For example, instead of supplies of shrimp running low by Friday evening, suppliers sell out by Wednesday afternoon. If you were the shopkeeper or seller, how would you react in this situation? You might try to get more shrimp from your distributors. But when you tell them you want more, they must increase orders from their sources of supply. In other words, the message that there isn't enough shrimp on the market to satisfy demand is passed all the way to the wholesalers and fishing fleet companies.

When information of a shortage is transmitted through the marketplace, the opportunity for profit-taking is presented. The fish companies will respond to the shortage by increasing their catch and supplying more shrimp, raising prices, or both. The result is that prices will be higher and more shrimp will eventually reach the market. As prices are raised to distributors and, in turn, passed along to consumers, the shortage is gradually reduced. How? The higher price is an incentive to suppliers to offer more shrimp. To consumers, however, the higher price is a disincentive, and they will buy less shrimp.

What if prices are raised too high? What if the middlemen (distributors) decide to increase their profit margins by adding 10 percent to their increased costs? People won't be able to buy as much, and a surplus of shrimp will develop. More shrimp are on the market than people want to buy. The result is that distributors will reduce their orders and/or decrease prices.

MARKET DYNAMICS

As implied by the foregoing discussion, market conditions are very dynamic. Indeed, one of the more fascinating aspects of economics is how changes in supply and demand result in new prices and sales. Returning to the diet soda market, we can use a basic supply-and-demand graph to examine how changes in the determinants of supply and demand result in changes in price and quantity sold. Remember: Equilibrium is the intersection of supply and demand—a point at which a single price equates quantity demanded and quantity supplied. Other things being equal, what would happen if soft drink firms around the country expected sales and profits to decline by 10 percent in the next six months? Would the supply curve shift? If so, which way?

If you said a shift to the left, you are correct. How do you know? Think of it like this: If suppliers have a pessimistic outlook about sales and profit, then they are going to cut back on production. The result must be less diet soda sold at each existing price. This is illustrated on the graph by drawing a new supply curve to the left and above the original curve. The new curve intersects the demand curve at a higher price and a lower quantity (see Figure 3–7.)

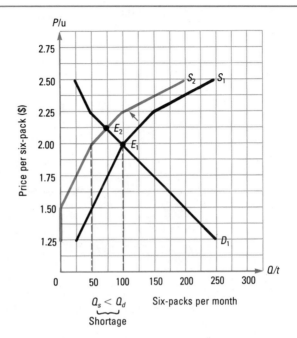

Situation: Firms expect declining sales and profits. Adjustments: Firms cut production and lay off workers, illustrated as a leftward shift of the supply curve (from S_1 to S_2). The market will be in disequilibrium initially, as $Q_d > Q_s$ at \$2. Gradually, firms raise price to \$2.13, the price which equates Q_s and Q_d at 75 six-packs.

A Note on Market Dynamics

Figure 3–7 shows the before and after equilibrium situations, E_1 and E_2. Although this is important, it is also interesting to examine the process by which the new equilibrium is reached. This is what is meant by market dynamics. Let's look at each stage.

FROM E_1 TO E_2:

1. Companies cut production.
2. Wholesalers and retailers receive smaller shipments.
3. Retail businesses and customers feel the *shortage:* businesses run out of diet soda before the next shipment is delivered; consumers buy substitutes.
    The shortage is illustrated as the horizontal distance between the two output lines, Qd and Qs (50 six-packs), measured at the original equilibrium price of \$2.

4. Recognizing the shortage, retailers increase price to $2.05. This has the effect of reducing the shortage from 50 six-packs to approximately 30 six-packs as suppliers stock more six-packs and consumers buy fewer six-packs.

5. This trial and error process continues indefinitely. For example, it is likely that price would be increased above the equilibrium level of $2.13, say to $2.25. This would generate a surplus of 50 six-packs, where the quantity of six-packs supplied exceeded the quantity demanded. Retailers would then run a sale on diet soda.

THINKING IT THROUGH

"Talk is cheap 'cause supply exceeds demand!" Perhaps you have heard this cliché. On the surface, it makes sense. If the supply of something exceeds demand, then the price should be low. Is this old saying technically correct?

Finding examples for which supply and demand analysis may be applied is as easy as naming a product, service or resource. Indeed, in the following CASE-IN-POINT, we further address the important issues of supply and demand as they relate to the job market. As you read the case, think about how and why shortages and surpluses develop in the markets for specific types of skills (labor).

CASE
• IN •
POINT

Job Skills in Short Supply

Supply and demand is of no greater importance than in the job market. Current and projected manpower shortages are of primary concern to businesses as they strive to maintain competitive advantages with their domestic and overseas rivals.

"Imbalances always exist between what colleges and universities are turning out and what employers are taking in. Today is no exception. . . . Just which kinds of expertise employers find scarce . . . changes rapidly, as schools and students react to the shifting job market." The most severe current shortages are concentrated in three areas: cutting edge technologies, electrical engineering, and mixed degrees. "Specialists are needed in optics, laser technology, electromagnetics, avionics, and composites technologies. The latter involves the development, and application to manufacturing, of new materials. An example is the use in aircraft structures of composites that are stronger than any material used in the past."

The demand for electrical engineers is increasing in both conventional manufacturing and in high-tech fields, and the shortage is likely to get much worse because of severe faculty shortages in graduate schools.

"The thing that is in shortest supply for us would be people with a technical undergraduate degree and an M.B.A." says James Fish, manager of management development and personnel recruiting for Ford Motor Co. A company spokesman at Chase Manhattan Bank wants "to see more liberal arts majors who also have accounting skills or some other analytical proficiency, such as statistics."

Other shortages are most evident in manufacturing engineering, personal computers, banking (especially retail banking), marketing (especially research), statistics, and teaching. "Shortages exist in both business and engineering graduate schools. The American Assembly of Collegiate Schools of Business notes that '16% of all authorized, doctorally qualified, tenure-track positions in business schools are vacant.' A study last year by the American Electronics Association of all engineering schools in California found a 22% vacancy rate in full-time positions." The state of California projects that there will be 80,000 teaching vacancies in the state by 1990. This extreme shortage of teachers is evident nationwide.

Many professions like teaching, nursing, and engineering experience cyclical patterns of shortage and surplus. When a shortage of teachers becomes evident, for example, most states generously support expanded teacher-training programs and local school districts vote tax and/or bond issues to increase salaries to retain existing teachers and attract new people to teaching. The shortage is gradually eliminated, and the market begins to show signs of a surplus of teachers. Undergraduate and graduate schools are slow to respond to the signals, however, since jobs are at stake and there are thousands of students nearing completion of their training.

"The chief of the division of occupational outlook for the Bureau of Labor Statistics noted recently that 'until the last couple of years or so,' people worried about a shortage of computer programmers and systems analysts. 'But colleges are producing so many now that there might be concern they're overproducing.'" Such are the vagaries of the market. (*WSJ*, October 7, 1986)[5]

Questions to Consider

1. *How would you appraise the job market in your community? What resources are available to help you in this task? (Hint: One excellent resource is the annual* Occupational Handbook, *published by the Department of Labor.)*

2. *Have you matched your skills and talents with current job prospects? Have you visited your college's counseling center to request an occupational inventory test? Have you visited your college's job placement office?*

---

[5] Excerpted from two articles in *The Wall Street Journal:* "Although the Scarcities are Fewer, Some Job Skills are in Short Supply," October 7, 1986; and "Academic Careers Rebound as Some Professional Schools See a Decline," December 30, 1986.

Summarizing: Changes in Supply and Demand

As consumer incomes rise and fall, as costs and prices change, and as expectations change regarding prices, incomes, and profits, consumers and businesses make decisions about what and how much to buy and produce. As we have seen, these changes in the determinants of supply and demand result in *shifting* curves, as opposed to *movements along* the existing curves. The following diagrams summarize the process of adjustment, noting the effect on price and quantity—if known.

Figure 3–8 illustrates five supply and demand diagrams, each of which records a different supply and demand shift and corresponding changes in price and quantity. Panel A illustrates the market for cellular phones. If consumer tastes for such devices become more favorable, the result is increased demand, shown as D_2 on the graph. Relative to D_1, D_2 intersects S_1 above and to the right of the original equilibrium. This means that price is higher and quantity is greater.

Panel B illustrates the market for prime beef. The demand for prime beef has decreased in recent years, and this is illustrated as a leftward shift of the demand curve from D_1 to D_2. The D_2 demand curve intersects S_1 at a new equilibrium E_2, located below and to the left to the original equilibrium E_1. The result is a lower price and less quantity.

Panel C depicts the market for bicycles. Because of brisk sales in recent years, market profitability has attracted a number of new producers. This is shown as a rightward shift of the supply curve from S_1 to S_2, resulting in a lower price and greater quantity (comparing E_1 and E_2).

Panel D illustrates the market for cigarettes. There has been a decrease in the supply of cigarettes, illustrated as a leftward shift of the supply curve from S_1 to S_2. The new S_2 curve intersects D_1 at E_2, a higher price and lower quantity than the original equilibrium E_1.

Panel E shows the market for microcomputers. Both supply and demand curves shift to the right, indicating the greater number of producers (and other supply-increasing determinants) and an increased number of consumers (as well as other demand-increasing determinants). Unlike the situation with other panels, the result here depends upon the relative amounts by which each curve has shifted. As shown in Panel E, S_2 and D_2 have increased by equal percentage amounts, resulting in a greater quantity and no change in price. However, if we had shown a greater shift in supply relative to increased demand, the result would be a lower price as well as increased quantity.

FIGURE 3–8, a-e. Market Adjustments

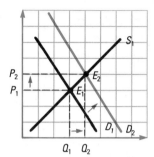

Panel A: Cellular phones

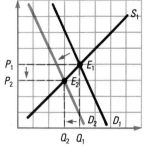

Panel B: Prime beef

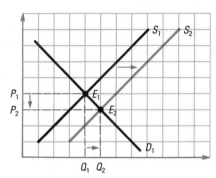

Panel C: Bicycles

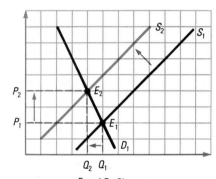

Panel D: Cigarettes

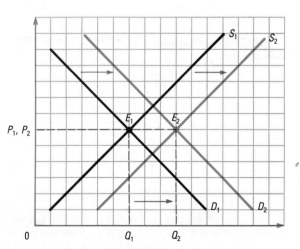

Panel E: Microcomputers

Shifting demand and supply curves result in new equilibrium prices and quantities.

THE MARKET AND GOVERNMENT REGULATION

In this section, we use the principles of supply and demand to analyze three important economic issues: the minimum wage, rent ceilings, and occupational licensure. Common to each case is the impact of government regulation on the respective markets.

Minimum Wages

$4.25/hr

Minimum wage *is a government-established minimum below which wages may not go.*

In 1938, Congress enacted the first national **minimum wage.** This policy seemed to be the correct action since we were in the middle of the nation's worst depression. "Something had to be done to shore up purchasing power among the masses," said Adolphe Berle, one of FDR's chief advisors. Let's see how economists view the issue of the minimum wage.

What effect does the imposition of a minimum wage have upon the market for unskilled labor? Figure 3–9 illustrates the supply and demand for unskilled labor. The equilibrium wage is $3 per hour; the equilibrium number of unskilled workers is 1.5 million. The government then legislates a legal minimum wage of $3.35 per hour. This effectively establishes a floor below which wages for a wide range of labor may not go. What happens?

The minimum wage, higher than the market wage, creates two opposite forces. First, as shown in Figure 3–9, more people will be willing to work at $3.35 (point *F* on the supply curve: a quantity supply of 1.8 million). Second, employers will be willing to employ fewer unskilled workers at $3.35. This is shown as point *E* on the demand curve (a quantity demand of 1.3 million). The result is a *surplus:* the quantity supplied exceeds the quantity demanded at the minimum wage, measured as the horizontal distance between *E* and *F* at the $3.35 wage. The result is additional unemployment of 500,000 people.

FIGURE 3–9

The Minimum Wage

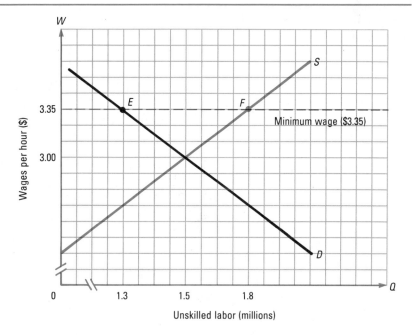

Before the minimum wage is enacted, 1.5 million workers are employed in unskilled jobs at the market wage of $3. The market is in equilibrium. After the minimum wage is enacted, at $3.35, unskilled jobs are eliminated and 500,000 workers are unemployed. This is shown as the horizontal distance from E to F, measured on the horizontal axis.

Rent Ceilings

Scenario: Tenant organizations and community action groups lobby city officials to do something about the rent gouging by landlords. City governments respond with rent control ordinances, usually with rent ceilings. Designed to combat unreasonable rents and too frequent and unreasonable rent hikes, a **rent ceiling**—or maximum rent above which property owners may not charge—appears to be a humane gesture offered to help those who have limited housing options. What are the effects of rent ceilings, in both the short run and the long run?

Rent ceiling *is the maximum rent above which property owners may not charge.*

Figure 3–10 illustrates the supply of and demand for housing in a low-income community. We begin before the imposition of rent controls, with market conditions represented by D_1 and S_1. The equilibrium rent is $250 per month; 30,000 housing units are rented at this rent. Assuming the local government imposes a rent ceiling at $250, no impact is felt initially. As time passes, however, and the demand for housing increases from D_1 to D_2, the effect of the rent ceiling takes its toll.

When property owners advertise a vacancy, many more people want to rent than there are housing units available. Normally, this shortage

FIGURE 3–10
Rent Ceilings

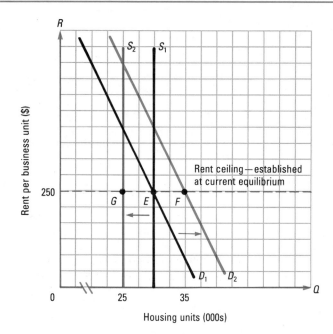

We begin with a free market equilibrium rent of $250 and 30,000 housing units. When the rent ceiling is imposed at $250 (the current market rent), no change occurs initially. However, as demand increases from D_1 to D_2, a housing shortage develops, shown as the distance from E to F (5,000 units). Ultimately landlords fail to repair buildings and city officials order buildings demolished. This is illustrated as a leftward shift (decrease) in supply. This aggravates the shortage, shown now as the distance from G to F (10,000 units).

would lead to increasing rents. But, with the rent ceiling in effect, rents do not rise and the shortage persists. Some families respond by doubling up: two bedroom apartments are now occupied by as many as 10 people.

No new apartments are built. Owners refuse to repair existing buildings, and apartments fall into disrepair. Tenants complain and city officials investigate. Nothing is done. Owners reap special tax benefits and sell to new owners.

Within 10 or 15 years, local residents and urban planners unite in efforts to bring the "headache ball" to the run-down buildings—demolition. This is illustrated as a leftward shift of the housing supply curve (from S_1 to S_2), further aggravating the housing shortage. The best of intentions—to aid lower-income tenants—results in dilapidated housing.

> **THINKING IT THROUGH**
>
> What is the alternative to rent controls? How else can city governments assist low-income tenants? Should city government be involved at all?

Occupational Licensure

You just got your master's degree in counseling and guidance. Always an entrepreneur, you decide to go into business for yourself as a marriage counselor. In 28 states (as of 1988), you must first obtain a license from the state in which you intend to practice. Also, consider the next-door neighbor who is a hairdresser at the popular New Wave Salon. He wants to strike out on his own. Can he just hang out his shingle and cut hair? Not in 36 states.

"Almost without exception, the demand for occupational licensing comes not from a mistreated public but from the occupational groups." In California and other states, even tree experts have been licensed. Why? According to the chairman of the Illinois State Tree Expert Examining Board, the purpose of licensing tree services is "to protect the public against tree quacks, shysters, and inexperienced persons."[6]

> **THINKING IT THROUGH**
>
> From medicine and counseling to hairdressing and real estate, governments have enacted state statutes and local ordinances requiring people to apply for a license to practice their trades. For what purpose? To what end? What effect does licensure have upon the prices for such services? What effect upon the incomes of the practitioners?

IMPORTANT TERMS TO REMEMBER

---

[6] Dwight R. Lee and Robert F. McNown, *Economics in Our Time* (Chicago: Science Research Associates, Inc., 1983), p. 95.

minimum wage, p. 82   shortage, p. 74
quantity demanded, p. 64   supply, p. 70
quantity supplied, p. 70   surplus, p. 75
rent ceiling, p. 83

CHAPTER SUMMARY

1. The law of demand is defined as the inverse relationship between price and quantity demanded, other things being equal.

2. The supply schedule or curve is a direct relationship between price and quantity supplied, other things being equal.

3. There are five determinants of demand, or other things being equal: income, tastes and preferences, prices and availability of substitutes and complements, expectations about future prices and income, and the number of consumers in the market.

4. The determinants of supply, also known as "other things being equal," are costs of production, technology, prices of related goods, expectations, and the number of suppliers.

5. Changes in one or more of the determinants of demand or supply will cause the demand or supply curve to shift to a new position. This shift is also referred to as a change in demand or a change in supply.

6. Changes in price cause a movement along the demand and supply curves; changes in the determinants cause a shift of the demand or the supply curve.

7. The supply curve may be upward sloping (for increasing cost conditions), horizontal (for constant cost conditions), or downward sloping (for decreasing cost conditions).

8. Government regulation of market supply and/or demand takes two basic forms. First, the government may attempt to influence market price by setting price ceilings (as in the case of the housing market) and price floors (as in the case of the minimum wage). Second, the government may attempt to restrict or forbid output (in the case of issuing licenses to practice a trade or illegal drug traffic).

DISCUSSION AND REVIEW QUESTIONS

1. News item: A severe frost has damaged Florida's citrus crop. Prices of oranges, grapefruits, and lemons have increased by 25 percent over the last month, from 60 cents a pound to 75 cents a pound.
    Draw a supply and demand diagram illustrating the initial equilibrium price of 60 cents per pound and the new equilibrium of 75 cents per pound.

2. In reference to the above question, describe in detail how the new price of 75 cents per pound is reached.

3. Broccoli and asparagus are substitute vegetables. If the price of broccoli increases, what will happen to the demand for and price of asparagus. Assuming that an increase in demand caused the price of broccoli to increase, draw two supply and demand diagrams illustrating these market conditions.

4. Analyze this headline: "Demand for software declines as prices rise." Is this technically correct? Why or why not? If incorrect, how would you rephrase the headline?

5. Does the presence of competition promise lower prices for the consumer?

6. Is equilibrium a common market situation? Why? Why not?

7. For each example in the following market situations, draw a graph with a typical supply and demand curve. (Make a big *L* and put an *X* in the middle. Label the curves, S_1 and D_1, and the axes: *Price* on the vertical, and *Quantity* on the horizontal.)

   a. As more women join the work force, demand for cosmetics has increased. Other things being equal, what will happen to product price and sales? (Draw the supply and demand curves for cosmetics and show the increase in demand for cosmetics.)

   b. Condominiums are the rage! As contractors build more condos and apartment owners convert to condos, what effect will this condo rage have on rental units and rents? (Draw the supply and demand curves for apartment units and show the decrease in the supply of rental housing. Note: Should the supply curve be vertical? Why or why not?)

   c. Coffee and tea are substitutes. If the price of coffee decreases by 30 percent, what will happen to the demand, price, and sales of tea?

   d. You just read this headline in the newspaper: "Yogurt Increases Your Life Span." Content: Medical research shows that people who eat a regular diet of yogurt live 10 years longer than people who do not eat yogurt. What will happen to the demand for yogurt, its price, and sales?

8. With your understanding of markets, it is helpful to apply the principles of supply and demand to some common economic problems. Don't worry about not having enough information. Policymakers are always complaining about this! Note: There are no "right" answers.

   a. Your college parking lot is always full between 9 A.M. and 12 noon and between 5 P.M. and 9 P.M. Students are always complaining about the lousy parking situation. If you had the authority, what would you do to solve the parking problem?

   b. As head of the Environmental Protection Agency (EPA) you are responsible for, among other things, conserving the nation's natural resources. Your staff of eminent statisticians estimate that, as a nation, we could reduce fuel consumption by 15 percent if major traffic jams could be eliminated. What would you propose? For example, how would you reduce the number of cars on the road during peak commuter time?

A BRIEF LOOK
AHEAD

The next chapter takes you one step further into microeconomics. With a solid foundation of supply and demand behind you, notice that Chapter 4 takes a closer look at demand. Utility theory examines consumer behavior and explains why the demand curve is downward sloping—why lower prices result in increased consumption. And price elasticity of demand describes how responsive consumers are to changes in price.

PART

II

Microeconomics

Consumer Behavior: Utility Theory and Consumer Demand

Mickey Pallas, International Center of Photography

In the previous chapter, you explored the operation of the market via supply and demand. In this chapter, you will take a more detailed tour of the demand side. The broad outlines of the marketplace presented in Chapter 3 are explained to help you understand how and why we buy goods and services and how sensitive we are to changes in price. Two main topics are presented: utility theory, which addresses the topic of consumer choice, and price elasticity of demand, which looks at the responsiveness of consumers to price. The FOCUS and CASES-IN-POINT are designed to highlight some of the more interesting aspects of consumer behavior and market phenomena.

After completion of this chapter, you should be able to do the following:

1. Diagram, describe, and explain the law of diminishing marginal utility.
2. Explain the concept of consumer equilibrium and utility maximization.
3. Explain the relationship between the law of diminishing marginal utility and the law of demand.
4. Distinguish between the substitution effect and the income effect of a price change.
5. Explain how utility theory, the substitution effect and income effect account for the downward sloping demand curve.
6. Diagram and explain the relationship between individual demand and market demand.
7. Using the total revenue method and the elasticity formula, and given a schedule (table) of prices and quantities demanded, identify whether demand is elastic, inelastic, or unit elastic.

Pet Rocks, Hula–Hoops, and "Consumeritis"

Hula-hoops were the craze in the late 1950s and for brief periods ever since. In the late 1970s pet rocks caught consumers' fancies. And, although less frivolous, stonewashed jeans were the big item in the 1980s. Why would people buy pet rocks? Hula-hoops? What's so special about stonewashed jeans?

Consumers mainly want value in what they buy. But many people also like eccentric fun things like pet rocks. An acquaintance of mine related the following: "I remember a party where the hostess, holding her pet rock for display before a circle of friends, expounded on its virtues. 'This may seem like just an ordinary rock, but looks are deceiving. After all, everyone here is just fascinated with the crazy thing,' exclaimed the young woman." She went on to say that pet rocks were for the moment and without any useful function whatsoever. "Why buy them?'' you ask. Why else but for the sheer amusement created when owners share the item with their friends and for the pleasure of knowing that you have a hot new item.

Consumers buy things because the things bought increase satisfaction. Indeed, a well-known psychological theory says that people satisfy their needs according to a hierarchy. People first satisfy their most basic needs, like food and shelter, and only then do they try to fulfill needs like love, affection, status, and self-actualization.[1]

Some economists are critical of using scarce resources for such trendy items as pet rocks and hula-hoops. They claim that advertising literally creates a demand for these goods, and that consumers have acquired a uniquely capitalistic disease called *consumeritis*—buying things for the snob appeal or to emulate their friends and neighbors (i.e., the "bandwagon effect").[2]

---

[1] The Hierarchy of Needs Theory was developed by Abraham Maslow.

[2] Thorstein Veblen was a well-known economist and social critic at the turn of the twentieth century. Veblen argued that the middle-class consumer, in his or her endless quest for wealth, position, and standing, engaged in "conspicuous consumption." People do not consume merely to satisfy physical or even spiritual, aesthetic, or intellectual wants, Veblen said. Instead, they want to consume in a way that displays their wealth. (This is sometimes simply referred to as *snob appeal*.) Those who observe this display in turn engage in a process of emulating their peers, often called "keeping up with the Joneses." Of course, this pattern sets up a bandwagon effect, in which one person after another joins in the parade of conspicuous consumption. In other words, many consumers buy a particular good or service only because it seems that so many other people have done so.

THINKING IT THROUGH

Do pet rocks provide the same kind and degree of satisfaction as food or shelter. Why? Should society (i.e., governments) be concerned about how consumers spend their incomes? What is the real issue: what we buy or the economic freedom to buy whatever we want? Do you think that you have consumeritis? If you bought a pet rock (or some similar product), why did you buy it? Finally, how would you measure your satisfaction from the goods or services you buy?

THE LAW OF DEMAND REVISITED

Why do people buy more when the product price decreases? What determines the shape and slope of demand curves? For more than a hundred years, economists have pondered these questions. Two main explanations may be offered to account for buying more at lower prices and vice versa: utility theory and the substitution and income effects. We will discuss utility theory first.

Utility

When you go shopping for food, clothes, records, and other things, do you think about how the purchase contributes to your overall satisfaction? How do you evaluate a new car versus a European vacation in terms of your level of satisfaction? Is price a measure of quality (i.e., the higher the price, the better the quality)? Do you consciously evaluate what you buy and consider whether it is providing the intended satisfaction, or is the whole process imbedded deep in your subconscious? These and other questions are central to our discussion of utility in this chapter.

As we pointed out in Chapter 3, tastes and preferences are important determinants of demand. Indeed, changing consumer tastes were largely responsible for the sudden surge in pet rock sales, boom boxes, and fashion sneakers. In trying to describe and explain consumer behavior, economists take these tastes and preferences as given. Economists are interested in why you buy products like pet rocks, but not from the standpoint of psychological motivation; that is, economists prefer to leave the questions about how your tastes are formed to psychologists. Economists assume that consumers know what they like, including pet rocks, and the only reason for buying the product is to increase satisfaction (or utility).

Utility *is the psychological satisfaction and need-fulfillment from the consumption of a service or product.*

Marginal utility *is the change in total utility resulting from buying one additional unit of the item.*

Law of diminishing marginal utility *means that with each additional consumption of a good or service, the extra satisfaction (marginal utility) declines.*

Total utility *is the accumulated units of satisfaction from consumption.*

Utility is a term used by economists to define the psychological satisfaction and need-fulfillment from the consumption of a service or product. Demand for stonewashed jeans, tickets to a ballgame, and legal services exists only because the products and services have a value; that is, they provide satisfaction. And it is the marginal (or extra) utility we derive from buying things that is the basis for demand. **Marginal utility** is defined as the change in total utility resulting from buying one additional unit of the item (change in total utility divided by the change in the number of items purchased).

The Law of Diminishing Marginal Utility

You just finished playing a strenuous game of racquetball. You need water! Your first drink provides immense satisfaction, but with each additional sip you derive less additional satisfaction than the previous drink. The satisfaction derived from the first, second, third, and additional drinks is referred to as marginal utility. This common phenomenon illustrates the **law of diminishing marginal utility**—with each additional consumption of a good or service, the extra satisfaction (or marginal utility) declines.

Here is another example of this everyday occurrence. You've just awakened at 6 A.M. to resume studying for your economics exam. Drowsy and still bleary eyed, you find that drinking your first cup of coffee (or some substance with caffeine) provides great satisfaction. You begin to concentrate and absorb the material. However, each additional refill provides less and less additional satisfaction. Your marginal utility is diminishing. Indeed, you may have experienced going beyond the saturation point, in which drinking too many cups produces negative marginal utility: you become so jittery that you are unable to concentrate at all.

This is easy to illustrate graphically. Figure 4–1 shows two graphs, one for total utility and one for marginal utility of cups of coffee. In order to illustrate the relationship between demand and utility, the scene is now the college cafeteria. At the college, you have the opportunity to find classmates to commiserate about the upcoming test.

The first cup of coffee provides 10 utils of satisfaction. (Think of a util as an artificial measure of satisfaction.) The height of the first bar in Figure 4–1a represents the marginal utility from the first cup. When you decide to buy a refill, the marginal utility diminishes to nine utils, shown graphically as the height of the second bar. Similarly, each additional cup provides less and less additional satisfaction. Finally, when you purchase the fifth cup, marginal utility is zero.

How is marginal utility related to total utility? **Total utility** is the accumulated units of satisfaction from consumption. It is calculated by adding the marginal utilities for all units of the product consumed. Al-

FIGURE 4–1

Total and Marginal
Utility

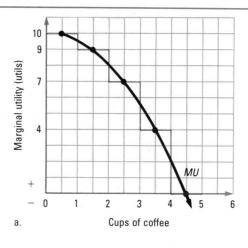

a.

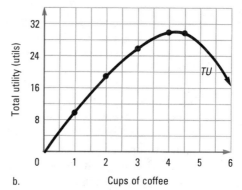

b.

though marginal utility is declining with the purchase of the first four cups of coffee, total utility increases. However, as you can see in Figure 4–1b, the total utility curve is approaching its peak. In other words, it is increasing at a decreasing rate. With each additional cup, the extra satisfaction you derive is less than the preceding cup, and thus the increase in total utility is correspondingly smaller. Finally, marginal utility reaches zero when you buy the fifth cup. It contributes nothing to total utility, and total utility peaks out.

THINKING IT THROUGH

What will happen if you buy a sixth cup? What is the relationship between marginal utility and total utility?

Another example may help further to illuminate this intriguing law of diminishing marginal utility and the relationship between total utility and marginal utility. Consider my brother-in-law Gary. Perhaps you are more disciplined than my brother-in-law, but each Thanksgiving family get-together provides the opportunity for Gary to feast like there is no tomorrow. Groaning about the quantity of food he has consumed, he retires to the nearest sofa. Where would you locate Gary's last morsel consumed on the total utility curve? On the marginal utility curve?

Behind the Demand Curve

Utility theory helps us understand consumer demand by focusing on the decisions at the margin. Will the next purchase increase satisfaction as much as the previous item or the purchase of still another good? How does price enter the picture? Figure 4–2a is a copy of the previous marginal utility graph. Figure 4–2b illustrates your demand curve for coffee at the college cafeteria. With these two graphs, we can see the relationship between marginal utility and the demand curve.

Because we buy things to increase our satisfaction, the marginal utility curve is a rough approximation of demand. The height of the marginal utility curve for each cup of coffee corresponds to the quantity demanded–price coordinates on the demand curve. For example, the first cup of coffee provides 10 utils of satisfaction. Looking at the demand curve in Figure 4–2b, you are willing to pay 50 cents for this first cup. In other words, you value the first cup of coffee at 50 cents. (This is what you are willing to sacrifice to get your caffeine.) However, because your marginal utility diminishes to nine utils for the second cup, you are not willing to pay the same amount that you paid for the first cup. Because you value the second cup less than the first, you are willing to give up less money to get it. The same holds true for the third and fourth cups. The fifth cup provides zero marginal utility, and thus you will not pay for it.

THINKING IT THROUGH

Your marginal utility from the fifth cup is zero and negative for the sixth and additional cups. Will you drink more coffee? Under what circumstances would you take another cup?

The demand curve for coffee (and other goods and services) is rooted in the marginal utility we derive from consumption. Indeed, if we were to draw a smooth curve connecting the midpoints of each of the mar-

FIGURE 4–2 Marginal Utility and Demand

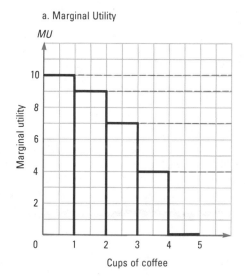

a. Marginal Utility

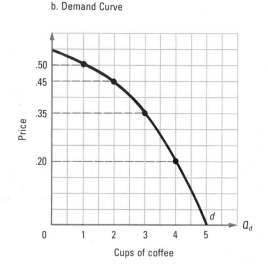

b. Demand Curve

ginal utility bars in Figure 4–2a, the resulting marginal utility curve would resemble the demand curve.

Although the law of diminishing marginal utility says that we derive less additional satisfaction from each extra item purchased, it is the marginal utility to price ratios of all the goods and services in a consumer's market basket that determine the pattern of consumption. And, because we generally buy more than one item at a time, it is more realistic to consider how the consumer spends a certain amount of money in order to maximize utility.

Utility Maximization

Just in case you're wondering, very few of us—not even economists—consciously evaluate each consumption decision in terms of the law of diminishing marginal utility. However, as self-interested rational consumers, we do seek to increase our level(s) of satisfaction from the goods and services purchased every day. In economic terms, we try to maximize utility.

Utility maximization means that the ratios of marginal utility to price for all goods and services consumed are equal.

Utility maximization means that the ratios of marginal utility to price for all goods and services consumed are equal. In other words, utility maximization is a state of consumer equilibrium. Given a fixed income and fixed prices, we spend our dollars in order to realize an equilibrium of marginal utility per dollar for all items purchased. Let's see how this works. Here is the setting.

White Castle (WC) is a chain of hamburger havens dating back more than 60 years. Headquartered in Columbus, Ohio, White Castles are scattered all over the Midwest and in a few cities in New York and New Jersey. Though no serious competitor to MacDonalds, WC's sales exceeded $500 million in 1987. Built upon a "can-do," innovative management philosophy, WC remains a strong cult institution to its burger denizens. Indeed, it serves up its 3-inch square burgers at the incredible price of 30 cents.[3]

Anxious to chomp into these delectible morsels, you and your companion pull into the nearest WC. With $3 to your name and with the prices of the basic burger and soft drinks set at 30 cents and 50 cents, respectively, you plan to spend all of your $3. Table 4–1 illustrates a table of your marginal utilities per item purchased. Remember that each number represents the amount of additional satisfaction derived from consuming one additional hamburger and/or soft drink. In order to maximize utility, you buy the good whose Marginal Utility/Price

TABLE 4–1	Burgers ($.30)			Soft Drinks ($.50)		
The White Castle Feast and Diminishing Marginal Utility	Purchase	TU	MU	Purchase	TU	MU
	1	90	90	1	150	150
			75			100
	2	165		2	250	
			60			0
	3	225		3	250	
			30			− 150
	4	255		4	100	
			0			− 200
	5	255		5	− 100	
			− 45			− 250
	6	210		6	− 350	

This table illustrates the total and marginal utilities associated with the consumption of burgers and soft drinks at White Castle. The marginal utility, or the extra satisfaction from consuming one additional burger or soft drink, steadily declines in conformity with the law of diminishing returns. The consumer will maximize utility—reach consumer equilibrium—when the *MU/P* ratios for each item are equal. This state of equilibrium is reached when the consumer buys five burgers and three soft drinks.

---

[3] So strong is WC's cult appeal that Fountain Hill, an Arizona town with a population of 2,700, ordered 10,000 fully cooked frozen burgers by mail in 1980. White Castle capitalized on this unique sale with a publicity blitz. It has been so successful in this air express burger business that, in a nine-month period in 1983, WC shipped over 300,000 burgers from a single store in Reynoldsburg, Ohio. WC's success has not gone unnoticed. Beginning in 1987, Burger King introduced its Burger Bundles, a WC look-alike at a competitive price. And, not to be outdone by burgers, Kentucky Fried Chicken launched its new line of Chicken Littles. Is this what Alvin Toffler meant by the term *overchoice* in his book *Future Shock?*

(*MU/P*) ratio is greatest. If two ratios are equal, you buy one of each, providing that your income is sufficient.

The great WC feast begins. You order a burger and soft drink, spending 80 cents. The first hamburger contributes 90 utils of satisfaction; the soda provides 150 utils of satisfaction. Having devoured the first burger in a few moments, you then order a second burger and wash it down with your soda. Why not also buy a second soda? Because the *MU/P* ratio of the second burger (75/30 cents, or 250) exceeds the *MU/P* ratio of the second soda (100/50 cents, or 200), you derive greater additional satisfaction (marginal utility) per expenditure on the second burger.

You've now spent $1.10, but you're still hungry and thirsty! Because the *MU/P* ratios are equal for the third burger and second soda (60/30 cents = 100/50 cents), you buy one of each. Total spent: $1.90. With $1.10 left to spend and still ready for more, you buy a fourth burger. The *MU/P* ratio of the fourth burger is 30/30 cents or 100, which exceeds the *MU/P* ratio of the third soda. You've spent $2.20 and decide to go for one more burger and soda. When you do so, you reach the maximum total utility for burgers and sodas, as the fifth burger and third soda purchase provide no change in total utility; marginal utility is zero. You have reached consumer equilibrium, in which the *MU/P* ratios for burgers and sodas are equal, and you have also maximized total utility!

What would happen if the price of soft drinks at White Castle decreased to 40 cents? The lower price upsets the *MU/P* ratio, making the *MU/P* ratio of soft drinks exceed the *MU/P* ratio of burgers. Three things could happen to restore equilibrium. First, buy more soft drinks. Because another soft drink will reduce the marginal utility, the *MU/P* ratio will decline. Second, buy fewer burgers. If you reduce burger consumption, the *MU/P* ratio of burgers will increase and be closer to the *MU/P* ratio of soda. And third, hope for a lower price of burgers. This, too, may or may not restore equilibrium, depending upon the new *MU/P* ratios.

Consumer equilibrium is a very elusive state, possibly as remote as achieving an equilibrium of quantity demanded and quantity supplied. Indeed, it would be very unlikely to reach consumer equilibrium in our daily consumer behavior. In the White Castle case, for example, if you had $2 or $4 instead of $3 to spend, you would have been unable to attain equal *MU/P* ratios for burgers and sodas.

Although it is implausible for consumers to realize a state of consumer equilibrium, we still try to obtain the greatest marginal utility per dollar spent. Many, perhaps most, consumers regularly shop for sale items, return items if dissatisfied, wait for discounts and sales to be announced before purchasing something, and so forth. All of this behavior seems to support the idea of maximizing utility.

The Income and Substitution Effects

Why do consumers buy more at lower prices? Less at higher prices? Besides the law of diminishing marginal utility, economists explain the downward slope of the demand curve in terms of the substitution and income effects. Two things happen when the price of a good changes. First, the **income effect** measures the change in consumption of the good attributed to a variation in real income caused by a change in price. *Real income,* or purchasing power, is what your dollar income can buy after adjusting for price changes. A lower price raises the purchasing power of your income or total expenditures on an item. Assume for the moment that the price of gasoline is $1 per gallon and that you spend $500 per year on gasoline. You thus buy 500 gallons. If the price falls to 50 cents per gallon, your $500 can now buy 1,000 gallons. Your real income (or purchasing power), or how much you can buy with the same $500, has doubled in terms of gasoline purchases. Of course, some of us would continue to buy 500 gallons and spend $250 on other items, such as entertainment. But, in terms of explaining the law of demand, the important point is that a lower price raises real income and enables us to buy more. Conversely, higher prices reduce real incomes and force us to economize and buy less of the higher-priced item and perhaps other goods as well.

Income effect *measures the change in consumption of the good attributed to a variation in real income caused by a change in price.*

THINKING IT THROUGH

Some of us economize better than others. Assuming that your dollar income remains unchanged, do you make a conscious decision to reduce consumption when prices increase on goods you regularly buy? Or do you try to maintain current levels of consumption, either by using installment credit or by reducing saving? Does it depend upon the individual product or service? Why?

Substitution effect *is the change in consumption caused solely by a change in the price of the good relative to the prices of other goods.*

The **substitution effect** is the change in consumption caused solely by a change in the price of the good relative to the prices of other goods (substitutes and complements); thus, if the price decreases relative to other goods, the substitution effect measures the increase in quantity demanded attributed to the lower price. For example, if the price of gasoline declines from $1.00 to 50 cents, driving your car becomes less expensive relative to the bus and other modes of transportation. Because the price is lower, relative to other goods, consumers will buy more gasoline.

To summarize thus far, we know that people will buy more of a good as its price declines for two basic reasons. Take the case of compact discs (CDs). First, the law of diminishing marginal utility tells us that additional consumption of CDs brings smaller and smaller increments of satisfaction; thus, other things being equal, we will buy more CDs only if prices fall. (Lower prices raise the *MU/P* ratio.) Second, as the price of CDs declines, our real income increases, which enables us to buy more CDs with the same amount of income (the income effect). Moreover, as CD prices come down, we will buy more because the price of CDs is lower relative to substitute goods (cassettes and LPs)—the substitution effect.

We know from the law of demand that people buy more at lower prices than at higher prices, other things being equal. Moreover, because we have widely diverse tastes and incomes (and other demand determinants), any two or three individuals have very different demands for the same product. How are individual demand curves related to market demand? Just how sensitive are consumers to changes in price? What determines our responsiveness to price changes? If the price of Big Macs declines by 10 percent, how many more burgers will consumers buy? And, given the income effect of lower burger prices, how many more french fries and sodas will be sold? We now turn to these questions to better understand consumer demand.

INDIVIDUAL DEMAND AND MARKET DEMAND

If your economics instructor assigned you and your classmates to determine the market demand for one-scoop ice cream cones in a specific market (a two-square-mile area), based upon a well-defined sample of individuals, during a given week in the summer, how would you do it? Although time-consuming research is required to gather the data, the solution is really quite simple: *Market demand is merely the sum of individual demands.* Once you have chosen the method of selecting your sample and the sample size, you would ask each person in the sample how many ice cream cones they would buy at different prices during the week.[4] Adding each individual's quantity for each price would then produce the market demand schedule. Please see Table 4–2 and Figure 4–3 on the following pages.

To illustrate the relationship between individual demand and market demand, the demand schedules for Sally, Ramon, and George are illustrated in Table 4–2. To arrive at the market demand, just add the quan-

---

[4] Along with this data, you might also obtain information regarding the determinants of demand, like income, tastes and preferences, prices of substitutes (like frozen custard), and so forth. Although more difficult to obtain, this information would be useful in ascertaining the effect of a cold spell on ice cream sales or a special sale on frozen custard cones.

TABLE 4–2 Individual and Market Demand Schedules	**Price**	**Sally** Q_d	**Ramon** Q_d	**George** Q_d	**Market** Q_D
	$1.50	2	1	1	4
	1.20	3	2	2	7
	.90	4	2	3	9
	.75	4	3	4	11
	.60	4	4	5	13

The market demand curve is the horizontal summation of each individual's quantity demanded (Q_d) at each corresponding price. For each price, the individual quantities demanded are added. For example, at a price of $1.50, the quantities of ice cream cones consumed, 2, 1, and 1, are added to arrive at the market quantity demanded of 4.

tities demanded for each price. The data are plotted as demand curves and shown in Figure 4–3.

As you can see in the figure, the market demand curve smooths out the irregularities of the various individual demand curves. In Sally's case, the number of cones demanded is constant at 90 cents and lower prices. Unlike Sally, Ramon purchases more at lower prices, especially after the 90 cent threshold. On the other hand, George's consumption of cones increases steadily with lower prices. There is just no accounting for tastes!

Ice cream shops, like all businesses, are interested in market demand. And business firms are especially interested in how consumers (as a group) respond to changes in price. In the next section, we turn our attention to the relationship between percentage changes in price and percentage changes in quantity demanded.

ELASTICITY AND TOTAL REVENUE

If your hardware store runs a sale on paint, how will consumers respond? Specifically, if paint prices are cut by an average of 20 percent, will the store's paint sales rise by more than, less than, or equal to 20 percent? If the store raises the price on electric drills, will it suffer a big decline in sales revenue?

This relationship between a price change and the corresponding change in total revenue enables us to determine how responsive consumers are to price changes. **Price elasticity of demand** is the responsiveness of consumers to changes in price, measured by changes in total revenue (price times quantity sold).

There are three types of demand elasticity: elastic, inelastic, and unit elastic. Demand is **elastic** if total revenue increases in response to a lower price, or total revenue decreases in response to a higher price. If price falls and total revenue also declines, or if price increases and total

Price elasticity of demand *is the responsiveness of consumers to changes in price, measured by changes in total revenue.*

Elastic demand *refers to a total revenue increase in response to a lower price.*

FIGURE 4–3 Individual and Market Demand Schedules

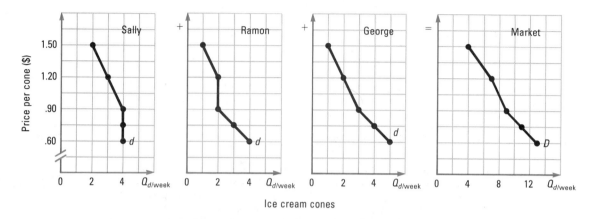

Ice cream cones

The market demand is determined by adding each individual's Q_d for each price. For example, at a price of $.90 per cone, Sally, Ramon, and George buy 4, 2, and 3 cones, respectively; the market Q_d is 9 cones, the sum of the individual quantities demanded.

Inelastic demand *refers to the situation in which if price falls, total revenue also declines, or if price increases, total revenue also increases.*

Unit elastic demand *refers to the situation in which when prices change, either increasing or decreasing, total revenue remains unchanged.*

revenue also increases, then demand is **inelastic.** The third case is unit elasticity. When prices change, either increasing or decreasing, and total revenue remains unchanged, demand is **unit elastic.**

The logic of these three cases may be seen in the following Table 4–3, illustrating April 1990 sales of Frank's Water Bed Outlet.

As we have just seen, comparing the direction of price change and the direction of change in total revenue indicates whether demand is elastic, inelastic, or unit elastic. For example, if Frank reduces the price on water beds from $600 to $500, total revenue increases from $12,000 to $14,000; thus, the demand for water beds in this price range is elastic. Let's pursue the logic of this relationship.

The only way that total revenue can increase at a lower price is if the quantity demanded increases by a greater percentage than the percentage decrease in price. In this example, quantity demanded (unit sales) increases by 33 percent (the change in sales [8] divided by the average of the two unit sales figures [24].) Price decreases by 18 percent: the change in price ($100) divided by the average price ($550).

What happens if Frank lowers the price again to $400? Because total revenue remains unchanged at $14,000, demand must be unit elastic in this price range (from $500 to $400). Consumers increase consumption by 22 percent, exactly the same percentage that price decreases. If Frank tries a "fire sale" and cuts prices to $300, however, he encounters the inelastic portion of the demand for water beds. This time, a price cut results in declining total revenue. The moral in this (other things

TABLE 4–3
Frank's Water Bed Outlet
Monthly Sales, April
1990

Price	Unit Sales	Total Revenue	
$600	20	$12,000	
			Elastic
500	28	14,000	
			Unit elastic
400	35	14,000	
			Inelastic
300	40	12,000	
			Inelastic
200	50	10,000	

Elasticity of demand may be determined easily by observing the relationship between a price change and its corresponding effect on total revenue. Frank's demand curve is represented by the first two columns in the table, Price and Unit Sales. Total Revenue is calculated by multiplying the price times the unit sales.

For example, when price decreases from $600 to $500 and unit sales rise from 20 to 28, total revenue increases from $12,000 to $14,000. This means demand is elastic in the price range from $600 to $500. The logic of this is as follows. Since elasticity is a measurement of how responsive consumers are to changes in price, and since the quantity demanded (or unit sales) must have increased by a larger percentage than the percentage decrease in price, consumers are quite responsive to price changes. The term *elastic* is used to define such behavior. Similarly, when the percentage increase in quantity demanded is less than the percentage decrease in price, then total revenue must fall and demand is said to be inelastic. Consumers are not very sensitive to changes in price.

TABLE 4–4
Price, Total Revenue,
and Elasticity

Price Change	Change in Total Revenue	Demand Is
↑/↓	↓/↑	Elastic
↑/↓	↑/↓	Inelastic
↑/↓	No Change	Unit Elastic

Elasticity of demand may be determined by observing what happens to total revenue when price changes. When price and total revenue change in opposite directions, demand is elastic. When price and total revenue change in the same direction, demand is inelastic. And when price changes and total revenue does not change, demand is unit elastic.

being equal) is not to cut prices if demand is inelastic. Instead, raise prices.

These price–total revenue relationships are summarized in Table 4–4. As indicated in the table, demand is elastic if prices and total revenue move in the opposite direction. On the other hand, demand is inelastic if prices and total revenue move in the same direction. Finally, if there is no change in total revenue regardless of price change, demand is unit elastic.

The total revenue test of elasticity is a quick way to ascertain consumer responsiveness to changes in price. However, price elasticity of demand is also calculated using a formula, a method which provides more information. By calculating an elasticity coefficient, we can determine exactly by how much or little quantity demanded will respond to a price change. This approach to elasticity is discussed in Appendix B.

Read the following CASE-IN-POINT to reinforce your understanding of elasticity.

CASE
• IN •
POINT

Tempest in Tampa

Tempest, a well-known midwestern brewery, faced a tough decision.[5] Recently, through a number of bold advertising and pricing initiatives, its competitors made serious inroads into Tempest's Tampa, Florida, market. In crisis-management style, top level executives called national marketing managers together for a meeting.

The evidence was painfully clear. Tempest's competitors had seized nearly 20 percent of its Tampa market. Although upset and uncertain about the loss of market share, Tempest managers remained confident and optimistic about one thing—the historic pattern of its customers' brand loyalty.

However, upper management was more interested in the immediate problem—declining sales and profits. "One way to turn the tide is to raise price," said the Pacific Northwest marketing manager. "Our office projections indicate that, with a solid brand-loyal customer base, a 10 percent price hike would actually boost sales revenue by 20 percent." Although disagreement was expressed, top management followed this advice and raised prices by 10 percent. Within a short three months of the price hike, Tempest lost an additional 15 percent of the market.

Questions to Consider

1. *Concerning the preceding CASE-IN-POINT, consider the following:*
   a. *Did the marketing manager assume that the demand for Tempest beer was elastic, inelastic, or unit elastic? Explain.*
   b. *When the 10 percent price increase was made and total revenue fell by 15 percent, it was painfully obvious that demand was elastic. Make up your own figures to illustrate this situation.*

2. *Do you know of a similar situation in which prices were changed without specific information about the target market? What happened?*

---

[5] The name of the brewery has been changed to protect the innocent.

Determinants of Elasticity

Among all of the products we buy and the services we enjoy, what causes these variations in elasticity? Why do we virtually ignore changes in the prices of salt and matches on the one hand, yet react strongly to changes in the prices of fresh tomatoes, foreign travel, and Chevrolets?

Determinants of elasticity *include the number and availablility of substitutes, total expenditures for the good, whether the product or service is considered a luxury or a necessity, and the time period.*

There are four main **determinants of elasticity** of demand:

1. the number and availability of substitutes.
2. total expenditures for the item.
3. whether the product or service is considered a luxury or a necessity.
4. the time period.

The fewer the substitutes, the lower the expenditures, the more it is considered a necessity, and the shorter the time period involved to adjust to the price change, the more inelastic the demand. Salt meets these conditions quite well, as does water. (For many goods, the number of substitutes is probably the most important elasticity determinant. Insulin and other lifesaving drugs have virtually no substitutes, for example.) However, the demand for dry breakfast cereals and electronic calculators is relatively elastic, as is foreign travel. In the case of foreign travel, the price is high, domestic travel for many people is a good substitute, and it is regarded as a luxury.

How does the time period play a role? Let's use gasoline as an example. If the price of gasoline increases, how do motorists respond? In the short run, although they will cut back a little, consumers have very little recourse but to keep filling up. Everything from our commuting arrangements to diehard personal habits prevent us from reducing consumption very much. As the weeks and months pass, however, alternative transportation (substitutes) may be found, and we will further reduce our reliance upon the automobile. This is exactly what happened in the 1970s when the United States imposed an embargo on imported oil.

Also related to the time determinant is the important role played by the availability of close substitutes. The longer the time period under consideration, the greater is the probability that alternative products or services will be developed. For example, when San Francisco and Washington D. C. completed their mass transit facilities, thousands of regular automobile commuters gratefully switched to BART and METRO. The result was a decline in gasoline consumption.[6] This helps to explain why the long-run elasticity of gasoline is greater than the short-run elasticity.

---

[6] This example combines two different but related events. First, the demand for gasoline decreased (the curve shifted to the left). Second, because commuters now had more choice, the demand for gasoline became less steep, that is, demand for gasoline became less inelastic.

Another interesting relationship to explore is the difference in elasticities between product categories and specific types of products and even brand names. For example, the category *food* may be broken down into food types, like meat, vegetables, fruit, and so forth. In turn, each of these types may also be broken down into the assorted varieties of meat and vegetables. Meat consists of beef, chicken, liver, lamb, and so forth. We can even reduce this variety of meat types by grade, brand, and other criteria. The point is this: the demand for food is almost perfectly inelastic (vertical).[7] However, the demand for meat is less inelastic than food, and the demand for beef is even less inelastic than meat. Indeed, the demand for a 12-ounce filet mignon steak (at home or at a restaurant) is very elastic.

Graphical Views.   It is often helpful to view these relationships graphically. The determinants of elasticity govern the relative steepness or flatness (shape) of the demand curve. Figure 4–4 illustrates the three types of elasticity.

Figures 4–4a and c illustrate the most common demand curves. Figure 4–4a depicts the demand for fresh tomatoes. In the price range from $1.05 to $ .95 per pound, the elasticity coefficient is 4.0 (If the price declines by 10 percent, from $1.05 to $ .95, the quantity demanded increases by 40 percent, from 8 to 12 pounds. Remember, the percentage change calculations are based upon the averages of price and quantity over the relevant range of change.)

Figure 4–4c illustrates the relatively inelastic demand for coffee. Research indicates that the elasticity of demand for coffee is approximately 0.25. This means that a 20 percent hike in coffee prices will reduce the amount sold by only 5 percent. Evidently, U.S. consumers do not regard tea as a close hot-beverage substitute.

Our third case is depicted in Figure 4–4b. Because unit elastic demand is such a rare case, the demand for automobile tires is used to approximate unitary elasticity. If we take a little liberty and average the short-run and long-run elasticity coefficients, we have a unit elastic demand. If tire stores increase the prices of tires by 10 percent, motorists will reduce their consumption by a like amount. This raises an intriguing question. What substitutes are there for new tires? Recaps and retreads are alternative products, but are these good substitutes? Are they as safe? Whether we would buy them or not is quite irrelevant. The fact is that many consumers only purchase retreads because the price is afford-

---

[7] Food is probably the closest case for a perfectly inelastic demand. But even food has substitutes—albeit imperfect. Hunger is a substitute for food for millions of Americans. If you have some doubt about this, travel to Appalachia, Indian reservations, and inner cities!

FIGURE 4–4 Demand Curves and Elasticity

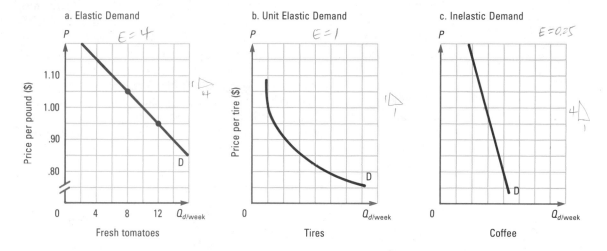

able. The upshot is that they must sacrifice a measure of safety promised with the new tires. Consumer surveys have also indicated that people drive less as tires (and other auto accessories) increase in price.

THINKING IT THROUGH

Using the determinants of elasticity as a guide, how would you classify the following products and services according to elastic, inelastic, or unit elastic demand?

- Tickets to a one-night performance of The Grateful Dead.   E
- Beer.   u⁻
- Budweiser beer.   I

Before we examine an alternative way to determine elasticity, read the following CASE-IN-POINT on elasticity and the farm problem.

CASE
• IN •
POINT

The Root of the Farm Problem: Inelastic Supply and Demand

Farmers confront the harsh facts of economic life every day. If natural disasters like floods and droughts presented the only problems, perhaps farmers would adjust and cope. However, the unpredictability of government subsidies compound the problem. And to make matters worse, the very nature of the product itself is perhaps the most serious problem.

As we have seen, the demand for food and most food groups is highly inelastic. Although the substitution effect works for food groups just like it does for other consumer items, there is a limit to the quantity of food we will consume, regardless of how low the price goes.[8] On the supply side of the market, a similar situation exists. The supply is also inelastic. Once the crop has been planted, changes in price will produce very little change in quantity supplied. (Of course, farmers may draw upon surpluses of some grains in storage.)

The result of this peculiar market situation, which has highly inelastic demand and supply, is that very small changes in demand or supply result in very large changes in market price and farm incomes. For example, over the last 50 years, agriculture has experienced rapid technological improvements. These innovations in farming methods and management greatly increased productivity, resulting in a much larger output per acre. On the demand side of the market, population growth (and consumer appetites) did not keep pace with this agricultural revolution. The result is all too predictable: lower farm prices and lower farm income.

Enter the government! To ensure a plentiful domestic food supply, to generate enough grain exports to help pay for our imports of oil and other goods, and probably to lend support to troubled farmers, the federal government provides subsidies to farmers. These subsidies come in various forms: outright payments per bushel, crop retirement and acreage allotment schemes, loans based upon crop collateral, and so forth. Some of these programs encourage more production because the subsidies are linked directly to output: the more produced, the higher the subsidy. Other programs result in less production.

Questions to Consider

1. *Draw a graph illustrating the market for bushels of corn. The demand and supply curves should be inelastic. Then, show on the diagram what happens to price when the supply curve shifts to the right. To compare price changes, draw in a new demand curve which is very elastic.*

2. *The American Soybean Association spends millions advertising the multitude of ways to use soybeans in our diets. If this ad campaign worked, what would this do to the demand for soybeans? Is the only effect an increase in demand or would the demand curve become more elastic? Inelastic?*

3. *Could the government do something to make the demand for food more elastic? Why or why not?*

---

[8] U.S. households spend a smaller percentage of their budgets on food than all other nations. The United States ranks lowest with 10.9 percent of income spent on food, followed in order by Canada (12.3 percent), the Netherlands (12.7 percent), the United Kingdom (13.5 percent), and Australia (14.0 percent). (Note: If you like curious statistics, did you know that Americans eat 75 acres of pizza every day!) (Source: Joan Lunden, "Good Morning America," July 6, 1987.)

determinants of elasticity,   p. 106
elastic demand,   p. 102
income effect,   p. 100
inelastic demand,   p. 103
law of diminishing marginal
    utility,   p. 94

marginal utility,   p. 94
substitution effect,   p. 100
total utility,   p. 94
unit elastic demand,   p. 103
utility,   p. 94
utility maximization,   p. 97

CHAPTER
SUMMARY

1. Utility is a term which describes the amount of satisfaction consumers
    derive from the purchase of a product or service. Marginal utility is the
    extra satisfaction, measured in utils (an artificial unit of satisfaction), re-
    ceived from the purchase of one additional unit of the good or service.
    When total utility is maximum, marginal utility is zero.

2. The law of diminishing marginal utility describes how extra satisfaction
    declines with each additional item consumed.

3. Utility maximization (or consumer equilibrium) occurs when the marginal
    utility to price ratio for all products and services consumed is equal. Al-
    though this is an ideal state, like the market equilibrium of quantity de-
    manded and quantity supplied, consumers do strive to maximize utility.

4. The substitution effect says that consumers will buy less of an item and
    more of its substitutes when its price increases. Related to the substitu-
    tion is the income effect. Because an increase in product price results in
    a decrease in purchasing power, consumers find that they not only have
    less to spend on the product in question, but they have less real income
    to spend on all goods.

5. The market demand curve is found by adding each individual demand
    curve: for each market price, the corresponding quantities demanded are
    totaled.

6. The total revenue method may be used to determine whether demand is
    elastic, inelastic, or unit elastic. If price and total revenue change in the
    same direction, demand is inelastic. For example, if price increases and
    total revenue increases, then it must be true that quantity demanded
    changes by a smaller percentage than product price. Demand is elastic if
    price and total revenue change in the opposite direction. For example, if
    price decreases and total revenue increases, then the percentage increase
    in quantity must be greater than the percentage decrease in price. Finally,
    demand is unit elastic if total revenue remains unchanged in response to
    a price hike or a price reduction.

DISCUSSION AND
REVIEW
QUESTIONS

1. Situation: You and a friend are discussing which movie to see. You open
    a bag of jelly beans, pour them on the table, and begin munching as you
    review this week's movie fare. Initially, you eat one jelly bean after an-
    other without regard to color or flavor. After eating several dozen jelly
    beans, however, you begin to slow your intake. Then you begin to hunt

for your favorite color or flavored jelly bean. Use the law of diminishing marginal utility to explain your behavior while eating jelly beans.

2. Diagram, describe, and explain the relationship between individual demand and market demand.

3. The theory of demand tells us that lower prices generally mean that we will buy more of the cheaper good, less of higher-priced substitutes, and more of complements. However, when the price of soda declined in our White Castle example, why would you buy fewer burgers? Does this mean that a lower-priced good (soda) will not increase demand for its complement (burgers)? How can you reconcile this contradiction?

4. The marginal utilities for coffee and doughnuts are shown in the table below. If the price of coffee is $.50 a cup and the price per doughnut is $.40, and your money available is $2.80, how many cups of coffee and doughnuts will you purchase in order to reach consumer equilibrium? Record the order of consumption. Hint: Consume in order of the highest *MU/P* ratio until your income is gone or you can no longer buy either with your remaining money.

Purchase	Marginal Utility of Coffee	Marginal Utility of Doughnuts
1	100	60
2	75	45
3	50	30
4	25	10

5. Water is indispensable. Diamonds are attractive, but we all could live without them. Despite these facts, diamonds are very expensive, but water is cheap. This apparent contradiction is known as the *paradox of value*. How can you explain why diamonds have such a greater market value than water? Are there circumstances in which this would not hold true?

6. Construct a demand curve using the data from Question 1 in Appendix B. Then, using the demand schedule for strawberries from Question 1, Appendix B, make a third column for total revenue. Use the total revenue approach to determine whether demand is elastic or inelastic between each pair of prices. Label the demand curve accordingly.

7. At a board of trustees meeting for your college, the question of increasing tuition was brought up. "If the college fails to raise tuition, we will face a budget deficit next year," said the college president. As usual this remark generated a heated discussion. One board member responded, "Raising tuition would prevent many lower-income students from attending college. Besides, there's no guarantee that we'll generate enough revenue to meet our expenditures next year. The last time we increased tuition, we lost revenue."

What do the college president and board member assume about the elasticity of demand for education? Using the determinants of elasticity, and assuming the college is a public community college in a large city, do you think that demand is elastic, unit elastic, or inelastic? What if the college is an Ivy League school (e.g., Harvard, Princeton, Yale, etc.)?

A BRIEF LOOK AHEAD

You have studied the demand curve with utility theory and examined price elasticity of demand. Chapter 5 deals with the supply curve. By studying the costs of production and how costs vary with output, you will gain an understanding of the forces that shape the supply curve.

APPENDIX A

Consumer Surplus

Have you ever wondered why you leap at the purchase of one item, hesitate to buy another, and refuse even to consider others? If we think about it, at one time or another all of us have experienced these feelings. For example, all of us have had the exhilarating experience of getting a real bargain. It may have been buying a high quality, deeply discounted brand name sweater, a special round-trip airfare to Paris, or living room furniture on a clearance sale. Or, wanting a personal computer but unable to afford one, you postpone the purchase until prices come down, or perhaps you negotiate a good deal on a car. Whatever the occasion, whatever the item involved, all of us look for the best value in the services and products we buy. And there are those times when we feel like we got exactly what we wanted at a really good price. Our sense of satisfaction is immense.

Consumer surplus *means the extra (or surplus) satisfaction derived from buying a good or service.*

Consumer surplus means the extra (or surplus) satisfaction derived from buying a good or service. It is the difference between the market price and the demand price (the price we are willing to pay). When you feel like you got a terrific bargain, you are probably willing to pay more for the good or service. Right? This feeling of extra satisfaction is referred to as consumer surplus. Take a look at Figure A4–1. Here we have a typical supply and demand diagram of the microcomputer software market.

The market demand represents the total of thousands of individual consumer demand curves. As shown in the diagram, some consumers are willing to pay more than $600 per unit of software. However, when Software Unlimited sells its products at $300, buyers purchase the goods well below the higher demand prices ($400, $450, etc.). As a result, buyers obtain a consumer surplus, measured by the triangle *ABE*, the area between the demand curve and the current market price. If you went to the store prepared to pay $500 for the software, but discovered that the actual market price was $300, then you would earn $200 of consumer surplus. Although this is a highly subjective measurement, in terms of utility theory this area represents the *excess satisfaction* you derive from buying the product at $300 instead of a higher price.

The sale price of $300 is a measure of the value consumers place on the product, but because they are willing to pay more, they derive surplus benefits or satisfaction. This concept helps to explain why consumers deluge de-

FIGURE A4–1

Consumer Surplus in the Market for Microcomputer Software Software Unlimited, Inc.

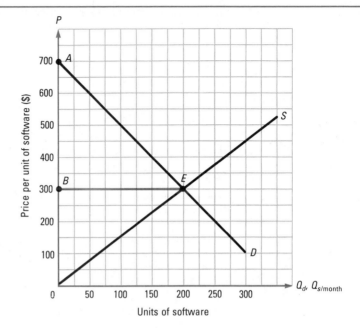

Consumer surplus is the difference between the price people are willing to pay (the demand price) and the market price. At the equilibrium price of $300, consumers realize a surplus (bargain) represented by the triangle ABE. This is the area bounded by the demand curve, the vertical axis, and the price line (BE).

partment stores during bargain-basement sales. The opportunity to purchase goods at prices much lower than normal results in a significant increase in satisfaction—a greater consumer surplus.

QUESTIONS AND PROBLEMS

1. Explain the idea of consumer surplus.
2. Using Figure 4–2b, the demand curve for coffee in your college cafeteria, identify the area of consumer surplus for a price of 35 cents per cup.
3. What happens to the area of consumer surplus when the product price declines? Increases? How does this help to reinforce and explain the law of demand?

APPENDIX B

Price Elasticity of Demand

All businesses dearly want to know how consumers will respond to changes in price. Think about the sales advertised in your local newspaper or on television. Department stores often run sales on hundreds of articles at the same time, ranging from clothing to compact disc players. From department stores to banks, from ice cream stores to fast-food restaurants, managers constantly seek ways to increase sales.

The Concept of Elasticity

A concept which applies to many situations, elasticity measures the cause and effect relationship between two variables. Specifically, it is a measurement of the percentage change in one variable to another. For example, if the temperature increases from 80 degrees to 100 degrees, how will the percentage increase in temperature affect the attendance at a community pool? If you increase the speed at which you are driving, from 60 to 70 MPH, how will the percentage increase in MPH affect the percentage change in gas consumption (MPG)?

Instead of being interested in temperature and attendance or speed and MPG, economists are interested in the responsiveness of quantity demanded to price. If prices of microcomputers are reduced by 10 percent, how will consumers respond? If banks raise interest rates by 5 percent, what will happen to the amount of funds demanded? Will people reduce the amount of funds borrowed by more than, less than, or equal to 5 percent? In other words, what is the price elasticity of demand?

Price elasticity of demand
measures the percentage change in quantity demanded to a percentage change in price.

Price elasticity of demand measures the percentage change in quantity demanded to a percentage change in price, other things being equal. It is a measure of consumers' responsiveness, or sensitivity, to price changes. Let's use another ice cream store, Sheila's Ice Cream Delights, to see how to calculate the price elasticity of demand. Figure B4–1, a market demand curve for ice cream cones during the week of July 15 to 21, illustrates a number of prices and quantities purchased.

The demand for ice cream slopes downward and to the right as usual. At lower prices for Sheila's one-scoop delights, people buy more cones, and at higher prices, people buy fewer cones. So Sheila's problem is to determine what price to charge for her basic one-scoop cone. Let's assume that Sheila is now charging $1.50 per cone. Should she lower her price to $1.20? Raise the price to $1.80? How will consumers respond?

The formula for computing the price elasticity of demand is

$$E = \frac{\% \text{ Change in Quantity Demanded}}{\% \text{ Change in Price}}$$

To compute the price elasticity of demand, we need to calculate the percentage change in quantity demanded and the percentage change in price. Percentage change in quantity demanded is found by dividing the change in quantity by the average of the beginning and ending quantities. The numerator may thus be rewritten as

$$\frac{\text{Change in } Q_d}{(Q_1 + Q_2) \div 2}$$

FIGURE B4–1

Demand for Ice Cream Cones
Sheila's Ice Cream Delights
July 15–21

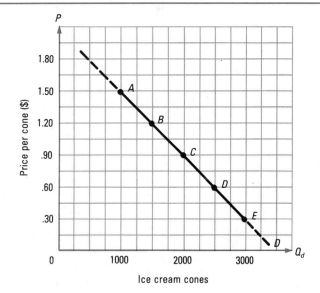

Q₁ is the beginning quantity and Q₂ is the ending quantity; dividing by two produces the desired average quantity. The same procedure is used to compute the percentage change in price. The denominator may be rewritten as

$$\frac{\text{Change in } P}{(P_1 + P_2) \div 2}$$

P_1 is the beginning price and is paired with Q_1; P_2 is the ending price and is paired with Q_2. Beginning at point A, ice cream lovers are buying 1,000 cones (Q_1) at a price of $1.50 ($P_1$). If Sheila lowers her price to $1.20 ($P_2$), people will buy an additional 500 cones, or 1,500 (Q_2). Substituting the numbers into the formula, we get the following:

$$\frac{\dfrac{500}{(1{,}000 + 1{,}500) \div 2}}{\dfrac{\$.30}{(\$1.50 + 1.20) \div 2}} = 1.82 \qquad \text{ELASTICITY} \\ \text{COEFFICIENT}$$

The average quantity is found by adding 1,000 and 1,500 and then dividing by 2: 2,500 ÷ 2, or 1,250. The percentage change in quantity demanded is then computed by dividing the change (500) by the average (1,250): 500 ÷ 1,250, or .4. The average price is found by adding the two prices, $1.50 and $1.20, and dividing by 2: $2.70 ÷ 2, or $1.35. The percentage change in price is computed by dividing the change in price ($.30) by the average price ($1.35): $.30 ÷ $1.35, or .22. Now, dividing the percentage change in quantity demanded (0.4) by the percentage change in price (.22), we arrive at the price elasticity of demand for Sheila's single-scoopers: 1.82 percent. (Ignore all minus signs in elasticity formulas. All figures have been rounded to the nearest hundredth.)

What does this mean? Or, as some of you may be thinking, so what? This elasticity number tells Sheila that, in the price range from $1.50 to $1.20, a 1 percent change in price will produce a greater 1.82 percent change in quantity demanded. Because the percentage increase in quantity is greater than the percentage decrease in price, demand is elastic. Translated into operating revenue for Sheila, this means that if she raises price anywhere in this price range, dollar sales (total revenue, or price times quantity) will decrease. Not exactly good news! However, she also knows that lowering price will increase total revenue, since the percentage increase in quantity is greater than the percentage decrease in price. This is music to Sheila's ears![9]

THINKING IT THROUGH

If Sheila raised her price by 10 percent, what would be the percentage change in quantity demanded?

Having explored the responsiveness of consumers to price changes at Sheila's Ice Cream Delights, we turn now to a general discussion of price elasticity of demand. The following table summarizes the various responses to changes in price. The beauty of this is that there are only three main cases: demand is elastic, inelastic, or unit elastic.[10]

If consumers are price sensitive, when price changes, the amount they buy will change by a greater percentage than the percentage change in price. This is referred to as elastic demand. Conversely, if people react minimally to a price change, so that the percentage change in quantity demanded is less than the percentage change in price, then demand is inelastic. The third possibility occurs when consumers' percentage responsiveness in quantity demanded equals the percentage in price. This means that demand is unit elastic.

---

[9] It is premature to advise Sheila about whether to raise or lower price from this information alone. Since we do not have any information concerning her costs of production (wages and salaries, fringe benefits, materials, and other miscellaneous costs which vary with output), we are unable to determine the effect upon her profit and loss picture.

[10] There are two other logical possibilities. Perfectly elastic demand is horizontal (parallel to the quantity axis); in this case, the coefficient of elasticity cannot be determined. Perfectly inelastic demand is vertical (parallel to the price axis); in this case, the coefficient of elasticity is zero. Although these cases are interesting brainteasers, these cases are so exceptional that, for practical purposes, we will not consider them here.

TABLE B4–1	Relationship of % change in Q_d to % change in P	Coefficient of Elasticity	Demand Is
Price Elasticity of Demand	% change in:		
	$Q_d > P$	$E > 1$	Elastic
	$Q_d < P$	$E < 1$	Inelastic
	$Q_d = P$	$E = 1$	Unit Elastic

Demand is elastic, inelastic, or unit elastic. When the percentage change in quantity demanded is greater than the percentage change in price, demand is elastic. (Consumers react to the price change by changing their consumption by a greater percentage amount.) When the percentage change in quantity demanded is less that the percentage change in price, demand is inelastic. And when the percentage change in quantity demanded is equal to the percentage change in price, demand is unit elastic.

Examples. As you may suspect, the coefficient of elasticity varies greatly. The demand for salt is highly inelastic, as is the demand for bread, eggs, and electricity for household use. For other products and services, consumers are much more responsive to price changes. For example, the demands for restaurant meals and for foreign travel are relatively elastic. Between these cases of elastic and inelastic demand are items for which demand is nearly unit elastic, like private education. See Table B4–2 on the next page for a representative sample of goods and services and their respective estimated elasticity coefficients.[11]

What does it mean to say that the price elasticity of demand for salt is 0.1 or that the coefficient of demand elasticity is 4.0 for foreign travel? As we have seen before, this coefficient enables us to anticipate the responsiveness of consumers to changes in price. For example, if the price of salt increases by 10 percent, the coefficient reminds us that the quantity demanded will decline by one-tenth (10 percent) of the change in price, or 1 percent. This is extremely inelastic and suggests that consumers are almost oblivious to price changes for this universal condiment.

In the case of foreign travel, the 4.0 coefficient tells us that the percentage change in quantity demanded will be four times greater than the percentage change in price; thus, if the price of foreign travel declines by 15 percent, we can expect a 60 percent increase in expenditures on travel.

A good example of how much more responsive we are to price changes for specific types of a product category is also shown in the table. The elasticity

[11] H. S. Houthakker and L. Taylor, *Consumer Demand in the United States: Analyses and Projection,* 2nd edition (Cambridge, Mass.: Harvard University Press, 1970); P. S. George and G. A. King, *Consumer Demand for Food Commodities in the U.S. with Projections for 1980* (Berkeley Calif.: University of California Press, 1971); and D. R. Bohi, *Analyzing Demand Behavior* (Baltimore: Johns Hopkins Press, 1981).

TABLE B4–2
Elasticity Estimates

Products/Services	Estimated Coefficient
Salt	0.1
Matches	0.1
Gasoline	
short-run	0.2
long-run	0.7
Coffee	0.25
Bread	0.15
Eggs	0.32
Beef (all)	0.64
Steak	2.54
Electricity (household)	0.13
Medical care	0.31
Physician services	0.6
Tires	
short-run	0.9
long-run	1.1
Private education	1.1
Radios and televisions	1.2
Restaurant meals	2.27
Foreign travel	4.0
Chevrolet automobiles	4.0
Fresh tomatoes	4.6

The range of price elasticity coefficients is very great for the goods in our market baskets. The table shows some of the elasticity estimates for 20 items; for two items, there are short-run and long-run estimates. Any coefficient less than one (1) means that the demand is inelastic; if the coefficient equals one, demand is unit elastic; and when the coefficient is greater than one, the demand is elastic. The determinants of demand help to explain why certain products have very low price elasticities while others are relatively high. Demand for a good such as salt or matches is inelastic because there are very few substitutes; salt is regarded as a necessity, and total expenditures on the item are small (relative to one's income).

---

of demand for beef is 0.64, but the demand for steak is 2.54. And the elasticity of demand for medical care (in general) is 0.31, while the elasticity coefficient is 0.6 for physician services—a subset of medical care.

QUESTIONS AND PROBLEMS

1. Given the following table of prices and quantities demanded for baskets of fresh strawberries, calculate the elasticity of demand coefficients between each pair of prices and quantities (e.g., between $1.20 and $1.00; between $1.00 and $ .80, etc.).

Demand for Strawberries at
the Farmers Market

Price	Quantity Demanded
$1.20	70
1.00	100
.80	140
.60	200

2. The price elasticity of demand for Chevrolet automobiles is estimated to be 4.0. What will happen to quantity demanded for Chevys if the price is increased by 10 percent? Reduced by 10 percent? What do you think are the most important determinants of elasticity for Chevrolets? Why?

IMPORTANT
TERMS FOR
APPENDIXES
A AND B

consumer surplus,   p. 112

price elasticity of demand,   p. 114

Supply and the Costs of Production

Karen Leeds, The Stock Market

This chapter continues building our microeconomic foundation. Chapter 4 examined the forces shaping consumer behavior to understand demand. In this chapter, we study the supply curve and the costs of production. How does a manufacturing firm determine the mixture of resources required to produce its desired output? How does a service business identify the combination of inputs necessary to satisfy its clients? How do costs vary with output? These and other questions constitute the basis for this chapter.

As in other chapters, graphs and tables are very important here. You may not yet feel that graphs are very helpful, but you have my guarantee that close attention to graphs will really pay off!

After the completion of this chapter, you should be able to do the following:

1. Describe and explain a production function, and give an example.
2. Diagram and explain the law of diminishing returns.
3. Distinguish between short-run and long-run production periods.
4. Explain the average-marginal rule.
5. Explain the relationship between marginal product and marginal cost.
6. Diagram, describe, and explain breakeven analysis.
7. Distinguish between economies of scale and diseconomies of scale.
8. Explain how the time period influences the elasticity of supply.
9. Identify and differentiate among increasing costs, constant costs, and decreasing costs.

Oh, That Pasta Salad!

My wife's pasta salad ranks right up there with the dishes served at the best Italian restaurants! Served cold, among other ingredients, it consists of vermicelli, thinly sliced zucchini, shredded carrots, marinated artichoke hearts, a smattering of sliced green olives, mozzarella cheese, with a very light touch of olive oil. This is a recipe for the gods, and the outcome would please the most discriminating palate.

Gayle's Pasta Salad

4 ozs. vermicelli or spaghetti	2 ozs. sliced green olives	3/4 tsp. dry mustard
1 6-oz. jar, marinated artichoke hearts	1 cup shredded mozzarella cheese	1/2 tsp. dried oregano, crushed
1/2 of a small zucchini, sliced	2 tbsp. grated Parmesan cheese	1/2 tsp. dried basil, crushed
1 carrot, shredded	2 tbsp. olive oil	1 clove garlic, crushed
2 tbsp. white wine vinegar		

Break pasta in half. Cook pasta according to package directions; drain and set aside. Drain artichokes, reserving marinade; coarsely chop artichoke hearts. Halve the zucchini slices. In a large bowl, combine the cooked pasta, artichokes, zucchini, shredded carrot, olive slices, mozzarella cheese, and Parmesan cheese. In a screw-top jar, combine the reserved artichoke marinade, olive oil, vinegar, mustard, oregano, basil, and garlic; shake well. Pour dressing over pasta mixture; toss to coat evenly. Transfer salad to a covered container; chill several hours. Makes 8 to 10 small servings.

Good for virtually all occasions, this epicurean delight seems to be most welcome as a light dinner on a warm summer eve. Enjoy!

PRODUCTION

Production function *lists economic resources in measured proportion in order to produce a quantity of output.*

Gayle's pasta recipe is a **production function.** It lists the ingredients in measured proportion in order to produce a quantity of output. Input and output—that is what a production function is. Whether making a pasta salad, manufacturing automobiles, or providing legal services, each activity consists of combining inputs in order to produce some output.

Of course, the combination of inputs (economic resources) to provide a given quantity of output may vary considerably. In the production of wheat, for example, one bushel can be harvested by one farmer with only primitive hand tools. Another farmer can produce one bushel with dozens of farm hands and the most modern equipment. Consider my wife's pasta again. If the salad is too tangy for your tastebuds, you might consider eliminating the green olives, or perhaps substituting slices of salami if you would like to add meat. In any event, she can produce 8 to

10 servings by herself with only a few rudimentary kitchen utensils. The same salad may be served from an elaborately outfitted restaurant kitchen, with a chef and several assistants.

As you may suspect then, the combination and type of inputs is determined largely by the scale of operation; that is, if one is serving hundreds of diners, day in and day out, then a household kitchen just will not do the job. Similarly, if one is growing wheat as a livelihood, a sickle is a poor substitute for a harvesting machine. In other words, the commercial producer must always seek the most efficient combination of resources and methods of production.

The production process involves the combination of land, labor, and capital in order to produce a good or service. To understand this process, let's use a barbering-hairdressing business. Like a one-horse farm, our hairdressing salon is a small operation, staffed only by the single proprietor and equipped with six customer chairs, scissors and razors (electric and manual), combs, and other essentials. We'll call it One Cut Above.[1] The proprietor Terry plans to hire additional hairdressers as business improves. And, as the short-run (weekly) production schedule in Table 5–1 shows, Terry's plans have been realized.

As the word spread about One Cut Above, Terry hired George, a second hairdresser. Before George came Terry cut 40 customers. When she had to turn customers away, however, George picked up the clippers. Together, Terry and George handled 90 customers. Business was still brisk, so Terry hired Alice, a third hairdresser. When Alice joined the team, One Cut Above serviced even more customers, 55 more than Terry and George could handle. As Terry continued to hire additional hairdressers in response to increased demand, Pierre, Lynn, and Wally entered the business. Even though the salon serviced more customers, each additional employee added fewer additional haircuts.

Marginal product *(of labor) is the change in (or contribution to) total product per extra unit of labor.*

As you can see from Table 5–1, total product is the number of haircuts provided. **Marginal product** is the change in (or contribution to) total product per extra unit of labor; thus, each additional hairdresser's marginal product is the extra number of haircuts which they provide.

The Law of Diminishing Returns

Law of diminishing returns *says that as additional units of a variable resource are added to fixed inputs, the extra output will eventually decrease.*

Marginal product increases at first, reaches a peak, and then decreases. This illustrates the **law of diminishing returns,** also called the law of diminishing marginal productivity. Stated simply, this law says that as additional units of a variable resource (such as labor) are added to fixed inputs, the extra output (marginal product) will eventually decrease. If

---

[1] The name is purely fictional and no reference to any real business is intended.

TABLE 5–1	Labor (number of hairdressers)	Total product (number of haircuts or customers)	Marginal product (change in customers per unit of labor)
Short-Run Production	0	0	—
Schedule			40
One Cut Above	1	40	
			50
	2	90	
			55
	3	145	
			50
	4	195	
			35
	5	230	
			15
	6	245	

Total product increases steadily as Terry hires additional hairdressers. Marginal product *(MP)*, however, shows the change in total product for each additional hairdresser hired. *MP* is calculated by dividing the change in total product by the change in the quantity of labor. In this example, because the labor employed increases by one person at each level, the *MP* is simply the change in total product.

this sounds unusual for a hair salon, imagine how the additional fourth, fifth, and sixth hairdressers actually get in each other's way.[2]

In order to gain a better understanding of the law of diminishing returns and the relationship between total product and marginal product, please see Figures 5–1 and 5–2 on the next page.

With each additional hairdresser employed, the total product curve increases throughout, reaching a total of 245 haircuts with six hairdressers. However, as shown in the companion Figure 5–2, the slope of the total product curve changes with each extra hairdresser hired. When marginal product is increasing, total product is increasing at an increasing rate. When marginal product reaches a peak (with the third hairdresser), total product increases at a constant rate. Finally, when the law of diminishing returns sets in, marginal product is decreasing and total product is increasing at a decreasing rate.

It may help if you realize that the law of diminishing returns, as applied to producers, is a concept similar to the law of diminishing marginal utility (as applied to consumers). Each law deals with at least one variable input in combination with fixed inputs. And each law explains how, once a saturation point is reached, diminishing returns set in. For

---

[2] This may occur as a result of having only one of everything: one cash register, one broom, and so forth. Some customers will decide to try other barber shops and hairdressing salons as the waiting time increases. Not even an appointment schedule handles the load.

FIGURE 5–1
Total Product

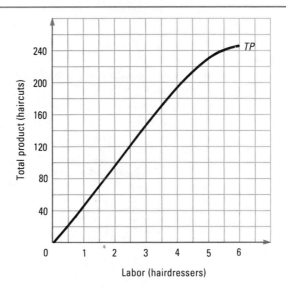

Output increases with each additional employee, initially increasing at an increasing rate for the first three hairdressers, then at a decreasing rate for the fourth, fifth, and sixth hairdressers.

FIGURE 5–2
Marginal Product

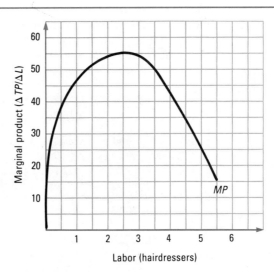

Diminishing returns set in with the employment of the fourth and additional hairdressers.

the consumer, each additional purchase results in less and less extra satisfaction. For the producer, each additional input results in less additional output. Moreover, each law is confined to the short run, a subject to which we now turn.

Short Run versus Long Run

Short run *is defined as a length of time so short that the scale of operations cannot be changed.*

It is important to distinguish between two major time periods in production. The **short run** is defined as a length of time so short that the scale of operations cannot be changed. This generally means that the size of the physical facility (store or plant) is fixed. Given a specific square footage, the business is unable to expand to meet increased demand. As Terry's business expands and she adds the sixth hairdresser, she has reached her capacity to produce in the short run.

Long run *is a time period long enough that all inputs (or economic resources) may be changed, including the size and scale of operations.*

The **long run** is a time period long enough that all inputs (or economic resources) may be changed, including the size and scale of operations. In the long run, Terry would be able to buy or lease the adjacent office, break down the wall, and expand One Cut Above into a 10 or 12-chair operation. On the other hand, she could buy or lease another store. In other words, there are virtually no constraints on the production function.

Although we may be tempted to think in terms of weeks, months, and years, the calendar has nothing to do with defining short run or long run. For some businesses, the short run may be as little as two or three months. One Cut Above may be able to expand its operations in a few weeks. For others, it may be as long as a year or more. Defense contractors, like McDonnell Douglas and Boeing, may require a year or more to build an extra plant to produce fighter jets. Because the conditions vary so much from one business to another, no fixed calendar time period is used as the definition.

THINKING IT THROUGH

Imagine an underutilized family farm operation, consisting of 500 acres, two farm laborers, and standard equipment. If the owner hires a third, fourth, and fifth laborer, what will happen to farm output? Explain how the law of diminishing returns is applied to this situation.

COSTS OF PRODUCTION

Costs are incurred because resources are scarce and have alternative uses. Increased production of CDs, for example, means that resources have been bid away from the production of alternative goods, such as tapes and records. Moreover, as we have seen before, the cost of doing anything is the value of the best unused alternative. The opportunity cost of attending your economics class, for example, is whatever you give up to do so. It may be a job, extra sleep, or relinquished study time.

Opportunity Costs: Explicit Costs and Implicit Costs

Explicit costs, *are payments made to suppliers of resources who do not have a share in the ownership of the business.*

Although all activities entail opportunity costs, it is important to distinguish between two major categories of cost. **Explicit costs,** also known as accounting costs, are payments made to suppliers of resources who do not have a share in the ownership of the business. Always found on the company's books, they include the wages and salaries paid to employees, rent for the building, payments for supplies, inventory, utilities, insurance, and related operating expenses. Explicit costs are often called out-of-pocket costs.

Implicit costs *are the costs to the business owners in using their labor and other resources in their business instead of other activities.*

Besides out-of-pocket costs, a business also has costs associated with resources which it itself owns. **Implicit costs** are the costs to the business owners in using their labor and other resources in their business instead of using them in other activities. Proprietors who own and contribute their labor, buildings, and other capital in the operation of the business give up the opportunity of earnings elsewhere. In our example with One Cut Above, because Terry is contributing her own labor along with the other hairdressers she has employed, her implicit wage is the income she could earn in working for someone else. Moreover, the money invested in the hairdressing salon carries an implicit opportunity cost as well. For example, if Terry invests $20,000 to equip the business, she sacrifices the opportunity of earning interest income on this money. Although implicit costs rarely appear in a company's accounting, they are essential costs of doing business. Because alternative uses of resources are so important in decision making, economists generally use the term *cost* to mean both explicit and implicit cost, and we will use the same convention throughout this book.

Profits

We normally think of profit (or loss) as the difference between sales revenues and expenses. Although this is generally correct in an accounting sense, because of the distinction between explicit and implicit costs, there are different measures of profit.

Normal profit is the income of the entrepreneur. It is an implicit cost of production, similar to the implicit wage Terry could earn by working for someone else or the implicit interest income from using her $20,000 to purchase a bond instead of tying up her money in the hair salon. Normal profit represents the minimum payment required to keep the business owner-entrepreneur in business. If Terry fails to earn a normal profit, she will close shop and do something else with her skills, time, and money.

Accounting profit is found by subtracting only explicit costs from total revenues (selling price times the quantity sold, or dollar sales). Unlike accounting profits, **economic profit** is calculated by subtracting from total revenues the total costs—implicit costs and explicit costs. Since normal profit is included in implicit costs, when a firm breaks even, that is, when it just covers its total costs, it is still earning a normal profit. If its total revenue exceeds total costs, it is earning an economic profit (above and beyond the normal or minimum profit). Table 5–2 summarizes these cost, revenue, and profit concepts for Terry's hair salon.

As illustrated in the table, subtracting total explicit costs of $98,800 from Terry's total receipts of $140,530 yields an accounting profit of $41,730. When implicit costs are deducted, Terry's economic profit is $20,930. This is in excess of her normal profit and is thus not a cost. In our next section, we will explore costs in still greater detail.

Terry's Short-Run Costs

Besides the concern about delivering quality haircuts at a competitive price, Terry is most interested in the costs of her services. Specifically, how do her costs vary with output? Table 5–2 illustrates the short-run costs associated with operating One Cut Above.

Short-run costs are broken down into fixed costs and variable costs. **Fixed costs** do not change with output; they are constant. Examples of fixed costs are rent, insurance premiums, interest payments on loans, depreciation, and related expenses which will not vary with the volume of business. In Table 5–3 (page 130), we can see that, regardless of the number of haircuts provided, One Cut Above has total fixed costs of $400. Even when Terry closes shop for vacation, she still incurs her fixed costs. When we add in Terry's implicit costs, however, her total fixed costs rise to $800 per week. (The implicit costs are based upon Terry's opportunity cost of working elsewhere [$18,800], and her alternative interest income from investing $20,000 in a security [returning $2,000 per year]. These implicit costs of $20,800 [$400 per week] must be added to her explicit fixed costs of $400 to paint a true picture of her total opportunity costs.)

Unlike fixed costs, **variable costs** are expenses which change as output changes. Wages and salaries, fringe benefits, and supplies are some common examples. According to Table 5–3, total variable costs are $0 when output is zero; the costs increase to $300 when Terry begins cutting hair and increase by $300 for each additional hairdresser. **Total cost** is the sum of fixed costs and variable costs. The total costs of providing 90 haircuts is $1,400, the sum of fixed costs ($800) and variable costs ($600).

Economic profit *is calculated by subtracting from total revenues the total costs—implicit costs and explicit costs.*

Fixed costs *are costs that do not change with output.*

Variable costs *are expenses which change as output changes.*

Total cost *is the sum of fixed costs and variable costs.*

TABLE 5–2

Calculating Economic Profit

One Cut Above

Total receipts (P = $11.75 × 230 haircuts		
× 52 weeks)		$140,530
Less:		
Explicit costs (payments to outsiders)		
Lease of building	10,400	
Insurance	7,800	
Depreciation	2,600	
Wages	62,000	
Supplies	5,000	
Utilities	8,000	
Miscellaneous	3,000	
Total explicit costs		98,800
Equals:		
Accounting profit		41,730
Less:		
Implicit costs (payments for Terry's resources)		
Wage	18,800	
Interest	2,000	
Total implicit costs (or normal profit)		20,800
Equals:		
Economic profit		$20,930

Accounting profit = Total receipts − Explicit costs
Economic profit = Total receipts − Total costs (explicit + implicit)
Remember that normal profit is the same as implicit costs; thus if Terry breaks even, that is, if her *TR* = *TC*, then she still makes a normal profit. Economic profit is excess—above and beyond the normal profit.

Marginal cost is the extra cost per unit of output, calculated by dividing the change in total cost by the change in output.

Average and marginal costs are additional cost concepts which also provide very useful information. First, **marginal cost** is the extra cost per unit of output. It is calculated by dividing the change in total cost by the change in output. Marginal cost is the answer to this question: Given that we are producing 90 haircuts, what will it cost to provide the next haircut? When One Cut Above hires its third hairdresser, output increases from 90 to 145 haircuts and its total cost increases from $1,400 to $1,700. The marginal cost of providing each of these 55 extra haircuts is $5.45, $300 divided by 55. And because we are interested only in the extra cost, fixed costs do not enter into the marginal cost calculation. Indeed, we just as easily could use the variable costs in our calculations.[3]

Besides the family of total costs, average costs are perhaps the most common measures of a firm's production costs. The *average fixed cost* (AFC) is calculated by dividing the total fixed costs by the output. At

---

[3] It is *very* important to remember that marginal cost is the *per unit* extra cost. This is why we must divide the change in output into the change in total cost. If output changed by one unit, of course, then marginal cost would simply be the change in total cost.

TABLE 5–3

One Cut Above Short-Run Costs of Production

Labor (number of hairdressers)	Output (number of haircuts)	TOTAL FIXED COST TFC	TOTAL VAR COST TVC	TOTAL COST TC	MARG COST MC	AVG FIXED COST AFC	AVG VAR COST AVC	AVG COST AC
0	0	$800	$0	$800		—	—	—
					7.50			
1	40	800	300	1100		20.00	7.50	27.50
					6.00			
2	90	800	600	1400		8.89	6.67	15.56
					5.45			
3	145	800	900	1700		5.51	6.21	11.72
					6.00			
4	195	800	1200	2000		4.10	6.16	10.26
					8.57			
5	230	800	1500	2300		3.48	6.52	10.00
					20.00			
6	245	800	1800	2600		3.27	7.34	10.61

The formulas:

$$TC = TFC + TVC$$
$$MC = \Delta TC \div \Delta Q$$
$$AFC = TFC \div Q$$
$$AVC = TVC \div Q$$
$$AC = TC \div Q$$

This table shows One Cut Above's short-run production costs. Note that the fixed costs include implicit costs, such as Terry's relinquished opportunity of working elsewhere and the interest income which she sacrifices because her $20,000 is invested in her business instead of a bond or certificate of deposit.

Average cost (AC) *is the cost per unit of output, calculated by dividing the total costs by the quantity of output.*

an output of 40 haircuts, the *AFC* = $20 ($800 ÷ 40). *AFC* declines steadily with increasing output because the total fixed costs are spread over larger and larger output. *Average variable cost (AVC)* is computed by dividing the total variable costs by the output. *AVC* is $6.67 at an output of 90 haircuts ($600 ÷ 90). **Average cost** *(AC)* is defined as the cost per unit of output, and it is calculated by dividing the total costs by the quantity of output. Average cost is the answer to the question, What is the cost per unit of providing 90 haircuts? Dividing the total cost ($1,400) by the number of haircuts (90) gives the average cost, $15.56. Unless stated otherwise, the term average cost *(AC)* always refers to average total costs to distinguish it from *AFC* and *AVC*.

Although average cost may seem to be a more complete picture than marginal cost, marginal cost is more important for decision making. If we want to know what it will cost a business to produce another unit of output, does it really matter what the fixed costs are? Economists think not, for two very good reasons. Since fixed costs must be borne whether the company is closed or open for business, and because fixed costs will not vary with the volume of activity, fixed costs should not enter into the decision-making process. By ignoring fixed costs marginal cost yields exactly the information we seek.[4]

The following series of graphical illustrations will help to review these important cost concepts. Figure 5–3 shows the total curves: fixed costs, variable costs, and total costs.

Total fixed cost *(TFC)* is illustrated as a horizontal curve at $800. Total variable cost *(TVC)* begins at zero and increases by $300 for each additional hairdresser hired, reaching $1,800 for the sixth hairdresser and 245 haircuts. Note in particular the changing slope of the *TVC* curve. Initially increasing at a decreasing rate, the *TVC* curve flattens out and then increases at an increasing rate. This relationship of how *TVC* varies with output is a reflection of the law of diminishing returns. As total product (output) begins to increase at a decreasing rate with the fourth worker, *TVC* begins to increase at an increasing rate. We will explore this relationship further in a few pages.

Total cost, the sum of *TFC* and *TVC,* rises from $800 (the *TFC*) to $2,600. With this diagram, Terry is able to identify the total costs of operating her business for each output level. She also can determine the cost of any intermediate output between 0 and 250, like 150 or 160.

FIGURE 5–3

How Costs Vary with Output: Total Fixed and Variable Costs *(TFC, TVC, TC)*

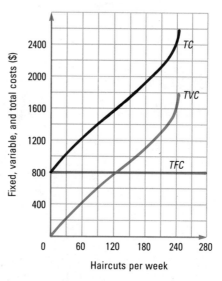

Total fixed costs are constant at $800 (explicit and implicit costs; *TFC* is thus parallel to the output axis. Unlike *TFC,* total variable costs *(TVC)* change as output varies. Total cost = *TFC* + *TVC.* Initially increasing at a decreasing rate, both curves flatten out and then increase at an increasing rate. This is a reflection of the law of diminishing returns.

---

[4] It is ironic at least that the very concept economists champion most—marginal cost—also is the cost concept used least by most businesses. We will explore this puzzle in the next chapter.

The average variable cost, average cost, and marginal cost curves are illustrated below in Figure 5–4.

Whether we use *AVC* or *AC*, this graph enables us to see the dramatic decline in the cost per haircut. For example, the *AC* decreases from $27.50 when Terry was working alone, to $15.56 after George was hired, to the lowest average cost *(AC)* of $10 when the fourth hairdresser is working, only to rise thereafter. The *AVC* is also a U-shaped curve, declining initially before increasing. Why does *AC* fall so quickly, bottom out at 230 haircuts, and then increase? Two factors account for the shape of the average cost curves. First, as Terry hires the second, third, and additional hairdressers, she is spreading the fixed costs over more units of output. In other words, the average fixed costs start at $20 when Terry cuts 40 customers and decline all the way to $3.27 when 245 haircuts are provided.

Marginal cost is a second factor that explains why *AVC* and *AC* decline as output increases. When *MC* is less than *AC*, the *AC* will fall. This is true so long as the extra cost of providing another haircut is less than the average cost. As soon as *MC* exceeds *AC*, the *AC* increases. This enables us to state a general *marginal-average rule:* the marginal cost curve will intersect the average cost curve from below at the minimum *AC* and then rise above it. (The same is true for *AVC*.) As the following example illustrates, this marginal-average rule may be applied to any situation.

FIGURE 5–4
Average Costs and Marginal Cost
One Cut Above

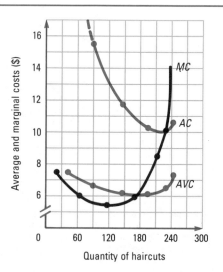

Average variable cost *(AVC)* and average cost *(AC)* continue to decline so long as marginal cost *(MC)* is less than the average (lies below the *AC* curve). When *MC* exceeds the average, *AC* increases. When Terry hires a sixth hairdresser, *MC* > *AC* and *AC* turn upward.

Consider the case of Michelle, an undergraduate student majoring in economics. Taking 15 credit hours per semester, Michelle has completed 60 credit hours in her freshman and sophomore years. Table 5–4 illustrates her individual semester grade point averages (GPA) and her cumulative GPA.

Using this table, we can easily see the marginal rule at work. In Michelle's first semester, she earns a 3.0 GPA; this is her marginal GPA (see Column 4). Since this is her first semester, her average GPA (Column 7) is the same as her marginal GPA. (Note that the average GPA is calculated by dividing cumulative grade points earned, Column 6, by the cumulative credit hours, Column 3.) After Michelle's social life perked up, she earned a 2.0 GPA in the second (spring 1988) semester. Because this marginal (or extra) GPA (2.0) is less than her average (3.0), the cumulative average declines to 2.5. But when Michelle took her first economics course in the fall 1988 semester, she found the inspiration to earn a 4.0. This semester's performance pulled up her average GPA to 3.0. When she repeated with a 4.0 GPA in the S'89 semester, her average GPA increased again (to 3.25). In other words, as long as Michelle's marginal GPA exceeded her average GPA, the average rose. When the marginal GPA fell below the average, the average fell.

THINKING IT THROUGH

What will happen to Michelle's average GPA if her next (marginal) semester's GPA is 3.25, the same as her current cumulative average? Can you think of other examples of the marginal-average rule?

TABLE 5–4
The Marginal-Average
Rule
Michelle's GPA

Semester (1)	Credit Hours (2)	Cumulative Hours (3)	Semester GPA, or Marginal GPA (4)	Semester Grade Points (5) (2) × (4)	Cumulative Grade Points (6)	Cumulative or Average GPA (7) (6) ÷ (3)
F87	15	15	3.00	45	45	3.00
S88	15	30	2.00	30	75	2.50
F88	15	45	4.00	60	135	3.00
S89	15	60	4.00	60	195	3.25

Michelle's college record nicely illustrates the marginal-average rule. After she earned a 3.0 GPA in her first semester, her second semester's performance fell to a 2.0. The result was that her average GPA fell from 3.0 to a 2.5. But in her third and fourth semesters, she earned a 4.0, resulting in an increase in her average GPA to 3.0 and 3.25. Whenever her semester or marginal GPA decreased, the average GPA fell; when the marginal GPA increased, so did her average.

Marginal Product and Marginal Cost

Another important relationship to consider is the relation between *MP* and *MC*. Table 5–5 consolidates the information in Tables 5–1 and 5–3.

Marginal product is the change in the number of haircuts provided by each additional hairdresser. Marginal cost is the additional cost per haircut attributed to hiring each additional hairdresser. As Table 5–5 indicates, when marginal product is increasing, marginal cost is decreasing. When *MP* reaches a maximum (55) and then declines with the hiring of the fourth, fifth, and sixth hairdressers, marginal cost reaches a minimum ($5.45) and then increases thereafter. Why is this? Why does *MC* move in directions exactly opposite to *MP?*

To see why this is so, ask yourself what marginal product measures. When Terry opens business at One Cut Above, she cuts 40 customers. After George goes to work, together they provide 90 haircuts, so George's *MP* is 50 haircuts. Meanwhile, the marginal cost declines from $7.50 to $6.00. The increased productivity of the second hairdresser translates directly into a lower marginal cost. In other words, rising productivity is equivalent to lower costs of production.[5] This is one of the reasons why it is so important for business to search for more efficient

TABLE 5–5	Labor (number of hairdressers)	Marginal Product of Hairdressers	Marginal Cost of Hairdressers
Marginal Product and Marginal Cost Relationship One Cut Above	0		
		40	$750
	1		
		50	6.00
	2		
		55	5.45
	3		
		50	6.00
	4		
		35	8.57
	5		
		15	20.00
	6		

The relationship between marginal product *(MP)* and marginal cost *(MC)* is inverse; that is, as *MP* increases, *MC* decreases; as *MP* decreases, *MC* increases. This is because *MP* is a measure of a firm's efficiency. When *MP* increases the firm obtains more additional output than it got from hiring the last worker. This extra boost of productivity is translated into a lower marginal cost, or the extra cost of producing one more unit of output (or haircuts in our example.)

---

[5] The same relationship holds true for average product $(AP = TP / L)$ and average cost $(AC = TC / Q)$. As *AP* increases, *AC* decreases; when *AP* peaks out, *AC* reaches its minimum, and when *AP* decreases, *AC* increases. One is the mirror image of the other.

ways to combine economic resources and for improved methods of production. Whether we deal on the microeconomic level of a hair salon or the broader micro and macro issues of international trade, increasing productivity has sweeping implications for everything from lower inflation at home to an improved competitive international posture.

BREAKEVEN ANALYSIS

Perhaps the most common analytical tool associated with pricing, costs, and sales is breakeven analysis. If Terry wants to know how many haircuts her shop must provide in order to cover her total costs, breakeven analysis offers an answer.

Breakeven refers to the quantity of output at which total revenues equals total cost.

Breakeven refers to the quantity of output at which total revenue equals total cost. It is also expressed in dollar terms: the total sales revenue that will cover all of the company's costs (fixed—explicit and implicit—and variable). In order to calculate the breakeven point (in dollars or units), Terry first must compute total revenue (sales)—the price times the number of haircuts (or unit sales) provided. If we assign TR to represent total revenue, P for price, and Q for unit sales, then $TR = P \times Q$. As we have seen already, total cost is the sum of fixed and variable costs. Letting TC stand for total cost, TFC for total fixed cost, and TVC for total variable cost, then $TC = TFC + TVC$. The breakeven point in units is that output (number of haircuts) at which $TR = TC$.

TABLE 5–6 Breakeven (Profit and Loss Analysis) One Cut Above	Output (number of haircuts)	Total Cost (TC)	Marginal Cost (MC)	Average Cost (AC)	Price (P)	Total Revenue (TR)	Economic Profit or Loss
	0	$800		—	$13.00	0	($800)
			$ 7.50				
	40	1100		$27.50	12.75	$ 510.00	(590)
			6.00				
	90	1400		15.56	12.50	1,125.00	(275)
BREAKEVEN → 144			5.45			*TR = TC*	
TC = TR	145	1700		11.72	12.25	1,776.25	76
			6.00				
	195	2000		10.26	12.00	2,340.00	340
			8.57				
PROFIT MAXIMIZED → 230	2300			10.00	11.75	2,702.50	403
			20.00				
MC = P	245	2600		10.61	11.50	2,817.50	218
					12.25		

Terry breaks even at an output of approximately 144 haircuts. Her economic profit is $403 at an output of 230 haircuts, the output that maximizes her profits.

FIGURE 5–5
Breakeven Chart

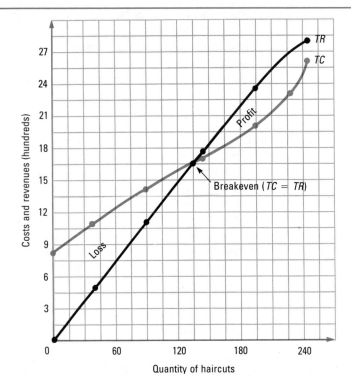

The breakeven point, defined as the quantity of output where $TC = TR$, occurs at about 135 haircuts. If Terry's salon does less business, she will experience an economic loss; at more than 135 haircuts—at least for the forseeable future—Terry's salon will turn an economic profit. (Note: Because TR is showing signs of peaking out, and because TC is increasing at an increasing rate, Terry is likely to see declining profits and another breakeven point beyond 230 haircuts.)

For purposes of our example, we will assume that the haircutting business is a *monopolistically competitive market;* that is, there are many small firms each of which provides a similar service. Moreover, each firm tries to differentiate its product from its competitors by advertising and by offering unique services (such as a free manicure), coupons featuring price discounts, and so forth. Much more will be said about this and other markets in the next chapter.

Table 5–6 summarizes the relevant information from Table 5–3, with the addition of price and profit and loss columns. Note also that average cost is included as well, since we may also calculate total cost by multiplying the average cost times the number of haircuts provided. Declining average prices reflect Terry's interest in expanding services.

FIGURE 5–6
Breakeven Chart

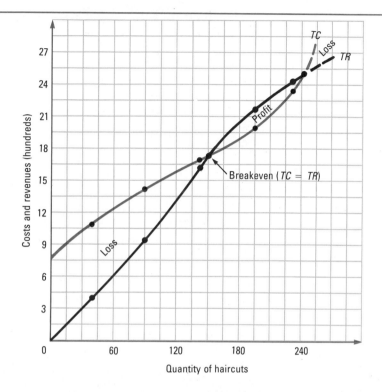

When market demand for haircuts decreases, leading to lower prices, the *TR* curve now intersects *TC* at approximately 150 haircuts. Terry's best profit output is still 230 haircuts, although her economic profit is reduced to $173.

Before her first customer, Terry incurred an economic loss of $800 (equal to her fixed costs). When she cut 40 customers, she reduced her loss to $590. As she hired additional hairdressers, she continued to reduce her losses until she reached the breakeven point at approximately 144 haircuts and three hairdressers (including herself). Hiring two more hairdressers and raising output to 230 haircuts enables her to reach the best economic profit of $403.

Although the data in the table speak for themselves, the breakeven point is more clearly shown graphically. Figure 5–5 illustrates the same data and gives us a clear picture of Terry's costs and revenues. Figure 5–5 shows three clearly delineated areas of loss, breakeven, and profit. Terry experiences an economic loss until her shop has about 144 customers. This is her breakeven point, where the *TR* curve intersects the *TC* curve. Her best short-run outcome occurs at an output of 230 haircuts where she maximizes her economic profit.

But what happens when market conditions change? Figure 5–6 illustrates the effect of a decline in market demand for haircuts, perhaps because a new fashion for longer hair is sweeping the nation. The upshot is that the demand for haircuts decreases, resulting in a new and lower set of prices.

Earning one dollar less for each haircut translates directly into a more narrow range of profitable output. As Figure 5–6 shows, Terry's new breakeven output is approximately 150 haircuts, and she makes an economic profit of only $173.

Fixed costs, variable costs, total costs, marginal cost, average cost, total revenue, accounting profit, economic profit, breakeven—Enough already! Take a breather and test your understanding of the following CASE-IN-POINT. This summarizes the salient information about costs of production and a company's profit and loss picture.

CASE
• IN •
POINT

The Food Mart

Bo Smith is the owner of The Food Mart. Located in a residential neighborhood, Bo's grocery store operation has been in business for just a few years. Bo has $25,000 of his own money invested in his store (providing for the building, equipment, start-up inventory, etc.). His explicit fixed costs were $20,000 last year, and total variable costs paid to his suppliers and employees came to $30,000. Bo's total sales last year were $80,000.

In a moment of weakness, feeling overworked and not making nearly as much money as he planned, Bo estimated that he could have earned $20,000 working for the A&P. Similarly, if he hadn't tied up his $25,000 in the store, Bo figures that he could have drawn at least 8 percent interest on these funds ($2,000). Relating his tale of woe to a customer, Bo confessed, "It's times like these that make you wonder about the joys of owning your own business!"

Questions to Consider

1. *What is Bo's accounting profit? What is his economic profit?*
2. *Assuming constant marginal costs (a linear total cost curve) and a linear total revenue curve, construct a breakeven chart for The Food Mart which shows two total cost curves. (One should show explicit costs and the other should show implicit plus explicit costs.) Using your graph, what is Bo's breakeven point, measured in dollar sales, using only the explicit costs? What is the breakeven using implicit and explicit costs?*

COST CONDITIONS

As we have seen already, a company's costs vary considerably over its range of output. Terry's average and marginal costs changed significantly from start-up to breakeven and to her profit-maximizing output. How do these costs help determine the shape of the firm's supply curve? Do all supply curves have a positive slope? Under what circumstances may a supply curve be vertical? Horizontal? Can a supply curve have a negative slope?

The supply curve for an individual product at a constant price provided by a specific business is generally horizontal. In the case of our hairdressing salon, if Terry charged a single price of $12 per haircut, demand would determine the quantity of haircuts supplied. However, if we were to include other hairdressing services, like a simple trim, perms, coloring, highlighting, and straightening, all at different prices, then the supply curve would be upward sloping. And in the extreme short run—from today to tomorrow, for example—the supply curve may even be vertical. Terry and George can cut only 90 customers per week when only they are working. If business suddenly picks up, she will have to turn customers away, since she will be unable to find another hairdresser on such short notice. Of course, one way some businesses deal with this situation is to raise prices, but that is a matter for the next chapter.

As we have just seen, the time period plays a critical role in supply. In the short run, a business is limited to adding more labor (another shift) and using existing equipment and facilities more intensively. Ultimately, the company faces decreasing productivity and rising unit costs. Unable to expand output further in response to increased demand, it is commonplace for companies to raise prices in order to cover their increased costs and to try to maintain profit levels.

Elasticity of Supply

Elasticity of supply *measures the responsiveness of quantity supplied to changes in price.*

A useful tool when dealing with a firm's ability to expand output is our old friend elasticity. **Elasticity of supply** measures the responsiveness of quantity supplied to changes in price. (Sound familiar? Just substitute *quantity demanded* for *quantity supplied* and we have our original elasticity of demand definition.) Supply elasticity enables us to describe and explain how the time period is a major determinant of production. As with Terry's hairdressing salon, any company in the short run is very limited in its ability to expand production. And, the shorter the time period, the less responsive business is to increased demand and higher prices. Figure 5–7 illustrates this situation.

FIGURE 5–7

Elasticity of Supply

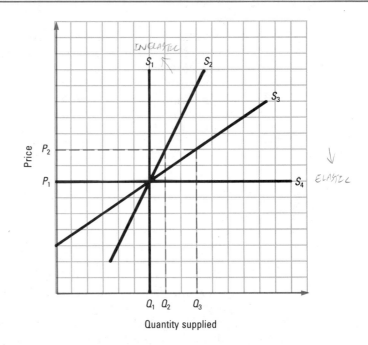

Quantity supplied

This graph illustrates four supply schedules, S_1 to S_4, with increasingly greater elasticity of supply. From S_1, which is perfectly inelastic, to S_4, a perfectly elastic supply curve, the price increase from P_1 to P_2 causes increasingly greater increases in quantity supplied.

We have four supply curves, S_1, S_2, S_3, and S_4, representing increasingly more elastic supply conditions in the short run. S_1 is vertical and thus is perfectly inelastic. If price increases from P_1 to P_2, the quantity supplied remains fixed at Q_1. Consider the supply of original Picasso paintings. Fixed in supply, regardless of how great the demand or how high the price, additional paintings will not become available. Of course, when demand is strong in the face of inelastic supply, the opportunity for profits often leads to black-market operations. In the case of the art market, dealers must always be on the alert for counterfeit works.[6] As with any illegal activity, the risks are great, but so are the rewards.

The second supply curve, S_2, is more elastic than S_1 and thus more output can be coaxed out if the price goes high enough. As prices in-

---

[6] A similar situation exists whenever the government acts to prohibit or regulate the supply of a product or service. Drugs and prostitution are two such examples today, as was alcohol during Prohibition. The housing market offers another example. Let's assume that there are several types of apartments for rent—studio, one-, two-, and three-bedroom apartments, condos, townhouses, and so forth. Because the landlord or contractor cannot increase production (quantity supplied) of housing units available in the short run, the supply curve is generally considered vertical. This is reflected in the CASE-IN-POINT in Chapter 3.

crease from P_1 to P_2 on the S_2 supply curve, quantity supplied increases from Q_1 to Q_2. Oil drilling in the United States is a good example. When the price per barrel of oil went over \$30 in the 1970s, everyone, from Exxon geologists to the secretary of the Department of the Interior speculated on extracting oil from the oil shale in the Rocky Mountains. Many unproductive wells were activated, and oil exploration began in earnest. When the OPEC bubble deflated (temporarily) and oil prices tumbled in the mid-1980s, wells were capped, whole divisions of oil companies in the gulf states were cut out, and the United States resumed importing more than half of its oil. The moral of this story is simple: Business does not do that which is unprofitable.

S_3 illustrates still another possibility. More elastic than S_2, when price increases from P_1 to P_2 on the S_3 supply curve, the quantity supplied increases from Q_1 to Q_3. When the economy is recovering from an economic slump, many businesses have a lot of unused production capacity. Machinery and equipment are idle, and departments may be operating at only 60 to 70 percent of optimum. When business activity picks up again in this situation, companies are positioned to recall laid-off workers and greatly expand output. Moreover, since firms are utilizing their existing capital more fully than before, labor productivity (output per employee per hour) increases. This increased level of efficiency translates into lower unit costs of production and increased profits. Indeed, this situation sets up a fourth case, illustrated as the supply curve S_4. Here we have a perfectly elastic supply curve (parallel to the quantity axis). In this situation, the firm will supply whatever quantity market demand dictates with no change in market price.

THINKING IT THROUGH

Why is it unlikely for a firm in the short run to operate on a perfectly elastic supply curve? Of the two extreme cases, perfectly inelastic and perfectly elastic supply, which is more plausible? Why?

Long-Run Costs

In the long run, a firm has sufficient time to build a new plant or expand its capacity within its existing plant. This presents an entirely new dimension for our discussion of the supply curve. As a firm increases production in the short run, its average costs of production ultimately increase. Because these cost pressures jeopardize its ability to price its product competitively and make a reasonable profit, the firm is faced with the decision to expand. Once the company decides to reach for

Economies of scale *means decreasing average costs of production.*

greater sales (increased market share), it may buy or build additional plants and thus realize **economies of scale,** or decreasing average costs of production.

Many factors may be cited for the presence of economies of scale. Specialization and division of labor, the substitution of capital for labor and the use of other cost-reduction techniques, and the application of new production methods and other knowledge derived from research and development, in the long run, contribute increased productivity and lower unit costs. Figure 5–8 below illustrates these effects. Here we have a series of five short-run average cost curves *(SAC)* and one long-run average cost curve *(LAC)*. Each *SAC* represents a new plant or the expansion of an existing plant. A firm operating in the short run is stuck on SAC_1 and will eventually experience rising unit costs. In the long run, however, it may decide to build another plant in order to seize these economies of scale. When the firm does so, it then operates on a new and lower short-run cost curve, SAC_2. In other words, the typical business, be it a single proprietor or a major corporation, is guided by its self-interest and rational behavior to seek improved sales and profits by driving down its costs of production.

As evidence from industry indicates, firms do not enjoy permanent economies of scale. For example, as our hypothetical firm continues to reach for lower unit costs by expanding its operations and building new

FIGURE 5–8

Long-Run Average Cost

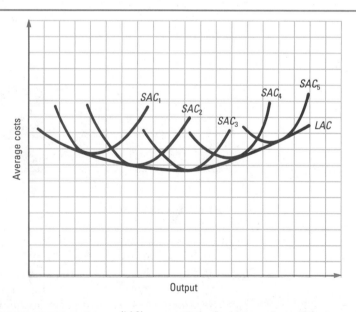

The long-run average cost curve *(LAC)* represents the firm's expansion path from one short-run average cost curve to another *(SAC_1 − SAC_5)*. Economies of scale cease with the building of the fourth plant. From that point on, the firm incurs diseconomies of scale.

plants, it moves from SAC_2 to SAC_5. If we sketch in a long-run average cost curve tangent to (just touching) the approximate minimum points on each short-run average costs curve, the firm eventually experiences **diseconomies of scale,** or increasing average costs. Why is this? What can be done to prevent it?

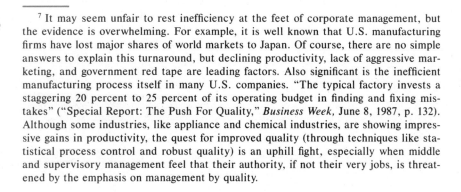
Diseconomies of scale *refers to increasing average costs.*

When the firm expands beyond its minimum long-run average cost, that is, when it decides to build the fourth plant, it has exceeded its *optimum size,* the point at which its average cost is at a minimum. Although optimum plant (or firm) size varies greatly from industry to industry, and though it is difficult to generalize about the relationship between a firm's size and its optimum scale of operations, diseconomies of scale appear to be common in the trucking industry. In very large corporations, there are many levels in the organization between production (plant) workers and decision-making management personnel. Indeed, centralization may go so far as to cause breakdowns in communication, resulting in costly delayed decisions. As firms add more internal services as they expand, some companies become top-heavy in middle and upper management. Indeed, one of the trends among Fortune 500 companies in the 1980s was to reduce corporate fat, cutting out layers of middle management. Some firms like Southwestern Bell Telephone have undergone extensive decentralization in a quest for greater operating efficiency. On the other hand, the U.S. Steel Corporation and other steel firms are highly centralized organizations, and top management seems to be uncertain about any economies from decentralization. To be sure, the battle against rising costs is always an uphill struggle, and it seems that diseconomies are the price paid for inefficient management.[7]

The following CASE-IN-POINT offers some evidence on the size of a firm's operations and its optimum scale. Because there is so much variation from firm to firm and from industry to industry, it is important to study individual companies within an industry with the hope of finding a general pattern.

---

[7] It may seem unfair to rest inefficiency at the feet of corporate management, but the evidence is overwhelming. For example, it is well known that U.S. manufacturing firms have lost major shares of world markets to Japan. Of course, there are no simple answers to explain this turnaround, but declining productivity, lack of aggressive marketing, and government red tape are leading factors. Also significant is the inefficient manufacturing process itself in many U.S. companies. "The typical factory invests a staggering 20 percent to 25 percent of its operating budget in finding and fixing mistakes" ("Special Report: The Push For Quality," *Business Week,* June 8, 1987, p. 132). Although some industries, like appliance and chemical industries, are showing impressive gains in productivity, the quest for improved quality (through techniques like statistical process control and robust quality) is an uphill fight, especially when middle and supervisory management feel that their authority, if not their very jobs, is threatened by the emphasis on management by quality.

CASE
• IN •
POINT

L-Shaped Average Cost

Although the short-run average cost curve is U-shaped, reflecting the law of diminishing returns, the long-run average cost curve seems to be L-shaped. "Seems to be?" you ask.

For over 50 years, economists have described the short-run and long-run average cost relationship as depicted in Figure 5–8. However, empirical evidence gathered over many years strongly suggests that most firms in most industries do not experience long-run diseconomies. Table 5–7 below shows the research findings for six industries.

These findings strongly suggest that the *LAC* curve looks like the lazy L-shaped curve shown in Figure 5–9, not a U-shaped curve.

Each number in the table represents the size distribution of a representative firm's actual average cost as a percentage of the industry's minimum average cost. For example, small commercial banks have average costs more than 16 percent greater than large commercial banks, and small hospitals experience long-run costs that run nearly 30 percent higher than large hospitals. However, the pattern is not universal. For example, small and medium-sized trucking firms enjoy greater economies than large trucking operations. In general, although medium and large firms tend to have lower long-run average costs than smaller firms, the difference is not very significant. Nonetheless, there is absolutely no support for the traditional U-shaped long-run average cost curve.[8]

Questions to Consider

1. *What industry characteristics may account for constant returns to scale in the long run? Explain what factors may account for the long-run economies for larger firms in banking or hospitals. Why don't such cost advantages operate for the larger trucking firms?*

TABLE 5–7
Average Cost Ratios

	FIRM SIZE		
Industry	Small	Medium	Large
Commercial banking	116.1	104.7	100.0
Electric power generation	113.2	101.0	101.5
Hospitals	129.6	111.1	100.0
Life insurance (Canada)	113.6	104.5	100.0
Railroads (east)	100.0	127.9	119.9
Trucking	100.0	102.1	105.6

---

[8] Source: Walter Nicholson, *Intermediate Economics and Its Applications* (Hinsdale, Ill.: Dryden Press, 1986), pp. 194–96.

FIGURE 5–9

L-Shaped Average Cost

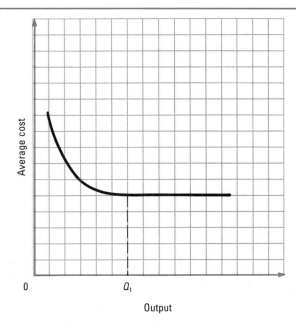

This represents a typical long-run average cost curve. Its lazy L-shape is based on many studies of cost conditions of actual business firms. The output range 0 Q_1 is the zone for which the firm enjoys economies of scale. Beyond Q_1, the firm experiences constant returns to scale.

2. *Each of the industries in the evidence cited are older well-established product and service groupings. How would you classify fast-food restaurants? Private (college) education? Computer software? Do these industries differ from those listed in the table? How? Why?*

Long-Run Supply

Where does that leave us? Incorporating what we know about a firm's cost conditions, we may have three long-run supply curves: upward sloping (based upon increasing costs), perfectly elastic supply (based upon constant costs), and downward sloping (based upon decreasing costs). Please see Figures 5–10a–c as we take each of these in turn.

Increasing Costs. Figure 5–10a illustrates a firm's long-run supply curve, labeled *LRSC*. In this situation, demand for the company's bicycles has increased faster than its ability to produce. The upshot is diseconomies of scale. Because its long-run average costs are rising, it finds it necessary to increase price in order to maintain its profit margin.

FIGURE 5–10 Long-Run Cost Conditions

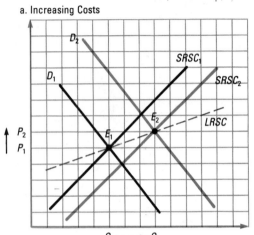

a. Increasing Costs

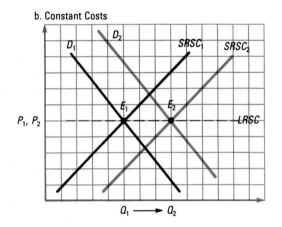

b. Constant Costs

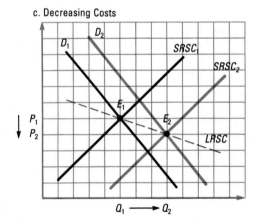

c. Decreasing Costs

Constant returns to scale occur if a firm's long-run average costs remain constant over a major range of output.

Constant Costs. If a firm's long-run average costs remain constant over a major range of output, the firm experiences **constant returns to scale.** As shown in Figure 5–10b, the increase in demand for bicycles is matched by an equal increase in supply. The *LRSC* is perfectly elastic, parallel to the horizontal axis.

Decreasing Costs. A firm may also experience economies of scale in the long run, although this is a most unusual case. A good example is the semiconductor industry. If improved technological change ushers in a major decline in average costs of production, a company's supply of memory chips may increase more than the increase in consumer demand. As illustrated in Figure 5–10c, the upshot is a downward sloping *LRSC*. Because this says that a firm is willing to offer more units and even a lower price, if the firm is to continue making good profits, its average costs of production must have declined at least as much as the product price.

<table>
<tr><td rowspan="10">IMPORTANT
TERMS TO
REMEMBER</td><td>average cost, p. 130</td><td>implicit costs, p. 127</td></tr>
<tr><td>breakeven, p. 135</td><td>law of diminishing returns, p. 123</td></tr>
<tr><td>constant returns to scale, p. 146</td><td>long run, p. 126</td></tr>
<tr><td>diseconomies of scale, p. 143</td><td>marginal cost, p. 129</td></tr>
<tr><td>economic profit, p. 128</td><td>marginal product, p. 123</td></tr>
<tr><td>economies of scale, p. 142</td><td>production function, p. 122</td></tr>
<tr><td>elasticity of supply, p. 139</td><td>short run, p. 126</td></tr>
<tr><td>explicit costs, p. 127</td><td>total cost, p. 128</td></tr>
<tr><td>fixed costs, p. 128</td><td>variable costs, p. 128</td></tr>
</table>

CHAPTER
SUMMARY

1. A production function, much like a cooking recipe, lists all inputs necessary to produce a specific quantity of output.

2. Businesses face the law of diminishing returns in the short run. When a company hires or buys additional resources in combination with fixed inputs, the extra output produced, attributable to the extra resource used, eventually decreases. Marginal product increases, reaches a peak, and then decreases.

3. The production process and costs of production are divided into two time periods. In the short run, companies do not have time to change the plant or store size. Firms have fixed costs in the short run. In the long run, there are no restrictions on business capacity, and all costs are variable.

4. Fixed costs, like rent and depreciation, do not change as output varies. Variable costs, like wages and supply expenses, will vary with the volume of business.

5. Total cost = Total fixed cost + Total variable cost, or $TC = TFC + TVC$.

6. Average cost = Total cost divided by the quantity produced, or $AC = TC \div Q$.

7. Marginal cost = the change in total cost divided by the change in output, or $MC = \Delta TC \div \Delta Q$.

8. Marginal cost is a near-perfect reflection of marginal product. As marginal product *(MP)* increases, marginal cost *(MC)* decreases; when *MP* reaches its maximum point, *MC* is at its minimum; and when *MP* decreases—that is, when diminishing returns set in—*MC* increases.

9. Breakeven (in units) occurs at that output where $TR = TC$. Total revenue is computed by multiplying selling price times the units sold $(TR = P \times Q)$. If a firm breaks even, it is still earning a normal profit since

implicit costs are a part of total costs. If *TR* exceeds *TC,* the firm makes an economic profit.

10. Economies of scale mean declining long-run average costs; diseconomies of scale occur when the long-run *AC* increases.

11. The elasticity of supply is a measure of the responsiveness of companies to changes in price. It is computed by dividing the percentage change in Q_s by the percentage change in *P*.

12. Short-run supply curves are generally upward sloping, reflecting increasing costs and diminishing returns. There are some instances in which supply may be perfectly inelastic (vertical) or perfectly elastic (horizontal).

13. Long-run supply curves generally take one of three shapes: upward-sloping, to reflect the case of increasing costs; perfectly elastic supply, to reflect the case of constant returns to scale (or constant *AC*); and downward-sloping, to reflect the case of decreasing costs.

DISCUSSION AND REVIEW QUESTIONS

1. If you were a graduating high school senior making plans to go away to college next year, you would make a budget showing your expected expenses. Your list consists of tuition, books, lodging, meals, commuting to and from school, and personal expenses. Construct a budget showing your explicit and implicit costs of attending college.

2. We have seen that production costs rise more sharply in the short run than in the long run. How does the law of diminishing returns account for this phenomenon? Does the law of diminishing returns also apply to the long run? Explain.

3. Movie houses used to be very large elaborate theaters, with a capacity of seating 1,000 or more people. Most went broke years ago. Today, it is common to find movie chains which operate a multitheater complex with three or more small theaters under the same roof. One concession offering candy, popcorn, and soda services the movie-goers in all the theaters. Explain how this change in the production function illustrates diseconomies and economies of scale.

4. The table below shows costs and revenues associated with operating an apple orchard in Muskegon, Michigan.

Ollie's Orchard

Output (bushels of apples per year)	Total Fixed Cost	Total Variable Cost	Total Cost	Total Revenue	Profit/Loss
0	$25,000	$ 0			
1,000	25,000	10,000			
2,700	25,000	20,000			
5,000	25,000	30,000			
7,000	25,000	40,000			
8,300	25,000	50,000			
9,000	25,000	60,000			
9,300	25,000	70,000			

    a. Complete the table assuming that Ollie sells apples for $12 per bushel.

    b. On a sheet of graph paper, plot the *TFC, TVC, TC,* and *TR* curves.

    c. What is Ollie's breakeven output? _____ What is the breakeven revenue? _____ .

    d. Judging from your diagram, at what (approximate) output does Ollie maximize profits?

5. You are interested in proving the marginal-average rule. Use the following information about your college's star basketball player to do so.

Games	Points Scored
1	30
2	10
3	35
4	25

6. Figure 5–7 on page 140 illustrates several supply curves. Assigning price values of $10 to P_1 and $12 to P_2, and quantity supplied values of 60, 70, and 90, to Q_1, Q_2, and Q_3, respectively, calculate the elasticity of supply coefficient for each supply curve (S_1 through S_3) for the price increase from $10 to $12. As with the elasticity of demand calculations, use average prices and quantities in your calculations here as well.

7. On a piece of graph paper, draw a set of highly inelastic supply and demand curves. Through the same equilibrium price (which we arbitrarily label as $3), draw a set of highly elastic supply and demand curves. Label the first set D_1 and S_1; label the second set D_2 and S_2. Let's assume that this is the market for wheat. If the government establishes a support price for wheat at $4 (above the current equilibrium), under which set of supply curves will the resulting surplus be greater? Which set of curves (D_1 and S_1, or D_2 and S_2) do you think most accurately describes the wheat market? Why?

A BRIEF LOOK AHEAD

The next chapter continues our treatment of microeconomics. Decisions about how much to produce to maximize profits, in the short and long run, will be examined both in the context of perfect competition and the more realistic framework of what we will call market competition. Also, actual business pricing practices will be compared with economic theory through several real-world companies.

6

Competition, Prices, and Profits

Richard Sobol/ Stock, Boston

This chapter focuses on the pricing and output decisions of businesses in perfectly competitive markets. However, because the degree of competition varies extensively from industry to industry, we will also build a market classification scheme in order to understand the type of market in which a company sells its products and services. Once we identify the type of product market, we will then ask whether the firm is a price taker (with no control over price) or a price searcher (with varying degrees of control over price). We will also examine the differences between short-run and long-run pricing decisions.

After completion of this chapter, you should be able to do the following:

1. Identify, describe, and explain the characteristics of the four market models: perfect competition, monopolistic competition, oligopoly, and pure monopoly.

2. Describe and explain how a company in the short run selects the output and price necessary to maximize profits in pure competition; and identify the profit maximizing rule for a purely competitive firm.

3. On a graph showing demand, average cost, and marginal cost, identify the profit-maximizing price, output, and area of profit.

4. Distinguish between short-run and long-run profit maximization conditions.

Texas Instruments: Anyone Remember the TI–99/4A?

Setting prices in practice is no easy task. Just ask executives at Texas Instruments (TI) to describe the pricing of the company's 99/4A home computer. The 99/4A was introduced in 1979 at a price of $1,100. However, sales volume failed to meet TI's expectations, and the 99/4A price was reduced to $399 in December 1981. In 1982, again recognizing that the price was too high, TI reduced its price to $299. Then, in September 1983, TI slashed the computer's price to $199 using customer allowances and dealer price discounts. Commodore, TI's chief rival in home computers, countered with an identical price reduction and then three weeks later dropped the price of its competitive model another $40. TI retaliated by lowering its price to $150. TI, Commodore, and a host of other home computer firms accelerated the price war by again cutting prices to $99 in mid-May 1983. When this happened, TI scrapped its plan to introduce its lower priced 99/2 model, which was originally scheduled for introduction at a price under $100. Finally, on October 28, 1983, TI announced it would reduce its price on the 99/4A to $49.95 and stop production of the model. Industry analysts estimated that TI had almost 1 million unsold units at the time of the announcement. Losses on the 99/4A amounted to several hundred million dollars in 1983.[1]

How does a company find a price to make a profit? As the FOCUS on TI indicates, this is no easy task. TI continued to search for a price to sell surplus home computers, only to discover that consumer perception of questionable quality or product viability was far more important. Price cutting and discounts just did not attract enough people to the TI personal computer.

TI's chief competitors, especially Commodore, countered with price cuts, setting up a cutthroat price war. Price competition proved to be TI's undoing as it discontinued production and left the PC market. TI's experience with the 99/4A PC is the outcome for thousands of companies every year. The market is littered with unwanted products and with firms who failed to survive the competitive struggles of the marketplace.

A similar example in the personal computer industry is the Osborne computer, developed by eccentric entrepreneur Adam Osborne in 1982.

---

[1] Erin N. Berkowitz, Roger A. Kerin, and William Rudelius, *Marketing* (St. Louis: Times Mirror/Mosby, 1986), p. 311.

Initially a tremendous success, Osborne's computer was hailed as a small business coup. His product design, packaging, promotion, and pricing were successfully integrated to yield almost immediate consumer acceptance. The success was short-lived, however, as Osborne was unable to meet demand. Deliveries of computers to dealers were delayed, and quality control slipped badly as Osborne pushed production quotas harder and harder. Frustrated dealers cut orders, and fickle consumers switched to other brands. Even steep price cuts did little to prevent the consumer exodus and the ultimate bankruptcy. Like TI, Osborne discovered that pricing had little to do with sales.[2] Consumers just did not want to get stuck with a computer no one would service and for which no software was being developed. Unlike TI, Osborne did not have an extensive financial base to absorb the financial loss and the failure of the product.

COMPETITION

Competition *refers to the absence of market power.*

What is competition? *Webster's Ninth New Collegiate Dictionary* defines competition as "rivalry: the effort of two or more parties acting independently to secure the business of a third party by offering the most favorable terms." Although this is a useful definition, competition in a market context requires more than rivalry. And if there are only two or three firms in a market, competition is much less vigorous than in markets with a greater number of firms; thus, we will use the term **competition** to mean the absence of market power. In other words, if a company does not possess market power, then it is unable to influence the price of its product(s) or service(s). A monopolist, on the other hand, is the only seller of the product and has the greatest control over price.[3] It is between extremes, however, that we find the vast majority of businesses, from mom-and-pop hardware stores to the gigantic auto, oil, and steel firms. (See the Appendix for a description of the relative size and legal forms of business organizations.)

---

[2] One could argue that pricing was very important. TI's initial price may have been too high—a tactical error. If TI had chosen a lower price to capture more of the market, it may have discouraged competitors from entering the market. Of course this what-if analysis is like Monday-morning quarterbacking. If only TI had known in 1979 what it knew in 1983, the results might have been different.

[3] All firms price their products according to profit objectives. However, for firms that possess market power, other nonprofit objectives are considered as well, since even monopolists are interested in avoiding consumer wrath and government inquiries.

Market Characteristics

Nonprice competition *refers to the means other than price reduction to increase sales.*

Over the last 50 years, economists have developed several characteristics to define the nature and degree of competition in a given market. In addition to the *number of firms* in a market, other characteristics are the *type of product or service,* the *extent of and access to market information,* the *ease of entry into the industry,* and the *degree of nonprice competition.* **Nonprice competition** refers to the means other than price reductions to increase sales, such as advertising and sales promotion activities. With these five primary characteristics, we can develop a more discrete market classification scheme. A few specific examples will be helpful to consider first before we plunge into the general model.

Consider the automobile industry. There are three major firms—General Motors (GM), Ford, and Chrysler. Together, they account for more than 98 percent of domestic manufacturing sales. Although the automobile can be seen as merely a standard means of transportation, it is really highly differentiated by design, color, warranty, and special add-on features. All of these combine to make the Chrysler luxury sedan very different from the Ford or GM counterpart. Moreover, as if these easily recognizable differences weren't enough, the Big Three spend millions of advertising dollars annually to further differentiate one car from another.[4] Moreover, each auto firm is a multibillion dollar company producing over one million cars annually in highly automated plants. The capital requirements to enter and compete in the industry, combined with the huge advertising outlays necessary to attract and win consumer acceptance, serve as overwhelming barriers to a new firm considering entry into this market.

The real estate industry consists of hundreds of firms offering a wide range of listing and selling services. Firms like Coldwell Banker, Better Homes and Gardens, and Century 21 are industry leaders, but there are

---

[4] Advertising is designed to increase overall demand, but it is also designed to segment essentially one market into many smaller markets based on consumer appeal.

hundreds of smaller firms as well. Unlike the highly differentiated automobile product, real estate services are virtually homogeneous. Whether you go to a Coldwell Banker with scores of agents or to a sole proprietor-broker agency, one offers a range of services virtually indistinguishable from the other.[5] And, unlike the prohibitively high cost of entering the auto industry, virtually anyone can start selling real estate. Although all states have licensing requirements, the test is not so rigorous as to seriously restrict entry. Indeed, in Los Angeles, California, there are 20 licensed real estate agents per 100 people. Imagine! Every fifth person you see is likely to be in real estate.

From the auto industry to real estate, from the local electric company to independent truckers, there is a vast difference in the nature and degree of competition. Figure 6–1 shows a breakdown of the range and type of competition into four distinct market structures. Specific industries are placed along the continuum according to industry characteristics like the number of firms and product type. Examples of each market type are also included.

Market Structures

Pure competition *is a market structure with a very large number of firms, each producing a homogeneous product with few barriers to entry and little if any nonprice competition.*

Pure Competition. Agriculture often is cited as the classic example of **pure competition.** It is a market structure in which there are a very large number of firms, each producing a homogeneous product with few barriers to entry and little if any nonprice competition. There are thousands of wheat farmers across the country, so many that no single farmer is able to exert any influence on market price. Why? Because each producer's output is such a small percentage of the total market output, even if several farmers withheld their supply of wheat, product price would not be affected. Farmers are thus **price takers**—they sell at the price determined by the market forces of supply and demand. And, since the products of one farmer are the same as others, nonprice competition does not exist. After all, if Farmer Jones advertises his wheat, he also promotes the wheat of his rival farmers.

Price takers *are firms that sell at the prices determined by supply and demand.*

Another characteristic of pure competition is the amount of information known about price and other market conditions. In agricultural markets, all farmers have nearly perfect information regarding price. Commodity exchanges, like the Chicago Exchange, list daily the prices of grains and other farm production.

---

[5] Of course, it is true that branch agencies of the very large firms will probably offer some services unavailable at the smaller firms. For example, computer analysis of market value, many more selling agents to show your property, and perhaps more access to innovative financing alternatives are generally offered by the larger well-established companies. This does not necessarily mean, however, that the larger firm will sell your home faster.

FIGURE 6–1 A Continuum of Market Structures

Market Structures

CHARACTERISTICS	PURE COMPETITION	MONOPOLISTIC COMPETITION	OLIGOPOLY	PURE MONOPOLY
	Price Takers	◄ – – Price Searchers – –►		
Number of firms	Very large	Many	Few	One
Ease of entry	Very easy	Easy	Very difficult	Rare
Type of product	Homogeneous	Differentiated	Homoegeneous or differentiated	Unique
Control over price	None	Some	Extensive	Most
Nonprice competition	None	Considerable	Extensive	Some or none
Examples	Agriculture; New York and American Stock Exchanges	Real estate, service (gas) stations, and financial institutions	Auto, oil, steel, and airlines	U.S. Postal Service, and public utilities

Even though individual farmers are price takers, various governmental programs designed to aid farmers greatly modify or interfere with the operation of the market pricing mechanism. Crop subsidies, acreage retirement plans, and related agricultural support directly or indirectly affect price, thereby nullifying the perfectly competitive nature of the market. Moreover, there is some degree of nonprice competition in agriculture. Perhaps you have seen the television commercials from the U.S. Dairy Association promoting the beneficial effects of drinking milk. In order to increase sales of milk and share the promotion costs, the trade association urges individual farmers to join and support their common cause.

Other industries also approximate purely competitive markets. The New York and American Stock Exchanges, for example, provide instant information regarding stock prices, and the products (stocks, bonds, and other marketable securities) are homogeneous. Moreover, much like farmers who sell to grain and livestock brokers, stock and bond transactions are handled by licensed securities brokers and dealers through the organized market exchanges.[6] Moreover, brokerage firms are regulated by the Securities and Exchange Commission, so their conduct, like agribusiness, is controlled by more than market forces.

THINKING IT THROUGH

Many farmers will join a trade association in order to promote their common welfare, but some will not join. How does this illustrate the free-rider problem involved in the provision in public goods? If you were a dairy farmer, what incentive would there be for you to join? If you didn't join, wouldn't you get the same benefits as the members?

Pure competition then really does not exist, except as an ideal type of market structure. Why study it, you may ask, if it does not exist? Economists have always studied pure competition as a way to shed light on real market structures. If we know how firms behave in pure competition, operating in a well-defined market environment, then we may compare actual business behavior under less than purely competitive conditions. As we will see later in our discussion of the government's antitrust policies, if it is deemed desirable to have very competitive markets, then we need to define certain noncompetitive behaviors and measure the potentially adverse effects on the economy.

Monopolistic Competition.   Service (gasoline) stations and many retail businesses, like clothing and hardware stores, are examples of **monopolistic competition.** In this market, there are many sellers of differentiated goods and services and a considerable amount of nonprice competition. Gasoline stations offer widely disparate services. Some have only self-serve pumps while others offer full-serve features, plus an assortment of services from towing to full vehicle repair. Some clothing stores are elegantly furnished, staffed with knowledgeable salespeople, and stocked with fashionable apparel. Others are very spartan—few if any sales personnel, limited selections, in very plain surroundings. Advertising also plays a major role in product differentiation. Everyday our newspapers are loaded with ads featuring new lines of clothes, special

Monopolistic competition *is a market structure having many sellers of differentiated goods and services and a considerable amount of nonprice competition.*

---

[6] Although recent trends indicate that banks and other financial institutions may be allowed to buy and sell securities and thereby compete with brokerage firms, we still live with the legacy of the Great Depression and the collapse of hundreds of insolvent banks. Indeed, many economists are concerned that, because third world countries have defaulted on loans, the U.S. banking industry is already in a precarious position. They warn that to permit banks to become full-fledged securities dealers would only add to their financial problems.

sales, Mother's or Father's Day promotions and the like; thus product packaging, presentation, and advertising are important ways to differentiate one product or business from another, whether the differences are real or imaginary.

There are relatively few barriers to entering monopolistically competitive markets. Although you may incur more start-up costs with a gasoline station or a clothing store than with a small farm, your costs are considerably less than with building a factory to produce televisions or laser discs.

Price searchers *are firms that set their own prices.*

Because control over price is limited by the extensive number of firms in the market, monopolistic competitors are **price searchers;** that is, they are keenly aware of their competitors' prices, evidenced by how quickly they adjust prices in accord with their chief rivals. Indeed, many of us have experienced the impulse to buy a blouse or sweater only to discover the next day that the same item is on sale. Wait another few days and still another price tag appears.[7]

THINKING IT THROUGH

How do these price fluctuations in monopolistic competition differ from perfect competition? Wheat prices increase and decrease, just like shirt prices. What's the difference?

Oligopoly *is a market structure with a few firms producing either a homogeneous or differentiated product or service.*

Oligopoly.   The automobile industry is an example of **oligopoly.** In an oligopolistic market, there are relatively few firms who produce either a homogeneous or differentiated product or service. In the case of autos, the product is differentiated in many ways. Perhaps the most important way is through advertising and other forms of nonprice competition. The Big Three automakers spend millions of dollars to segment the market—promoting each model car to a specific well-defined consumer group. Think about the television commercial showing the whole family piling in and out of the station wagon. Consider the young man or woman (25 and single?) tearing off through the countryside in a red, sleek, and sporty looking convertible. Of course, differentiation is also managed through design changes, service packages, warranty programs, and the endless array of special options and features you can add.

Barriers to entry are prohibitive in oligopoly. Recent estimates of building an auto assembly plant run around $100 million. And that is

---

[7] During recent inflationary periods, many hardware stores simply gave up marking prices on their merchandise. The combination of rising costs and competitive pricing placed a tremendous burden on the proprietors as they tried to keep current on thousands of different articles.

just the fixed-cost component. Initial operating (variable) costs would be extremely high, since a brand new business is unlikely to capture enough sales to capitalize on economies of scale. Compounding the problem is the obligatory product-promotion costs. No wonder that there are no firms about to challenge the Big Three, not to mention the Japanese, European, and other foreign competitors.

Pricing control in oligopolistic markets is extensive. Unlike agricultural markets, where prices literally are determined by supply and demand, the automobile firms set their prices, although they are sensitive to market conditions. And, like retailers, gasoline stations, and other monopolistically competitive firms, oligopolists search for prices after careful consideration of their competitors' prices. However, because there are only a few dominant firms operating in the industry, each firm exercises much more control over price. Indeed, it is not uncommon for auto firms to post a price increase even in the face of declining sales. This would be less likely to occur in monopolistic competition (like gasoline stations) and unheard of in agriculture.

Pure Monopoly.   A **pure monopoly** has only one seller of the product or service; thus, by definition, the firm is the industry. The product or service is therefore unique, and entry into the industry is virtually blocked. Although there are no other competitors, some degree of nonprice competition exists, primarily in the form of public relations. California's Pacific Gas & Electric or New York's Consolidated Edison may have no direct competition from other gas or electric companies, but they still spend a lot of money to enhance the company image as an efficient and socially responsible corporation with your best interests at heart.

There are actually three basic types of monopoly: government monopolies, natural monopolies, and private unregulated monopolies. The U.S. Postal Service is an example of a *government monopoly*. Established by the federal government to provide mail services, it is the principal source of first, second, and third class mail delivery.[8] Public utilities, such as gas, electricity, water, and sewer, are **natural monopolies.** These services are franchised by state and local governments to individual companies and then regulated by governmental agencies and commissions. A natural monopoly exists when one firm can produce for the whole market at a lower average cost than two or more firms. Production or distribution aspects of the service entail very large capital outlays, such as laying gas, sewer, or water-main lines. In order to real-

Pure monopoly *is a market structure with only one seller of the product or service.*

Natural monopolies *exist when a single firm can produce for the whole market at a lower average cost than two or more firms.*

---

[8] United Parcel Service (UPS) and courier services do compete with the postal service for packages, boxes, and related bundles, but only the U.S. Postal Service can deliver letters to your residence or place of business.

ize economies of scale, the firm must have a very large volume of output over which to spread its high fixed costs.[9]

A third type of monopoly is the *private unregulated monopoly*. Examples of such firms include Alcoa, when it controlled 95 percent of the world's supply of bauxite—a material necessary in making aluminum; and Xerox, when it developed the photocopying process known as Xerography; and Polaroid, when it introduced instant photographic development.[10] Although Alcoa, Xerox, and Polaroid were free to price their products according to their respective profit objectives, the federal government must approve postage rate increases, and the New York State Utility Commission similarly must review all rate hikes for Con Edison.[11]

Although in layman's terms competition may mean nothing more than the number of firms in the industry, other factors play a very important role. Some people believe that monopolists charge excessive prices for their products and services because there is so little effective competition. The fewer the firms, the less competitive is the industry, and the higher is the price. Conversely, the greater the number of firms, the greater is the incidence of price competition, and the lower the price. In other words, if there is only one firm available to supply natural gas to your home, that company must be charging unfair (excessive) prices. Right? Not necessarily. Not only are there alternative energy sources, but the state and federal regulatory commissions serve to review all price changes.[12] Moreover, pure monopolists know that government antitrust bodies are also watching their behavior. Remember the promises of lower telephone rates as a result of breaking up AT&T? After the breakup, prices of local telephone calls increased in every state in the country. Breaking up Ma Bell's operating companies into several "Little Bells" did not result in lower prices to the consumer.

---

[9] Of course, the local electric and gas companies are actually in competition with one another, since natural gas and electricity are substitutes in heating and cooling. Although consumers are reluctant to make such substitutions because of the high conversion cost, higher energy prices will provide immediate motivation. Indeed, when heating oil prices quadrupled in the 1970s after the OPEC oil embargo, thousands of households in the East converted to natural gas and electricity.

[10] Alcoa was a legitimate pure monopolist in the aluminum industry. Xerox and Polaroid had patent protection provided by the federal government, ensuring a temporary monopoly period.

[11] In Alcoa's case, because it owned or controlled the natural resources required to make aluminum and thus controlled the world's supply of aluminum, the United States, in a landmark antitrust case in 1940, forced Alcoa to sell off a percentage of its aluminum interests.

[12] In this case, your real gripe may be that the commission is dominated by people who do not adequately represent consumer interests. This takes us into the political arena and away from pure economic theory—a subject we will address increasingly as we move along.

Ironically, only long-distance telephone charges declined, further evidence of the difficulty in making predictions about the relationship between monopoly and so-called fair or unfair prices.

As we have shown in the foregoing continuum of market structures, competition is a relative term. The nature and degree of competition varies widely from industry, and it is often difficult to classify an industry into a specific structural cubbyhole. A good example of this is the airline industry.

The airline industry has long been identified as an oligopoly. And, like trucking and shipping, because it involves travel and transportation in the public airways, it also has been regulated by the Federal Aviation Administration (FAA) and the Civil Aeronautics Board (CAB) since the 1930s (although the CAB no longer exists). From 1978 to 1986, however, the airline industry went through a convulsive period of deregulation. Many decisions regarding airfares, routes, and schedules formerly made by the FAA and CAB were turned over to private airline management. The upshot was increasing competition: more airlines, more routes, and lower prices. In other words, although still classified as an oligopoly according to strict definitions, the industry was more competitive in 1985 than in 1975.[13] On the continuum of market structures, as shown in Figure 6–1, even though it was described and defined as an oligopoly, firms behaved more like monopolistic competitors.

The trucking industry, or at least a significant part of it, also helps to illustrate the difficulty of fitting an industry neatly into a specific market structure. The following CASE-IN-POINT is about independent truckers, "the last American Cowboys."[14]

CASE
• IN •
POINT

Cowboy Truckers

The next time you are out on the highway, take a close look at the trucks that are passing you. You will see many that belong to large firms, such as PIE and Yellow Freight, that haul large numbers of small shipments, mostly of manufactured goods, all over the country on regular schedules. Many other trucks will bear the names of companies like Sears or Sun Oil, for which transportation is only a sideline. These firms use their own trucks to haul

---

[13] One unintended consequence of airline deregulation was a marked increase in merger activity. By late 1987, the top eight airlines accounted for 94 percent of all passenger miles. The competitive environment proved too rich for new and some old firms alike, resulting in bankruptcies and buyouts. The irony is that the airline industry may becoming less competitive as a result of the economic freedom spawned by deregulation.

[14] "'Last Cowboys' Hit the Road to Capitol Hill," *St. Louis Post-Dispatch,* June 23, 1983; Edwin Dolan, *Microeconomics,* 3rd ed. (Hinsdale, Ill.: Dryden Press, 1983).

their own products. Largely as a result of government regulatory policy, the markets these trucks operate in are far from perfectly competitive.

If you look closely, though, you will see that about one truck in four looks a little different. The tractors, often brightly painted and highly chromed, are likely to have sleepers attached to them. The refrigerated trailers, usually with no identifying name, are filled with agricultural produce moving to market. These are the trucks of independent owner-operators. Exempt from federal regulation so long as they haul only fresh farm goods, they work in a market that comes about as close to pure competition as any to be found in the U.S. economy.

Each firm in this market consists of a man or woman who typically owns and drives just one truck. Each clearly contributes only a tiny fraction of the total market output.

The owner-operator's product is about as homogeneous as one can imagine. For the shipper of fresh produce, one refrigerated truck is about as good as another, so long as it is headed in the right direction. And most operators will go anywhere the traffic takes them.

Although there is no such thing as *perfect* information in this imperfect world, a widespread information network keeps independent truckers reasonably well-informed of where the loads are and what rates are being paid. A key element in this network is the truck broker—an information specialist who matches the needs of farmers for trucks with the needs of owner-operators for loads in return for a 5 or 10 percent commission. A call to a broker from a truck stop can give the trucker a tip that rates have moved a few dollars per load, so the time has come to switch from hauling Florida citrus to hauling California lettuce.

Finally, entry into this market is relatively easy. Some people go into business with a used truck and an investment of as little as $5,000. Most operators buy their trucks on credit and have less than $20,000 invested in their businesses. Experts can be hired to help the prospective trucker obtain the necessary state licenses and permits. Some independent truckers complain that entry is, in fact, too easy and that too many operators soon go broke. But statistical studies suggest that the turnover rate is no higher than in other markets dominated by small businesses.

The people who run the giant trucking companies that haul manufactured goods often look down their noses at the independent truckers with their loads of apples and potatoes. They call them "gypsies" or worse. But this highly competitive market succeeds every day in putting fresh produce on the dinner table in every town.

Questions to Consider

1. *The trucking industry is divided into two distinct market structures: one dominated by several large firms and another very close to pure competition. Does this make the overall industry monopolistically competitive? Why or why not?*

2. *Using the characteristics of pure competition, how do independent (gypsy) truckers compare with real estate agents?*

PRICING IN PURE COMPETITION

Economic theory assumes that all firms maximize profits; that is, companies will produce that output (goods or services) at a price which will generate the greatest total profits. In order to understand how this is done, let's return to our example of Ollie's Apple Orchard (from page 148).

Ollie is a perfect competitor. His apple orchard is one among thousands in the state of Michigan. Although Ollie swears his apples are heaven sent, in fact his apples are just like all other apples. The product is homogeneous. Moreover, entry into and exit from the apple market are easy. Although it takes several years before an orchard begins to bear a good crop of apples, a person can acquire several good acres of land for $10,000. Information about prices and other market conditions is readily available through local farmer organizations and the markets where apples are sold. Before discussing how to find Ollie's profit-maximizing output, let's take a brief look at the relationship between Ollie's Orchard and the general apple market.

Figure 6–2a illustrates the market demand for and supply of apples. The intersection determines the market equilibrium—the price at which Ollie and his competitors sell bushels of apples. Figure 6–2b shows the individual apple grower's demand curve (d_1). Because Ollie and all of the other growers are price takers, they each face a perfectly elastic (horizontal) demand curve at the market price of $12.

Market demand and the price at which individual apple growers sell their fruit are inexorably linked. Changes in market conditions are transmitted directly to each individual; thus if the determinants of demand or supply change, the market demand or supply curve will shift, resulting in a new market price and a new demand curve for Ollie. For example, if the price of oranges increases, a determinant of consumer demand for apples, the market demand for apples will increase (shift from D_1 to D_2). The upshot will be a higher equilibrium price of $14 and a new demand curve (d_2) for Ollie. When we add the familiar average and marginal cost curves to Figure 6–2b in the next section, we will be able to identify the specific number of bushels Ollie should sell in order to maximize profits. For now, it is helpful to examine the relationship between some old and new revenue concepts.

Table 6–1 illustrates Ollie's cost and revenue picture in the short run. Columns 1–5 present familiar information regarding Ollie's short-run

FIGURE 6–2a Market Demand FIGURE 6–2b Individual Grower's Demand

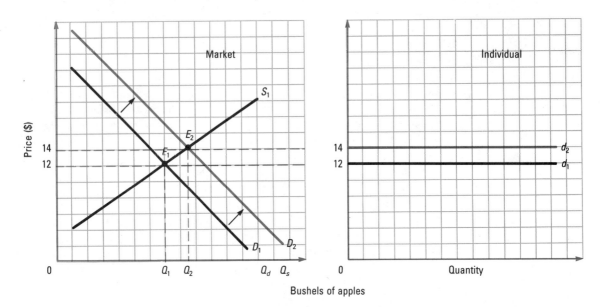

Bushels of apples

The market equilibrium price of $12 increases to $14 as a result of increased market demand, illustrated as a rightward shift of the demand curve from D_1 to D_2. This may have been caused by a change in any of the determinants of demand (e.g., an increase in the price of oranges or perhaps a change in consumer tastes.) The new market price is immediately translated into a new demand curve for Ollie and all individual growers of apples, shown as an upward shift in the individual demand curve from d_1 to d_2.

Average revenue *is the revenue per unit of output.*

Equation: $AR = \dfrac{TR}{Q} = \dfrac{P \cdot Q}{Q} = P$

Marginal revenue *is the extra revenue earned from selling one more unit of output. Equation:*

$MR = \dfrac{\Delta TR}{\Delta Q}$

costs; Column 6 shows the price per bushel *(P)*, which is also equal to average revenue *(AR)* and marginal revenue *(MR)*. (Friendly note: From here on, all cost and revenue concepts will be abbreviated. It's hard to remember what they all mean at first, but as you work with them it's much easier.) What is *AR*? What is *MR*? Why is $P = AR = MR$?

First, **average revenue** is defined as the revenue per unit of output; *AR* is just another term for price. Why? If total revenue *(TR)* is computed by multiplying *P* times *Q*, and *AR* is calculated by dividing *TR* by *Q*, then $P = AR$. Symbolically,

$$TR = P \times Q, \text{ and}$$
$$AR = \frac{P \times Q}{Q} \cdot \text{ The } Qs \text{ cancel, leaving}$$
$$AR = P.$$

Next, $P = MR$ in perfect competition (only). **Marginal revenue** is defined as the extra revenue earned from selling one more unit of out-

TABLE 6–1

Costs, Revenues and Profits
Ollie's Orchard

Output (Bushels of Apples) (1)	Total Fixed Cost (2)	Total Variable Cost (3)	Total Cost (4) (2) + (3)	Marginal Cost (5) Δ(4) ÷ Δ(1)	Price (= MR = AR) (6)	Total Revenue (7) (6) × (1)
0	$25,000	$ 0	$25,000			$ 0
				$10.00	$12.00	
1,000	25,000	10,000	35,000			12,000
				5.88	12.00	
2,700	25,000	20,000	45,000			32,400
				4.35	12.00	
5,000	25,000	30,000	55,000		MR>MC	60,000
				5.00	12.00	
7,000	25,000	40,000	65,000			84,000
				7.69	12.00	
8,300	25,000	50,000	75,000	MR=MC @ Qs = 8300		99,600 MAX PROFIT = 24,600
				14.29	12.00	
9,000	25,000	60,000	85,000			108,000
				33.33	12.00	
9,300	25,000	70,000	95,000	MR<MC		111,600

put. Ollie's *MR*, the extra revenue earned from selling one more bushel or peck, is calculated by dividing the change in *TR* by the change in *Q*. And, since the change in *TR* is influenced only by changes in *Q* in perfect competition (firms are price takers, unable to change prices themselves), then we may write symbolically

$$MR = \frac{\Delta TR}{\Delta Q} = \frac{P \times \Delta Q}{\Delta Q}$$

Canceling the ΔQs we are left with $MR = P$.

THINKING IT THROUGH

It is always helpful to understand the logic of such relationships, but it's also interesting and practical to prove it for yourself. Using the information in Table 6–1, show that $P = AR = MR = \$12$.

Knowing the market price, how does Ollie identify the profit maximizing output?

The Profit-Maximizing Rule

Profit maximization means that total economic profits are maximum. The long way to determine this is to find the greatest difference between *TR* and *TC*. Although this approach is accurate, it is very time consuming. Subtracting *TC* from *TR* for the output levels illustrated in Table 6–1 may not seem so bad, but what if our output ranged from 0 to 9,300 in increments of 100? Fortunately, there is a much faster way.

The **profit-maximizing rule** states that firms should produce that output where *MR* equals *MC*. And, since *P* = *MR* in perfect competition, we can simplify the rule. Under conditions of perfect competition, a company should produce until *P* = *MC*. Looking at Columns 5 and 7 in Table 6–1, Ollie notes that the *P* = *MC* rule means that he should produce 8,300 bushels. Why does this guarantee profit maximization? Let's prove that this is indeed Ollie's best profit (maximization) output. Please refer to Table 6–1 as we go. We have three approaches to look at this problem.

The profit-maximizing rule states that firms should produce that output where MR equals MC.

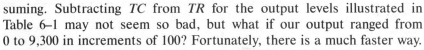

The Total Revenue/Total Cost Approach.

How much profit (loss) does Ollie realize at 7,000 bushels of output? *TR* is $84,000 ($12 × 7,000), *TC* is $65,000, so the total profit is $19,000. At the 8,300 output level, *TR* is $99,600, *TC* is $75,000, so the profit is $24,000. At 9,000 bushels of output, *TR* is $108,000, *TC* is $85,000, and profit is $23,000. Moreover, at all outputs less than 7,000, Ollie makes even less profit; thus, total profits are maximized at 8,300 units of output.[15]

The Marginal Revenue/Marginal Cost Approach.

We can also demonstrate that producing 8,300 bushels of apples will maximize profits using the *MR* / *MC* approach. Since *MR* is the extra revenue from selling one more bushel of apples, and *MC* is the extra cost of producing one more bushel of apples, as long as *MR* > *MC,* Ollie knows that he is adding more to revenue than to cost by producing more apples. Stated differently, total profits continue to increase with additional production and sales so long as *MR* > *MC*. Not until *MR* < *MC* does Ollie have no incentive to continue production. When the extra cost of producing one more bushel exceeds the extra revenue from selling that bushel, total profits will decline. We can confirm this relationship by looking again at Table 6–1. The *MR* (or price) is constant at $12. *MC* decreases until the production of 5,000 bushels, after which it steadily increases. Let's assume that Ollie is producing 7,000 bushels, and he wants to know whether to produce an additional 1,300 bushels for a total output of 8,300. Because the *MR* ($12) exceeds the *MC* ($7.29) for these additional 1,300 bushels, his total profits will increase. As a profit maximizer, Ollie would go for it. You will note that *MR* > *MC* at 8,300. Although this is

---

[15] It is worth noting that Ollie's production of apples is in batches; that is, for the sake of our example, the bushels of output shown in Column 1 are the only outputs which he can produce. If Ollie could produce 8,200 or 8,400 bushels, he very well might be able to squeak out even more profit. Batch production is actually a more common situation in manufacturing or processing, like chemicals, paints, and semiconductors.

TOTAL PROFITS CONTINUE TO INCREASE AS LONG AS MR > MC

not the pure profit-maximizing output, because Ollie can produce only those outputs shown in the table, he will stop at 8,300 bushels. To go further would mean the decision to produce 9,000 bushels, and that will yield less profit.

Graphical Approach.   A third approach involves a slight modification of Figure 6–2b. By plotting the *AC* and *MC* curves on this diagram, we can determine a graphical solution. Figure 6–3 below illustrates Ollie's short-run cost and revenue picture.

First, the graph shows the conventional marginal cost—average cost curve configuration: *MC* intersects *AC* from below at minimum *AC*. Second, Ollie's demand curve (d_1) is perfectly elastic, a reminder of the fact that he is a price taker, unable to set the price at which he sells apples. Applying our profit-maximizing rule—produce that output at which *MR* = *MC*—Ollie can easily identify the output at which his profits are maximum. The procedure works like this.

FIGURE 6–3

Profit Maximization—
Graphically

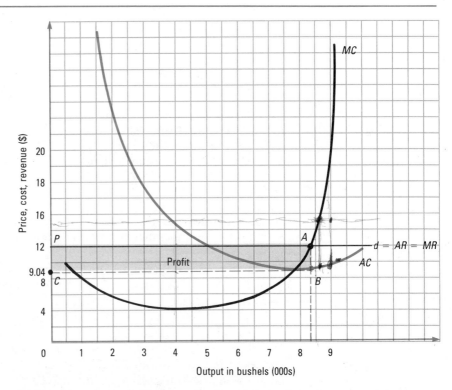

This figure illustrates a graphical view of profit maximization. Using the profit-maximization rule, Ollie should continue producing until *MR* = *MC*. This occurs at an output of 8,300 bushels, marked by the output line segment *AB*. The shaded area represents his total profit, the profit per unit *(AR − AC)* times the 8,300 bushels of output.

1. Locate the intersection of the demand curve (MR or AR = 12) and the MC curve, labeled point A in Figure 6–3. (Note: The demand curve may also be referred to as the *price line*.)
2. Draw a plumb line from point A directly down to the quantity axis (a line perpendicular to the horizontal axis, parallel to the vertical axis). This determines the output that maximizes profits. For lack of any other name, we will call this the *output line*.
3. To estimate total profits, note that the output line intersects the AC curve at point B. At this intersection, draw a plumb line to the vertical or price axis. For lack of any special name for this, we will call this line the cost line. This determines the AC or cost per unit, 9.04.
4. The rectangle *PABC*, formed by the demand curve, the output line, the cost line, and the vertical axis, is the area of profit.

We already know from the total revenue/total cost approach that total profit is $24,600$ at $8,300$ bushels. This is confirmed in our graphical view by using the average revenue and average cost figures. The profit per unit is computed by subtracting AC from $AR;$ to get total profits, the profit per unit is multiplied by the units sold.

1. Profit per unit = Average revenue − Average cost
2.96 = 12 − 9.04
2. Total profit = Profit per unit × output
$24,568$ = 2.96 × $8,300$

This figure is slightly less than our actual total profits ($24,600$) because of rounding the AC value (9.03614). Don't let this bother you: this graph does not show the extreme detail required. Imagine trying to design a vertical scale to show a value of AC = 9.03614 (or 9.04).

Short-Run Losses

Not all apple growers are created equal; that is, some apple-growing operations are not as efficient as Ollie's operation, as we can verify in Figure 6–4.

What if conditions exist which result in costs higher than we have shown for Ollie? For example, poor irrigation and inadequate disease control may cause the loss of dozens of trees. In these circumstances, the short-run average cost *(SAC)* lies above the demand or AR curve. This means that price fails to cover AC, and the farmer incurs an economic loss. Even in this situation, however, the profit-maximizing rule is followed in order to minimize losses. As Figure 6–4 shows, farmers will produce $8,300$ bushels and suffer a $16,600$ loss. (AC = 14, AR = 12, so the loss per bushel is 2.) In the short-run the farmer can survive such losses if the price is greater than his average variable cost. Let's see why. Please see Table 6–2 on page 170.

FIGURE 6–4 Short-Run Losses

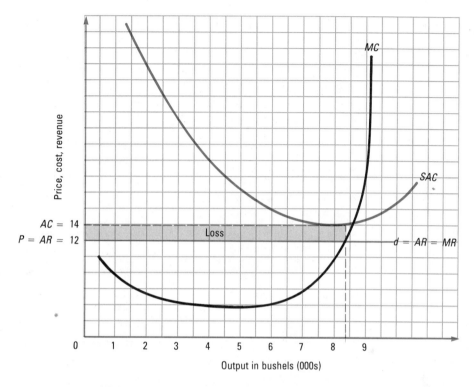

Ollie's short-run average cost curve shifts upward because of adverse conditions, i.e., a crop disease requiring extensive chemical treatment. The result is that *SAC* lies above the demand price at all output levels. In the short run, Ollie can minimize losses by continuing to produce 8,300 bushels.

Table 6–2 illustrates *AVC; AC;* three demand curves, labeled Price-1, Price-2, and Price-3; and the profits or losses associated with each demand price. In any market, only three possible situations may exist for producers: profit, breakeven, or loss. Because economic theory assumes that all businesses attempt to maximize profits, firms will produce the output where *MR = MC*. And, as we have just seen, the same profit maximizing rule holds true for firms trying to minimize losses. Thus, when the demand price (Price-1) is $12, Ollie will produce and sell 8,300 bushels and realize a profit of $24,600.

What happens if prices of oranges and other substitutes for apples decrease? As consumers switch to these products, the market demand for apples shifts to the left, price comes down, and apple growers now face a lower demand price, perhaps $9. Should Ollie and his competitors

TABLE 6–2

Costs, Prices, and
Profit/Loss
When to Shut Down?

Output	AVC	AC	Price-1 (AR = MR)	Profit-1	Price-2 (AR = MR)	Profit-2	Price-3 (AR = MR)	Profit-3
0	—	—		($25,000)		($25,000)		($25,000)
			$12		$9		$5	
1,000	10.00	35,00		(23,000)		(26,000)		(30,000)
			12		9		5	
2,700	7.41	16.67		(12,600)		(20,700)		(31,500)
			12		9		5	
5,000	6.00	11.00		5,000		(10,000)		(30,000)
			12		9		5	
7,000	5.71	9.29		19,000		(2,000)		(30,000)
			12		9		5	
8,300	6.02	9.04		24,600		(300)		(33,500)
			12		9		5	
9,000	6.67	9.44		23,000		(4,000)		(40,000)
			12		9		5	
9,300	7.53	10.22		(95,000)		(95,000)		(95,000)

Only three possible situations exist for producers: profit, breakeven, and loss. However, Ollie will remain in business in the short run even if he makes a loss. All profit maximizers must also be loss minimizers as well. As shown above, Ollie will keep producing when the price falls to $9 because he minimizes his losses: a $300 loss is much better than a $25,000 loss. However, if price falls to $5, he will do better to shut down. (The price or marginal revenue figures are shown between output levels because *MR* represents the change in revenue over a range of output.) Using the *AVC* data, we can develop a shut-down rule. Whenever $P < AVC$ in the short run, the firm can minimize its losses by closing. As the data above show, if price should fall to $5 per bushel, the smallest loss is $30,000; thus he can reduce his losses by $5,000 if he shuts down.

stay in the apple business? At a price of $9, yes. Whether picking apples or vacationing in the Bahamas, Ollie always incurs fixed costs of $25,000; thus, if Ollie shuts down, he will realize a loss equal to his fixed costs ($25,000). In the short run, Ollie will minimize his losses by continuing to produce 8,300 bushels of apples.

What if the demand price falls to $5? Should Ollie still remain in business? At $5 per bushel, the $P < AVC$, so Ollie does not even cover his average variable costs, let alone his average fixed costs. Using our loss-minimizing rule, produce where $P = MC$, Ollie would realize a loss of $30,000. Because this exceeds his fixed costs of $25,000, Ollie should shut down.

Shut-Down Rule.   A general rule regarding shut down in the short run is this: if $P < AVC$, shut down. If $P \geq AVC$, continue to produce. The logic of the **shut-down rule** is simple. If you can cover your fixed costs, you are better off staying in business. However, if you cannot cover your fixed costs (including your implicit costs), you are better off doing something else, like trying to sell your apple orchard.

The **Shut-Down Rule** *states that in the short run if P < AVC, shut down; if P > AVC, continue to produce.*

The Long Run

As we have seen in Chapter 5, the long run means that all inputs and costs are variable. Firms have the time to introduce laborsaving capital equipment, expand the size of their operations, even acquire new land and buildings. Existing firms exit and new firms enter the industry. Indeed, one of the most important characteristics of the long run is the entry of new firms into the industry. And perhaps nowhere is this more evident than in agriculture.

Ollie and his competitors have done well—in fact, perhaps too well. At the demand price of $12, short-run profits are so good that in the long run other farmers will be attracted to the apple orchard business. As new trees are planted and reach bearing age, the annual apple crop will increase. As Figure 6–5a shows, the supply of apples increases, illustrated as a rightward shift of the market supply curve.

The first noticeable result of increased supply is a lower price: P_2 ($9.04). Quantity sold also increases to Q_2. This market change is transmitted immediately to Ollie and all other individual farmers. The upshot is that Ollie's profit-maximizing output is reduced to about 8,150 bushels. The profit maximizing rule $(P = MC)$ now requires that Ollie produce and sell fewer apples at a lower price. And, since $AC = AR$ (= $9.04), Ollie is breaking even. Although economic profit is reduced to zero, he is still making a normal profit, enough to justify remaining in the apple business.

As illustrated in Figure 6–5b, the long-run equilibrium occurs at the intersection of price, long-run average cost (LAC), and long-run marginal cost (LMC). Economic profits disappear because of the increased competition from new entrants. Although Ollie is a survivor at breakeven, farmers less efficient than Ollie will have gone bankrupt. If AC exceeds the long-run demand price (AR), then the apple grower will realize a loss and be forced to leave the market.

Competition, by its very nature, means change. In the short run, changes in business operations are as common as sunshine. Such changes might include hiring and firing, searching for less expensive and more reliable parts and services, expanding and contracting output to meet demand, and so forth. It is in the long run, however, that major transformations occur. For example, the introduction of robotic technology and just-in-time production scheduling have permanently changed the way automobiles are assembled in the United States. And, new products that appear to be mere trends in the short run often become well-established industries. The microcomputer industry is a prime example. From a few firms producing personal computers in the early 1970s, this new product spawned a brand new industry in a brief 10 years. Moreover, a whole host of complementary products, like software, printers, and add-on memory boards, have further augmented the microcomputer revolution.

FIGURE 6–5
Long-Run Equilibrium

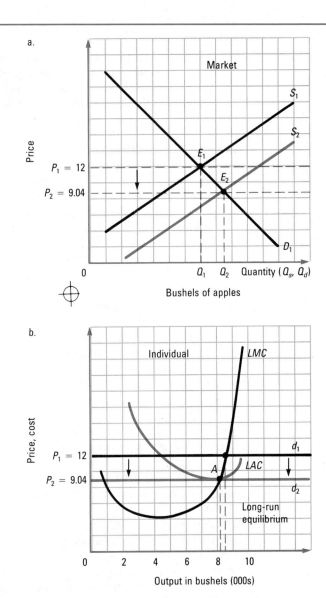

In the long run, economic profits are eliminated as new firms are attracted to the industry. Because of short-run profits, more apple growers enter the market, shifting the supply curve to the right. This results in a lower price of $9.04 (P₂) in the long run and a corresponding decrease in price for each individual grower (shift from d_1 to d_2 in Figure 6–5b). The demand price of $9.04, the long-run average cost (LAC) and long-run marginal cost (LMC) all meet at the long-run equilibrium (point A).

Another industry characterized by rapid change is the retail merchandise industry. In closing our chapter on competition, prices, and profits, read the following case about Wal-Mart, one of the fastest growing retail operations in the United States.

Hypermarts: The New Retail Thrust

Picture a store the size of four football fields end to end, or more than three . . . [huge supermarkets]. Fill the 220,000-square-foot space with discounted food and general merchandise, everything from clothing to electronics and toys. Sounds like the ultimate in one-stop shopping, right?

The answer is a resounding "yes," at least according to Sam M. Walton, founder and chairman of Wal-Mart Stores, Inc., the $16-billion-a-year Arkansas-based retail businessman.

Four Hypermart-USA stores recently opened in St. Louis, Missouri; Arlington and Garland, Texas; and in Topeka, Kansas. Each store will combine a full-line discount store and a supermarket. The stores also will lease space to a dry cleaner, fast-food restaurant, photo finisher, and other service businesses.

Each store will have a total of 500 employees; be open from 7 A.M. to 11 P.M. seven days a week; be decorated in patriotic red, white and blue, and post large directories in aisles to make finding merchandise easier, according to Stacey Duncan, a Wal-Mart spokeswoman.

Most retail observers say the success of the stores won't be known for . . . years. Based on Wal-Mart's uncanny knack for getting shoppers to fork over billions of dollars, the betting is that its newest division should be successful. In just 25 years, the company has grown to more than 1,100 stores in 23 states. Annual sales totaled $11.9 billion in fiscal 1986. . . .

Wal-Mart's business strategies have been simple. It builds stores big, furnishes them simply but fills them with up-to-date merchandise with low price tags. It also saturates its markets, servicing the stores from big distribution centers.

Walton's Hypermart success will depend upon several factors. Douglas J. Tigert, a retail marketing professor at Babson College in Boston, thinks that a prime factor is location. "They're most likely to succeed if they're built in low-overhead, rural areas where consumers don't have as much access to large discount stores and if merchandise is priced below low-cost leaders in each market. The stores must make at least $50 to $60 million, or $225 a square foot annually, to break even." Another crucial factor, Tigert said, is how quickly Walton and his staff master the nuances of retailing food. "He's had little prior experience. It's going to take him a while to go down the learning curve."

Probably the greatest hurdle in Walton's way, the experts say, is the possibility that the stores will cannibalize, or steal, sales from Wal-Mart's existing divisions, especially its Wal-Mart Discount Stores and Sam's Wholesale

Clubs. Both operate big stores with discounted general merchandise and some food. . . .

In spite of the difficult odds, retail observers think Walton has a better chance than any competitor to make his hypermarkets fly. Don Spindel, an analyst at A.G. Edwards, Inc., thinks that Walton . . . will fine-tune the concept so it appeals to American consumers. "He's a brilliant merchandiser."[16]

Questions to Consider

1. *Despite Sam Walton's enormous merchandising success, many retail observers think that Walton is bucking tradition. "Americans have gotten used to buying their soft goods and groceries in different places. They already have plenty of places to do so," says Robert Hughes, executive director of* Supermarket Business, *a trade publication.[17] Would you shop at a Hypermart? Why or why not?*

2. *The history of hypermarkets in the United States is one of failure. Euromarche, a French company, built several huge hypermarkets in the Midwest in the 1970s, and none succeeded. Then, as if this rejection was insufficient evidence, the same firm opened a 200,000 square foot store called Bigg's in Cincinnati in 1984. "The store, with 50 aisles and 600 employees, lost more than $7 million in its first two years and is still losing money."[18] Given this record, and knowing that many retail marketing experts think that hypermarkets should be built in low-overhead, rural areas, why is St. Louis a site? Indeed, why build them at all?*

IMPORTANT TERMS TO REMEMBER

average revenue, p. 164
competition, p. 153
marginal revenue, p. 164
monopolistic competition, p. 157
natural monopoly, p. 159
non-price competition, p. 154
oligopoly, p. 158

price searchers, p. 158
price takers, p. 155
profit-maximizing, p. 166
pure competition, p. 155
pure monopoly, p. 159
shut-down rule, p. 170

CHAPTER SUMMARY

1. Competition is defined generally as the absence of monopoly power. However, competition in the marketplace varies widely and is classified into four separate market structures.

   a. Pure competition is made up of a very great number of firms, each with no control over price, a standardized or homogeneous product

---

[16] Excerpted from Barbara B. Buchholz, "Wal-Mart Is Expecting a Lot from Hypermarkets," *St. Louis Post-Dispatch*, August 30, 1987.

[17] "Wal-Mart Is Expecting a Lot from Hypermarts," *St. Louis Post-Dispatch*, August 30, 1987.

[18] Ibid.

or service, and ease of entry into and exit from the industry. All firms are price takers because market supply and demand determine the price. Although perfect competition does not exist, agriculture and independent trucking serve as close examples.

b. Monopolistic competition is a market structure with many firms, a highly differentiated product, some barriers to entry and considerable nonprice competition. Firms are price searchers and thus exert some control over price. Retail businesses, like hardware, clothing, and general merchandise discount stores, are monopolistically competitive markets.

c. Oligopoly is a market dominated by a few large firms (three to eight, or perhaps a few more). Depending upon the industry, the product may be homogeneous or highly differentiated, as in the difference between the steel and auto industries. There are very high barriers to entry, like expensive start-up capital outlays and advertising, and extensive nonprice competition. Firms exert extensive control over price.

d. Pure monopoly is a market in which the seller is the industry. The product or service is unique, although there may be substitutes in other industries (e.g., natural gas and electricity). Entry into the market is very difficult because of high barriers, some natural (large economies of scale) and some artificial (patent protection, resource ownership and/or control, and franchises).

2. Profit maximization means that firms will produce that output where the marginal revenue equals the marginal cost *(MR = MC)*. Perfectly competitive firms may realize economic profits in the short run, but in the long run, as new firms are attracted to the industry, economic profits are competed away. In the long run, firms break even; there are no economic profits.

DISCUSSION AND REVIEW QUESTIONS

1. Compare and contrast the four types of market structures, and cite an example of each from the real world. If pure competition does not exist, why study it?

2. Using Table 6–1 on page 165 and the profit-maximizing rule, answer the following:
   a. How many bushels of apples should Ollie produce if the price is $15 per bushel?
   b. What will be Ollie's profit at this output?
   c. Draw a diagram which illustrates the area of profit (similar to Figure 6–3, p. 167).
   d. What is the reasoning behind the *MR = MC* rule?

3. Draw a breakeven chart (with *TFC, TC,* and *TR*) using the information from question 2 a above. Verify that all three approaches, tabular, *TR-TC* breakeven chart, and the *MR-MC* graph, all provide the same answer.

4. George and Yvette Mercurio bought a small hardware store. In their first year of operation, total implicit costs were $50,000; explicit costs were $100,000, and their total revenue was $125,000. What is their economic

profit or loss? Normal profit or loss? Using our guidelines or rules for shut-down, should they sell out or remain in business? Explain why a company will stay in business in the short run even if it is not making a profit. Draw a diagram illustrating this short-run loss situation, and explain the shutdown rule.

5. Small real estate firms and gypsy truckers are approximate examples of pure competition. Although real estate commissions are fairly standardized in most markets, recently some real estate firms have embarked upon discount fees for their services in order to build their businesses. Does the presence of large national chain real estate agencies, like Coldwell Banker and Century 21, prevent a purely competitive environment in real estate? Are real estate agents and brokers really free to charge whatever they choose, or are they subject to market-determined prices? What about gypsy truckers? Do they have the freedom to set their own charges for shipment of goods or are such rates set by market forces?

6. Explain the difference between a firm's short-run profit maximization position and its long-run equilibrium position. Why are all economic profits eliminated in the long run for a purely competitive firm?

A BRIEF LOOK AHEAD

The next chapter resumes with an in-depth examination of pricing in imperfectly competitive markets. Because nearly all business activity occurs in markets that are monopolistic and oligopolistic, that is where the emphasis is placed. We will ask whether firms really maximize profits and whether companies actually price their products and services according to the $MR = MC$ rule. The practice of price discrimination, collusion, and bid rigging will also be examined.

APPENDIX

Forms of Business Organization

There are many ways to describe businesses in America, but the most conventional method is to classify businesses into their legal forms of organization: proprietorship, partnership, and corporation.

There are three main forms of business organization. The typical *sole proprietor* or *proprietorship* is a small business in the personal and business services industries. As the owner and manager of the business, the sole proprietor has *unlimited liability*. This means that one's personal assets, as well as business assets, are at risk in the event of bankruptcy. Although licenses, permits, and other forms of government approval are often required, as with barber shops and hair salons, hardware stores, and service stations, many sole proprietors can start their businesses without formal application to government. Lawn care and home improvement businesses come and go every day.

Partnerships are also common in business and personal services, especially in law and medicine. Such businesses generally are formed with one or more general partners and several limited partners. The limited partners possess *limited liability:* their financial liability is limited by their investment contribution to the firm. Like sole proprietors, general partners have unlimited liability. Routine management decisions are made by the general partners, although the limited partners have voting rights to resolve questions regarding expansion, mergers, and dissolution.

The *corporation* is characterized by separation of ownership, control, and management. The business must apply to the state to be chartered as a corporation. Most corporations are financed by issuing stock (ownership shares) and bonds (indebtedness or IOUs). Stocks come in two main forms: common and preferred. Both offer voting rights to the holders, one vote per share, but in the event of bankruptcy the preferred stockholders are paid off before common stockholders if there is sufficient cash to get that far. In fact, creditors and bondholders are first and second in line before stockholders. The chief advantage of the corporate organization is limited liability, a feature which enables the corporation to attract investors.

One way to understand business organizations is to examine the size distribution of all businesses according to number of firms and total sales. Tables A6–1 and A6–2 provide this profile of U.S. businesses for the mid-1980s.

As shown in the tables, proprietorships and partnerships, nearly all of which are small businesses, constitute 83 percent of all firms. Although these small businesses make up more than four fifths of all business organizations, they account for less than 10 percent of total sales. On the other hand, while corporations represent only 17 percent of the total number of business organizations, they account for nearly 90 percent of total business sales.

TABLE A6–1

Size Distribution of Businesses, by Number, Total Sales, and Average Sales

	Total Number of Firms	Total Sales	Average Sales per Firm
Proprietorships	12,185,000	$ 523,000,000,000	$ 42,922
Partnerships	1,461,000	272,000,000,000	186,174
Corporations	2,812,000	7,026,000,000,000	2,498,578
Total	16,458,000	7,821,000,000,000	

TABLE A6–2

Percent Distribution of Businesses

	Number (percent of total)	Sales (percent of total)
Proprietorships	74.0	6.7
Partnerships	8.9	3.5
Corporations	17.1	89.8

Imperfect Competition:
Pricing and Profits

Al Francekevich

This chapter resumes our discussion of business-pricing practices. We will examine the economic theories of imperfect market structures (monopolistic competition, oligopoly, and monopoly) and determine how firms establish price and maximize profits. A second major purpose of this chapter is to present alternative profit objectives and pricing tactics. We will ask if firms actually price their products according to conventional economic theory. In other words, can firms estimate demand for their products so accurately that they actually succeed in maximizing profits? Do supermarkets, hardware stores, and private schools price their products and services according to the profit-maximizing rule?

After completion of this chapter, you should be able to do the following:

1. Explain why price exceeds marginal revenue under conditions of imperfect competition.

2. Diagram, describe, and explain how firms determine the profit-maximizing output and price under conditions of monopolistic competition, oligopoly, and monopoly.

3. Explain why it is difficult to determine price, output, and profits in oligopoly.

4. Identify and distinguish among the different types of monopoly.

5. Diagram and distinguish between profit maximization and sales maximization.

6. Diagram, compare, and contrast the long-run equilibrium positions of a perfectly competitive firm and an imperfectly competitive firm.

7. Explain how markup pricing differs from conventional economic theory.

Pricing: You Had Better Know Your Rivals Well

A midwestern electromechanical components manufacturer recently found itself in a tough spot. With a stagnant market share and industry prices edging downward, the company's profit margins were taking a terrible beating, and there was no relief in sight. In an effort to increase sales and restore its margins, the marketing vice president ordered prices to be cut by an average of 7 percent. Within three weeks, however, the move had provoked severe price cuts from the company's major competitors and set off a full-scale price war. Prices swiftly declined in a kind of death spiral that soon had everyone in the industry doing business at a loss.

What the vice president failed to realize was that conditions in the industry were ripe for a price war. Not only is the industry a high-fixed-cost, high-contribution-margin business, but there was substantial excess capacity at the time. Moreover, the major competitors were desperate to hold their own market-share positions. Ironically, the unfortunate executive who had started it all failed to anticipate his competitors' reaction to the price cut. Worse still, he saw his company as the victim of an unprovoked attack. This misapprehension was natural enough: all the information the company had about current price levels in the industry was what it had learned from the bids on orders lost to competitors. Where pricing was concerned, the company had weighed its options with all the weights on one side of the scale.[1]

As the FOCUS shows, price competition can be ruthless. How does a company know what price to charge? Should it increase or decrease price? How much? Should it increase (decrease) price on all products or just for the products with the strongest sales history? How does it know if the demand is price elastic or price inelastic?

These and other price-related questions go to the heart of the issue raised in the FOCUS. With the company's profit margins following a downward price trend, the vice president looked at its product price and sales history and determined that demand was elastic. (The price elasticity of demand was estimated to be 1.5.) Accordingly, a 7 percent de-

---

[1]Adapted from Elliot B. Ross, "Making Money with Proactive Pricing," *Harvard Business Review* 62, no. 6 (November–December, 1984), pp. 1–2.

crease in price would increase sales by 10.5 percent. This was just what the economic doctor ordered.

Competitors were not to be outdone, however. Going for the financial jugular, competitors retaliated almost immediately by slashing prices. The upshot was a devastating price war leading ultimately to losses for all of the industry's firms.

In retrospect, the electrical parts company knew it had made a mistake. Each firm in the industry was very protective of its market share and viewed the initial price cut as outright aggression. All of the elasticity of demand calculations had little to do with the outcome. Each competitor reacted defensively.

Of course, price is but one of many ingredients in the equation leading to a successful transaction. Equally important is nonprice competition, such as product quality, advertising, after-sale product support, warranties, and related elements. To what extent had our company differentiated its product(s) from its competitors? Were its support services dependable? Answers to these and other questions will be addressed as we examine different market structures.

IMPERFECT COMPETITION

In the previous chapter, we defined competition as the absence of market power. We also noted that pure competition does not exist, except as an ideal with which we may compare actual behavior. What then is imperfect competition?

Imperfect competition
means that firms possess
the ability to set prices
without strict reliance
upon supply and
demand.

Imperfect competition means that firms possess market power—the ability to set prices without strict reliance upon supply and demand. And, since pure competition does not exist, by definition all competition is imperfect. Unfortunately, this implies that there is something inherently wrong with existing market structures. As applied to firms in various market structures, the word imperfect suggests a flaw, that something is faulty. If we define these flaws to mean control over market price, nearly all markets are imperfect. One way out of this imperfect maze for now is to understand that few if any markets ever were (nor probably ever will be) perfect. Like the concept of market equilibrium, however, pure competition is a useful concept. It helps us understand more about real business behavior. It serves as a yardstick by which we can measure the extent to which real companies deviate from the ideal case. Our problem is deciding how pricing control adversely affects consumers and impedes efficiency and deciding what to do about it. Then, if we can agree upon specific criteria of unacceptable business conduct (like price fixing), making public policy to regulate and control undesirable business behavior is much easier.

Demand and Marginal Revenue

Although the term *imperfect competition* is not very instructive, it is useful in one important sense. Unlike pure competitors, who face perfectly elastic demand curves, all imperfect competitors confront downward-sloping demand curves. This means that the price elasticity will change all along the curve.[2] Moreover, this has great significance to the way in which imperfectly competitive firms price their products.

Under our purely competitive model, we showed that price *(P)* equals marginal revenue *(MR)*. (See page 165 if you would like to review this equality.) In all imperfectly competitive markets, however, price will always be greater than marginal revenue. This in turn means that instead of having a demand curve representing price *and* marginal revenue, all imperfectly competitive firms will have a demand curve and a separate marginal revenue curve. Let's see how this works; please refer to Table 7–1 and the corresponding Figure 7–1.

The individual firm's demand (quantity-price) relationship in imperfect competition is the same as that for the purely competitive firm with one important difference: it slopes downward and to the right. This is because firms can only sell more at lower prices. As before, to find total revenue *(TR)*, we multiply price times the quantity of output (or sales), only this time *TR* changes because both price *and* the quantity of output

TABLE 7–1

Demand and Marginal Revenue

Sales (Output)	Price (AR)	Total Revenue (TR)	Marginal Revenue (MR)
0	$100	$ 0	
			$90
10	90	900	
			70
20	80	1,600	
			50
30	70	2,100	
			30
40	60	2,400	
			10
50	50	2,500	
			− 10
60	40	2,400	
			− 30
70	30	2,100	

---

[2] The single exception to this is a demand curve in the shape of a rectangular hyperbola. Such a curve is negatively sloped, but has a constant elasticity of unity (= 1). Any change in price results in an equal and opposite percentage change in quantity demanded.

FIGURE 7–1

Demand and
Marginal Revenue

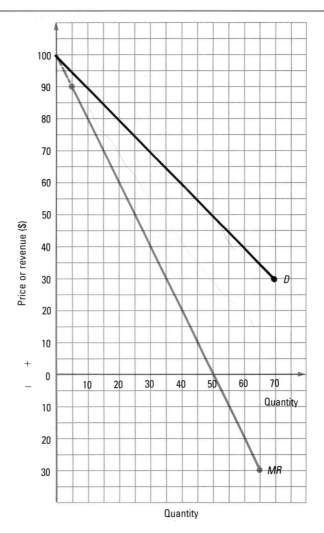

The demand curve slopes downward and to the right in all imperfectly competitive markets. This means that marginal revenue will always be less than price.

(sales) change. To find *MR*, we also proceed as we did before: divide the change in *TR* by the change in sales. For example, if price is reduced to $90, the change in *TR* is $900 and the change in sales is 10; thus, *MR* = $900 ÷ 10 = $90. So when *P* = $100, *MR* = $90. Why the difference? Why is *P* > *MR*?

If we compare the level of sales at two different prices, we can see why *P* > *MR*. If the firm's price is $90, it sells all 10 units at this price. But if its price was $80, the firm would sell more but make less on each item sold. In order to derive *MR,* we must subtract from the $80 price the $10 it would lose in selling each of the first 10 units at $90; thus, $80 minus $10 equals $70, the extra revenue received from selling the additional ten units.

To summarize, firms in purely competitive markets have demand curves which are perfectly elastic, and the price is equal to marginal revenue. Under imperfect competition, firms face downward-sloping demand, and the price always exceeds marginal revenue.

Elasticity and Marginal Revenue

Another important relationship exists between marginal revenue *(MR)* and the price elasticity of demand *(E).* Based upon our work in Chapter 4 with the total revenue approach of determining elasticity, it is a short step to this *MR − E* relationship.

Table 7–2 and Figure 7–2a and b illustrate new data and graphs. Because the sales change by units of one, *MR* is calculated simply as the change in *TR.* (There is no need to divide the change in *TR* by the change in sales.) Figure 7–2a shows the *TR* curve rising, reaching its peak at 4 and 5 units, and then decreasing. Figure 7–2b depicts the demand curve and marginal curve.[3] Let's explore the relationship between *TR* and *MR.*

	Sales	Price	Total Revenue (TR)	Marginal Revenue (MR)	Elasticity
TABLE 7–2 Marginal Revenue and Elasticity	1	$16	$16		
				$12	Elastic
	2	14	28		
				8	Elastic
	3	12	36		
				4 > 0	Elastic
	4	10	40		
				0 $= 0$	Unit elastic
	5	8	40		
				−4 < 0	Inelastic
	6	6	36		
				−8	Inelastic
	7	4	28		
				−12	Inelastic
	8	2	16		

---

[3] The *MR* figures are plotted at the midpoints of sales. For example, *MR* of $12 is plotted at 1.5 units instead of at 2 units; *MR* of $8 is at 2.5 units, and so on.

FIGURE 7–2a

Total Revenue

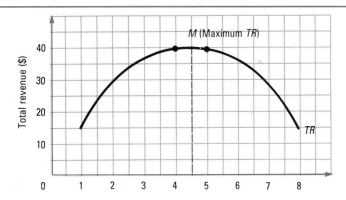

Over a range of output, the typical total revenue curve rises, reaches a maximum, and then declines.

FIGURE 7–2b

Marginal Revenue, Demand, and Elasticity

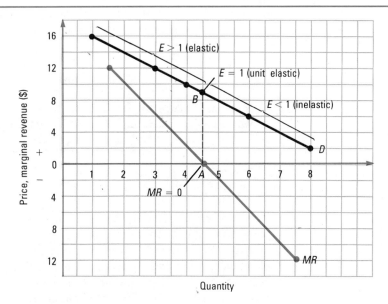

When *MR* is positive, demand is elastic; when *MR* = 0, demand is unit elastic (at point *B*); and when *MR* is negative, demand is inelastic.

First, although *TR* rises, reaches a maximum, and falls, *MR* declines steadily. Second, *MR* is positive as *TR* increases, but when *MR* = 0, *TR* is maximum, and when *MR* becomes negative, *TR* decreases. How does this relationship between *TR* and *MR* relate to elasticity?

Let's begin with our company selling three units at a price of $12. To sell more, the price is cut to $10, and total revenue increases from $36 to $40. Since *TR* increased in response to a price cut, we know that demand is elastic. Note also that *MR* is positive.

What if our company again cuts its price? If price is reduced to $8, *TR* remains unchanged at $40 and *MR* = 0. As you will recall, if *TR* does not change when price changes, demand is unit elastic. Another price cut to $6 results in a decrease in *TR* to $36 and a negative *MR*. In this case, demand is inelastic. We can summarize all of this as follows:

when *MR* > 0, demand is elastic,

when *MR* = 0, demand is unit elastic, and

when *MR* < 0, demand is inelastic.

Using either Table 7–2 or Figure 7–2b, our company now can easily identify the range of its elasticity of demand just by referring to marginal revenue. Extending a perpendicular line from *MR*'s intersection of the quantity axis (at point *A*) to the demand curve (at point *B*) determines the price and quantity at which demand is unit elastic. At all higher prices, demand is elastic; at all lower prices, demand is inelastic.

THINKING IT THROUGH

How does knowledge of elasticity help a business price its products? Would you increase price if you knew that demand was elastic? Why?

Pricing in Imperfect Competition

Because pure competition does not exist, nearly all businesses have some control over the prices of their products and services. From small neighborhood grocery stores to larger retail discount chains, from large chemical processing firms to even larger oil refining and distribution companies, all possess some degree of market power. And while the power of an Exxon or Dupont is much greater than a mom-and-pop grocery store, even small businesses demonstrate market power if they have limited or no competition in the relevant geographical area. With this introduction, let's begin our survey of pricing in imperfect competition. You may find it helpful to refer to Figure 6–1, page 156 as we discuss these market structures.

Monopolistic competition
is a market structure with thousands of firms producing a differentiated product or service with some price control.

Monopolistic Competition. Closest to the model of pure competition is **monopolistic competition.** Although this market structure is the most prevalent form of competition in terms of sheer numbers of businesses, it is oligopoly that is responsible for the majority of U.S. production. Most monopolistically competitive firms are sole proprietors and partnerships; virtually all oligopolists are organized as corporations.

Each monopolistically competitive industry consists of thousands of firms producing a differentiated product or service with some degree of control over price. Some barriers to entry exist, mainly in the form of nonprice competition and efforts to differentiate the product. Gasoline stations, whether the full-service or self-service variety, illustrate this type of market structure. Some stations offer only gasoline at self-service pumps; others provide a complete service facility, including towing and mechanical repairs, car wash, and a wide selection of automobile accessories.

Another distinguishing characteristic of monopolistic competition is *excess capacity,* an underutilization of production and service facilities. Think of the last time you pulled into the station to fill up. If we were not experiencing a gasoline shortage, the chances are that most of the pumps were free. And in many locations, if you looked across the street, you would find a similar situation: other underutilized stations. At non-commuter times, gasoline stations have a surplus of what we may loosely call *pump slots*. Of course, the real test of excess capacity is whether the firm survives in the long run; that is, does the firm have sufficient sales to earn at least a normal profit?

THINKING IT THROUGH

Excess capacity is commonplace among firms in monopolistic competition. Why are there so many gas stations? Whose interests are served, the oil company franchising or licensing the dealers and independents, or the owner-operators themselves? Among all of the businesses you frequent, which ones appear to have excess capacity?

One implication of excess capacity is higher average costs than would prevail in perfect competition. Advertising and other product differentiation efforts also raise the per-unit cost of operations. The upshot is that average costs sometimes exceed price. And though firms have some control over price, raising price to cover unusually high unit costs will only drive customers to more efficient lower-priced competitors. If this persists into the long run, firms will be forced to shut down. How many gasoline stations have you seen bite the financial dust?

Table 7–3 and the accompanying Figure 7–3 help to illustrate these pricing and profit conditions. Using our profit-maximizing rule, our business should produce and sell four units at a price of $10 in order to maximize profits ($13).[4]

In Figure 7–3 the profit area is marked by the rectangle *ABCD*. The business identifies the profit-maximizing output at that point where $MR = MC$. The steps are as follows:

1. Locate the point where $MR = MC$.[5]
2. Extend an output (reference) line up to the demand curve (point *B*) and down to the quantity axis (point *Q*), an output of 4 units.
3. Where the output line cuts the *AC* curve, at point *C*, draw a perpendicular line to the price axis (to point *D*); where the output line intersects the demand curve (point *B*), draw another perpendicular line to the price axis (to point *A*).

The area bounded by points *ABCD* is the area of profit.

From Table 7–3, we can easily see that total profits are maximized at 4 units of output. By subtracting *TC* from *TR* at each output or sale, we can calculate the profit and loss. The same information is depicted graphically in Figure 7–3. Since price is average revenue *(AR)*, subtracting *AC* ($6.75) from *AR* ($10) gives us the profit per unit ($3.25). Multiplying the profit per unit times the number of units sold gives us the total profit ($3.25 × 4 = $13).

This situation will not persist for long, however, as economic profits will attract new businesses into the market. As this occurs, the supply

TABLE 7–3	Sales	Price	TR	MR	TC	MC	AC	Profit
Pricing and	1	$16	$16		$15		$15.00	$1
Output in				$12		$5		
Monopolistic	2	14	28		20		10.00	8
Competition				8		3		
	3	12	36		23		7.67	13
				4		4		
	4	10	40		27		6.75	13
				0		6		
	5	8	40		33		6.60	7
				−4		10		
	6	6	36		43		7.17	−7
				−8		15		
	7	4	28		58		8.29	−30
				−12		23		
	8	2	16		81		10.13	−65

---

[4] Production and sales of three or four units both yield the same maximum profit. If the business is interested in increasing sales, then it should produce and sell four units.

[5] The $MR = MC$ intersection in our example gives us exactly four units of output. But if the output line to the quantity axis falls in between two quantities, say between six and seven, then the company will produce six units; thus, $MR > MC$.

FIGURE 7–3

Pricing and
Output in
Monopolistic
Competition

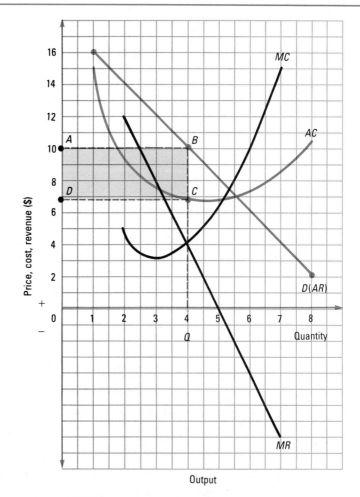

Profit maximization occurs at an output of 4, determined by the intersection of *MR* and *MC*. Where the output line *(BC₄)* cuts the *AC* curve determines the average cost of producing 4 units. The shaded area represents the profit, calculated by multiplying the profit per unit (price less average cost, or $3.25) times the output (4), or $13.

of goods will increase, pushing price down to the average cost. Figure 7–4 illustrates the long-run equilibrium position.

Although the *MR* = *MC* profit-maximizing rule still applies, this time *AR* = *AC* at the profit-maximizing output. Firms are still making a normal (or accounting) profit, but economic profits are reduced to zero, so firms are just breaking even (in the economic sense, *AR* = *AC* and *TR* = *TC*).

Oligopoly. Beer, breakfast cereals, chewing gum, cigarettes, coffee, tires, and tubes—the list goes on and on. These and hundreds of other

FIGURE 7–4
Long-Run
Equilibrium in
Monopolistic
Competition

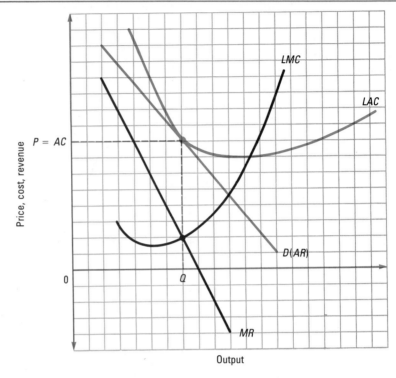

Short-run profits attract new firms into the industry. The result is that market share per firm declines, average costs increase, and economic profits are erased. The long-run equilibrium is illustrated at point *A* where the price line meets the tangency of demand and *LAC*. (A tangent is a line which touches but does not intersect another line or curve.)

manufacturing industries are dominated by the four largest firms. The story about how they came to dominate their industries is interesting, but it is a story too long to tell in this book. Instead of relating the history of oligopoly, in the next few pages we will focus on the pricing practices of the largest firms in the United States.

Eastman Kodak, GM, Hallmark, Kellogg, Philip Morris, IBM, and Exxon Corporation are the "Who's Who" of U.S. manufacturing. Each of these companies is the recognized leader of its industry. However, because each industry has several other large firms, each firm remains alert to its rivals' new products, advertising, and price initiatives. For example, although Anheuser-Busch is the top firm in the malt beverages industry with about 40 percent of total barrels of beer shipped in 1986, it is keenly aware of Miller, Coors, and other breweries. Likewise, even though Kellogg's sales of cold breakfast cereals comprised 43 percent of the industry's total sales in 1986, it is always cognizant of the packaging, advertising, and pricing of its chief rivals, General Foods, General Mills, and Ralston Purina.

Characteristics.   The product type in **oligopoly** may be highly *differentiated*, like cereals, autos, and beer, or it may be *homogeneous*, like the metallurgical, cement, and explosives industries. Barriers to entry into the industry are extensive, be they **natural barriers** like high capital requirements and raw material ownership or **artificial barriers** like patents, licenses, and franchises. Regardless of entry barriers and product type, however, the chief characteristic of oligopoly is **mutual interdependence.** Because there are relatively few firms, each company is very sensitive to the decisions made by its rivals, especially regarding price. As the FOCUS points out, changes in price are easily misunderstood, often leading to disastrous results.

Figure 7–5 below illustrates the pricing dilemma faced by our electro-mechanical parts firm presented in the Chapter FOCUS.

A few simplifying assumptions are made to analyze the firm's pricing. First, there are 10 firms in the industry, each producing between 8 and

Oligopoly *is a market structure with only a few dominant firms, either a highly differentiated product or a standardized product, and high barriers to entry.*

Natural barriers *to entry consist of high capital requirements and raw material ownership.*

Artificial barriers *to entry are things such as patents, licenses, and franchises.*

Mutual interdependence *means that in oligopoly each company is very sensitive to the decisions made by its rivals, especially regarding price.*

FIGURE 7–5
Oligopoly Pricing

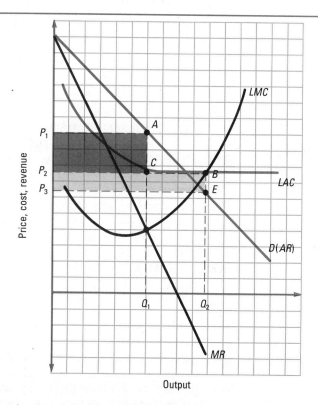

Even in oligopoly, where a few firms dominate the industry, cutthroat pricing and price wars can easily develop. At P_1 the oligopolist makes an economic profit, shown by the area P_1ACP_2. If firms begin a price war, however, prices are reduced to P_2, resulting in long-run breakeven. At Q_2 output, if conditions really deteriorate, a price war may develop leading to losses for all firms in the industry (at a price of P_3). Naturally, because these outcomes are so undesirable, there is extensive motivation for firms to collude in order to reduce price competition.

12 percent of total industry output. Second, they produce a standardized product of uniform quality. And third, each firm prices its products independently of the others. What will happen? The tendency is for prices to drift downward from P_1 to P_2, for output to increase from Q_1 to Q_2, and for economic profits to be erased. The long-run equilibrium will be at point B, much like the condition for monopolistic competition. Indeed, for our electromechanical firm and its rivals, prices wound up at a price like P_3 where all industry firms were losing (area $P_2 BEP_3$).

This tendency of firms to move from an economic profit at Price P_1 to breakeven at P_2 or economic loss at P_3 is attributable to the fewness of firms and the high degree of pricing interdependence. The demand curve for each firm is relatively elastic (or at least that is the perception of the competitors), so that for every 1 percent cut in price, sales will increase by more than 1 percent. The temptation is strong to cut price and, once done, competitors must either match the price cut or lose some of their customers. With this kind of pattern, it is easy to understand the motivation to collude on pricing or otherwise cooperate instead of engaging in price competition.

Price Leadership. The fewness of competitors and consequent mutual interdependence regarding price in oligopoly makes it very difficult to identify exactly how firms set price. Because there are so few firms, and because each firm wants to avoid price wars, there is a tendency toward cooperation. This takes two main forms.

Price leadership is when the biggest or most assertive firm announces changes in price and other firms merely follow suit.

Price leadership, in which the biggest or most assertive firm announces changes in price and other firms merely follow suit, is a very common practice in oligopoly. Because all firms are anxious about their rivals' reactions to price changes, one firm often emerges as the price leader. When this firm increases or decreases price, the other firms quickly imitate. As long as the copiers have not engaged in any formal agreements, this is perfectly legal behavior. For example, if Anheuser-Busch increased the price per six-pack by 10 percent, it would be expected that Miller and other competitors also would increase prices by like amount. To do otherwise might suggest price warfare, a war that smaller firms would not likely win.

Collusion describes any agreement among business firms whose purpose is to limit competition.

Gentlemen's agreement is an agreement by which firms promise not to price compete against one another.

Collusion. **Collusion** is a general term used to describe any agreement among business firms whose purpose is to limit competition—that is, restrict output and raise prices. Although many countries permit or encourage collusive arrangements, any action whose intent or effect is the restraint of trade in the United States is illegal. Nonetheless, in the face of cutthroat price competition, the temptation to strike informal gentlemen's agreements, if not formal cartels, is overwhelming. A **gentlemen's agreement** is an informal accord among industry firms to carve up the market—an agreement by which firms promise not to price compete against one another.

Cartel *is a formal (some-times written) agreement to restrict output and increase prices.*

Cartel. A **cartel,** or formal (sometimes written) agreement to restrict output and increase prices, is the most insidious form of collusive behavior. Expressly prohibited by federal statutes, the cartel persists as one of the domestic oligopolists' main defenses against price wars at home and competition abroad. Although most well-known cartels are international in scope, U.S. cartels have been disclosed among Seattle bakeries, national electrical equipment manufacturers, and regional breweries. However, none is more notorious than OPEC.

OPEC's sole economic objective is to restrict production and drive up the price of oil. It was initially very successful—the price per barrel of oil quadrupled between 1973 and 1974. However powerful the cartel seemed at first, the agreement gradually crumbled by the early 1980s as members cheated by increasing the production of oil. Although the few numbers of Middle Eastern countries involved made it easy to strike the initial agreement, there was a great incentive for the smaller members to defect from the agreement. Formally promising to uphold the production quotas, the same countries then increased production in order to capture increased sales and profits.[6] Is this behavior mere greed, or is there something else behind it? Read the following CASE-IN-POINT for one view.

CASE
• IN •
POINT

Why Cartels Fail

While publicly proclaiming the virtues of solidarity, OPEC's oil sheiks privately selected alternatives that were in their own financial interest. But there is also another reason why cartels fail.

The main reason cartels like OPEC failed was not greed, but because of OPEC's belief that it could maintain artificially high prices through collusion. OPEC developed a high-price umbrella under which nonmember producers were willing to undercut OPEC prices, thereby reducing the available market for OPEC's high-priced products.

According to Professor Peter F. Drucker, famed author, management consultant, and keen business observer, only two monopolies (or cartels) have

---

[6] OPEC's inability to coerce compliance with production quotas or to discipline its member nations led to its loss of influence. This behavior is a classic example of what is called the *free rider* problem. Any voluntary agreement is prone to crumble as some *volunteers* decide that they can improve their position by acting independently. Have you ever tried to get coffee drinkers to share the cost of office coffee? Ever been a member of a union whose benefits go to members and nonmembers alike? OPEC's power is once again being felt, however, as lower oil prices in the mid-1980s increased oil consumption.

worked in modern industrial history. They were Nobel's dynamite dynasty and AT&T, until its recent dismemberment. The management of these enterprises understood that a monopoly works, and can only work, by lowering prices each year, and not by raising them as OPEC was doing. Rather than attracting competition, the prices and pricing strategies of Nobel and AT&T deterred effective competition for nearly 100 years.

Would-be competitors knew that in the face of these truly monopolistic strategies, it would be difficult to match prices next year and impossible in five years. These monopolists simply passed on their increasing productivity in the form of lower prices, rather than creating an OPEC-like canopy for the competition. Xerox learned this lesson the hard way after its pricing decisions assured the arrival of lower-priced imitators.[7]

Questions to Consider

1. *The author argues that greed is an insufficient explanation of the free rider problem. Do you agree or disagree? Why? (Perhaps the word* greed *is too strong? What if* self-interest *instead of* greed *is used to describe such actions? Would that make a difference?)*

2. *Most cartels fail because members want to undercut prices and reap gains not otherwise possible if they adhered to the cartels' production quotas. The author argues that this did not occur with other cartels, like AT&T. However, AT&T was not a cartel; it was a national monopoly sanctioned and regulated by the federal government. Is there a difference between a monopoly and a cartel? Explain.*

Pure monopoly *is a single seller of a product or service for which there are no close substitutes.*

Monopoly. **Pure monopoly** is a single seller of a product or service for which there are no close substitutes. It is the only firm in the industry. If our definition is national in scope, then pure monopoly, like pure competition, does not exist. There just are not any industries in which only one firm produces 100 percent of industry output, nor are there industries that have no close substitutes. Even for a public utility like natural gas, consumers may substitute other forms of energy. Moreover, monopoly is not a monolithic structure. If we move from the national level to state and local geographic areas, then we can identify two distinctly real types of monopoly: private unregulated monopoly and natural monopoly (or private regulated monopoly).[8] In each case, the firm, as the only

---

[7] "Why Cartels Fail," *The Wall Street Journal,* December 30, 1986.

[8] A special case can be made for the publicly owned and regulated monopoly, like the U.S. Postal Service. Indeed, if we look to nations like Great Britain, we can find many examples of government owned-and-operated businesses, sometimes called *state monopoly.* The steel, coal, and natural gas industries, to name a few, have been nationalized (taken over by the government) and denationalized several times in Great Britain.

provider of goods or services in the industry, enjoys considerable discretion regarding price and output.

Private unregulated monopoly *is an industry in which there is only one firm, or one firm dominates the market.*

One common variety of monopoly is the **private unregulated monopoly.** In many large cities, there is only one newspaper firm, and it is common to find only one cable television company operating in a community. In each case, the business has a local (or geographic) monopoly.

There are no national monopolies which are free of government regulation, but there are countless examples of local monopolies. Indeed, the odds are that you have encountered a local monopoly in your travels. The general store which sells the only soap, toilet paper, and deodorant for miles around is very common. With no effective local competition, the business can (and does) charge what the market will bear.[9]

Geography is thus a major factor in monopoly power. If several firms selling similar merchandise are close enough so that consumers may easily compare prices, then no monopoly exists. Separate these same businesses by a distance too great for customers to traverse easily and each firm acquires monopoly power. Please see Figure 7–6 on the next page for an illustration of monopoly pricing and profits.

Like a firm in monopolistic competition, our monopolist faces a downward-sloping demand curve. Using the profit-maximizing $MR = MC$ rule, the firm will produce and sell 500 units at a price of $3, generating an economic profit of $750. Unlike monopolistic competition, whose short-run profits may be erased as new competitors make a grab for market share, the monopolist may well be able to retain its economic profits in the long run. This largely depends upon the ability of the firm to prevent new firms from entering the industry. One tactic mentioned in the previous CASE-IN-POINT is to pass on cost savings to customers in lower prices. Of course, this is easier said than done. AT&T, who pioneered major technological innovations leading to regular cost reductions, was able to deter effective competition. Other monopolists, like Alcoa before World War II, lock out potential competition because they own or control resources required to manufacture the product. Still others have an assurance of monopoly power because of government patents, licenses, and franchises. One way or the other, firms will try to corner the market.

Natural monopoly *is a firm which may produce at a lower average cost than if two or more firms shared the market.*

Natural Monopoly. Electricity, natural gas, water, and local telephone services also are examples of industries with a single seller. **Natural**

---

[9] On a recent vacation in the Grand Tetons of Wyoming, our family encountered prices more than 30 percent above at-home prices for identical merchandise. Some of this is attributable to higher transportation costs. The local shopkeeper, whom we came to know well over the 10 days in camp, said "People will pay a lot for things like toothpaste and toilet paper, even on a camping trip." In other words, inelastic demand for these products enables owners to increase sales revenue and profits by raising prices.

FIGURE 7–6
Monopoly Pricing

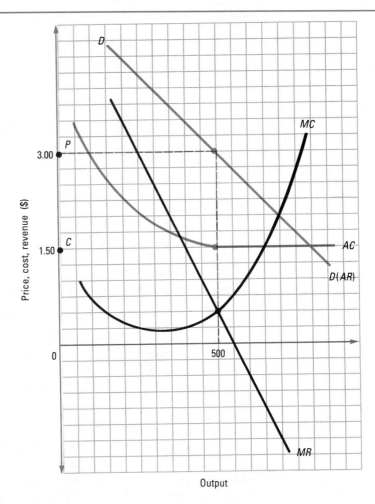

The monopolist will produce 500 units at a price of $3.00, determined the intersection of *MR* and *MC*, and make an economic profit of $750 (calculated by multiplying the profit per unit of $1.50 times the 500 units sold).

monopoly is a firm (and local industry) which experiences long-run economies of scale, such that it may produce at a lower average cost than if two or more firms shared the market. In other words, because of very high fixed costs and high capital requirements, delivery of these services would carry very high average costs if several firms competed in the same market. Only by permitting one firm the privileges of monopoly rights, franchised by the city or state, is it possible to spread these high fixed costs over many more customers and thus take advantage of economies of scale. Figure 7–7 illustrates this situation.

FIGURE 7–7

Natural Monopoly and
Economies of Scale

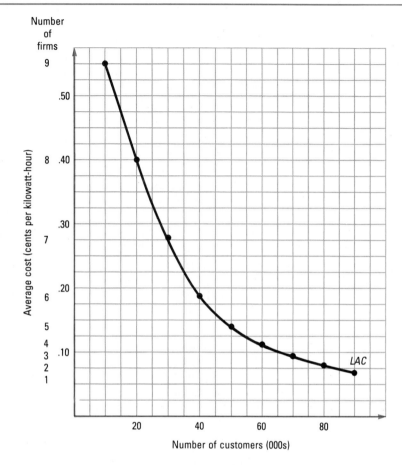

Economies of scale for many public utilities are such that the long-run average cost curve declines steadily, as shown above. If nine firms shared the market for electrical power, the cost per KWHR would be $.55. However, if only one firm supplied electricity to the entire customer base, the cost per KWHR would be $.07.

The long-run average cost *(LAC)* curve is depicted as we have discussed earlier in Chapter 5. Note in particular its L-shape in order to conform with research findings. The horizontal axis measures the number of customers. The vertical axis measures the cost per kilowatt hour (kwhr) and the number of firms associated with each per unit cost. If we assume that there are 90,000 customers in the service area, and if we further assume that the market is divided evenly among nine firms (10,000 customers per firm), Figure 7–7 shows that the cost per kwhr would be 55 cents. However, if one firm serviced the entire customer base, the cost per kwhr would be 7 cents. The difference is dramatic, enough to justify authorizing only one firm to provide such services.[10]

Sometimes monopolies exist exclusively at the pleasure of local government. Bus companies and transit authorities are common examples. Bus service is important to thousands of people who do not own automobiles. And, from a social welfare perspective, bus service and other forms of public transportation are essential to control urban congestion and pollution. However, because long-run costs generally exceed the bus fare, local governments elect to subsidize a company to provide the service.

Price Discrimination

Price discrimination is the act of charging different prices to different customers.

A very common practice employed by oligopolists and monopolists is **price discrimination**—charging different prices to different customers without cost differentials accounting for the difference in prices. Colleges and universities uniformly practice price discrimination when they charge higher tuition for out-of-state students than they charge for residents.

Two conditions must hold true if a firm is to engage successfully in price discrimination. First, resale must be impossible or highly improbable. Why? What if movie theaters priced discount (special promotion) tickets at $1.50 and regular adult tickets at $4.00. What would prevent a patron from acquiring several discount tickets at $1.50 and reselling at $3.00? This is the reason for having color-coded tickets.

A second requirement for successful price discrimination is that the market for the service or product is capable of being segmented. Market segmentation is the process of dividing the whole market into submarkets based upon age, income, elasticity (sensitivity to changes in price), and related factors. For example, airlines practice extensive market segmentation, with special fares for children, senior citizens, off-season travelers, business commuters, and so forth.

What is gained from price discrimination? Using elasticity of demand as the basis of segmentation, if the firm can identify one group with inelastic demand and another with an elastic demand, then it can charge a higher price for the group with an inelastic demand and a lower price with an elastic demand. In this way, the firm makes more profit than if it charged one price for both groups.

---

[10] Because only one firm is designated as the local monopolist, the city or state must regulate prices, service, and profits.

> ### THINKING IT THROUGH
>
> According to our definition, if doctors charge different prices for the same physical examination to two different patients, is this price discrimination? How about electric and natural gas companies that charge different rates for business and residential users? Is this price discrimination? Why or why not?

Pure Competition versus Imperfect Competition

We have repeatedly stated that studying pure competition is useful because it helps us to better understand and evaluate actual business behavior in regard to standards of general economic performance. One common measure of such performance is the efficiency by which firms allocate resources.

Resource allocation in pure competition is ideal. Purely competitive firms produce that output where $P = MC$. Price represents the value which consumers place on the last unit purchased, the marginal utility. Marginal cost is a measure of the value of society's resources in producing the last unit. When price equals marginal cost, no other arrangement can improve resource allocation. However, if price either exceeds or is less than marginal cost, then resources are either underallocated or overallocated to the production of the good. Because imperfectly competitive firms produce that output where $MR = MC$, and because $P > MR$, it follows that $P > MC$. This results in an underallocation of resources since consumers value the last unit produced more than it costs to produce it. Economic efficiency would be improved if there was more competition, leading to lower prices and greater output, thereby bringing price and marginal cost closer together.

Since all market structures are imperfect, it just does not make good sense to assert that all forms of imperfect competition are somehow harmful to the economy. However, once said, we can argue that certain types of imperfect competition result in outcomes which are disadvantageous to the consumer. Specifically, in those industries without substantial economies of scale and in which only a few firms dominate, one can argue that output is restricted for the purpose of driving up prices and profits. Figure 7–8 conveys the story graphically.

This graph illustrates a familiar set of curves: demand, marginal revenue, average cost, and marginal cost. Using the customary $MR = MC$ rule, a firm with monopoly power will produce 400 units at a price of $2,000. With a per unit cost of $1,200, the firm realizes an economic

FIGURE 7–8
Perfect Competition
versus Monopoly

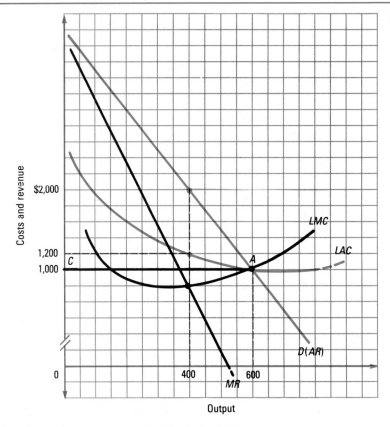

If a monopolist was converted to a pure competitor, price would be lower, output greater, and economic profits would be eliminated. The monopolist would produce 400 units at a price of $2,000 and make an economic profit of $32,000. The pure competitor, however, would face an elastic demand curve (segment *CA*) and produce 600 units at a price of $1,000, determined by the intersection of *LMC* and *CA* at point *A*.

profit of $32,000. If our firm did not possess power to influence market price, its demand curve would be *CAD*, perfectly elastic until the point where marginal cost cuts the demand curve, and downward sloping thereafter. It would produce 600 units at a price of $1,000, determined by the intersection of marginal cost, average cost, and the demand curve. Unlike the oligopolist or monopolist, the pure competitor would not make an economic profit. What this says is that if a pure competitor acquires market power, we can expect less output, higher prices, and economic (excess) profit. As we have seen, this is not the most socially beneficial outcome since the price paid by consumers exceeds the marginal cost of producing the goods. This means that an insufficient quantity of resources is being allocated to production. Society is deprived of additional output, and the reason is the presence of monopoly power. We will explore the issue of market power and antitrust in the next chapter.

In the next section, we continue our discussion of pricing behavior with two important differences. Instead of assuming that all businesses try to maximize profits, first we will examine the alternatives to profit maximization and second, we will explore several alternative pricing strategies and practices.

ALTERNATIVES TO PROFIT MAXIMIZATION

Satisficing *is the decision to select a satisfactory profit level instead of trying to maximize profits.*

One alternative to profit maximization is called **satisficing.** Instead of trying to reap the maximum profits from the sale of goods and services, management will select a profit level which it considers satisfactory. The motivation for this kind of profit goal varies, but one popular reason to satisfice instead of maximize is the desire to avoid unwanted government scrutiny. Another reason involves the high cost of determining the marginal cost for each product. For example, steel companies produce thousands of varieties of steel. And retail businesses, from hardware to fast-food operations, have so many items for sale that it is too expensive to identify marginal cost data for each product line.

Because satisficing strategies vary from company to company, there is no satisficing rule comparable to the profit-maximizing rule. One variation of satisficing is illustrated in Figure 7–9. Instead of seeking profit maximization, some firms will adopt a goal of sales maximization subject to a minimum level of profits. Interested in building its market share through aggressive pricing and marketing tactics, the company will price its products according to the profit level selected. Let's see how it works.

Let's assume that our hypothetical firm manufactures bicycles and that management has decided that it must make a minimum economic profit of $10,000. Figure 7–9 shows two diagrams: (a) the breakeven chart illustrating the firm's total revenue and total cost, and (b) the profit curve, derived from the breakeven chart. Profit maximization is most clearly shown in Figure 7–9b: profits are maximized at the output of 400 bicycles where the profit curve peaks. This is also shown in the breakeven chart in Figure 7–9a as the greatest distance between the *TR* and *TC* curves. Using Figure 7–9b, we can easily determine how much the firm should produce and sell and still earn its minimum profit. The intersection of the satisfactory profit line and the profit curve (at point *A*) determines the satisfactory profit output, 500 bicycles.

It is a simple step for the firm to identify the price. Since total revenue is price times quantity, the company just divides the total revenue of $50,000 by 500 (the number of bicycles) to determine its price, $100.

FIGURE 7–9a
Breakeven

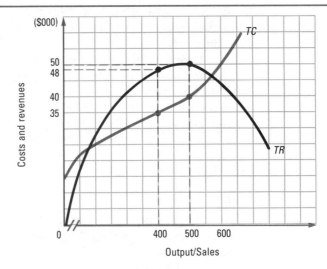

FIGURE 7–9b
The Profit Curve

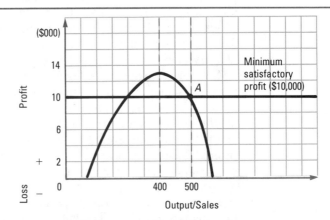

Profit maximization occurs at an output of 400, where the total profit curve peaks out. If a firm elects a satisficing strategy, however, such as $10,000, it will produce 500 units (point A, where the profit curve intersects the minimum satisfactory profit line).

What price would it charge if it were maximizing profits? Just divide the total revenue ($48,000) by the number of bicycles (400). The profit-maximizing price is $120.

Do Firms Maximize Profits?

The answer to this question largely depends upon whom you ask. Although economists seldom are in complete agreement on any given issue, there is widespread consensus in the economics profession that businesses try to maximize profits. Economists think that it would be irrational to do otherwise. Is it not in business interests, they ask, to make as much profit as they can?

However, if we ask business personnel the same question, the answer is nearly always a resounding no! They may want to maximize, but the information required to do so simply is too difficult and expensive to obtain. For example, profit maximization requires that firms estimate sales demand at all prices for all product lines. Moreover, marginal cost data is needed for each product as well. Because such data is nearly impossible to obtain, or because obtaining it results in prohibitive costs, most businesses do not use the profit-maximizing rule.[11]

Instead of charging a single price which reaps maximum profits, businesses use a wide range of pricing tactics. These tactics range from price skimming and penetration pricing to markup pricing formulas. Let's take a look at these alternative pricing strategies.

Price Skimming. When businesses market a new product, they often practice **price skimming,** charging the highest price the market will bear. Firms who adopt this tactic usually have identified a market cluster of customers with inelastic demand. These customers typically regard the high price as a promise of quality. For example, firms initially priced videocassette recorders at more than $1,500 and the Trivial Pursuit game at $39.95. Three years later, these same products were selling at prices less than half their original prices. This is a common practice in the book-publishing industry as well, when companies replace bestselling hardbound novels with paperbacks.[12]

Price skimming *is charging the highest price the market will bear.*

Penetration Pricing. Exactly the opposite of price skimming, **penetration pricing** is the strategy of charging a low enough price to attract the largest possible number of customers. Texas Instruments used penetration pricing when it introduced its hand-held calculators and digital watches.

Penetration pricing *is the strategy of charging a low enough price to attract the largest possible number of customers.*

---

[11] This does not mean, however, that business ignores marginal analysis. For example, companies are very interested in knowing if their advertising expenditures are generating increased sales (shifting the demand curve). Although difficult to identify, some firms use techniques like discount coupons in their ads in order to determine which of their customers are responding to advertisements.

[12] The inherent danger of price skimming is that other firms may be attracted to the market. In the short run, however, this may not be a serious problem, inasmuch as patent and copyright law will protect against product imitation or market invasion. The examples of price skimming and penetration pricing are borrowed from Eric N. Berkowitz, Roger Kerin, and William Rudelius, *Marketing* (St. Louis: Times Mirror/Mosby, 1986), pp. 313–14.

Although neither price skimming nor penetration pricing employ profit maximization as the chief goal, both pricing strategies focus on the demand side of the market. Each strategy considers consumer tastes and sensitivity to price as important determinants of the product price.

Markup Pricing.   Unlike pricing strategies which emphasize demand considerations, many retail establishments focus on the supply side and the costs of production. Firms using **markup pricing** set price by adding a fixed percentage markup of product costs to their production and marketing costs. For example, if a hardware store's cost of a power drill is $20, and if it adds a 25 percent markup on cost, it would set the price at $25. Other similar examples abound. "Construction companies submit job bids by estimating the total project cost and adding a standard markup for profit. Lawyers and other professionals typically price by adding a standard markup to their costs."[13]

Markup pricing *sets the price by adding a fixed percentage markup of product costs to the production and marketing costs.*

Markup pricing is very common throughout retail industries. Fast-food restaurants, supermarkets, furniture, clothing and hardware stores all add a percentage markup on the cost of a full-product line. Of course, these markups range widely from grocery to department store operations. For example, "Some common markups (on price, not cost) in department stores are 20 percent for tobacco goods, 28 percent for cameras, 34 percent for books, 41 percent for dresses, 46 percent for costume jewelry, and 50 percent for millinery."[14] Markups also vary according to product type and sales volume. Grocery stores typically use higher markups for so-called discretionary goods (like paper products, deli foods, and candy) and lower markups for staples (like bread, milk, sugar, and flour).

Nowhere is markup pricing practiced more extensively than in the grocery business. The following CASE-IN-POINT illustrates pricing strategies in one of the most competitive industries in America.

CASE
· IN ·
POINT

Kroger: Where a One Percent Error Is Too Much

A supermarket chain is always a breath away from disaster because it's such a high-volume, low-margin industry. The target for most supermarket chains such as Kroger, Safeway, and Jewel is to make one penny of profit on each dollar of sales.

In recent years, that hasn't been easy, partially because consumers aren't buying the way they traditionally have bought—and the way supermarket

---

[13] Philip Kotler, *Principles of Marketing,* 3rd ed. (Englewood Cliffs, N.J.: Prentice-Hall, 1986), p. 381.
[14] Ibid.

chains count on them to buy. Typically, a supermarket lures prospective buyers with sale-priced, low-profit staples like milk, bread, coffee, and detergents. Once in the store, these consumers are expected to buy the higher-profit items like quality meats, produce, convenience foods, and nongrocery items. But in recent years, sales of the high-profit items have often been down. The differences in supermarket markups on staple versus discretionary items show the problem:

Staple Item	Markups (percent)	Discretionary Items	Markups (percent)
Dairy products	23	Stationary and school supplies	47
Soaps and detergents	17	Hosiery	42
Oils and shortenings	17	Candy and gum	32
Flour	16	Frozen foods	28
Coffee and sugar	10	Health and beauty aids	28
		Snacks	27

Faced with increasing competition among chains, higher operating costs, and more sophisticated consumers who shop for bargain prices among a number of stores, what should supermarket chains do to continue making a profit?

Kroger chose as its basic strategy for the 1980s and 1990s to broaden its appeal by combining higher-priced specialty items with low-cost private label goods. Many Kroger stores now have specialty deli, seafood, and bakery shops; and nonfood items such as clothing, motor oil, hardware, and toys account for 60 percent of their shelf space. Kroger's own private-brand items, which give higher margins than do national brands, are being stressed to compete with national brands at the high end of the price scale and generic products at the low end.[15]

Questions to Consider

1. *Based upon Kroger's strategy for the 1990s, combining higher priced specialty items with low-cost private label goods, it sounds like Kroger is turning into a hypermarket. If you could buy motor oil, screwdrivers, and toys along with groceries in the same store, would you do it? Why might some consumers prefer to shop at hardware stores for hammers? At auto stores for oil?*

2. *Is one-stop shopping the wave of the future? If so, what does this mean for the small specialty stores?*

No matter how firms price products, the acid test is whether consumers want them and are willing to part with their money. Businesses

---

[15] Berkowitz, et al., *Marketing*, p. 319.

therefore ultimately must deal with consumer demand—ways to differentiate their products from their competitors, the tastes and preferences of consumers, the prices and availability of substitutes and complements, and the other determinants of consumer demand.

<table>
<tr><td>

IMPORTANT TERMS TO REMEMBER

</td><td>

artificial barriers, p. 191
cartel, p. 193
collusion, p. 192
gentlemen's agreement, p. 192
imperfect competition, p. 181
markup pricing, p. 204
monopolistic competition, p. 186
mutual interdependence, p. 191
natural barriers, p. 191

</td><td>

natural monopoly, p. 195
oligopoly, p. 191
penetration pricing, p. 203
price discrimination, p. 198
price leadership, p. 192
price skimming, p. 203
private unregulated monopoly, p. 195
pure monopoly, p. 194
satisficing, p. 201

</td></tr>
</table>

CHAPTER SUMMARY

1. Imperfect competition is a catchall term that refers to market structures and firms which have enough market power to set prices. These structures include monopolistic competition, oligopoly, and monopoly.

2. Besides the ability to influence product price, there are two important characteristics which distinguish imperfect competition from pure competition: First, price exceeds marginal revenue (and marginal cost) in imperfect competition. Second, elasticity measurements are closely related to marginal revenue *(MR)* so that when $MR > 0$, demand is elastic; when $MR = 0$, demand is unit elastic; and when $MR < 0$, demand is inelastic.

3. Monopolistically competitive industries, like retail food stores, are characterized by many sellers, a highly differentiated product or service, few barriers to entry, and excess capacity. While short-run economic profits are common, new firms attracted to the industry often result in the elimination of economic profits.

4. Oligopoly is a market structure with only a few dominant firms, either a highly differentiated product (like autos) or a standardized product (like cement), and high barriers to entry. The barriers to entry may be natural (like economies of scale) or artificial (like patents and licenses).

5. Mutual interdependence is the chief characteristic of oligopoly. Because there are so few firms, each firm is very sensitive to the prices set by its competitors.

6. Because of mutual interdependence, oligopolists engage in several pricing strategies in an effort to deter price competition and price wars. These strategies include price leadership, collusion (or conspiracy), gentlemen's agreements, cartels, and price discrimination.

7. Pure monopoly is a single seller of a product or service which has no close substitutes. Although pure monopoly does not exist on a national level, close approximations in the real world are local private unregu-

lated monopolies (like newspaper firms) and natural monopolies (like public utilities).

8. Price discrimination is practiced extensively by oligopolists and monopolists. Price discrimination involves charging different prices to different customers for the same product or service.

9. Because businesses find it difficult and/or too expensive to obtain estimates of demand and marginal cost data, satisficing is a common alternative to profit maximization. Some firms choose to maximize sales subject to a minimum or satisfactory level of profit.

10. Alternative pricing strategies to the profit-maximizing rule involve price skimming—charging a high price on a low volume of sales and thus making a high profit per unit, penetration pricing—charging a low price to tap the mass market (the opposite of price skimming), and markup pricing—charging a price computed by adding a fixed percentage (markup) to the average costs of production and marketing.

DISCUSSION AND REVIEW QUESTIONS

1. The chapter FOCUS presents a real situation in which oligopolistic price cutting set off a price war, resulting in losses for all firms in the electromechanical parts industry. How else might the firm have handled its problem?

2. Jan's Apparel, a new retail clothing store, just opened in a nearby shopping mall. As a monopolistic competitor, Jan wishes to maximize profits.
   a. Complete the table below for *MR, MC, AC,* and profit.
   b. Diagram the demand, *MR, MC,* and *AC* curves, and identify Jan's short-run profit-maximizing price, output, and profits on the graph.
   c. What is likely to happen to Jan's economic profits in the long run?

Output	Price	TR	MR	TC	MC	AC	Profit
0	$50	$0	45	$50	5	—	-50
1	45	45	35	55	10	55	-10
2	40	80	25	65	15	32.5	15
3	35	105	15	80	20	26.7	25
4	30	120	5	100	25	25	20
5	25	125	-5	125	30	25	0
6	20	120		155		25.8	-35

3. How do Domino's, McDonald's, and your local grocery store establish prices for various products? Do they maximize profits according to the *MR = MC* rule? Do they satisfice? Do they use a markup formula? Ask your grocer and local managers of Domino's and McDonald's.

4. Price discrimination is commonly practiced by many businesses. Insurance companies charge a higher premium on the same car to male drivers under 25 years of age than to either female drivers (of any age) or to males over 25 years of age. Is this price discrimination? Doctors and dentists

often charge low-income patients less than higher-income patients. Draw the demand curves for these patient groups. Does the medical profession increase patient revenue by practicing price discrimination?

5. Advertising is used by businesses to differentiate their products from their competitors' and increase demand. Advertising also serves as one of the most effective barriers to entry in many industries. For example, firms advertising during the Super Bowl have paid $500,000 for a one-minute commercial. Do you think that this is money well spent? How does the company know if its advertising dollars actually generate new sales?

6. Congress has passed special legislation permitting certain growers of fruit (oranges, lemons, and raisins, for example) to form marketing agreements by which they may limit production and establish production quotas. If two thirds of the farmers formally vote for such an arrangement, the Department of Agriculture will require all farmers to abide by the agreement. Is this agreement a cartel? What is the effect on price, output, and profits? Do you think that fruit growers are a special case, or should nonagricultural businesses also be permitted to form such agreements?

A BRIEF LOOK AHEAD

This chapter explored the pricing behavior of imperfectly competitive firms, and showed the effect of market power on price, output, and profits. The next chapter looks at the national policy implications of market power. Our problem is deciding if and how pricing control adversely affects consumers and impedes efficiency and what to do about it. Then, if we can agree upon specific criteria of unacceptable business conduct (like price fixing), making and enforcing antitrust policy to regulate and control undersirable business behavior is much easier.

Industrial Organization
and Antitrust

Paramount Communications Inc.

IS OUR NEW NAME
REPLACING GULF+WESTERN INC.

Paramount Communications Inc., a leader in entertainment and publishing,
is a global communications company. We are now poised for even greater growth
as we concentrate our resources and energies on worldwide expansion.

Our operations include the following well-known names:

Entertainment	Publishing
Paramount Pictures	Simon & Schuster
Paramount Television	Prentice Hall School
Paramount Home Video	Prentice Hall College
Famous Music	Prentice Hall Professional Information
Wilshire Court Productions	Pocket Books
Famous Players Theaters	Silver Burdett & Ginn
Madison Square Garden Center	Allyn & Bacon
Madison Square Garden Network	Appleton & Lange
MSG Television Productions	Globe Book Company
New York Knicks	Coronet/MTI Film & Video
New York Rangers	Judy Instructo
Miss Universe Pageants	Modern Curriculum Press
Interests in:	Webster's New World
Cinamerica Theaters	J.K. Lasser
United International Pictures	Arco
Cinema International Corporation	Betty Crocker
CIC Video	Frommer
United Cinemas International	Summit Books
USA Network	Poseidon Press
International Advertising Sales	Fireside
Pending interest in TVX Broadcast Group:	Touchstone
WTXF-TV (Philadelphia)	Brady Computer Books
WDCA-TV (Washington, D.C.)	S&S Audio
KTXH-TV (Houston)	Woodhead-Faulkner
KTXA-TV (Dallas)	Harvester/Wheatsheaf
WLFL-TV (Raleigh-Durham)	Macdonald Children's Books

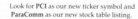

Look for **PCI** as our new ticker symbol and
ParaComm as our new stock table listing.

Paramount Communications Inc.

15 Columbus Circle   New York, N.Y. 10023-7780
212-373-8000

Paramount Communications

This chapter is devoted to a field of economics known as industrial organization. Concerned with the structure, conduct (behavior), and performance of business firms, it follows naturally from the preceding chapters on pure and imperfect competition. We will examine the structure of U.S. industry, types of mergers and merger activity, antitrust legislation, court cases, and the issues surrounding antitrust legislation and enforcement.

After completion of this chapter, you should be able to do the following:

1. Describe the pattern and trend of aggregate and industry concentration.
2. Describe and explain the concentration ratio as a measure of market (monopoly) power, and explain the limitations of this measure.
3. Identify and distinguish among three merger types: horizontal, vertical, and conglomerate.
4. Describe the key provisions of the Sherman Act, the FTC Act, the Clayton Act, the Celler-Kefauver Act, the Miller-Tydings Act, and the McGuire Act.
5. Describe the patterns of merger activity following each piece of antitrust legislation.
6. Compare and contrast the structuralist and the behaviorist positions regarding antitrust.
7. Identify and explain some of the issues surrounding antitrust.

Merger Mania: Are We Building Monolithic Capitalism?

"Another Record-Setting Merger," "How Much Longer Can the Merger Mania Last?"—from headlines plastered across the first pages of newspapers and in major stories in *Newsweek* and *Time* magazines, we learn about the largest merger wave in U.S. history. Du Pont bought Conoco in 1981 for $7.4 billion; U.S. Steel bought Marathon Oil Corporation for $6.5 billion in 1982; Southern Pacific and Santa Fe railroads merged in 1983 at a $5.2 billion price tag; and Chevron swallowed Gulf Oil for a cool $13.4 billion in 1985. Although these were some of the biggest deals, there were thousands of others. Over the seven year period from 1980 to 1987, there were 18,782 mergers with a reported value of $667 billion. Of these acquisitions, 106 were takeovers involving firms worth $1 billion or more. This amounts to more than 25 percent of the current market value of all traded stocks.[1] We are moving from competitive capitalism to monolithic capitalism.

Why the flurry of mergers? What's behind this merger mania? Company executives cite a number of reasons internal to the corporation, such as economies of scale, diversification, increased research and development capability, and profitability. But it is uncertain whether increased efficiencies result from conglomerate mergers, and there is little evidence that bigness leads to more inventions and innovations.

Among the many forces shaping industrial structure, two main external or environmental factors account for this merger wave. First, deregulation of private industry has spawned big consolidations in railroads, airlines, communications (including newspapers), oil and natural gas, and in trucking. Second, the Reagan presidency actively opposed antitrust enforcement. Indeed, Reagan's appointees to the Antitrust Division of the Justice Department and to the Federal Trade Commission generally agree that the antitrust laws should be abolished. Deregulation and a policy of benign neglect regarding antitrust enforcement together constitute an ideological position: get the government off the backs of U.S. business and let the private marketplace work.

While it may be conceded that government regulations are often unreasonable and costly to implement, it is unlikely that corporate giantism is the answer to U.S. problems in the area of international competition. Gargantuan size does confer economic and political power, but does it contribute to increased efficiency? Does bigness provide comparative production advantages? Are product development and technical improvements in the production process somehow enhanced by sheer size? If the record of the last 20 years is a guide, the answer to these questions is a resounding no!

---

[1] Walter Adams and James W. Brock, *The Bigness Complex: Industry, Labor and Government in the American Economy* (New York: Pantheon Books, 1986).

There is little doubt that U.S. corporations have acquired a merger addiction. However, there is widespread disagreement among economists about the alleged dangers of this merger activity. Many economists take the view that competition is a sufficient safeguard against excessive market power, and antitrust laws merely impede the efficient allocation of resources. What's all the fuss about? is the essence of the question. Many other economists, as reflected in the FOCUS, think that giant mergers generally are motivated by a desire for bigness in and of itself, without any benefits of increased efficiency or technical progress. Indeed, some economists think that economic and political power is the underlying motive for periods of merger mania.

What is the function of antitrust? Are antitrust laws really necessary? As with nearly all policy issues, there are no right and wrong answers to these questions. In order to understand the issues involved, however, we need to look at the structure of U.S. industry and examine the measures of aggregate and industry concentration.

Industrial Organization and Market Concentration

What percentage of all manufacturing assets is owned by the largest 100 firms? The largest 200 firms? How has this concentration changed over time? With this kind of data, we can get a clear picture of aggregate (or overall) concentration. Table 8–1 shows the ownership of assets for selected years between 1950 and 1984 of the largest 100 and 200 manufacturing firms. The aggregate concentration of the 200 largest corporations increased from 47 percent in 1950 to 61 percent in 1984. Perhaps even more important, in 1984 the 100 largest manufacturing firms held 49.2 percent of all manufacturing assets, more than the largest 200 manufacturers owned in 1950. Although many more observations may be made regarding this data, the important point is that aggregate concentration has increased since World War II. To see how this is played out in individual industries, we now turn to specific industry measures of concentration.

TABLE 8–1		Year	100 Largest	200 Largest
Aggregate Concentration		1950	39.2	47.3
Trends: Ownership of		1955	44.3	52.5
Assets by the 100 and		1960	46.5	55.0
200 Largest Manufactur-		1965	48.0	57.6
ing Companies,		1970	49.1	59.8
1950–1984		1975	44.0	58.1
		1984	49.2	61.0

SOURCE: *Statistical Abstract of the United States.*

TABLE 8–2

Market Concentration Ratios, Selected Industries, 1947–1982

Industry	Four-Firm Ratios			Eight-Firm Ratios		
	1947	1967	1982	1947	1967	1982
Motor vehicles and car bodies	71	92	92	NA	98	97
Aluminum	100	D	64	X	100	88
Cigarettes	90	81	D	99	100	D
Tires and tubes	70	70	66	89	89	86
Farm machinery	NA	44	53	NA	56	62
Photographic equipment and supplies	61	69	74	76	81	86
Aircraft and parts	72	69	64	92	89	81
Dry breakfast cereals	79	88	86	91	97	D
Telephone, telegraph equip.	NA	92	76	NA	96	83
Motor vehicle parts	NA	60	61	NA	68	69
Radios and TVs	NA	49	49	NA	69	70
Household refrigerators and freezers	NA	73	94	NA	93	98
Machine tools (metal cutting)	20	21	30	30	33	44
Primary lead[a]	D	D	100	100	100	D
Copper[a]	87	77	D	99	97	D
Women's handbags and purses	7	10	30	13	17	38
Roasted coffee	52	53	65	68	71	76
Metal cans	78	73	50	86	84	68
Malt beverages	21	40	77	30	59	94

[a] = Value added is used instead of value of shipments.
D = Data withheld by companies to avoid disclosure.
NA = Not available.
X = Not applicable.
SOURCE: *1982 Census of Manufactures,* Bureau of the Census, MC82-S-7, March 1986.

Because market structure is used as one measure of monopoly (or market) power, the government's investigatory and enforcement arms maintain regular data banks of industry concentration. Table 8–2 presents concentration ratios for selected industries.

A **concentration ratio** indicates the percentage of total industry assets or sales of the top four or eight firms in the industry. (In goods-producing industries, it is common to use the total value of shipments.) As Table 8–2 indicates, although concentration ratios vary widely by industry, concentration increased between 1947 and 1982 in many industries. Some changes were dramatic. For example, in the malt beverage (beer) industry, shipments of the largest four firms increased from 21 to 77 percent between 1947 and 1982. In cigarettes and several metallurgical industries, like lead and copper, the four-firm concentration ratio approached or equaled 100 percent. (Information is often withheld by companies in such industries in order to avoid disclosure.) On the other hand, there is also evidence of declining concentration in a number of industries, such as metal cans, aircraft and parts, and tires and tubes.

Concentration ratio *indicates the percentage of total industry assets or sales of the top four or eight firms.*

Still another way to view the degree of concentration is to look at the distribution of industries according to the four-firm concentration ratio. Please see Table 8–3 below.

Of the 441 industries reported in the Census of Manufactures, 18 (4 percent) had concentration ratios in excess of 80 percent. In the 60–79 percent range of concentration, the census identified 54 industries, 12 percent of the total. And there were 120 industries in the concentration range from 40 to 59 percent, representing 28 percent of the total. What does this data suggest? First, even though aggregate concentration has increased over the last 45 years, and even though concentration has increased significantly in many industries, a majority of industries remain unconcentrated. As the data in Table 8–3 shows, 249 industries, or 56 percent of all manufacturing industries, are in the range from 0 to 39 percent, a range generally regarded by antitrusters and the courts as unconcentrated. Second, these unconcentrated industries account for 64 percent of the total value added of total shipments. (Value added is the difference between the sale price of the goods shipped and the costs of production incurred by the firm in making the goods [labor, raw materials, and other supplies.]) Thus, although a majority of individual industries are unconcentrated, collectively they control nearly two thirds of all the value added in manufacturing.

Limitations of the Concentration Ratio. As we have already seen, the concentration ratio is defined as the share of industry shipments made by the top four or eight firms. Although it is used extensively by the courts in antitrust cases as evidence of market power, there are a number of inherent problems with its use. For example, the concentration ratio is based upon voluntary corporate reporting of ownership or control of plants (directly or through subsidiaries) in an annual questionnaire from the U.S. Bureau of the Census. Naturally, if a corporation has control of a plant but does not report it, then the concentration ratio will be understated.

	Four-Firm Concentration (percent)	Number of Industries (census)	Cumulative Percentage	Percentage of Value Added (percent of total)
TABLE 8–3 Distribution of Manufacturing Industries by Concentration Ratios, 1982	80–100	18	4	6
	60– 79	54	16	12
	40– 59	120	44	18
	20– 39	163	80	44
	<20	86	100	20
	Total	441	100	100

SOURCE: Richard G. Lipsey, Peter O. Steiner, and Douglas D. Purvis, *Economics,* 8th ed. (New York: Harper & Row, 1987), p. 262.

Another source of understatement exists because the ratio is a national measure, thereby possibly concealing higher ratios for regions, states, or smaller markets. If the relevant market is smaller, either regional or local, the concentration ratio for the nation will understate the actual degree of concentration. In other words, the definition of the industry is critical in determining the degree of concentration. For example, the four-firm ratio for newspapers is 22 percent nationally. However, since the relevant market in most cases is a city or metro area, and because most cities have only one major daily newspaper, the actual concentration ratio is much greater. Indeed, if the relevant market is local, the ratio is 100 percent in all cities with only one newspaper.

A third source of understatement relates to product perishability, transportation costs, and other factors which limit the market area. For example, even though the national four-firm ratio in the cement industry is 6 percent, the relevant market is local (concrete mix is not shipped great distances); thus, the concentration ratio is actually much larger.

Sources of overstatement are also important. First, because all imports are excluded, the ratio is overestimated. If oil, auto, and computer imports were included, the ratios for these industries would be lower. And, second, because some industry definitions are very narrow, some products that consumers or producers treat as good substitutes are excluded. For example, metal cans and glass containers are classified as different industries, although there are many uses for which the two are perfectly substitutable. Defining the relevant market in antitrust cases is one of the most difficult problems for the courts.

Merger Types

Horizontal merger *is the combination of two or more competing firms in the same industry.*

There are three types of mergers: horizontal, vertical, and conglomerate. The **horizontal merger** occurs when two or more competing firms in the same industry merge. A classic case would be the merger of GM and Ford, or Avis and Hertz. In the deregulated airline industry, the recent mergers of Texas Air with Continental, Eastern, and People Express were typical of the horizontal consolidations of the 1980s. If structure matters, then it is interesting to note that while 12 airline carriers controlled 85.5 percent of air travel in 1986, one year later only 8 airlines controlled 94 percent. The antitrust statutes are designed to prevent any merger where the effect is to lessen competition by monopolizing and restraining trade.

Vertical merger *is the consolidation of a firm and its supplier or wholesale or retail outlet(s).*

A **vertical merger** is a consolidation of a firm and its supplier or wholesale or retail outlet(s). The Firestone Tire & Rubber Co. is a fully vertically integrated firm. It owns rubber plantations in Brazil and elsewhere, it owns tire and tube processing plants, it has its own fleet of trucks to deliver products to wholesalers and retailers, and it owns retail outlets. Because the Sherman and Clayton acts were invoked to curtail horizontal integration, most firms that wanted to expand by merger were forced to choose vertical integration.

Conglomerate merger
occurs when two or more firms in different industries merge.

A **conglomerate merger** occurs when two or more firms in different industries get together. If GM purchased Russell Stover Candies, a firm in a totally unrelated product line, this would be a conglomerate merger. Conglomeration has resulted in the creation of some of the nation's largest firms. Ling-Temco-Vought (LTV), with sales in excess of $8 billion in 1985, operates in dozens of industries, such as aerospace and missiles, processed foods, electronic equipment, sporting equipment, pharmaceuticals, and chemicals, to name just a few. And International Telephone and Telegraph (ITT), one of the most well-known conglomerates, has assets exceeding $14 billion, two thirds of which was acquired by merger with companies in totally unrelated industries.

ANTITRUST LEGISLATION

Historical Background

> People of the same trade seldom meet together, even for merriment and diversion, but the conversation ends in a conspiracy against the public, or in some contrivance to raise prices.[2]

So wrote Adam Smith in 1776. Could this be the United States' foremost champion of laissez-faire capitalism? Even Adam Smith, proponent of free market economies, could sense the ever-present danger of businesses to collude for the purpose of profit taking.[3]

One hundred years after Smith wrote about the tendency of businesses to conspire against the public, the warning came true. A transformation occurred in the U.S. economy in the late 19th century. In a brief 30 years, the United States turned from a predominately agrarian rural society into an industrial, rapidly urbanizing society. As population growth created an insatiable demand for more goods and services, the economy grew. Although businesses responded with mass production efforts, fierce price competition for markets ensued, often leading to

---

[2] Adam Smith, *An Inquiry into the Causes and Nature of the Wealth of Nations,* ed. E. Cannon (Chicago: University of Chicago Press, 1976), p. 144. Originally published in 1776.

[3] Actually, Smith's observation (or, more appropriately, warning) makes sense if understood in the context of late-18th-century United States. In *The Wealth of Nations* Smith explained how mercantilism, a practice by which England controlled much of its colonies' commerce, denied the colonists the economic freedom to pursue their own self-interests, resulting in countless inefficiencies. Desiring to show the folly of a state-controlled economy and the need to throw off the shackles of mercantilism, Smith also was perceptive enough to realize the consequences of such freedom. The dilemma survives to this day.

Trusts *are combinations of competitors to fix prices and control the market.*

combinations of competitors to fix prices and control the market. These efforts to cartelize markets were known as **trusts,** what we would call today *shared monopolies*. Businesses in the same industry would form a trust arrangement in which all production and sales decisions would be governed by a common board, consisting of the upper management of each member firm. Although separate companies, each firm passed control of its operations to the board in exchange for an end to price competition, the elimination of risk, and the assurance of a profit.

It has been estimated that these trusts controlled over 40 percent of U.S. manufacturing industries in 1900. Who were these firms? The list is very familiar, since they have survived to this day, albeit in different form: U.S. Steel, U.S. Rubber, American Can, U.S. Gypsum, General Electric, International Nickel, International Paper, United Fruit, National Lead, National Biscuit Company, International Salt, to name a few.

Competition is rooted in, and derives its vitality from, decentralized economic power. In order to preserve a decentralized economic system, the antitrust laws were designed to maintain a competitive environment and inhibit and prevent price collusion. Capitalism is at its best when competition is effective, translated as low costs of production, low prices, new products, and technological progress. But capitalism is at its worst when it is degraded by the concentration of power and the abuses which often ensue.

Countless examples of price fixing, bid rigging, and related anticompetitive behavior have been uncovered by the Justice Department in the last 30 years. Here are a few examples:

- An international quinine cartel cornered the world market in the early 1960s and raised the price from $.37 to $2.13 per ounce.
- In the period from 1953 to 1961, pharmaceutical companies conspired to fix prices of the antibiotic tetracycline, charging $51 for a bottle of 100 tablets. After congressional hearings and an indictment, the same drug firms sold the same quantity of tetracycline for $5 in 1971.
- In 1969, it was discovered that in 22 cities competing newspapers conspired to fix advertising rates and pool their profits.

Price fixing *is an agreement by firms to subdivide markets and charge those prices agreed to by the conspiring parties.*

Suppression of competition through formal trust organizations was common at the turn of the century. More common still, however, is the overt act of **price fixing**—an agreement by firms to subdivide markets and charge those prices agreed to by the parties involved in the conspiracy. No more blatant an example of this exists than the electrical conspiracy discussed in the following CASE-IN-POINT.

The Infamous Electrical Conspiracy

In February of 1960, in the biggest criminal antitrust case in history, General Electric (GE), Westinghouse, Allis Chalmers Corporation and 25 other electrical equipment producers were indicted and found guilty of a massive price-fixing conspiracy.

Over the preceding 10 to 15 years, these companies held clandestine meetings in which they agreed not to compete against one another. Despite flagrant violations of antitrust laws and great risk of prosecution if caught, they engaged in bid rigging, price fixing, and successfully eliminated all price competition in the industry. How did they do it?

In the market for turbine generators used in hydroelectric power plants, a $400 million market, the government required companies to submit sealed bids. The government would then award the contract to the company with the lowest bid. To circumvent this process, the conspirators simply agreed beforehand to share the business according to a system of rotation. For example, GE would submit a low bid for $142,490 and the others would submit higher bids. The government would award the contract to GE. On the next job, it was Westinghouse's turn. It would submit the lowest bid, and so it went for nearly 15 years. Prices charged amounted to as much as 50 percent above competitive levels, and illegal profits exceeded $100 million.

Questions to Consider

1. *The electrical conspiracy was an open-and-shut case of illegal activity. Why did the executives of GE, Westinghouse, Allis Chalmers, and other firms do it?*

2. *The conspiracy was initially discovered by a reporter for the Knoxville News-Sentinel. The reporter obtained a document from the Tennessee Valley Authority (TVA) which showed that Westinghouse won a contract for transformers on a bid of $96,000. The document also listed the bids of Allis Chalmers, GE, and Pennsylvania Transformers—all identical quotations of $112,712. The reporter then found other contracts with similar identical bids. When he wrote a series of articles about the pattern, Senator Estes Kefauver, the chairman of the Senate Subcommittee on Antitrust and Monopoly, saw them and launched an investigation. This led to a grand jury indictment and subsequent prosecution. Why would the companies submit identical bids? Were they just careless?*

What Is Antitrust?

Antitrust *refers to any legislative or judicial action taken to arrest monopolistic behavior and the restraint of trade.*

Although the word **antitrust** was originally applied exclusively to any effort to curtail the growth and influence of the trusts, today antitrust means any legislative or judicial action taken to arrest monopolistic behavior and the restraint of trade. In 1890, Congress responded with the first national antitrust legislation, the **Sherman Antitrust Act.** There were two main provisions of the law.

The **Sherman Antitrust Act** *made every contract or combination (merger) in restraint of trade illegal.*

Section 1. Every contract, combination in the form of trust or otherwise, or conspiracy, in restraint of trade or commerce among the several States, or with foreign nations, is hereby declared illegal.

Section 2. Every person who shall monopolize, or attempt to monopolize or combine or conspire with any other person or persons, to monopolize any part of the trade or commerce among the several States, or with foreign nations, shall be deemed guilty of a misdemeanor.

The Sherman Act did little to prevent practices which tended to reduce competition or were conducive to creating monopolies. It did not apply to cases which were *only likely* to lead to the destruction of competition and which fell short of an actual monopoly or combination in unreasonable restraint of trade. Moreover, because the Sherman Act was so general, each alleged violation was handled on a case-by-case basis. Indeed, it was felt that the lack of specificity in the Sherman Act opened the proverbial Pandora's box of mergers. More and more mergers were ruled by the courts as out of jurisdiction. This led to the Federal Trade Commission and Clayton Acts.

The **Federal Trade Commission Act** *created the FTC and classifies as illegal any unfair or deceptive practices or methods of competition.*

There are two main provisions of the 1914 **Federal Trade Commission Act.** First, it created the Federal Trade Commission (FTC), to be composed of five commissioners, appointed by the president and confirmed by the Senate. A second provision stated that "Unfair methods of competition in or affecting commerce, and unfair or deceptive acts or practices in or affecting commerce, are declared unlawful." This section went on to charge the FTC with the responsibility to investigate suspicious conduct and, if unfair methods of competition were found, to issue complaints and hold hearings to ascertain guilt or innocence. The FTC would then issue a cease and desist order to all corporations determined to be in violation of the law(s). And, if the corporation persisted in the violation, the FTC is empowered to assess fines for each violation.

The **Clayton Act** *prohibited corporations from acquiring the stock of another corporation engaged in interstate commerce where the effect would be to monopolize or reduce competition.*

Designed to close the loopholes evident in the Sherman Antitrust Act, Section 7 of the **Clayton Act** of 1914 was by far the most important. Section 7 specifically prohibited corporations from acquiring the stock of another corporation engaged in interstate commerce where the effect would be to "substantially lessen competition . . . or tend to create a monopoly." By prohibiting stock acquisition, legislators hoped to plug the stock loophole in the Sherman Act. Like its predecessor, the Clayton Act did not slow the pace of merger activity. Prohibited from acquiring the stock of competing companies, firms responded by acquiring the assets instead.

Another section of the Clayton Act prohibits interlocking directorates, wherein the officer of a corporation sits on the Board of Directors of a competing company. A third provision outlawed price discrimination which was not based on difference in the grade, quality, or quantity of the product sold, or differences in transportation costs. A fourth provision prohibited tie-in sales, a practice whereby a business, as a condition of sale of a product, required the client to purchase a related product or service. For example, in a 1947 case the Supreme Court declared that International Salt Company illegally required its customers who had leased a patented salt-processing machine to purchase all salt used in the machine from International Salt. Such tie-in sales were deemed destructive of competition.

The wording of Section 7 was carefully chosen in order to address the Supreme Court's decisions in two famous cases, the *Northern Securities Company* case in 1904 and the *Standard Oil* case in 1911. The Northern Securities Company, created in 1901 by New York financier J. P. Morgan, James Hill, and other railroad owners, was a huge holding company composed of the Great Northern Railway Company and the Northern Pacific Railway Company. The court declared that the combination was a **per se violation** of the Sherman Act, whereby the agreement itself constituted a violation, and no further evidence was required to declare the combination unlawful. The court held that "every contract, combination . . . or conspiracy in restraint of trade . . . is made illegal by the [Sherman] act."

> **Per se violation** *is a judicial decree that finds a merger or the agreement to merge by itself illegal.*

At the turn of the 20th century, the Rockerfellers and other prominent oil magnates had formed a giant holding company called The Standard Oil Company of New Jersey, consisting of 33 companies in the petroleum drilling, refining, and distribution business. As it did with the *Northern Securities* case, the Justice Department filed suit against The Standard Oil Company of New Jersey for per se violations of the Sherman Act. Unlike the Northern Securities decision, however, this court decision declared that the Sherman Act effectively denied companies the right of contract by prohibiting any merger through monopolization or attempts to monopolize. Enunciating the **rule of reason,** the court held that not all mergers were per se violations and that only in cases involving *unreasonable restraints* of trade would the proposed merger be prohibited. In effect, the court established a new test in which the government had to prove corporate *intent to monopolize* or restrain trade.[4] Moreover, the court raised the issue of the inherent ef-

> **Rule of reason** *was the Supreme Court decision that not all mergers were per se violations; only cases involving* unreasonable restraints *of trade would be prohibited.*

---

[4] With tongue in cheek, Justice Harlan, in a dissent, wrote, "You may now restrain such commerce, providing that you are reasonable about it; only take care that the restraint is not undue." Ironically, Justice Harlan's sarcasm became the standard by which future mergers would be judged. Years later, citing the Sherman Act, the Court ruled that the rule of reason itself was unreasonable. Instead of investigating each and every restraint of trade, the Court adopted the practice of ruling whether a particular merger was a per se violation.

The *per se* violation was a decision made by the Supreme Court to avoid the rule of reason requirement to balance the anticompetitive effects against the procompetitive

fect of the proposed merger, thereby suggesting that the structure of the industry (degree of market concentration) is likely to affect potential competition and overall economic performance (price, output, and profits).

In 1950, 36 years after the passage of the Clayton Act, Congress enacted the **Celler-Kefauver Act.** The most important part of this bill was an amendment to Section 7 of the Clayton Act. It said that "No corporation engaged in interstate commerce shall acquire . . . the stock . . . or any part of the *assets* of another corporation engaged also in commerce, where *in any line of commerce in any section of the country,* the effect of such acquisition may be substantially to lessen competition, or tend to create a monopoly . . . ." (The italicized words show the changes to Section 7 of the Clayton Act.) The purpose of this legislation was preventive, and its purview extended to all mergers—horizontal, vertical, and conglomerate. Like its predecessors, the Sherman and Clayton Acts, the Celler Act also failed to curtail merger activity.

> The **Celler-Kefauver Act** *plugged the asset loophole in the Clayton Act, making it illegal to acquire stock or the assets of another firm in order to monopolize.*

The Congress has also weakened antitrust legislation through numerous acts designed to aid specific industries. For example, the *Webb-Pomerene Act* of 1916 granted specific permission to businesses that exported goods and services to form agreements, share markets, and otherwise collude. *The Shipping Act* of 1916 exempted from antitrust laws all common carrier rate agreements approved by the Maritime Commission. And in 1937, Congress specifically approved the formation of agricultural marketing cooperatives (cartels) in the area of citrus fruits and nuts.

With the dawning of discount retail chains, supermarkets, and other mass merchandising operations in the 1920s and 1930s, small businesses complained that they were unable to compete against the high-volume, lower-price strategy of the discount firms. Congress responded with the *Miller-Tydings Act* in 1937. This bill exempted from the Sherman Act all resale price maintenance agreements in fair trade states. These resale agreements were contracts by which the retailer consented to sell at a price agreed to with the manufacturer.[5]

---

effects of every questioned restraint of trade. The court felt that certain agreements had such *obviously* pernicious effects on competition that it would be inefficient and unneccesary to become involved. A prolonged and complicated investigation into the entire history of the company and the industry to determine whether or not a particular restraint was unreasonable was seen as a waste of court time. (*Northern Pacific Railway Co.* v. *United States*, 1958.) Per se violations involve price fixing, agreements not to compete with rival firms, boycotts, and tying arrangements (whereby a seller of a product may condition its sale upon the buyer's purchasing a second product from the seller.)

[5] A fair trade state is one in which the legislature has passed a law permitting producer-seller price agreements.

The *McGuire Act* of 1952 further reduced price competition at the retail level by clarifying the Miller-Tydings Act. In the McGuire Act, the Congress said that if any manufacturer entered into a resale price maintenance agreement with any retailer in a fair trade state, every retailer in that state must comply with that agreement.[6]

THINKING IT THROUGH

A trade association is an organization of businesses in the same industry or market. Do you think the McGuire Act boosted trade association membership and activity? Why or why not?[7]

The courts have also rendered decisions which have greatly weakened antitrust statutes. In 1953, the Supreme Court pronounced professional baseball exempt from antitrust laws. Why? According to the majority opinion, baseball does not constitute interstate commerce and thus falls outside the purview of all antitrust legislation. Professional football also obtained an exemption, although this tour de force took a legislative route. If baseball and football are exempt, why not basketball? Soccer? Hockey? Do these professional organizations play and entertain only within their home-state boundaries? When Wade Boggs travels to Oakland to play ball, is this not interstate commerce?

Growth by Merger

How did America's largest corporations become so big? Economist George Stigler asked this question in a little different way. "If big businesses are not more efficient, how did they get so big? The answer is that most giant firms arose out of mergers."[8] Although many companies grew large because of cost-saving improvements in production, new and improved products, and aggressive marketing, the majority of firms reached Fortune 500 status by merger. One antitrust specialist notes that "a vast merger movement commenced shortly after passage of [the

---

[6] Curiously enough, in the preceding year, the Supreme Court ruled that such agreements only covered the parties that signed the agreement. With the congressional override in the McGuire Act, each retailer was forced to abide by an agreement that it had no party to.

[7] A vice president of a company charged with antitrust violations said that the only reason for a trade association is to fix prices. Indeed, more than 40 percent of all criminal antitrust litigation has involved trade associations. (Mark Green, et al., *The Closed Enterprise System* (New York: Bantam Books, 1972), p. 161.

[8] Quoted in Adams and Brock, *The Bigness Complex*, p. 152.

Celler-Kefauver Amendment] in 1950. . . . . [M]erger activity reached a frenzied pace in 1967–1970, when more than one in five manufacturing and mining corporations with assets exceeding $10 million was acquired."[9] The pace of merger activity slowed and then soared in the early 1980s. As we have already noted, recent merger activity is at an all-time high, with a record-level $179 billion of mergers in 1985.[10]

Merger Patterns

Indeed, one of the oddities of antitrust history is the occurrence of a flurry of merger activity *after* enactment of antitrust legislation. Let's take a brief tour of merger activity over the 100-year period since the passage of the Sherman Act.

There have been four major merger waves. First, eight years after the Sherman Act was signed into law, U.S. firms went on a merger kick. Between 1898 and 1902, there were over 2,600 major consolidations, an average of 561 per year, compared to an average of 46 per year in the preceding three years. Similarly, between 1925 and 1929, there were 4,583 mergers, culminating with a peak of 1,245 mergers in 1929. These mergers, like those following the Sherman Act, occurred after the enactment of the Clayton and Federal Trade Commission Acts. The third major merger movement occurred after the Celler Act took effect. In the 1955 to 1959 period, there was an average of 1,169 mergers per year; in the 1960 to 1966 period, 1,664 mergers were consummated per year; and in the period from 1967 to 1969, there was an average of 3,605 mergers per year. Not only was there a lot of merger activity in this latter period, but the consolidations represented some of the nation's largest firms. Between 1962 and 1968, for example, "110 of Fortune's 500 largest firms disappeared by merger. Moreover, between 1948 and 1968 over 1,200 manufacturing companies with assets of $10 million or more were merged with other firms."[11]

A fourth major merger movement began in the late 1970s and continued throughout the 1980s. As indicated in the chapter FOCUS, nearly 19,000 mergers occurred in the seven-year period from 1980 to 1987, for an average of 2,714 mergers per year. These mergers and acquisitions were so large that, beginning in 1985, the total market value of mergers exceeded the total amount of private expenditures on research and development and net new investment. The opportunity cost of the billions spent to accomplish the reshuffling of corporate assets is the billions not spent on plant and factory improvements and research and development.

---

[9] Ibid., p. 203.

[10] Ibid.

[11] Green, et al., *The Closed Enterprise System*, p. 11.

If U.S. productivity gains are lackluster, and if more efficient methods of production are wanting, it is little wonder that U.S. firms are having trouble competing in international markets.

TWO ANTITRUST BLOCKBUSTERS

Two recent court cases illustrate the complexity of antitrust issues. Perhaps the most famous occurred in 1974 when the Justice Department sued AT&T for monopolizing the communications market. Specifically, AT&T was charged with suppressing competition. Through its 80 percent control of local telephone service, it had prevented other firms from establishing long distance (LD) services by denying these firms the links with AT&T lines. Monopoly profits from LD services and its Western Electric (equipment manufacturing) subsidiary enabled AT&T to establish and maintain artificially low rates on local telephone services.

In a negotiated settlement eight years later, AT&T agreed to divest (free) itself of its 23 operating companies (New Jersey Bell, Southwestern Bell, Pacific Telephone, etc.). AT&T retained its LD service, and it obtained permission to enter other unregulated businesses such as the data communications field. The local operating companies kept the yellow page directories.

What looked like a boon to the consumer quickly turned into what some observers called the "boondoggle of the century." The consumer must have been perplexed in the aftermath of the breakup. When AT&T's LD monopoly position was broken, permitting MCI, Sprint, and others to enter the market, LD rates fell. However, local telephone rates soared almost immediately, since the new independent local telephone companies no longer had AT&T's financial tranfusions. Also disappointing was the quality of long distance service and telephone equipment from the new firms.

In one of the longest antitrust cases on record, in 1978, a federal court dropped a suit against IBM. Years earlier, Memorex charged that the world's largest computer maker had monopolized its markets, alleging a prima facie per se violation of the Sherman Act. Invoking the rule of reason, the court thought otherwise and proceeded to obtain the necessary documentation and evidence of wrongdoing. Years and three tons of documents later, the case was ready for trial. The judge "allowed the jury to take into the jury room some 3,000 exhibits and the trial transcript, including the judge's 90-page instructions and five days of final arguments by opposing lawyers." When the jury's decision split 9 to 2 in favor of Memorex, the judge interceded and dismissed the case. The judge declared that not only was there insufficient evidence to declare for Memorex, but "the magnitude and complexity of the case . . . render it . . . beyond the competency of any jury to understand and decide rationally." One of things the jury had to decide was the engineering specifications of IBM designs and whether its electronic interfaces performed as promised.[12]

COMPETITION AND ANTITRUST: THE ISSUES

As big business gets bigger, does the market system work as well? Does the presence of fewer and/or larger firms in an industry always mean that there is less competition? Does a merger between two giant firms in unrelated industries generate more efficient production, distribution, marketing or improved technology and new products and innovations in production? We may summarize these and related antitrust issues by looking at two dominant schools of thought.

Structuralists *argue that the structure of an industry determines the behavior of its firms and its performance in the economy.*

The conventional economic concern is rooted in two different but related arguments. First, one group of economists whom we will call **structuralists** argue essentially that the structure of an industry determines the behavior (or conduct) of industry firms and the overall performance of the industry in the economy. The structuralists generally use concentration ratios to measure how the industry is structured. For example, in the oligopolistic photographic equipment and supplies industry, the four largest firms in 1982 shipped 74 percent of all industry output. As the structuralists see things, because there are only a few large photo equipment and supply firms, and because these firms dominate the industry, the probability of collusion is very high. Moreover, potential competition is reduced by the presence of large firms that may easily buy out or drive out smaller firms; thus, the structuralists say, high industry concentration leads inexorably to unfair competition and a restraint of trade. The upshot is unfavorable industry performance, indicated by restricted output, excessive prices, and abnormally high profits. The structuralists also argue that concentrated oligopolies have a poor record of research and development (inventions and innovations), resist technological change, and thus impede economic growth.

Behaviorists *reject the structure-conduct-performance model in favor of a case-by-case approach regarding alleged antitrust violations.*

A second group of economists may be called **behaviorists.** They reject the structure-conduct-performance model as too simplistic. Instead, the behaviorists argue that it is important to examine only the conduct of individual oligopolists and ask if the firm's actual behavior (decisions and activities) are detrimental and/or illegal. In other words, sheer size is an insufficient reason to suspect or believe that some type of collusion exists in the industry. For example, although IBM completely dominates the mainframe computer industry, having more than 70 percent of total industry shipments, the behaviorists contend that there is no evidence

---

[12] Richard A. Shaffer, "Those Complex Antitrust Cases," *The Wall Street Journal,* August 29, 1978.

of an industry cartel, price fixing, or other illegal conduct by IBM. Moreover, IBM has a demonstrated history of commitment to new product development and an emphasis on technological improvements to promote increased efficiency and productivity. The behaviorists think it would be unfortunate to penalize such a firm for its size.

Many economists have dubbed the behaviorists the "Chicago School," after the University of Chicago. Former professor and now Judge Richard Posner, Appellate Court Justice Robert Bork (President Reagan's Supreme Court appointee who was rejected by the Senate), and George Stigler, a Nobel laureate in economics, among others, adhere to a laissez-faire philosophy. They argue that private markets do a much better job of resource allocation than government, and the antitrust laws erect almost insurmountable barriers to the efficient operation of a corporation. As Robert Bork has warned, antitrust "should never attack [oligopolies and other concentrated market] structures, since they embody the proper balance of forces for consumer welfare."[13] Antitrust policy, according to Bork, should concern itself solely with horizontal mergers and then only when concentration exceeds 60 or 70 percent of the market.[14] Moreover, Bork thinks that the government should keep its hands off all vertical and conglomerate mergers. According to Bork, vertical integration and conglomeration cannot reduce competition.[15]

In defense of bigness and conglomeration, the behaviorists have offered two main arguments. First, they claim that technological progress (inventions and innovations) requires large corporations because of the huge costs involved in research and development (R & D). (We will call this the *innovation argument*.) Second, the behaviorists assert that economies of scale are a function of firm size: the larger the firm, the lower will be the average costs of production. (We will call this the *efficiency argument*.) Let's take each of these in turn.

Joseph A. Schumpeter, a renowned author and Professor of Economics at Harvard University, wrote in 1950 that large corporations "must be accepted as a necessary evil . . . [of] the economic progress . . . inherent in its productive apparatus."[16] John Kenneth Galbraith, prolific author and former Harvard University economics professor, observed that "the modern industry of a few large firms [is] an excellent instrument for inducing technological change [and] . . . financing technical development."[17] Years later, Galbraith further solidified this size-

---

[13] Robert H. Bork, *The Antitrust Paradox* (New York: Basic Books, 1978), p. 164.

[14] Ibid., p. 221.

[15] Ibid., p. 226–27.

[16] Joseph A. Schumpeter, *Capitalism, Socialism and Democracy,* 3d edition (New York: Harper and Row, 1950), p. 106.

[17] John Kenneth Galbraith, *American Capitalism* (Boston: Houghton Mifflin, 1952), p. 86.

technology relationship when he declared, "The imperatives of technology and organization, not images of ideology, are what determine the shape of economic society."[18] In Galbraith's view, the modern industrial economy is increasingly dependent upon large firms that must replace the market with planning. Indeed, to Galbraith, "size is the general servant of technology," and advanced technology requires large organizations capable of extensive planning.[19]

Strong assertions and sweeping generalization aside, what evidence is there to support the innovation argument? Do the giant firms invent more products per R&D dollar than small firms and individual inventors? A very well-known study researched the origins of 70 important 20th-century inventions. The findings were conclusive: more than one half of the inventions were developed by independent inventors. For example, xerography was invented by a physicist who had no connection with Xerox; air conditioning was developed by several independent inventors; and stereophonic sound was invented by two ham radio buffs on their own time.[20] The list goes on and on.

Comprehensive evidence from numerous studies supports the innovative superiority of small firms and independent inventors. The National Science Board of the National Science Foundation conducted a study of 310 major technical innovations between 1953 and 1973. Classified by the size of firm, the board found that only 34 percent of the innovations came from the largest firms (10,000 or more employees). The smallest firms, with fewer than 5,000 employees, were responsible for 60 percent of the total number of inventions. In conclusion, the board reported that "for the whole 1953–1973 period, the smallest firms produced about 4 times as many innovations per R&D dollar as the middle-size firms and 24 times as many as the largest firms."[21]

Behaviorists and other proponents of large firm size also argue that *technical efficiency* requires bigness and more concentrated industrial structure. In this simple equation, the bigger the firm, the more efficient the firm. (Unlike economic efficiency, which refers to the production of goods and services that satisfies society's wants to the greatest degree, technical efficiency deals with cost-effectiveness—producing the greatest output, given existing resources, or minimizing the use of existing resources in order to produce a given output.) Yale Brozen, a scholar at the University of Chicago and author of dozens of articles and books on antitrust economics, claims that bigness per se leads to operating effi-

[18] John Kenneth Galbraith, *The New Industrial State* (Boston: Houghton Mifflin, 1967), p. 7.

[19] Ibid., p. 33.

[20] John Jewkes, David Sawers, and Richard Stillerman, *The Sources of Invention*, 2nd edition (New York: W. W. Norton, 1969), p. 54.

[21] Adams and Brock, *The Bigness Complex*, p. 52.

ciencies and, in turn, that these economies of scale result in bigness. "Concentration occurs and persists," says Brozen, "where that is the efficient structure for producing and distributing a product and for adapting to changing technical possibilities, shifting demand, and increasing regulatory requirements." In a thoroughly unqualified assertion, he concludes, "concentration persists only where it brings efficiencies or is the consequence of superior management."[22]

There is no doubt that many manufacturing processes require large plant size. As shown in Chapter 5, if economies of scale are to result, the plant unit must be large enough to spread high fixed costs over more output. However, these economies are realized at the plant level and not necessarily for the very large firm with many plants. While there is general agreement about large plant operating efficiencies, there is considerable disagreement about the need for large administrative units.

Perhaps the most telling evidence on this issue comes from the steel industry. The seven largest U.S. steel companies, all ranked among Fortune 500's industrial corporations, collectively ship nearly 70 percent of raw steel production.[23] All seven complain bitterly about their inability to compete against imported, "cheap-labor" steel. If these imports are not restricted, according to the big steel magnates, they will be forced to continue their massive layoffs and plant closings. To the giant steel firms, quotas and protective tariffs are the solutions to the U.S. trade deficit and competitiveness problems.

However, the U.S. International Trade Commission cites the recent emergence of mini-mills, small steel companies producing only a few products such as wire rods and bars. These mini-mills undersold imported wire rod by $50 per ton (15 percent) and large U.S. steel firms by an average of 20.7 percent.[24] This strongly suggests that large, multi-plant steel firms, like U.S. Steel and LTV, are much less efficient than the smaller, newer, technologically efficient mini-mill plants. And Frederick M. Scherer, a widely recognized antitrust expert, has found virtually no evidence to support the contention that mergers generally reduce the per unit costs of production. In his broad-based study, Scherer concluded that "with few exceptions, the minimum optimal plant scale revealed in studies of American manufacturing industries has been small relative to industry size. . . . [E]conomies of scale do not . . . necessitate high national concentration levels for U.S. manufacturing industries."[25]

---

[22] Yale Brozen, *Concentration, Mergers, and Public Policy* (New York: Macmillan, 1982), pp. 56–57.

[23] Adams and Brock, *The Bigness Complex,* p. 34.

[24] Ibid.

[25] Frederick M. Scherer, *Industrial Market Structure and Economic Performance,* 2nd edition (Chicago: Rand McNally, 1980), pp. 94, 95.

THINKING IT THROUGH

Which school of thought do you support—the structuralists or the behaviorists? Why?

The growth of international trade is another concern with implications for antitrust policy and government regulation in general. The volume of world trade in 1980 was more than six times the 1970 volume. The United States experienced similar growth, as the combined value of exports and imports as a percentage of gross national product (GNP) increased from 3.9 percent to 9.1 percent. Its growth, however, was lopsided in favor of imports. And, more recently, imports have continued to increase much faster than export activity, raising the question about the need for U.S. firms to compete better in foreign markets. If U.S. firms are to compete against international cartels and foreign companies heavily subsidized by their governments, and the federal government persists in prohibiting domestic cartels, how can the U.S. firm hope to level the playing field? If the U.S. government vigorously enforces its antitrust laws by preventing mergers among competing as well as noncompeting firms, are we making it easier for foreign corporations to grab U.S. markets? One solution offered by several economists is to abolish the antitrust laws. Radical as it may seem, a growing number of economists and legislators find the idea intriguing.

CASE
▪ IN ▪
POINT

Let's Abolish the Antitrust Laws!

Lester Thurow, Professor of Economics and Management at the Massachusetts Institute of Technology, argues that we should abolish the antitrust laws. Moreover, Thurow contends that the United States, in an increasingly global economy, should reduce barriers to free trade. In other words, if competitive markets are the desired outcome (as implied by the antitrust statutes), instead of increased regulation and expensive litigation, we would all be better off if we were to eliminate tariffs and quotas. Even in the case of clear-cut collusion, Thurow argues that the costs of regulation and antitrust actions exceed the benefits. For example, several years ago the Federal Trade Commission (FTC) investigated the dry-breakfast-cereals business and found that the firms had engaged in anticompetitive behavior. The FTC estimated that the oligopoly (Kellogg, General Foods, and other firms), through a combination of collusive arrangements, charged consumers $1.2 billion more than they would have paid for cereals in a more competitive industry between 1958 and 1972. With tongue in cheek, Thurow points out that this monopoly power translates to 0.1 cent per breakfast! Surely, this is "much ado about nothing!"[26]

Questions to Consider

1. *Behaviorists in general, and economists of the Chicago School, in particular, share Thurow's point of view. Essentially laissez-faire in their approach, they argue along the lines laid down by Adam Smith more than 200 years ago, namely, that the so-called invisible hand of competition is the best possible method of regulation. Enforcement of antitrust laws unfairly penalizes the efficient firm, imposes exorbitant legal costs on the private corporation resulting in a gross misallocation of resources, and interferes with the profit motive as the principal means by which the private marketplace works. Do you think competition in the private markets is sufficiently brisk that we can abolish the antitrust laws? Why or why not?*

2. *Thurow's argument is twofold: First, the costs of enforcing antitrust legislation exceed the benefits to society. For example, what do you think it cost the FTC to estimate the costs of cereal food industry collusion? A second and related argument is that antitrust laws and barriers to free trade generally are obstacles to doing business with other nations. Conceding the possibility that the abolition of antitrust laws will improve our competitiveness in international markets, is that sufficient reason to do so? Will domestic industries become so concentrated that price competition may be severely reduced?*

3. *If America's huge trade deficit is the problem, perhaps the solution lies in adopting the policies of our trading partners. In other words, how about increasing all forms of government assistance to firms doing business internationally? Such aid could take the form of large export subsidies, or reinstituting the investment tax credits for firms that plow back profits into efforts to drive down the costs of production, improve quality control, and so forth. What do you think? Which might do a better job—less government and more free market operation, or more government and less market freedom?*

IMPORTANT TERMS TO REMEMBER

antitrust, p. 219
behaviorists, p. 226
Celler-Kefauver Amendment, p. 222
Clayton Act, p. 220
concentration ratio, p. 214
conglomerate merger, p. 217
Federal Trade Commission (FTC)
  Act, p. 220

horizontal merger, p. 216
per se violations, p. 221
price fixing, p. 218
rule of reason, p. 221
Sherman Act, p. 220
structuralists, p. 226
trusts, p. 218
vertical merger, p. 216

---

[26] Adapted from Lester C. Thurow, "Let's Abolish the Antitrust Laws," *The Wall Street Journal*, December 13, 1985, p. 33.

CHAPTER SUMMARY

1. Aggregate (overall) concentration of America's 200 largest manufacturing firms, measured by assets owned, has increased from WW II to the present. Although general market concentration clearly has increased over the last 40 years, there is a lot of variation in the four-firm concentration ratios from industry to industry—the percentage of total industry shipments accounted for by the top four firms.

2. The consolidation of two or more firms may be classified as follows:
   a. Horizontal: firms in the same industry (e.g., Anheuser-Busch and Miller brewing companies).
   b. Vertical: firms in the same channel of distribution, from raw materials to retail outlets (e.g., GM and U.S. Steel).
   c. Conglomerate: firms in unrelated markets (e.g., IBM and Merrill Lynch).

3. The Sherman Act (1890), America's first antitrust law, declared illegal any combinations (especially trusts) in restraint of trade and any conduct which monopolizes or attempts to monopolize.

4. Court interpretations of the Sherman Act fall into two broad categories:
   a. Per se violations: where an existing agreement between corporations is a clear and flagrant violation (like price-fixing or geographic division of markets).
   b. Rule of reason: wherein the conduct of the corporation and/or the potentially damaging effect on competition is questionable, the antitrust prosecutors must prove that the conduct is unreasonable.

5. The Clayton Act closed the Sherman Act's stock loophole. It also outlawed tying contracts, interlocking directorates, and price discrimination. The Federal Trade Commission Act created the Federal Trade Commission and charged it with investigating unfair trade practices.

6. The Celler-Kefauver Act amended the Clayton Act, plugging the asset loophole, and extended the prohibition against all mergers (horizontal, vertical, and conglomerate) whose effect may be to lessen competition. One of the ironies of antitrust history is the occurrence of a major increase in merger activity following each piece of antitrust legislation.

7. Conglomeration has been the predominant form of merger since the mid-1950s, chiefly because the effects of such mergers on competition are as unclear as the laws.

8. There are two main schools of thought regarding antitrust.
   a. The structuralists use a structure-conduct-performance model. They say that if the industrial structure is concentrated, then it is much easier for firms to collude (illegal conduct), leading to adverse performance (higher monopoly-like prices and profits and restricted output).
   b. The behaviorists (or Chicago School) argue that the structure-conduct-performance model is too simplistic. They say that only per se violations should be prosecuted; all the rest are simply a waste of time and money.

9. Prevailing evidence strongly denies any justification of mergers based on scale economies or research and development capability. Most mergers

do not result in greater operating efficiency, and most mergers do not contribute to new product development or more technological innovations. In general, available evidence suggests that efficiency and innovation are more closely associated with smaller firms.

DISCUSSION AND REVIEW QUESTIONS

1. The concentration ratio is often used to measure market structure, with implications for certain anticompetitive effects (especially if the ratio exceeds some threshold, like 50 percent). What are the inherent weaknesses of the concentration ratio?

2. Provide examples of the three types of mergers, and explain which of these mergers may be challenged and why.

3. The airline mergers in the mid-1980s resulted in a substantial increase in market concentration. Why weren't these mergers challenged or blocked? Are they per se violations, or do they come under the rule of reason?

4. List and describe the main provisions of the four leading antitrust laws: the Sherman Act, the Clayton Act, the FTC Act, and the Celler-Kefauver Act.

5. Compare and contrast the structuralist and behaviorist positions regarding antitrust enforcement.

6. Make a case for or against the abolition of the antitrust laws. In your argument, be sure to address the issues of economies of scale, technological innovations, and international competition.

A BRIEF LOOK AHEAD

The next chapter looks at the several subjects related to the economics of labor: wage determination, poverty, and income distibution. Here we will examine the factors responsible for wage differentials, such as age, education, occupation, race, sex, and geographic region. Other things being equal, why do men earn more than women? Whites more than blacks? Also considered is the subject of poverty in the United States: Who are the poor and what are the forces responsible for poverty?

9

Labor Markets, Wage Determination, and Income Distribution

Comstock

This chapter seeks to answer three major questions: What determines how many employees a firm hires? What determines how much a person is paid? What determines wage differentials and the distribution of income?

We all know that a major league ball player makes more than a teacher or secretary, but why? Is it because of personal characteristics such as skills, training, education, and experience? Unionization? Strength of product demand? En route to addressing this question, we will revisit the familiar terrain of supply and demand and the law of diminishing returns to help provide a perspective. Moreover, we will examine several important institutional and behavioral phenomena, like credentialism, unionism, and discrimination. Why do men earn more than women, everything else being equal (education, occupation, experience, etc.)? Why do whites earn more than nonwhites, everything else being equal? Although there are no easy answers to these and related questions, understanding the forces which produce the distribution of income in the economy is crucial to an understanding of the labor market.

After completion of this chapter, you should be able to do the following:

1. Describe and explain the concept of comparable worth.
2. Explain the concept of backward-bending supply of labor and why men are more inclined to substitute leisure for work than women.
3. Compare and contrast monetary attributes of occupations with nonmonetary characteristics, and explain how these attributes affect wage differentials.
4. Define the concept of derived demand and explain how it is related to labor demand.
5. Using marginal productivity theory, diagram, describe, and explain how a business firm determines how many workers to hire.
6. Compare and contrast hiring decisions in perfectly competitive and monopolistic markets.
7. Describe the pattern of income distribution in the U.S. economy.
8. Describe the demographic characteristics of the poverty population.

Market Worth or Comparable Worth?

Electricians make more money than secretaries. Postal workers make more than hairdressers. Wages and salaries are determined primarily by the neutral market forces of supply and demand. But imagine a different system, a system by which earnings were set by the government.

Equal pay for equal work and the doctrine of comparable worth (equal pay for jobs of equal value) have become major issues in the workplace. Involved is the issue of equity: if an employer values two different jobs of equal importance, is it equitable to pay more for one than the other? Some people think not and would prefer that market-determined wages be replaced by a system which recognizes comparable worth.

In 1973, a personnel firm was hired by the governor of the state of Washington to ascertain whether the pay scale for state employees was equitable. The firm assigned points for each job in four different categories: knowledge and skills, mental demands, accountability, and working conditions. When finished, it found many disparities. For example, truck drivers and laundry workers each were assigned 97 points, but laundry workers earned only 70 percent of what truck drivers earned. Indeed, traditional female jobs paid 20 percent less than traditional male jobs despite being of comparable worth.[1] Although an employee's union filed a suit resulting in a district court order to raise state earnings in order to eradicate allegedly unwarranted wage differentials, a federal appellate court overturned the ruling, arguing that no discrimination was found. Although temporarily suspended, the issue is still being pressed. The Democratic party has made the doctrine of comparable worth a plank in its platform, and many women's groups continue to lobby for federal legislation.

It is said that people are paid what they are worth. But what determines labor value, or worth? Wages and salaries are paid by individual employers, but the market value of labor is set in the market place by supply and demand. Of course, wages and salaries also are subject to federal and state laws covering occupational licensure, affirmative action, minimum wages, and related nonmarket forces. What, then, actually determines wages and salaries? Why do private and parochial teachers average lower salaries than their public school counterparts? Why do pediatric physicians earn less than general internists? Before addressing these and related questions, it is important to understand the economic theory of wage determination.

---

[1] Data from *The Margin* 2, no. 1 (The University of Colorado, January 1987).

THE SUPPLY OF LABOR

What is the relationship between earnings and the hours of labor supplied to the market? Will you work more or less if paid more? Conventional economic theory says that the quantity of labor (or hours) supplied is directly related to earnings: as wages rise, the hours of labor (or the number of workers) will increase. Figure 9–1 illustrates this relationship.

This graph is the familiar looking upward-sloping supply curve which we developed in Chapter 3. The chief difference is that here we are dealing with labor. The vertical axis thus measures wages, and the horizontal axis measures quantity of labor (or hours) supplied.

There are two major characteristics about this relationship: It is direct (meaning that as wages rise, the quantity of labor increases); and the supply curve intersects the wage axis above zero. The latter means that, on the average, workers will not work below a given base wage, say $1.00. This base wage is entirely arbitrary, but common sense tells us that nearly all of us have some wage below which we will not accept employment.

Because there is a natural limit to the number of hours one can work, and because (in all industrial societies) there has been a long-term decline in the average workweek, it is reasonable to conclude that people have substituted leisure for work. But how much? (*Leisure* is broadly

FIGURE 9–1
Conventional Labor
Supply Curve

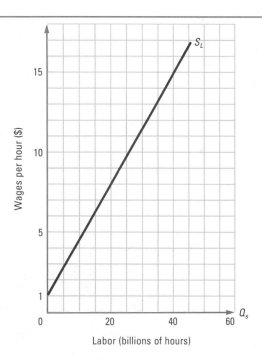

defined as any form of nonmarket activity, such as volunteer [unpaid work], recreation and personal fitness activities, going to a movie or ballgame, visiting friends, etc.)

The Backward-Bending Supply Curve of Labor. For a long time, economists have speculated about a **backward-bending supply curve of labor.** Figure 9–2 illustrates this relationship wherein number of hours worked (or quantity of labor supplied) will decrease as wages rise. Assume that workers are paid $10 per hour. At this wage, they offer 36 hours to the market. If wages are increased to $12, hours offered rise to 40. Total wages increase from $360 to $480. The next hourly wage increase to $14, however, results in a decrease in hours worked, back to 36. Total wages still rise (to $504), but workers have substituted leisure for work. Although this may make good sense, does it really happen?

Research Findings. Recent empirical research shows a dramatic difference between men and women. For adult men, the labor supply curve is backward-bending. Of five studies, three report a negatively sloped supply curve throughout; two others show a positively sloped supply

Backward-bending supply curve of labor *shows that, after a certain number of hours of work at a specified wage, people reduce the number of hours worked as wages rise.*

FIGURE 9–2
Backward-Bending
Supply of Labor

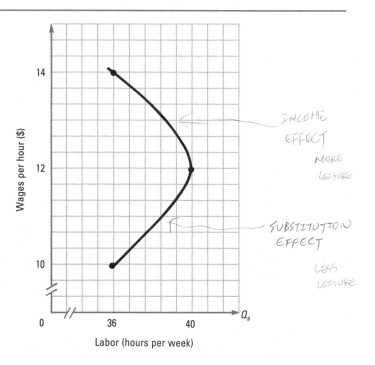

curve at lower wages and a negatively sloped curve at higher wages.[2] What does this mean?

There are two effects operating whenever a monetary change occurs: a substitution effect and an income effect. When wages rise, the **substitution effect** says that we will substitute hours of work for hours of leisure. However, an **income effect** also operates and may even overwhelm the substitution effect. As earnings rise, we may be so much better off that we decide to work less. For every wage hike, the income and substitution effects work in opposite directions: the substitution effect pushing you to work longer hours; the income effect pulling you back toward more leisure.

Substitution effect says that as wages rise we will substitute hours of work for hours of leisure.

Income effect means that as earnings rise, we will work fewer hours and substitute leisure and so forth.

Wage Elasticity of Supply. The studies referred to above indicate that, on the average, the male wage elasticity of supply is -0.1.[3] For a 10 percent increase in wages, a negative 0.1 coefficient of wage elasticity means that men will reduce their working hours by 1 percent. Thus for a 40-hour workweek, a 10 percent wage hike will result in a decrease to 39.6 hours. Twenty-four minutes may not be a lot for one worker, but this adds up to a lot of hours if spread across the entire economy.[4]

The same research efforts found that women have a $+0.9$ wage elasticity coefficient. For women, a 10 percent increase in earnings will, on the average, yield a 9 percent increase in hours worked.[5] Given a 40-hour workweek, a 10 percent increase in earnings will generate a 3 hour and 36 minute increase in the average workweek.

Why do men and women respond differently to changes in earnings? Although this question lends itself to a complex answer, drawing upon social and psychological research, two basic economic explanations may be offered here. First, because men earn more than women on the average, the income effect is likely to be stronger for men. Second, since over 90 percent of adult men work full time, the trade-off men face is simple: work or leisure. Given an increase in wages, many men will opt

---

[2] Bruce E. Kaufman, *The Economics of Labor Markets and Labor Relations* (Hinsdale, Ill.: Dryden Press, 1987), p. 51.

[3] Ibid., pp. 51–52. The wage elasticity of supply is computed by dividing the percent change in wages by the percent change in hours worked. The resulting coefficient of elasticity may be positive or negative. If it is negative, as it is for men, it means that the labor supply curve is downward sloping (wages and hours of labor supplied are inversely related).

[4] In 1986, of 60.9 million men in the labor force, 54.8 million (90 percent) worked full time. If we use a 40-hour workweek, they worked about 2.2 billion hours. A 1 percent reduction translates to a loss of 22 million hours, the equivalent of 110,000 person-years of labor.

[5] Kaufman, *The Economics of Labor Markets and Labor Relations*, p. 52.

to reduce their workweek. Women, on the other hand, have a third choice, partly because only 72 percent work full time. In the traditional family, women still do most of the household work: cleaning, cooking, laundering, and so forth. The upshot is that when women receive a wage advance, especially women who work part time (fewer than 35 hours per week), they may substitute paid employment for unpaid household work.

Thus far we have looked at the supply of labor and how responsive workers are to wages. We turn now to the formal theory of wage determination and the demand for labor in order to understand how firms hire labor and what determines the wages paid.

THE DEMAND FOR LABOR

Derived demand *is a firm's demand for a resource derived from the demand for its product or service.*

How does a business know how many workers to hire? How does a company know what wage or salary to pay? Because product demand is central to labor requirements, we may begin to answer these questions with the concept of **derived demand.** Derived demand means that the firm's demand for labor is derived from the demand for its product or service. The demand for teachers (a labor resource), for example, is determined by the demand for education (the service). Similarly, the demand for carpenters, electricians, and other construction workers is determined by the demand for residential and commercial construction. This common sense notion is also true for all other economic resources or factors of production. For example, the demand for land to raise soybeans is derived from the demand for the final products containing soybeans, that is, soybean oil and soybean meal.

Hiring Decisions and Marginal Productivity Theory

As we saw in the two previous chapters, economic theory holds that companies are in business to maximize profits. Using our marginal rule, firms will maximize profits when they produce the output where marginal revenue equals marginal cost. Businesses employ a similar rule in deciding to hire the number of workers which will maximize profits or minimize costs. Whether the firm is hiring labor or deciding how many bicycles to produce or patients to see, the decision is based on a marginal revenue and marginal cost principle. Firms will maximize returns by hiring labor until the extra revenue contributed by the next (or last) worker equals the cost of hiring the worker.

Case I: Pure Competition in Labor and Product Markets. Tried 'N True Tennis Rackets (TNT), a new company to your community, produces a high-quality tennis racket at a bargain price. It hires its labor and sells its product in perfectly competitive markets. To simplify proceedings, we also assume that TNT hires only full-time workers. In order to hire the cost-minimizing (profit-maximizing) number of workers, it must compare the marginal revenue product of labor (MRP_L) and the marginal resource cost of labor (MRC_L). Please refer to Table 9–1 below as these concepts are developed.

Marginal Resource Cost (MRC). The extra cost of hiring the last worker is referred to as the **marginal resource cost (MRC).** It is calculated by dividing the change in total labor costs by the change in quantity of labor hired. Whether operating in pure or imperfect competition, the *MRC* is calculated in the same way. Looking at Table 9–1, note that the wage is constant regardless of the amount of labor hired. (Wages are for one eight-hour day.) Beginning with three workers, each person is paid $100 for a total wage bill of $300. If TNT hires another worker, it pays the fourth worker the same wage. In perfect competition, the wage equals the *MRC*.

Marginal Revenue Product (MRP). A worker's contribution to total revenue is called the **marginal revenue product (MRP),** and it represents the firm's demand curve for labor. It is computed by multiplying the worker's marginal physical product (units of output) times the marginal revenue from selling the last unit of output. Whether the firm is operating in purely competitive or imperfectly competitive markets, the

Marginal resource cost (MRC) *is the extra cost of hiring the last worker.*

Marginal revenue product (MRP) *is a measure of a worker's contribution to total revenue and it represents the firm's demand curve for labor.*

TABLE 9–1: Case I
Tried 'N True Tennis Rackets Marginal Productivity Theory and Hiring Labor

Labor	Wage	Total Wage Cost	MRC*	Output	MPP	Price	TR	MR	MRP*
3	$100	$300		6		$90	$540		
			100		5			90	450
4	100	400		11		90	990		
			100		4			90	360
5	100	500		15		90	1,350		
			100		3			90	270
6	100	600		18		90	1,620		
			100		2			90	180
7	100	700		20		90	1,800		
			100		1			90	90
8	100	800		21		90	1,890		

(NOTE: Data are on daily basis; that is, the $100 wage and *MRC* figures are for one eight-hour day. Asterisks (*) head the critical columns, *MRP* and *MRC*.)

Case I: TNT hires labor and sells rackets in purely competitive markets.

Under purely competitive resource and product markets, TNT will hire labor *MRP* = *MRC*. Thus seven workers will be hired. (Under pure competition the wage is equal to the *MRC*, since all workers are paid the same wage.) The *MRP*, computed by multiplying *MPP* times *MR* (or price in pure competition), declines throughout because of declining marginal physical product (the law of diminishing marginal returns).

MRP is calculated in the same way.[6] From Chapter 5 on the costs of production, we know that hiring more labor (with other factors of production being fixed) results in a decrease in the marginal product of labor (the law of diminishing returns). Each additional laborer hired contributes less to a firm's total output. Four workers produce 11 rackets. The fifth worker contributes an additional five rackets; the sixth worker produces three more rackets. Multiplying the *MPP* of the sixth laborer, three, times the marginal revenue *(MR)* of $90 yields the marginal revenue product of labor *(MRP$_L$)*, $270. Repeating this procedure for each worker, that is, multiplying each worker's *MPP* times the corresponding *MR* for each level of output (sales), yields TNT's labor demand curve.

The Hiring Decision Rule.   In order to maximize profits or minimize costs, a firm will hire labor (or any resource) until the *MRP* equals the *MRC*. This is the **rule for hiring labor** or using other economic resources. In our example, TNT will hire seven workers. Although the seventh worker's *MRP* of $180 exceeds the *MRC* of $100, the firm will go no further since the eighth worker will add more to cost than to total revenue.

Rule for hiring labor *says that in order to maximize profits or minimize costs, a firm will hire labor (or any resource) until the* MRP *equals the* MRC.

This relationship is easily represented graphically.[7] Figure 9–3 illustrates a purely competitive labor market. In pure competition, there are no artificial barriers to wage determination, such as unions and minimum wage legislation. Panel A shows the total labor market. The supply curve S_1 is upward sloping to the right, indicating that more workers will be willing to work at higher wages than at lower wages. The demand curve D_1 is downward sloping to the right, indicating that employers will hire more workers at lower wages than at higher wages. The intersection of supply and demand determines the equilibrium wage, $100 ($W_1$).

Panel B illustrates our firm, TNT. The daily wage offered each worker ($100) by the firm is taken from the general labor market. The firm's demand curve for labor, or marginal revenue product *(MRP$_L$)*, is determined by the marginal productivity of labor and the marginal revenue (or price) from selling its output. The firm's marginal resource cost curve *(MRC$_L$)*, w_1, is perfectly elastic. As Figure 9–3B shows, the equality of *MRC* and *MRP* occurs at the intersection of the two curves, at point *e*. By drawing a line perpendicular to the quantity axis, we can

---

[6] The *MRP* is also computed by dividing the change in total revenue by the change in the number of workers hired. In our example, because labor increases in increments of one worker, the *MRP* is simply the change in total revenue.

[7] You know, of course, that a picture is worth a thousand words. But did you hear the latest news? With all the concern about budget deficits, trade imbalances, dollar depreciation, and other market uncertainties, a picture is now worth only 400 words!

FIGURE 9–3 Marginal Productivity Theory and Hiring Decisions

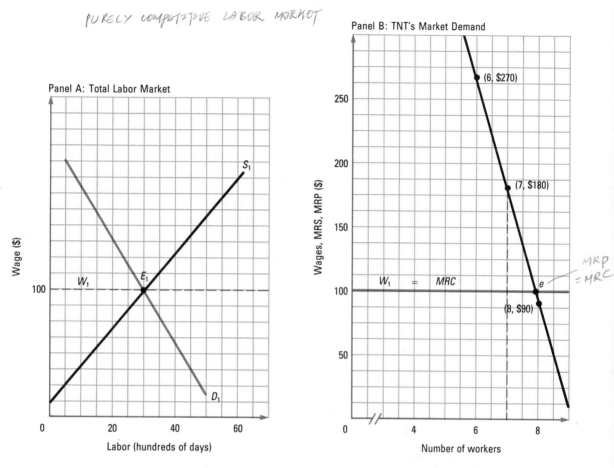

PURELY COMPETITIVE LABOR MARKET

Panel A: Total Labor Market

Panel B: TNT's Market Demand

see that approximately 7.8 workers is the optimum amount of labor. However, since TNT only hires full-time employees, it must stop at seven workers, where *MRP* still exceeds *MRC*. This will ensure that the firm will be employing the optimum (or best profit) number of laborers.

Case II: Imperfect Competition in Product Market Only. What if our firm hires in a competitive labor market, but sells in a monopolistic market? This might exist if a firm like Wilson hired labor from all around a metropolitan area, but operated the only store (or sold to the only store) selling tennis rackets. In such a situation, our fictional company faces a situation like that illustrated in Table 9–2, Case II.

The important difference between this situation and Case I is that TNT must now decrease product price in order to sell more rackets. The

TABLE 9–2: Case II

Tried 'N True Tennis Rackets Marginal Productivity Theory and Hiring Labor

Labor	Wage	Total Wage Cost	MRC*	Output	MPP	Price	TR	MR*	MRP*
3	$100	$300		6		$120	$720		
			100					98	490
4	100	400		11	5	110	1,210		
			100					73	290
5	100	500		15	4	100	1,500		
			100					40	120
6	100	600		18	3	90	1,620		
			100					(10)	(20)
7	100	700		20	2	80	1,600		
			100					(130)	(130)
8	100	800		21	1	70	1,470		

(handwritten annotations: "=WAGE" pointing to MRC column; "MRP=MRC @ 6+" pointing to the MRP value 120)

(NOTE: Data are on daily basis; that is the $100 wage and MRC figures are for one eight-hour day.)

Case II: TNT hires labor in purely competitive markets and sells rackets in monopolistic markets.

Case II presents a slight variation from Case I. Here TNT is selling rackets in monopolistically competitive markets and thus faces a downward-sloping product demand curve. This means that it must lower prices to sell more rackets. As a result, MRP declines more rapidly, and the firm hires only six workers. (Note that the same decision rule is used: hire until, or so long as, MRP = MRC.)

upshot of this minor change is that the *MRP*, the firm's demand curve for labor, will decline more rapidly. Since the $MRP_L = MPP_L \times MR$, if product price and marginal physical product both decline, then the *MRP* will decline more rapidly than if only product price is constant. As a result, the quantity of labor at which $MRP_L = MRC_L$ occurs sooner. According to Table 9–4, TNT will hire six workers, one fewer than when it sells in purely competitive markets.

Case III: Imperfect Competition in Both Markets. Our third case, illustrated in Table 9–3, is much more realistic. TNT now hires its labor and sells its rackets in imperfectly competitive markets. In addition to declining product price, TNT must pay more for each additional worker it wants to hire. The result is that MRC_L exceeds the wage. Why? TNT not only pays each additional worker more, it also pays all workers (doing the same work) the same wage. For example, if it wants to hire a fourth worker, the actual marginal resource cost is $110: $95 for the fourth worker, plus $5 for each of the other three workers ($15). The upshot is that TNT will hire even fewer workers in monopolistic labor markets. Using its hiring rule, TNT now will hire only five workers.

Examples of Resource Monopoly. As in the product market, it is very unusual to encounter conditions of pure competition in the labor (or any

TABLE 9–3: Case III Tried 'N True Tennis Rackets Marginal Productivity Theory and Hiring Labor

Labor	Wage	Total Wage Cost	*MRC	Output	MPP	Price	TR	MR	*MRP
3	$90	$270		6		$120	$720		
			110					98	490
4	95	380		11	5	110	1,210		
			120					73	290
5	100	500		15	4	100	1,500		
			130					40	120
6	105	630		18	3	90	1,620		
			140					(10)	(20)
7	110	770		20	2	80	1,600		
			150					(130)	(130)
8	115	920		21	1	70	1,470		

(handwritten annotations: "↗ WAGE", "MRC ↗ WAGE", "MRP=MRC @ 5†")

(NOTE: Data are on daily basis; that is, the $100 wage and *MRC* figures are for one eight-hour day.)

Case III: TNT hires labor and sells rackets in monopolistic markets.

Under monopolistic conditions (or imperfect competition) in both the resource and product markets, not only does *MRP* decline rapidly (because of declining product price and declining marginal physical product), but the *MRC* now exceeds the wage rate for all labor hired. The result is that firms will hire only five workers, determined by the hiring rule *MRP* = *MRC*. Because wages are no longer constant, but must be increased to acquire additional workers, when the firm hires another worker, it must not only pay more for the extra worker, but it must also pay the same wage to all other workers. In hiring the fifth worker, *TNT* pays $100 plus $5 for each of the other four workers. The *MRC* of the fifth worker is thus $120 ($100 + [$5 × 4]).

other resource) market. The chief difference is that employers have more power to control the wages that they pay labor. One example of such employer control exists in the so-called company town, in which nearly all people in the community work for one corporation. The famous Pullman Motor Car Company is a classic historic case, but numerous contemporary examples exist as well. The headquarters of Phillips Petroleum, for example, is located in Bartlesville, Oklahoma. Phillips employs over 80 percent of the town's labor force. Obviously, Phillips has more control over wages and salaries than its counterpart in Houston or Los Angeles, where several oil firms and thousands of other companies compete for skilled labor. Geography is thus an important factor contributing to monopolistic labor markets.

Another factor contributing to employer control over wages occurs when a firm hires highly specialized labor. "For example, marine engineers with many years of experience in designing nuclear submarines must work for the one or two companies that produce such vessels. Because other jobs would not make use of these workers' specialized training, alternative employment is not particularly attractive. Similarly, experienced telephone circuit designers may find they have to work for AT&T if they wish to capitalize on their skills. As a nonlabor example, the McDonald's Corporation for many years bought more than 50 percent of all frozen french fried potatoes produced in the United States."[8] With that kind of leverage, McDonald's probably exerted considerable control over the prices paid for french fries.

Still another factor contributing to wage control is collusion. The most notorious example of collusion in hiring in recent years has been in professional baseball and football. Through their respective organizations, the players have charged that the owners conspired to hold down salaries by preventing the free movement of players among the various teams. How? Read the following CASE-IN-POINT about free agency in professional baseball.

<table>
<tr>
<td>
CASE
▪ IN ▪
POINT
</td>
<td>

Collusion at the Old Ballpark?

Professional baseball is exempt from antitrust laws (determined not to be interstate commerce), and that seems to be chief issue surrounding players' rights to quit a team and sign with another at will. It all started in 1972 when Curt Flood, a centerfielder with the St. Louis Cardinals baseball team, challenged the so-called reserve clause. Once drafted by a team, the reserve clause required that a player deal only with that team or give up major league baseball. Once signed, he was owned by that team for the rest of his career. He could be sold or traded, but he could not offer his services to other teams. Curt Flood lost his case in the Supreme Court, but two other players won the right of free agency in 1975 through arbitration rulings.

The reserve clause was thrown out in 1975, and a modified system of "free agency" took its place. Under the free agency guidelines, baseball players who signed with a team before 1976 were able to become free agents and sign with another team in 1977; players signing after 1976 could obtain free agent status after six years.

The effect on players' salaries was startling. Average salaries for all players jumped from $51,500 in 1976 to $77,000 in 1977.[9] The effects are even more dramatic in recent years. Average player compensation exceeded $200,000 in 1980 and $410,000 in 1986. Economists have compared the players' *MRPs* and salaries before and after the reserve clause and found striking differences. For example, while the *MRP* of a star pitcher in the late 1960s was estimated to be $3,970,000, these big ticket players earned *only* $612,000, less than a sixth of their contribution to team revenues. After the reserve clause bit the dust, the gap closed fast. Rollie Fingers, a highly sought-after pitcher in the late 1970s, had an estimated *MRP* of $304,000. When he became a free agent in 1977, he signed for $332,000. Others have done even

</td>
</tr>
</table>

---

[8] Walter Nicholson, *Intermediate Microeconomics and Its Application*, 4th ed. (Hinsdale, Ill.: Dryden Press, 1987), p. 419.

[9] Timothy Tregarthen, "Players Head for the Courts," *The Margin* 3, no. 3 (The University of Colorado, November 1987), p. 8.

better. Reggie Jackson signed a contract worth $975,000 with the California Angels in 1982. And more recently, the New York Yankees signed slugger Jack Clark away from the St. Louis Cardinals for over $1 million and $500,000 in bonus incentives.

The owners, though pleased with big crowds, were unhappy at the prospect of paying ever higher salaries to acquire free agents. That was when, according to the Major League Baseball Players Association (MLBPA), the team owners engaged in collusion by agreeing to end competitive bidding for free agents. The evidence seemed overwhelming: only the top players received any offers at all. For example, Andre Dawson became a free agent in 1986 after leaving his $800,000 post with the Montreal Expos. He got one offer on the last day of the so-called open bidding period. It was for $650,000 with the Chicago Cubs, less than half of what he was seeking. He went on to be the Most Valuable Player in the National League that year! In September 1987, major league baseball owners were found guilty of collusion and conspiracy by independent arbitration.

Questions to Consider

1. *How did the team owners exploit baseball players under the reserve clause? How does free agency level the playing field between owners and players?*

2. *How would you estimate a star pitcher's marginal revenue product?*

3. *In 1987, all baseball teams reduced their rosters from 25 to 24 players. The MLBPA alleges that this is further evidence of collusion. What do you think?*

Having explored the supply and demand for labor, we now turn to an examination of the relationship between employment and earnings. What are the factors which influence earnings? For example, how do earnings vary with the level of education attained? Which occupations command the highest earnings? And what is the relationship between earnings and sex and race?

EMPLOYMENT AND EARNINGS: SOME EVIDENCE

Education and Earnings

It is a well-known fact that earnings rise with the level of education attained. Indeed, recent data reported in a U.S. Census Bureau study shows a dramatic difference between monthly earnings of those

TABLE 9–4
Schooling Pays
Dividends

Education	Average Monthly Earnings, 1987
Professional degrees (medicine, law, etc.)	$3,871
Doctoral degrees	3,265
Masters degrees	2,288
Bachelors degrees	1,841
Associate degrees	1,346
Vocational training	1,219
Attended college: no degree	1,169
High school diploma	1,045

Ranking 1987 average monthly earnings by educational attainment, it is very clear that the greater the degree of education attained, the higher the average monthly income. This is not to say, however, that more education means higher income for all persons. There are too many other variables, such as intelligence, motivation, ambition, experience, and related factors that also are directly related to higher earnings.

SOURCE: "Schooling Pays Dividends on the Job," *St. Louis Post-Dispatch.*

who have only completed high school and those who have either some years of college or a college degree. The table above, Schooling Pays Dividends, illustrates the monthly income by level of educational attainment.

Judging from the figures in the above table, education clearly has its rewards. "There's a hard lesson shown just in the listing of degrees, irrespective of field," said Robert Kominski of the Census Bureau in a recent interview. "The piece of paper, and different kinds of . . . paper, mean something. They mean something to employers, and to the success of individuals, they represent different levels of learning and development of skills."[10] Translated into lifetime earnings, even without taking into account faster and larger increases for people with higher levels of education, a "piece of paper" obviously pays handsome rewards.[11]

Education and Human Capital

Human capital *refers to any investment in one's earnings capacity, such as education and health.*

Economists refer to education as **human capital.** Indeed, any investment in one's earnings capacity is referred to as human capital. As we have just shown, education is an investment which pays solid dividends.

---

[10] "Schooling Pays Dividends on the Job," *St. Louis Post-Dispatch*, November 14, 1987.

[11] Even this fact, however, must be qualified. If product demand is weak or declining, one's education has little bearing on whether a job may be found, let alone how much one can earn. Possessing a doctorate in Sanskrit may offer precious few job opportunities. The moral is that one must find a field for which there is market; having skills for which there is limited demand is nearly as bad as having no skills at all.

Other forms of human capital are also important. For example, many corporations invest heavily in on-the-job training (OJT) programs. In recent years, as businesses have stepped up efforts to automate their office operations, microcomputer literacy has become a virtual necessity for most office jobs. IBM, AT&T, and Hewlett-Packard Co. are only a few of the U.S. companies that realize that such employee training results in substantial paybacks in the form of increased productivity.

THINKING IT THROUGH

Besides OJT and formal education, what other types of things might be included in human capital?

Occupation and Earnings

Which occupations provide the best earnings? Which occupations pay the least? We already know that, on the average, professionals (doctors and lawyers) are the highest paid, but what about manufacturing, mining, and retail services? Table 9–5 shows median weekly earnings in selected occupations according to sex for 1985.

There are several interesting observations to make about this data. First, women are concentrated in the lowest-paid occupations such as services, and underrepresented in the top-paying professional and managerial occupations. Second, on the average, the female to male earnings ratio tends to be significantly lower in occupations in which women are underrepresented. Third, even in the highest paid occupations such as dentistry and economics, where women are underrepresented but still have a significant share of the occupation, women still earn much less than men. Considering these patterns, it is anomalous that women earn 87.4 percent and 84.2 percent of men's earnings in geology and petroleum engineering, respectively, two occupations in which women are woefully underrepresented.

There are similar if not more graphic occupational wage differentials between whites and nonwhites. While the nonwhite to white earnings ratio has risen disproportionately during upturns of the business cycle, it also has demonstrated greater sensitivity to recessions. Much of this movement may be attributed to unemployment. Many minorities were the last hired, and, when sales slump, they are the first to be laid off. This periodic disruption of employment clearly has an adverse effect on earnings and results in a delayed improvement in the nonwhite to white earnings ratio.

TABLE 9–5

Median Weekly Earnings in Selected Occupations by Sex, 1985

Occupation	Earnings of Men	Earnings of Women	Percent Female	Female-Male Earnings Ratio
Highest Paid:				
Medical science teachers	$891	$635	27.3%	71.3%
Judges	801	433	14.7	54.1
Petroleum engineers	779	656	9.1	84.2
Airline pilots	768	298	2.1	38.8
Economists	702	404	36.5	57.5
Geologists	689	602	16.7	87.4
Dentists	672	403	38.5	60.0
Purchasing managers	625	405	22.2	64.8
Average	741	480	20.9	64.8
Lowest paid:				
Sales workers, apparel	226	157	77.4	69.5
Waiters and waitresses	209	152	82.8	72.7
Gardners and groundskeepers	202	191	1.3	94.6
Cashiers	201	164	80.1	81.6
Hotel clerks	185	183	65.9	98.9
Service station and garage workers	169	137	2.8	81.1
Teachers' aides	163	174	94.6	106.7
Household cleaners and servants	133	135	95.2	101.5
Average	186	162	62.5	88.3

Several observations may be made about this data. First, men are concentrated in the highest paid occupations, and women are concentrated in the lowest paid occupations. Second, in the lowest paid jobs where women tend to be overrepresented, on the average, men still earn more than women for the same work. Third, even in those occupations where women have a higher than average representation, such as dentistry and economics, women still earn considerably less than men.

SOURCE: *Employment and Earnings,* Bureau of Labor Statistics.

As educational attainment of nonwhites begins to approach levels reached by whites, much of the pay disparity is likely to disappear. However, because this is a protracted process, the government has made certain legislative initiatives to accelerate the process. Manpower development (job training) and related Great Society programs launched in the Johnson administration have helped to reduce such disparities. More recently, affirmative action has resulted in modest improvements. Indeed, significant progress has been made in reducing the disparity between nonwhite and white females. In the period from 1960 to 1985, the nonwhite to white female earnings ratio increased from about 60 percent to nearly 95 percent. Not nearly as much improvement has occurred between nonwhite and white males. Starting at roughly the same spot in 1960, the earnings ratio for males increased to about 70 percent in 1985. Although significantly better than the 1950s, change has been slow, especially given the social awareness, public expenditures, and private initiatives.

Accounting for Wage Differentials

Why do such glaring wage differentials exist? Pay disparities between men and women and between whites and nonwhites may be attributed to five factors: (1) personal characteristics and abilities (differences in education, training, experience, intelligence, job preferences, talents, and initiative), (2) working conditions and differences in job quality, (3) presence of institutional rigidities (unions, minimum wage legislation, and occupational licensing), (4) geographic immobility (refusal to relocate or, because of the lack of information, the inability to relocate), and (5) discrimination (the illegal variety, based on sex, race, age, etc.), not necessarily in that order. Let's take each of these in turn.

Personal Characteristics. Born into this world and endowed with a basic intelligence—a capacity for learning and adapting—we are not all created equal. We learn at different rates, we are interested in different activities, we possess different values, and so on. Our families may be very wealthy and provide us with every conceivable advantage and economic opportunity over children from families with poor or modest means. At the risk of stating the obvious, each of us is unique.

Working Conditions. In general, given equal ability to perform a job, nonmonetary factors will result in the payment of **compensating wage differentials.** These payments adjust for the perceived unattractive quality of the work. Steel workers who risk life and limb erecting I-beams high into the sky are paid a compensating wage differential—an amount over what their coworkers make who work on the ground. Similarly, because corporate executives generally prefer life in the states to assignments in other countries, business firms usually offer an incentive salary for work in so-called undesirable locations. The extra pay counteracts the negative elements of the job and brings the salary or wage in line with that paid to those who work only in their native countries.

Compensating wage differentials *are payments that adjust for the perceived unattractive quality of work.*

THINKING IT THROUGH

Why do grade school teachers, who spend four or five years in college preparing for their careers, earn less than trash collectors?

Unionism and Wage Differentials.   Labor unions, formed to represent the interests of workers, are cartel-like organizations. Although they sell resources to companies, their chief purpose is generally the same as the firms that hire the labor. Just as firms seek to maximize profits, unions, whether they are craft or industrial types, endeavor to maximize wages for their members.[12] The steamfitters, pipefitters, and electrical workers are organized as **craft unions;** all members share the same skill. The United Auto Workers, however, is an **industrial union;** its membership consists of all skill levels.

Craft unions *are worker organizations in which all members share the same skill.*

Industrial unions *represent workers whose membership consists of all skill levels.*

Unions' magna carta is the *National Labor Relations Act (NLRA).* Passed in 1935, this legislation endorsed and supported the practice of collective bargaining. Although unions had already won the right to bargain collectively in the courts, antiunion businesses still engaged in unfair labor practices such as union busting. What the *NLRA* really accomplished was to prohibit antiunion practices such as management threats to fire or demote workers engaged in union activity and refusal by management to bargain in good faith. The *Norris LaGuardia Act of 1932* had already outlawed the infamous *yellow dog contract* by which companies required prospective employees, as a condition of employment, to swear that they would not join a union.

By 1947, the public sentiment backing unionism had changed. Union membership burgeoned from 3.5 million in 1935 to 14 million within a brief span of 13 years. Strikes were more common and were perceived as disruptive. The upshot was the Taft-Hartley legislation of 1947. Whereas the intent of the *NLRA* was to ensure the rights of workers to organize, the *Taft-Hartley Act* was designed to protect the rights of workers *not* to organize. Indeed, it is often regarded as management's magna carta. Its main provision was the prohibition of the **closed shop,** a contract clause requiring a worker to join the union before they could be hired. The legislation permitted the **union shop,** whereby an employee had to join the union within 30 days after being hired, unless the states passed **right-to-work laws** to the contrary. As of 1985, 20 states had passed legislation barring the union shop. Unions have tried to survive in this environment by creating an **agency shop** provision, whereby workers must pay dues even if they are not members of the union.

Closed shop *is a contract clause requiring workers to join the union before they can be hired.*

Union shop *is a contract provision whereby an employee must join the union within 30 days after being hired, unless state laws are to the contrary.*

Right-to-work laws *are state statutes which bar the union shop.*

Agency shop *is a contract provision whereby workers must pay dues even if they are not union members.*

Unionism varies widely across American industry. From the highly organized railroad (82.8 percent) and postal service (82.4 percent) industries, to the least organized banking (2.8 percent), agriculture (3.8

---

[12] It should be noted that there is no consensus among economists about this objective of wage maximization. One alternative to wage maximization is to maximize employment, or some optimum combination. This is increasingly a troubling issue for unions given the movement of manufacturing plants to the southern states where organized labor is less powerful and where right-to-work laws are more prevalent. As recently demonstrated by the UAW, job security is a growing concern.

percent) and textile (17.9 percent) industries, union membership ranges by 80 percentage points. Membership has slipped in recent years because of increased service-sector growth relative to the goods-producing industries, a decline in the heavily unionized smokestack industries (coal and steel), and growing import competition. As of 1984, the total union membership as a percent of total employment was 18.8 percent, down from 23 percent in 1980.[13]

The impact of unionism on wages and union-nonunion wage differentials is a subject of a great deal of research. As you may suspect, the union-nonunion differential varies extensively from industry to industry and from region to region. The differential is greatest in the construction trades, where it has been estimated that unionized plumbers and electricians earned wages 55 percent to 70 percent above their nonunion counterparts. For all occupations across all industries, the average union wage differential ranges between 10 and 17 percent.[14] Workers unable to find work at union wages swell the ranks of nonunion labor, resulting in lower wages.

Unions employ many strategies to win wage concessions and improved working conditions, but the strike is the most powerful weapon. A union's bargaining power and its probability of success in negotiations depends upon five key factors: the type of product, the nature of production, general economic conditions, the strength and size of the union, and the militancy and perseverance of the union and company.[15] The strike, or the threat of strike, and the probability of a favorable settlement for the union is more likely under these conditions: the more perishable the product, the more labor-intensive the production process, the more prosperous the general economic conditions, the larger and stronger the union, and the more militant the union.

Labor Immobility and Wage Differentials.   On the average, wages in the North are higher than in the South. Some economists have suggested that a North-South (or regional) wage differential is attributed to labor immobility. For example, average earnings of wage and salaried workers in Flint, Michigan, are more than double the earnings of workers in Miami, Florida: $15.59 per hour in Flint versus $7.20 in Miami in August 1987. Similar variations exist around the country: Lynchburg, Virginia: $8.55; St. Louis, Missouri: $11.57; Dallas, Texas: $9.76; and Philadelphia, Pennsylvania: $10.85.

If labor immobility is the cause, is it because workers do not know about the jobs (imperfect information)? Is it because they prefer their

---

[13] Kaufman, *The Economics of Labor Markets and Labor Relations,* pp. 420–21, 426.

[14] David Hyman, *Modern Microeconomics: Analysis and Applications* (St. Louis: Times Mirror/Mosby, 1987), p. 476.

[15] Kaufman, *The Economics of Labor Markets and Labor Relations,* pp. 468–69.

current job in familiar surroundings? Indeed, the reason may not be immobility at all. A number of studies have determined that cost-of-living differences fully account for the wage differentials. When living costs are taken into account, the money wage differentials are erased. Moreover, if the disamenities of urban life are considered, such as pollution, congestion, and crime, one could argue that labor immobility is an unlikely explanation of regional wage differentials.[16]

Discrimination and Wage Differentials.   Like unionism, discrimination has the effect of restricting the supply of labor. **Discrimination** occurs when, given two or more groups of workers of equal productivity, employers hire or pay one group of workers more than another group. The most frequently cited types of discrimination are those based on age, handicap, race or ethnic background, religious affiliation, and sex.

Discrimination *occurs when employers hire or pay one group of workers more than another equally productive group.*

Discrimination takes many forms. It may be segregation in low-paying jobs, unequal pay for equal work, or being passed over at promotion time. Whether the employer has a prejudice against women, minorities, and teenagers, or whether the employer argues that these groups have proven to be less productive than white males over 21, the effect is the same, and the act constitutes a violation of federal law.

To be sure, discrimination exists in many forms. Read the following CASE-IN-POINT to gain a new perspective on discrimination.

CASE
▪ IN ▪
POINT

Height and Weight in the MBA Market

Getting an MBA will boost your earnings. Being a man will boost them more. A new study suggests that being a tall, slender man will raise them more still.

Each extra inch of height raises the salaries of male MBAs by $600 a year on the average. Being 20 percent or more overweight, on the other hand, cuts male salaries by a whopping $4,000.

University of Pittsburgh professors Josephine Olson, Irene Frieze, and graduate student Deborah Good examined the 1983 salaries of a sample of people who had received MBAs between 1973 and 1982 to determine factors significant in salary determination. Factors that were important determinants of salary included the number of years a person had worked before getting an MBA, the number of years spent working only part-time, and the number of years unemployed or not working. The researchers also considered height and weight.

"The average man in our sample was 71 inches tall and earned $42,480 in 1983," Ms. Olson says. "Earnings went up $600 for every inch over that height, and were $600 lower for every inch below it. Being overweight reduced earnings by $4,000 a year."

---

[16] Hyman, *Modern Microeconomics; Analysis and Applications,* pp. 453–54.

The height and weight evidence suggests a possible form of discrimination—against shorter and heavier men. "The height and weight variables didn't seem to matter for the women—they earned less than the men on average already," Ms. Olson reports.

The study found that female MBAs were earning about $3,000 less per year than male MBAs with similar experience. Being a woman is, apparently, a lot like being a fat man.[17]

Questions to Consider

1. *Keeping in mind that the authors of this report are women, are they being facetious when they report that "Being a women is, apparently, a lot like being a fat man"? What do they mean by this?*

2. *Do the findings in this study prove that employers discriminate against heavy and/or short men? Is it possible that short and overweight men are less productive than tall lean men?*

INCOME DISTRIBUTION

In closing this chapter on labor markets and wage determination, it is useful to summarize our discussion by looking at the general distribution of income and the extent of poverty in society. We begin with the income distribution. Table 9–7 illustrates the percentage distribution of families by income level and race from 1970 to 1985.

Because there are a lot of numbers to contend with, we will concentrate on a few salient trends and comparisons. First, note that each group exhibited an increase in the percentage of families at both ends of the income distribution. In a 15-year period, for whites, blacks, and Hispanics, the percentage point increase in the number of families earning more than $50,000 was 5.7, 2.5, and 3.2, respectively. Although blacks and Hispanics closed the income gap on whites somewhat, both minorities were still well underrepresented in this highest income category. At the other extreme, all three groups also experienced an increase in the percentage of families earning less than $5,000 annually. Black and Hispanic families, however, joined the ranks of the lowest income group in far greater proportion to their populations.

Second, if we collapse the income ranges into larger income groups, we can observe some other interesting trends. In the $15,000–$34,999 range, the vast so-called middle-income group, we see a secular decline in the percentage of families. Although all groups experienced a declin-

---

[17] "Height and Weight in the MBA Market," *The Margin* 2 no. 3 (The University of Colorado, March 1987).

TABLE 9-6 Percent Distribution of Families by Income Level and Race, 1970–1985

	Number of Families (000s)	<5,000	5,000-9,999	10,000-14,999	15,000-19,999	20,000-24,999	25,000-34,999	35,000-49,999	>50,000	0-24,999	OVER 25,000	15,000-34,999	Median Income (in 1985 dollars)	Black/White Median Income Ratio	Hispanic/White Median Income Ratio
					Percent of All Families						**SUMMARY**			**Medians**		
White															
1970	46,535	3.2	7.1	9.2	10.5	12.2	23.7	20.2	13.9	42.2	57.8	46.4	$28,358		
1975	49,873	2.7	7.7	9.9	10.8	11.3	21.7	21.0	14.9	42.4	57.6	43.8	28,518		
1980	52,710	3.0	7.6	9.9	11.0	10.7	21.2	20.5	16.1	42.2	57.8	42.9	28,596		
1985	54,991	3.7	7.5	9.7	10.3	10.4	19.2	19.7	19.6	41.6	58.5	39.9	29,152		
Black															
1970	4,928	9.9	17.4	16.2	14.0	11.6	15.8	10.7	4.5	69.1	31.0	41.40	17,395	0.61	
1975	5,586	8.5	20.3	14.7	13.2	11.7	15.5	11.2	4.9	68.4	31.6	40.40	17,547	0.62	
1980	6,317	11.4	19.3	15.3	12.2	10.2	14.9	11.3	5.5	68.4	31.7	37.30	16,456	0.58	
1985	6,921	13.5	17.1	14.3	13.0	9.0	14.3	11.8	7.0	66.9	33.1	36.30	16,768	0.58	
Hispanic															
1970	2,499	6.5	15.7	16.8	14.2	12.1	18.9	10.8	4.9	65.3	34.6	45.20	19,090		0.67
1975	3,235	7.1	15.6	15.7	14.1	11.4	16.8	12.7	6.4	63.9	35.9	42.30	19,212		0.67
1980	3,305	7.1	15.5	15.7	13.1	12.9	16.2	12.9	6.7	64.3	35.8	42.20	19,399		0.68
1985	4,206	8.3	17.0	14.9	12.1	11.3	16.0	12.5	8.1	63.6	36.6	39.40	19,027		0.65

Each group, black, Hispanic, and white, experienced an increase in the percentage of families at both ends of the income distribution. Although both minority groups closed the income gap on whites, both blacks and Hispanics were still well underrepresented in the highest income category. In the middle-income range, $15,000 to $34,999, each group had a lower percentage in 1985 than in 1970, although whites saw their share fall by the greatest amount (6.5 percentage points). With respect to median income data, only white families experienced an increase over the 15-year period. There was also a corresponding decrease in the black/white and Hispanic/white median income ratios.

SOURCE: *Statistical Abstract of the United States*, 1987, Table 731, p. 436.

ing share of the middle income range, it was most pronounced for whites, who saw their share fall by 6.5 percentage points. If this sounds peculiar, ask yourself where these families shifted. Because a greater percentage of white families started (in 1970) in this range, most of the movement was into the highest range (over $50,000). For black and Hispanic families, in part because they were more concentrated in the lower reaches of the middle range, their upward movement was more evenly distributed in the the two highest income ranges.

A third observation pertains to the median income figures. The data are in real (or constant 1985 dollar) terms, which means that they have been adjusted to remove the influence of inflation.[18] Although no group showed dramatic changes, it is noteworthy that white families enjoyed a modest increase in real income, while black and Hispanic families experienced a slight decline. These relative income movements are reflected in the last column of the table, the median income ratios. The ratios compare black and Hispanic family incomes to white family incomes. Over the 15-year span, the black/white median income ratio slipped 3 percentage points, and the Hispanic/white ratio dropped 2 percentage points. This slippage is not surprising, given the significant increase in the lowest income category. Indeed, the family shares in the lowest two income classes (from $0–$9,999), 11.2 percent, 30.6 percent, and 23.3 percent respectively for whites, blacks, and Hispanics, correspond roughly to the poverty levels for each group.

POVERTY

Poverty is an economic straitjacket. But poverty is much more than an economic problem. Although defined by the government in monetary terms for practical reasons, the character of poverty is deeply emotional and psychologically debilitating, and it is etched with personal despair and disillusion. Millions of people move in and out of the ranks of poverty every year.

Poverty is extremely difficult to define and perhaps even more difficult to measure. First, *poverty is relative*. One person's poverty in the United States may actually constitute affluence in Bangladesh. Second, *poverty is personal*. Because people possess different values, aspirations, and expectations, they regard their positions in society in different ways. Some people, for example, tend not to compare themselves with others,

---

[18] The median income figures are in constant 1985 dollars. This permits us to make meaningful comparisons from one year to the next. Since the money value of income is eroded by higher prices, economists generally prefer to express monetary values in real (or constant dollar) terms. This is accomplished by dividing any previous year's income figure, (e.g., $28,596 for 1980), by a price index. We will explore this important topic further in Chapter 11.

have modest expectations, even refuse government assistance. Others are frustrated because they are not participating in the good life, the so-called *American dream*. Indeed, many people may feel impoverished because of media bombardments which parade the good life—fancy cars, exotic travel, and luxurious homes. The message seems to say, *Spend your way to happiness* or *More money means more happiness*.

A third problem is that if the government intends to do something to reduce poverty, it must define poverty. In other words, government must develop an **absolute measure of poverty.** Accordingly, the Department of Agriculture (DA) has developed a definition, used now for over 20 years. By survey techniques, it was determined that poor (and lower-income) families spend approximately one third of their budgets on food. The DA then estimated the cost of a minimally nutritious and balanced diet for a family of four (two adults and two children). It also developed similar food budgets for single individuals and all other households. The final step was to multiply this food budget times three. The result was the poverty level (before taxes and any government assistance). Although criticized as too simplistic, unrealistic, and arbitrary, it remains the official definition of poverty. A family of four was poor in 1986 if it had a cash income of less than $11,203.[19]

> **Absolute measure of poverty** *is determined by estimating the cost of a diet for a family of four (two adults and two children) and multiplying by three.*

Who Are the Poor?   In 1985, 33.1 million persons were poor, 14 percent of the population. Broken down by race, there were 22.9 million poor whites, 8.9 million poor blacks, and 1.3 million Hispanics and peoples of other races. Another way to view the poverty data is to ask what percentage of each group is poor. In order to understand the composition of the poor, a brief profile of Americans in poverty will clarify the picture. (All figures are for 1985.)

- About a third of blacks, one fourth of Hispanics, and one tenth of whites are poor.
- About 50 percent of black female household heads are poor.
- Nearly 40 percent of the poor are children.
- Twelve percent over 65 years of age are poor.

A recent study by a private research group found that the number of poor families has grown 35 percent from 1979 to 1986, and one third of the increase is attributed to "a decline in the effectiveness of government anti-poverty programs." The number of poor families with children increased to 5.5 million from 4.1 million in 1979.[20]

---

[19] One serious problem is in calculating the cost of acquiring the food items to obtain a nutritious diet. The official method assumes that each householder does extensive comparison shopping to obtain the best buys, and it makes no allowance for soda, chips, and other luxuries.

[20] "Poor Families With Children Rose 35% Since 1979, Analysis Finds," *The New York Times,* September 8, 1987.

Related poverty characteristics are such things as unemployment, high school dropout rates, infant mortality, and violence. Although there are many other measures of life in poverty, these provide further insight. Violence seems to be endemic to poor communities, and one measure of the impact of violence is the number or rate of homocide victims. The homocide rate per 100,000 people, as reported by the FBI's serious crime count index, was 51.4 for black males and 8.6 for white males. Infant mortality is another characteristic of poverty. In 1983, the rate of infant deaths per 1,000 live births for blacks was 19.2; for whites, it was 9.7. Education is also critical to one's earnings capability, and dropping out of high school often leads to chronic unemployment, a major cause of poverty. In 1985, 12.6 percent of black youths and 10.3 percent of white youths dropped out of high school. Finally, if one is not working, the chances of joining the ranks of the poor are greatly increased. Approximately 35 percent of the poor were unemployed in 1985.

Any discussion of poverty must address the disproportionate share of minorities, children, and females. Looked at from the perspective of statistical odds, the picture is pretty grim. If you are Hispanic, there is a one-in-four chance that you are poor; if black, the odds increase to one-in-three. The odds are even worse if you are a black female household head: there is a 50 percent chance that you will be poor.

Why Are the Poor Poor?   Why do minorities and female household heads constitute such a high proportion of the poor? As we have already seen, part of the explanation is related to productivity factors and labor force participation. Unemployment rates are highest among minorities, especially black and Hispanic youth. Moreover, minorities are concentrated in those occupations with the lowest earnings. But this is only part of the picture, since nearly 40 percent of the poor are employed.[21]

---

[21] This statistic (taken from the *Monthly Labor Review*, February 1986) is somewhat misleading. The Bureau of Labor Statistics defines employment as anyone over 16 years of age who works at least one hour for pay during the survey period. Thus, many people are counted as employed who work part-time because they cannot find full-time work. A related issue is the number of people working below, at, or slightly above minimum wage. In 1986, there were 5.1 million workers earning minimum wages ($3.35 per hour) or less (3.5 million exactly at the minimum wage and 1.6 million less than $3.35). Thirty-seven percent were teenagers and 23 percent were aged 20–24; 40 percent were 25 and over. Another 9.6 million workers earned between $3.35 and $4.35 per hour (25 percent were teenagers and 25 percent were between 20 and 24; 50 percent were over 25 years of age). (*Monthly Labor Review*, July 1987, pp. 34–38.) How does this relate to poverty? If one works 40 hours per week, 52 weeks a year at the minimum wage, the annual earnings are $6,968. This is $4,235 below the poverty line for a family of four. If you get a $1 per hour raise, you will earn $9,048, or $2,155 below poverty. In order to escape poverty (as the head of a family of four), a person would have had to earn $5.40 per hour in 1986, assuming no paid vacations and a 52-week workyear.

> ### THINKING IT THROUGH
>
> If 40 percent of the poor are employed, and 35 percent of the poor are unemployed, what about the remaining 25 percent? How are they classified?

Other productivity factors such as years of education, credentials (diplomas and degrees), skills, on-the-job training, and job experience are also important. Even if we take these into consideration, however, we cannot fully explain poverty and the distribution of income. After all, the marginal revenue product is zero for someone who is unemployed.

If we factor out all productivity-related variables, we are left with three main reasons. First are personal abilities and family characteristics. Not all of us can become surgeons, engineers, or lawyers, let alone star athletes. If the head of household has a college degree and works in a white-collar job, the odds are one-in-three that the child will follow a similar path. It is no secret that middle-and-upper-class families place a much higher value on education than lower-class families. But family, class, and other environmental factors are not the whole picture. Personal abilities must also be figured in. Intelligence, talent, initiative and hard work, discipline, and ambition are important ingredients in accounting for differences among individuals. Have you ever asked yourself why or how two people from impoverished and underprivileged families have totally different economic experiences? One person may become a successful businessperson while the other bounces from job to job, making ends meet with government aid. Although it is difficult to attribute cause and effect, there is little doubt that individual differences play a major role in accounting for poverty.

A second factor is family wealth. Although we all have heard that "There's no substitute for hard work," one can also say that "There's no substitute for a fat inheritance." In other words, money begets money, the rich marry the rich, and propertied wealth is highly concentrated. In 1985, 2 percent of all families accounted for 17 percent of all property income, nearly $565 billion of interest, dividend, and rental income. This very unequal distribution of nonwage income is also reflected in the distribution of wealth. In 1985, 12 percent of Americans had no assets at all, and another 22 percent held less than $10,000 in asset wealth. The richest 12 percent of Americans, on the other hand, owned nearly 40 percent of all personal wealth.

The third factor is discrimination. As we have shown throughout this chapter, white males earn more than any other demographic group. If minorities and women have the same education as white males, and other productivity factors are equal as well, then discrimination looms large in any accounting of income differentials and poverty.

IMPORTANT TERMS TO REMEMBER

absolute measure of poverty, p. 258
agency shop, p. 252
backward-bending supply curve
   of labor, p. 238
closed shop, p. 252
compensating wage differentials,
   p. 251
craft unions, p. 252
derived demand, p. 240
discrimination, p. 254

human capital, p. 248
income effect, p. 239
industrial unions, p. 252
marginal resource cost, p. 241
marginal revenue product, p. 241
right-to-work laws, p. 252
rule for hiring labor, p. 242
substitution effect, p. 239
union shop, p. 252

CHAPTER SUMMARY

1. The supply of labor is extremely heterogeneous. Although age, sex, and race are the most obvious and publicized features, intelligence, talents and abilities, skill levels, and experience are but a few of the rich background characteristics.

2. The supply curve of labor is backward-bending, reflecting the substitution effect at lower wages and the income effect at higher wages.

3. Marginal productivity theory and the theory of wage determination tells us that firms will hire workers to the point where the marginal revenue product of labor equals the marginal resource cost. In purely competitive markets, the firm will pay the worker a wage equal to the *MRP*. However, in imperfectly competitive markets, the firm pays a wage less than the *MRP* and hires fewer workers than under purely competitive conditions.

4. Productivity-related factors such as education, training, and experience are important factors in explaining wage differentials in the economy, but nonproductivity factors may be at least as important. Unionism, discrimination, minimum-wage legislation, and geographic location play a significant role in shaping earnings.

5. One major factor accounting for wage and salary differentials is the distribution of income and wealth in the economy. Median family income figures reveal that minority families earn approximately 60 percent of white family incomes.

6. Poverty remains a major problem in U.S. society. Although the majority of the poor are white, a significantly higher percentage of black and Hispanic families are poor. Moreover, poverty is concentrated among children and female headed households.

1. The backward-bending supply curve of labor says that, after a certain wage level is reached, increased wages will cause workers to substitute leisure for work. At what wage or salary on your present job would you begin to trade-off leisure for work? Why is the wage elasticity of supply positive for women and negative for men?

2. Using the data in Table 9–2 (TNT hiring labor in competitive markets but selling rackets in monopolistic markets), sketch in the new *MRP* curve in Figure 9–3. Confirm graphically that the firm will hire six workers.

3. *Monopsony* is the technical term for a firm which is the only buyer or employer of a resource. Compared to pure competition in the resource markets, why are fewer workers hired when companies possess monopsonistic power? Besides professional sports and the company town, what are other examples of imperfect competition in the resource market?

4. What are the factors which account for wage differentials between men and women and between whites and minorities?

5. Does the income distribution shown in Table 9–7 support the claim that we are becoming a nation of haves and have-nots? Is the famous U.S. middle-class gradually disappearing?

6. Do you think that the definition of poverty is satisfactory? Why? If not, what changes would you make?

7. All of us like creature comforts, but some of us are more concerned than others about acquiring material possessions. What do you make of the following formula for happiness?

$$\text{Happiness} = \frac{\text{Material consumption}}{\text{Desire}}$$

What does this say? How can you become happier according to this formula?

The next chapter is the bridge between microeconomics and macroeconomics. We will examine the differences between private and public goods, how and why markets may fail, the field of economics known as public choice, and the role of benefit-cost analysis in decision making.

10

Public Choice and Benefit-Cost Analysis

Marc PoKempner, TSW-Click/Chicago

As we have demonstrated in the previous chapters, choice is a basic subject of economics. What is (should be) produced by private business and what is (should be) provided by government? How are (should) such decisions (be) made? Why are decisions to produce goods such as education and health services made predominately by government? Why do some markets fail to provide their important allocation and information functions? These are the questions that will guide us in this final chapter devoted to microeconomics.

This chapter is also an initial foray into the macroeconomic realm. Because government services constitute about 30 percent of total economic activity, we should understand how and why resources are allocated in this way. Public choice theory helps to do that by focusing on the behavior of voters and officeholders as they express their preferences for more, the same, or fewer provisions from the public sector. And analysis of the costs and benefits of governmental activity helps to determine the most desirable level of collective goods and governmental regulation.

After completion of this chapter, you should be able to do the following:

1. Distinguish between public goods and private goods and provide examples of each.
2. List three kinds of market failures, and describe and explain how and why they occur.
3. Identify and give an example of the free rider problem.
4. Explain and provide an example of how private consumption and production decisions can generate spillover effects (negative and positive externalities).
5. Describe and explain benefit-cost analysis, and use this analytical tool to determine whether an economic activity is meritorious.

Would You Vote for It?

There were no vacancies in Florida's prisons in 1989. Nonetheless, as criminal activity mounts, the courts continue to sentence convicted felons to years in prisons. However, because the prisons are full, many prisoners are released long before their sentences have expired. Why? Basically to make room for the newcomers. The upshot is that thousands of people sentenced to 10 or 20 years for serious crimes are paroled after 5 or fewer years. Floridians are upset.

In early 1989, the governor of Florida proposed a sales tax increase to finance the expansion of prison facilities. The governor noted his opposition to more taxes, but said that law-abiding citizens had no choice: if the public wanted safer streets, it had to pay for it. It was estimated that a middle-income family would pay an additional $100 in sales taxes annually.

Unlike an individual consumer's decision to buy a car, take a vacation, or dine out, the provision of more prisons is a collective decision. The governor of Florida may proclaim the importance of more or better prisons, but the decision to provide more prisons often rests ultimately with the electorate, especially if more taxes are required. Because goods such as prisons, parks, and highways cannot be sold in the private marketplace, the government must provide them for the general population and finance them with tax receipts. And when such collective goods and services require more revenue, government often must submit the tax increase to the voters for approval. Majority rule thus replaces individual consumer choice and the market.

MARKETS AND MARKET FAILURE

Market *is an exchange mechanism through which buyers and sellers execute an economic transaction.*

A **market** is an exchange mechanism through which buyers and sellers execute an economic transaction. The New York Stock Exchange, a roadside produce stand, and an automobile showroom are clearly recognized as common examples of private markets. But how do these markets actually work? Although we have covered this subject earlier, it is useful to review the highlights here.

Market Functions

Markets operate through the principles of supply and demand, transmitting information about price and product availability. If the demand for a product increases, other things unchanged, we would expect product price to increase. Why? Let's examine this scenario in the market for fresh grapes.

It is a Saturday morning in the summer at the Farmers' Market in Anytown, U.S.A. A plentiful supply of grapes is available in a number of stalls. Then, the crush hits. For some unknown reason, people are buying grapes like there is no tomorrow. By ten o'clock, half the market's supply has been sold. Vendors begin to post new signs, increasing the price of grapes per pound from 59 cents to 89 cents. Sales slow down, but by noon there are hardly any grapes available. Once again, the sellers increase price, this time to $1.19 per pound. Some consumers buy at this new price, but others begin to complain, and still others walk away in disgust. There are some grapes left at the close of the day, but not nearly as much as usual for the next day. What happened?

As Figure 10–1 shows, the increased demand (from D_1 to D_2) created a shortage of grapes at the opening market price of 59 cents. However, as grape sales far exceeded the usual Saturday pattern, sellers realized that there were not enough grapes to satisfy the quantity demanded, and they accordingly increased the price to 89 cents. This resulted in some relief, illustrated in Figure 10–1 as a reduced shortage, but there was still an insufficient amount to meet demand. Traffic at the grape stalls did not decrease substantially until the vendors increased the price to $1.19 per pound. Of course, we should not be surprised at this result since this new price created a surplus. At the $1.19 price, vendors now were supplying more grapes than consumers were willing to buy.

THINKING IT THROUGH

What will probably happen when the market opens the next day? Will vendors maintain the $1.19 price? Why or why not?

Although all markets provide the important functions of processing and conveying information, allocating scarce resources among competing and alternative uses, and sending signals to buyers and sellers, some markets are more efficient and informative than others. Indeed, in some cases markets fail to provide these allocation and information functions because of monopoly and other forms of imperfect competition. Markets also fail to inform buyers and sellers and allocate resources efficiently because some goods and services cannot be sold in the marketplace. In the next section, we will explore in greater detail how and why markets fail and how governmental intervention tries to improve resource allocation.

FIGURE 10–1
The Local Grape Market

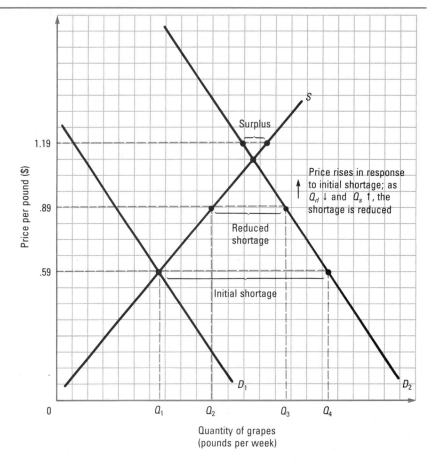

The initial shortage (Q_4–Q_1) in the grape market can be seen at the market opening price of $.59. The shortage was created when consumer demand for grapes increased suddenly, from D_1 to D_2. Vendors increased prices to $.89 and the shortage decreased. Consumers decreased consumption and the sellers offered more grapes on the market. There was still excess quantity demanded, so vendors raised prices to $1.19. This time they went too far, shooting past the equilibrium price. The result was a small surplus. At least they had some grapes for the next day, thanks to the efficient allocation and information functions of the market.

Market Failures

Market failure *occurs when too few or too many resources are allocated to production.*

A **market failure** occurs when too few or too many resources are allocated to production. There are three basic sources of market failure: (1) imperfect competition, (2) public goods, and (3) externalities.

Imperfect Competition. First, as we have already seen in the last few chapters, imperfect competition clearly results in allocative inefficiency. Because price exceeds marginal cost—that is, because society is willing to pay more than it costs society to produce an extra unit of the good—resources are underallocated to production. This is especially true under conditions of monopolistic competition and oligopoly, where more competition would result in increased output and lower prices. On the other hand, under some conditions of natural monopoly, such as a bus system or other modes of public transportation, the price may be less than the marginal cost. In this case, resources are underallocated to the service.

Public Goods. A second source of market failures is public goods, such as national defense, prisons, and highways. In order to understand public goods, however, for purposes of comparison it is useful first to examine the characteristics of private goods. Let's say that you go to see a new film at a local theater. Although the service (entertainment) provided by the business is made available to many people at the same time, it is a private good because the benefits you derive from watching the film are yours alone. Moreover, the ticket is sold in the marketplace. The purchase of a private good (an admission fee to the movie) sets up what is called the *exclusion principle:* those who do not buy the good

Private goods *are* divisible *and yield* private benefits.

are excluded from the benefits of the good or service. **Private goods** thus have twin properties: they are *divisible* and they yield *private benefits*. In other words, private goods can be packaged so that only those who pay enjoy the benefits from consumption. A *pure private good* is one in which the sharing of benefits from consumption is logically impossible, as in the case of a piece of chewing gum.

Public goods *and services are* indivisible *and yield* collective benefits.

Unlike private goods, **public goods** and services are *indivisible* and yield *collective benefits*. Moreover, they are not sold in the private marketplace.[1] One important reason why some things are done by government is that they would not otherwise be done at all. National parks and wildlife refuges are two such cases. A second reason is that some goods and services are by their very nature indivisible; that is, it is either impossible or extremely difficult to sell individual units of the item to individual consumers in the marketplace. Such services as a lighthouse, national defense, prisons, and police and fire protection are indivisible. Another property of public goods is that they provide collective benefits. When a good is indivisible and yields collective benefits, such as national defense, offering the service to just one person automatically means that everyone shares equally in the benefits (whether you want to or not). Moreover, the marginal cost of providing the good to additional citizens is zero.

---

[1] Imagine the federal government selling national defense or property repairs resulting from hurricanes and tornado damage! Although many of us would voluntarily buy such services just as we buy private insurance, the amount raised would unlikely finance the desired level of protection.

Some goods fall in between the extremes of purely private and purely public categories. For example, national parks are public goods (amenities) financed by everyone's tax dollars, as are zoos, museums, and wildlife sanctuaries. Although not everyone enjoys the benefits, at least not every year, such goods represent options available to all of us. And since there is no market whereby we can pay for the option to use Yosemite National Park or San Diego Zoo, there must be a mechanism to pay of the goods.[2]

Externalities.   Although private goods production involves private costs to the producers and provides benefits exclusively to those buying the good, not all private goods yield exclusive private costs and benefits. For example, when a chemical company dumps waste into a local river or sends noxious gases into the air, it creates costs for the general community. When there are such spillover effects, an **externality** exists: the actions of a private business or household generate costs or benefits above the private costs and benefits associated with production or consumption. When someone other than the buyer(s) and seller(s) bears some of the costs or receive some benefits of production or consumption, an externality exists. If the activity imposes costs upon a third party, then there is an **external cost** or (negative externality); if the activity creates benefits to third parties, then there is an **external benefit** (or positive externality).

Although pollution is an obvious case of an external cost, whereby private producers shift private costs of production to others, the presence of externalities is widespread and may well entail external benefits as well as external costs. For example, the federal government may decide to reroute a major interstate highway. Although some local restaurants and motels may suffer a loss of business, perhaps forcing them to close, others may experience an unanticipated boom in business. When a company opens a new plant in a community, new jobs are created, incomes are generated, existing businesses prosper and new businesses are created. Such economic multipliers are positive externalities.

Private consumption also generates external costs and benefits. When a homeowner decides to erect a fence, plant trees, and otherwise beautify the property, the neighboring homeowner may find that his vegetable garden is blocked from necessary sunlight. When you decide to mow your lawn at 8 A.M. Sunday morning, you deprive your neighbors of the

Externality *refers to the actions of a private business or household generating costs or benefits above the private costs and benefits associated with production or consumption.*

External cost *(or negative externality) exists if the activity imposes costs upon a third party.*

External benefit *(or positive externality) exists if the activity creates benefits to third parties.*

---

[2] Because of budget problems, some states and localities charge user fees to citizens for admission to parks, zoos, museums, and other public goods. However, these fees defray only a small portion of the operating costs. Without public tax support, it is unlikely that the goods would be provided at all, since the user fees would be truly exorbitant. For example, the daily adult admission to Epcot Center, one of several famous Disney attractions in Orlando, Florida, was $28 per person in 1989. Imagine paying $28 to go to the zoo!

pleasure of sleeping in. On the other hand, your neighbors may be eternally grateful when you resod your front lawn. Runoff of rainfall is greatly reduced, resulting in drier basements for the surrounding homeowners. Whether private business, consumer, or government agency, such private and public actions all generate costs and benefits to others.

The Free Rider Problem and Taxation

Free rider problem *exists when people enjoy the benefits of consumption without sharing in the cost of providing the good.*

Because it is impossible to withhold the benefits of national defense and other public goods from anyone, there is virtually no incentive for individuals to pay for public goods. Even if some people voluntarily contribute, most will not since the good will be provided anyway. In other words, a **free rider problem** exists when people (try to) enjoy the benefits of consumption without sharing in the cost of providing the good. Moreover, the problem will persist as long as the benefits exceed the costs. The following CASE-IN-POINT illustrates a free rider problem that you may have experienced.

CASE
• IN •
POINT

What Me? A Free Rider?

The situation is a wholesale furniture supply office. Most of the 20 employees are coffee drinkers and, as is customary, the job of making coffee is delegated to the secretary. Unfortunately, collecting money wasn't part of the job description.

The word goes out that coffee may be bought for 20 cents per cup or $5 per month (a real bargain). A sign announcing the price is placed above the coffee table. In the beginning, all goes well: $65 is collected in monthly fees, and the coin collection jar is brimming with silver.

As months roll by, however, funds are depleted faster and faster until there is insufficient money to replenish the supplies. A friendly word and a more threatening note from the secretary produce more coins in the jar and an additional $10 monthly dues. Then, one cold Monday morning when Frank appeared for work, something was different. Everyone was going about their normal business. The phones were ringing off the desks. Mail was piled high. It all seemed so dreadfully normal for a Monday, except . . . And then it hit him: no wonderful coffee aroma, and no coffee. The cupboard was bare; the coffers were empty. Frank didn't have to look further, and he certainly didn't want to ask the secretary what happened. He knew. He had paid only $10.40 for coffee in a six-month period.

Questions to Consider

1. Our culprit Frank is a classic free rider. He and others in the office wanted a free ride—coffee without paying for it. Does this mean that the office coffee was a public good? Or did Frank and others treat a private good as a public good?

2. *How would you solve the coffee supply problem if you were the secretary? If you were the office manager would that make a difference in your solution?*

Examples of the free rider problem exist in all walks of life. The open-air concert enables many people to enjoy the music without paying admission. The chemical plant that dumps waste products into the passing river treats the river as its property, forgetting that it is a public resource that actually belongs to everyone. Motorists toss trash on the roadside from their automobiles (perhaps because they perceive the benefits of this method of disposal greater than the probability of being caught littering). Even the seemingly harmless behavior of taking a shortcut across a lawn that bears a "Please Keep Off the Grass" sign is a free rider problem. The trespasser simply is enjoying benefits without paying for them.

What is it that prompts some of us to behave as free riders? What property or characteristic of certain goods or transactions enables one person to impose costs (or benefits) on others without their consent?

The answer is that either no one owns the resources or that property rights are not clearly defined. In the case of the open-air concert, no one owns the air space through which the music travels. Because the concert is held out-of-doors, it is impossible to exclude nonpayers from the music (whether the externality is a cost or a benefit). The chemical plant may be producing pesticides and fungicides and related agricultural insect repellants, but it also produces waste. When it dumps these by-products (pollutants) into the river, it contaminates common property—property owned by the people. How to remedy such misallocations of resources often involves the government—as caretaker of the commons.[3] But more will be said on this a little later.

---

[3] The free rider issue as it relates to ill-defined property rights was conveyed in an obscure little ditty from the late 1960s, during an era of considerable concern about the environment.

> The law protects the felon who steals the goose from the commons, but lets
> the greater felon loose who steals the common from the goose.

In other words, one can get off scot-free if the violation involves public (common) property. But if the action involves private property, there is an enormous corpus of law on the subject. The law is clear about individuals' and property rights, even that of the felon. But the law is virtually silent regarding public property, often called the commons (from our English heritage).

THINKING IT THROUGH

As the homeowner of a home near a major airport, you (and your neighbors) are tiring of the excessive noise pollution caused by aircraft taking off and landing. Do you have any rights regarding the airspace used by the airlines? What is your recourse?

Although our CASE-IN-POINT about the office coffee is a somewhat trivialized example of the free rider problem, it does illustrate the issue of how to raise sufficient revenue to pay for a good or service. Unions face such problems in right-to-work states, since they cannot compel workers to join the union and pay dues as a condition of employment. And the government faces this problem in the provision of public goods which carry significant collective benefits. If the service is indivisible and nonexclusive, there must be a coercive system of cost-sharing to finance the activity.

Once it is determined that an activity is to be undertaken, the government has three alternatives to pay for it: levy taxes on the general population, borrow, or charge user fees (as with many toll roads, bridges, and museums). Indeed, when Californians passed the famous Proposition 13 in 1981 to dramatically reduce property taxes, user fees became the only viable option for the state and local governments to continue offering their array of services. Libraries began charging for book lending, zoos initiated admission fees, and summer school became a pay-as-you-go operation.

PUBLIC CHOICE, PUBLIC GOODS, AND BENEFIT-COST ANALYSIS

Public choice is the economic analysis of political behavior, of voters, officeholders, and others who provide public goods.

Public choice is the economic analysis of political behavior, of voters, officeholders, and others who provide public goods. Public goods are provided mainly by governments, and the process is as much political as economic. Just as we cast dollar votes in the marketplace for goods and services, we vote our elected representatives into local, state, and national legislative bodies in order to implement programs, solve problems, and generally serve our interests. In other words, we vote for public goods.

In the electoral contest, political candidates compete for our votes just as producers of automobiles compete for our dollars in the product market. Taking this analogy just a little further, it is possible to suggest that office holders are much like firms with a market share to protect.

Politicians campaigning for reelection behave like companies marketing a new product. The business firm tries to maximize profits; the office seeker tries to maximize votes. And vote maximization is accomplished by selling yourself, your ideas, and the promise of something new or better for your constituents.[4]

This is where public promises and public goods enter the picture. A prime example is the Great Society program and the War on Poverty inaugurated by the Johnson administrations during the 1960s. Promising to create a society in which no citizen would go without the basic necessities of life or be denied the opportunity of gainful employment, Johnson managed to guide many bills through Congress. By 1968, however, a short five years after Johnson became president, the electorate expressed a desire for a change, sweeping Nixon into the oval office in a landslide.

Many decisions regarding private goods which have external effects also involve governmental regulation. The Food and Drug Administration (FDA), for example, establishes and monitors standards regarding all foods and drugs sold commercially. Because drugs and foodstuffs often contain ingredients which may be harmful, the government may withhold the product from the market until it has had time to conduct tests.

When a new drug is invented, or when a chemical preservative is created for foodstuffs, the FDA goes into action. For example, sodium nitrate is a preservative used in cured meats to prevent the growth of potentially lethal botulism (in ham, salami, corned beef, hot dogs, sausage, etc.). Although the FDA has established permissible limits regarding the use of nitrates, because there is no substitute, it has chosen not to ban nitrates. However, there is evidence that nitrate consumption leads to cancer in laboratory animals.

In its decision not to ban nitrates, the FDA weighed two significant points. First, banning nitrates would mean banning many meats. The FDA evaluated the costs and benefits. Banning nitrates obviously would eliminate the risk of cancer from meat consumption. But would consumers consume enough meat to run such a risk? The FDA said no. Second, the FDA discovered that many consumers are informed of the cancer risk (at least to laboratory animals) and choose to consume the nitrate-treated meats anyway.

Another case involving the FDA concerned the use of saccharin and cyclamates as noncaloric sweeteners in soft drinks and other consumables. The FDA received a Canadian report in 1977 that saccharin had unacceptably high levels of carcinogens and banned the substance in all

---

[4] "Porkbarrel" and "boondoggles" are the unkind descriptions provided to some governmental activities. Subsidies to tobacco growers, tax exemptions for local real estate developers, or a dam here and there to placate local interests are common examples.

foods. But the public was outraged. Dieters, diabetics, and others who wished to control their sugar consumption objected to the ban. Within months, the Congress responded with a moratorium on the FDA ban.

The irony in the FDA ban and subsequent rescission is that the FDA had previously banned cyclamates (in the late 1960s), an ingredient used in artificial sweeteners suspected of causing cancer. When the FDA banned cyclamates, production of saccharin increased substantially. The cyclamate ban actually stimulated increased usage of saccharin, a substance known to cause cancer.

The important point to be made about such regulatory actions is that there is no clear right or wrong answer; making such determinations is fraught with uncertainty. As we have indicated before, it is one thing to marshall evidence which links the use of a substance with cancer. But it is quite another thing to argue that its use should therefore be banned. Other research may show little if any harm from use of the substance, especially if the amount consumed is not excessive. In other words, the decision often comes down to how much damage will be caused, to how many people, and with what degree of certainty. This is where benefit-cost analysis enters the picture.

Benefit-Cost Analysis

Cigarettes are known to cause cancer, heart disease, and many other maladies. Should the government ban cigarettes and other tobaccos? Although it might try to do so, America's experience with Prohibition has taught legislators a few lessons about making widely used substances illegal. Instead of an outright ban, the government has placed excise taxes on tobacco and alcohol. Such taxes raise the price and discourage some consumption, although the primary purpose of the tax is to generate tax revenues. The irony is that the government also subsidizes tobacco growers, which lowers production costs and serves as a direct inducement to raise more tobacco. It seems that lawmakers just can't make up their minds.

The process of calculating costs and benefits is also a routine part of consumers' lives. Should you go to college? Should you return to school to get an MBA? Should you go to the party tonight or study for the economics test? Should you buy or lease an automobile? These and countless other questions often keep us awake at nights calculating costs and benefits.

Benefit-cost analysis is a decision-making tool that estimates all costs and benefits associated with an economic activity.

Benefit-cost analysis is a decision-making tool requiring the estimation of all costs and benefits associated with an economic activity. If the net benefits (total benefits minus total costs) are positive, then it is a good indication that you will be better off by going ahead. However, if the net benefits are negative, then alternatives should be considered. If you are considering whether to return to school, for example, then you know that this may involve giving up your job (and income). Obviously, this is a major cost of your decision. However, you also know that your future and lifetime income may be substantially greater by investing now in more education. What should you do? Regardless of whether the net benefits are positive or negative, you have a rational basis for your decision.

Benefit-cost analysis is easily illustrated graphically. Figure 10–2 shows the marginal benefit *(MB)* and marginal cost *(MC)* curves associated with additional education. **Marginal benefit,** much like marginal utility, is shown as a downward-sloping line. This reflects the idea that additional benefits decline with each additional semester's or year's coursework. **Marginal costs** are upward sloping, reflecting the idea that, over time, each additional semester's or year's coursework will cost more. (Remember that marginal costs include all costs, out-of-pocket plus opportunity costs.) Where the *MB* and *MC* curves intersect determines the optimum amount of education.

Marginal benefit *is the extra benefit received from an additional unit of consumption or production.*

Marginal costs *are the extra costs associated with additional units of consumption or production.*

FIGURE 10–2

Marginal Costs and
Marginal Benefits

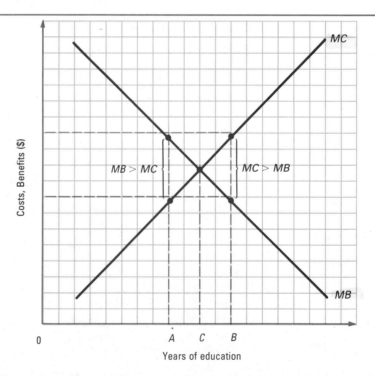

Should you go to college and, if you do, should you go for a master's degree? Benefit-cost analysis helps address this question by identifying all of the relevant costs and benefits associated with the decision to go to school. Marginal benefit (*MB*) is a downward-sloping line, reflecting the fact that with very little education (to the left of point *A*, for example) marginal benefits are very high. Marginal cost is an upward-sloping line, reflecting the idea that at very low levels of education the opportunity cost of going to school is also quite low. Point *C* represents the optimum amount of education, a master's degree.

As Figure 10–2 shows, you will optimize your educational investment at point *C*, representing a master's degree. If you continue your education beyond the master's, the marginal costs exceed the marginal benefits, and net benefits are negative. In other words, in your field of endeavor, education beyond the master's does not produce positive net benefits. What happens if you stop short of obtaining the master's degree? Because marginal benefits exceed marginal costs, you should continue your education.

Benefit-cost analysis is used extensively in private business to ascertain the desirability of one investment activity over another. For example, should a computer firm manufacture its own memory chips or buy them from other businesses? Of course, the private business is interested in obtaining the greatest profit from its operations, regardless of its decision. In the public sector, however, the issue involves the economy as a whole—the welfare of the entire society, not individual economic enterprises.

Although benefit-cost analysis is often used to evaluate private investment decisions, it also has a very important role in public policy decisions. In matters of public policy, such as federal housing, transportation, and the environment, benefit-cost analysis is used to determine whether *society as a whole* will be better off as a result of undertaking a particular project. Much like your economic problem of whether to go to college or to continue working (or some combination), costs and benefits of *public* projects are estimated in a similar fashion. Should the government ban nitrates, cyclamates, and saccharin? Or should it curtail the use of such substances? Should the government require automobile drivers to wear safety belts or automobile companies to install airbags or other passive restraint devices? Should the government pass a law to require insurance for all drivers? For all of these proposed initiatives, if the benefits exceed the costs, the project will be deemed efficient (and perhaps socially desirable—but determined by the electorate in a democracy). If the costs exceed the benefits, the project is not efficient (although it still may be deemed socially desirable).

Because the government does so many things, such as providing public goods and services; redistributing income; and regulating pollution, product safety, and unfair business practices (among other things), benefit-cost analysis has sweeping implications for the public sector. Like private businesses that desire to maximize profits, government officials want to provide those public goods whose benefits exceed the costs. Unlike private business, however, government officials want to do those things which promise the greatest net benefit *to society as a whole*. For example, will a new mass transit system generate benefits (reducing traffic congestion and pollution) in excess of its costs (construction, traffic snarls during construction, property taken out of use, etc.)? Although legislators and Department of Transportation officials may be committed to the social desirability of the project, benefit-cost analysis focuses on the issue of efficiency—the allocation of resources. Regardless of the commitment or so-called social desirability of the project, if the benefit-cost ratio is negative, then alternatives should be investigated.

One of the recurring problems faced by federal and state governments are the related issues of automobile safety and reckless driving. Consider the following CASE-IN-POINT involving the measurement of costs and benefits concerning our driving behavior.

Requiring Safety Devices May Increase Reckless Driving

Two different but related measures are taken by governments to increase automobile safety. One strategy focuses on forcing motorists to drive more safely; the other strategy attempts to make automobiles safer. Let's take each of these in turn.

Will cracking down on speeding motorists, drunk drivers, and other reckless drivers reduce traffic fatalities and make our roads safer? Assume that even tailgaters and speeders calculate costs and benefits of their driving behavior, especially if the expected costs of imprudent driving are quite high. For example, most states charge much higher fines for people who greatly exceed the speed limit. To raise the costs of speeding, imagine a schedule of fines that graduated from $50 to $1,000 for speeding violations, a mandatory driving school, and, for the greatest violators, mandatory license suspension. Under such a system, it is reasonable to predict that drivers will be more careful behind the wheel. They will calculate the costs and benefits of having an accident to themselves and to the other people in the car. They are careful because the costs of being less careful are greater than the benefits that can be achieved. If these statements are reasonable, the reader should agree that one reason for the large volumes of accidents on highways is that the expected cost to the drivers is relatively low. This is simply another application of the law of demand.

The second strategy to reduce fatalities concerns automobile safety. Cars driven without brakes, lights, horns, and so forth, are dangerous. The government thus requires that vehicles are equipped with such braking and warning devices. But what of other safety devices? Are we more safe if safety belts are required? What about passive restraint systems, such as air bags? If we are surrounded by safety devices, will we drive as cautiously? This raises an intriguing behavioral anomaly.

The use of air bags, collapsible bumpers, and other safety devices considerably reduces the probability of death and severe injury from an accident. If the government makes such equipment mandatory, it is reducing the expected cost of an accident (personal injury and property damage) and of reckless driving. Will our driving behavior be the same? Unlikely. Because our vehicles are safer (e.g., collapsible bumpers, passive restraint systems, etc.), we are likely to feel safer and thus drive more recklessly. If this analysis is accurate, the irony is that safety regulations may actually increase the probability of accidents and casualties.

Questions to Consider

1. *If automobile safety devices may actually increase reckless driving, does it follow logically that governments should therefore repeal laws which require such equipment?*

2. *The government can raise the cost of driving recklessly, but it can do little to reduce the benefits of such behavior. For example, how would you behave if you were late for class, work, or an important meeting? How would such situations affect your benefit-cost calculations?*

As we have seen, benefit-cost analysis is a useful tool in identifying the efficiency implications (and even the desirability) of many public goods, public policies, and government regulations. From prisons to highways, from air pollution standards to automobile safety regulations, the government tries to ascertain the costs and benefits of its actions to society as a whole. Of course, since public action itself carries a considerable cost, it is important that governmental intervention be cost effective. The regulatory history of the trucking industry illustrates this quite well.

The Regulation and Deregulation of Trucking

The Period of Regulation. Until 1980, the government closely regulated the trucking industry through the Interstate Commerce Commission (ICC). Created in 1887 with minimal powers, the ICC quickly grew to become a major regulatory agency with jurisdiction over railroad, trucking, and domestic water carriers. But its operations also came under criticism as serving the interests of the regulated far better than the interests of the public at large. In the words of one regulatory scholar,

> The ICC was set up by Congress as an agency of experts to protect and represent the public interest in matters of transportation in interstate commerce. In fact the agency is predominately a forum at which transportation interests divide up the national transportation market.[5]

---

[5] R. Fellmuth, *The Interstate Commerce Commission* (New York: Grossman Publishers, 1970), p. 1. The Interstate Commerce Commission (ICC) was established in 1887 to enforce the Act to Regulate Commerce (enacted in 1887). Although the ICC originally was limited to hearing complaints regarding price discrimination and other alleged violations of railroad owners, by World War I it had became a genuine regulatory body, effectively preventing monopoly pricing over routes that lacked competition. The Motor Carrier Act of 1935 brought motor carriers (trucks) under the ICC's jurisdiction.

Although critics attacked the ICC's rate-setting practices, the primary objection concerned the practice of licensing entry.[6] The ICC had regulated the entry of new trucking firms prior to 1980 by requiring licenses to operate. If a new firm wanted to enter the industry, it had to prove that existing service was inadequate. The result was that very few applications were approved, and rates thus were kept much higher than would have occurred under conditions of open competition. Moreover, specific routes were attached to each trucking license. This practice prevented existing firms from altering routes in response to changes in demand and frequently resulted in empty trucks on backhauls.

Deregulation.   In 1980, Congress passed two bills which deregulated the trucking and railroad industries. With respect to the trucking industry, the Motor Carriers Act accomplished two major changes: (1) loosening entry requirements, and (2) permitting firms more freedom in setting rates. Instead of requiring new firms to prove inadequate service from existing carriers as a condition of entry, the Motor Carriers Act shifted the burden of proof to those objecting to the new license. This greatly relaxed the conditions for entry, resulting in a considerable increase in ICC permits.

Firms were also accorded greater freedom to set their own rates without ICC approval. The new rule permitted trucking firms to increase or decrease their rates by as much as 10 percent without ICC intervention.

What were the costs and benefits of deregulation? Perhaps the most obvious benefit was greater competition, as measured by a greater number of carriers, lower rates, and increased ton-mile service. One clear benefit was the greater ease of entry. Prior to deregulation, applicant firms had to prove inadequate service before the ICC would grant permission to enter the industry. The only other way to gain entry was by purchasing an existing license from an established firm (much like liquor and other licenses are handled in many states). The average price of operating licenses was $398,000 in 1975. After deregulation, the average price was $15,000.[7] Obviously, deregulation turned the valuation of licenses over to the market system, which quickly discounted the value of such licenses.

Although new firms benefited from a relaxation of controls, the financial condition of many firms was damaged by deregulation. And the least

---

[6] The ICC established price floors in trucking, which kept prices considerably higher than would exist without regulation. This practice ostensibly was adopted to protect trucking from so-called unfair competition from the railroads.

[7] T. Gale Moore, "Rail and Trucking Deregulation," in *Regulatory Reform: What Actually Happened,* eds. Leonard W. Weiss and Michael W. Klass (Boston: Little, Brown and Co., 1986), pp. 14–36.

competitive carriers, protected for decades by noncompetitive rates and entry restrictions, went bankrupt.

Just as the Congress has determined that society would be better served with less regulation of transportation (that is, the costs of regulation exceeded its benefits), in other matters of governmental regulation, it is important to examine the alternative policies available to improve the benefit-cost ratio. Because pollution is perhaps the most common application of such policies, we will conclude our discussion of benefit-cost analysis with this example.

POLICY ALTERNATIVES: WHAT CAN BE DONE?

The government has many options available to curtail and otherwise control the amount of pollution. The various alternatives may be viewed along a continuum, as shown in Figure 10–3.

At one extreme, it can nationalize the industry.[8] Although this approach has been taken in Great Britain and other countries, state ownership is an extremely unpopular option in the United States. Another method is to pass laws which prohibit pollution. Like nationalization, this approach also is deemed to be very impractical. A zero level of pollution, or what might be called the *principle of perfection,* is widely regarded as technically impossible and outrageously expensive. At the other extreme of approaches, the government could do nothing whatsoever. Indeed, many government critics claim that there is no clear environmental policy and that the government is doing very little to improve the quality of air and water.

Also shown in Figure 10–3 are the alternative policies actually used by governments at all levels: regulation and market incentives (such as taxes and subsidies). Perhaps the most common strategy is to regulate, that is, establish permissible standards of pollution based upon benefit-cost analysis and identify acceptable equipment to reduce polluting activities. (A similar though less effective strategy is *jawboning*, whereby the president and the responsible regulatory agency try to elicit voluntary compliance, essentially a form of self-regulation.)[9]

---

[8] Nationalization is the formal process by which the government purchases the firms and assumes complete control of the industry. Great Britain has done this in the coal and steel industries, although it has also denationalized each. However, municipal and state governments in the United States do operate gas and electric companies. Governmental ownership, however, would seem to offer few guarantees of a clean environment: the city of Cleveland has been cited as the primary polluter of Lake Erie.

[9] Does jawboning or moral suasion do any good? Even if some respond to the public appeal, doesn't this approach aggravate the free rider problem?

FIGURE 10–3
**Continuum of Pollution
Control Strategies**

National- ization	Outright prohibition	Direct forms of regulation	Market incentives			Do nothing
			Taxes	Subsidies	Pollution licenses	

The figure lays out a continuum of pollution strategies or policies, ranging from nationalization to doing nothing. Regulation (via the *EPA* and other federal agencies) is the most prevalent pollution policy. With regulation, the government sets permissible standards, checks for compliance, and provides enforcement through penalties (fines and public tongue lashings).

Regulation. The Congress established the Environmental Protection Agency (EPA) to provide exactly such a regulatory apparatus. Two pioneer environmental analysts have described this regulatory approach:

> Congress sets broad environmental objectives, often phrased in ambiguous language, and then instructs the EPA to develop and enforce any policies necessary to achieve the goals of the law.[10]

Southern California's smog problem illustrates very well the regulatory process and the use of benefit-cost analysis. During the early 1970s the city of Riverside, California, sued the Environmental Protection Agency (EPA) to make Los Angeles (LA) stop the pollution of the air over Riverside. Smog in the greater LA area was (and is) a serious health hazard, caused chiefly by the very great number of automobiles. To meet the provisions of the federal Clean Air Act of 1970, the EPA estimated that 80 percent of LA's automobiles would have to be barred from the road. Because the automobile is an essential mode of transportation for most LA residents, such a drastic curtailment of automobile usage would have meant the loss of over 400,000 jobs. Such a ban obviously was considered unacceptable, and the EPA entered into a compromise with LA whereby the federal standards were relaxed to a degree. Figure 10–4 helps to illustrate the costs and benefits associated with this case.

Marginal social benefits (MSB) are the additional private and public benefits received from one additional unit of economic activity. *MSB* declines as pollution abatement and the percentage of clean air increase. This inverse relationship reflects the fact that with very dirty air (point *A*), reducing air pollution is extremely urgent and thus the marginal benefits are very high. On the other hand, if pollution abatement has produced very clean air, then the amount of smog is less dangerous, and thus the marginal benefits of further abatement are very low (point *C*). **Marginal social costs (MSC)** reflect the total opportunity costs of clean

Marginal social benefits (MSB) *are the additional private and public benefits received from one additional unit of economic activity.*

Marginal social costs (MSC) *are the total opportunity costs involved in consumption or production of a product or service.*

---

[10] J. J. Seneca and M. K. Taussig, *Environmental Economics*, 3rd ed. (Englewood Cliffs, N.J.: Prentice-Hall, 1984), p. 195.

FIGURE 10–4

Marginal Costs and
Marginal Benefits of
Cleaner Air

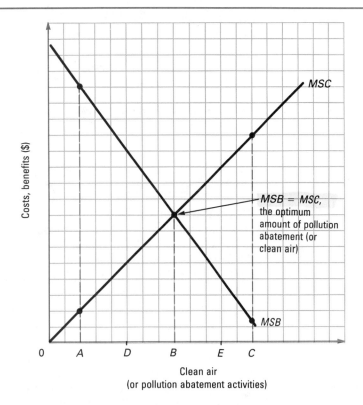

Clean air
(or pollution abatement activities)

Much like our earlier benefit-cost analysis of education, we can also ascertain the net benefits of pollution abatement programs to produce cleaner air. The marginal social benefits *(MSB)* curve shows that with very dirty air, such as point *A*, a very small increase in pollution abatement provides very high marginal benefits. Conversely, with a very clean environment (such as point *C*), any additional pollution abatement will yield very small marginal benefits. The marginal social cost *(MSC)* curve slopes upward. This reflects the fact that with very dirty air (point *A*) it is very cost effective to introduce pollution abatement. However, once the air is much cleaner (point *C*), additional abatement programs are very expensive. The optimum amount of clean air (or pollution abatement) is at point *B* where the *MSC* = *MSB*.

air, private costs plus externalities. The *MSC* increases as pollution abatement increases. Why? When there is very dirty air (point *A*), there are many relatively inexpensive ways to increase the percentage of clean air. However, as abatement programs expand and most efforts have been exhausted, further improvements in air quality will cost increasingly more (point *C*). The socially optimal amount of pollution abatement (or clean air) is obtained at point *B*, where the *MSB* and *MSC* intersect.

THINKING IT THROUGH

If the city lands at point D and remains there, why is this an unsatisfactory level of abatement? What if the pollution authorities push abatement programs to point E? Is there such a thing as too much clean air?

Market Incentives.   Instead of establishing standards of compliance and mandating specific results, most economists prefer to use the pricing mechanism and market incentives to accomplish social objectives. By taxing those activities that generate external costs, such as a chemical plant dumping wastes into a river, and subsidizing others that provide external benefits, such as those who own large tracts of forested land, market prices will reflect the full social costs of production and thus provide a more efficient allocation of resources. To see how this works, let's look at vinyl chloride production.

Many chemical plants manufacture vinyl chloride, a chemical gas used in the production of a variety of plastic products, flooring, and wire insulation. There is positive proof that vinyl chloride is a carcinogen (a cancer-causing agent). Although the EPA has taken actions to regulate usage through a set of standards, production continues. Environmental and consumer groups want stronger action.

What if a tax was imposed on chemical producers of vinyl chloride equal to the estimated external costs? Figure 10–5 illustrates the before and after conditions of the vinyl chloride market. The equilibrium price and quantity before taxation is P_1 and Q_1, respectively. The demand (D_1) or *MSB* (or marginal social benefits) is downward sloping as usual. The two supply curves, S_1 or *MPC* (marginal private costs) and S_2 or *MSC* (marginal social costs) also take their normal shape. (The marginal social costs are the total of private costs plus external costs.) Because vinyl chloride production results in costs to others besides the chemical firm, *MPC* understates the actual social costs of production. If the firm realized its full social costs of production, it would produce at Q_2, where the *MSC* = *MSB*. However, because costs are understated, the firm produces Q_1. The result is overproduction of vinyl chloride $(Q_1 - Q_2)$.

If a tax equal to the external costs is imposed, indicated by the vertical line labeled *tax*, a socially optimum level of production will result (Q_2). The tax raises the firm's costs of production, resulting in higher prices and lower output. Of course, how the burden of the tax falls on producers and consumers depends upon the elasticity of demand.[11]

---

[11] Another market incentive approach favored by economists is to issue licenses to pollute, effectively charging firms for the privilege of polluting. President Bush even wants to permit firms to sell their pollution licenses.

FIGURE 10–5

Taxation to Eliminate
External Costs

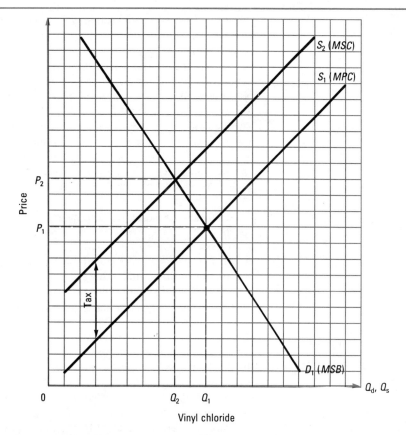

Vinyl chloride

Vinyl chloride is a chemical gas known to cause cancer. As a result, there are major external costs which the chemical producers avoid, shifting these costs to the community as a whole. This is reflected in the two supply or cost curves, S_1 (MPC) and S_2 (MSC). Marginal private cost includes only the firm's internal costs of production; marginal social cost includes both the private costs plus the external costs, the latter measured by the vertical distance between the MPC and the MSC curves. As usual, the demand (or marginal social benefit—MSB) curve is downward sloping. The free market price and output are P_1 and Q_1, respectively. This market outcome conceals the external costs of production reflected by the MSC curve. Government can make the chemical firms internalize these externalities by imposing a tax, indicated by the vertical line labeled "Tax." The result will be higher price and less vinyl chloride production (and less production of those goods containing vinyl chloride).

IMPORTANT TERMS TO REMEMBER		
benefit-cost analysis, p. 275		market failures, p. 268
external benefits, p. 270		marginal social costs, p. 282
external costs, p. 270		marginal social benefits, p. 282
externalities, p. 270		market, p. 266
free rider problem, p. 271		private goods, p. 269
marginal benefit, p. 276		public choice, p. 273
marginal cost, p. 276		public goods, p. 269

CHAPTER SUMMARY

1. Private goods are divisible: they are sold to individuals in the private marketplace and thus are subject to the exclusion principle. They also provide private benefits from consumption. Because public goods cannot readily be sold in the marketplace, they are indivisible and provide collective benefits. Examples of private goods are Big Macs at McDonald's, articles of clothing, and tennis rackets. National defense, public education, and libraries are examples of public goods.

2. The free rider problem occurs whenever individuals or organizations are able to realize the benefits of consumption, yet avoid sharing in the costs of providing the good. Because there is no way of selling public goods like national defense in the marketplace, the government must ensure adequate revenue to pay for the product or service through public taxation and borrowing.

3. Externalities, or so-called *spillover effects,* are the external costs and benefits which arise from private production and consumption. Pollution is a classic example of a negative externality—one which imposes heavy external (social) costs. A positive externality is associated with vaccines and immunizations since there are significant external (social) benefits from the reduced risk of epidemics to society at large.

4. Public choice is the economic analysis of political behavior. Public choice thus involves the study of government's provision of public goods and services and the voting behavior of citizens in their support of and rejection of public goods. Just as consumers vote with their pocketbooks in the marketplace to obtain private goods and services, citizens vote indirectly for public goods by electing those representatives to office who promise to supply certain programs.

5. Benefit-cost analysis is an important tool used by private business and government agencies to identify the relative worth of an economic activity. Although difficult to measure, for government it is an especially useful alternative to outright bans, limitations, and related regulatory standards.

6. In controlling for external costs such as pollution, the government has many possible strategies in its policy arsenal. The most prevalent methods used are direct regulation and market incentives, although outright bans on some products and activities are also commonplace.

DISCUSSION AND REVIEW QUESTIONS

1. Distinguish between private goods and public goods, and explain why there is a free rider problem associated with the supply of public goods.

2. Classify each of the following goods and services as private goods or public goods, and explain your reasoning. If you think that the properties of a good could make it private or public, explain why.

   a. Police protection   **f.** A sunset
   b. A public university   **g.** A "Saturday night special" (handgun)
   c. A private university   **h.** A St. Patrick's Day parade
   d. Polio vaccine   **i.** A private golf course
   e. A personal computer   **j.** A toxic waste dump

3. Evaluate the following argument for reducing pollution:
    "There have been many remedies offered to reduce pollution, but the solution always seems to be 'Let the government do it.' But governments pass laws which are riddled with loopholes, impose petty fines, and consistently grant variances from pollution standards to the greatest culprits. A much better approach is to use the market system and price pollution just like other goods (or bads). In other words, corporations who pollute should pay for the privilege of sending sulfur dioxide into the air and dumping sewage into waterways. By forcing companies to internalize the negative externalities, prices of goods which entail considerable spillover effects would be higher. Consumers would thus buy less of these goods, companies would seek ways to reduce such costs, and the environment would be cleaner. Moreover, only by getting the government out of the pollution control business can we eliminate the politics of pollution."

4. When you vote for a candidate for public office, do you generally "vote your pocketbook"—that is, view the goods and services which the candidate promises to deliver in terms of your economic self-interest? Do you also consider the candidate's qualifications for office, such as knowledge of public affairs, experience in public office, and voting records?

5. How is your use of aerosol spray cans (paint, deodorant, etc.) an example of pollution and the free rider problem?

6. In early 1989, many newspapers headlined a tragic story regarding Florida's overcrowded prisons. A second-degree felon was released from a Florida prison with two thirds of his sentence remaining. On the same day, eight men were sentenced to the same prison for writing bad checks. A few weeks later, the paroled felon shot two Miami policemen.

    One of Florida Governor Martinez's economic advisors proposed a novel solution for Florida's overcrowded prisons. Instead of building more prisons, the advisor suggested allocating prison space to courts based on the crime rates in the court jurisdictions. This would enable judges to control how prisons are used and to determine who should go to prison and who should receive some other kind of punishment.

    This proposed allocation system implies that, if prison capacity is unchanged, only the most serious offenders will serve time in prison. How does this proposal solve the problem of overcrowded prisons? Do you think that this market approach to sentencing offers a more rational use of Florida's prison space?

7. Using benefit-cost analysis, explain why there is congestion on highways.

8. The chief benefit of leaded gasoline is a cheap boost to the octane rating (the antiknock properties of gasoline). But the external costs are considerably greater. Leaded gasoline causes lead poisoning which leads to mental impairment (especially in children) and very high costs of treatment and care. In response to overwhelming evidence, President Reagan executed an executive order in 1984, which called for the ultimate elimination of lead in gasoline. The ban of lead in gasoline is expected to reduce by 90 percent the level of lead in the environment by 1992. Explain how a tax on leaded gasoline might have accomplished a similar outcome.

A BRIEF LOOK AHEAD

This chapter closes our journey through microeconomics and opens the door to another passage. In the next nine chapters you will venture into the world of the macroeconomy.

Have you ever tried to do a jigsaw puzzle, make a gourmet dinner, or build a model airplane? Micro is to macro as pieces of the puzzle are to the completed puzzle, as ingredients of the dinner are to the finished product, and as the parts of the airplane are to the fully constructed model. Rather than concentrating on microeconomics, the behavior of individual business owner-managers, consumers, and workers, from here on we will look at the broad picture. We will shift our focus from how the individual consumer makes decisions to the expenditure patterns for all consumer households. Instead of studying the pricing and output decisions of single firms, we will examine the rate of inflation and the gross national product. And rather than asking how many workers a single firm will hire, we will concentrate on employment and unemployment for the entire economy.

III

Macroeconomics

The Macroeconomy: Goals and Measures of Economic Activity

Rygiel Studio

If asking the right questions is at least as important as getting the right answer, we have plenty of questions to guide us in this pivotal chapter. For starters, as we posed at the end of the last chapter, how do the micro pieces relate to the macro whole? How do the millions of separate production and consumption decisions of households and businesses blend into a coherent macroeconomic picture? What happens when economic activity slows down? What exactly is a recession? What causes a downturn in economic activity, and how can we tell if an economic slump is brewing? What signs indicate a weak or a strong economy over the next few months? If unemployment rises by a fraction of a percent, does this foretell an economic downturn? What causes the economy to recover from a recession?

These are some of the principal questions guiding us during our initial macroeconomic journey. As we address these questions and get some answers and directions, we will have more insight into the nature of the boom and bust patterns of the U.S. economy.

After completion of this chapter, you should be able to do the following:

1. Define inflation and describe how the consumer price index is used to measure the change in the price level.

2. Define and describe how the unemployment rate is calculated.

3. Define and describe the macroeconomic goals specified in the Employment Act of 1946.

4. Define, describe, and explain the expansion and contraction phases of the business cycle (recovery, peak, recession, and trough stages).

5. Identify the economic indicators which may signal an approaching recession.

6. Distinguish among leading, coincident, and lagging economic indicators.

The Roller-Coaster Economy

The path of the economy's performance often looks like a roller coaster. The stock market turns down, business inventories rise, net exports decline, employment increases, the help wanted index dips, and on and on. Such indicators are the signs we look to for clues about the future performance of the economy. Even to economists it's pretty confusing, es-

'There's Only One Economic Indicator I Go By'

© 1980, Engelhardt in the *St. Louis Post-Dispatch*. Reprinted with permission.

pecially since the key indicators often move in opposite directions. Some move up, some down, and others remain unchanged. What does it all mean?

As the cartoon character's lament suggests, when you're out of work or when inflation eats up your budget, you don't need charts and graphs to tell you that you're experiencing economic distress.

Of course, as the fallacy of composition tells us, what is true for the individual is not necessarily true for the economy. While millions of individuals experience extreme hardships, the macroeconomy may be perking right along. But somehow, knowledge of the economy's fine performance is small consolation to someone who was laid off and can't find work. And when the economy does go into its periodic slumps, it translates into human misery. As a very old and perverse joke goes, when your neighbor loses his or her job, it's a recession; when you get laid off, it's a depression.

Inflation and unemployment are vital economic signs for all of us. Perhaps more than any other indicators, these two measures of economic conditions are watched very closely. Because they are reflections of our general macroeconomic health, and because they are viewed by many as harbingers of the future, we begin our discussion of economic fluctuations with these important measures of economic activity.

INFLATION: WHAT IS IT AND HOW IS IT MEASURED?

Inflation *is a rise in the general level of prices on all goods and services or on a representative sample of goods.*

All of us have read headlines such as "Coffee Prices Soar and Inflation Surges." But how often do you hear that inflation occurs when the prices of lettuce or videodisks increase? Although higher prices on individual products and services certainly contribute to inflation, they do not by themselves constitute inflation. **Inflation** is defined as a rise in the *general level* of prices (on all goods and services or on a representative sample of goods).

What happens when there is an inflation? We know that, other things being equal, the dollar buys less when prices rise. In other words, common sense tells us that our incomes just do not go as far. Adding a little mathematics to our common sense will help us get a better understanding of this process.

Price Indexes

Whenever we want to measure degrees of change from one period to another, index numbers are typically used. An index number helps measure how a variable changes over time, such as raw material inventory, U.S. exports to Canada, and consumer prices. Inflation is measured by a **price index,** a ratio of prices in the current year to prices in the base year. The resulting number is then multiplied by 100 in order to express it as a percentage. This means that the price index in the base year is always 100 since the current year price and the base year price are the same. (The term *current year* refers to any year for which the index is calculated and not necessarily the calendar year at this moment; thus the current year could be 1960, 1990, or any other year.)

Let's construct a price index for a single product—gasoline. The first thing to do is get the data: record the price per gallon of regular unleaded gasoline at specific intervals (weekly or monthly). Next, decide on the base period, January 1, 1990, for example. If this base price per gallon is 84 cents, and the price on May 1, 1990, is 89 cents, dividing the current price 89 cents by the base price 84 cents will yield the index number, 1.0595. Then, multiply the number times 100 to express the index as a percentage. Rounding to a whole number, we arrive at a price index of 106. This means that gasoline prices have risen 6 percent above the base period price. Although this is a lot of work to compare only two prices for an individual product, it has great value in more complex calculations.

Now that we have a price index, we can return to the question of the dollar's worth. Suppose that the price index on all goods increases from 100 to 200. What will happen to the value of the dollar? Because the price level doubled, the dollar is worth half as much, or 50 cents. Let's try another. What if the price index increases from 100 to 400? The dollar is worth 25 cents (one fourth its base value) because the price level quadrupled. What if the price index decreases from 100 to 50? Here the dollar doubles in value to $2 because the price level fell by 50 percent. So far all of this is good old-fashioned common sense. But what happens to the value of the dollar if the price index increases from 100 to 172? The method to compute the dollar's worth involves dividing 100 by the price index (expressed as a formula, $V = 100/PI$); $100/172 = \$.58$. Although you may not have realized it, this formula is the mathematical equivalent of the intuitive process we used in reaching the previous solutions.[1]

We know that inflation erodes the value of the dollar, but how can we measure the degree of price changes? In the next section, we turn to the most widely used measure of inflation, the consumer price index.

---

[1] This idea was borrowed from Ralph T. Byrns and Gerald W. Stone, *Great Ideas for Teaching Economics,* 3rd ed. (Glenview, Ill.: Scott, Foresman, 1987), p. 100.

The Consumer Price Index

"Consumer Price Index Tops 300," "The CPI Shows Smallest Gain in Five Years," "CPI Increases at a 4% Annual Clip"—all over the country, such news makes the headlines nearly every month. We begin our study of inflation measures with something that you already know something about—the consumer price index.

Consumer Price Index (CPI) *is a measure of the average change in the prices paid by urban consumers for a fixed market basket of goods and services.*

The Consumer Price Index (CPI). The **consumer price index (CPI)** is a measure of the average change in the price paid by urban consumers for a fixed market basket of goods and services. Many employers, including the government, use the CPI to adjust wages and salaries for inflation. For example, the Postal Service workers' union has a cost-of-living-allowance (COLA) clause in the contract that calls for an automatic adjustment (upward only) equal to the percentage change in the CPI. Many industrial unions have similar inflation protection, and, depending upon the political climate, social security benefits are often CPI adjusted.

The Bureau of Labor Statistics (BLS) is responsible for compiling this important measure of inflation. Since the early 1980s the BLS has prepared two versions of the CPI, one for all urban household units and one for all wage and clerical workers. Because the urban CPI measure represents about 80 percent of the nation's household units, and the wage and clerical CPI measure covers less than 40 percent of consumer units, we will use the urban CPI. Also, effective February 1988, the BLS began publishing the CPI using an updated base year. Instead of using 1967, a fine year except for the fact that most people have forgotten prices paid more than 20 years ago, the BLS now uses a three-year average as the base year (1982 to 1984). The BLS selects a three-year average because it thinks that, for the time period in question, an average of several years better represents price movements than does any single year. The last multiple-year average base year index was 1957 to 1959.

Because of the rich diversity and number of products on the market, the BLS classifies consumer purchases into seven categories and then identifies a market basket of 364 items. Each item in the basket is weighted so that it is representative of consumer expenditure patterns. Shoppers from the BLS price the goods and services in the basket each month at over 21,000 establishments in 91 urban areas, and the current prices are then compared to the base year prices in order to calculate the overall CPI. Table 11–1 illustrates the price indexes for all consumers and for each product/service category.[2]

---

[2] The categories are Food and beverages, Housing, Apparel and upkeep, Transportation, Medical Care, Entertainment, and Other goods and services. Although the vast

TABLE 11–1		November 1988	Percent change 1987–88
Consumer Price Index, November 1988 (1982–1984 = 100)	All items	120.3	5.90
	Food and beverages	120.3	5.90
	Housing	119.9	4.99
	Apparel and upkeep	119.9	13.22
	Transportation	110.7	8.21
	Medical care	141.8	16.23
	Entertainment	122.2	9.50
	Other goods and services	141.0	16.14

The CPI is figured by pricing 364 representative items in a market basket every month. With a base year of 100, the index permits us to quickly calculate the percentage difference between the current period and the base year. For example, although all items cost 20.3 percent more in November of 1988 compared to the base year, the prices of medical care increased by 41.8 percent. This means that if a physician's service cost $100 in 1982–84, its average price was $141.80 in 1988. If you earned an average of $2,500 in the base year, how much would you need to earn in 1988 in order to maintain your purchasing power? Since the CPI rose by a factor of 1.203, multiplying $2,500 times 1.203 gives us the monthly income of $3,007.50—just to stay even with your base year income.

SOURCE: Bureau of Labor Statistics, *Monthly Labor Review* 112, no. 1 (Washington, D.C.: U.S. Government Printing Office, January 1989), Table 30, p. 105.

The Price Level versus Relative Prices.   As you can tell from the table, the 1988 cost of living increased by 20.3 percent over the base year period (1982 to 1984). Of course, there is considerable variation in price changes across the economy. This illustrates the important difference between inflation, which measures the change in the average price level, and changes in **relative prices,** the price of one item in comparison to the average prices of all goods. For example, relative to all other goods in the base year, the price of medical care increased by nearly 42 percent, while transportation prices increased only minimally over this period.

Relative prices *are comparisons of a product price to the average prices of all goods.*

Weakness of the CPI.   Any statistical measure is subject to inherent shortcomings, and the CPI is no exception. There are three specific weaknesses: First, it is important to avoid making generalizations based

majority of items are excluded, the market basket is very representative of urban consumer expenditures. Included among the items are such things as women's suits, men's shirts, watches, physicians' and dental services, coffee, milk, ground beef, new and used cars, gasoline, newspapers, magazines, toys, and admissions (to entertainment events). The market basket is adjusted periodically (usually every 10 years or so) and the last revision occurred in 1987. It is based on consumer expenditures in the 1982–84 period. Periodic revisions of the expenditure weights are necessary so that the CPI reflects changes in prices and demographics. For example, the retired population is increasing faster than any other age group, and this has a dramatic effect on items such as entertainment and medical care.

upon the CPI. Although the Consumer Price Index measures how the average price level changes, it consists of only 364 items purchased by moderate-income urban households. The CPI thus does not accurately account for the price changes on goods purchased by rural or low- and upper-income Americans. Second, because of changes in consumer tastes and preferences, demographic patterns, and prices of substitute and complementary goods, the expenditure weights change over time. If the weights are not changed frequently, then the index becomes less reliable. For example, as a result of the surge in gasoline prices following OPEC's restriction of oil supplies, Americans switched to smaller, more fuel-efficient cars, formed car pools, and took shorter vacations. Even though we spent less of our budgets on gasoline, the expenditure weights did not change for several years. The CPI thus overstated the actual cost of living.

A third shortcoming occurs because quality changes in the products and services we buy are not easily captured by the index. Although we pay more for medical care today, for example, some of the higher price is related to a higher quality of medical care. The same may be true for automobiles and tires. However, because the CPI accounts only for price variations, it overstates the actual cost of living.

These weaknesses notwithstanding, the value of the CPI and other price indexes is that we can quickly determine the degree of price level changes. Since the CPI is a percentage value, we know that an index of 120.3 means that prices in November 1988 were 20.3 percent higher on the average than the base year (1982 to 1984 = 100). Translated into more concrete terms, if you paid an average of $100 for a vacation in the base year period, you would pay approximately $120 in 1988—20 percent more.

Your take-home pay is a nominal figure (no pun intended). Since what and how much you can buy is also governed by the prices you pay, it is your *real income* that is important. To keep things simple, assume that you started working in 1983, earning $2,000 a month. (We also assume that the price index for 1983 equals 100.) Over the years, you have done well, changing jobs to take advantage of special opportunities. Your 1988 salary is $3,000 a month. You know that you do not have 50 percent more purchasing power, so how do you stand? In order to determine your 1988 real earnings, divide your nominal salary ($3,000) by your personal CPI (120.3) and multiply times 100. The resulting real income is $2,485, just 24.25 percent higher than your 1983 income. Although your real income is higher, inflation eroded more than half of your nominal income. Such calculations can be a depressing exercise.

The CPI numbers can also be used to compute rates of inflation. The technique is similar for any rate of change calculation and involves two simple steps: First, subtract the prior year value from the current year value. Second, divide the difference by the prior year value. Here is the formula:

$$\text{Rate of inflation} = \frac{CPI_{cy} - CPI_{py}}{CPI_{py}}$$

where

cy = current year, and

py = prior year.

Using actual data for November of each year, the CPI was 113.6 in 1987 and 120.3 in 1988. Subtracting 113.6 from 120.3, we get 6.7. Then, dividing 6.7 by 113.6, we calculate the rate of inflation from 1987 to 1988, 5.9 percent. Knowing the rate of consumer price inflation (for moderate-income Americans), you can then subtract this inflation rate from your percentage increase in earnings to determine your real increase in wage or salary. For example, if you got a 5 percent increase in salary in 1988, your purchasing power actually declined by 0.9 percent.

Clearly, inflation is an important measure of economic activity. Sustained increases in the price level can not only erode one's real income but, because the inflation experience affects our expectations, it can also distort normal decison making. For example, if you expect inflation to continue, will you postpone that long-planned-for winter vacation to the Virgin Islands, or will you act now before the price level rises again?

Like inflation, jobless statistics get national headlines every month. In the next section, we examine this important measure of economic activity: how the statistics are compiled and what they mean.

COUNTING THE EMPLOYED AND UNEMPLOYED

Each month the Bureau of Labor Statistics (BLS) and the Bureau of the Census jointly conduct a survey of 55,800 U.S. households. Representative of the U.S. population 16 years of age and older, the sample gathers information about the employment status of household members. In addition to learning whether household members are working, looking for work, discouraged, or not in the labor force, the survey identifies job type and industry affiliation, length of service (or unemployment), and assorted demographic information.

Who gets counted among the employed? The unemployed? In compiling the unemployment statistics that you read about each month, the BLS must carefully define each population group that it is measuring. To be counted as **employed,** the household member must be at least 16 years of age and must have worked at least one hour for pay during the survey week or at least 15 hours (without pay) in a family business. Also included as employed are those who are temporarily absent from their regular jobs because of illness, vacation, industrial dispute (e.g., strike),

Employed *are all people 16 years of age or older who have worked at least one hour for pay during the survey week or at least 15 hours without pay in a family business.*

Unemployed *are those who do not have a job but are actively seeking work.*

or similar reasons. This means that all part-time, temporary workers, even if they want full-time work, are counted among the fully employed. To be counted as **unemployed,** one must not have a job, but actively be seeking work. (Although anyone can say that they are looking for work, in order to qualify for federal and state welfare assistance, one must be registered at the state's employment office, on a list at a union hiring hall, or otherwise demonstrate that a serious job search is being undertaken.) Also unemployed are those who are waiting to be recalled from temporary layoff and people waiting to start a new job within the next 30 days (and not in school).

Civilian labor force (CLF) *consists of the total number of employed and unemployed, excluding resident armed forces.*

Unemployment rate *is determined by dividing the number of unemployed by the civilian or total labor force.*

The total number employed and unemployed make up the labor force. In November of 1988, there were 124.5 million people in the labor force, 117.9 million employed and 6.6 million unemployed. (Note: This data includes the armed forces. Excluding the armed forces produces another category called the **civilian labor force**—civilian employment plus unemployment.) To determine the total **unemployment rate,** the BLS divides the number of unemployed by the labor force; thus, the unemployment rate in November 1988 was 5.3 percent (6.6 million unemployed divided by the 124.5 million people in the labor force). This figure, splashed all over the headlines of our newspapers each month, is closely monitored by Washington's policymakers, Wall Street investors, and businesses that try to determine the direction of the economy in the months ahead. With the exception of the rate of inflation, the unemployment rate is probably the single most watched statistic emanating from Washington.

THINKING IT THROUGH

Unemployment statistics are important economic indicators. But sometimes they may be misleading. Is it possible for the unemployment rate to increase even if no one loses jobs and more people are working?

All those who are neither working nor looking for work are lumped into a category called *not in the labor force*. Table 11–2 summarizes these and other labor force numbers. Starting at the top, the 1987 U.S. population stood at 243.8 million. Subtracting the *institutional population* (those in school, prisons, mental hospitals, and other institutions) from the total population determines the *noninstitutional adult population* (184.5 million). This latter population "comprises all persons 16 years of age and older who are not inmates of penal or mental institutions, sanitariums, or homes for the aged, infirm, or needy, and members of

TABLE 11–2

Labor Force Composition, 1987

Total population	243,773,000
Less: Institutional population	59,283,000
Equals: Noninstitutional adult population	184,490,000
Less: Not in labor force	62,888,000
Equals: Labor force	121,602,000
Less: Resident armed forces	1,737,000
Equals: Civilian labor force	119,865,000
Civilian employed	112,440,000
Civilian unemployed	7,425,000
Civilian unemployment rate	6.2%
Unemployment rate, including the armed forces	6.1%
Labor force participation rate	65.9%

Definitions:
a. The noninstitutional population includes the resident armed forces.
b. The civilian labor force (CLF) consists of the noninstitutional adult population that is employed and unemployed.
c. All those not working nor looking for work are classified as not in the labor force.
d. The civilian unemployment rate is computed by dividing the unemployed by the civilian labor force (excluding the resident armed forces).
e. If the resident military population is added to the labor force, dividing total civilian unemployment by the labor force gives us a total unemployment rate of 6.2 percent. [Note that this calculation assumes that there is zero unemployment in the armed forces.]
f. The labor force participation rate is calculated by dividing the labor force by the noninstitutional adult population.

SOURCE: *Economic Report of the President* (Washington D.C.: Superintendent of Documents, 1989), Table B-32, p. 344.; *Monthly Labor Review* (Washington D.C.: Superintendent of Documents, February 1988), Table 4, p. 86.

the armed forces stationed in the United States."[3] Subtracting the 62.9 million not in the labor force determines the labor force, 121.6 million in 1987. Most of those not in the labor force voluntarily choose not to work, a category the Census Bureau calls "at home" or "voluntarily idle," such as people who are retired and those who are attending school but not working. Also not in the labor force are those who are unable to work because of a long-term illness. Finally, some of the so-called *voluntarily idle* group are **discouraged workers,** people who have dropped out of the labor market because they no longer believe that they will find employment. Indeed, recent estimates indicate that approximately one million people are discouraged workers who, for a complex of reasons, have given up on the job search.

Because economic activity is largely influenced by efforts to manage the performance of the economy, it is important to understand the nation's economic goals. In the next section, we take a brief look at the Great Depression, post-World War II economic history and the macroeconomic goals that have guided administrations since 1946.

Discouraged workers *believe that they cannot find jobs and thus drop out of the labor force.*

[3] *Monthly Labor Review* 112, no. 3 (January 1988), p. 76.

MACROECONOMIC GOALS

Our modern macroeconomic dilemma is how to sustain full employment without inflation. In order to understand this problem, it is helpful to examine a few important economic events and issues of the post–World War II period.

The Last 50 Years: A Brief Economic History

The Great Depression! More than 10 years of economic slump came to an abrupt end with our entry into World War II. Thousands of idle and underutilized factories were shifted into full-time production. Millions of the unemployed joined the war effort, if not as new recruits, then in the new civilian army. Unemployment fell from 14.6 percent in 1940 to 4.7 percent in 1942 and to 1.2 percent in 1944, and real GNP (in 1982 dollars) nearly doubled, from $772 billion in 1940 to $1,380 billion in 1944.

With the end of World War II came the pleasant but difficult job of demobilization—returning to a peacetime economy. Millions of returning soldiers resumed their old jobs, many displacing the women who had joined the labor force in the war effort. As factories resumed civilian production, many businesses found a tremendous pent-up demand for goods and services that were unavailable during the war. Car production ceased entirely in 1944, for example, in order that all steel output could be allocated to military items. As the increased demand for goods sent prices skyward, the rate of inflation exceeded 19 percent in 1946. This so-called *bottleneck inflation* gradually cooled off as supply caught up to demand.

With the experience of massive unemployment, war, and rampant inflation behind them, members of Congress took decisive action to make the federal government responsible for economic stabilization. Resolved that a repeat of the 1930s should not be permitted, the Congress enacted the nation's first set of economic goals in the **Employment Act of 1946.** The law said that "it is the continuing responsibility of the Federal Government to use all practical means . . . to promote maximum employment, production, and purchasing power." Although no numerical targets were attached to the goals, economists and politicians translated the language into more specific objectives. By 1960, four distinct objectives were identified:

1. *Full employment*—Full employment describes that percentage of the labor force holding jobs which is consistent with stable prices, originally thought to be 96 percent. It does not mean 100 percent because millions of people voluntarily quit their jobs in order to seek new employment. Moreover, rather than stating the objective as a percentage of the labor force that is working, the goal is expressed as the percentage

Employment Act of 1946 *made the federal government responsible for designing economic policies to pursue and maintain full employment and price stability.*

of unemployment—4 percent. Reaching this goal in the last 20 years has proven to be so elusive that many economists think that 6 percent unemployment is a more practical noninflationary target. (More will be said about this a little later.)

2. *Price stability*—Although some inflation is indicative of rising demand and a healthy economy, too much inflation reduces purchasing power, causes a decline in exports, and generally creates an unfavorable climate of uncertainty. The general consensus today is that inflation should be held to approximately 3 percent (as measured by the price index for *all* goods and services).

3. *Economic growth*—If a nation is to enjoy a higher standard of living, economists emphasize the importance of a steady increase in production capacity and real GNP generally is used as the indicator of such performance. In order to sustain a fully employed economy, it is generally recognized that real GNP must grow by 3 to 5 percent each year.

4. *Balance of payments*—It is also considered desirable that the United States strive to balance its account with the rest of the world. In other words, the total receipts from abroad (from exports of goods and services, interest on loans, gold flows, etc.) should roughly equal the total outflows of dollars for imports, interest on foreign-held debt, and other transactions.

The legislation also created two research-advisory bodies, the Council of Economic Advisors (CEA) and the Joint Economic Committee of Congress (JECC). Consisting of a chairman and two associates, and a staff of research assistants, the CEA advises the president on economic issues and problems. The JECC, a committee consisting of an equal number of senators and representatives, holds hearings, commissions studies, and issues recommendations on a wide range of economic policy problems.

The Employment Act of 1946 was a major departure from the initial draft legislation. The original bill, entitled the Full Employment Act of 1945, would have required the president to use a method called *compensatory finance* to stabilize the economy. The formula required the president to submit a forecast of the output necessary to generate full employment. If the economy's actual output was less than the full employment output, the president was required to submit legislation to run a budget deficit large enough to raise output to the projected full employment level. Conversely, if actual GNP exceeded the projected full employment GNP, the president was required to run a budget surplus in order to bring actual output in line with the full employment level.

This interventionist formula of compensatory finance was reflected in the bill's strong philosophy. The act said, "All Americans . . . are entitled to an opportunity for useful, remunerative, and full-time employment. . . . [T]he Federal Government has the responsibility to assure continuing full employment, that is, the existence at all times of sufficient employment opportunities for all Americans."[4]

The congressional debates on the proposed legislation revealed three main objections. First, most legislators thought that it was impossible to sustain full employment without running the risk of excessive inflation. They also argued that it was impossible to produce accurate forecasts of full employment output. The third and most vociferous objection had to do with the broad statement of philosophy. Opponents argued that it was socialistic and would lead people to expect too much from the government. The bill's detractors won. The idea of employment as an entitlement and the concept of compensatory finance were deleted.

The extent to which the federal government should be the manager of the macroeconomy has resurfaced from time to time. The following CASE-IN-POINT highlights the most recent effort to amend the Employment Act.

CASE
▪ IN ▪
POINT

Some Ideas Die Hard

Some ideas die hard, especially when economic conditions provide fertile ground for reconsideration.

By historical standards, unemployment remained relatively low in the years after the passage of the Employment Act. Indeed, the unemployment rate averaged 4.6 percent from 1950 to 1970, very close to the 4.5 percent average for the 30-year period preceding the Depression. In the 1970s, however, unemployment began to rise, reaching more than 8.5 percent in 1975. In 1976, 30 years after the passage of the Employment Act, Senator Hubert Humphrey and Representative Augustus Hawkins resurrected the original 1945 bill and introduced the Full Employment and Balanced Growth Bill of 1976.

Like its predecessor, it suffered a similar unwelcome in the Congress. After two years of debate, in 1978, Congress passed and President Carter signed the bill—a watered-down reaffirmation of the goals of the Employment Act. Two potentially strong provisions—one setting a goal of achieving 3 percent unemployment for those aged 20 and over by 1983, the other setting an inflation goal of 3 percent by 1983 and 0 percent by 1988—were thoroughly emasculated by a subsequent provision allowing the president to modify the timetables for achieving these goals. What began as an effort to make the government a practitioner of compensatory finance ended by including a provision that encourages the government to adopt a fiscal policy that would reduce federal spending as a percent of GNP.

---

[4] U.S. Senate, Hearings before a Subcommittee of the Committee on Banking and Currency, *Full Employment Act of 1945*, 79th Congress, 1st sess., September 1945, Government Printing Office.

Questions to Consider

1. Do you think that specific quantitative goals, such as a 3 percent unemployment rate, should be legislated? Why or why not?

2. Evaluate the following debate between Senator Freemarket and Senator Intervention. Senator Intervention: "The only way to sustain high employment in the long run is to adopt legislation which requires the federal (state and local) government to guarantee public employment to everyone willing and able to work. In other words, employment should become a right of citizenship."
Senator Freemarket: "A job for everyone! Indeed! Guaranteed employment is actually a guarantee of bureaucratic nightmares. Forcing the government to create jobs and then fill them with the unemployed is a perfect recipe for inefficiency and inflation. What's more, how are we going to pay for this? With more taxes or bigger government deficits? No, thank you."

It is important to point out that the Employment Act is silent about how its objectives are to be fulfilled. Indeed, the language of the act is intentionally vague, permitting each administration to adopt policies that it deems appropriate for the current economic climate. There are, however, inherent contradictions within the broad outlines of the objectives. For example, the pursuit of full employment may trigger unacceptably high rates of inflation. Subsequent efforts to cool inflation may, in turn, cause higher than desirable levels of unemployment. Although full employment and economic growth are compatible, as are price stability and a balance of payments, the experience of the last 50 years has taught us that the simultaneous attainment of all four objectives is virtually impossible.

What are the signs of change? What is a recession? A depression? How do we get into economic tailspins? Perhaps even more perplexing, how do we sustain prosperity? We will begin our investigation of these fascinating questions by studying the business cycle.

ECONOMIC FLUCTUATIONS: PATTERNS AND TRENDS

*A **business cycle** is the recurring but irregular wavelike movement of the economy over a period of time.*

A **business cycle** is the recurring but irregular wavelike movement of the economy over a period of time. It is measured by real GNP, indexes of industrial production, or some composite index. As illustrated in Figure 11–1, every cycle consists of two distinct expansion and contraction waves, and these are further broken down into four stages: recession, trough, recovery, and peak. Although these are relatively commonsense terms, trying to define these stages in great detail, to quote an anony-

FIGURE 11-1

The Business Cycle

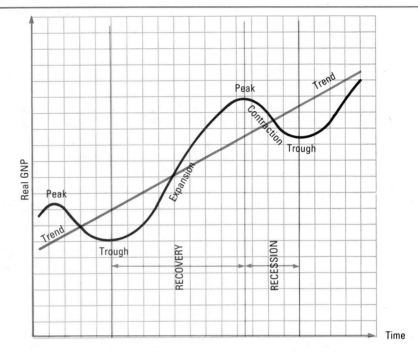

The business cycle is a periodic, recurring but irregular expansion and contraction of economic activity. The length of a cycle is measured from peak to peak or from trough to trough. Each cycle consists of four stages: recession, trough, recovery, and peak. The trend line smoothes out the fluctuations and shows the economy's overall expansion.

mous source, is like describing a martini. In other words, you have to experience them to really know them. However, knowledge does not absolutely require personal experience (the so-called *school of hard knocks*), so it behooves us to make a stab at defining and describing these fluctuations.

Business Cycle Stages

Deciding where to begin is one of the problems faced in describing any dynamic process. Hence we begin arbitrarily with expansion. Economic **expansion** consists of a period of increasing economic activity, illustrated in Figure 11–1 as the upward sloping portion of the curve. Real GNP and employment increase, and the stock market generally posts annual gains. Expansion consists of two stages: recovery and the peak. The **recovery** stage is a period of economic growth and job formation. Indeed, during the early stages of recovery, economic growth and employment gains are usually quite rapid. This is represented in Figure 11–1 as the steepest slope of the curve. (The average length of the eight

Expansion *consists of a period of increasing economic activity.*

Recovery *stage is a period of economic growth and job formation.*

Peak *of a business cycle is a point where real GNP reaches a maximum.*

Contraction *is a period of declining economic activity.*

Recession *is a period of declining real GNP over a period of at least six months.*

Trough *is the bottom of the contraction, where real GNP reaches its lowest level before turning upward in the next expansion.*

Depression *is a period of prolonged and deep unemployment and decreasing real GNP.*

Composite index of 12 leading indicators *is a series of business cycle signals which typically reach their cyclical peaks and troughs earlier than the corresponding turns of the business cycle.*

expansions from 1945 to 1983 is 45 months.) As the expansion wears on, the economy reaches its **peak**—a point where real GNP finally tops out. During this stage, there are signs of a downturn brewing, such as excessive inventory accumulation (higher-than-normal inventory to sales ratios), growing inflationary pressure, and a slowing of consumer and investment spending.

Economic **contraction** is a period of declining economic activity, shown as the downward sloping portion of the curve in Figure 11–1. The **recession** stage is a period of declining real GNP over a period of at least six months, characterized by increasing unemployment, declining real GNP, and usually a slowing of inflation. (Recessions have averaged 11 months in duration in the post–World War II period.) The **trough** stage is the bottom of the contraction, where real GNP stops declining (reaches its lowest level) before turning upward in the next expansion. Although there is no widely accepted definition of **depression,** if a recession lasts more than a year and unemployment remains at a stubbornly high level (more than 10 percent), the recession then might be officially called a depression.[5] Actually, there is considerable political pressure in recent history to avoid labeling a severe economic slump a depression. Certainly no president wants his administration associated with a depression.

Figure 11–2, a chart based upon data prepared by the Bureau of Economic Analysis (BEA, a division of the Department of Commerce), illustrates the actual course of the U.S. economy from 1968 to 1988. The BEA conducts business cycle research by collecting data on current economic conditions and reporting the data in several series of cyclical indicators. These economic time series consist of three main indexes: leading, coincident, and lagging.

The first index in Figure 11–2 is the **composite index of 12 leading indicators,** series which typically reach their cyclical peaks and troughs earlier than the corresponding turns of the business cycle. The leading index is the most watched measure because it anticipates future economic activity. It consists of such indicators as the average workweek in manufacturing, net business formations (formations less failures), manufacturers' new orders of consumer goods and materials, contracts and orders for plant and equipment, building permits, and Standard & Poor's Index of 500 industrial common stock prices. As we can see in the figure, the index turns down before each recession stage.

---

[5] The Great Depression lasted nearly a decade, and the economy experienced a full cycle of expansion and contraction within the 10-year slump. The U.S. economy has experienced eight cycles since 1945. Recessions range in duration from 6 to 16 months, with an 11-month average; expansions range in duration from 12 to 106 months, with an average length of 45 months.

FIGURE 11–2 Charting the Business Cycle with Economic Indicators

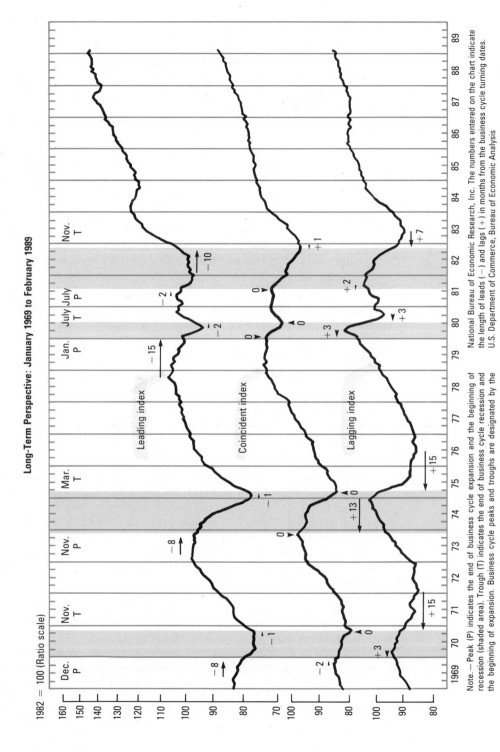

Long-Term Perspective: January 1969 to February 1989

1982 = 100 (Ratio scale)

Note.— Peak (P) indicates the end of business cycle expansion and the beginning of recession (shaded area). Trough (T) indicates the end of business cycle recession and the beginning of expansion. Business cycle peaks and troughs are designated by the National Bureau of Economic Research, Inc. The numbers entered on the chart indicate the length of leads (−) and lags (+) in months from the business cycle turning dates.
U.S. Department of Commerce, Bureau of Economic Analysis

The second index is the *composite index of coincident indicators,* series which historically roughly coincide with the business cycle turning points. Coincident indicators include such things as nonfarm employment, personal income less transfer payments, manufacturing sales, and industrial production. The third index is the *composite index of lagging indicators,* series which reach their peaks and troughs after the corresponding business cycle turns. Lagging indicators include the prime rate, the ratio of consumer installment debt to income, and labor cost per unit of output.

Although the leading indicators index has a good track record in predicting cyclical turns, they are far from perfect. As you can see from Figure 11–2, there have been numerous occasions in which the economy quickly rebounded from several months of declining leading indicators. In order to get a feel for the inherent uncertainty of economic forecasting, read the following CASE-IN-POINT.

CASE
• IN •
POINT

Signs of the Times

I am writing this in February 1988, a time in which speculation about recession abounds. Why? Let's look at the signs of the time. First, let's consider the good news. The U.S. economy experienced more than five years of uninterrupted growth between 1983 and 1988. More than 10 million jobs were created, the unemployment rate fell to a decade low of 5.8 percent, real GNP increased by 17 percent, and inflation slowed to the lowest point in over 25 years. Add to this a brisk if not ebullient stock market, and it is little wonder that consumer spending sustained a long period of expansion. Indeed, spending on imports did a lot to propel many foreign economies as well. And with the dollar depreciation from 1985 to 1988, some economists are counting on a much improved export picture.

As someone once said, all good things come to an end. And so together with all of this good news were the twin deficits in the federal budget and in international trade. The increasing debt burden at home and abroad resulted in federal interest payments equal to 15 percent of the national budget. Moreover, big institutional investors finally decided that it was time to take their capital gains and pull out of the market. In one day, the market plunged more than 500 points, wiping out nearly $1 trillion worth of paper assets. On the heels of this collapse, consumer spending slowed, and businesses were caught with large and growing stockpiles of unsold goods.

Other indicators of a turning point in the 1983 to 1988 expansion were also evident. Most ominous was the decline of the composite index of 12 leading indicators in each month of 1987's fourth quarter. Forecasters generally interpret such a decline as a warning sign of recession, and the performance of specific indicators confirmed the worst fears. First, business investment showed clear warnings. New orders for plant and equipment declined, and permits for residential and commercial construction fell off. The help wanted index, a measure of the demand for labor, also turned downward. But perhaps the most critical harbinger of future economic activity is consumer spending. Although personal consumption expenditures is not among the BEA's composite indicators, it is widely regarded as the economy's chief propellent.

As *Business Week* wryly observed in early 1988, "Consumers are getting tired."[6] Real consumer spending, expenditures adjusted for inflation, increased an average of 4.5 percent from 1983 through 1986. But this spending spree slowed to 0.6 percent in 1987 and even declined by 0.95 percent in the fourth quarter. The bloom on the stock market rose was clearly gone, and the consumer may have been taking the opportunity to rebuild the stock of savings in order to reduce record installment debt.

More optimistic economists are betting that exports will increase enough to compensate for the cutback by consumers, but this assumes that the manufacturing sector can meet the demand. U.S. firms may be more competitive as a result of cost-cutting efficiencies, but capital spending has gone primarily for machinery and equipment to reduce costs, not to increase capacity.

Is a downturn imminent? My crystal ball is a little cloudy, but the indicators certainly point to a recession. Of course, *when* is the important question; if we knew that, we could go to the bank on it.

Questions to Consider

1. *You are reading this case more than a year after it was written. What happened between the second quarter of 1988 and the fourth quarter of 1989? (Some good sources for such data are* Survey of Current Business, Business Conditions Digest, *and the* Economic Report of the President.*)*

2. *What is the current economic outlook? Besides the sources listed above, other good references are* Business Week, Fortune, *and* The Wall Street Journal.

---

[6] "Business Outlook," *Business Week,* February 15, 1988, p. 21. Normally a cautious observer of trends in the economy, *Business Week* proclaimed, "a slowdown is beginning to look inevitable." One year later, the editors were more cautious still about their forecasts, and with good reason. The economy continued its record-setting pace of job formation, and somehow this was obtained without much additional inflation. It would seem that the crystal-ball-gazing business is about the only activity in the doldrums.

IMPORTANT TERMS TO REMEMBER

business cycle, p. 304
civilian labor force, p. 299
composite index of 12 leading
   indicators, p. 306
consumer price index, p. 295
contraction, p. 306
depression, p. 306
employed, p. 298
Employment Act of 1946, p. 301
expansion, p. 305

inflation, p. 293
peak, p. 306
price index, p. 294
recession, p. 306
recovery, p. 305
relative prices, p. 296
trough, p. 306
unemployed, p. 299
unemployment rate, p. 299

CHAPTER SUMMARY

1. A price index is a ratio of the price in the current year to the price in the base year.

2. Inflation is defined as a rise in the general level of prices. One measure of inflation is the consumer price index.

3. Among other things, a price index, such as the consumer price index, is used to express nominal income as real income by dividing the nominal (or current) wages by the price index.

4. The civilian labor force consists of the employed and the unemployed. To be counted as employed, one must be 16 years or older and have worked at least one hour for pay during the survey week or 15 hours without pay in a family business. To be counted as unemployed, one must be 16 years or over, not holding a job currently, but actively seeking work.

5. The Employment Act of 1946 made the federal government responsible for pursuing four economic objectives: full employment, price stability, a healthy rate of economic growth, and a balance of payments.

6. The Full Employment and Balanced Growth Act of 1978 (the Humphrey-Hawkins amendment) reaffirmed the goals of the 1946 act and added specific numeric targets: 3 percent unemployment by 1983 and 0 percent inflation by 1988.

7. Using 4 percent unemployment and 3 percent inflation as the targets of economic policy, the historical record shows that in only three years (1952, 1953, and 1967) has the United States attained both goals.

8. The business cycle is a periodic but irregular expansion and contraction of the economy. The four stages are recovery, peak, recession, and trough.

9. The expansion and contraction waves of the cycle are measured by three indexes: the composite indexes of 12 leading indicators, coincident indicators, and lagging indicators.

10. Leading indicators, such as new orders for plant and equipment, anticipate turns in the business cycle.

DISCUSSION AND
REVIEW
QUESTIONS

1. What is a business cycle? Describe the economic fluctuations in the U.S. economy in the period from 1970 to 1990.

2. What are leading indicators? What are some examples?

3. What is the difference between inflation and the inflation rate?

4. Assume that your weekly wage was $600 in 1988. You have earned two raises since and your current wage is $700. If the current consumer price index is 130, what is your real income?

5. There are many gray areas in counting the employed and unemployed. For each of the following cases, decide whether the person would be counted as employed, unemployed, or not in the labor force. Also explain why.
   a. A 16-year-old full-time student working 20 hours a week at a fast-food restaurant.
   b. A 72-year-old doing miscellaneous home repair jobs in the underground economy.
   c. An electrical worker who is on strike.
   d. A recently laid off clerk who has found another job that will begin in two weeks.

6. List and describe the goals of the Employment Act of 1946.

7. Evaluate this statement: "The Employment Act of 1946, often hailed as a bold legislative initiative, was actually a conservative compromise, a reaction against big government."

A BRIEF LOOK
AHEAD

The next chapter takes you a little deeper into the macro world. We will look at three main topics: the various parts of the macroeconomy depicted in circular flow diagrams, the national income and product accounts maintained by the government, a new measure of inflation and the difference between current dollar and constant dollar (or inflation adjusted) GNP.

APPENDIX

Constructing Your Personal CPI

Are you better off or worse off than you were 1, 5, or 10 years ago? Although U.S. workers are actually earning less in real terms than they did in 1981, how do you stand? Building your personal CPI may help you to get a fix on your cost of living.

Economists at Citibank have developed a step-by-step procedure to follow. First, collect your receipts for everything and put them in the seven categories used by the Bureau of Labor Statistics (see Table 11–3 on the next page). Second, total your expenditures in each category. Third, divide each category

TABLE 11–3
Your Personal Consumer
Price Index

Category	National CPI Nov. 1988	Your Expenditure Weights	Your Personal Indexes
Food	120.3	0.20	24.06
Housing	120.2	0.38	45.68
Transportation	119.9	0.18	21.58
Apparel	119.9	0.08	9.59
Medical care	110.7	0.06	6.64
Entertainment	141.8	0.03	4.25
Other goods and services	141.0	0.07	9.87
Total	124.8		121.7

To calculate your personal price index, multiply your expenditure weight times the national price index numbers for each category. Adding the index numbers gives you a total personal CPI of 121.7, approximately three index points below the national average.

total by the total outlays for the period. (One month is enough, but the procedure calls for a three-month period in order to give you a good idea of expenditure patterns.) Don't include personal income or social security taxes, savings, gifts, or life insurance; these are excluded in the official CPI.

For example, assume that you spent $4,000 in the first quarter of the year: $800 for food, $1,520 for housing, $720 for transportation, $320 for apparel, $240 for medical care, $120 for entertainment, and $280 for other goods and services. Your percentages by category are then, respectively, 20, 38, 18, 8, 6, 3, and 7. (The approximate national percentage figures are, respectively, 18, 44, 18, 6, 5, 4, and 5.) The fourth step is to calculate your personal indexes. Multiply the national (or regional) price index figures times your expenditure weights. Finally, add the column of numbers to get your total personal price index. Table 11–3 below shows the results.

With a personal CPI of 121.7, you are a little better off than average, primarily because you are spending less on categories like housing. By calculating your personal CPI a few times each year and comparing it to the national or regional CPI, you will gain some idea of how you are doing in the battle of the budget.

DISCUSSION QUESTIONS

1. Why might it be important to use a regional consumer price index instead of the national CPI? In other words, why would living in Chicago, Miami, or Phoenix make a difference?

2. Under what circumstances is the national CPI a more appropriate measure of inflation?

The Macroeconomy: National Income Accounting

Elizabeth Crews/ Stock, Boston

We continue our macro journey with the interrelationships among house-holds, businesses, government, and international trade, what economists call the circular flow of goods and services. We then examine the official system of national economic accounts, what gets counted and what does not, noting that billions of dollars of economic activity escape the national income ac-counts. We also will study the two ways in which GNP accounts are main-tained, some of the inherent weaknesses of GNP as a measure of current economic activity, and carefully examine the distinction between nominal (current dollar) and real (constant dollar) GNP.

After completion of this chapter, you should be able to do the following:

1. Describe and explain the circular flow of goods and services.
2. Distinguish between stocks and flows and give examples of each.
3. Explain why national income is always equal to national product.
4. Describe the role of financial markets in the economy.
5. Describe and give examples of the underground economy.
6. Distinguish between the expenditures and incomes approaches to GNP.
7. Explain the values added method of calculating GNP.
8. Identify, describe, and explain what is excluded from GNP and why.
9. Distinguish between nominal GNP and real GNP, nominal wages and real wages, and nominal interest rates and real interest rates.
10. Calculate the implicit price index.

The Macro Puzzle

The macroeconomy is much like abstract art. Although intriguing in a mysterious way, for many viewers it's a puzzling conglomeration of figures, lines, colors, and textures. Like appreciating an abstract work of art, we may comprehend the macroeconomy (the system as a structure), but it is often difficult to understand (or predict) how one part affects or relates to another part.

Take the stock market. Who could have predicted the October 19, 1987, debacle (ominously referred to as a "financial meltdown" and "Black Monday")? On that fateful day, the market plunged 508 points and lost nearly 20 percent of its value in a six-hour trading day. And once it had happened, who would have thought that the decline would have caused so little economic disruption?

The international economy is a perfect example of the fascinating yet puzzling nature of macroeconomics. From 1980 to 1985, the dollar increased in value by more than 50 percent against the Japanese yen, German deutsch mark, and other currencies. With an appreciated dollar, the price of our exports rose dramatically, and the price of imports fell. (Since transactions are denominated in the currency of the selling country, when the dollar increases in value Americans can buy more marks with the same dollar. However, Germans find that the mark buys fewer dollars.) The upshot was a growing trade deficit as exports declined and imports soared.

Nearly all economists agreed that the solution to the trade deficit was relatively simple: the dollar must depreciate in order to make our exports more price competitive and our imports more expensive. They reasoned that if dollar appreciation caused a trade deficit, then dollar depreciation would restore trade balance if not a surplus.

And that's what is so puzzling. Even after the dollar fell in value, reaching an all-time low against the yen in late 1987, the deficit actually worsened (despite a falling dollar and expanding exports). Although U.S. exports increased substantially in 1988, the dollar depreciation did not come close to restoring a trade balance. Naturally, lots of explanations were offered (from hindsight). While some analysts attributed the problem to a U.S. import addiction, others argued that not enough U.S. businesses were interested in exporting. Still others were confident that the deficit would come down but that the correction would require more time. There was no shortage of explanations. To paraphrase the famous British scholar George Bernard Shaw, if you put all the economists in the world end to end they wouldn't reach a conclusion.

Because the macroeconomy is so vast, it is often difficult to comprehend so many unpredictable developments. And drawing clear cause-and-effect relationships is even more challenging. It's like a bowl of jello: push on the surface here and you get ripples nearly everywhere. In order to make sense of such abstract and complex interrelationships, it is helpful to break down the macroeconomy into its logical components. By first studying the component parts and gradually building the interrelationships, we will gain a practical understanding of how the economy works.

THE CIRCULAR FLOW OF GOODS AND SERVICES

The domestic economy is divided into two sectors, private and public (or government), and the private sector may be further divided into households and businesses. The rest of the world, or foreign sector, constitutes a fourth and increasingly important aspect of our economy. Indeed, the $160 billion trade deficit in 1987 is a constant reminder that the domestic and international parts of the economy are highly interdependent. We begin with a very simplified picture of the circular flow.

Model I: The Basic Circular Flow

Figure 12–1 illustrates the basic circular flow model with the private sector by itself. To keep things simple, we assume that there are no financial markets, no international trade, and no government. Although very remote from reality, the abstraction is useful because we are able to isolate and understand the basic relationships more easily.[1]

First, we assume in Model I that businesses sell all that they produce and households spend all that they earn; thus, neither saving nor investment occurs. Moreover, since government does not exist, there is neither government spending nor taxation. Second, two basic flows are shown: the counterclockwise flows of resources (in the lower half) and goods and services (in the upper half). Balancing the flows of resources and products are the clockwise flows of payments (wages and other pay-

---

[1] Because it is important to keep a sense of humor in all things we do, read the following story about the power of assumptions.

Did you hear about the three people marooned on a desert island? A physicist, an engineer, and an economist were shipwrecked. Only a few provisions were saved—articles of clothing and canned food. Weak with hunger but having no implements, they put their heads together about how to open the cans of food. "The solution is simple," said the physicist. "First, find a sharp object. Second, make a simple slingshot. Third, calculate the velocity of the object required to apply sufficient impact force to open the can." When the others stopped laughing, the engineer proposed her idea. "Look, all we need to do is design an implement sharp enough to open the can. Let's find a piece of sea glass. Then we can rub the glass in the sand—it's a natural medium to sharpen an object." The others groaned, whereupon the economist offered his solution. "Assume that we have a can opener!"

FIGURE 12–1 The Circular Flow: Model I

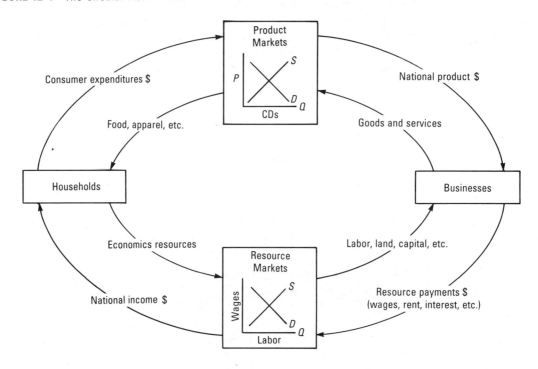

ments for resources in the lower half and consumer expenditures for products in the upper half). In the lower flow, business firms are on the demand side of the resource market, where they hire labor and buy other resources from households. (Of course, businesses actually buy from other businesses, but for the time being we assume that all resources are provided by households.) Businesses are on the supply side of the product market, where they offer goods and services for sale.

Stocks versus Flows.   Since we have been discussing flows, it is important to distinguish between flows and stocks. A **flow** is measure of an activity or a process that occurs over a period of time, such as the number of houses built in the month of July, the dollar value of U.S. exports to Canada in 1988, and your monthly saving. In contrast to a flow, a **stock** is a measure of accumulation at a moment in time. The total number of houses in your community on December 31, 1988, is a stock. (Indeed, we often refer to this measure as the housing stock.)

A bathtub analogy is useful in distinguishing flows and stocks. The water that pours into the tub from the spigot is a flow because it is measured by quantity per some time period, such as quarts, gallons, or

A **flow** *is measure of an activity or a process that occurs over a period of time.*

A **stock** *is a measure of accumulation at a moment in time.*

liters per minute. The amount of water in the tub, however, is a stock. It is the amount of water accumulated at some moment.

Another example of the difference between stocks and flows can be found in accounting. Income statements and balance sheets are used to profile a firm's financial picture, but they show quite different things. The income statement is a flow because it is a measure of the firm's revenues and expenses over a year. The balance sheet, on the other hand, is a stock because it represents the assets, liabilities, and net worth on a given date, usually the end of the calendar year. A flow is like a moving picture; a stock is a photograph or snapshot.

THINKING IT THROUGH

Wealth vs income—which one is a stock and which one is a flow? Why? Is the amount of money in your bank account a stock or a flow? Why?

The Flows of National Income and Product

National income *is the total income earned (wages, rent, interest, profit, and depreciation) in producing goods and services.*

Two important concepts are central to understanding the circular flow. **National income** is the total wages, salaries, tips, commissions, dividends, rent, interest, and profits earned in producing goods and services. National income is illustrated in Figure 12–1 in the lower half of the diagram and is often referred to as the income flow. Although all of national income is spent in our example, actually it is used in four ways: spending on goods produced at home, spending on foreign goods (imports), saving, and taxes. **National product** is the total market value of all goods and services produced; it is represented in the upper, or product, flow of the diagram.[2] It is obtained by taking the total quantity of each product and service, multiplying by the corresponding market prices, and then adding them all up. The national income is equal to the national product by definition. Indeed, national income and national product are two sides of the same coin. Let's see why.

National product *is the total market value of all goods and services produced.*

Because all earnings are spent on goods produced, and because all production is sold, national income must be equal to national product (the market value of goods and services produced). This equality holds true even if we drop these assumptions used in Model I. A microeconomic example will help to make this point more concrete. In our basic circular flow, a company's total sales revenue is equal to its contribution

---

[2] The term *national product* probably looks familiar to you, although it is referred to more generally in the media as gross national product. The word *gross* is added in order to indicate that business depreciation is included. More will be given on this subject in a few pages.

to national product (because it sells all that it produces). Profits and losses are incomes just like wages and salaries. Indeed, profit or loss is always the balancing item between a firm's selling price and its costs of production. If a new computer firm has costs of $100,000 and revenues of $120,000, then its profit of $20,000 is a part of national income. If its costs rise to $130,000 with no change in revenues, then it realizes a loss of $10,000. But the loss is a negative contribution to national income, so the value of production (its contribution to national product) is still equal to its contribution to national income.

Aggregate Production and Aggregate Expenditures

Aggregate production (AP) is the total market value of goods and services produced. The word aggregate means total and is used in order to distinguish it from its microeconomic counterpart, as in the market supply of potato chips. It is also used in order to draw a comparison with another important concept, aggregate expenditures. Unlike the microeconomic demand for soda or health care, **aggregate expenditures (AE)** is the *total* amount of spending on *all* goods and services produced. It includes all personal consumption expenditures, business investment spending on plant and equipment, commercial and residential construction, and planned changes to inventory (increases and decreases), all government purchases of goods and services, and net exports (exports less imports).

> **Aggregate production (AP)** *is the total market value of goods and services produced.*

> **Aggregate expenditures (AE)** *is the* total *amount of spending on* all *goods and services produced.*

Let's take a look at some of the relationships among the various concepts we have discussed. First, we know that national income always equals national product, or aggregate production. Second, since there is no saving and no taxes, there is but one use for national income: all of it is spent. Third, aggregate expenditures consist only of personal consumption expenditures (household spending). Then, by definition, aggregate expenditures equal aggregate production, and there is neither inventory accumulation nor inventory depletion. The economy is in equilibrium.

Model II: The Circular Flow with Saving and Investment

Figure 12–2 introduces some reality to our basic circular flow model. Relaxing our original assumptions, we now permit households to save and businesses to invest. Moreover, we introduce financial markets as a medium for the placement of savings and a source of borrowed funds. How does this modify our basic aggregate production and expenditures relationships?

First, aggregate expenditures now consist of consumption and investment spending. Second, national income is now used for saving as well as consumption. We know that aggregate expenditures must equal aggre-

FIGURE 12–2 The Circular Flow: Model II

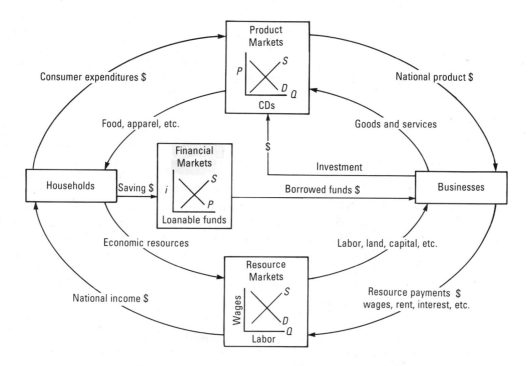

gate production in equilibrium, but will this occur? It all depends upon the relationship between saving and investment. If investment exactly matches saving, then aggregate expenditures will equal aggregate production. However, if investment exceeds saving, then aggregate expenditures will exceed aggregate production, and the economy will be in disequilibrium. Disequilibrium will also result if saving exceeds investment.

Unplanned Inventory: The Missing Ingredient. When businesses plan to increase the stock of goods, it is called *planned inventory*. **Unplanned inventory** is the unintended addition to or the depletion of the stock of goods produced. More simply, it is the difference between aggregate production and aggregate expenditures. In equilibrium unplanned inventory is zero, since everything produced is sold. In disequilibrium, however, unplanned inventory will be positive (inventory accumulation) or negative (inventory depletion). If *AE* exceeds *AP*, then buyers are purchasing more than is being produced, resulting in a decrease in the level of inventory. A common example is in the automobile industry where firms strive to maintain an inventory of cars, generally 15 to 30 days. If

Unplanned inventory *is the unintended addition to or the depletion of the stock of goods produced.*

companies sell more cars than anticipated, they will experience an un-planned depletion of inventories. If this situation persists, firms will hire an extra shift of workers or put existing workers on overtime in order to replenish the stock of cars. Conversely, if *AP* exceeds *AE,* then buyers are purchasing fewer cars than sellers anticipated, and unplanned inventory accumulation will occur. Faced with this situation, firms will lay off a shift or temporarily close a plant in order to restore the desired level of inventory.

On Disequilibrium. The most common state for the economy is disequilibrium. Indeed, the occurrence of equilibrium is about as probable as you or I winning the $6 million lottery. Why? There are over 65 million households and nearly 15 million business firms. Imagine what must happen for equilibrium to occur. The production plans of 15 million firms must mesh exactly with the spending plans of 65 million households. To say that this is improbable is the understatement of the year. If equilibrium does occur, it is a fleeting moment in time.

Although disequilibrium is a natural occurrence, the word carries negative connotations. Indeed, because it is used in medical diagnoses to describe generally unfavorable health, we transfer the association to the economic world. However, economic disequilibrium is neither good nor bad; these are entirely inappropriate descriptions of disequilibrium. If aggregate expenditures exceed aggregate production, it merely means that people are buying more goods and services than are being produced. This is a growth situation. Using a microeconomic example again, imagine a photofinishing store, Instant Image, that promises to turn out prints in 24 hours or less. Instant Image had been doing well and recently experienced a surge in demand for its business. Besides more orders, the first signs of increased demand were diminished supplies of photo paper and chemicals. When it placed orders for more supplies, it discovered that other businesses also experienced shortages. What did Instant Image do? What any self-respecting for-profit business does in this situation: raise prices. It also hired an additional worker and sought other suppliers. The upshot was higher prices, more jobs, and more production. And this was repeated throughout the industry.

Translated at the macro level, shortages and increased demand will lead to similar results. When aggregate expenditures exceed aggregate production, the economy is poised for expansion. Because delivery of materials is often untimely, because it is often difficult for businesses to find skilled labor, and because firms may not have the production capacity to accommodate increased demand, inflationary pressure tends to build up. The upshot is higher prices for individual products and services and a greater rate of inflation. Conversely, when aggregate production exceeds aggregate expenditures, surpluses will cause the economy to contract, resulting in a lower rate of inflation, less production (national product), and fewer jobs.

Model III: The Circular Flow with Government and Foreign Trade

Relaxing the initial assumptions further, we can develop a model of economic activity which more accurately represents the real economy. In Figure 12–3, we introduce the public (government) and foreign sectors, resulting in several important changes.

First, national income now is distributed in four ways: personal domestic consumption, spending on imports, saving, and taxes. The latter three terms (imports, saving, and taxes) are called **leakages.** They are dollar flows of income which are not spent on domestic production, but diverted temporarily out of the circular flow. Savings are routed to the financial markets (banks, savings and loans, credit unions, and direct placement in financial assets such as stocks and bonds). Imports are flows of dollars out of the United States in payment for foreign goods and services. And you get only one guess where your tax dollars go. The diversions are temporary because these flows are closely matched by corresponding **injections.** Injections are inflows of dollars to the circular flow, consisting of investment spending, exports, and government purchases.

Second, aggregate expenditures now consist of four components: consumption, planned investment, government spending, and net exports. **Net exports** is the difference between exports and imports, a negative flow if imports exceed exports. Because government is now in the picture, we must account for several additional flows. Governments (federal, state and local) purchase goods and services in the product market and hire and buy resources in the resource market. Moreover, they finance their expenditures by taxation and borrowing (issuing debt). Governments also transfer (redistribute) tax revenue to households. These **transfer payments** are one-way flows of tax revenue from government to individuals. Examples are federal food stamps, Aid to Families with Dependent Children (AFDC), educational grants and stipends, and housing subsidies.

With the introduction of the foreign sector, consumers and businesses now spend their money on imported goods and services, and businesses sell their products outside the United States (as exports). With all of these additional flows, it is even more unlikely for equilibrium to occur. With the introduction of government and international trade, it is now required that the total of planned investment, government spending, and exports equals the total of saving, *net taxes* (taxes less transfers), and imports.

Leakages *are dollar flows of income not spent on domestic production.*

Injections *are inflows of dollars to the circular flow, consisting of investment spending, exports, and government purchases.*

Net exports *is the difference between exports and imports.*

Transfer payments *are one-way flows of tax revenue from government to individuals.*

FIGURE 12–3 The Circular Flow: Model III

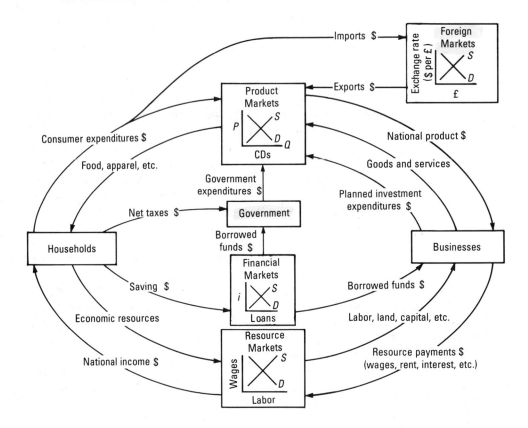

Changes in unplanned inventory are the first signals of imbalances between production and sales. Because such imbalances cause businesses to make employment, production, and pricing decisions, variations in unplanned inventories play a pivotal role in macroeconomic adjustments. Table 12–1 summarizes the three possible relationships between aggregate production and expenditures and the probable resulting actions.

In equilibrium, where *AP* equals *AE*, unplanned inventory is zero. Because sales match production plans, there will be no tendency for changes in prices, employment, or production. Two disequilibrium cases may occur. First, if *AP* exceeds *AE*, then sales fall short of production. This is a contractionary situation for the economy. As unplanned inventory accumulation occurs, firms lay off workers, cut production, and re-

TABLE 12–1

Aggregate Supply and Demand Relationships: Unplanned Inventory and Macro Adjustments

Aggregate Conditions	Change in Unplanned Inventory	Effect on Employment, Production and Prices
$AP > AE$	+ (accumulation)	↓
$AP < AE$	− (depletion)	↑
$AP = AE$	0	no change

If aggregate production (AP) exceeds aggregate expenditures (AE), then there will be an increase in inventory and, other things being equal, downward pressure on employment, production, and prices. If AP is less than AE, however, inventories will be depleted and firms will expand production, employment, and raise prices. In the case of equilibrium ($AE = AP$) there will be no change in inventory and accordingly no tendency for changes in prices, employment, or production.

duce prices. Although some businesses will decide to lay off workers, cut production, and leave prices alone, others will cut prices in hopes that sales will rebound. Regardless of the individual microeconomic actions, however, for the macroeconomy, we can expect three results: fewer jobs, less production, and a lower price level. A second disequilibrium condition occurs when AE exceeds AP. This represents an expansionary situation. As firms experience unplanned inventory depletion, they will take three possible actions: raise prices, hire more workers, and increase production. Some firms may elect to raise prices without making any output adjustments, possibly to determine if the imbalance is only temporary. Then, if the higher price does not significantly reduce sales, they may expand production. Other firms will respond immediately by increasing production. Taking all of the individual actions into account, the macroeconomy will experience more jobs and output at a higher price level.

The Actual Numbers: 1988

Thus far we have illustrated three versions of the circular flow of goods and services. Although Model III is by far the best representation of reality, we still are dealing in rather abstract terms. Let's look at the following CASE-IN-POINT in order to identify the actual 1988 flows of income and product, expenditures, saving, taxes, and transfers discussed in the various models.

CASE
• IN •
POINT

The Actual Income and Product Flows

How are the concepts we have discussed related to the real world? What were the actual numbers in the economy? Let's summarize the data and see what happened.

TABLE 12–2

Aggregate Production
and Expenditures, 1988
(all figures in billions
of 1988 dollars)

Economic flow		1988 Value
Aggregate production		$4,863.1
Aggregate expenditures (Final Sales)		4,814.6
Personal consumption		
expenditures	$3,227.2	
Planned investment	717.5	
Government purchases	964.1	
Net exports	−94.3	
Unplanned inventory accumulation		48.6
Total leakages:		
Saving	814.2	
Taxes less transfers	821.7	
Imports	614.5	
Total	2,250.4	
Total injections:		
Investment (planned		
and unplanned)	766.1	
Government purchases	964.1	
Exports	520.2	
Total	2,250.4	
Federal budget deficit (−)/surplus		−143.3
All government deficit (−)/surplus		−88.4

Subtracting final sales (aggregate expenditures from total production [GNP]) determines the change in inventory. For 1988, there was inventory accumulation of $48.6 billion. Total leakages (saving + net taxes + imports) will always equal (by definition) the total injections (total investment—planned plus unplanned— + government purchases + imports).

SOURCE: Bureau of Economic Analysis, U.S. Department of Commerce, *Survey of Current Business* 69, no. 1 (January 1989), Tables 1.1, 1.2, 2.1, pp. 8–12. (Figures may not add because of rounding.)

First, aggregate production, or gross national product, was $4,863.1 billion. That was a whopping sum of production: $4,863,100,000,000. (In prose, this was four trillion, eight hundred and sixty-three billion, one hundred million dollars worth of goods and services.) Second, aggregate expenditures, the total of all planned spending by households, businesses, government, plus net exports, was $4,814.6 billion. The inequality means that the economy was in disequilibrium: $AP > AE$ by $48.6 billion. Because more was produced during the year than was purchased, the economy experienced unplanned inventory accumulation.

Also illustrated are leakages and injections. As you can observe, no pair of flows are equal. Saving exceeds total investment, government purchases exceed taxes less transfers, and imports exceed exports. However, even though there are inequalities for each pair, total leakages equal total injections. This will *always* be so because total investment includes changes in unplanned inventory. The latter item serves as the balancing term here just as it does between aggregate production and aggregate expenditures.

Questions to Consider

1. *If Americans had purchased fewer imports in 1988, how would this have affected the flows?*

2. *We pointed out earlier that when AP > AE, the economy generally experiences a contraction—declining production and employment. In 1988, however, both jobs and output increased. How can you account for this?*

Summarizing the Flows.   In order to put the various flows into perspective, we can summarize the relationships in two statements.

1. Aggregate production $\equiv$ aggregate expenditures
     + unplanned inventory investment.
2. Total leakages $\equiv$ total injections or,
     Saving + [taxes − transfers] + imports $\equiv$
     Total investment [planned + unplanned] + government purchases
      + exports.

First, note that these statements are identities, indicated by the $\equiv$ sign. This means that they are equal by definition. (If we said that $AP = AE$, this would hold true only if unplanned inventory investment is zero.) Second, remember that disequilibrium occurs because production (AP) is not equal to final sales or aggregate expenditures (AE), and the difference is unplanned inventory investment. Third, the same relationship holds for leakages and injections. Saving, taxes, and imports represent flows of national income not spent. These leakages are matched by expenditure flows or injections of exports, government purchases, and investment. If only planned investment is counted, then leakages exceed injections. However, since inventory accumulation represents current economic activity (the production of goods and services), it must be accounted for in the total, and this brings total injections into line with total leakages.

Government budget data is also shown in the CASE-IN-POINT for comparative purposes. Although the federal government posted a $143.3 billion deficit in 1988, all governments together ran a $88.4 billion deficit. This means that state and local governments collectively operated with a surplus of $54.9 billion in 1988.

The circular flow of income and product has provided a view of the interrelationships in the macroeconomy and how some of the microeconomic pieces fit together. But if we are to understand macroeconomic activity, it also is important to examine the ways in which the government collects and reports information concerning income, expenditures, and production. In the next section, we look into the system of national income accounting.

THE NATIONAL INCOME AND PRODUCT ACCOUNTS

In 1930, shortly after the United States plunged into its deepest depression, it became painfully obvious to the government that it had no reliable measurement of the nation's economic activity. It seemed, to use a depression-born phrase, that "we were going to hell in a hand-basket." A task force was formed headed by well-known economist-statistician Simon Kuznets. By 1932, the government had designed a national income accounting system. How is the data collected? What are the accounts and what do they show?

Gross National Product

Gross national product (GNP) *is the total market value of all final domestic goods and services produced in one year.*

The principal account is **gross national product (GNP)**—the total market value of all final goods and services produced in one year. This definition contains several key words. First, GNP represents *market value,* that is, the price at which the product or service is sold. It also measures *final goods.* In other words, it counts only sales to end users and excludes all intermediate products. Third, GNP measures production, *not sales.* If we counted all sales occurring within a year, many items would be represented more than once. Finally, the time period is *one calendar year,* January 1 through December 31.

Two Approaches to GNP

There are two basic methods used to determine the nation's total annual production: the expenditures approach and the income approach. As we observed in the circular flow model presented in the previous chapter, these represent two sides of the same coin. Total expenditures on goods produced are always equal to the total income earned in making those goods.

The Expenditures Approach. The simplest way to identify the GNP is to add all expenditures on final goods and services produced. Table 12–3 illustrates the expenditures method.

Total expenditures consist of four elements: personal consumption expenditures, gross private domestic investment, government purchases of goods and services, and net exports. The data presented are in nominal, or current 1988 dollar terms. The word *nominal* means that current-year (1988) prices are used, as opposed to base-year prices. More will be given on this a little later.

The Income Approach. An alternative method is to add up all the incomes earned directly in producing goods and services. Then, by adding

TABLE 12–3

Gross National Product, 1988 Expenditures Approach

	Nominal GNP
Gross national product	$4,863.8
√ Personal consumption expenditures	3,227.2
Durable goods	451.1
Nondurable goods	1,047.4
Services	1,728.7
√ Gross private domestic investment	766.1
Fixed investment	717.5
Nonresidential	487.8
Structures	142.9
Producers' durable equipment	344.8
Residential	229.8
Changes in business inventories	48.6
√ Government purchases of goods and services	964.1
Federal	380.5
State and local	583.6
√ Net exports	94.3
Exports	520.2
Imports	614.5

The expenditures approach to GNP consists of adding expenditures by consumers, businesses, government, and the difference between exports and imports.

SOURCE: Bureau of Economic Analysis, U.S. Department of Commerce, *Survey of Current Business* 69, no. 1 (January 1989), Table 1.1 and 1.2, p. 8.

in a few more items, we arrive at GNP. Table 12–4 on the next page illustrates the income approach.

Adding all resource payments (wages, salaries and other labor earnings, rental income, interest income, dividends, proprietor income, and corporate profits) yields an account called national income (NI). When indirect business taxes (taxes levied on sales and property) and the net surplus from governmental enterprises are added in, we get net national product (NNP). Finally, by adding capital consumption allowances to NNP, we get GNP.

As we have emphasized all along, the two approaches result in the same dollar total. However, you may have noted that there is an item called *statistical discrepancy*. This is the balancing item which the government adds to or subtracts from the income side in order that the two sides are equal. Basically, the government cannot find the discrepancy and thus includes it as an adusting entry. The error is remarkably small, amounting to less than one tenth of 1 percent of GNP.

TABLE 12–4		Compensation of employees	$2,906.2
Gross National Product,		Rental income	19.5
1988 Income Approach		Net interest	391.9
		Proprietors' income	324.7
		Business profits	323.8
	NI	National income	3,965.0
		Plus: Indirect business taxes	
		and other adjustments	391.8
	NNP	Net national product	4,356.8
		Plus: Capital consumption allowances	506.4
	GNP	Equals: Gross national product	4,863.1

The income approach to GNP adds all incomes earned (and not necessarily received) in the production of goods and services. To this total of national income, we add indirect business taxes and other adjustments plus capital consumption allowances to reach GNP.

SOURCE: Bureau of Economic Analysis, U.S. Department of Commerce, *Survey of Current Business* 68, no. 12 (December 1988), Tables 1.9 and 1.14, p. 5.

Value Added Approach

Value added *is an approach to compute GNP by adding to the value of the product at each stage of production.*

A variant of the expenditures approach is referred to as **value added**. Instead of adding total expenditures only on final goods, this approach adds the value added to the product at each stage of production. The sum of the values added will equal the expenditure by the end user. Let's see how this works.

Joanne and Harvey operate a specialty furniture store featuring custom-made kitchen cabinets. Each set of cabinets sells for $6,000. The costs associated with this operation, from raw material to final product, are shown in Table 12–5.

The saw mill and logging company sells the oak timber for $1,000 to Lumberyard Inc., which, in turn, cuts the raw timber into finished lumber. The lumber is sold to Unique Cabinets, Inc., for $1,500, which then fashions a customized set of kitchen cabinets. The finished cabinets are sold to the Posh Furniture Wholesalers for $3,500. The wholesaler distributes cabinets nationwide and sells the cabinets to J & H retail outlets for $4,500. In the spirit of value added and making a good living, J & H sells the cabinets to you for $6,000. The final market value is thus $6,000, which is exactly equal to the sum of the values added in the course of cutting trees, making lumber, fashioning cabinets, and distributing the product to retail stores for final sales. Instead of focusing on *intermediate goods* and tracing each value added transaction, the Department of Commerce uses expenditures on *final goods* as the current market value of the product.

TABLE 12–5	Stage of Production	Product or Service	Price	Value Added
Value Added Approach to GNP	Forest Inc.	timber	$1,000	$1,000
	Lumberyard Inc.	lumber	1,500	500
	Unique Cabinets, Inc.	finished cabinets	3,500	2,000
	Posh Wholesaler	distribution	4,500	1,000
	J & H	Retail sales	6,000	1,500
		Total value added		6,000

The sum of all values added at each stage of production, from raw materials to final retail sale, will equal the final expenditure to the end user. Because the value added method entails so many steps and is thus prone to many reporting errors, the Department of Commerce uses the expenditures approach.

The Various National Accounts

There are five principal accounts maintained by the Department of Commerce. Besides GNP, NNP, and NI, the government also calculates the personal income (PI) and disposable income (DI) accounts. Table 12–6 summarizes the five accounts, indicating what items are added and subtracted to go from one account to another. It may seem like an incredible amount of detailed information to remember, but each item is central to the macroeconomy. Let's summarize some of the flows.

The difference between GNP and NNP is capital consumption allowances, an overdressed term meaning depreciation. Second, in moving from NNP to NI, three items are subtracted and one is added. The largest item subtracted is indirect business taxes, consisting of excise, property, and sales taxes. These taxes amounted to $389.1 billion in 1988. Two other items subtracted are business transfer payments ($30.7 billion) and the statistical discrepancy (−$12 billion). (Because the statistical discrepancy is the balancing item between the expenditures and incomes approaches to GNP, it is not a reported or calculated amount. And, because it was negative in 1987, the incomes reported exceeded total expenditures.) The single item added is the difference between government subsidies and the surplus from government enterprises such as the postal service, buying and selling securities, and revenue from the TVA and similar operations. The result is **national income,** the total income earned (by persons and corporations) in the production of goods and services. (Note that although excise, sales, and property taxes are costs of production, they do not represent earnings paid to a factor of production.)

National income *is the total income earned by persons and corporations in the production of goods and services. (Also see page 319.)*

Personal income (PI) *is the total income received by persons, excluding corporate flows.*

While national income represents total income earned by corporations and persons in the production of goods and services, **personal income (PI)** is the total income received by persons, excluding corporate flows. We can use a simple little rule in moving from NI to PI: subtract all income earned but not received, and add all income received but not earned. Three flows are subtracted: corporate profits ($323.9 billion), net interest ($391.9 billion), and contributions for social insurance ($444.7 billion), a euphemism for social security taxes. Four flows are added: government transfer payments to persons ($555.3 billion), personal interest income ($576.3 billion), personal dividend income ($96.3 billion), and business transfer payments ($30.7 billion). As an example of our rule, social security contributions are income that you do not keep even if you do receive it, and transfer payments represent income received even though no economic activity occurred to earn it. The last account is **disposable income (DI),** defined as the total earnings of households after payment of personal income taxes or, more simply, after-tax income.

Disposable income (DI) *is the total earnings of households after payment of personal income taxes.*

THINKING IT THROUGH

An interesting observation about the GNP data is that personal income is greater than national income. Why?

What Does and Doesn't GNP Measure?

GNP measures annual production of final goods at current market prices. That sounds pretty comprehensive, and that is one reason why it is gross. Let's look at the various ways in which the GNP account overstates or understates U.S. economic activity. The following CASE-IN-POINT discusses the underground economy, an example of perhaps the most glaring omission from the national accounts.

CASE
· IN ·
POINT

The Vast Underground Economy

By midnight on April 15, the deadline for individual income tax returns, more than $660 billion (15 percent) of 1987 income went unreported to the IRS. A combination of high tax rates, inflation, and a distrust of government have produced a vast and growing underground economy. By conservative estimates, more than 20 million people work in the underground economy.

No matter what you call it—the cash, subterranean, or **underground economy,** it all refers to the same thing: unreported income from legal and illegal

Underground economy *refers to the unreported income from both legal sources and illegal sources.*

TABLE 12–6

National Income and Product Accounts, 1988

Gross national product	$4,863.1
Less: Capital consumption allowances	506.4
Equals: **Net national product**	4,356.8
Less: Indirect business taxes	389.1
Business transfer payments	30.7
Statistical discrepancy	(12.0)
Plus: Subsidies less current surplus of government enterprises	16.0
Equals: **National income**	3,965.0
Less: Corporate profits	323.9
Net interest	391.9
Contributions for social insurance	444.7
Plus: Transfer payments to persons	555.3
Personal interest income	576.3
Personal dividend income	96.3
Business transfer payments	30.7
Equals: **Personal income**	4,063.4
Less: Personal taxes	590.4
Equals: **Disposable income**	3,473.0

This table illustrates the items subtracted and added to reach the nation's five principal income and product accounts.

SOURCE: Bureau of Economic Analysis, Department of Commerce, *Survey of Current Business* (Washington, D.C.: U.S. Government Printing Office), 69 no. 1 (January 1989, Table 1.9, p. 10 and Table 2.1, p. 12.

sources. Various studies estimate the size of the underground in a range from 10 to 20 percent of GNP. Taking 15 percent as the median, the underground amounted to $666 billion in 1987.[3]

When we think of the *underground,* most of us probably conjur up Hollywood-type images of unsavory and sleezy characters dealing in drugs, gambling, prostitution, and kiddie-porn. Most of this activity consists of organized crime, highly sophisticated networks often operating behind a facade of legitimate business. Of course, such operations could not succeed without the hundreds of thousands of people who have dropped out of the visible, above-ground, legitimate economy. For example, one study found that 30 percent of Boston's and Chicago's youth are involved in gambling operations and peddling dope. When asked why they were doing these things, they responded that it was much more lucrative.

Narcotics, prostitution, and other illegal activities are clearly big business in the United States. The income from these is not reported for obvious reasons. However, only about a third ($220 billion) of all subterranean activity comes from these illegal sources. Two thirds ($446 billion) of the underground economy consists of people working in legal activities who, in order to evade taxes, conceal all or part of their incomes from the IRS. We all may know of the moonlighting plumber who takes only cash for the job, the dentist who

---

[3] For 1987, the cash economy ranged from $445 billion to $890 billion. These are projected figures based upon the study "A Monetary Perspective on Underground Economic Activity in the United States," *Federal Reserve Bulletin*, March 1984, pp. 177–90.

pressures his patients to pay cash, or the street vendor who, although working full time, reports not a dime to the government.

Although tax evasion is a powerful motive, so is the eligibility for unemployment benefits and welfare payments. Of the estimated 20 million underground workers, as many as one million may be listed as officially unemployed. The good news about this is that the national unemployment rate may be substantially overestimated. The bad news is that many people work officially just long enough to be eligible for benefits, whereupon they no longer report their incomes. Pretending to be unemployed, they collect benefits until no longer eligible, whereupon they begin reporting income again. Although this on-the-books and off-the-books strategy is a well-known phenomenon, it is extremely difficult to monitor and even more difficult to control.

Questions to Consider

1. *Why doesn't the government just make a good guess about the size of the underground economy and include it in the GNP?*

2. *Would the underground economy be smaller if income taxes were lower? What if a much higher percentage of tax returns were audited? Would that make a difference? What would you do to reduce the size of the underground economy?*

As the CASE-IN-POINT on the underground economy shows, there is a great deal of work (illegal and legal) that does not get counted in the GNP. Indeed, the GNP does not accurately measure actual current annual production because it excludes about $650 billion of underground activity (in 1987). The government declines to estimate the size of underground production because the data are notoriously unreliable. However, the government does make *guesstimates* of owner-occupied housing and adds to GNP what it calls *imputed rent*. This represents the consumption value of housing, the opportunity cost of holding the house in its present use as your residence. These numbers are far from reliable since they are based on estimated assessed property valuations, and most of these are not current. If the government can guess about imputed rent, perhaps it could make a conservative guess about the size of the underground and include it in GNP. At least it would formally recognize what everyone knows—that millions of people earn billions of dollars annually in illegal and criminal activity.

A second criticism of GNP accounts is that all voluntary and unpaid domestic household work is excluded from GNP. Billions of hours of labor are volunteered annually in charitable organizations. Day care centers, Boy and Girl Scout Associations, the American Cancer Society, the American Heart Association, parent-teacher organizations, to name a few, are largely dependent upon the spirit of voluntarism in the United States. By some estimates, this activity represents more than eight million volunteers and amounts to nearly 10 percent of GNP. Moreover, the work of a housewife or househusband in the home is excluded. Imagine—if you marry your housekeeper, you will reduce GNP!

Third, because sales of used goods generally do not entail current production, these transactions also are excluded from GNP. If you sell your 1985 Isuzu to your neighbor Mary, and Mary sells the car to her friend George, neither sale is counted in GNP. Purely financial transactions are also excluded because they merely represent a swap of paper assets. For example, if I purchase a $5,000 General Motors bond through a broker at E. F. Hutton, this transaction also is excluded (unless the broker earned a commission, a fee for service. However, if I invested the $5,000 in a no-load mutual fund, the transaction would not be reflected in GNP).[4]

THINKING IT THROUGH

If Jose bought a used painting from an art dealer, would this transaction be counted? What if the dealer acquired the painting for $10,000, spent $2,000 in restoration, and sold it for $20,000?

Fourth, because GNP is expressed in nominal values (or current year prices), we are not able to make direct comparisons between this year's GNP and the GNP of earlier years. Even if GNP increases between 1990 and 1991, it is possible that we are producing less. Why? Take a simple example of a one-product economy. The nation of Ratcha produces 100 Ratchafratchits at $10, a 1990 GNP of $1,000. In 1991, Ratcha produces 90 Ratchafratchits at $12 each, so GNP increases to $1,080—an 8 percent increase in GNP. On closer inspection, however, we find that Ratcha is really worse off, since it is actually producing 10 percent less in 1991. If we express 1991 output in 1990 prices, we find that Ratcha's real (constant dollar) GNP is $900 ($10 times 90). Although it is obvious that production has declined in our simple economy of Ratcha, it is much less obvious in real world economies which produce millions of goods. The difference between nominal and real GNP is so important that we will return to this subject in a few pages.

Fifth, changes in the quality of goods and services are not reflected automatically in GNP. We pay less for personal computers today than

---

[4] If a fund carries a load, then there is a service charge; no-load funds do not carry sales charges, fees, or commissions, at least none that are obvious to the buyer.

we did five years ago. We pay much more for health care today than we did in 1960. Is the higher price of health care compensated for by improved quality—more reliable tests, improved drugs, and more effective surgical operations? Although this is difficult to determine, government statisticians try to estimate such quality effects in GNP.

Sixth, GNP includes the production of so-called *bads,* such as pollution. It also includes the production of goods to counteract, neutralize, and control the negative externalities associated with production of such bads. In other words, GNP counts Dow Chemical's pollution-control equipment, produced to monitor and reduce the air pollution resulting from its own chemical plants (and probably the factories producing pollution-control devices). Many observers think that it is ironic that we count so many so-called bads along with the goods.

With all its shortcomings, GNP is probably the best way of summarizing the nation's economic activity. The important thing to remember, however, is that GNP should not be used as a measure of economic well-being. When you know that GNP increases, you know only one thing: the current value of goods produced has increased this year.

Nominal and Real Values

The data in Tables 12–3 and 12–4 are expressed in nominal terms (current year prices). In other words, goods produced in 1988 are expressed in 1988 prices. Although this method provides an accurate picture of economic affairs in the current year (1982, 1985, or 1988), what if we want to compare 1988 GNP with 1982 GNP? The GNP in 1988 is much greater, but is it because of more output, higher prices, or other combinations? In other words, the influence of higher prices complicates the job of comparing annual GNP data by masking variations in actual production.

In order to gauge how we stand today compared to an earlier period, it is necessary to express each year's output in terms of prices in some fixed year. Such a year is called the **base year,** some year in the recent past that is representative of economic activity. The government uses different base years for its various statistical reporting. For example, although for the national income accounts the Department of Commerce uses 1982 as the official base year, until very recently the Bureau of Labor Statistics (BLS) has used 1967 as the base year for calculating the consumer and producer price indexes. In 1988, the BLS changed the base year to 1982–1984.

Nominal GNP (NGNP) is current year output expressed in current year prices (e.g., 1988 production times 1988 prices). **Real GNP (RGNP)** is current year output expressed in base year prices (e.g., 1988 production times 1982–1984 prices). Let's see what the figures are in the period from 1982 to 1988. Table 12–7 summarizes the data.

Base year *refers to any year in the recent past which is representative of economic activity.*

Nominal GNP *is current year output expressed in current year prices.*

Real GNP *is current year output expressed in base year prices.*

TABLE 12–7

Nominal versus Real
GNP, 1980–1988
(1982 = 100)

(1) Year	(2) Nominal GNP (NGNP) ($ billions)	(3) Real GNP (RGNP) ($ billions)	(4) Year-to-Year Percent Change NGNP	(5) Year-to-Year Percent Change RGNP	(6) = (4) − (5) Difference (Percent Change in Price Level)
1980	2,732.0	3,187.1			
1981	3,052.6	3,248.8	11.7	1.9	9.8
1982	3,166.0	3,166.0	3.8	−2.5	6.3
1983	3,405.7	3,279.1	7.6	3.6	4.0
1984	3,765.0	3,489.9	10.5	6.4	4.1
1985	3,998.1	3,585.2	6.2	2.7	3.5
1986	4,235.0	3,713.3	5.9	3.6	2.4
1987	4,526.7	3,847.0	6.9	3.6	3.3
1988	4,863.1	3,995.1	7.4	3.8	3.6

Real GNP expresses current year output in base year prices (e.g., 1987 output in 1982 prices). This enables us to compare directly the production in one year to another without the influence of inflation. As shown above, RGNP growth was far less than NGNP growth. Another important relationship indicated in the table is that the percentage change in NGNP always equals the percentage change in RGNP plus the percentage change in prices.

SOURCE: Bureau of Economic Analysis, Department of Commerce, *Survey of Current Business* 69, no. 1 (Washington, D.C.: U.S. Government Printing Office, February 1989), Table 1.1 and 1.2, p. 2; Council of Economic Advisors, *Economic Report of the President* (Washington, D.C.: U.S. Government Printing Office, 1989), Table B–1, pp. 308–9 and Table B–2, pp. 310–11.

If we use the NGNP data, the U.S. economy grew by a healthy 53.6 percent over this seven-year span, producing a GNP in 1988 worth $1,695.8 billion more than the GNP in 1982. Dividing each figure by the respective U.S. population figures, the per capita GNP increased by $6,200. Were each of us that much better off?

Column three indicates that our real growth was actually about half of the nominal growth. Over the 1982 to 1988 period, RGNP increased by $829 billion, and per capita RGNP increased by approximately $2,600. As the RGNP data reveal, we did experience real growth, but not nearly as much after we factor out inflation.

The data in Table 12–7 also show that the economy experienced a recession in 1982. Indeed, unemployment reached a post-World War II high of 10.3 percent early in the year. Although NGNP increased by 3.8 percent, this figure contains both price and output changes, and thus we cannot determine the change in production by itself. When price changes are removed from the data, the RGNP actually decreased by 2.5 percent. This decline in output is concealed in the nominal data since prices increased by more than the decline in production. Column six shows this percent change in the price level, computed by subtracting Column five from Column four.[5] Furthermore, since an increase in

---

[5] Subtracting −2.5% from 3.8% yields a +6.3% since the subtraction of a negative value is the same as addition: 3.8% − (−2.5%) = 6.3%; a minus times a minus equals a plus.

spending (aggregate expenditures) will lead to changes in price, output, or both, it is important to note that the percentage change in NGNP is always equal to the percentage change in RGNP plus the percentage change in prices. Of course, the objective of any national policy is to maximize RGNP growth and minimize inflation.

The GNP Deflator. The relationship between nominal and RGNP may be examined by studying the **GNP deflator** (officially known as the implicit price index)—a ratio of prices in the current year to prices in the base year for all goods and services. Looking back to Table 12–7, the GNP deflator is calculated by taking the ratio of Column two data to Column three data, that is, the nominal GNP (NGNP) to real GNP (RGNP), and then multiplying times 100. (Remember that it is necessary to multiply times 100 in order to express the index as a percentage. Note also that all indexes are serial numbers; they do not carry dollar signs.) For example, the GNP deflator for 1988 is found by dividing $4,863.1 billion by $3,995 billion, yielding 1.217. This tells us that prices in 1988 were approximately 21.7 percent higher that in 1982. (Although the government uses many more decimal places for greater accuracy, such as 1.2172662, the index number is generally expressed to one or two decimal places.) Multiplying 1.217 times 100 gives us 121.7, a more common expression for index numbers. The reason for doing this is that we can perform a simple subtraction of the base year price index (always equal to 100) from the 1988 price index to find out by how much the price level has increased.

GNP deflator is a ratio of prices in the current year to prices in the base year for all goods and services.

THINKING IT THROUGH

Why is the base year price index always equal to 100?

In order to see how this works, let's express the relationship as a formula.

$$GNP \text{ deflator} = \frac{NGNP}{RGNP} \times 100, \text{ or,}$$

$$GNP \text{ deflator} = \frac{P_{cy} \times Q_{cy}}{P_{by} \times Q_{cy}} \times 100$$

where
  P = prices of goods and services,
  Q = quantity of goods and services produced,

cy = current year, and
by = base year.

Substituting actual years,

$$GNP \text{ deflator} = \frac{P_{1988} \times Q_{1988}}{P_{1982} \times Q_{1988}} \times 100$$

The quantity of each good produced in 1988 is multiplied by its 1988 price, and then each $P \times Q$ subtotal is added to give us the 1988 NGNP. To get the 1988 RGNP (in 1982 dollars), the quantity of each good produced in 1988 is multiplied times its price in 1982. The individual $P \times Q$ subtotals are then added. The NGNP is then divided by the RGNP and multiplied by 100.

Manipulating the Formula.   With this basic relationship, and knowing any two values, we can easily solve for the third. For example, if we know that the NGNP in 1990 is $5,000 billion and the GNP deflator is 132, all we have to do is divide the NGNP figure by the price index to get RGNP: $5,000 ÷ 132 = $37.878 billion. Since this looks a little low (we know that prices rose only 32 percent), we realize that we then must multiply by 100 to express the answer in correct form: $3,787.8 billion.

In other words, just manipulate the basic formula to solve for the unknown variable. There are three variations of the basic relationship.

$$GNP \text{ deflator} = \frac{NGNP}{RGNP} \times 100$$

$$RGNP = \frac{NGNP}{GNP \text{ deflator}} \times 100$$

$$NGNP = \frac{RGNP \times GNP \text{ deflator}}{100}$$

This may look like a lot to remember, but all you have to know is one expression, such as the GNP deflator formula, to get the others.

IMPORTANT TERMS TO REMEMBER

aggregate expenditures, p. 320
aggregate production, p. 320
base year, p. 336
disposable income, p. 332
flow, p. 318
GNP deflator, p. 338

gross national product, p. 328
injections, p. 323
leakages, p. 323
national income, p. 319; 331
national product, p. 319
net exports, p. 323

CHAPTER SUMMARY

1. The circular flow of goods and services diagram is a model which outlines the relationships among households, businesses, government, and the rest of the world regarding resource, product, and income flows.

2. A flow is a measurement of some activity over time, such as annual consumption and investment expenditures, monthly income and saving, and quantity demanded per week. On the other hand, a stock is the accumulated value of something at some instant in time. Examples of stocks are capital assets, the money supply, and wealth.

3. National income equals national product by definition. Since every price is an income, the value of what is produced (its market value) is equal to the sum of incomes earned in producing it.

4. Financial markets play an important middleman role in the economy by taking the savings from households and making loans available to investors.

5. Gross national product is the total market value of all final goods and services produced in one year. It is computed according to the expenditures or incomes approaches. The expenditures approach adds all expenditures by households, businesses, government, and spending on net exports to arrive at GNP. The income approach adds all incomes earned in the production of goods and services.

6. The value added approach is a variation of the expenditure approach. This method adds the contribution to the value of the item at each stage of production and distribution, from raw material to final sale.

7. There are five main national income and product accounts:
   a. GNP: the market value of all final goods and services produced in one year.
   b. NNP: GNP less capital consumption allowances (depreciation).
   c. NI: the total income earned by households and businesses in the production of goods and services.
   d. PI: the total income of persons, excluding all business income but including transfer payments.
   e. DI: after-tax income.

8. Although GNP is a useful measure of the economy's current production valued at this year's prices, it should not be considered a measure of the nation's economic well-being for several reasons. It excludes all underground economic activity, all voluntary activity, and all secondary and financial transactions. However, it includes the production of goods that generate both negative and positive externalities—social costs and benefits that are associated with private production and consumption.

9. Nominal GNP (NGNP) measures current year output at current year prices. In order to eliminate the influence of prices from one year to the

next, the real GNP expresses the current year output in base-year prices. The base year is some fixed reference year.

10. The underground economy represents economic activity which is not counted in GNP—the illegal variety such as gambling, drugs, and prostitution, and that which involves legal employment that is not reported.

11. Price indexes are ratios of current-year prices to base-year prices. The GNP deflator, which measures the changes of prices for all goods and services, is found by dividing the NGNP by the RGNP and multiplying times 100. The GNP deflator uses current year quantities in its calculations.

DISCUSSION AND REVIEW QUESTIONS

1. Why does national income equal national product?

2. Diagram and describe the circular flow of goods and services (Model III).

3. Estimates of the underground run as high as 25 percent of GNP. How does the opportunity cost concept help to explain why so many impoverished youth make crime a career choice.

4. One index of underground activity is the growing popularity of cash transactions, measured by the ratio of currency (paper money) to the total money supply. For example, $100 bills in circulation increased by twice the rate of all currency in recent years. How else would you measure the growth or size of the underground?

5. For each of the transactions listed below, which are included and which are excluded from 1990 GNP and why?
    a. Joanna, age 13, earns $8 for an evening of babysitting.
    b. E. F. Hutton sells $10 million worth of a client's bonds.
    c. It is February 14, 1990, and you buy a new 1989 Buick from a dealer.
    d. IBM sells $40 million of personal computers to a French firm.
    e. Food stamps worth $100 are received by Ms. Smith.
    f. U.R. Mobile purchases a brand new mobile home.
    g. Eric pays $400 in rent to his landlord.

6. Distinguish between nominal and real GNP. Why are these two values always the same in the base year?

7. The country of Bliss produces three goods and services, yogurt, yogurt machines, and psychological therapy (for the Blissful citizens who are fed up with yogurt). The prices and quantities produced in 1985 and 1990 are illustrated in the table below.

TABLE 12–8
GNP in Bliss

Item	1985 P	Q	NGNP	RGNP	1990 P	Q	NGNP	RGNP
Yogurt	$ 1.20	5,000			$ 1.00	6,000		
Yogurt machines	200.00	50			150.00	60		
Therapy	50.00	1,000			70.00	1,200		
Totals	———	———			———	———		

a. Complete the table.

    b. Calculate the GNP deflator for 1990; use 1985 as the base year.

8. The country of Oblivion produces only two goods, Right-on tennis rackets and tennis balls.

TABLE 12–9
GNP in Oblivion
(1985 = 100)

Product	P	Q	NGNP	RGNP	P	Q	NGNP	RGNP
			1985				**1990**	
Right-on	$1.50	1,000	_____	_____	$3.00	800	_____	_____
Tennis balls	3.00	400	_____	_____	3.50	450	_____	_____
Totals			_____	_____			_____	_____

(NGNP = Nominal Gross National Product; RGNP = Real Gross National Product; P = product price; Q = quantity of output.)

    a. Complete the table.
    b. Calculate the GNP deflator for 1990; use 1985 as the base year.
    c. Are Oblivious citizens better off in 1990?

A BRIEF LOOK AHEAD

In the next chapter, we will resume our discussion of the macroeconomy. Our primary attention will be given to the economic theories developed by John Maynard Keynes in order to describe, explain, and predict economic fluctuations and changes in income and employment. Although macroeconomic theory is undergoing a major reevaluation, special emphasis is placed upon Keynesian economics as the mainstream economic thought.

Keynesian Economics and National Income Determination

Culver Pictures

The purpose of this chapter is to introduce you to Keynesian economics, a macroeconomic theory of how income and employment are determined. Although the theory was developed more than 50 years ago by John Maynard Keynes, and though there have been many challenges to his ideas, the basic Keynesian explanation of economic fluctuations and the determination of income and employment probably remains today the mainstream macroeconomic view. Armed with the knowledge of business cycles, the relationships of the circular flow of goods and services, and national income accounting, you will find that the journey into macroeconomic theory will be more clear.

After completion of this chapter, you should be able to do the following:

1. Use aggregate supply-aggregate demand analysis to describe and explain the Great Depression.
2. Compare and contrast classical economics and Keynesian economics.
3. Diagram and describe the Keynesian Cross model.
4. Define and describe the multiplier effect.
5. Use the multiplier formula to compute changes in nominal income resulting from increased spending.

The Last Depression

The last Depression occurred when most Americans were not yet born. Memories are strong and vivid, however, among millions of people who lived through the Great Depression of the 1930s. And one of the most striking recollections is recorded in Studs Terkel's *Hard Times,* a unique account of the period as seen through the eyes of those Americans who survived the period.

One reminiscence speaks to the shock of the Great Depression. As song lyricist E. Y. (Yip) Harburg recalls while living in New York City in the early thirties, "We thought American business was the rock of Gibraltar. We were the prosperous nation, and nothing could stop us now. . . . There was a feeling of certainty. If you made it, it was there forever. Suddenly the big dream exploded. The impact was unbelievable."

While gloomy statistics effectively capture the severity of the economic collapse, the personal experiences and psychological impact of the Depression are often more meaningful. Many had no job, no place to sleep, and did not know where the next meal was coming from. Bread lines and soup kitchens were available, but would they be there tomorrow? "Fellows with burlap on their shoes were lined up all around Columbus Circle [in New York City], and went for blocks and blocks around the park, waiting."

It was not the best of times for most Americans. Peggy Terry grew up in Oklahoma and remembers when her father took her to see one of the Hoovervilles—entire communities of homeless named for (and blamed on) President Hoover. "Here were all these people living in old rusted-out car bodies. I mean that was their home. There were people living in shacks made of orange crates. One family with a whole lot of kids was living in a piano box. This wasn't just a little section; this was maybe ten-miles wide and ten-miles long. People living in whatever they could junk together." And, contemplating the implications of the depression, Peggy said, "I think that's the worst thing that our system does to people, is to take away their pride. It prevents them being a human being. . . . You wake up in the morning, and it consciously hits you—it's just like a big hand that takes your heart and squeezes it—because you don't know what that day is to bring: hunger or you don't know."

As bad as it was, few people blamed themselves. Indeed, most blamed the system or Hoover. As Peggy Terry tells us, "[T]hey cussed [Hoover] up one side and down the other. . . . I'm not saying he's blameless, but I'm not saying either it was all his fault. Our system doesn't run by just one man, and it doesn't fall by just one man, either."[1]

---

[1] Studs Terkel, *Hard Times: An Oral History of the Great Depression* (New York: Pantheon Books, 1970), pp. 21, 56–7. Terkel's history, based upon hundreds of inter-

Depression memories and Depression realities—is Peggy Terry right? If we cannot attribute the collapse of the economy to one man, how and why did the system fail us? In the pages that follow, we will attempt to explain the forces responsible for the Great Depression and, in turn, examine the emergence of a new view of the macroeconomy. We will focus primarily on the Keynesian revolution and the reasons why classical economics was supplanted by Keynesian economics. Other prominent theories will be presented in later chapters.

A MACRO SUPPLY AND DEMAND MODEL

We have devoted considerable time to supply and demand in our study of microeconomics. We learned that, other things equal, the quantities demanded and supplied depend upon the product price. The demand curve is thus *downward* sloping to the right, reflecting this inverse relationship. Similarly, the supply curve is *upward* sloping to the right, indicating a direct relationship between price and quantity supplied. Moving from the micro marketplace to the macroeconomy, we can still draw upon this very useful supply and demand model.

Micro versus Macro. Unlike the micro model wherein we measured individual product price, we use the price level to measure changes in average prices for all goods and services in the macro model. And, instead of dealing with the quantity of the *individual* good in the micro supply and demand graph, we will measure the real GNP (of all goods and services). Instead of asking how changes in the demand for eggs affect the price of eggs and the quantity on the market, we now ask how changes in total spending or aggregate demand affect the price level and real output.

Aggregate demand (AD) *is an inverse relationship between the price level (as measured by the GNP deflator) and real GNP.*

Figure 13–1 illustrates the **aggregate demand (AD)** curve for all goods and services. It is an inverse relationship between the price level (as measured by the GNP deflator) and real GNP, with the price level measured on the vertical axis and real GNP on the horizontal axis. The aggregate demand curve tells us that, other things being equal, we will buy more goods at a lower price level than at a higher price level. If the price level rises from point *A* to point *B,* then our ability to purchase goods and services declines. Similarly, if the price level falls, our real income is greater, and we are able to purchase a greater quantity of goods and services.

views, is a stirring account of the Depression told through a mosaic of memories. It does not purport to be a collection of facts, nor does it pretend to be a sociological treatise. It is the story of the Great Depression as experienced and recalled by Americans who lived through this dark decade.

FIGURE 13–1

The Aggregate Demand
Curve

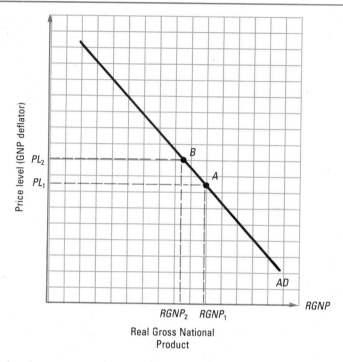

Like the micro demand curve, the *AD* curve slopes downward to the right, reflecting the inverse relationship between the price level and RGNP. If the price level rises from *PL*₁ to *PL*₂, we move up along the *AD* curve from *A* to *B*, indicating that with the same nominal income less RGNP can be purchased.

Aggregate supply (AS) *is the total amount of goods and services that is supplied at various price levels.*

The other side of the story is the **aggregate supply (AS)** curve, depicted in Figure 13–2. Although similar to the supply curve of a specific product, aggregate supply is the total amount of goods and services that is supplied at various price levels. The *AS* curve is horizontal over a large range of real output, then slopes upward gradually over a second range, and finally turns vertical. The lazy J-shape of the *AS* curve is important because it reflects the economy's ability to produce with varying degrees of inflationary pressure. On a micro level, factors such as diminishing returns, economies and diseconomies of scale, the availability of skilled labor, and related production variables play a vital role in determining how much and how efficiently a firm can produce. On a macro level, the nation's capacity to produce is governed by a similar set of opportunities and constraints.

The three zones represent the ability of the economy to produce under different degrees of inflationary pressure. The closer the economy gets to its capacity to produce, represented by the vertical portion of the *AS* curve in Zone III, the greater the pressure on prices to rise.

FIGURE 13–2

The Aggregate Supply
Curve

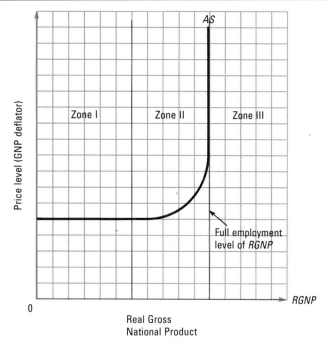

The *AS* curve is a J-shaped curve passing through three zones. Each zone represents a different degree of inflationary pressure. In Zone I RGNP can increase with no change in the price
level; in Zone II, the price level increases as RGNP increases; and in Zone III, the economy
reaches its production possibilities, so any effort to expand output results in pure inflation in
the short run.

Drawing upon the production-possibilities model as an analogy, Zone III
corresponds roughly to a location on the frontier. We are doing all we
can. If all (or the vast majority) of the nation's resources are utilized,
then any effort to do more will result in strains. Such strains often result
in inflation.

Zone I represents the other extreme (e.g., depression). Here we find
the economy operating well inside its production-possibilities frontier.
Efforts to expand production result in pure output gains. Inflationary
pressure is minimal or nonexistent because there is so much unused
capacity. Finally, Zone II depicts the economy in its more customary
state. The economy is neither at full employment nor in stark depression; efforts to increase output result in both a higher price level and
more real GNP.

Figure 13–3 shows the combined *AD-AS* model. By putting these two
together, we can illustrate the economic collapse during the 1930s. Point
A illustrates the economy in 1929. Then the bottom fell out. By 1933,
unemployment had reached nearly 25 percent, the price level had fallen

FIGURE 13–3
AD-AS Model and the
Great Depression

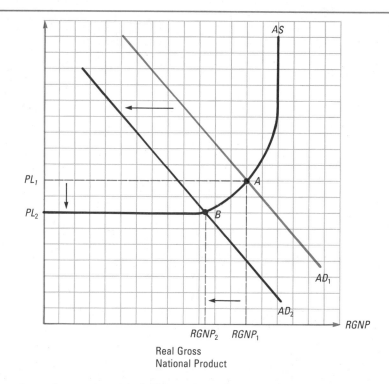

The collapse of economic activity is illustrated as a downward shift of the aggregate demand curve (from AD_1 to AD_2), resulting in a lower price level (PL_2) and reduced real output ($RGNP_2$).

by approximately 15 percent, and real GNP had declined by more than 30 percent. This is shown in Figure 13–3 as a leftward shift of the aggregate demand curve, from AD_1 to AD_2. The new intersection of AS and AD_2 at point B illustrates the economy operating at a lower price level and a lower level of real GNP.

The foregoing discussion is useful because it compares the most-watched policy variables, inflation and real GNP (or, with the help of some additional analysis, unemployment). Even more helpful is to use the model with actual numbers. The following CASE-IN-POINT offers this perspective.

CASE
• IN •
POINT

Aggregate Demand and Aggregate Supply

Another example, this time with actual values illustrating increased aggregate demand, is shown in Figure 13–4. Beginning at point A, where AD_1 intersects AS, the economy is producing a real GNP of $3,000 billion worth of goods and services. (This is determined by dividing the nominal output of $4,500 billion by the price level [index] of 150 and multiplying by 100. We arbitrarily assume that the base year price index of 100 is associated with a real output of $2,500 billion.) If the current administration tries to stimulate the economy through tax cuts and increased government spending to reach the full employment output level of $3,500 billion, this is shown by the shift of aggregate demand from AD_1 to AD_2. Our model indicates that its goal can be attained only if the price level increases to 165, representing a 10 percent rate of inflation. (Multiplying 165 times $3,500 and dividing by 100 gives us a nominal GNP of $5,775 billion). The rate of inflation is calculated by subtracting the beginning price level of 150 from the new price level of 165 and dividing by the beginning price level of 150: $(165 - 150)/150 = 10$. Although this is a purely hypothetical example, the Johnson adminstration experienced a similar set of circumstances.

Changes in nominal GNP are thus divided between a change in the price level (or inflation) and a change in real GNP. The goal of macroeconomic policy is to maximize the gains in real output and minimize the increase in the price level, a subject that occupies center stage in the remaining chapters of the book.

FIGURE 13–4
The AS-AD Model

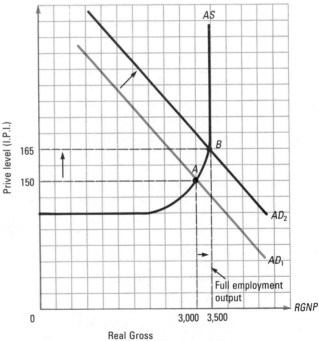

Beginning at point *A,* with a price level of 150 and a RGNP of $3,000 billion, the administration decides to increase employment and RGNP by cutting taxes and increasing spending. The upshot is a higher price level and more RGNP. *AD* shifts to the right (from AD_1 to AD_2) as a result of more spending, intersecting *AS* at point *B.*

Questions to Consider

1. *Although we have yet to consider the policies available to control inflation and unemployment (stagnant and/or declining real GNP), the analysis thus far suggests that decreased AS and increased AD (especially at full employment) is inflationary. Knowing this and little more, what would you suggest to keep the economy on an even keel?*

2. *What would happen to the price level and real GNP if, starting from point B, aggregate demand increased? What would happen to the price level and real GNP if aggregate demand decreased from point B?*

THINKING IT THROUGH

Would you be willing to live with a 10 percent inflation rate in order to reduce unemployment and increase real output?

CLASSICAL ECONOMICS VERSUS KEYNESIAN ECONOMICS

Classical economics *is the economic idea that the private marketplace provides incentives for businesses and consumers to maintain full employment.*

Say's Law *states that general overproduction is impossible because the act of supplying goods created its own demand.*

Until the Great Depression, recovery followed recession in what most economists thought was a reliable and consistent pattern. Some recessions and depressions lasted longer than expected, but recovery from the downturns came about without any direct government intervention. But in the period from 1929 to 1933, the economy went from bad to worse. Real GNP declined by nearly a third and the rising unemployment rate showed no signs of reversing itself. In early 1933, one out of every four people in the labor force was jobless. In the face of these grim economic conditions, President Hoover promised that recovery "was just around the corner." In fact, about the only thing just around the corner was another bread line. Why did Hoover believe that the economy would recover on its own? What were the so-called *self-correcting mechanisms* in the economy?

The main body of economic thought at this time was called **classical economics.** Economists thought that the private marketplace would provide incentives for businesses to lead the economy out of the depression. The principal idea was called **Say's Law,** named after Jean Baptiste Say, a late-18th to early-19th-century French philosopher. Say argued that general overproduction was impossible because the act of supplying goods created its own demand. In a barter economy, Say explained that when a merchant brought a cow to market, for example, the cow would be exchanged for perhaps 200 yards of cloth. In turn, the cloth would be exchanged for other articles. In other words, Say argued that there was a circular flow of production, income, and expenditures, in which what was produced would generate income (or articles of value), and all of the income would be spent on (or traded for) existing goods. By definition, each transaction meant that supply created its own demand; thus general overproduction was impossible. Say and his disciples argued that in a money economy nothing would change: money merely acted as a medium of exchange.

By 1930, classical economists had developed a much more detailed explanation of Say's Law of markets. How could they hope that the market would automatically bring about recovery? The key was wage and price flexibility. They argued that if unemployment was increasing, wages would decline. This decline in wage costs, they thought, would provide the incentive for businesses to hire more workers. In a short time, the economy would be returned to prosperity.

A similar logic was supposed to work in the financial markets. If the supply of loanable funds exceeded the demand for funds (or if saving exceeds investment demand), then interest rates would decline. With lower interest rates, the cost of borrowing money was cheaper. And, in the same mechanistic fashion, businesses would borrow more to invest in machinery, equipment, and buildings.

You may be thinking how could they think businesses would borrow more just because interest rates were lower or how could they think that businesses would hire more workers just because of lower wages? If you are, then you are thinking like a Keynesian.

John Maynard Keynes (1886–1946) studied mathematics and economics at Cambridge University in England. He served in a post in the British Treasury and went to Paris as a representative at the Treaty of Versailles. He was a prolific author whose list of books and essays would fill an entire chapter in this book. And his most famous work, *The General Theory of Employment, Interest, and Money* (1936), revolutionized economic thought. Indeed, Keynes turned classical economics upside-down, and in the process created a whole new set of theories which came to be known as **Keynesian economics.** In order to provide the setting in which this revolution occurred, let's look further into the economic conditions of the late twenties and thirties.

Keynesian economics *is a macroeconomic theory built on the premise that aggregate demand (expenditures) is the main determinant of income and employment.*

The collapse of agriculture and investment spending led in 1933 to a record unemployment rate of 25 percent. In the years from 1929 to 1933, the economic policies of the Hoover administration were a miserable failure. Shocked by the severity of the Depression, Hoover was still determined to balance the federal budget. In 1932, he pushed a bill through Congress which cut government spending and raised taxes. This action only served to magnify the problems: unemployment increased. Reluctantly, Hoover yielded to circumstances and launched the Reconstruction Finance Corporation—a government agency created to subsidize private industry and create jobs. But this was too little and too late![2]

In 1933, Franklin Delano Roosevelt swept into office with a national mandate to restore prosperity. A practical man, President Roosevelt surrounded himself with brilliant advisors. Together they launched the New Deal—an alphabet soup of government agencies and programs designed to create jobs. The AAA, NRA, WPA, CCC, and countless other programs put millions of people back to work. Although the economy showed signs of improvement, it took World War II to end America's worst depression.

In England, Keynes was hard at work on a project that would revolutionize economic thought and forever transform the U.S. economy. His first task was to dispel the classical notions that no longer explained reality. As we have seen, the classical ideas held that the economy contained a self-regulating mechanism which guaranteed high employment. Keynes showed the fallacy of such thinking. At a time when most conventional thinkers assumed that the economy would return to full employment within a short time, Keynes explained why the economy went into a long stall at a high unemployment rate. His idea was really quite simple: *look at total spending (aggregate expenditures)* if you want to understand what is happening to the economy. Private investment had been declining since the late 1920s. This decrease in investment spending led to a decrease in jobs and income which, in turn, led to a decrease in consumer spending. Instead of getting better, Keynes said, things only got worse because little was being done to halt the downward cycle. Decreased income led to less spending; less spending meant lower business sales; reduced sales caused businesses to cut production and lay off workers; more unemployment meant less income and less spending, and so on, ad infinitum. This process became known as the multiplier effect.

Keynes applied the same logic to *financial markets*. If interest rates were declining in this economic environment, Keynes asked, why would businesses invest more? His answer? Only if businesses had favorable expectations regarding sales and profits would they increase investment. In other words, it wasn't that wage and interest costs were insignificant. Rather, it was the more important role played by *aggregate expenditures* that explained why businesses were not hiring more workers and building more factories. Why expand production and hire workers when consumers were spending less? Why borrow money to build new factories if sales are declining?

---

[2] The Federal Reserve was also of little help. Instead of creating a climate of easy credit to stimulate the economy, they raised the discount rate, the amount charged on loans to commercial banks.

To reverse the downward trend, Keynes argued that it was necessary for the government to increase spending. **Aggregate expenditures** (or total planned spending), he said, consists of consumption, planned investment, government, and net exports. If private spending (consumption and investment) is down, what else is there to do but compensate for the declining private spending with increasing public (government) spending. It was this idea, that government must take the responsibility for the health of the nation's economy, which was to reshape the U.S. economy if not revolutionize U.S. capitalism.

In the next section, we will examine more closely the fine points of Keynesian economics. What determines the level of income and employment? Why is aggregate demand the engine of the economy? How does the multiplier process work?

Keynesian Economics

The core of Keynesian economics is *aggregate expenditures*—the total planned spending on goods and services produced. Indeed, in the General Theory, Keynes posed two important questions. He first asked, *what determines the level of income and employment in society?* His answer, in two big words, was aggregate expenditures. In other words, it was the spending of consumer households, businesses, and governments that provided the incentive for private businesses to hire workers and produce goods. If total spending was insufficient, then unemployment would result. Even worse, if aggregate expenditures were declining, then employment would go into a kind of free fall to which there would be no clear bottom.

The second question followed logically from the first one. What determines aggregate expenditures? Keynes' answer seemed paradoxical. He said that national income, the total income earned in producing goods and services, determines how much people spend. With these two relationships, Keynes established what computer programmers would call a closed loop. Figure 13–5 illustrates this relationship in a simple schematic drawing. The important feature is the *interdependence of spending and income*. Spending depends upon income, which, in turn, depends upon spending. In a computer program, this leads to endless repetition of whatever is contained in the loop. In the economy of the 1930s, this led to a seemingly endless downturn of economic activity. Unlike the classical economists who promised a return to full employment equilibrium in time, Keynes said that equilibrium was possible with high unemployment. In other words, the economy could come to a rest at a level of real GNP far below our potential output. Since declining aggregate expenditures is the same thing as declining sales, businesses will respond in very predictable ways. They will cut production, lay off workers, and possibly reduce prices. With fewer people working,

FIGURE 13–5
The Simplified Keynesian
Model

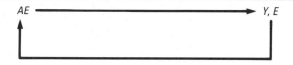

AE = Aggregate expenditures
Y = National income and product
E = Employment

This schematic illustrates the central role of aggregate expenditures in Keynesian economics. *AE*, which determines the level of national income and product (GNP), is determined by national income and employment. The closed-loop character of income and expenditures is the basis for the multiplier effect.

less will be spent, which returns us to the beginning of the closed loop character of the economy. In short, spending is the key. We now turn to examine spending more carefully.

The Consumption-Income Relationship. Because personal consumption expenditures account for nearly two thirds of aggregate expenditures, Keynes began his analysis with household spending (or, briefly, consumption). Following his convention, we will let the letter C represent consumption and Y_d stand for disposable income.[3] In his study of consumer behavior, Keynes developed what he called the *fundamental psychological law* of consumer spending. To paraphrase Keynes, people will increase spending as their incomes increase, but not as much as the increase in their incomes. In other words, with more disposable income we spend some and save the rest. Although not an earth-shattering revelation, the implications of this simple observation are enormous.

Table 13–1 and the corresponding Figure 13–6 illustrate a hypothetical consumption *(C)* − disposable *(Y_d)* relationship for an individual household. We begin at the micro level (for an individual family) in order to discuss what happens when income is zero.

The figures in Columns two and three represent average weekly incomes and consumption, respectively; Columns four and five show the *changes* in Y_d and C. For example, the change in Y_d between 1985 and 1987 is $200 ($600 − $400), and the corresponding change in C is $160 ($560 − $400). But it is Column 6 that Keynes was interested in.

---

[3] If you are wondering why we use the letter Y for income, the choice is really quite arbitrary, except that I is used to represent investment. Subscripts are also used to define different types of income and investment. For example, the subscript n attached to Y, as in Y_n, means national income; Y_d means disposable income, and so on. Moreover, since most economic relationships are measured in dollar terms, economists are prone to express whatever they can quantitatively.

TABLE 13-1

The Consumption-Income Relationship (weekly income and consumption figures)

Year	(1) Disposable Income (Y_d)	(2) Consumption (C)	(3) Change in Disposable Income (ΔY_d)	(4) Change in Consumption (ΔC)	(5) Marginal Propensity to Consume (MPC) (5) ÷ (4)	(6)
1985	$400	$400				
			$100	$80	0.8	
1986	500	480				
			100	80	0.8	
1987	600	560				
			200	160	0.8	
1988	800	720				
			50	40	0.8	
1989	850	760				
			50	40	0.8	
1990	900	800				
			100	80	0.8	
1991	1000	880				

The marginal propensity to consume is the ratio of the change in consumption to the change in income. For example, between 1990 and 1991, our hypothetical consumer increases spending *(C)* by $80 out of $100 additional income *(Y)*. The *MPC* is thus 80 ÷ 100, or 0.80, or 4/5, or 80%.

The Marginal Propensity to Consume.   Keynes' fundamental psychological law tells us that when income increases, people will spend some, but not all of the increase in income. In other words, on the average, consumers will spend a certain percentage of extra income, defined as the **marginal propensity to consume (MPC).** The *MPC* is calculated by dividing the change in consumption by the change in disposable income. Expressed symbolically, we may write this as follows:

Marginal propensity to consume (MPC) *is the ratio of extra consumption to extra income,* $\dfrac{\Delta C}{\Delta Y}$

$$MPC = \frac{\text{Change in } C}{\text{Change in } Y_d} = \frac{\Delta C}{\Delta Y}$$

where Δ means "change in."

Between 1985 and 1987 and for each other pair of years, the MPC is 0.80 (or four fifths).

$$MPC = \frac{560 - 400}{600 - 400} = \frac{160}{200} = \frac{4}{5} \text{ or } 0.80.$$

Although the *MPC* is a constant 0.80 throughout this example, the *MPC* actually varies considerably from year to year. We use a constant value in order to simplify the relationship.[4]

---

[4] It is important to note that these are averages. You and I may spend 105 percent of our extra income, while our neighbors and friends may spend only two thirds of additional income.

FIGURE 13–6

Consumption-Income
Relationship

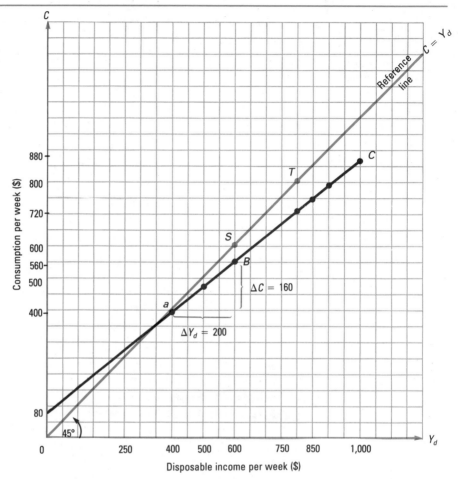

The consumption schedule illustrates the relationship between consumer spending and disposable income. The intersection of the C schedule and the 45-degree line (at point a) illustrates equilibrium—all income is spent. As income increases from \$400 to \$600, consumption increases from \$400 to \$560, indicating that the $MPC = 0.80$.

The same relationship is also illustrated graphically in Figure 13–6. First, a 45-degree reference line is included in order to compare spending and income. Because the reference line bisects the 90-degree angle, we know (from geometry) that every point on the line is an equal distance from each axis. Since we measure C on the vertical axis and Y_d on the horizontal axis, this means that $C = Y_d$ at every point on the line. For example, points S and T represent spending and income levels of \$600 and \$800 respectively.

The line labeled C is the consumption schedule. It is drawn by plotting the Y_d, C pairs of values from the table and then connecting the points. The *MPC* may also be illustrated on the graph. First, although any two points may be used, let's use points *a* and *b* representing the years 1985 and 1987. The *MPC* is the vertical distance between the two points divided by the corresponding horizontal distance. The horizontal distance is the change in income; the vertical distance is the change in consumption.

The graph is useful because we can see the $C - Y_d$ relationship more clearly, and it also enables us to make simple straight-line projections. For example, assuming that consumers continue to spend 80 percent of additional income, how much will be spent if income increases to $1,200 in 1992? Multiplying the *MPC* times the change in income gives us the change in consumption. The amount of additional spending caused by increased income is called **induced consumption.** By adding the induced consumption spending to the old (1991) level of *C,* we arrive at the new level of spending. In equation form,

Induced consumption *is the amount of additional spending caused by increased income.*

> 1. $\Delta C = MPC \times \Delta Y_d$, and
> 2. New $C_{1992} = $ Old $C_{1991} + \Delta C$

Substituting the actual data,

> 1. $\Delta C = 0.80 \times 200 = 160$
> 2. New $C_{1992} = 880 + 160 = 1,040.$

Following the same line of reasoning, we may ask what will happen if the family breadwinner becomes unemployed. Assuming that the year is 1985 and income falls to zero, how much will our household spend? Multiplying the *MPC* of 0.80 times the change in income ($400) determines the change in consumption, $320. Subtracting the change of $320 from the 1985 level of *C* ($400) indicates that our hypothetical family will continue to spend $80 per week.

Autonomous consumption *is the amount of consumer spending that does not depend upon income.*

Autonomous consumption is the term used to describe this phenomenon—the amount of consumer spending that occurs when income is zero. In other words, it is that portion of consumption which does not depend upon income.[5] Total spending thus consists of two parts, autonomous consumption (one which is independent of income) and induced consumption (which depends directly upon income [$MPC \times \Delta Y$]).[6]

---

[5] It may be helpful to think of this as spending to maintain a *subsistence* standard of living.

[6] For those of you who are mathematically inclined, you may have observed that the *MPC* is the slope of the *C* schedule. Knowing this and that the *C* schedule intersects the vertical axis at the autonomous consumption value, we may write a simple equation for the *C* schedule: $C = a + b Y_d$, where a = autonomous consumption and b = the *MPC*.

THINKING IT THROUGH

What sources of money would you draw upon if you were unemployed? What might you (or others) do if these sources are tapped out?

Our initial discussion of consumption is based upon an individual household instead of total consumer spending. Although it is perfectly logical to show zero income for a household, it makes no sense at all to discuss zero income for the whole economy. After all, how can national or disposable income fall to zero? For the rest of this chapter, we focus exclusively on the macroeconomy.

The Consumption Schedule: Movements versus Shifts

As with the supply and demand models discussed throughout the book, an important distinction exists between a movement along a curve and a shift of the curve. The same is true for consumption.

Changes in disposable income cause consumers to spend more or less. This is represented as a movement along the existing schedule. For example, as shown in Figure 13–7, if income increases from $3,000 billion to $3,100 billion, with an *MPC* of 0.80 consumption increases by $80 billion, from $3,000 billion to $3,080 billion, or from point *a* to point *b*.

Of course, *nonincome factors* also influence consumer spending. Changes in *wealth, taxes and transfers,* and *expectations* (regarding prices and income) also lead to changes in consumption. However, instead of a movement along the existing curve, the *C* schedule will shift up or down (away from or toward the horizontal axis). The reason is that the conditions operating under the old consumption-income relationship have changed. For example, research has shown that consumers with substantial wealth (in the form of stocks, bonds, and property) will spend more freely than families with limited financial assets. If stock prices increase, people are wealthier and often spend more of their current income. The additional spending is in the form of more autonomous consumption since the stimulus is not related to changes in disposable income. This is shown in Figure 13–7 as a shift from *C* to C_1. If consumers are optimistic about the economy, and they expect their incomes to increase and prices to remain stable, a similar upward shift will occur in the *C* schedule.

Changes in taxes will also affect consumption. Taxes may be classified into two categories: lump-sum and income taxes. We deal here only with lump-sum taxes, such as property and sales, since personal income and social security taxes vary with income. When lump-sum taxes in-

FIGURE 13-7
Consumption: Movement
Versus Shifts

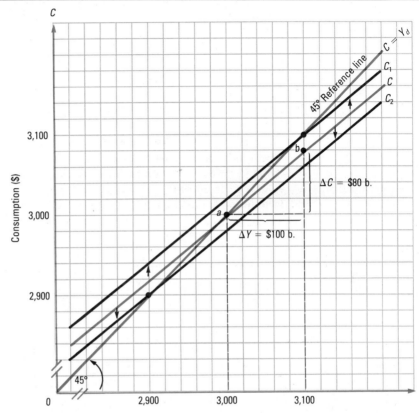

Changes in income cause changes in consumer spending, shown as movements along the existing C schedule. For example, as income increases from $3,000 to $3,100, consumption increases from $3,000 to $3,080 (by $80), a movement from point a to point b on the same schedule. Nonincome factors, however, will cause the C schedule to shift. For example, lower stock prices or expectations of a gloomy economy will cause the C schedule to shift downward, from C to C_2. Conversely, higher bond prices and other favorable wealth effects will cause an increase in spending, shown as an upward shift of the schedule from C to C_1.

crease, autonomous consumption will decline (by an amount equal to the *MPC* times the change in taxes). This is represented as a downward shift of the C schedule from C to C_2. We will deal with income taxes in the next chapter.

Investment Expenditures

A second element of private aggregate expenditures is investment. It was here that Keynes devoted substantial care to explain why business investment played a key role in economic fluctuations.

As we noted earlier, Keynes parted company with the classical economists over explanations of investment behavior. Although he recognized the importance of interest rates as the price of borrowed funds, Keynes said that business expectations were often more important. If sales and profits expectations were gloomy, cheap money would not be a sufficient incentive for businesses to invest. Thus, as consumers spent less on goods produced, businesses would not only cut production and lay off workers, they also would cancel plans to invest in plant and equipment.

To put this in perspective, Figure 13–8 illustrates the market for loanable funds. Saving (the supply of loanable funds) and investment (the demand for loanable funds) are each depicted as functions of the interest rate. We begin with the market interest rate at 10 percent and a $60 billion surplus of loanable funds. Classical economists argued that the excess supply of funds would depress interest rates. As rates declined,

FIGURE 13–8
The Market for Loanable
Funds

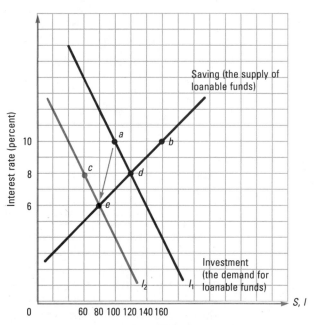

Beginning with a 10 percent interest rate, Saving (the quantity supplied of loanable funds) exceeds Investment (the quantity demanded for loanable funds). Classical economists predicted that equilibrium would be restored as interest rates fell. However, during the Great Depression, even falling interest rates failed to provide adequate incentive for business investment. Keynes explained this reluctance to invest by pointing out that business expectations of sales and profits were at least as important as the interest rate; thus, instead of returning to equilibrium, investment may shift downward in response to a grim economic outlook, resulting in a multiple contraction of income.

businesses would borrow more money and invest the funds in all sorts of productive assets. Although this adjustment might require years, equilibrium was inevitable.

Keynes agreed that the cost of funds was important, but he also knew that sales and profits (and expectations about future earnings) were often more important. Let's assume that businesses have an average expected rate of return of 8 percent. If this expected yield on investments is less than the market rate of interest (cost of borrowed funds), then the project would not be undertaken, and the money would not be borrowed. Moreover, if the business outlook is gloomy, businesses will scale back their investment plans. This is shown in Figure 13–8 as a leftward (and downward) shift of the investment demand curve, from I_1 to I_2. The 8 percent interest rate now cuts the I_2 demand curve at point *c*. Since saving is still greater than investment, the surplus of loanable funds will create further downward pressure on interest rates. Not until interest rates reach 6 percent will equilibrium be restored. Instead of moving down the I_1 curve to an equilibrium position at point *d,* the economy winds up at point *e* at a much lower level of investment expenditures. And, as Keynes pointed out, this decline in investment spending will trigger a decline in consumption and an even greater decline in national income.

THE INCOME-EXPENDITURES MODEL (WITHOUT GOVERNMENT)

In order to maintain continuity with our earlier work, we will begin our discussion by returning to Model II of the circular flow of goods and services (Figure 12–2, page 321), in which the economy was depicted without government and without international trade. In this example, recall that equilibrium requires that planned expenditures $(C + I_p)$ equal aggregate supply $(C + S)$. Since we can cancel the consumption element on each side of the identity, equilibrium may be stated as the equality of I_p and S. Let's compare these relationships by incorporating our national income and product data from the last chapter.

Figure 13–9 illustrates aggregate private expenditures $(C + I_p)$ as block A and aggregate supply as block B. (Remember that aggregate supply is just another term for national product, and that by definition national product = national income.) In order to equate GNP with NI, we also assume that capital consumption allowances and indirect business taxes are zero.

Because production exceeds total planned expenditures, the economy is in disequilibrium. The total production of goods and services ($2,600 billion) exceeds the total planned expenditures of $C + I_p$ ($2,500 billion). The difference of $100 billion is the amount by which saving exceeds planned investment. This shortfall is the amount of unplanned

FIGURE 13–9

Aggregate Production *(AP)* Exceeds Aggregate Expenditures *(AE)*

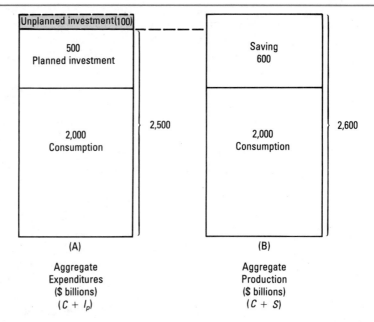

Aggregate (private) expenditures *(C + I$_p$)* is depicted as Block A and aggregate production *(C + S)* is shown in Block B. Since *AP > AE* (or *S > I$_p$*), the economy is in disequilibrium, and business firms will cut production, lay off workers, and reduce prices. (The difference between *AP* and *AE* is the unplanned inventory investment, shown as the shaded rectangle at the top of Block A.)

inventory accumulation, represented by the shaded rectangle at the top of the aggregate expenditures block.

How will producers react to this situation? As we have shown previously, firms will respond by reducing output, laying off workers, and possibly reducing prices. As this retrenchment spreads throughout the economy, will national income fall by exactly $100 billion? As Keynes was quick to observe, although the economy would certainly contract, national income would fall by some multiple of the $100 billion. Let's see how it works.

The Multiplier Effect

*The **multiplier effect** refers to the process by which a change in spending results in a greater (magnified) change in income.*

In the simplest terms, the **multiplier effect** refers to the process by which a change in spending results in a greater change in income. In order to understand why this is so, we can trace the logic of the multiplier process through two basic propositions.

First, *every expenditure is an income.* Actually, this is a basic rule of double-entry bookkeeping dating back hundreds of years. For example, when you spend $300 on a compact disk player, the proprietor receives

$300 of additional income. Your expenditure is his income. Of course, the process also works for decreases in spending. If businesses or consumers reduce expenditures, this is the same as declining sales and income.

Second is *the marginal propensity to consume.* Although this is ground we have covered, it is useful to emphasize the fact that on the average people will increase spending when they receive additional income. The ratio of the extra consumption to extra income is the marginal propensity to consume *(MPC).*

Marginal propensity to save (MPS) *is defined as the ratio of extra saving to extra income,* $\dfrac{\Delta S}{\Delta Y}$

A closely related concept is the extra saving out of extra income, known as the **marginal propensity to save (MPS).** Since there are only two things we can do with disposable income, spend or save, the fraction of extra consumption *(MPC)* and the fraction of extra saving *(MPS)* must *always* total 1, or 100 percent. For example, if you receive an additional $1,000, and you spend $700 and save $300, your *MPC* = 0.7 (or 70 percent) and your *MPS* = 0.3 (or 30 percent). By definition, the *MPC + MPS* = 1.

Table 13–2 illustrates the multiplier effect (or process). We resume with our previous example in which production exceeds expenditures by $100 billion. Businesses respond to this by reducing investment by $100 billion, and this starts our chain reaction. The *MPC* is 0.8 (or 4/5). The time periods are divided into quarters of the year.

The process begins as the $100 decrease in investment reduces income by $100 (following our first proposition that every expenditure is an income). The change in consumption is − $80, 80 percent of the reduced income. Since the change in consumption plus the change in saving equals the change in income, saving declines by $20. (We can also

TABLE 13–2	Time Period (3 month periods)	Change in Income	=	Change in Consumption	+	Change in Saving
The Multiplier Process (all figures in billions of dollars)	1	− 100.00		− 80.00		− 20.00
	2	− 80.00		− 64.00		− 16.00
	3	− 64.00		− 51.20		− 12.80
	4	− 51.20		− 40.96		− 10.24
	Total after one year	− 295.20		− 236.16		− 59.04
	Total of all other periods	− 204.80		− 163.84		− 40.96
	Total Change	− 500.00		− 400.00		− 100.00

The multiplier describes a process by which a change in spending causes a greater change in income. In our example, business investment declines by $100 billion, which starts the process. Since every expenditure is an income, the decrease in investment is translated immediately as a decline in income. Since the *MPC* is 0.8, consumer spending declines by $80 billion. This sets off round two: as income falls by $80 billion, consumption declines by 80 percent, or $64 billion. Adding all of the changes in income, the original $100 billion decreases in investment spending causes a $500 billion decrease in income.

compute the change in saving by multiplying the MPS times the change in income: $0.2 \times -100 = -20$.)

The multiplier process continues in Period 2 as the $80 decrease in consumption results in an equal decrease in income. Multiplying the *MPC* (0.8) times the changes in income ($-$80$), determines the 2nd period decrease in consumption, $-$64$. Because the iterative process continues round by round, there is no need to describe each additional period. The changes in income, consumption, and saving become increasingly smaller, gradually approaching zero. Indeed, the numbers become so small that it is useful to round them off to the nearest dollar. If we add all of the individual changes in income, the total final change in income is $500, five times the original change in investment. Instead of wading through the table to prove this, let's look at a shortcut method.

The Multiplier Formula

Although a table clearly shows the round-by-round multiplier process, such repetitive (and monotonous) operations are calculated much faster by a computer. For us mortals, it is far more efficient to use a formula to find the effect of a change in spending upon income.

*The **multiplier** is the ratio of the final change in income to the original change in spending (aggregate expenditures or AE) or the reciprocal of the marginal propensity to save (MPS).*

The **multiplier** is the ratio of the final change in income to the original change in spending (aggregate expenditures or *AE*). As such, the multiplier is a coefficient or number that tells us how much greater will be the change in income compared to the original change in spending. Since we know the final change in income, dividing $500 by $100 gives us 5 as the value of the multiplier. Expressed as a formula, we can write

$$m = \frac{\Delta Y}{\Delta AE},$$

where m is the value of the multiplier, *Y* is the final change in income, and AE is the original change in spending. (Note: ΔAE is used here to include changes in any one or more of its components, consumption [*C*], planned investment [I_p], government [*G*], or net exports [*NX*].) Substituting the actual values, we can solve for the multiplier.

$$m = \frac{500}{100} = 5$$

This is fine if we know the value, but generally the change in income (or the change in spending) is the unknown value. In this case, we have two unknowns, *m* and *Y*, and we cannot solve for *m*; thus the need for another definition of the multiplier.

*The **multiplier** is also defined as the reciprocal of the marginal propensity to save (MPS).* The reciprocal of any number is that number inverted. For example, the reciprocal of 2/5 is 5/2, or 2½; the reciprocal of 1/4 is 4/1, or 4. If we know the *MPC*, we can easily find the *MPS*, since *MPC* + *MPS* = 1. Just subtract the *MPS* from 1. In our example, the *MPC* is 0.8. Subtracting 0.8 from 1 gives us an *MPS* of 0.2. The reciprocal of 0.2 is 5. Expressing the values as fractions, the *MPC* is 4/5; 1 − 4/5 = 1/5; and the reciprocal of 1/5 is 5.[7]

Expressing this formula symbolically,

$$m = \frac{1}{MPS}$$

Substituting the value for MPS, we can solve for *m*.

$$m = \frac{1}{0.2} \text{ or } \frac{1}{1/5} = \frac{5}{1} = 5.$$

If the question is "with an *MPC* of 0.8, how much will income change if spending decreases by $100?" first find the multiplier (1/*MPS*) and then solve for the change in income.

(1) $$m = \frac{1}{MPS} = \frac{1}{0.2} = 5.$$

(2) $$m = \frac{\Delta Y}{\Delta AE} = \qquad 5 = \frac{\Delta Y}{-100}; \Delta Y = -500.$$

If you prefer, you can easily rearrange the second expression in order to put the unknown *(Y)* on the left side of the formula. Rewriting the formula, we get

$$\Delta Y = m \times \Delta AE.$$

Of course, you can also rewrite the basic expression in terms of Δ AE:

$$\Delta AE = \frac{\Delta Y}{m}$$

However you write the formula, the relationship is the same.

THINKING IT THROUGH

If the MPC is 0.75, by how much will income change if investment increases by $50?

---

[7] If you haven't worked with decimals and fractions recently, do not despair! To convert a decimal to a fraction, just read its value: 0.8 is read as "eight tenths." Expressed as a fraction, eight tenths is 8/10. Reducing to the lowest common denominator, 8/10 = 4/5. Also, if you want to express a decimal as a percent, just multiply it times 100: 0.8 x 100 = 80%.

The Keynesian Cross Model

Keynesian Cross model *relates aggregate expenditures to aggregate production, showing the three possible outcomes: a shortage, a surplus, and equilibrium.*

We are now ready to develop the complete **Keynesian Cross model,** also known as the *income-expenditures model* or the *theory of national income determination.* The material we have already covered in Chapters 11 and 12 provide a perfect takeoff point for the Keynesian Cross model.

The circular flow of goods and services enabled us to examine the relationship between aggregate expenditures and aggregate production. We saw that there are only three possible outcomes: a shortage (in which $AE > AP$), a surplus (in which $AP > AE$), and equilibrium (where $AE = AP$). If a nation's planned expenditures exceed its output, the economy experiences inventory depletion. This sets the stage for an expansion of output and employment as businesses gear up to meet demand. Conversely, inventory accumulation occurs when aggregate production exceeds aggregate expenditures. As a result, as we saw in Figure 13–9, the economy is likely to experience a multiple contraction of income (output and employment).

To build the Keynesian income-expenditures model, we need the same basic ingredients: AP and AE. We start with AP because it is the reference against which we measure the planned expenditures. Moreover, all output and income measures are expressed in nominal terms, for example, nominal GNP, income and expenditures.

Aggregate Production

From Figure 13–6, we know that the 45-degree line establishes an equality between expenditures and income. In Figure 13–10, however, this reference line takes on special significance. Since national income equals national product, the aggregate production schedule represents the collective production plans of businesses. In other words, this curve tells us that businesses plan to produce the quantity of goods and services that they think will be purchased. If we select an arbitrary national income level such as $2,000 billion on the horizontal axis, this amount of output will equal the total expenditures or national product on the vertical axis.[8]

---

[8] Individual businesses intentionally produce more or less than they plan to sell because of unintended or unplanned changes in inventory. But this is on the microeconomic level. On the macroeconomic level, however, we assume that such differences disappear, and that on the average firms try to produce what they think they will sell. From a theoretical perspective, this is much more appealing than the alternative assumptions—that firms will produce more/less than their expected sales.

FIGURE 13–10

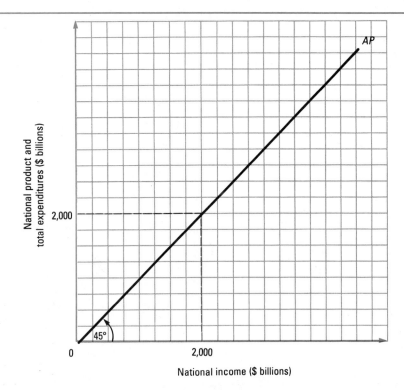

The 45-degree reference line shows the identity of national income and national product (and total expenditures). It serves as the aggregate production *(AP)* curve because business will produce that quantity of goods that they think will be purchased.

Aggregate Expenditures

Although *AE* consists of consumption, planned investment, government purchases, and net exports, we confine ourselves to private expenditures for the moment. Figure 13–11a illustrates a consumption schedule with an *MPC* of 0.75 and autonomous consumption of $500 billion. Where the consumption schedule intersects the aggregate production (45-degree) curve at equilibrium point E_1, consumers spend all that they earn ($C = Y_n = \$2,000$ billion. (Since government is temporarily out of the picture, there is no distinction between national income and disposable income.) At income levels greater than the equilibrium, consumers save a portion of their incomes. At the $3,000 billion level of income, for example, consumers save $250 billion and spend $2,750 billion. This amount of saving is represented graphically as the vertical distance cd between the *AP* curve and *C* schedule. At income levels less than equilibrium, consumers spend more than they earn. This is illustrated on the graph at $1,000 billion income, where consumers spend $1,250, $250

FIGURE 13–11a

The Consumption
Schedule

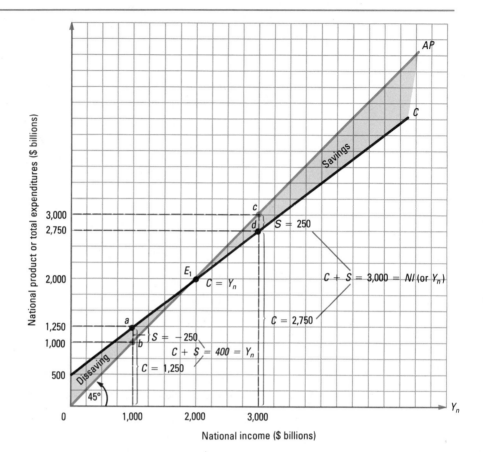

Comparing the consumption schedule with the *AP* schedule (45-degree line), we can illustrate saving and dissaving. At income levels greater than equilibrium ($2,000), where $C = Y$, income exceeds consumption. For example, at the $3,000 income level, $C = $2,750 and $S = $250 (represented graphically as the vertical distance *cd* between *AP* and *C* schedule). At income less than equilibrium, consumers spend more than their incomes—what economists call dissaving. This is shown at an income of $1,000, where $C = $1,250 and $S = -$250 (represented graphically as the vertical distance *ab* between *AP* and the *C* schedule).

more than they earn, a concept economists call *dissaving* (shown as the distance *ab*).

Planned investment expenditures (I_p) is the second part of private demand, the income spent on machinery, equipment, and buildings.[9] To keep this simple, we assume that I_p is a constant $250 billion. In Figure 13–11b, planned investment is added to the consumption schedule to give us the $C + I_p$ schedule. Because I_p is a constant value, $C + I_p$ is parallel to the *C* schedule throughout.

[9] Remember that *unplanned* investment is the increase or decrease in inventories resulting from the imbalance between *AP* and *AE*.

FIGURE 13–11b Consumption + Planned Investment and Disequilibrium Conditions

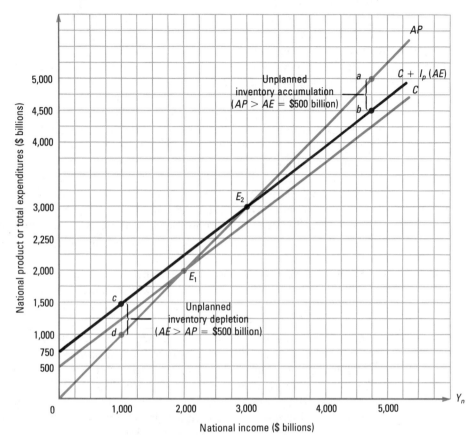

Unplanned inventory depletion is the amount by which aggregate expenditures *(AE)* exceed aggregate production *(AP)*, represented as the distance *cd* at the $1,000 income level. When *AE > AP*, businesses will increase output, hire workers, and raise prices. Unplanned inventory accumulation is the amount by which *AP* exceeds *AE*, also measured at a specific income level. For example, at the $5,000 billion income level, *AP* = $5,000 billion at point *a* and *AE* = $4,500 billion at point *b*; the distance *ab* represents the amount of unplanned inventory accumulation ($500 billion). In response, businesses will cut employment and production and lower prices.

Equilibrium and Disequilibrium Revisited. The intersection of the *AP* curve and the $C + I_p$ schedule determines equilibrium. As discussed in Chapter 12, if planned expenditures equal aggregate production, unplanned inventory investment must be zero. Of course, considering how unlikely it is that the plans of 15 million businesses will mesh perfectly with the plans of some 65 million households, the probability of equilibrium is very remote. Equilibrium is important, however, because there is a much greater tendency for the economy to move toward equilibrium than away from it.

Disequilibrium is a normal economic situation: aggregate expenditures are either less than or more than aggregate production. These conditions are illustrated in Figure 13–11b. Unplanned inventory accumulation occurs when $AE < AP$. The gap is measured graphically as the vertical distance between AP and $C + I_p$ (AE) at any income level greater than equilibrium, for example, the distance ab ($500 billion) at the $5,000 billion income level. This condition is recessionary because businesses will reduce production and lay off workers when their production exceeds sales. Investment will decline and, with fewer people working, consumer spending will decrease.

The other state of disequilibrium occurs when aggregate expenditures exceed aggregate production, shown in Figure 13–11b as the vertical distance cd ($500 billion) between AP and the $C + I_p$ (or AE) schedule at the $1,000 billion level of income. Because there is unplanned inventory depletion (that is, sales exceed production), businesses are motivated to increase output and hire more workers.

Before we added planned investment, our equilibrium income was $2,000 billion at E_1. When we add I_p, however, the equilibrium level rises to $3,000 billion at E_2. Why not increase to $2,250, by the amount of investment? What's going on here?

As we can see in Figure 13–11b, $AE > AP$ at the $2,000 level of income. In other words, total planned expenditures of consumption ($2,000) and investment ($250) exceed the aggregate product (or AP) ($2,000). This is an expansionary condition. As the $250 billion of increased spending is received as new income, the multiplier effect is invoked. New income is spent, and this generates additional rounds of income and spending. Let's take a closer look at this important process.

The Multiplier Revisited: A Graphical Approach

Figure 13–12 illustrates the multiplier process in graphical form. Earlier, we discussed the multiplier effect attributed to a surplus situation (in which $AP > AE$). Here we examine the opposite situation: $AE > AP$. This graph is nearly identical to Figure 13–11b, except that the scale has been increased in order to see the changes more clearly.

Beginning at the original equilibrium point E_1, after planned investment is added, aggregate expenditures ($C + I_p$) exceed the aggregate production ($C + S$). The distance Ea represents the amount by which $AE > AP$ (or planned investment exceeds saving). Because this represents additional spending, and because every expenditure is an income, the extra income received (ab) is equal to that which is spent (Ea). ($Ea = ab = $250.) Since the $MPC = 0.75$, income recipients will spend 75 percent of the $250, or $187.50, shown as line segment bc. This process

FIGURE 13–12

The Multiplier Process

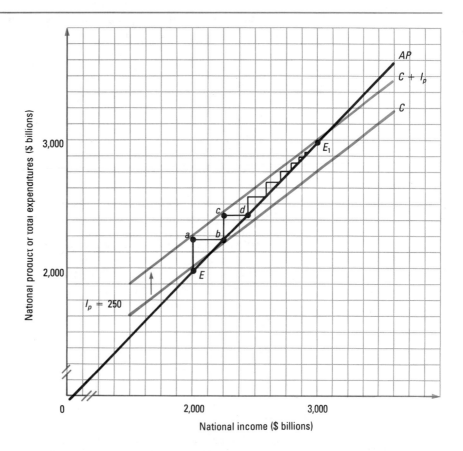

Starting with an equilibrium position at point E, adding investment spending triggers the multiplier process. Investment of $250 billion (distance Ea) is received as new income (distance ab). With an MPC of 0.75, people will spend $187.5 billion (0.75 × 250), or distance bc. Since every expenditure is an income, this process continues until the new equilibrium E_1 is reached. The new income level is $3,000, $1,000 more than the beginning ($2,000) level. Multiplying the original change in spending (250) times the multiplier (4) gives us the change in income, $1,000. Adding the change ($1,000) to the old income level ($2,000), gives us the new equilibrium, $3,000.

is repeated again and again until the new equilibrium E_2 is reached. The multiplier process is represented graphically as the stair-step sequence from E to a, a to b, b to c, c to d, and so forth.

Using our multiplier formula, m = $\Delta Y \div \Delta AE$, we can easily confirm our graphical solution.

1. $\Delta Y = m \times \Delta AE$.
2. $\Delta Y = 4 \times \$250 = \$3,000$
3. New $Y = $ Old $Y + \Delta Y$.
4. New $Y = \$2,000 + \$1,000 = \$3,000$.

Although our example implies that the economy comes to a rest at the new equilibrium E_2, nothing could be further from the truth. The actual dynamics of the multiplier process does not begin with one equilibrium, only to await the next jolt of extra spending. Indeed, unanticipated changes in aggregate expenditures occur daily. Here are some examples:

- The dollar increases in value, demand for U.S. goods decreases, and imports increase.
- Mortgage interest rates fall, leading to a surge in home buying.
- Congress enacts a mass transit bill calling for $5 billion of additional spending this year.
- Automakers eliminate rebates and other sales incentives on new car sales, sending consumer spending into a tailspin.
- Lower installment credit rates cause consumers to increase spending on durable goods like autos and household appliances.

Such changes are nearly impossible to predict and build into the nation's economic outlook. As we move closer to one projected equilibrium, a change in spending may quickly propel us beyond or reverse our direction and usher in a recession.

Read the following CASE-IN-POINT to gain a special insight into the multiplier process.

CASE
• IN •
POINT

Macro or Micro—It's Still a Multiplier

Marachi was a sleepy little nonindustrial community located on the banks of the Osage River in Oregon. The area's economy was primarily agricultural, although a local state university provided employment for nearly 20 percent of the town's residents. And then it happened.

Cow Chemical Chemical (CCC), a national chemical firm, purchased a large plot of land on the outskirts of town along the river. It then set about wooing the town council for rezoning and building permits to erect a chemical plant. Although environmental groups objected, the promise of jobs and more business for the community convinced the town's leaders to approve the project.

Within six months, the community was transformed. CCC contracted with a construction firm in Eugene to spearhead the project. Although most of the construction crew was imported, several local firms became major subcontractors. Mobile trailer parks popped along the river, and temporary housing was built to accommodate the workers. Local businesses felt the crush almost immediately. Several restaurants and bars expanded, two new gasoline stations were opened, and a real estate developer began plans for a shopping center.

The town council formed a committee to examine the impact on public services. New roads were needed, and existing arteries had to be expanded. New sewers and a second water treatment plant were needed, and the police and fire departments required additional support. The school board even leased trailers and erected temporary buildings to handle the increased number of schoolchildren. Faced with a growing demand for new and improved services, the council increased property taxes and submitted three bond issues to the voters to fund new schools, roads, a bridge, and a recreational park.

Local merchants were humming with business, and new businesses seemed to just pop up every day: a bank, three real estate offices, two bars, a furniture store, two hardware stores, a lumber mill, three fast-food eateries, and so forth. Then two of CCC's major suppliers applied for permits to build plants in the community. Overjoyed at the sudden prosperity, the council swiftly approved. Within a span of eighteen months, Marachi had become an economic magnet attracting an endless array of new business. Marachi had become a boom town.

Questions to Consider

1. Although Marachi's experience is on the local level, it nevertheless serves as an example of the multiplier process or, more simply, economic growth. Do you know of a community that underwent such an expansion? What would happen if the government let contracts to build a new airport in your community? Trace the local multiplier effect from the beginning.

2. The positive aspects (positive externalities) of economic growth are fairly obvious, especially to local businesses. But what are some of the negative externalities associated with economic growth such as Marachi experienced?

As we have seen, the multiplier effect describes the process by which economic growth occurs. Increased spending provides new income, and a major portion of this additional income is spent on new consumption. The new round of spending may even trigger new business and public investment. Such growth is desirable because it is the source of a higher standard of living. However, just as the multiplier works to induce expansions, it also magnifies economic contractions. Smoothing out such variations in the economy is one of the objectives of economic policy, a subject we take up in the next chapter.

IMPORTANT TERMS TO REMEMBER

aggregate demand *(AD)*, p. 347
aggregate expenditures *(AE)*, p. 355
aggregate supply *(AS)*, p. 348

autonomous consumption, p. 359
classical economics, p. 352
induced consumption, p. 359

CHAPTER SUMMARY

1. The aggregate demand-aggregate supply model is a useful tool to analyze the effect of changing macroeconomic conditions on the price level and real *GNP*. For example, if aggregate demand increases, other things being equal, we know that the price level (*GNP* deflator) will increase along with increases in real output; thus, changes in nominal *GNP* are divided between changes in the price level and changes in real *GNP*. Of course, our goal is to maximize growth of real *GNP* and minimize the increase in the price level.

2. Classical economics, the prevalent view of economic affairs during the 1930s, held that the economy would tend automatically toward full employment. If demand decreased, falling wages and prices would restore full employment. When the Depression came, however, it was obvious that this process did not work. It was John Maynard Keynes who explained that falling wages and prices only exacerbated the conditions. Falling wages resulted in declining national income, which in turn resulted in less spending and more unemployment. To counteract this downward spiral, Keynes said that government would have to step in to increase aggregate demand. With extra spending, businesses would hire more workers who, in turn, would spend more on new consumption.

3. The heart of Keynesian economics is aggregate expenditures. Two ideas summarize the Keynesian economic framework: (1) aggregate expenditures determine income and employment, and income, in turn, determines aggregate expenditures; and (2) the marginal propensity to consume is the ratio of changes in consumption to changes in income. Working together, these behaviors constitute the multiplier effect.

4. The round-by-round process of extra spending and extra income is defined as the multiplier effect. The multiplier itself is defined as the ratio of the final change in income to the original change in spending. It is also calculated by taking the reciprocal of the marginal propensity to save.

5. When aggregate private expenditures exceed total production, consumption and planned investment expenditures exceed the production plans of business. The difference between *AE* and *AP* is the unplanned inventory depletion, measured as the vertical distance between *AE* and *AP*. Another disequilibrium state occurs when $AP > AE$, the output exceeds the planned expenditures of households and businesses. The difference between *AP* and *AE* is the unplanned inventory accumulation, measured as the vertical distance between *AP* and *AE*.

DISCUSSION AND REVIEW QUESTIONS

1. Use the aggregate demand-aggregate supply model to describe and explain an inflationary economy.

2. What are the differences between classical economics and Keynesian economics?

3. What is the main idea of Keynesian economics?

4. Ms. Macro increased her annual personal consumption expenditures from $12,000 to $13,500 when her income rose from $13,000 to $15,000. What is her marginal propensity to consume *(MPC)?* Her marginal propensity to save (MPS)?

5. What is the relationship between the *MPC,* the *MPS,* and the multiplier? As the *MPC* increases, what happens to the value of the multiplier? Why?

6. Describe the multiplier process in detail.

7. If the equilibrium level of income is $3,200 billion, with an *MPC* of 0.80, by how much will income increase if investment spending increases by $10 billion? *P.365*

8. Illustrate the multiplier effect in Question 7 above, using a table such as Table 13–2.

9. Draw a diagram illustrating the multiplier effect in the foregoing two questions. Use Figure 13–12 as a guide.

A BRIEF LOOK AHEAD

One clear legacy of the Great Depression years is the increased knowledge about managing the nation's economy. And it is John Maynard Keynes to whom we all owe a debt of gratitude for identifying a lack of aggregate demand as the chief reason for the Depression. It was in the 1930s that the federal government learned how to use fiscal and monetary policies to help moderate the extreme fluctuations of the business cycle. It is only appropriate that we now turn to an examination of policy economics. We begin with fiscal policy.

Fiscal Policy

Les Moore, Uniphoto

This chapter begins our examination of economic policy, specifically how the federal government conducts fiscal policy in order to pursue the goal of maximum employment with price stability. Among the topics we will consider are macroeconomic goals; making economic policy in a political arena; examples of fiscal policy in action; differences among tax, transfer, and expenditure policies; and the everpresent concern with deficit spending. Because our primary focus is how fiscal policy affects economic performance, most of the chapter is devoted to both actual federal programs and hypothetical situations and how new spending and tax initiatives influence national income, unemployment, and the price level.

After completion of this chapter, you should be able to do the following:

1. Describe how the federal budget becomes law.
2. Distinguish between discretionary fiscal policy and automatic stabilizers.
3. Identify the correct change in government expenditures to close the GNP gap.
4. Use the tax multiplier to compute the effect of changes in taxes on national income.
5. Define and explain the balanced budget multiplier.
6. Distinguish between the actual budget deficit and the high-employment budget deficit.
7. Describe and explain the reasons why deficit spending is a cause for concern.
8. Identify and explain (fiscal) policy lags.
9. Describe and explain the U.S. historical record of unemployment and inflation in the last several decades.

The Federal Budget: A Statement of National Priorities

The Federal Budget is an expression of whom the government would help and whom it would tax to mold the kind of society that it and the majority of the electorate desire. It is also often a tool for speeding up a weak economy or cooling off a strong one.

Although the Reagan-era budgets produced a long economic expansion, reduced inflation, and rapid job formation, most economists are worried about the huge deficits and mounting debt. One concern is that the national debt resulting from the deficits will keep the economy from growing as fast as it could, perhaps through the 1990s. Government borrowing competes with the borrowing that businesses do to expand, and this competition pushes interest rates higher than they would otherwise be. High rates, in turn, discourage private borrowing.

Large deficits in years of strong economic growth also inhibit the government's ability to turn to deficit spending at the time conventional wisdom says it should: when the economy falls into a recession and the unemployed and others hurt by such a downturn would need government aid.

Furthermore, the Reagan era's disputes over the deficits precluded much planning for the use of the government's resources 5, 10, and 20 years from now. For example, the U.S. economy has shrunk as a share of the world's industrial economies from 40 percent in 1960 to 35 percent in 1988, and yet the U.S. military role remains as large as it was after World War II. Rarely in a budget debate does Congress or the administration ask whether other industrial countries ought to share more of that burden.

For another example, the growth of the country's elderly population, which is supported in part by social security, far exceeds the growth of the work force, which is taxed for Social Security. Questions about the working population's ability to pay rarely come up. "If you are going to deal with the budget properly," said James R. Jones, a former Democratic congressman from Oklahoma and former chairman of the House Budget Committee, "those are the kinds of questions that have to be asked."[1]

Deficits certainly are not new to the United States. In earlier times, deficit spending usually occurred during times of emergency, such as depression and war. During World War II, for example, the government amassed a $250 billion debt, more than the 1945 GNP. However, since Vietnam and especially during the 1980s, deficits appear to be out of

[1] "Deficits Fill A Vacuum," *New York Times*, February 19, 1988.

control. Why do governments run deficits? Is deficit spending inflationary? What is the consequence of large deficits? What is the proper role of government in managing the economy, and how activist should the government be in stimulating jobs and subduing inflation? These and related questions will guide us in our tour of fiscal policy.

FISCAL POLICY

Fiscal policy *is the change in taxes, transfers, and expenditures designed to affect income and employment.*

Fiscal policy is the change in taxes, transfers, and expenditures designed to affect income and employment. The president and the Congress are responsible for making fiscal policy, and its broad economic purpose is to fulfill the goals of the Employment Act. In a nutshell, fiscal policy is the manipulation of the budget (revenues and expenditures) in order to achieve our macroeconomic objectives.

A Political Process

Although we are primarily interested in the economic dimensions of fiscal policy, it must be emphasized that fiscal policy is made in the political arena. A budget or other legislation that begins as a cohesive plan based upon clear economic objectives is then subjected to bargaining and special deals, a process often having little to do with the macroeconomy. Although not all bills suffer from so-called *pork barrel* politics, the final bill often bears little resemblance to the proposed legislation.

The Budget Process. The complete budget process consists of four major stages and takes 20 months or more. The first stage is the president's budget. The process begins with the executive branch sometime in January of the year preceding the new *fiscal year*. (The U.S. government operates on a fiscal year that runs from October 1 through September. The 1991 fiscal year thus runs from October 1, 1990, through September 30, 1991. In other words, the fiscal year is named for the year in which it ends.) Table 14–1 summarizes the budget process in brief, from inception to final approval.

The Office of Management and Budget (OMB), one of the most important agencies in Washington, prepares the federal budget for the president to submit to Congress. To track the time line, we will assume that the president is beginning to prepare the 1992 budget. From January to March 1990, the OMB and the president develop guidelines for all federal agencies. Between April and July, the agencies submit their budget requests to the OMB. August and September find the OMB holding hearings with federal agencies' officials. Between November and December the OMB presents the revised budget to the president. With the advice of OMB, the Department of the Treasury, and the Council of

	Time Period	Activities
TABLE 14–1 The Federal Budget Process—An Overview	January–March	The Office of Management and Budget (OMB) and the president develop guidelines for all federal agencies.
	April–July	The federal agencies submit their budget requests to the OMB.
	August–October	The OMB holds hearings with agency directors and reviews the agency funding requests.
	November–December	After reviewing any appeals from federal agencies, and after consultation with the Department of Treasury, the Council of Economic Advisors, and other key economic advisory elements, the OMB submits the revised budget to the president.
	January (new year)	The president submits the budget for the new fiscal year to Congress.
	February–May	Congressional budget committees review the entire budget with the Congressional Budget Office (CBO), a body much like the OMB. The proposed budget is broken out by agency and program and given to the various congressional committees.
	May–June	The congressional budget committees present the first concurrent budget resolution, which consists of recommended outlays for all functional areas of government (defense, agriculture, etc.). All authorization bills are also submitted with the concurrent resolution.
	July–September	Congress puts the finishing touches on the authorization bills and draws up detailed appropriation bills. These bills then are submitted to the budget committees of the House and Senate for a second concurrent resolution.
	September–October	Each separate appropriations bill is sent to the president for signature. If vetoed by the president, the bills are returned to committee, or the Congress may override the veto with a two thirds vote.
	October 1	The new fiscal year begins for all federal agencies.

Economic Advisors (CEA), and after considering requests for more money for missiles from the Department of Defense and more highway funds from the Department of Transportation, and so forth, the president submits the budget for the new fiscal year to Congress in January 1991.

Stage two begins with a thorough congressional review of the president's budget and ends with the first concurrent budget resolution. From February to May 1991, the House and Senate budget committees review the entire budget with the Congressional Budget Office (CBO), a body much like the OMB. The proposed budget is dissembled by program and agency and sent to the respective committees and subcommittees. The congressional budget committees present a first budget resolution to the full House and Senate sometime in May or June. This resolution consists of recommended outlays for the government's major functional areas of spending (agriculture, national defense, income security, and 16 others). It also contains target levels for total outlays, revenues, the national debt, and the deficit (or surplus). "The first resolution is the foremost expression of Congress's spending priorities and . . . seldom significantly changed later in the budget process."[2] All authorizing bills, legislation which creates or continues a federal program or agency, are also submitted along with the first concurrent resolution.

After the first budget resolution is passed and before October 1, Congress is expected to finish all authorization and appropriation bills. It is in this third stage that negotiations and compromises among various committee factions, between the House and Senate, and between the Congress and the president ultimately produce a complete set of appropriations bills. Unlike the budget resolutions, the appropriation bills include the actual federal funds committed to programs and agencies. Following shortly thereafter is the second concurrent resolution, the fourth and final stage. Although this resolution sets the absolute spending ceiling and revenue floor, it is little more than an accounting exercise. Very minor adjustments are made to the first resolution based upon changes in the economy, for example, more or less inflation than anticipated.

Each appropriations bill is sent to the president for signature in September. If vetoed, the bill is returned to Congress which may override the veto by a two thirds vote in each body, or revise the bill. If the budget has not been signed by the president by October 1, Congress must then pass a continuing budget resolution by which it enables the government to continue spending at last year's level until a new appropriation is passed. In any case, a new fiscal year begins October 1, 1991.

The end result is a patchwork of programs sometimes barely resembling the original budget proposal submitted by the president. Moreover, the goals of macroeconomic policy are lost in the bargaining process. Compromises, deals, and good old-fashioned horse trading replace any semblance of budget formulation with the Employment Act in mind. For better or for worse, however, the budget emerges as a statement of the nation's priorities for the new fiscal year.

Fiscal Policy: Automatic and Discretionary

Discretionary fiscal policy *refers to* changes *in taxes, transfers, and governmental expenditures.*

When people speak of fiscal policy, they generally mean *changes* in taxes, transfers, and expenditures. This type of action is called **discretionary fiscal policy** since it requires a specific action by the president and Congress. For example, the 1986 Tax Reform Act made sweeping changes to the tax code, reducing rates, eliminating deductions, and introducing new tax guidelines. The final bill was signed by President Reagan more than a year after it was first proposed to Congress. An-

---

[2] Stanley E. Collander, *The Guide to The Federal Budget* (Washington D.C.: The Urban Institute, 1983), p. 17.

other example is the 1981 Tax Reduction Act. Among other things, this bill cut tax rates by 25 percent over three years, introduced the Individual Retirement Account (IRA), and phased in the indexation of taxes.[3]

Automatic stabilizers, another type of fiscal policy, consist of federal and corporate income taxes, transfer payments (chiefly unemployment compensation and welfare), and certain expenditures. Unlike discretionary fiscal policy, automatic stabilizers require neither legislation nor specific action by Congress or the president. As their name suggests, they are automatic. Let's see how they work.

A good example is the federal income tax. In a *progressive income tax system,* tax rates and tax liability increase as income increases, and decrease as incomes decrease; thus, if the economy experiences rapid growth, national (and personal) income will increase, and tax revenues will automatically rise. Conversely, if the economy dips into a recession, national income will decline. Because the tax base is smaller, tax revenue declines. Even if the Congress is recessed and the president is vacationing at Camp David, the automatic stabilizers will continue to work.

Transfer payments are ideal examples of automatic stabilizers. If unemployment increases, more people are eligible for unemployment compensation, food stamps, housing subsidies, Aid to Families with Dependent Children and related transfers; thus, federal outlays increase automatically as unemployment rises. Conversely, as unemployment declines and fewer people are eligible for welfare payments, federal outlays automatically decline. Moreover, certain trigger bills have been enacted that will not be activated unless certain economic conditions exist. In other words, the program has been authorized, but no funds have been appropriated. If the unemployment rate rises above 7 percent, however, one such authorization bill calls for $500 million to be appropriated for manpower training.

The value of automatic stabilizers is that they cushion the economy against extreme fluctuations. To use a simple example, assume that the federal budget is balanced: outlays equal receipts. If the economy goes into a slump, tax revenues automatically fall, and transfer payments and government expenditures automatically increase. The result is a budget deficit. The fact that government outlays now exceed receipts means that the budget is helping to stabilize the economy and counteract the built-in recessionary forces. As the budget swings into a deficit position, there is a net increase in injections. Since the government is now putting more dollars into the circular flow than it is withdrawing, the effect is to dampen the severity of the recession.

---

[3] Tax indexation means that the tax tables are adjusted annually to eliminate the effect of inflation. Without indexation, when people earn more income, they are pushed into higher tax brackets even if they are earning the same real income. Tax indexation adjusts the lower and upper limits of the income classes by the amount of inflation.

> ### THINKING IT THROUGH
>
> How will a budget surplus slow economic expansion and reduce inflationary pressure?

In order to examine the purpose and mechanics of fiscal policy, we now return to the Keynesian model, relating expenditures and income. In this discussion, government is added to the private sector model (from the previous chapter) in order to discuss the effects of government spending and taxes on income.

The Keynesian Cross Model Revisited

The Keynesian Cross model depicts the relationship between total planned expenditures ($C + I_p$) and planned production (AP). Since the budget is nothing more than planned spending, we can add government's budgeted expenditures to consumption and investment. As Figure 14–1 shows, the result is an aggregate expenditures curve which consists of $C + I_p + G$, where G represents the appropriations for the new fiscal year ($250 billion). The intersection of AE and AP determines the equilibrium national income, $4,000 billion. Before government expenditures were added, equilibrium national income was $3,000 billion (at E_1). When government spending of $250 billion is added, the economy's new equilibrium rises to $4,000 billion, depicted as point E_2. The familiar multiplier effect magnified a $250 billion injection into $1,000 billion of additional income. Let's review this process.

The additional spending of $250 billion produces a like amount of new income. With a marginal propensity to consume (MPC) of 0.75, we know that $187.5 billion will be spent. As this additional spending is received as new income, 75 percent (or $140.625 billion) will be spent. This process continues until the changes in income and spending become very small, approaching zero.

Using our multiplier formula, $\Delta Y = m \times \Delta AE$, we can quickly confirm the final change in income. The multiplier is the reciprocal of the marginal propensity to save (MPS). Since we know that $MPC = 0.75$, it follows that $MPS = 0.25$. The reciprocal of 0.25 (or 1/4) is 4. Substituting the values into our formula, we get

$$\Delta Y = m \times \Delta AE$$
$$= 4 \times 250 = \underline{\$1,000 \text{ billion}}$$

All of this is familiar territory. But what if unemployment is excessive, say 8 percent, at the E_2 level of income? In other words, what if

FIGURE 14–1

Keynesian Cross with
Government

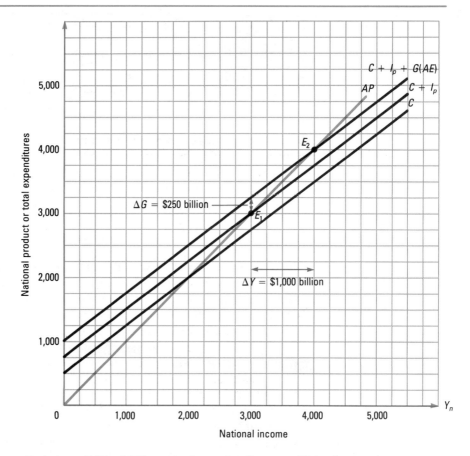

Beginning at E_1 ($Y = 3,000$), we can observe the effect on equilibrium income when government expenditures are added to the picture. With an *MPC* of 0.75 and a multiplier of 4, government spending of $250 billion increases national income by $1,000 (4 × $250).

the economy is operating considerably below its estimated full employment potential? How can the government stimulate growth of output and employment? Similarly, what if inflation is considered excessive? How can the government cool off an overheated economy?

Fiscal Policy: A Problem-Solving Process. In order to answer these questions, it is useful to consider fiscal policy as a problem-solving process consisting of several steps. These steps consist of identifying the problem, stating the objective(s), collecting all pertinent data, evaluating alternatives, and selecting the best alternative.

Fiscal Policy via Expenditures. Applied to our previous example, our policy steps are

1. The problem: high or excessive unemployment, translated as a GNP gap.
2. The objective: reduce unemployment to 6 percent by closing the GNP gap.
3. The relevant data: MPC = 0.75; the actual income level = $4,000 billion; the target (or full employment) level of GNP = $4,500 billion; the GNP gap = $500 billion. The **GNP gap** is the difference between the target (or full employment) level of income and the current or actual level of income.
4. Alternative solutions include the following:
    a. Increase expenditures.
    b. Reduce taxes.
    c. Increase transfer payments.
5. Decision: increase spending (on health, highways, defense, parks, etc.) by $x billion.

GNP gap is the difference between the target (or full employment) level of income and the current or actual level of income.

Our fiscal policy is to increase federal expenditures by enough to reduce unemployment and close the GNP gap of $500 billion. The remaining problem is to determine the actual amount of spending required. *This is where the multiplier formula comes into play.* We know that the desired change in income (GNP) is $500 billion, the *MPC* is 0.75, and the multiplier is 4. Dividing the desired change in income ($500 billion) by the multiplier (4) gives us the required change in government spending, $125 billion. Expressing this information in our familiar formulas and substituting the known values,

$$\Delta AE = \frac{\Delta Y}{m} = \frac{\$500 \text{ billion}}{4} = \$125 \text{ billion}$$

Figures 14–2 and 14–3 illustrate the solution graphically. Beginning with Figure 14–2 at the $4,000 billion level of income, where $C + I_p + G = AP$ (at E_1), government spending increases by $125 billion. Note in particular that this new aggregate expenditures curve lies above the previous schedule by exactly $125 billion (as shown by the vertical arrows). The same information is illustrated in Figure 14–3, except that the $C + I_p + G$ curves have been collapsed into single aggregate expenditure schedules (AE_1 and AE_2). Note that AE_2 is exactly $125 billion above the AE_1 curve, the amount of increased government spending. AE_2 intersects AP at E_2 at the $4,500 billion income level, $500 billion more than the E_1 level of income.

Fiscal Policy via Taxes. Reductions in taxes trigger a similar multiplier process and accomplish the same end result as increased expenditures. There is one important difference, however. When government increases spending, the full amount of additional expenditures is received as new income. However, when taxes are reduced, the first effect is to increase

FIGURE 14–2 Effect of Increased Government Expenditures

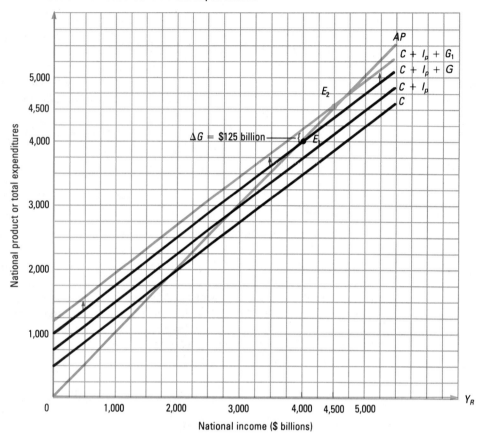

Starting at E_1 at $4,000 billion national income, $(C + I_p + G = AP)$, increased government spending of $125 billion, with an MPC = 0.75, results in increased national income of $500 billion and a new income level of $4,500 billion at E_2.

income. There is no initial spending. And, since we do not spend 100 percent of additional income, some part of the tax cut is saved. This reduces the first round of spending and, in turn, reduces the final change in income. Using the same numbers in our previous example, if Congress cuts taxes by $125 billion, families would find themselves with $125 billion of additional income. With an *MPC* of 0.75, consumers will spend $93.75 billion and save $31.25 billion. In other words, one fourth of the tax cut is not spent. What effect will this have on the outcome?

Using our multiplier formula again, we know that the original change in spending is $93.75 billion (not $125 billion). We also know that the spending multiplier is 4; thus, the final change in income is $375 billion

FIGURE 14–3

Effect of Increased
Government
Expenditures

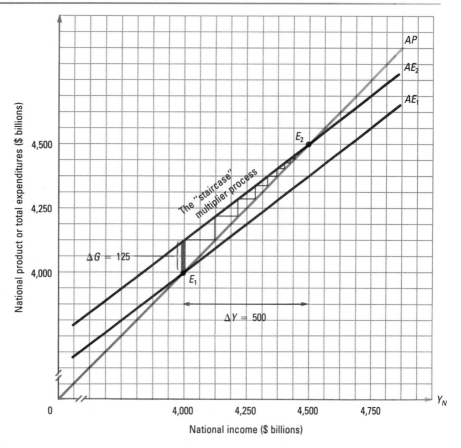

The objective of fiscal policy is to increase government spending by an amount sufficient to close the *GNP* gap and reach the new equilibrium of $4,500. With an *MPC* = 0.75 and a multiplier of 4, we can determine that the required increase in expenditures is $125 billion ($\Delta G = \Delta Y \div m = 500 \div 4$ = $125 billion).

($\Delta Y = \Delta AE \times m$, or $93.75 billion $\times$ 4). This change in income is $125 billion less than occurred when government expenditures were increased, exactly one fourth of the $500 billion. Why? Because consumers saved one fourth of the tax cut (additional income), this income was leaked from the circular flow and thus did not contribute (initially) to additional income, production, and employment. All of this means that tax policy is less powerful than expenditure policy.[4]

How much of a tax cut is required to do the same job as increased government expenditures? To answer this question, it helps to ask still

---

[4] The taxes we are dealing with are lump-sum taxes, such as income tax rebates (a one-time change), and taxes which are independent of income, such as property, sales, and excise taxes.

another question: *What change in consumer income would result in increased consumption of $125 billion?* Since we are working with an *MPC* of 0.75, we can express this as follows: 75 percent of what number equals 125? Dividing 125 by 0.75 gives us the answer, 166.67 (rounded off). In other words, if Congress cuts taxes by $166.67 billion, it will have the same effect as a $125 billion increase in expenditures.

We can simplify this process somewhat by developing a tax multiplier. Briefly, the **tax multiplier (*m_t*)** may be defined as the regular expenditures multiplier minus one, and negative. Written as a formula, $m_t = -(m - 1)$. Using our same example, since the expenditures multiplier is 4, the tax multiplier is -3. ($m_t = -(m - 1) = -(4 - 1) = -4 + 1 = -3$.) *The tax multiplier is one less than the expenditures multiplier and negative.*

Of course, the rate at which people spend additional income (*MPC*) is the critical determinant of the tax and expenditures multipliers. To illustrate this point, Table 14–2 shows the tax cuts and *alternative* corresponding increased government expenditures required to reach the desired change in income with different *MPC*s. In each example, we assume that the desired change in income is $500 billion. With an *MPC* of 0.5, the multiplier is 2; thus $250 billion of increased spending is required to reach the $500 billion change in income. However, if the tax policy is used, since one half of additional income is saved, the tax multiplier is -1; thus, it is necessary to cut taxes by $500 billion to increase income by $500 billion if the *MPC* = 0.5.

Using another example, with an *MPC* = 0.80, the expenditures multiplier is 5, and increased income of $500 billion can be attained by increasing government spending by $100 billion. If tax policy is used, the multiplier is lower (-4), and the necessary tax cut is $-$ $125 billion. Modifying our original multiplier formula in order to account for tax policy, we can substitute ΔT for ΔAE; thus,

$$\Delta Y = T \times m_t$$

where
ΔT = change in taxes, and
m_t = tax multiplier.

Rewriting this expression to solve for *T*,

$$\Delta T = \frac{\Delta Y}{m_t}$$

Using our original data in the previous example,

$$\Delta T = \frac{\Delta Y}{m_t} = \frac{500}{-3} = 166.67.$$

TABLE 14–2

Fiscal Policy: Comparing Tax and Expenditures Policies

MPC	Expenditures Multiplier	Tax Multiplier	Change in Government Expenditures	Change in Taxes	Change in Income
0.50	2	−1	250.00	−500.00	500.00
0.67	3	−2	166.67	−250.00	500.00
0.75	4	−3	125.00	−166.67	500.00
0.80	5	−4	100.00	−125.00	500.00

This table indicates that expenditure policy is more powerful than tax policy. Because consumers will save a portion of a tax cut, not all of the additional income is spent. The result is a smaller multiplier effect, as illustrated in the table. The tax multiplier is always one less than the regular expenditures multiplier and negative.

Fiscal Policy via Transfers.   Changes in transfer payments are also classified as fiscal policy. On the theoretical side, transfers are similar to tax policies. Like tax policy, their effect is less powerful than government expenditures because transfer recipients have the opportunity to save a portion of additional income before it is spent. Unlike taxes, welfare payments, unemployment compensation, and AFDC are received by families and individuals whose *MPC*s are very high. Because such payments go to individuals and families who do not have other primary sources of income (unlike general taxpayers), recipients are likely to spend (nearly) all of any increase in payments.

If we work on the assumption that transfer recipients spend 100 percent of their additional incomes, then a transfer policy has the same effect as increased expenditures.[5] Increased AFDC payments of $125 billion, for example, will increase recipients' incomes by a like amount. If they spend all of it, unlike general taxpayers, $125 billion enters the income stream. Using our multiplier formula, the result is the same as if the government spent $125 billion on the Pershing missile program. All of the transfer payments are spent, leading to a multiplied $500 billion increase in income.

The Balanced Budget Multiplier.   A misconception about budgetary policy is that a balanced budget is neutral, that is, it neither stimulates nor retards economic activity. In fact, a balanced budget change is a positive stimulus to growth. Let's see why.

Assume first that the budget is currently balanced. Assume further that the government decides to build mass transit facilities in five cities at a total cost of $50 billion, and that it finances the programs by in-

---

[5] Because unemployment compensation payments are a major kind of transfer payments, and because many unemployed workers have substantial savings and perhaps other sources of income, the *MPC* is probably somewhat less than 100 percent.

creasing taxes by $50 billion. Both outlays and tax receipts go up by $50 billion. Although the budget remains balanced, the economic effect (on income and employment) will not be neutral.

Using an MPC of 0.8 (any value may be used), the expenditures multiplier is 5 and the tax multiplier is −4. From these multipliers we can determine that the **balanced budget multiplier** is *always equal to 1* (5 + (− 4) = 1). The balanced budget multiplier is used whenever there are equal changes in expenditures and revenues, and the final change in income will always be equal to the original change in expenditures. Expressed in our multiplier formulas,

$$\Delta Y = (\Delta AE \times m) + (\Delta T \times m_t).$$

The change in expenditures (ΔAE) times the expenditures multiplier (m) plus the change in taxes (ΔT) times the tax multiplier (m_t) equals the change in income. Substituting our values, we get

$$\Delta Y = (50 \times 5) + (50 \times -4)$$
$$= 250 + (-200) = \underline{\underline{50}}.$$

The logic is straightforward. We know that increased expenditures will have a positive effect on income and that increased taxation will have a negative effect on income. We also know that tax policy is less powerful than expenditures policy because consumers do not spend all of their extra income (from the tax cut); so, when expenditures and taxes change by equal amounts, up or down, the net effect on income will be positive or negative and equal to the change in spending.

THINKING IT THROUGH

If the budget is balanced and the government reduces spending and taxation by $25 billion, with an MPC of 0.8, what will be the change in income?

Fiscal Policy: The Political Football. If we do not concern ourselves with politics, the choice of a specific fiscal program is virtually irrelevant. It just doesn't matter what we do. Increasing government expenditures by $125 billion on a program to improve highways and bridges, $166.67 billion of reduced taxes, or $125 billion of expanded benefits to the unemployed all accomplish the same thing: raise income (GNP) by $500 billion, the amount necessary to reach the desired full employment level of GNP.

Enter politics and normative economics! A tax cut to one legislator is eminently preferred to increased expenditures or greater transfer payments to another lawmaker. Why? Some legislators are opposed to a larger federal role in the economy and thus favor tax reductions over increased federal outlays as a way of stabilizing the economy and helping people. Indeed, the issue of government intervention and the size of government is often more important than the issue of unemployment. Others think that increased transfers and expenditures are the only sensible approaches, since they would prefer to specify how and on what programs the money is spent and the kind of assistance received by individuals. It's an age-old philosophical debate: What is the proper role of government in the economy?

Fiscal Policy, Fine Tuning, and Policy Lags

Fine-tuning is an aggressive policy approach to regulate the economy.

In the 1960s, economists (of the Keynesian stripe) thought that fiscal policy could be used to fine-tune the economy, much like you would adjust the resolution of your television set. Rooted in the principles of compensatory finance, **fine-tuning** calls for raising taxes and cutting expenditures during an overheated (inflationary) economy, and cutting taxes and increasing expenditures during hard times. However, initial success with the 1964 tax cut provided a measure of confidence that was not to last. Two deep recessions (1974–75 and 1981–82) and prolonged periods of inflation in the 1970s and early 1980s were bitter disappointments to the fine-tuning proponents. What went wrong?

As we have just seen, conflicting political preferences often frustrate responsive decision making. But the formulation of effective fiscal policies also is difficult because of inherent problems involving forecasting and long time lags between adoption of the policy and its effect. The following CASE-IN-POINT summarizes some of the chief concerns.

CASE
▪ IN ▪
POINT

Is Fiscal Policy Destabilizing?

The attempt to use fiscal (and other economic) policies to smooth the economy has produced a pattern of successively higher peaks in inflation at each business cycle peak. As shown in the accompanying chart, Figure 14–4, higher inflation rates did not result in a reduction in unemployment rates as suggested by the experience of the 1960s. (During the 1960s, there was a relatively steady decrease in unemployment along with higher rates of inflation.) Three basic reasons may be offered for the destabilizing effects of fiscal policy.

First, it is extremely difficult to obtain reliable information and discern trends in preliminary data. With hindsight, peaks and trends of economic fluctuations are easy to spot. Identifying trends as they occur, however, is more difficult because there are large random components in the data, many changes in monthly data which are not statistically significant, and initial data

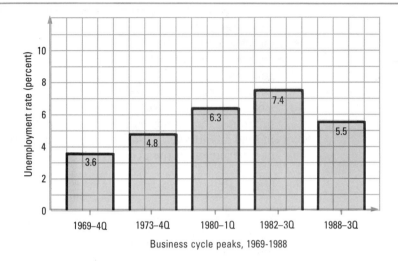

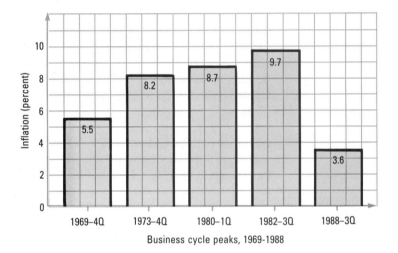

are often revised substantially. These difficulties and the time it takes to collect and disseminate the data make early recognition of trends even more difficult. For example, an analyst using business-cycle rules for identifying significant trends in the leading index of economic indicators would not have been able to identify in advance either the 1974 to 75 or the 1981 to 82 downturns, the two most severe recessions of the postwar period.

Second, when combined with inevitable time lags in making policy, these problems present even larger problems. Fiscal policy takes time to enact, and after enactment often requires three to six months to take effect. Fiscal policies often reach their peak effect on an average between 9 and 18 months, with wide variation around the average. If a policy is made on erroneous information, the effect may be worse than neutral.

A third factor complicating effective fiscal policymaking (and virtually all other economic policy) is the difficulty in making accurate forecasts. Given the lags and the fact that the average postwar contraction lasts only 11 months, to be effective, discretionary policy requires accurate forecasts of turning points at least four quarters ahead. Unfortunately, the record in the 1970s and 1980s indicates that neither federal government nor private forecasters have been able to forecast on an average whether the economy will be in boom or recession four quarters ahead.

Much of the error in these forecasts involves problems in estimating the course of fiscal policy. Some estimates indicate that as much as one half of the error of forecasts relates to unexpected changes in other economic policies. Much of the remaining error results from random shocks, such as changes in oil prices or in labor force productivity, and random fluctuations in decisions of government and private citizens at home and abroad.[6]

Questions to Consider

1. *If the index of leading economic indicators pointed to an imminent recession, and policymakers cut taxes based upon that reading, and then the reading proved wrong (after revisions of data and reevaluation of the indicators), what might happen?*
2. *Might discretionary fiscal policy actually be more destabilizing than if the govenment did nothing? Why?*

As alluded to in the foregoing CASE-IN-POINT, time delays are extremely important impediments to the effective formulation, execution, and ultimate effects of discretionary fiscal policy. Although such problems are not peculiar to the decision-making process, because of the enormous consequences of bad fiscal policy, it behooves us to take an even closer look at these problems.

Policy Lags. As we explained in our discussion of the budget, one of the characteristic problems in designing economic policy is that it is a political process, and fiscal policy is no exception. Economic goals tend to get lost in the internecine squabbles between the Congress and the president. And, compounding this highly politicized policymaking process are the policy time lags, the time between initial identification of the problem and the time when the policy begins to take effect.

First, there is the **recognition lag.** It takes time to identify and define the problem. A specific case in recent years concerned the federal defi-

Recognition lag *is the time it takes to identify and define the problem.*

---

[6] Council of Economic Advisors, *Economic Report of the President* (Washington, D.C.: Superintendent of Documents, U.S. Government Printing Office, 1989), pp. 40–43.

cit and whether taxes should be raised. President Reagan, who marshalled forces to cut taxes in 1981 and again in 1986, made his opposition to increased taxation very clear. Then, during the 1988 presidential campaign, George Bush hooked his political wagon to the no-new-tax brigade.[7] Although expenditure cuts might be made, it seemed that every agency and program, from defense to social security, was sacrosanct. Many critics (chiefly democrats) maintained that the deficit must be cut and higher taxes were the only reasonable way to do it. Regarding the need for a tax hike (or other deficit-reduction measures), a consensus was clearly lacking. And the recognition lag was compounded by the Bush administration's philosophical opposition to higher taxes.

Administration lag *is the time required to formulate the actual policy, guide it through Congress, and obtain presidential approval.*

A second delay in policymaking is an **administation lag,** the time required to formulate the actual policy and guide it through the maze of congressional committees and government agencies to the president for approval. When President Johnson proposed a surtax on personal income in 1967 to sop up some inflationary purchasing power, Wilbur Mills, the chairman of the powerful House Ways and Means Committee, locked up the bill in committee. For every dollar of increased taxation proposed, Mills wanted a dollar-for-dollar reduction in federal spending. But President Johnson contributed to the delays as well. In December 1965, the president received a strong surtax recommendation from his Council of Economic Advisors, but it was June 1967 before he recommended the proposal to Congress. Although this may have been as much a recognition lag as an administration lag, it took more than two years between initial recommendation and final approval of the surtax.

Impact lag *is the time required for the multiplier effect to change employment, income, and production.*

A third policy delay is the **impact lag.** Once the law is enacted, it takes time for the multiplier effect to change employment, income, and production. Although the arithmetic calculations give the impression of instantaneous changes, the process does not happen overnight. Indeed, depending upon how rapidly households and businesses spend additional income, the multiplier effect generally takes two years or more. Even if a tax or expenditure change works as planned—that is, the marginal propensities to consume turn out to be exactly what the policymakers assumed—the multiplier process will take time. This should not be surprising, since the process of new business formations, new employment, and other growth conditions do not occur in a matter of a few weeks.

---

[7] The 1988 campaign between George Bush and Michael Dukakis may be remembered mainly for its lack of substance. Rather than lively discussions of important issues, the candidates hurled hateful accusations back and forth. And though Bush's political slogan, "Read my lips—no new taxes," was a popular rallying cry, it is one campaign promise that may prove rather hard to keep.

To summarize and illustrate the effects of these policy lags, consider the Council of Economic Advisors' assessment of a discretionary tax reduction in the mid-1970s.

> The Tax Reduction Act of 1975 was a one-time tax cut designed to stimulate aggregate demand and fight the recession. Unfortunately, it was passed in March 1975, which was the recession trough, and the tax cut probably had its initial effect well after the expansion had begun, and its peak at a point well into the expansion, when inflation pressures were already starting to build.[8]

Other Problems.   Aside from the policy lag issues, discretionary fiscal policy may be completely ineffective in stabilizing the economy. "For example, the temporary income tax surcharge enacted in June 1968 failed to dampen consumer spending. Consumers responded by reducing personal saving, rendering negligible the impact of the tax surcharge in reducing inflationary pressures in the economy."[9] Of course, the surtax was hardly a big surprise. Given the two years or more of media coverage, consumers had ample time to adjust their expenditures and saving decisions.

Another problem is that the expected multiplier effect of increased spending may be frustrated by changes in consumer and business spending behavior. For example, consumers may thwart the effectiveness of a tax cut if they are convinced that government is doing very little to reduce the budget deficit. Believing that the government will have to raise taxes in the future to reduce the deficit, consumers may decide to save most of the tax cut. Of course, if the marginal propensity to save increases, the multiplier and the ultimate increase in income will be smaller.

As we have seen, the attempt to use discretionary fiscal policy to stabilize the economy is highly problematic. In many instances, fine-tuning has proven to be more harmful than helpful because of the inherent difficulties in forecasting business-cycle turning points, the long and variable policy lags, and the difficulty in discerning temporary and permanent effects on employment, output, and the price level. Despite such problems with fiscal policy, however, Congress and the president must continue to address the issues of unemployment, inflation, budget deficits, and other macroeconomic concerns. Indeed, in recent years, the budget deficit is becoming a common topic of dinnertime conversation.

---

[8] Council of Economic Advisors, *Economic Report of the President* (Washington, D.C.: Superintendent of Documents, U.S. Government Office, 1989), p. 43.

[9] Ibid., p. 75–76.

THE BUDGET AND THE DEFICIT

The odds are pretty good that you read something about the huge size of the U.S. government's federal deficit in the last week. In virtually every news medium, on network news, in *Newsweek* and *Time,* in your local newspaper and on radio talk shows, the economic news is dominated by concern with the federal deficit. As recently as 1979, however, the deficit was *only* $16 billion. Since 1979, the top has blown off: it rose to $146 billion in 1982, to $176 billion in 1983, finally to top $200 billion in 1986. So confusing are these figures that early in President Reagan's first term of office, David Stockman, the president's economic guru at the Office of Management and Budget, glumly reported that "None of us really understands what's going on with all these numbers."[10] How did the deficit get so big? Why is there reason to worry?

Growth of the Deficit

As we have just noted, deficits may arise because the government chooses to do so (as with discretionary fiscal policy) or because automatic stabilizers reduce tax revenue and increase outlays when the economy suffers a downturn. Table 14–3 illustrates the relationship between the deficit, unemployment, and GNP.

When Kennedy became president in 1961, he inherited a recession from Eisenhower. Unemployment rose to 6.7 percent, and the automatic stabilizers caused the budget to swing from surplus to deficit. Under Gerald Ford's interim presidency following Nixon's resignation, the economy dipped into its worst recession since the 1930s. With unemployment rising to an average of 8.5 percent in 1975, tax revenues fell and transfers soared, producing a $69.4 billion deficit. Near the end of the Carter years, unemployment gradually fell below 6 percent again (to 5.8 percent by 1979), and the deficit fell to near its pre-recession level.

The behavior of the deficit during the most recent recession of 1982 to 83 under Reagan is more difficult to evaluate. Because of the Economic Recovery Tax Act of 1981 (ERTA), it is questionable what share of the rising deficit is attributable to discretionary tax cuts and what was caused by automatic stabilizers. However, one clue is transfer payments to persons, and they increased significantly. From $247 billion in 1980, transfers rose to $282.1 billion in 1981, to $316.3 billion in 1982, to $340.1 billion in 1983 to only $344.3 billion in 1984. This more than $80 billion increase over a four-year period is evidence of the contracyclical power of automatic stabilizers.

---

[10] Quoted in William Greider, "The Education of David Stockman," *The Atlantic Monthly* (December 1981), p. 28.

TABLE 14–3

Economic Activity and the Deficit (selected years)

Year	GNP	Unemployment (in percent)	Surplus or Deficit (−)	Change in Deficit	Deficit/ Surplus, percent of *GNP*
1960	$ 515.5	5.5	$3.0	$ − 4.1	0.6
1961	533.8	6.7	− 3.9	6.9	− 0.7
1962	574.6	5.5	− 4.2	0.3	− 0.7
1963	606.9	5.7	0.3	− 4.5	0.0
1964	649.8	5.2	− 3.3	3.6	− 0.5
1965	705.1	4.5	0.5	− 3.8	0.1
1970	1,015.5	4.9	− 12.4	12.9	− 1.2
1973	1,359.3	4.9	− 5.6	− 6.8	− 0.4
1974	1,472.8	5.6	− 11.6	6	− 0.8
1975	1,598.4	8.5	− 69.4	57.8	− 4.3
1979	2,508.2	5.8	− 16.1	− 53.3	− 0.6
1980	2,732.0	7.1	− 61.3	45.2	− 2.2
1981	3,052.6	7.6	− 63.8	2.5	− 2.1
1982	3,266.0	9.7	− 145.9	82.1	− 4.5
1983	3,405.7	9.6	− 176.0	30.1	− 5.2
1984	3,765.0	7.5	− 170.0	− 6	− 4.5
1985	3,998.1	7.2	− 198.0	28	− 5.0
1986	4,208.5	7.0	− 205.6	7.6	− 4.9
1987	4,526.7	6.2	− 157.8	− 47.8	− 3.5

Changes in the level of economic activity, as measured by unemployment, are reflected in the absolute size of the deficit and in the change in the deficit from year to year. For example, during the 1974 to 75 recession, when unemployment increased from 5.6 percent to 8.5 percent, the budget deficit jumped from $11.6 billion to $69.4 billion. This primarily reflects the work of automatic stabilizers. As unemployment increased, fewer people were paying taxes, and more people were receiving unemployment compensation, food stamps, and assorted transfers. The same phenomenon in reverse is illustrated between 1975 and 1979. As unemployment declined, the automatic stabilizers caused income tax revenues to rise and transfer payments to fall, resulting in a smaller budget deficit.

SOURCE: *Economic Report of the President* (Washington, D.C.; U.S. Government Printing Office, 1987), Table B-1, p. 244; Table B-31, pp. 280–81; and Table B-76, p. 335; and *Survey of Current Business* (Bureau of Economic Analysis, U.S. Department of Commerce), 68, no. 12 (December 1988), Table 3.2, p. 8.

The burgeoning deficits in the 1980s may be attributed to three factors: (1) the tax cuts embodied in the ERTA of 1981, (2) the phasing out of bracket creep, and (3) unrestrained federal spending on defense, interest payments on the national debt, medicare, and social security. Between 1978 and 1986, federal expenditures on these items increased substantially. Indeed, the share of these items in GNP increased by 1.8 percent, 1.7 percent, 0.7 percent, and 0.5 percent, respectively, while nondefense spending (except on medicare, interest payments, and social security) declined by 1.8 percent. As Table 14–4 shows, total federal spending increased from 20.9 percent to 24.5 percent of GNP.

While federal spending was on the rise, tax collections showed considerably more variation over this time period. Initially, from 1978 to 1981, tax collections as a percent of GNP reached a post-World War II

TABLE 14–4
Federal Expenditures and Tax Receipts as a Percent of GNP

Year	GNP	Total Federal Tax Receipts	Percent of GNP	Total Federal Expenditures	Percent of GNP
1978	$2,249.7	$441.4	19.6	$ 470.7	20.9
1981	3052.6	639.5	20.9	703.3	23.0
1986	4208.5	826.2	19.6	1,030.2	24.5

Despite a tax cut and indexation, federal tax receipts did not increase as a percentage of GNP over the period from 1978 to 1986. Federal spending, however, increased from 20.9 percent to 24.5 percent over the same period. The result was a significant increase in the size of the deficit.

high of 20.9 percent, primarily because of bracket creep. The high inflation rates in those years resulted in large nominal wage gains, but in real terms most people saw their purchasing power fall. However, since the tax brackets were based on nominal income, people found themselves in higher tax brackets even though their real income (before taxes) had declined. This bracket creep was formally and finally fixed by indexing the tax brackets. Taking effect in 1985, indexation adjusted the tax brackets upward by the amount of inflation. With indexation, the Treasury lost a major source of additional (and often unbudgeted) revenue.[11]

Another major change in the ERTA of 1981 was the mandated tax cuts spread over the years 1982–1984. Marginal tax rates, rates paid on the last dollar earned, declined from a 1980 average of 24 percent to 22 percent in 1986.[12] The ERTA also reduced the top marginal tax rate from 70 to 50 percent, eased the eligibility requirements for individual retirement accounts (IRAs), and increased depreciation allowances and other investment incentives. As a result of indexation and lower tax rates, total federal tax receipts as a percent of GNP declined to its 1978 share (see Table 14–4).[13]

The growth of the deficit is thus attributable mainly to unrestrained federal spending, especially in the areas of defense and interest payments on the debt. The ERTA contributed to the higher deficit to the extent that it prevented revenue gains from the formerly higher tax rates and from bracket creep (beginning in 1985).

---

[11] The budget is a plan of operating expenses and revenues. When economic conditions change, (e.g., inflation increases or unemployment declines), the government may find it has more to spend. Unanticipated revenue from bracket creep, for example, produced the opportunity to spend more on authorized programs for which funds had not been appropriated.

[12] Council of Economic Advisors, *Economic Report of the President*, p. 80.

[13] If we break down total tax receipts from 1978 to 1986, we find that personal tax receipts declined .06 percent, corporate tax payments declined by 1.19 percent, and social security taxes increased by 1.29 percent. Combining social security and personal income taxes, the individual tax share in GNP was 15.2 percent in 1978, 16.96 percent in 1981, and 16.4 percent in 1986; thus, contrary to White House reports, five years after tax reform, individuals paid a higher percentage of taxes.

The Deficit: Reasons for Concern

There are three main reasons to worry about government deficits: (1) crowding out, (2) foreign ownership of debt, and (3) inflation. Before we discuss the consequences of government deficits, however, it should be mentioned that the biggest blue-chip corporations run massive amounts of red ink. Like the federal government, they too do not balance their budgets. Take AT&T for an example. Its 1985 indebtedness was more than 10 times its 1929 debt. Exxon, another Fortune 500 giant, increased its indebtedness from $170 million to over $5 billion in the same period.[14] Both companies operate like the government when its current-year expenditures exceed its operating revenues. While debt is always paid off as it matures, these firms do not use current earnings to do so. Rather, like the federal government, they issue new bonds, and with the proceeds from the new debt, they pay off existing bondholders. In other words, they roll over their indebtedness.

Federal Deficit Financing. When the government incurs a budget deficit, it has three ways to pay its bills. It may raise taxes, print money, or sell bonds.[15] Of course, these alternatives are not equally attractive. A tax hike, for example, is often viewed as an unattractive option by lawmakers; voting constituents have long memories—all the way to election day. Printing money is a similarly jaded alternative. We have learned from the school of hard knocks that printing money to finance deficits is very inflationary. Many examples may be cited, but nothing is more memorable than post-World War I Germany where, as a result of a massive infusion of deutsch marks, inflation reached the incredible height of 1,000,000,000 percent![16] As self-interested and rational individuals, legislators thus generally avoid printing money and tax hikes (especially during election years). Selling bonds to finance deficit spending is thus the preferred option and the overwhelming choice of nearly all governments.

Who Sells Government Debt and with What Effect? The Treasury Department is the fiscal agent for the U.S. government. One of its primary functions is to sell debt of all kinds to finance government expenditures.

[14] Robert L. Heilbroner and James K. Galbraith, *Understanding Macroeconomics,* 8th edition (Englewood Cliffs, N.J.: Prentice-Hall, 1987), p. 298.

[15] *Deficit financing* is the technical term by which the government goes about paying for its debt, via raising taxes, selling bonds, or, in the extreme case, printing money.

[16] History teaches us many lessons, and inflation is no exception. Most notable is that inflation is a chronic consequence of war. The price level shot up 100 percent during World War I. More current experiences, especially in less developed countries, is also illustrative. Bolivia's annual inflation rate averaged 360 percent over the period from 1960 to 1985.

When it does so, the supply of securities increases. (Government securities, or IOUs, go by different names: Treasury notes, bills, and bonds. No matter what the name, they all signify government indebtedness.) Figure 14–5 illustrates the effect of such sales.

The interest rate is the price of borrowed funds. Like other prices, interest rates move in a family way; that is, the higher cost of credit in one part of the economy impacts upon credit costs elsewhere, much like higher material prices run up prices of finished goods.

When the Treasury sells bonds, the supply of bonds increases relative to demand, shown as a rightward shift of the bond supply curve from S_1 to S_2. The result is that the market price of bonds falls from $1,000 to $960. Assuming for the moment that the sales involve 10-year bonds with a face value of $1,000, what does this do to the yield (the interest earnings on the bond)?

FIGURE 14–5

The Supply and Demand for Loanable Funds and the Crowding Out Effect

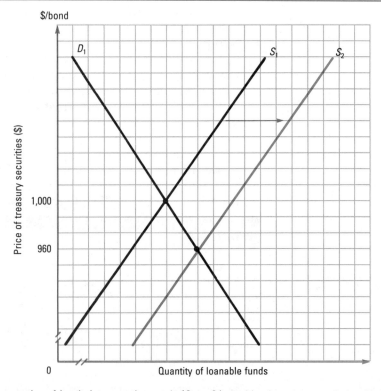

Treasury sales of bonds increase the supply (S_1 to S_2) resulting in a decrease in bond prices (from $1,000 to $960). If the face value of the bonds is $1,000 and the annual interest is $100, before the sale, the yield or interest rate is 10 percent. When the bond price falls to $960, the interest increases to 10.4 percent ($100 ÷ $960). As other rates rise, private investment is crowded out.

Assume that the bond returns $100 annually, or 10 percent of its face value ($100 ÷ $1,000 = 10 percent). When the Treasury offers additional securities for sale and the market price falls to $960, the yield increases to 10.4 percent. In other words, there is an inverse relationship between the bond price and its yield (or interest rate). As the price falls to $960, its annual yield increases to 10.4 percent ($100 ÷ $960 = 10.4 percent).

As bond yields rise, most other interest-bearing obligations do so as well, such as mortgage rates, retail installment rates, and ultimately the prime rate and discount rate.[17] As interest rates drift upward, businesses find it more difficult to justify borrowing funds for their various investment projects.

1. Crowding out.   When government enters the market for loanable funds, (some) private investment may be crowded out. When there is a decline in private investment because of the government's deficit financing, it is called **crowding out.** To the extent that planned investment is sensitive to interest rates, the crowding out effect may be substantial. If investment is highly interest elastic, for example, then a very small increase in interest rates may result in a major decrease in investment spending (e.g., a 5 percent increase in interest rates may decrease business expenditures on plant and equipment by 10 percent).[18] The process outlined above works like this:

Crowding out refers to a decline in private investment because of the government's deficit financing.

- The government runs a deficit.
- The government sells bonds to pay its bills.
- Bond sales result in lower bond prices and higher interest rates.
- Higher interest rates for borrowed money make some (many?) private investment projects unprofitable, resulting in a decrease in planned investment.

2. Foreign-held debt.   Another reason for concern is that a significant and growing share of the national debt is owned by foreign governments. High (real) interest rates in the early 1980s attracted record foreign purchases of U.S. debt. Since we cannot increase taxes on foreign incomes to finance U.S. debt, it means that we pay it off out of current production. Doing so means higher taxes and a corresponding reduced standard of living.

---

[17] The prime rate is the interest rate charged by banks to their best corporate customers. The discount rate is the interest rate paid by banks on loans from the Federal Reserve Banks.

[18] It should be noted that it is difficult to determine whether higher interest rates or some other investment determinant is responsible for a decrease in spending, such as sales and profits or expectations of future sales. In other words, we often have trouble identifying whether there was a movement along the investment demand curve or whether there was a shift of the curve.

3. Inflation. Some deficits are inflationary (and the key word is *some*). If the government runs a deficit when the economy is at full employment, inflation is a very likely outcome. Indeed, this is classic demand pull inflation, reminiscent of the later Vietnam years. The combination of the 1964 tax cut, Lyndon Johnson's Great Society programs, and Vietnam expenditures increased aggregate demand faster than aggregate supply. The upshot was inflation. We will discuss inflation in greater detail in Chapter 17.

Deficit spending during recessions (when unemployment is high and rising) is not only noninflationary, it is an effective way to stimulate the economy's private sector to create jobs. Essentially, then, there are good and bad deficits, and whether inflation ensues depends upon the prevailing economic conditions, not upon the deficit itself.[19]

But an important problem associated with deficit spending is how to define the deficit. Indeed, measurement of the budget deficit has been a continuing debate among economists for more than 20 years.

Measurement Problems. Closely related to the issue of policy lags is the question of measurement (actually a part of the administrative lag problem). The **actual deficit** is the amount by which the government's budget outlays exceed its receipts. However, because it is influenced by both automatic stabilizers *and* discretionary policy, the actual deficit may be an erroneous indicator of just how expansionary or contractionary is the federal budget. In the following CASE-IN-POINT, economist Robert Eisner explains why we should use a different deficit as the measure of fiscal policy.

Actual deficit is the amount by which the government's budget outlays exceed its receipts.

CASE
• IN •
POINT

The High Employment Budget

Actual budget deficits are not good measures of fiscal policy. The administration and Congress might be following a tight fiscal policy, keeping discretionary expenditures down and tax rates up, and yet a recession would create a substantial deficit. Indeed, by depressing aggregate demand, a tight fiscal policy might bring on a recession.

What is needed is a measure that is uncontaminated by what the economy does to deficits. In other words, we need to eliminate the influence of automatic stabilizers from the figures. Economists at the Bureau of Economic Analysis of the Department of Commerce developed just such a measure in

---

[19] This may be a bitter pill to swallow for some readers. If my guess is correct, our elders have told us repeatedly that government deficits are always inflationary.

*The **high employment budget deficit** presents estimates of what expenditures and receipts would be if the economy were operating at full employment.*

1955, called the **high employment budget deficit** or surplus.[20] It presents estimates of what expenditures and receipts would be *if* the economy were operating at full employment—generally taken to mean 6 percent in recent years. By doing so, we can eliminate the cyclical variations in employment, output, and income.

From 1955 to 1965, the actual budget was in deficit five times and in surplus six. The high employment budget was never in deficit. This reflects the fact that actual unemployment was more than the high-employment rate over this period. Actual tax revenues were thus less and government expenditures were more. From 1966 to 1969, actual unemployment was less than the high (or full) employment rate of 4 percent. (That is an interesting fact considering our current view of high employment. Ignoring the Humphrey-Hawkins Full Employment and Balanced Growth Act of 1978, we now cheerfully project unemployment in the 6 to 7 percent range.) The low unemployment of those years caused the three actual deficits to be less than the deficit associated with high employment, and the 1969 surplus to be greater.

The watershed for the upward drift (or surge) of deficits was 1970. In none of the last 20 years has the budget been balanced, let alone in surplus. When Richard Nixon announced in 1972 that "We are all Keynesians now," he underscored a widely accepted, albeit incorrect, interpretation that the deficits were evidence of expansionist fiscal policy. But the dilemma persisted. With larger budget deficits, why wasn't unemployment lower and the economy sizzling?

From hindsight the answer is quite simple. All of the attention was focused on the wrong deficit. By using actual deficits instead of the high-employment deficits as the economic thermometer, the analysts were getting mixed signals. As automatic stabilizers sent the actual federal budget into deficit during a slump, fiscal policy was interpreted as expansionary. Further discretionary fiscal action was thus deemed undesirable (e.g., inflationary). Meanwhile, the high-employment budget was either in surplus or showing a much smaller deficit. Furthermore, if the high-employment budget deficits were adjusted for inflation, then even smaller deficits show up.[21]

Questions to Consider

1. *What is the difference between the actual deficit and the high employment deficit? Why does the high employment budget give a better picture of fiscal policy?*

2. *If the goal is full employment and the high-employment budget is in deficit, should discretionary fiscal policy become restrictive? Why or why not?*

---

[20] Unfortunately, it goes by many other names as well: the full employment, standard employment, cyclically-adjusted, and structural budget.

[21] Robert Eisner, "Will the Real Deficit Stand Up?" *Challenge* (May/June 1986), pp. 13–21.

MACROECONOMIC GOALS—THE HISTORICAL RECORD

Along with the essentially political nature of the process, timing and measurement problems make the formulation of fiscal policy very difficult. Compounding the policy problem, as pointed out in Chapter 11, is the vague language of our goals as specified in the Employment Act of 1946. Perhaps even more troublesome is the inherent contradiction of attaining both full employment and price stability. Indeed, if we look at the record of inflation and unemployment over the last few decades, we can readily see how rarely we have succeeded in attaining maximum employment without inflation.

Figure 14–6 illustrates the historical record of unemployment and inflation over the period from 1950 to 1988. Two reference lines, a vertical line over 4 percent unemployment and a horizontal line indicating 3 percent inflation, divide the graph into four quadrants. Quadrant I thus defines the acceptable boundaries; any point inside or on the boundaries constitutes attainment of the Employment Act's objectives. And, as you can see, the United States realized its goals in only three years: 1952,

FIGURE 14–6 Unemployment and Inflation, 1950–1988

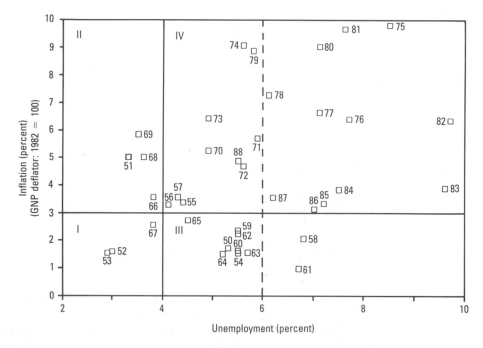

Using 4 percent as the unemployment objective and 3 percent as the inflation goal, in only three years (since 1950) has the United States realized its goals. If a 6 percent unemployment rate is used, the record improves slightly—to 11 years over the 39-year period.

1953, and 1967. Quadrant IV shows the other extreme, levels of unemployment and inflation in excess of the targets. Most notable is the stretch of consecutive years from 1970 to 1985 in which the United States experienced inflation and unemployment rates considerably above the consensus targets. Of course, if we use 6 percent unemployment as the noninflationary target, the record improves slightly. Still, in 10 of the years from 1970 to 1988, the United States failed to reach either of its main economic objectives.

Although lackluster by some standards, the most interesting feature of this period is the absence of hyperinflation or depression. From 1950 to 1988, neither inflation nor unemployment exceeded 10 percent. Indeed, the average unemployment rate was 5.7 percent, and the average rate of inflation was 4.3 percent. Should the government have done more? If it had been more activist in creating jobs, would inflation have been much worse? If it had pursued price stability in more earnest, would we have experienced longer or deeper recessions? There are no definitive answers to these questions. But such questions do raise the most important issues confronting the years ahead: What is the proper role of government in managing the economy? And, how activist should the government be in stimulating jobs and subduing inflation? These questions will guide us in the remaining chapters devoted to issues of economic policy and stabilization.

IMPORTANT TERMS TO REMEMBER

actual deficit,   p. 404
administration lag,   p. 396
automatic stabilizers,   p. 384
balanced budget multiplier,   p. 392
crowding out,   p. 403
discretionary fiscal policy,   p. 383
fine-tuning,   p. 393

fiscal policy,   p. 381
GNP gap,   p. 387
high employment deficit,   p. 405
impact lag,   p. 396
recognition lag,   p. 395
tax multiplier,   p. 390

CHAPTER SUMMARY

1. Fiscal policy is the change in taxes, transfers, and expenditures which affect income and employment in pursuit of the goals of the Employment Act.

2. The federal budget takes 20 months or more to create. The process consists of four stages, beginning with the president's budget proposal and ending with the second congressional budget resolution which establishes a spending ceiling and a revenue floor.

3. Fiscal policy, like the federal budget itself, is made by the Congress and the president. It is therefore a highly political process.

4. There are two types of fiscal policy:
   a. Automatic stabilizers: taxes and transfers which change automatically as national income rises and falls. The stabilizers help to

protect the economy from extreme fluctuations in income and employment.

    b. Discretionary fiscal policy: legislated changes to taxes and expenditures, such as the 1986 Tax Reform Act.

5. The GNP gap is the difference between the target (or full employment) income level and the current or actual income level. Fiscal policy objectives are often stated in terms of closing the GNP gap.

6. The lump-sum tax multiplier (m_t) is one less than the expenditures multiplier and negative. The balanced budget multiplier is always equal to one (1).

7. The federal deficit increased significantly in the 1970s and 1980s because of three main factors: the tax cuts in the Economic Recovery Act of 1981, the phasing out of bracket creep in 1985 (also part of the ERTA), and large increases in federal spending, especially on defense and interest payments.

8. The deficit is a major concern because of crowding out (lower private investment because of higher interest rates caused by federal deficit financing), foreign-held debt, and inflation.

9. The high employment budget measures expenditures and revenues at some target rate of unemployment such as 6 percent. Unlike the actual deficit, the high employment budget eliminates the effect of automatic stabilizers on the federal deficit and thus provides a better measure of current fiscal policy.

10. Using 4 percent unemployment and 3 percent inflation as the targets of economic policy, the historical record shows that in only three years (1952, 1953, and 1967) has the United States attained both goals.

DISCUSSION AND REVIEW QUESTIONS

1. Briefly describe the federal budgetary process.

2. Distinguish between and give examples of automatic stabilizers and discretionary fiscal policy.

3. Explain why changes in taxes are less powerful than changes in expenditures.

4. With an *MPC* of 0.80, by how much will national income decrease if government spending is decreased by $20 billion?

5. If the economy's marginal propensity to consume is 0.75, the current GNP is $4,000 billion, and the target GNP is $4,100 billion, by how much must government spending be increased to close the GNP gap?

6. Using the same information in Question 5, by how much must taxes be cut to close the GNP gap? If Congress wants to combine tax and spending policies, and it increases expenditures by $40 billion, by how much must taxes be cut in order to finish the job? (Hint: Calculate the change in income attributed to spending first, and subtract this change from the GNP gap to determine how much additional income must be created in order to reach the target.)

7. Describe and explain how the recognition, adminstrative, and impact policy lags make it difficult to make effective discretionary policy.

8. Why are federal budget deficits a potentially serious economic problem?

9. Briefly describe the record of unemployment and inflation during the past 20 or 30 years.

<table>
<tr><td>

A BRIEF LOOK
AHEAD

</td><td>

In the next chapter, we will examine the Federal Reserve System (Fed) and money markets. We will pay particular attention to how the Fed can control (increase and decrease) the amount of money in circulation. This, in turn, will lay the important groundwork for our discussion of monetary policy in Chapter 16.

</td></tr>
</table>

Money and Banking

Meryl Joseph, The Stock Market

The purpose of this chapter is twofold. First, we will examine money: its functions, the markets for money, money lenders (commercial banks, credit unions, savings banks, and savings and loan associations), and the state and federal agencies that regulate financial institutions—the Federal Reserve System, the Federal Home Loan Bank Board, and the National Credit Union Association. The second purpose is to examine how lending actually leads to the creation of new money (the multiple expansion of deposits).

After completion of this chapter, you should be able to do the following:

1. Describe and explain the functions of money.
2. Identify and define the measures of the money supply.
3. Identify and describe the institutions which make up the U.S. banking system.
4. List and describe the parts and organization of the Federal Reserve System.
5. List and describe the financial intermediaries and the national organizations which regulate them.
6. Describe and explain the financial innovations which occurred in the 1970s and 1980s.
7. Describe the Monetary Control Act of 1980 and explain its effects on financial institutions.
8. Using T accounts (simplified balance sheets), describe and explain how depository institutions (i.e., banks, savings and loans, etc.) create money (expand the money supply).

Currency Is Like a Rock in Yap

We use coins to get sodas from vending machines; we buy magazines at newsstands with dollar bills; and we pay our rent or mortgage (at least most of us do) with checks. Americans use coins, Federal Reserve notes (paper money), and checking accounts to buy things and pay our bills. But it wasn't always this way, here or elsewhere. Cigarettes were used as currency in World War II prisoner-of-war camps, and some less-developed nations use salt or shells. And for 2,000 years in Yap, Micronesia, the Yapese have used large stone wheels to pay for large purchases, such as canoes, land, and permission to marry.

Yap is a U.S. trust territory, and the U.S. dollar now is used for most purchases. But reliance on stone wheels continues today, much like the island's caste system and the traditional dress of loincloth and grass skirts. The Yapese lean the huge limestone wheels against their houses or prop up rows of them in village banks.

Stone currency clearly has its disadvantages. For example, Linus Ruuamau, the manager of one of the island's few retail stores, won't accept it in payment for general merchandise. And no bank managers are likely to accept limestone deposits. After all, the money would only gather moss.

But the use of stone wheels does have its advantages. For one, counterfeiting is extremely difficult, so the remaining 6,600 stone wheels provide a very stable money supply. Stone money also accords well with Yapese traditions. "There are a lot of instances here where you cannot use U.S. money," Mr. Gurtmag says. One is the settling of disputes. Unlike most money, stones sometimes can buy happiness, of a sort; if a Yapese wants to settle an argument, he brings his adversary stone money as a token. "The apology is accepted without question," Mr. Chodad says. "If you used dollars, there'd be an argument over whether it was enough."[1]

PART I: MONEY AND ITS INSTITUTIONS

Money is anything that is readily accepted as a medium of exchange.

Money is what money does. Have you ever heard that before? Yes or no, it is absolutely true. Think about it. Prisoners in P.O.W. camps used cigarettes as money. The Yapese use huge and cumbersome limestone wheels for major transactions like land purchases. But they also use U.S. dollars for most everyday transactions, since Yapese businesses will not accept the stones for payment.

---

[1] Art Pine, "Fixed Assets, Or: Why a Loan in Yap Is Hard to Roll Over," *The Wall Street Journal*, March 29, 1984.

What do we use for money? Coin, paper money (Federal Reserve notes), checks—right? But what else could be used? How about credit cards (or, more commonly, plastic)? Is a credit card money? To answer these and other questions, it is first helpful to examine the functions of money. Money is anything (even stone wheels) that is readily accepted as a medium of exchange.

THE FUNCTIONS OF MONEY

Think about what you use money for, and you will have listed its functions. Anything used as money must perform several useful functions:

1. Medium of exchange
2. Store of value
3. Unit of account (or standard of value)

Medium of exchange is perhaps the most important function of money.

Let's look at each of these. First, you buy goods and services with it; thus, it is a **medium of exchange.** For example, you applied for admission to your college, registered for this class in economics, paid your tuition and miscellaneous fees, and bought this book at the bookstore. What did you use for these last two transactions? Cash? Check? Credit? If you paid with cash or by check, you used money in exchange for a service and a product (the class and book). What about credit?

Paying for something with a *credit card* is actually only a means of putting off the inevitable. You have deferred payment for 30 days or more. When you sign the MasterCard or Visa receipt, in effect, you promise to make payment later. The college receives payment from the financial institution with whom you have established credit. It's a very convenient and efficient form of payment, especially if you pay up and avoid interest expenses. Interest charges can be prohibitive at the 15 to 22 percent rates charged by banks.

Store of value is the accumulation of unspent earnings.

Money is also a **store of value.** You have money in bank accounts, savings and/or checking. These represent storehouses of value that earn interest. But you can also put money in your lockbox at home, in your mattress, or in an old shoe. You can hoard it! Money's function as a store of value distinguishes it from **barter** systems in which people trade one good for another. In barter-based economies, it is extremely difficult to hoard. Imagine trying to hoard limestone wheels.

Barter means goods are traded directly for other goods.

Unit of account means that money is expressed in U.S. dollars, a common currency unit, enabling us to compare relative worth.

A third function of money is its role as a **unit of account** (often referred to as a *yardstick of value*). The things you buy are all expressed in common units, dollars and cents. You earn income, and this, too, is denominated in our currency. In this way, we are able to compare one item's worth to other things, especially if we express values in real terms.

Not only must money have a high use value, it must also be convenient for the user. Barter is just not convenient. Evidently, neither was the two-dollar bill! It has been introduced at least three different times. Instead of its catching on as a medium of exchange, consumers refused to spend it. Most people regarded it as such an oddity that it became a collector's item. It just didn't have a high use value. Can you think of another part of our money supply which has limited use value? Hint: It's popular in Las Vegas and Atlantic City.

Another part of the money supply which may be on its way out is the penny. Unlike the two-dollar bill, the copperhead has been around for a long time. However, as discussed in the following case, the penny has a high nuisance value.

CASE
▪ IN ▪
POINT

Do You Bend over for Pennies Anymore?

You see a penny on the ground. Do you still stoop over to pick it up? If a recent poll of 500 people in Atlanta, Georgia, is representative of public opinion, then the resounding answer is no. Not only do we ignore the copperhead shining up at us, but most of us find it a nuisance.

How often have you fumbled through your pockets or purses for a few of those pennies at the checkout counter? Think of the billions of such transactions each year which must waste millions of hours annually. But the cost extends beyond mere nuisance value.

"Consider the cost of minting and maintaining the penny supply. There are roughly 91 billion pennies circulating, and every year the U.S. Treasury produces 12 billion to 14 billion more, at a cost of about $90 million. Since this expenditure just produces a nuisance for society, it should be at the top of everyone's list of budget cuts."

Of course, some may claim that eliminating pennies would be inflationary. After all, you might argue, all of those $29.99 shirts would now be priced at $30. But if psychological pricing practices are important, why would retailers raise prices to $30? Rather, in a pennyless economy, they would lower the price to $29.95. Indeed, doing away with the penny would actually be disinflationary—if only one fifth of merchants reacted this way.

Sales taxes may pose a problem. If a 6 percent tax is levied on a $29.99 shirt, the final price is $30.79. If there are no pennies, one solution is to round the price to the next highest nickel, $30.80; or, if all prices are $xx.x0 or $xx.x5, let states and cities round the sales tax to the nearest nickel. The customer would lose a few pennies, four at the most. If the lost time and sheer nuisance of digging for pennies is really a bother, surely the benefits of abolishing the copperhead would exceed the extra costs.

"Let's get penny-wise and abolish the one-cent piece. The idea is so logical, so obviously correct, that I am sure the new Congress will enact it during its first days in office."[2]

Questions to Consider

"So logical"? "So obviously correct"? "Congress will enact ..."? What do you think? Should (or will) Congress take steps to abolish the penny, or might Congress be afraid of admitting that inflation has rendered the copperhead useless?

MEASURES OF THE MONEY SUPPLY

M1 *is the basic definition of the money supply—composed of currency in circulation, all checkable deposits, and traveler's checks.*

Checkable deposits *consist of* demand deposits *at commercial banks—often called checking accounts,* share drafts, *and* NOW accounts.

What does the money supply consist of? How much money is in circulation? Who keeps tabs on such information? You already know that you use money for transactions; thus, currency and checking accounts must be a part of the money supply. The basic definition of the money supply is called **M1**. It is composed of currency (coin and Federal Reserve notes) in circulation, all **checkable deposits**, and traveler's checks. It thus consists of the most liquid forms of money.[3] (Checkable deposits consist of *demand deposits* at commercial banks—often just called checking accounts, *share drafts* at credit unions and *NOW accounts* at savings and loan associations, also known as thrifts.) *NOW* means "negotiated order of withdrawal," a checking account that earns interest. Although *M1* is the smallest money supply measure, it is the most often used form of money. Of course, money is also held in other forms, like savings accounts. But is money in savings accounts regularly used for transactions?

How often do you go to your bank and withdraw money from a savings account to buy something or to pay rent or the electric bill? Because most people use their checking accounts and currency to purchase such goods and services, savings accounts are not a part of *M1*. However, if all passbook savings deposits, small denomination time deposits (less than $100,000), money market mutual fund accounts (and a few

---

[2] Alan S. Blinder, "Abolishing the Penny Makes Good Sense," *Business Week,* "Economic Watch," January 12, 1987, p. 29.

[3] Liquidity is a characteristic of financial assets. Liquid assets are readily and easily convertible to cash. Since *M1* consists of currency and checking accounts, and because checking accounts are nearly as good as cash with proper identification, the components of *M1* are the most liquid of all financial assets.

M2 is another definition of the money supply; M2 = M1 + time deposits less than $100,000, money market mutual funds, money market deposit accounts, and other highly liquid assets.

other liquid assets) are added to the *M1* money supply figure, we arrive at another definition of money: *M2*. And, by adding time deposits in denominations of $100,000 or more, repurchase agreements (longer than the overnight variety) and other miscellaneous assets, a third measure of the money supply is obtained, *M3*. Still another measure, *L*, counts everything in *M3* plus savings bonds, commercial paper, and other assets.[4] Please see Table 15–1 for the composition of the money supply as of October 1988; note the definitions of each component.

Why have different measures of the money supply? In fact, there are several other ways to define the money supply, but we will focus on *M1* and *M2*. Because money is what money does, and because *M1* has grown faster than nearly all other forms of money, the government has decided to define money according to its importance and frequency of use to handle transactions. After all, the role of money as a medium of exchange is probably its greatest value. However, since money held in various savings accounts amounts to more than three times the total of currency and checkable accounts, it is also important to have a measure of this money.

Federal Reserve System (FRS) is the nation's central banker and chief monetary authority in the United States.

Measurement of the money supply is the responsibility of the **Federal Reserve System (FRS),** the nation's central banker. But its functions and operations extend much further. It is the chief monetary authority in the United States, and it bears the primary responsibility for maintaining the stability of U.S. financial markets. We now turn to examine the structure and operations of the Federal Reserve System.

THE FEDERAL RESERVE AND THE BANKING SYSTEM

Why is there a need for a central bank? Why do most industrial nations have such an institution? A brief glance into the past is helpful in order to understand the Federal Reserve System.

In the late 1800s and early 1900s, commercial banks were regulated primarily by the states in which they did business. Most states were very permissive in their regulations, and banks enjoyed substantial freedom regarding lending practices—so much freedom, in fact, that many banks failed when the economy experienced a recession (or worse). Bank panics were common occurrences as depositors would make a run on the bank, withdrawing all their money for fear that the bank would go under. General business bankruptcies were bad enough, but bank failures were frightening. In order to provide greater control over commer-

---

[4] Commercial paper is an unsecured (no collateral) promissory note (or IOU) issued by a nonfinancial corporation. Interest rates on such notes are competitive with money market deposit accounts and money market mutual funds.

TABLE 15–1

The Money Supply: *M1, M2, M3,* and *L* October 1988 (all figures in billions of dollars)

Currency		$ 209.5
Plus: Transaction deposits:		
Demand deposits	$288.6	
Other checkable deposits	277.9	
Plus: Traveler's checks		7.4
Equals: *M1*		$ 783.4
Plus: Money market mutual fund shares		231.2
Plus: Money market deposit accounts		506.7
Plus: Savings deposits		431.3
Plus: Small-denomination time deposits (< $100,000)		1,009.9
Plus: Overnight repurchase agreements and other assets		76.0
Equals: *M2*		3,038.5
Plus: Large time deposits (> $100,000)		530.4
Plus: Long-term repurchase agreements		123.9
Plus: Miscellaneous assets		183.7
Equals: *M3*		3,876.5
Plus: Savings bonds		108.3
Plus: Short-term Treasury securities		281.3
Plus: Bankers acceptances		41.3
Plus: Commercial paper		309.2
Equals: *L*		4,616.6

Although the Federal Reserve uses four measures (different definitions) of the money supply, *M1* is the most closely followed. The components of *M1*, such as currency and all checkable deposits, are most commonly used by consumers and businesses for transactions ranging from lunches at local restaurants to bill payments.

Definitions:

Money market mutual fund shares: shares of short-term fixed-income securities, such as government Treasury bills, sold to the public; most brokerages (like E.F. Hutton and Merrill Lynch) have such funds in which you can purchase shares for as little as $500; the fund offers check-writing privileges (usually for amounts of $500 or more), and the interest rate is generally higher than conventional savings accounts.

Money market deposit accounts are virtually identical to the money market mutual funds; in 1982, banks and thrifts were permitted to compete with the big fund shares by offering their own version of money market funds.

Savings deposits offer security and (usually) immediate withdrawal privileges, although they carry lower interest than money market funds and depositors cannot write checks on their accounts.

Small-denomination time deposits are savings deposits with a twist: they are offered with a time frame attached, like six months, one year, five years, etc.; they also pay higher interest rates, but early withdrawal involves a penalty.

Repurchase agreements are special contract arrangements between a financial institution (bank or thrift) and a business (sometimes a consumer) in which the buyer agrees to buy a security and sell it back, often the next day, at a higher price; the difference between the buying and selling price is equivalent to an interest payment for the institution's use of the money.

SOURCE: *Economic Report of the President* (Superintendent of Documents, U.S. Government Printing Office, 1989), Tables B–67 and B–68, pp. 385–87.

cial banking, to provide for an elastic currency, and to provide confidence in the nation's banks, in 1913, the Congress established the Federal Reserve System.

Organization of the Federal Reserve System

The Federal Reserve System consists of five elements:

1. The Federal Reserve banks.
2. Commercial banks.
3. The Federal Reserve Open Market Committee.
4. The Board of Governors.
5. The Federal Advisory Council.

Federal Reserve Bank (FRB)
is a banker's bank, which
performs the same func-
tions for the commercial
bank that the financial insti-
tutions perform for its
depositors.

Federal Reserve District Banks.   The Federal Reserve Act of 1913 called for the creation of 12 *Federal Reserve Districts,* each with its own **Federal Reserve Bank (FRB)** (see Figure 15–1.) This decentralized central banking system was unique; all other industrial nations had only one central bank (e.g., the Bank of England, the Bank of France, etc.). But it was also quite customary for the United States. As a nation, we always have feared concentrations of power, and we have been especially suspicious of the concentration of power in governmental agencies.

What Are Federal Reserve Banks?   The Federal Reserve Banks are bankers' banks. If you think of the various functions and services provided by your commercial bank, a similar array of services is provided by the FRBs to commercial banks. For example, just as a commercial bank is a depository for your funds, the FRB also holds deposits for banks (called reserves). And, just as you can borrow from your commercial bank, the commercial bank can borrow from its FRB.

There are 12 headquarter Federal Reserve Banks, one in each district. However, in keeping with the legislative intent of the Federal Reserve Act, there are also 25 *branch banks*. These help to provide better service to the diverse economic regions within a Federal Reserve District. For example, although St. Louis is the headquarters for the eighth Federal Reserve District, there are branches in Memphis, Louisville, and Little Rock.

Commercial banks *receive*
deposits and lend money.

Commercial Banks.   Numbering more than 14,000 in 1988, commercial banks are the collective heart and soul of the Federal Reserve System. Whether chartered by the federal government or by the states in which they do business, all **commercial banks** share two essential functions: they receive deposits and they lend money.

Membership in the Federal Reserve System (Fed) is required only of national commercial banks—those chartered by the Comptroller of the Currency, and fewer than half of commercial banks are members of the Fed. Regardless of status, however, all commercial banks live with the same basic regulations determined by the Fed.

FIGURE 15–1 The Federal Reserve System Boundaries of Federal Reserve Districts and Their Branch Territories

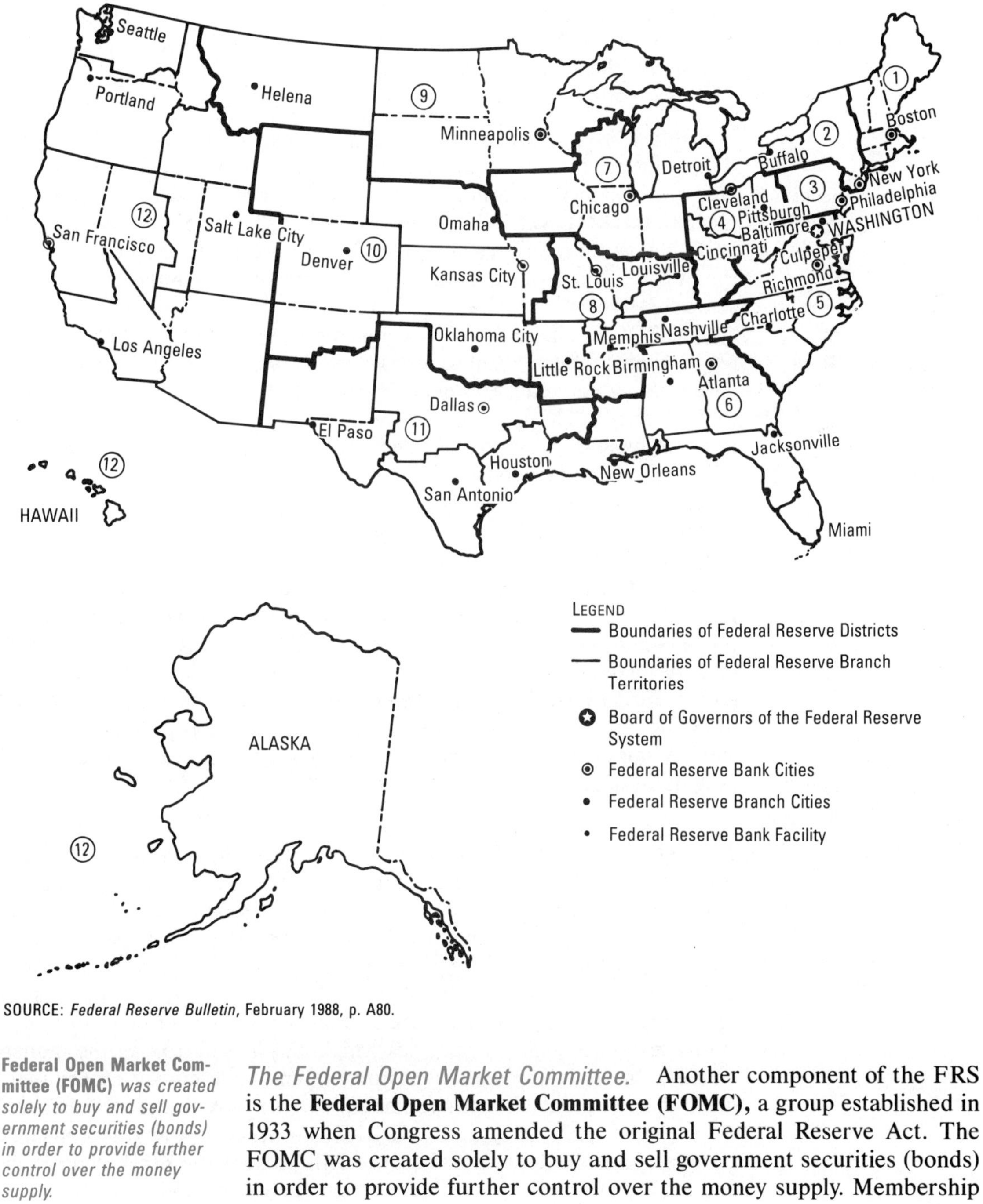

LEGEND
- **━** Boundaries of Federal Reserve Districts
- **─** Boundaries of Federal Reserve Branch Territories
- ✪ Board of Governors of the Federal Reserve System
- ◉ Federal Reserve Bank Cities
- • Federal Reserve Branch Cities
- · Federal Reserve Bank Facility

SOURCE: *Federal Reserve Bulletin*, February 1988, p. A80.

Federal Open Market Committee (FOMC) *was created solely to buy and sell government securities (bonds) in order to provide further control over the money supply.*

The Federal Open Market Committee.   Another component of the FRS is the **Federal Open Market Committee (FOMC),** a group established in 1933 when Congress amended the original Federal Reserve Act. The FOMC was created solely to buy and sell government securities (bonds) in order to provide further control over the money supply. Membership on the FOMC consists of the seven members of the BOG and five Federal Reserve Bank presidents. And, because the New York Federal Reserve District represents nearly 25 percent of the nation's deposits, the president of the New York Federal Reserve Bank has permanent membership on the committee.

The Board of Governors.   The Federal Reserve Act of 1913 and the Banking Act of 1933 (an amendment to the initial legislation) also created a regulatory apparatus headed by the **Federal Reserve Board of Governors (BOG).** The chief policy-making body of the system, the BOG has seven members appointed by the president and confirmed by the Senate. The terms are for 14 years with the appointed chairman to serve for 4 years.

Federal Reserve Board of Governors (BOG) *is the chief policy-making body of the system.*

The BOG is charged with several important duties. First, it has the responsibility of establishing **reserve requirements** for all depository institutions—a percentage of deposits that must remain as idle funds (not to be loaned). The reserve requirements are expressed as reserve/deposit ratios (e.g., 5 percent, 10 percent). For example, if a bank has $10 million in checking deposits and the reserve requirement is 3 percent, it is required to hold $300,000 in idle reserves.

Reserve requirement (rr) *(or reserve ratio) specifies the minimum percentage of deposits which an institution must hold by law.*

Another important function of the BOG is to set the *discount rate*—the rate of interest charged member banks when they borrow reserves from the Federal Reserve Banks. Additionally, the BOG, by virtue of its membership on the Federal Open Market Committee, conducts *open market operations*—buying and selling government securities for the purpose of influencing bank reserves, the money supply, credit availability, and interest rates. With these three tools, the reserve requirement, the discount rate, and open market operations, the BOG performs the extremely important job of formulating monetary policy, a subject we will take up in detail in the next chapter.

The Federal Advisory Council.   The principal function of the Federal Advisory Council is to advise the Board of Governors. It consists of 12 individuals selected by the Federal Reserve Banks (usually commercial bankers), one representative from each Federal Reserve District.

Although the Federal Reserve System is the most important of the U.S. financial institutions (from the standpoint of deposits and general monetary management), there are several other types of financial intermediaries and regulatory agencies which play a vital role in the money markets. In order to round out our understanding of money, money markets, and the regulatory environment, we will look first at the Federal Deposit Insurance Corporation (FDIC), an organization which insures commercial bank deposits. Then, we will present the other depository and lending institutions and discuss their regulatory bodies as well.

The Federal Deposit Insurance Corporation

Federal Deposit Insurance Corporation (FDIC) provides a federal role in bank regulation and economic stabilization, insuring individual deposits to $100,000.

A major part of the Banking Act of 1933 was the creation of the **Federal Deposit Insurance Corporation (FDIC).** Have you ever seen a bank panic? Have any of your relatives told you stories about the 1930s? Because there was no deposit insurance in those days, bank customers lived with the fear of losing all of their money if the bank failed. In order to restore confidence in the banking system, and to provide a federal role in bank regulation, the Congress established the Federal Deposit Insurance Corporation. Today the FDIC insures individual deposits to $100,000. The insurance fund is financed by a flat insurance premium of 1/4 of 1 percent of deposits.

When a bank does fail, the FDIC declares the bank illiquid, closes its doors, and conducts its routine examination of bank assets. How many banks actually fail? The FDIC oversaw the closing of 203 insured banks in 1987, a post–Depression high. By comparison with the previous seven years, the trend looks very ominous. A significant increase in closures occurred in 1987, from 145 in 1986, 120 in 1985, and only 10 in 1980. Indeed, commercial bank failures have risen each year since 1981, and in 1988, more than 200 banks closed their doors.

What does this mean? Do bank failures imply deeper problems than other business failures? Some financial analysts think so. As you might suspect, several observers fit into the camp of genuine prophets of doom, forecasting a financial collapse on the order of the Great Depression. Most economists, however, think that the bankruptcies continue to reflect a pattern of bank failures: a concentration in troubled oil and farm states. Others attribute most of the banks' problems to poor bank management, that is, extending loans to Third World countries and marginal farm owners whose repayment schedule was based upon some very questionable assumptions about price stability for oil and farm commodities.

THINKING IT THROUGH

There have been several "doom and gloom" books published recently, such as *The Coming Depression of 1990; The Great Stock Market Crash of 1989,* and so forth. Do bank failures suggest an economic collapse?

Other Financial Institutions

Financial intermediaries are institutions that receive deposits from the public and lend these funds to consumers and businesses.

Commercial banks are the nation's biggest **financial intermediaries**—institutions which receive deposits from the public and lend these funds to consumers and businesses. There are, however, many other bank-like institutions which have played an increasingly important role in financial markets in recent years. Although credit unions, savings and loans, and savings banks (called *thrifts* because they receive most of their deposits from consumer households) may not be perceived as major players, they have grown in stature and promise to play an ever larger role in the economy.

Credit Unions.   **Credit unions** (CUs) are tax-exempt cooperative societies formed to serve individuals working for the same employer or members of the same union. Although they are primarily organized around a single company or union, in recent years credit unions have extended their membership well beyond the immediate employee group.

Credit unions (CUs) are tax-exempt cooperative societies formed to serve individuals working for the same employer or members of the same union.

The first credit union was organized in 1909 in Manchester, New Hampshire. Numbering more than 15,000 today, CUs are the most numerous of all financial intermediaries. (Commercial banks are a close second with approximately 14,000.) Although states charter credit unions, most CUs are federally chartered. The regulatory body for federally chartered credit unions is the National Credit Union Association (NCUA), an organization whose functions mirror those of the Federal Reserve Board of Governors. Credit unions also have their own insurance agency, the National Credit Union Share Insurance Fund, administered by the NCUA. Like all other thrifts, this fund also provides deposit insurance up to $100,000 per depositor. And, like their counterparts, credit unions must hold reserves determined by the Federal Reserve authorities.

Savings and Loan Associations.   The first savings and loan (S&L) was established in 1831 (Oxford Provident Building Association of Philadelphia). **Savings and Loans** are bank-like financial intermediaries whose chief function is to receive deposits and make loans. Numbering about 3,000 in 1987, half are state chartered and half are federally chartered. Until late 1989, S&Ls were chartered and regulated by the Federal Home Loan Bank System (FHLBS), which was to S&Ls what the Federal Reserve is to commercial banks. The FHLBS consisted of 12 regional banks and a supervisory board in Washington, D.C. The regulation of the S&L industry is now in the hands of the *Office of Thrift Supervision*; this department of the U.S. Treasury was created in August 1989.

Savings and loans are bank-like financial intermediaries whose chief function is to receive deposits and make loans (mainly for homes).

Like banks and credit unions, the savings and loan industry also has its own insurance agency, the Savings Association Insurance Fund (SAIF). In the reforms made in 1989, SAIF replaced the Federal Savings and Loan Insurance Corporation (FSLIC), which was the original insurance fund. These and other changes to the S&L industry were part of a massive federal bailout of insolvent S&Ls. We will examine further this extremely important but relatively little publicized legislation in a few pages.

Savings Banks.   The original mutual savings banks were established in 1816 (the Provident Institution for Savings in Boston and the Savings Fund Society in Philadelphia). Today, there are approximately 800 savings banks, nearly all of which are concentrated in five eastern states. Thrift institutions like their sister S&Ls and CUs, **savings banks** (also called *mutual savings banks*) are structured as cooperatives or mutuals with their depositors owning the institution. Indeed, because their original purpose was to encourage savings and home ownership, like the S&Ls, it is difficult to distinguish savings banks and savings and loan associations. One difference is that savings banks do not have their own regulatory agency. They are regulated by the Federal Reserve Board, and their depositors are insured by the Federal Deposit Insurance Corporation.

Savings banks *are structured as cooperatives or mutuals with their depositors owning the institution.*

Commercial banks, savings and loans, credit unions, and savings banks are the four depository and lending financial intermediaries, but there are many other financial institutions which intermediate between savers and lenders. Insurance companies, pension funds, consumer finance companies, money market mutual funds, and mutual funds are each significant players in the financial markets. Indeed, as shown in Table 15–2, credit unions and savings banks constitute only 2.4 percent and 3.3 percent of the total assets in the financial industry, respectively. Although commercial banks and savings and loans account for about 47 percent of all assets, nonbank institutions represent 48.1 percent of the industry's assets. As mutual funds and insurance companies become more like banks and S&Ls, we can expect the ownership and distribution of assets to become more concentrated in nonbank institutions.

TABLE 15–2
Asset Rank of Financial Institutions

Institution	Asset Size*	Percent	Cumulative Percent
Commercial banks	$2,170	30.1%	30.1%
Savings and loans	1,160	16.1	46.3
Life insurance companies	900	12.5	58.8
Private noninsured pension funds	640	8.9	67.6
State and local government retirement funds	470	6.5	74.2
Mutual funds	410	5.7	79.9
Sales and consumer finance companies	400	5.6	85.4
Insurance companies	350	4.9	90.3
Money market mutual funds	290	4.0	94.3
Mutual savings banks	240	3.3	97.6
Credit unions	170	2.4	100.0

*Asset size figures are in billions of dollars.

Although credit unions are the most numerous of financial institutions, they account for only 2.4 percent of total assets. By contrast, commercial banks alone represent nearly one third of all assets. Perhaps even more interesting, nonbank institutions account for 48.1 percent of all assets in the financial industry.

SOURCE: Federal Reserve Flow of Funds Accounts.

One major reason for the greater role of thrifts and nonbank financial institutions is the deregulation of banking. Although starting in the 1970s, two pieces of legislation in the early 1980s have produced dramatic changes in the way financial institutions do business.

MODERN LEGISLATIVE INITIATIVES AND OTHER FINANCIAL INNOVATIONS

Perhaps the most far-reaching legislation occurred in 1980. The Depository Institutions Deregulation and Monetary Control Act of 1980 made sweeping changes throughout the banking industry, affecting not only commercial banks, but thrifts as well. But there were many other changes along the way; and there have been several changes since.

The Background

As we have said, under the Federal Reserve Act, all national banks were required to become members. State banks could also become members of the FRS provided that they met certain size requirements. Although membership conveyed certain benefits, like free check clearing and borrowing privileges, membership also exacted a price. Reserve requirements, the percentage of deposits held as idle funds, were much higher for Federal Reserve member banks than for state banks operating under charters issued by state banking commissions. Lured by lower reserve requirements and by more lenient regulations in the states, many state banks left the Federal Reserve System in the 1970s. The result was a significant drop in Fed membership and a corresponding decrease in the Fed's ability to conduct monetary policy.

Regulation Q was a provision of the Banking Act of 1933, now defunct, authorizing the Federal Reserve to set the maximum interest rates that commercial banks were allowed to pay on passbook accounts and time deposits.

Another problem faced by all financial institutions was **Regulation Q,** a provision of the Banking Act of 1933, which authorized the Federal Reserve to set the maximum interest rates that commercial banks were allowed to pay on passbook accounts and time deposits. (Since banks and thrifts also were prohibited from paying any interest on checking accounts, the effective ceiling interest rate was zero.)

Although designed to prevent what the legislators thought was aggressive (excessive) interest rate competition among banks during the 1920s, there is actually little evidence that this ever happened. Indeed, interest rates on regular savings and time deposits declined during the 1920s, so, what was the effect of Regulation Q?

Disintermediation.   When depositors put their savings in financial institutions, and these institutions in turn buy bonds, stocks, and mortgages, the process is called *financial intermediation.* Banks and others act as intermediaries between savers and borrowers. However, when depositors take their savings out of their accounts and buy such securities directly, it is known as *financial disintermediation*. And it was this process that ultimately resulted in the gradual elimination of Regulation Q.

When money markets were tight in the late 1960s and 1970s, Regulation Q kept interest rates on savings and time deposits well below other money market rates, such as money market mutual funds and Treasury bills. Eager to maximize interest income, households and businesses took their funds out of banks and S&Ls and bought bonds, commercial paper, T bills and other higher-earning assets. Such disintermediation resulted in reductions in lending and profits for all and threatened the survival of many.

One clear effect experienced by S&Ls, the primary mortgage lender for many home buyers, was a dramatic reduction in the availability of money for new home loans. As shown in Figure 15–2, the supply of loanable funds decreased, illustrated as a leftward shift of the supply

FIGURE 15–2

Supply and Demand in the Money Market

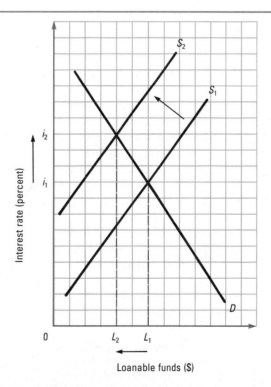

Regulation Q kept interest rates on passbook savings and time accounts below other interest-earning assets, such as Treasury bills and money market mutual funds. The result was financial disintermediation—depositors withdrew their funds and directly bought T bills and other higher-earning assets. This is shown as a decrease in supply of loanable funds (S_1 to S_2), higher interest rates (i_1 to i_2), and fewer loans (L_1 to L_2)

curve (S_1 to S_2), interest rates increased (i_1 to i_2), and fewer loans were made (L_1 to L_2). The demand for homes also declined as fewer and fewer people were eligible for loans at higher interest rates. The upshot often is a recession in the construction industry, a slump that gradually spreads like a cancer to the entire economy.

The effect of disintermediation was blunted to some extent by the Fed's elimination of ceilings on short-term (less than three-month) large certificates of deposit ($100,000 and over) in 1970. In 1973, the Fed eliminated ceilings on CDs of all maturities.

Greater relaxation of Regulation Q occurred in 1978 when commercial banks and thrifts were allowed to issue a six-month $10,000 certificate of deposit tied to the T bill rate. Useful as it was, this innovation excluded small depositors unable to accumulate $10,000. The answer to this problem was the Money Market Mutual Fund—an innovation which combined the funds from small savers ($500 or $1,000) and then bought large denomination certificates and other high yield alternatives. Small savers now could pool their funds in order to take advantage of higher money rates that had been denied them under Regulation Q.

The Monetary Control Act of 1980. A legislative solution to the problems in the commercial banking industry—the exodus of state banks, and the problems among thrifts finally was passed in 1980. Under the Depository Institutions Deregulation and Monetary Control Act of 1980 or the **Monetary Control Act,** the Congress and president launched two major reforms. First, the Fed's jurisdiction in setting reserve requirements was extended to all depository institutions—to thrifts as well as commercial banks. That took care of the membership problem.[5] All financial institutions were also permitted to offer NOW accounts (Negotiated Order of Withdrawal—a fancy term for interest-bearing checking accounts). Second, Regulation Q was abolished. All interest rate ceilings were phased out (by April 1986).

Monetary Control Act was a major banking system reform that extended the Fed's jurisdiction to all depository institutions and abolished Regulation Q.

Problems among savings and loan associations, however, did not vanish with these financial innovations. Many S&Ls experienced a profit squeeze because of outstanding low-interest mortgage loans and increasing pressure to pay higher and higher rates on deposits. To illustrate the problem, imagine Magnolia Savings and Loan in Anywhere, U.S.A. Most of its existing home loans were fixed rate mortgages made at less

---

[5] Before the Monetary Control Act, urban banks with large deposits were required to hold a higher percentage of required reserves than rural banks with small deposits. As of January 1, 1987, however, all depository institutions became subject to a uniform two-tiered system of reserve requirements. The Monetary Control Act requires reserves equal to 3 percent of the bank's first $25 million of checkable deposits and 12 percent of checkable deposits over $25 million. Although the BOG has the authority to make minor adjustments, it has not changed the reserve requirements since they went into effect.

than 10 percent interest. But, because of increasingly tight money markets, and because of the recent relaxation of Regulation Q, interest rates on many savings accounts were rising rapidly. As the interest expenses on its liabilities (deposits) rose, and the interest income on its assets (mortgages and other loans) remain fixed, the profit squeeze often turned into real financial distress or bankruptcy.

The Garn–St Germaine Act of 1982. Insolvent S&Ls and the growing concern that the situation would only further deteriorate led Congress in 1982 to pass the **Garn–St Germaine Depository Institutions Act**. Designed chiefly to rescue failing S&Ls, this legislation authorized savings and loans to offer money market deposit accounts so that they could more effectively compete with money market mutual funds. It also empowered S&Ls to make a wider variety of consumer and business loans, and made it easier for S&Ls to merge and for federal insurance agencies to make loans to troubled thrifts. Despite the Garn-St Germaine legislation, the savings and loan industry experienced greater financial trouble. As the following CASE-IN-POINT illustrates, the cure (deregulation) may have been worse than the disease (excessive regulation).

Garn–St Germaine Act of 1982 *was designed to rescue failing S&Ls, approving a broader variety of loans and money market mutual funds.*

CASE
• IN •
POINT

The Feds to the Rescue: The 1989 S&L Bailout

The 1980s witnessed a crisis of major proportions in the savings and loan industry. Widespread mismanagement, fraud, and bizarre real estate speculation produced bankruptcies and FSLIC takeovers at a cost of $100 billion. In 1988 more than one fourth of all S&Ls were insolvent or teetering on the edge of bankruptcy.

One source of failures was the financial deregulation of the banking industry in the early 1980s. A second source of failure was the combination of external events—such as a big decrease in oil prices and the collapse of real estate markets in Texas, and internal mismanagement and fraud, resulting in hundreds of bankrupt S&Ls and thousands of repossessed properties in the hands of the FSLIC.

In August 1989, President Bush signed into law Public Law 101-73. Although many details have yet to be finalized, the biggest bailout in U.S. history includes the following chief provisions:

- The newly established *Resolution Trust Corporation* in the U.S. Treasury will sell $50 billion of bonds to raise money to liquidate insolvent S&Ls. U.S. taxpayers will pay the interest charges on this debt over the next 30 years. The estimated cost is from $300 to $350 billion.
- S&Ls must adjust their loan portfolios so that at least 70 percent of their loans finance home mortgages and other residential loans.
- The FSLIC was replaced by the *Savings Association Insurance Fund (SAIF)* and merged with the FDIC.

- The FDIC fund is being shored up by doubling insurance premiums.
- S&L owners must invest 3–5.5 percent in their operations.
- The former regulatory agency, the Federal Home Loan Bank Board, was replaced with a new branch of the U.S. Treasury, the *Office of Thrift Supervision.*[6]

Questions to Consider

1. *No sooner had Congress passed the savings and loan salvage bill, than it began considering reform of the deposit insurance system. Specifically, the House Banking Committee wanted a reduction of the $100,000 deposit insurance limit. Although deposit insurance is designed to provide stability by preventing bank runs based on unfounded fears, does deposit insurance increase the amount of risk banks and other depository institutions are willing to take with depositors' money?*

2. *The bailout is predicated on several key assumptions about the economy over the next several years: long-term interest rates are expected to fall to 7 percent by 1991, real economic growth is expected to increase at 2.5 percent per year, and thrift deposits are expected to grow by 5 percent per year (even while the industry is contracting). What effect would a recession have on the thrifts and the success of the bailout plan?*

In order to consider the appropriate policies to deal with such issues as whether and how much regulation is required to stabilize financial markets, how much money should be in circulation, and related questions, it is important to understand how money is created. In Part II we will review this very important process.

PART II: THE CREATION OF MONEY

Financial institutions "create" money by making loans to their customers. (The more technical term for the creation of money is the **multiple expansion of checkable deposits.**) In order to see how this fascinating process works, let's follow the transactions of Paula Poulder and several banks, thrifts, and the Fed. First, we take a short detour and define a few important terms.

Multiple expansion of checkable deposits *(or creation of money) refers to the process by which loans from one bank become new deposits in other financial institutions, forming the base for excess reserves and new loans.*

The Bank Balance Sheet

A *balance sheet* shows the financial condition of a business on the date that the data is recorded. It shows assets, liabilities, and net worth. A

---

[6] "Success of S&L Bailout Bill Not Fully Guaranteed," *Congressional Quarterly*, August 12, 1989, pp. 2113–15; "Sticking It to The Taxpayers," *The Nation*, September 4/11, 1989, pp. 238–40; Robert Stonebraker, "Savings and Loans in Crisis," *The Margin* 5, no. 1, (September/October, 1989), pp. 19–21.

bank's *assets* are such things as its reserves (cash), buildings, land, and equipment, loans, and securities. Its *liabilities* are the things that the bank owes. A bank's chief liabilities are its customers' deposits, checking and saving. The difference between assets and liabilities is called *net worth*.

A simple version of a bank balance sheet is illustrated in the following T account. (Please see Table 15–3.) This is a very simplified T account; it shows only the most important assets and liabilities, and it omits net worth. For purposes of explaining how banks create money, all we need to show are three assets (reserves, loans, and securities) and one liability (checking accounts). The only requirement is that the left side of the T Account (assets) must always equal the right side (liabilities).

A Monopoly Bank

In order to keep our discussion relatively simple, we will begin by assuming that there is but one financial intermediary—a monopoly bank. All consumers and businesses have their deposits in and borrow money from Old Trusty National. To further simplify the process, we will present only new transactions (rather than illustrating the bank's current assets and liabilities). We begin with a new deposit to show the initial T account for Old Trusty.

Paula, a new resident of the community, opens a new account and deposits $1,000. Remembering that a balance sheet must balance, and that a bank's assets must equal its liabilities (plus net worth), Table 15–4 illustrates how Paula's demand deposit (DD) is recorded. Because the new deposit is owed to Paula, it is recorded as a liability. On the asset side, the money received is deposited in its reserve account at its Federal Reserve Bank. (As a practical matter, most banks will keep some of the deposit as vault cash. But whether on deposit at the Fed or kept on hand in the commercial bank, the deposit is still an asset called *reserves*.) The total reserves (or, in nonbank parlance, cash) are, by definition, equal to its liabilities.

TABLE 15–3 Bank Balance Sheet (T account)	Assets	Liabilities + Net Worth
	Total reserves (required reserves) (excess reserves)	Demand deposits
	Loans	
	Securities	

A T account illustrates a simplified bank balance sheet. Assets are always equal to liabilities plus net worth.

TABLE 15–4

A Monopoly Bank
Old Trusty National—
Initial Position

Assets		Liabilities + Net Worth	
Total reserves	$1,000	Paula's DD	$1,000
(required reserves)	(100)		
(excess reserves)	(900)		
Loans	0		
Securities	0		

The initial position of Old Trusty, our monopoly bank, is illustrated in the table after Paula deposits $1,000. The deposit is a bank liability, but it is also an asset—shown as total reserves of $1,000. Because the reserve requirement is 10 percent, Old Trusty must hold $100 in required reserves, leaving $900 in excess reserves.

Since we use a fractional reserve system of banking, Old Trusty is required to hold only a fraction of its deposit liabilities in idle reserves. This reserve requirement specifies the minimum percentage of deposits that an institution must hold by law (as established by the Federal Reserve). The actual dollar amount of **required reserves** is determined by multiplying the reserve requirement times the demand deposits. Letting rr represent the reserve requirement (a percentage value), RR the required reserves (in dollars), and DD the demand deposits, then

Required reserves (RR) *are the dollar amounts determined by multiplying the reserve requirement times the deposits.*

$$RR = rr \times DD.$$

In other words, the reserve requirement ratio is merely the ratio of required reserves to deposits. The difference between total reserves and required reserves is the amount of **excess reserves.** Letting TR represent total reserves and ER be excess reserves, then

Excess reserves *are the difference between total reserves and required reserves.*

$$TR = RR + ER$$

In our example, Paula's deposit is $1,000, and required reserves are $100. The reserve requirement is thus 10 percent. Excess reserves are $900, the difference between total reserves and required reserves. Old Trusty National is now able to make a loan. That is exactly what it does, and Table 15–5 illustrates what happens when it does so.

Harry Homeowner needs a home improvement loan. But he needs $9,000. Can Old Trusty make a loan of 10 times its excess reserves? Let's see what happens if Old Trusty does so. When a bank makes a loan, it generally wants to create an account in the borrower's name. We thus represent Harry's loan as a bank asset and as a new deposit liability of $9,000. As Table 15–5 shows, the assets (reserves plus loans) still equal total liabilities. Total reserves still equal 10 percent of deposit liabilities. So far, so good.

	Assets		Liabilities + Net Worth	

TABLE 15–5
A Monopoly Bank
Harry's Loan
	Total reserves
	  (required reserves)
	  (excess reserves)
		$1,000
		(1,000)
		(0)
			Paula's DD
			Harry's loan
				$1,000
				9,000

	Loans	9,000		
	Securities	0		

When Harry borrows $9,000 from our monopoly bank, the bank opens an account in his name with $9,000 on deposit. Harry's deposit is secured by a loan (a promissory note—an IOU.) of like amount. The bank can lend 10 times its excess reserves of $900 because there are no other banks. If Harry writes a $5,000 check, reducing its balance to $4,000, Old Trusty will lose neither deposits nor reserves. The party to whom Harry wrote the check will deposit the check back into Old Trusty. The transaction leaves the balance sheet unchanged.

But what would happen if Paula or Harry began writing checks, effectively destroying their deposits? Would Old Trusty's reserves decline, resulting in a reserve deficit position? Under other circumstances, yes, but because Old Trusty is a monopoly bank, this will not happen. Any check written on Harry's account, for example, would ultimately become a deposit in the same bank.[7] Thus, the total reserves and deposits in Figure 15–5 would remain unaltered even after Harry and Paula wrote checks. For example, if Harry wrote a $5,000 check to his roofing contractor, the contractor would deposit Harry's check in the same bank. Although Harry's account declines by $5,000, the contractor's account increases by $5,000; thus, total deposits and total reserves remain the same, and Old Trusty still complies with its reserve requirement.

What is the effect of Old Trusty's loan to Harry? The *M1* money supply, defined as nonbank cash and transaction accounts, has increased by 10 times the original deposit. With an initial deposit of $1,000, our monopoly bank was able to create $9,000 of new money. This may seem implausible or some kind of mathematical trickery, but it really is quite logical. Because banks create demand deposits when they make loans, and because demand deposits are money, making loans creates money. What is implausible is our assumption of a monopoly bank. So let's see how deposit creation occurs in the real world.

---

[7] As we will soon see, the same outcome will occur in our real-world multibank environment. Because all depository institutions are part of the consolidated banking system, the multiple expansion of deposits will be the same as if a monopoly bank handled all transactions. The important difference is that, unlike our monopoly bank, a single bank in a multibank system may make loans only in the amount of their excess reserves.

Deposit Creation in a Multibank Environment

In order to draw a comparison with the previous example, we will use the same numbers and reserve requirement as in our monopoly bank transactions. Suppose that Maria deposits $1,000 in her checking account in Citizens Bank. Table 15–6 illustrates the balance sheet. As before, we have broken down total reserves into required ($100) and excess ($900).

How much can it lend? Unlike a monopoly bank, the lending capacity of all commercial banks, S&Ls, and other depository institutions is limited to the amount of excess reserves. Knowing this, Citizens may lend exactly $900, but no more. Let's trace two transactions to see what will happen.

George applies for and receives a $900 loan from Citizens for a used car. In this case, the bank will most likely write a check to George for $900 out of its own (cash) reserves. Table 15–7 shows the balance sheet

TABLE 15–6
Citizens Bank—Initial Position

Assets		Liabilities + Net Worth	
Total reserves	$1,000	Maria's DD	$1,000
(required reserves)	(100)		
(excess reserves)	(900)		
Loans	0		
Securities	0		

The above T account illustrates the same initial position of Old Trusty, with one important difference. Citizens Bank is one of many depository institutions and thus can lend only the amount of its excess reserves.

TABLE 15–7
Citizens Bank—George's Loan

Assets		Liabilities + Net Worth	
Total reserves	$1,000	Maria's DD	$1,000
(required reserves)	(100)		
(excess reserves)	(0)		
Loans (George)	900		
Securities	0		

Here we show how Citizens Bank can make a loan without initially creating any new money. By writing a check to George out of its own (excess) reserves, it merely shifts assets from idle reserves to interest-earning assets (loans). The important point is that no new money is yet created because demand deposits remain unchanged.

TABLE 15–8

Bonafide Bank and Deposit Creation

Assets		Liabilities + Net Worth	
Total reserves	$900	Car dealer's DD	$900
(required reserves)	(90)		
(excess reserves)	(810)		
Loans	0		
Securities	0		

When the car dealer deposits George's check into its bank, deposits and reserves rise in Bonafide Bank. The money supply now has increased by $900. Moreover, Bonafide is in a position to make new loans in the amount of its excess reserves ($810).

after the loan is made. Notice that total reserves have declined by the amount of the loan, excess reserves are zeroed out, and George's loan of $900 appears on the asset side of the T account. In effect, Citizens merely rearranged its assets: shifting idle funds (from excess reserves) to an interest-earning loan. So far, however, there has been no change in the money supply. How can that be? Didn't we just say that making loans would create money?

George's used car dealer provides the answer. When the dealer deposits George's check in his account in Bonafide Bank, the money supply will increase by $900. Table 15–8 shows this transaction and illustrates that Bonafide now is positioned to make new loans.

Still assuming a reserve requirement of 10 percent, with a new $900 deposit, Bonafide must hold $90 in required reserves. This leaves $810 of excess reserves and, as we have seen already, enables the bank to make loans up to this amount. Assuming that it does so, the multiple expansion of deposits will continue.

Check Clearing

Check clearing is the process conducted by the Federal Reserve, the Federal Home Loan Bank, and other institutions, whereby reserves are transferred from one intermediary to another.

The missing ingredient thus far is how George's check is cleared. How does Citizens Bank learn of the transaction? **Check clearing** is the process conducted by the Federal Reserve, the Federal Home Loan Bank, and other institutions, whereby reserves are transferred from one intermediary to another.

In our example, we will assume that both banks have their checks cleared by the Fed. (Actually other financial regulatory agencies and nonbank institutions may also clear checks. And under the provisions of the Monetary Control Act, check clearing is a fee-for-service operation.) When the car dealer deposits George's check in Bonafide, the bank credits George's account for $900 and sends the check to the Fed. As illustrated in Table 15–9, the Fed's balance sheet, the Fed clears the check by adding $900 to Bonafide's reserve account and subtracting $900 from Citizens reserve account. Since Citizens and Bonafide keep a large share of their reserves on deposit at the Federal Reserve Bank, these reserves are liabilities on the Fed's balance sheet. The Fed then sends the check to Citizens Bank, the only party still to be informed about the transaction. Citizens reduces George's account (subtracting $900 from its liabilities) and reduces its (excess) reserve balance by the same amount on the asset side. All that has happened here is a simple transfer of reserves (excess) from one institution to another. The Fed merely acts as the clearinghouse.

Although we could extend this example of the lending- and deposit-creation transaction cycle through several additional banks, the basic point is already made. Lending results in new deposits, and since new deposits are money, lending creates money. But how much? To see how much money can be created from the initial excess reserve position, let's look at one more table.

The Multiple Creation of Deposits: Summing Up

As you are by now quite proficient at drawing T accounts and recording changes in reserves, loans, and deposits, you will be happy to know that we won't do any more of this. Instead of carrying the process on interminably, we can summarize what has happened thus far in a single table. Then, assuming that the process of deposit creation would continue until the new level of excess reserves is insignificant, we can show the total changes in deposits, loans, and reserves. Please see Table 15–10.

The first two rows of the table summarize the transactions already discussed. Rows 3–5 continue with the scenario, using the same assumptions. Each bank receiving new deposits holds 10 percent of the new deposit as required reserves, leaving a difference of 90 percent— the excess reserves. It is these excess reserves that provide the basis for the bank's lending operations and the multiple creation of deposits.

For example, if Bonafide lends $810 to Natasha for a school loan, the college will deposit the check in Bank 3. Bank 3 holds 10 percent and lends the rest ($729) to another worthy customer, and the process continues (see Rows 4 and 5). The Total "Change in Loans" is the increase in the money supply (*M1*)—all started with Maria's deposit in Citizens Bank. This is what is meant by the "Creation of Money."

Let's delve a little deeper. The "Sub-total" is calculated by adding up the first five rows of data in each column. The next row, "All other Banks," was calculated on a computer. The "Total" row was computed by adding the "Sub-Total" and "All Other Banks" figures for each column.

TABLE 15–9

Check Clearing at the Fed
Federal Reserve Bank
Balance Sheet

Assets	Liabilities + Net Worth	
	Citizens Bank	− $900
	Bonafide Bank	+ $900

The Fed clears a check by subtracting the check amount from the bank on whose account the check was drawn and adding the amount to the bank that received the deposit.

TABLE 15–10

The Multiple Creation of Deposits

Bank	Change in Deposits	Change in Loans (new money) (excess reserves)	Change in Reserves (required reserves)
1	$ 1,000.00	$ 900.00	$ 100.00
2	900.00	810.00	90.00
3	810.00	729.00	81.00
4	729.00	656.10	72.90
5	656.10	590.49	65.61
Sub-total	$ 4,095.10	$3,685.59	$ 409.51
All other banks	5,904.90	5,314.41	590.49
Total	$10,000.00	$9,000.00	$1,000.00

The table illustrates the multiple expansion of deposits. When Bank 1 receives a new deposit of $1,000, it holds $100 (because the reserve requirement is 10 percent), and lends $900. When the $900 loan becomes deposited in Bank 2, the money supply increases (by $900). Bank 2 may also increase its loans equal to 90 percent of the new deposit, or $810. As this loan is spent and deposited in Bank 3, the money supply increases again. The process continues until $9,000 of new money is created.

Knowing that a computer calculated these figures is OK, but that still leaves you in the dark. How then do you do it if you don't have a computer? This brings us to the wonderful world of shortcuts.

A Shortcut

No computers are really needed to do this work. In fact, one simple formula will do the trick. Our formula will tell us by how much the banking system can increase the money supply given two pieces of information: the reserve requirement ratio and the initial (Bank 1's or Citizens Bank's) excess reserves. And we know the value of each.

First, you know that the reserve requirement is 10 percent—10%, .10, or 1/10—depending on how you like to express the value. Second is the initial excess reserve position: this is the amount Citizens has available to loan after Maria deposits her $1,000. The initial excess reserves are $900. Next is the formula.

Deposit multiplier is the reciprocal of the reserve ratio, expressed as 1/rr.

The formula is similar to the Keynesian multiplier. *It says to multiply the change in excess reserves ($900) times the reciprocal of the reserve requirement ratio (10).* The result is $9,000. The reciprocal of the reserve ratio is called the **deposit multiplier.**[8] It may also be defined as the ratio of total checkable deposits to total reserves. In our case, the ratio is $9,000 : $900, or 10. Let *rr* stand for the "required reserve ratio," and let *ER* represent "excess reserves." Since *rr* refers to the required reserve ratio, then the deposit multiplier is shown as 1/*rr* (1 divided by *rr*). Hence the formula

$$\text{Change in } M1 = 1/rr \times \text{Change in } ER$$

This tells us to multiply the deposit multiplier times the change in excess reserves to find the change in the money supply (*M1*). Take a look back at Table 15–10, the table summarizing all of our transactions. The original deposit created excess reserves of $900. The reserve requirement is 10 percent. Plugging these values into our formula, we get

$$\text{Change in } M1 = 10 \times \$900, \text{ or}$$
$$\$9,000.$$

The total money supply thus increases by $9,000, and the total new deposits in the system (including Maria's original deposit) is $10,000. Now, referring to Table 15–10 again, we can easily calculate the amount of deposits for the category "All other banks." By subtracting the subtotal ($4,095.10) from the total ($10,000), we get $5,904.90.

One important caveat should be added. Deposit creation according to the formula assumes that banks lend all of their excess reserves and the public is willing to borrow the full amount that banks want to loan. In practice, banks and other financial institutions hold a certain quantity of excess reserves; thus, if for every new deposit dollar banks hold two or three cents in idle (excess) reserves, the multiplier process will be reduced.

---

[8] A short digression on reciprocals may be helpful. The reciprocal of a number is that number inverted. To invert a number, divide the number into one. Thus, if you have a number such as .5, and you want its reciprocal, just stand it on its head: 1/.5. Answer: 2. What if the number is a fraction, like 1/3? What is the reciprocal of 1/3? Divide 1/3 into 1 and you get 3 (1 / 1/3). If you have this number, .10, how do you find its reciprocal? Divide .10 into 1. Answer: 10. (If you prefer to work with fractions, but the reserve ratio is stated in decimal form, first convert the decimal to a fraction. For example, if the reserve ratio is .25, this means that 25 percent of deposits must be held as required reserves. Twenty-five percent is written as 25/100 or, reduced to the least common denominator, 1/4. Now, what's the reciprocal of 1/4? Just divide 1/4 into 1 (1 / 1/4) and you get 4.)

IMPORTANT TERMS TO REMEMBER

barter, p. 413
checkable deposits, p. 415
check clearing, p. 433
commercial banks, p. 418
credit unions, p. 422
deposit multiplier, p. 436
excess reserves, p. 430
Federal Deposit Insurance
  Corporation (FDIC), p. 421
Federal Open Market Committee
  (FOMC), p. 419
federal reserve banks, p. 418
federal reserve BOG, p. 420
federal reserve system, p. 416
financial intermediaries, p. 421

Garn-St Germaine Act, p. 427
M1, p. 415
M2, p. 416
medium of exchange, p. 413
Monetary Control Act, p. 426
money, p. 412
multiple creation of
  checkable deposits, p. 428
Regulation Q, p. 424
required reserves, p. 430
reserve requirement, p. 420
savings banks, p. 423
savings and loans, p. 422
store of value, p. 413
unit of account, p. 413

SUMMARY

1. Money is anything which is accepted as payment for goods and services. The basic money supply in the United States consists of currency (coin and Federal Reserve notes) and all checkable deposits. This definition is called *M1*. If we add savings deposits, money market funds, and other relatively liquid assets to *M1*, we obtain the *M2* definition of money.

2. The Federal Reserve System consists of five major parts: the member commercial banks, 12 Federal Reserve districts with 12 district head-quarter Federal Reserve Banks and 25 branch banks, the Board of Governors, the Open Market Committee, and the Federal Advisory Council.

3. Although only commercial banks are entitled to membership in the FRS, the Monetary Control Act of 1980 gave the Fed jurisdiction over all financial institutions in setting reserve requirements. In return for this new regulatory blanket, the legislation now permits all depository institutions to borrow from the Fed. More fundamental to the thrifts, the Monetary Control Act also authorized all banks and thrifts to offer NOW accounts (that is, checking accounts could now earn interest). It abolished Regulation Q, a Depression-born rule that enabled the Fed to set interest rate ceilings on passbook and time deposits.

4. The Federal Deposit Insurance Corporation (FDIC) also plays an important role in the banking system by insuring depositors up to $100,000 for commercial banks and mutual savings banks. The same kind of deposit insurance is provided for S&Ls and credit unions.

5. Depository institutions which receive funds (in checking and savings accounts) and make loans are known as financial intermediaries—commercial banks, mutual savings banks, savings and loans, and credit unions.

6. The Garn-St Germaine Act of 1982 was a legislative attempt to rescue failing savings and loan associations. It authorized S&Ls to offer a

greater variety of loans and the right to offer money market deposit accounts (MMDAs) to compete with the money market mutual funds (MMMFs).

7. The federal government came to the rescue of failing and insolvent S&Ls in 1989 in the biggest bailout in U.S. history. The FSLIC was replaced by the Savings Association Insurance Fund (SAIF) and merged with the FDIC, and the regulation of S&Ls was placed in the hands of the Office of Thrift Supervision in the U.S. Treasury Department.

8. The money supply is regulated by the Federal Reserve System (the Fed). The way in which the Fed controls money is through the reserves in financial institutions (credit unions, savings and loans, and commercial banks). The Fed establishes a reserve requirement which specifies the percentage of deposits that all banks are required to keep on hand (as idle funds). Banks may lend or invest excess reserves, the difference between its checkable deposits and its required reserves.

9. When banks lend excess reserves, they create money. Because lending takes the form of opening a new checkable deposit in the lender's name, the money supply increases by the amount of the loan. When the customer spends this money (writes checks), the checks are deposited in other banks by the people who received the check(s). Because these new banks now have excess reserves, they are in a position to lend all or any part of the excess reserves. This is what is called the multiple expansion of deposits or creating money. (Of course, money can also be destroyed. The change in the money supply [plus or minus] is determined by multiplying the reciprocal of the reserve ratio [the deposit multiplier] times the change in excess reserves.)

10. The Fed exercises control over the money supply through monetary policy. The chief monetary policy tools are open market operations (buying and selling securities), changes in the discount rate, and changes in the required reserve ratio.

DISCUSSION AND REVIEW QUESTIONS

1. List the following financial assets in order of liquidity: (a) time deposits, (b) NOW accounts, (c) currency, (d) 100 shares of IBM stock, and (e) U. S. treasury bonds. Which of the assets above are included in *M1*?

2. What are the differences among the *M1*, *M2*, *M3*, and L measures of the money supply? Why does the Fed have more than one measure?

3. If a banking system is fully loaned up, and the reserve requirement is 20 percent, by how much can Thrifty Bank lend or invest if it receives a new deposit of $10,000? Would it make a difference if, instead of receiving a new deposit, Thrifty sold $10,000 of its securities? How much can it lend in this case?

4. Assume that (a) all financial institutions in the banking system lend all of their excess reserves; (b) all institutions are fully loaned up; and (c) the reserve requirement ratio is 10 percent. Problem: If Hector deposits $5,000 in Greater-than-ever Credit Union, by how much may the supply

of money (*M1*) increase if Hector's deposit is a check written by his great aunt?

5. Working with the same general assumptions in the question above, solve this problem: Seung Li visits her local bank and deposits her $8,000 lottery winnings. By how much may *M1* increase if the $8,000 is transferred from the state lottery commission's savings account to Seung Li's checking account?

6. One way to define the deposit multiplier is the ratio of deposits to reserves. With a 10 percent reserve requirement, each dollar of reserves can support $10 of deposits; thus, if a banking system has total reserves of $20 billion, and a reserve requirement of 10 percent, its reserves can support a maximum of $200 billion of deposits.

    How many deposits can this hypothetical banking system's reserves support if the reserve requirement is reduced to 15 percent?

7. Credit cards, debit cards, teller machines, electronic transfers, and bill paying by phone, are only a few of the countless financial innovations introduced over the last several decades. Even vending machines are taking credit and debit cards! Are we moving to a cashless society, or will the obvious demand for cash transactions in the subterranean economy prevent the conversion to a truly cashless society?

8. Explain how the multiple expansion of deposits (and the deposit multiplier) is similar to the Keynesian multiplier effect (and the expenditures multiplier).

9. Describe and explain the main features of the S&L bailout bill. How are taxpayers involved in rescuing insolvent thrifts?

A BRIEF LOOK AHEAD

You have covered a lot of ground. You know how to define money and its functions, identify the composition of money supply measures, *M1*, *M2*, *M3*, and *L*, and distinguish among the various financial intermediaries and regulatory bodies. You also can describe and explain how money is created.

In the next chapter, we will look into the intriguing aspects of monetary policy. Specifically, we will examine how the Fed's buying and selling of securities, changes in the discount rate, and changes in the reserve ratio affect the money supply, the availability of credit, and interest rates. Moreover, we will show how and why the financial markets are so important to the general economic objectives of high employment and low inflation.

A Word to the Wise: Read and reread this chapter if you are unsure about particular concepts. It is essential that you are able to describe and explain how money is created, in great detail, before moving on to the subject of monetary policy.

Monetary Policy

Comstock

This chapter continues our discussion of money and banking and resumes our study of economic policy. The focus is on the Federal Reserve System and how the Fed manages the money supply, the availability of credit, and the general financial conditions in the economy. The emphasis is on monetary policy as it relates to the Employment Act, that is, how and why a specific monetary policy is made. We will examine how changes in the money supply affect spending, employment, and the price level.

After completion of this chapter, you should be able to do the following:

1. Define, describe, and explain the tools of monetary policy.
2. Identify and explain the equation of exchange.
3. Diagram and describe the transmission mechanism.
4. Describe how open market operations are conducted.
5. Prescribe the appropriate monetary policy to handle inflation and/or unemployment.
6. List and explain the advantages and disadvantages of monetary policy.
7. Describe and explain the interest theories (classical, Keynesian, and flow of funds).

Monetary Policy in Action

The time is early afternoon on a Wednesday in mid-June. The place is the trading room on the eighth floor of the Federal Reserve Bank of New York. The manager of the Open Market Account for Domestic Operations gathers with his trading room officers to reaffirm the judgment reached earlier to buy about $1.3 billion of Treasury bills. The banking system has a clear need for additional reserves to meet the increased public demand for currency and deposits expected as the end of the quarter and July 4 approach. . . . After a brief discussion, the manager gives final approval to the planned operation.

The officer-in-charge at the Fed's Trading Desk turns to the ten officers and securities traders who sit before telephone consoles linking them to three dozen primary dealers in U.S. government securities. "We're going to ask for offerings of all bills for regular delivery," she says. Each trader knows this means delivery and payment will take place the next day. Bill, one of the group, presses a button on his telephone console, sounding a buzzer on the corresponding console of a government securities dealer. "John," Bill says, "we are looking for offerings of bills for regular delivery." John replies, "I'll get back to you in a few minutes." Hanging up, John turns and yells, "The Fed is in, asking for bills for delivery tomorrow." Moments later information screens around the country and abroad flash the news. Salesmen begin ringing their customers to see if they have bills they want to offer. Meanwhile, John checks with the trading manager of his firm to see how aggressive he should be in pricing the firm's own securities.

Twenty minutes later, John rings back. "Bill, I can offer you $15 million of bills maturing August 9 at 9.20 percent, $40 million September 13 bills at 9.42, $25 million of September 20's at 9.46 and another 25 at 9.44. I'll sell $75 million December 13's at 10.12 and another 100 at 10.09. I can offer 50 May 16's at 10.28 percent. All for delivery tomorrow. Bill reads back the offerings and says, "Can I have these firm?" "Done," replies John.

Within 10 or 15 minutes each trader has written the offerings obtained on preprinted strips. The officer-in-charge arrays the individual dealer strips on an inclined board placed atop a stand-up counter. A quick tally shows that dealers have offered $7.8 billion of bills for regular delivery, that is, the next day.

The officer and a colleague begin comparing rates across the different maturities, seeking those that are high in relation to adjoining issues. She circles any bargains with a red pencil. Her associate keeps a running total of the amounts being bought. When the desired volume has been circled and cross-checked, the individual strips are returned to the traders, who quickly ring up the dealers to confirm all, part, or none of the offerings. Within 45 minutes of the initial offerings, all transactions have been completed, and the Trading Desk has bought $1,304 million of Treasury bills. Only the paper work remains.[1]

Such is monetary policy in action. On the day following the trading, the Fed will take delivery of the securities purchased from the banks that represent the dealers. With the exception of this delivery of actual paper, all other transactions are bookkeeping entries. The Fed pays for these securities by crediting $1,304 million to the banks' reserve accounts. This action creates reserves that did not exist before. With additional excess reserves, banks are now positioned to make more loans. And, as we have seen before, more lending generates a multiple expansion of deposits (increased money supply), more spending, production, employment, and usually higher prices. This process of how and why the Fed conducts specific monetary policies, what actions are appropriate under various economic conditions, and how the action is translated into more jobs and income is the main thrust of this chapter.

THE MONEY SUPPLY AND GNP—THE INTERRELATIONSHIPS

From our earlier work, we have established that spending (or aggregate demand) is the engine of the economy. As goes spending, so goes income, employment, and prices. This we know, thanks chiefly to John Maynard Keynes. But the amount of money in circulation also determines how much consumers and businesses spend. As the money supply increases, people have more money to spend. Conversely, as the money supply contracts, people have less money to spend.

Of course, economists have not always believed that money played an important role in the economy. The classical economists, for example, thought that money was merely a medium of exchange and thus a veil concealing the more important roles of wages, prices, and interest rates.

The Classical View: Savings and Investment

The demand for money had no place in classical economics, and the money supply was relevant only insofar as it affected prices.[2] Thus, instead of focusing on the relation between money and interest rates, the

---

[1] Paul Meek, Open Market Operations, Federal Reserve Bank of New York, August, 1985.

[2] We will discuss this relationship in detail a little later.

classical economists emphasized the flow of saving and investment. As we pointed out in Chapter 12, classical economists said that while saving varied directly with the interest rate, investment varied inversely with the interest rate. Thus, as shown in Figure 16–1, if the interest rate was above equilibrium (at 10 percent), the excess saving ($10 billion) would create downward pressure on interest rates. The temporary imbalance would soon be corrected as interest rates fell in response to the surplus. As interest rates came down, saving would decline, investment would increase, and equilibrium would be restored in the financial market.[3]

Of course, classical economics did not hold up in the face of the Great Depression. Keynes showed that saving and investment were influenced by income, sales, and expected earnings at least as much as by the interest rate. Moreover, Keynes observed that both the supply and demand for money could play an important role in the determination of aggregate demand, employment, and the price level. Just what that role is has become a central issue of macroeconomics in recent years.

The Supply of Money

Although the money supply and its creation is a subject with which we have dealt extensively in the last chapter, a brief review may be helpful. With the passage of the Monetary Control Act of 1980, Congress took steps to increase the Fed's ability to control the money supply and thereby improve its policy-making effectiveness. Although the jury is still out, most analysts think that the Fed is now able to control reserve levels and the money supply with greater accuracy.[4]

Money is created when banks lend money. First, the Fed requires that all banks hold a legal minimum level of reserves (called required re-

---

[3] Although economists have a tendency to speak of the interest rate, there are actually many different rates of interest: the prime rate, the federal funds rate, the discount rate, mortgage rates, the Treasury bill rate, and so forth. Because these rates generally move together (in the same direction), and because they all, more or less, reflect current money market conditions, economists tend to consolidate the various rates into a single trend rate. Although there is no such official trend rate, it does represent an important average. It is this average or trend rate of interest which is meant when no specific interest rate is mentioned.

[4] As implied in the FOCUS, the Fed does encounter difficulty in accurately predicting large flows of funds arising at certain times of the year. For example, tax payments are extremely difficult to predict accurately. Every April, the Fed undergoes its annual guessing game of how much money will be withdrawn to pay taxes or how much will be refunded. Quarterly tax payments by individuals and corporations are similarly difficult to assess. Moreover, the Fed is unable to predict (or control) the flow of foreign funds into the economy, nor the public's desire to hold more money in money market mutual funds and automatic transfer savings accounts. As it keys on M1 as the measure of the money in circulation, large flows of money in and out of M1 frustrate the Fed's ability to maintain its monetary targets.

FIGURE 16–1

The Interest Rate and
Savings and Investment

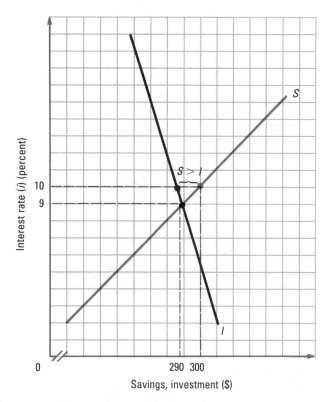

The classical economists stated that *S* and *I* were functions of the interest rate. If a surplus of funds existed (because *i* rates were too high), the excess supply would quickly be eliminated as *i* rates declined.

serves, calculated by multiplying the bank's deposits times the reserve requirement). Second, banks may lend anything over this minimum (called excess reserves). Third, when a loan is made, in the form of cash, a bank check, or a checking account in the borrower's name, the money supply will increase. Since all money is borrowed in order to spend, the money loaned by one bank winds up as new deposits in other banks.

This multiple creation of demand deposits carries with it powerful policy implications. Because financial institutions make loans based upon excess reserves, and because the Fed is able to influence bank reserves, the Fed exercises substantial power over how much is loaned and at what interest rate. For example, if the Fed wishes to curtail spending in order to reduce inflation, it will take action to reduce the amount of bank reserves. With fewer excess reserves, banks will lend less, and the money supply will decline. Since consumers and businesses depend, at one time or another, upon borrowed funds to finance their expenditures (a new house, car, building expansion, computers, and miscellaneous capital equipment), less money available for loans means higher credit costs. In other words, if the money supply declines, interest rates will increase, and households and businesses will borrow less money. Borrowing less translates directly into less spending and a multiplied reduction of income, production, and employment.

The Demand for Money

Easy money *is a current money market condition or monetary policy in which the Fed increases reserves in order to drive down interest rates.*

Tight money *is a monetary policy of slowing the growth of the money supply by reducing bank reserves in order to increase interest rates.*

Unlike the supply of money, the Fed is limited in its ability to regulate the demand for money. The Fed has no direct way in which to control the public's willingness to borrow (and hence spend). Of course, it can (and does) influence interest rates by tightening or loosening credit. For example, if the Fed adopts a policy of **easy money**, it will increase reserves in order to drive down interest rates. This will create the economic climate conducive to more borrowing. Conversely, it can adopt a **tight money** policy by slowing the growth of the money supply. This will gradually result in higher interest rates and thus make borrowing more expensive. It must be emphasized that both easy and tight money policies only increase the probability of more or less borrowing. As a famous cliche so aptly says, "You can lead a horse to water, but you can't make him drink." In other words, even if the Fed takes steps to create a favorable environment for more borrowing, there is no guarantee that the public will respond to the incentives.[5]

Transactions motive *means that because people want money for transactions they hold money in checking accounts and in cash.*

The demand for money refers to the purpose of holding money, and it was Keynes who originally conceived of different motives for holding money. Keynes said that people held money for three reasons: for transactions; for retirement, emergencies, and related big-ticket items; and for speculation. First, there is the **transactions motive.** People want money in order to spend it on goods and services. We thus hold money in checking accounts in order to pay our utilities, mortgage or rent, food, and related monthly bills. We also hold money in the form of cash in order to handle daily transactions, such as buying lunch, a birthday card, or a soda from a vending machine.

We also hold money for special occasions, such as vacations, our children's education, retirement, weddings, and miscellaneous rainy day

---

[5] Recent history is full of examples in which more borrowing occurred despite higher interest rates. Conversely, in spite of lower interest rates the public has continued to reduce its debt. One noteworthy example occurred in the 1970s when conventional mortgage rates (on housing loans) increased from an average of 8 to 14 percent. Confounding all forecasts, the public borrowed more money. With hindsight, we know what happened. Expectations of higher interest rates and higher home prices caused the demand for funds to increase in spite of higher financing costs. Of course, this had the unfortunate effect of tighter credit conditions and even higher interest rates.

Precautionary motive *means that we hold money for special occasions, such as vacations.*

Speculative motive *means that people also hold money for investment purposes.*

Velocity *is the average number of times the money supply is spent each year.*

contingencies. Keynes called this the **precautionary motive.** Unlike the transactions demand for money, people are likely to hold precautionary funds in less liquid, higher interest-earning assets. Thus, much like a commercial banker, every householder must balance the need for liquidity and profitability.

A third reason for holding money is the **speculative motive.** Keynes argued that people also hold money for investment purposes, specifically in bonds. (Many more options are available today, but the basic idea remains true.) Since bond prices fluctuate, investors must decide whether prices will rise or fall in the future. For example, people hold savings in very liquid money market mutual funds or deposit accounts in anticipation of higher bond prices or until bond prices actually begin to rise. As prices of bonds rise and interest rates fall, people will use their speculative (money market account) balances to buy bonds. They will hold the bonds in anticipation of higher bond prices. Conversely, if prices begin to fall, interest rates rise and investors will sell their bonds and hold the proceeds in speculative anticipation of rising bond prices.[6]

The quantity of money demanded varies inversely with the interest rate, other things being equal. Because the interest rate is the cost of borrowed funds, it is often said to be the price of money. In economic terms, the interest rate is the opportunity cost of holding money; thus, as the interest rate declines, the opportunity cost of holding money declines, and people hold money. In other words, the quantity of money demanded increases. Like all other demand curves, however, other factors or determinants also affect the amount of money demanded. The chief determinant of money demand is income, and there is a different money demand for each level of income. Figure 16–2 illustrates the demand for money at two different income levels, Y_1 and Y_2.

Generally, as national income increases from Y_1 to Y_2, the demand for money curve will shift from M_{d_1} to M_{d_2}. At higher income levels, people require more money for transactions, and for precautionary and speculative purposes. For any given level of income, however, such as Y_1, the amount of money demanded depends upon the interest rate. At high rates of interest, people would shift funds out of checking accounts into savings and bonds. **Velocity,** or the average number of times the money supply is spent each year, would thus increase to handle the load

---

[6] Of course, there are many alternative uses for savings, including stocks, mutual funds, certificates of deposit, gold, real estate, and so forth; thus, the speculative motive for holding money is considerably broader than bonds. A good example is what happened after the October 19, 1987, stock market crash. Many people experienced only a loss of paper gains; others suffered real losses since their entry into the market. The upshot was a kind of paralysis; and, as a kind of temporary holding action, many people shifted their funds into money market funds and savings accounts. The decision to wait and see what would happen in the market resulted in a substantial increase in the speculative demand for money.

FIGURE 16-2
The Demand for Money

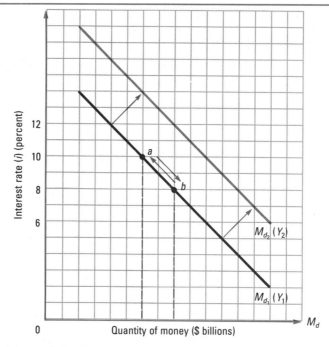

The demand for money is a downward-sloping curve, a reflection of the inverse relation between the rate of interest and the amount of money demanded, other things being equal. If
interest rates rise from 8 to 10 percent, people will shift funds into bonds and other interest-
bearing assets and hold a smaller amount in checking and speculative balances. If personal
income increases, from Y_1 to Y_2, the money demand curve will shift to the right, from M_{d_1} to
M_{d_2}, indicating that at the same interest rate people will want more money for transactions,
precautionary, and speculative purposes.

of transactions with smaller money balances. If interest rates came
down, people would be more willing to hold money in checking balances, and velocity would decrease.

Continuing with the Keynesian view of money, Figure 16–3 illustrates
the interaction of the supply of and demand for money. Because the
money supply is a stock, it is shown as a vertical line (M_{s_1}) at $700
billion. The equilibrium interest rate of 8 percent is determined by the
intersection of M_{s_1} and M_d. If the money supply increases by $10 billion
(to M_{s_2}), other things being equal, the result is a decline in the interest
rate from 8 percent to 7 percent.

It is the money supply over which the Fed exercises considerable control. Of course, the interesting question is how households and businesses obtain the funds (the extra money) to spend when the Fed
increases bank reserves. In other words, if householders want to buy a
new house or car, how do they get the money? What role do interest
rates have in the process? Two explanations are helpful in understanding

FIGURE 16–3
Interest Rates and the
Supply and Demand for
Money

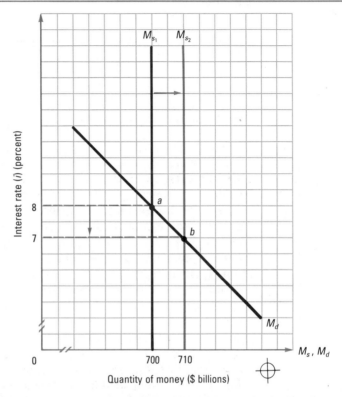

As the money supply increases from M_{s_1} to M_{s_2}, more reserves are created. This causes downward pressure on interest rates. Banks communicate this increase in the availability of credit by reducing interest rates from 8 to 7 percent.

this question. The first explanation, derived from the the quantity theory of money and the equation of exchange, indicates that there is a direct relationship between the supply of money and GNP; that is, if the money supply increases, GNP will increase by an equal percentage amount. The second explanation, the transmission mechanism, states that all changes in the money supply will affect GNP only through changes in interest rates.

The Equation of Exchange

Perhaps the oldest idea describing the relationship of the money supply and GNP is known as the **equation of exchange.** Briefly stated, it says that the amount of money spent equals the GNP. In equation form, this truism is expressed as

$$M \cdot V \equiv P \cdot Q$$

Equation of exchange *establishes the relationship between the money supply, velocity, and nominal GNP.*
$MV \equiv PQ$

where

    M = the supply of money ($M1$);

    V = the velocity of money, or the number of times the average dollar (in $M1$) is spent during the year;

    P = the price level, measured by the GNP deflator (implicit price index); and

    Q = the real GNP, or the quantity of goods produced in the current year expressed in base year prices.

The velocity of money may be thought of as the inverse of the demand for money. In other words, if velocity decreases, it means that we are spending our dollars less frequently, and this implies that we are holding onto our money for longer periods. For example, with a velocity of six, the money supply is spent (turned over) every two months. (To compute the turnover rate, divide the velocity into 12, the number of months in a year.) If velocity declines to four, people will reduce their rates of spending to three-month intervals from two-month intervals. This suggests that the public wants to hold its money balances for longer periods, perhaps because the economy is experiencing a recession.

Using a simple example, we can see that the left side of the equation of exchange always equals the right side. Assume that M = \$600 billion and that V = 1. Multiplying \$600 billion times 1 gives us total spending of \$600 billion. Now suppose that there are 600 billion units of goods and services produced and sold at an average of \$1 per unit. This, too, would give us total spending of \$600 billion.

Although these hypothetical numbers illustrate the basic identity of MV and PQ, let's see how the equation looks with real data. In 1987, the money supply ($M1$) was \$756.5 billion, and velocity was 5.95 (rounded off; the actual figure was 5.9518). The GNP deflator was 117.92 and real GNP was \$3,833.4 trillion.[7] Plugging these values into our equation, we can see each side equals the nominal GNP of \$4,502.5 billion.

$$M \cdot V \equiv P \cdot Q$$
$$756.5 \cdot 5.9518 \equiv 1.1792 \cdot 3,833.4$$
$$\$4,502.5 \text{ billion} \equiv \$4,502.5 \text{ billion}$$

Because the equation of exchange is a truism, it would appear to be relatively mundane. Since GNP is measured by total expenditures, the equation actually tells us that total spending equals total spending. For this reason, it is generally expressed as an identity, $MV \equiv PQ$.[8] But the

---

[7] This data is for the third quarter of 1987, taken from *Monetary Trends*, The Federal Reserve Bank of St. Louis, December 1987.

[8] An identity is an expression which is true by definition, as shown by the three bars instead of the typical equals sign. Another example of such a truism or identity is from our discussion of the circular flow of goods and services. National income is always equal (defined as equal) to national product.

beauty of the equation of exchange, like other equations and identities, is that it forces us to examine the relationships among the variables. One outcome was the quantity theory of money and ultimately an economic school of thought known as monetarism.

Monetarism *is a belief that economic stabilization can be attained by adherence to a strict monetary rule.*

Monetarism and the Quantity Theory of Money.   **Monetarism** is a belief that economic stabilization can be attained by adherence to a strict monetary rule. This rule states that the growth of the money supply should approximate the average growth of real GNP (RGNP), roughly 3 or 4 percent every year. Although not all monetarists advocate undeviating adherence to a strict rule, most monetarists think that the Fed's only responsibility should be to assure this average growth rate of the money supply.

An early pioneer of the importance of money in all economic relations was Irving Fisher (1867–1947), an economics professor at Yale University. Indeed, Fisher is thought of as the father of monetarism. Fisher used the equation of exchange to explain his idea that the price level and the rate of inflation were determined solely by changes in the money supply. This became known as the **quantity theory of money.** Fisher argued that in the short run, velocity and RGNP are very stable. (Indeed, for very short time periods such as a week, V and Q are effectively constant.) Thus, said Fisher, any change in M would be translated immediately into a change in P. Rewriting the basic equation of exchange, Fisher expressed this single cause theory of inflation as such:

Quantity theory of money *holds that any change in the money supply would be translated immediately into a change in the price level, assuming that velocity and real GNP are stable.*

$$P = \frac{M \cdot V}{Q}$$

Plugging in our data for 1987, we get

$$P = \frac{756.5 \cdot 5.9518}{3,833.4} = 117.92$$

If V and Q are fixed, then a percentage change in the money supply will cause an equal percentage change in the price level. For example, if the money supply increases by 10 percent ($75.65 billion) to $832.15 billion, then the price level will rise by 10 percent (11.792) to 129.71.

It should be pointed out, however, that neither velocity nor RGNP are fixed, unless perhaps if the time period is as short as one day. As the time frame is extended to a week, a month, a quarter, and so forth, then people are able to make more considered reactions and adjustments to changes in financial conditions; thus, increases in the money supply may be completely counteracted by declining velocity. Indeed, Fed attempts in recent years to slow the growth of *M1* were frustrated by increasing velocity. With less money available, consumers and businesses spent the existing money supply more often.[9]

---

[9] From 1945 until early 1982, velocity increased by an average of 3 percent per year.

What causes velocity to change? Although any factor which affects our ability to maintain our standard of living will likely affect our willingness to spend or hold (save) money, three main factors may be identified. First, general business conditions will have an effect. During recessions, people are more cautious and tend to spend money for only necessary things. The result is that velocity will decline as people increase their savings and postpone some expenditures. Second, inflation and price expectations are important determinants of velocity. If inflation is increasing, for example, we would expect people to spend their money faster. If they do not respond in this way, then their money balances will depreciate in value. The result is an increase in the velocity of money.

Interest rates also affect velocity. In general, velocity is directly related to interest rates. Higher interest rates raise the cost of borrowed funds and increase the reward for saving (or giving up liquidity). This, in turn, affects our spending behavior. As interest rates on savings accounts, money market accounts, and certificates of deposit rise, many people will shift more of their checking balances into savings, both short-term and long-term. The result is that $M1$ is reduced, and, as people spend existing checkable balances faster, the velocity will increase. Indeed, it is not uncommon for velocity to rise sufficiently to completely compensate for the decline in $M1$, with no significant change in NGNP.

Figure 16–4 illustrates the relationship between velocity and the federal funds rate (FFR—the rate banks charge other banks for very short-term loans). If we focus on the period from 1980 to 1986, we find the expected direct relationship between velocity and the FFR. Prior to 1980, however, velocity displays a steady rise despite erratic movement of the FFR. Why the difference?

In 1980, the Fed instituted changes in $M1$ so that all financial institutions with checkable deposits were subject to uniform reserve requirements. Because the FFR is a barometer of bank excess reserve positions, this reform resulted in a much closer relationship between the FFR and velocity. In other words, it was not until after 1980 that the FFR reflected credit availability of all depository institutions, not just those (member banks) subject to the Fed's reserve requirements.

The Transmission Mechanism

A rival explanation of the relationship between $M1$ and GNP was offered by John Maynard Keynes. Keynes argued that money is important in the economy, but only insofar as it affects interest rates. The name **transmission mechanism** is used to describe how changes in money are transmitted throughout the economy. Let's see how the linkage works.

In Keynes' view, increases in the money supply will *probably* reduce interest rates. Lower interest rates *may* stimulate more consumer and

Transmission mechanism *is used to describe how changes in money are transmitted throughout the economy:* $\Delta M \rightarrow \Delta i \rightarrow \Delta I \rightarrow \Delta GNP$

FIGURE 16–4

Velocity and the Federal
Funds Rate

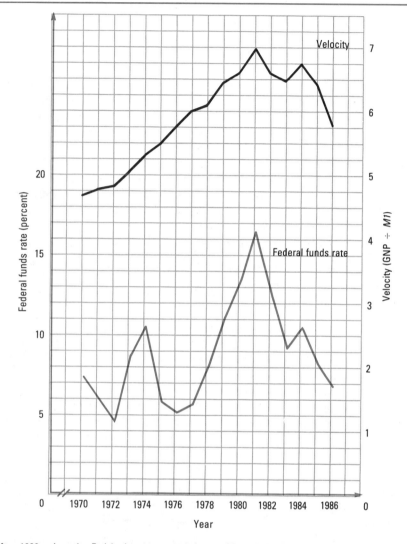

After 1980, when the Fed had greater control over *M1* and the FFR more closely represented excess reserve positions, whenever the FFR increased, velocity also increased. As people transfer money out of checking into less liquid assets, they spend their smaller money balances more quickly.

Conversely, as the FFR declined, velocity declined. This occurred because people tend to hold more money in *M1*, as the opportunity cost of holding money in transaction balances declines. As *M1* increases, people spend their checking balances less frequently.

business borrowing which, in turn, will be spent on real goods and services. Then, with increased aggregate demand, the multiplier effect will increase GNP by some multiple of the original change in spending. The same general process also works in reverse. For example, if the Fed takes steps to reduce bank reserves, and the money supply declines, interest rates *may* increase. With a higher cost of borrowing, some consumers and businesses would curtail their spending plans. This would result in a multiplied reduction in GNP. (The italicized words *probably* and *may* are important. Each is meant to emphasize the fact that the linkage is uncertain.)

Figure 16–5 illustrates the transmission mechansim in schematic form. Beginning with a change in the money supply, interest rates are affected. Since investment spending depends upon the cost of borrowing, aggregate demand may be influenced. (Of course, it was Keynes who first said that investment expenditures probably were more sensitive to sales and expectations of profits and sales than to intcrest rates.) If aggregate demand changes, then the multiplier effect will be invoked, and GNP will change by some magnified amount.

THINKING IT THROUGH

The transmission mechanism suggests that if *M1* is reduced, i will increase, aggregate demand will decline, and, through the multiplier effect, GNP will decrease. What links in this chain may not work as described? Why?

In Keynes' view of the economy, increasing amounts of money in circulation without a change in interest rate are negated by a decline in the velocity. The monetarists (or quantity theorists), to the contrary, argue that velocity is relatively fixed in the short run and thus does not com-

---

FIGURE 16–5

The Transmission Mechanism

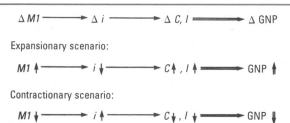

The transmission mechanism describes how monetary policy works in the Keynesian framework. Changes in *M1* may affect interest rates (*i*) which, in turn, may cause a change in aggregate demand (*C* and *I*). It is important to emphasize that this linkage is uncertain. For example, if personal income increases and the demand for money increases, then an increase in *M1* may not lead to a decrease in the interest rate. Moreover, even if interest rates decline, there is no assurance that people will borrow more money. As Keynes was quick to observe, investment was more sensitive to income (sales and profits) and expectations than to variations in the interest rate.

plicate the relationships. Fortunately, it is not important to us who is right or wrong. The most important thing is that we see that monetary policy matters. It is this subject to which we now turn.

THE MAKING OF MONETARY POLICY

The authority for making monetary policy rests with the Fed's Board of Governors and the Federal Open Market Committee (FOMC). The FOMC membership, as you know from the previous chapter, consists of the seven governors, the New York Fed's president, and four other FRB presidents, each from different districts. The committee meets about eight times a year in Washington, D.C., in order to fashion policies to make money and credit conditions conform to the broad goals of the Employment Act.[10] When the FOMC reaches consensus, a policy statement and more concrete directives are sent to the manager of the Open Market Desk at the New York Fed. It is the New York Fed that is responsible for executing the FOMC's directive by translating the directive into specific orders to buy and sell government securities. Because these open market operations are conducted so frequently, we begin our discussion of monetary policy with these transactions. From the FOCUS, you know how the open market operations work, but read the following CASE-IN-POINT to get a flavor of a policy directive sent to the New York Fed's Trading Desk.

CASE
• IN •
POINT

A FOMC Directive

At a meeting of the FOMC, the following directive was adopted and sent to the Open Market Desk of the New York Fed.

> In view of current market uncertainties and liquidity strains, open market operations until the next meeting of the Committee shall be conducted with a view to moderating pressures on financial markets, while, to the extent compatible therewith, maintaining bank reserves and money market conditions consistent with the Committee's longer run objectives of moderating growth in money and bank credit.[11]

If this sounds a bit vague, imagine how the manager of the Open Market Desk feels. Actually, the manager has much more to go on than this directive.

---

[10] The seven other Fed bank presidents also attend these meetings, although as nonvoting members.

[11] Alan R. Holmes, "A Day at the Trading Desk," *The New York Federal Reserve Bank Monthly Review,* October 1970, p. 236.

Before each meeting of the FOMC, the staff has circulated statistical summaries of bank reserves positions, a detailed analysis of alternative plans, their relation to employment and prices, and the interest rates and money market conditions likely to be associated with each plan.

The task of the Trading Desk is then to convert the policy directive into precise buy or sell decisions. The job is not to trade for profit, but to control the supply of bank reserves in line with the FOMC's directives.

Questions to Consider

1. *How would you interpret the FOMC's directive?*
2. *As the manager of the Trading Desk, what specific actions would you take?*

Open Market Operations

Borrowed reserves *are the funds obtained when financial institutions borrow from the Fed or from depository institutions.*

Nonborrowed reserves *are the funds obtained by banks when new deposits are received or when the Fed engages in open market purchases.*

Open market operations *are the Fed's purchases and sales of securities.*

Federal Reserve policies are designed to affect bank reserves, both borrowed and nonborrowed. **Borrowed reserves** are the funds obtained when financial institutions borrow from the Fed or from depository institutions. When banks receive new deposits or when the Fed engages in open market purchases, financial institutions obtain **nonborrowed reserves.** For either type of reserve, however, if you want to know what will happen to credit conditions and interest rates, look to changes in bank reserves. Let's look more carefully at how open market operations affect nonborrowed reserves.

Assume that the economy is tilting in the direction of a recession and that the Fed has expressed its desire to get the economy moving again. This is where **open market operations** come in: the buying and selling of government securities in order to regulate the excess reserves of depository institutions. The appropriate open market operation is to buy securities. As the buyer of securities, the Fed deals directly with bond dealers, brokers and banks, and indirectly with private businesses and the general public. Let's assume that Citicorp is the seller (a large bank headquartered in New York City). The transaction is actually relatively simple. The Fed credits Citicorp's reserve account at the Fed for the amount of the sale. The effect of the transaction is to increase the bank's reserves. Since deposits were not affected, and, regardless of its position before the transaction, bank reserves will rise by the full amount of the purchase. It is then positioned to make loans in the amount of its excess reserves. Lending by this bank will in turn generate new deposits, excess reserves, and new loans by other banks. The multiple creation of deposits is under way. The likely result is lower interest rates.

> ### THINKING IT THROUGH
>
> How would the transaction differ if a bond dealer with an account at Citicorp sold the securities? Assuming that the bank was loaned up prior to the transaction, would the bank have the same amount of excess reserves?

If the Fed decides to restrict the money supply, it will sell securities. Selling securities will result in a destruction of bank reserves. If Citicorp buys securities, the Fed will reduce its reserve account. The immediate effect is to drain reserves from the system. As reserves decline, the bank's lending ability is reduced. Because the bank has less excess reserves, the upshot is tighter credit conditions and upward pressure on interest rates.

Whether the Fed adopts a policy of easy money or tight money, the probable effect will be a change in interest rates. In turn, because many householders and corporate customers are sensitive to borrowing conditions, these changes in interest rates are translated into increased or reduced consumption and investment plans. Working through the multiplier effect, these changes in spending will impact upon employment and prices. One fairly recent example of just how effective tight monetary policy can be occurred in late 1979.

In the late 1970s, inflation accelerated to an unacceptably high rate. Paul Volcker, the chairman of the Fed at the time, repeatedly warned that if Congress refused to curtail spending and to take other actions to reduce the inflationary momentum, the Fed would have to take anti-inflationary action. When the consumer price index reached double digits, Volcker stepped in.

Reversing its practice of making monetary policy in order to closely regulate interest rates, the Fed adopted the monetarist position and focused almost exclusively on the money supply. By keying its policies to *M1*, the Fed effectively decided to permit interest rates to fluctuate freely. And since they were restricting growth of *M1*, interest rates did increase. From a relatively smooth trend range of 11–12 percent between September 1 and October 5, 1979, the Federal Funds Rate fluctuated up and down between 12 and 17.5 percent from October 9 to October 31.

High interest rates initially aggravated inflation, and both forces combined to usher in the worst recession since the 1930s. However unpopular in the beginning, the anti-inflationary policies ultimately worked. By early 1983, the inflation rate had fallen to the lowest level in over a decade, and the economy soon enjoyed a rapid recovery from the 10 percent plus unemployment.

The Discount Rate

Another policy tool available to the Fed is the **discount rate.** All financial institutions may borrow from the Fed, and the rate of interest charged for borrowed reserves is called the discount rate. Traditionally and by law, borrowing from the Fed is regarded as a privilege and not a right. Although the Fed is regarded as the lender of last resort, this important function is not a bail-out operation. However, the discounting function itself is a misnomer, as a former Federal Reserve staff economist at the New York Fed observes:

Discount rate is the rate of interest charged for borrowed reserves (loans) from the Fed to financial institutions.

> Behind the [discount] windows are a few offices and several desks, and, during business hours, a huge steamer trunk on casters. There is nothing outwardly impressive about the trunk; except for the casters and its bulk, it looks like one you might find in your Aunt Millie's attic. But on a day not so long ago . . . it contained approximately $5 billion of collateral, mostly in the form of commercial loan notes deposited with the Fed by the largest New York City banks. Banks that borrow from the Fed *must* (author's emphasis) put up suitable collateral to back the loan. Since most banks, if they must borrow, do so only at the end of the day, speed is essential in processing the loan before closing. Hence, collateral is deposited in advance. That's why the function needs a capacious trunk.[12]

Although the Federal Reserve Act of 1913 empowered the Fed to purchase or discount certain kinds of commercial securities, this power has not been used for several decades. Since the Fed wants to avoid the administrative problems involved in collecting from private borrowers, it has adopted the technique of making loans (called *advances*) that are secured by collateral. (*Collateral,* a catchall term that refers to anything of value, to the Fed, means acceptably liquid assets, such as government securities.) Moreover, short-term lending is the most common form of the Fed's advances.

When the Fed increases the discount rate, it raises the price of borrowed reserves to financial institutions. This has a twofold effect. First, by raising the discount rate, the Fed declares its opposition to an expansion of commercial lending. This *announcement effect* usually reinforces its open market sales of securities. The second effect is to discourage bank lending by increasing the cost of borrowed reserves. Although it takes time to dampen the demand for investment funds and is thus often a protracted process, the ultimate effect is to reduce lending. On the other hand, if the Fed reduces the discount rate, it makes borrowed reserves cheaper. In doing so, it also announces its desire to stimulate more loans and ultimately an economic expansion.

---

[12] William C. Melton, *Inside the Fed* (Homewood, Ill.: Dow Jones-Irwin, 1985), p. 6.

The Federal Funds and Other Money Markets

Federal funds *are very short-term loans of excess reserves from one financial institution to another.*

A much more important source of borrowed reserves is the federal funds market. **Federal funds** are very short-term loans of excess reserves from one financial institution to another. Ordinarily overnight loans, federal funds are often called *dollars with wings* since they fly around the system so often and so quickly. The name is unfortunate, however, since federal funds have nothing to do with the Fed or the federal government; they are excess reserves of private financial institutions.[13] And, although the federal funds rate (FFR) is nearly always higher than the discount rate, the borrowing bank avoids the additional paperwork connected with the Fed's discounting operation. Moreover, the FFR fluctuates with forces of supply and demand and thus more closely reflects current market conditions than does the discount rate.

Of course, banks and other depository institutions, nonfinancial corporations, and private individuals have access to many other money markets. Each business day *The Wall Street Journal* prints the prevailing interest rates on important U.S. and foreign money markets. Table 16–1 illustrates some of the principal money rates on Friday, April 7, 1989. One of the most interesting aspects of these financial markets are the relationships among maturity, risk, and liquidity. In general, the shorter the term, the lower the risk, and the more liquid the fund, the lower is the interest rate. For example, the U.S. Treasury paid 8.87 percent for 13-week bills, while conventional mortgage rates averaged 10.45 percent on 30-year fixed rate loans. Treasury bills are highly liquid, reasonably short-term obligations (13 or 26 weeks), and they have the full faith and credit of the U.S. government behind them. On the other hand, conventional fixed rate mortgages are often 30 years to maturity and carry considerably more risk. A lot can happen in 30 years. The important point, however, is that the financial markets offer a rich array of alternative sources to obtain or invest funds.

The Reserve Requirement

The **reserve requirement** *(rr)* is the formal legal required percentage of deposits which institutions must hold in idle reserves, either in their own vaults or on deposit at the Fed.

A third tool of monetary policy is the **reserve requirement (rr)**. Under the Monetary Control Act of 1980 and subsequent amendments, the Congress established a three-tier system of reserve requirements. The first $2 million of checkable and nonpersonal time deposits are free of requirements; from $2 million to some minimal benchmark (originally $25 million and increased thereafter according to an index tied to *M1*), the *rr* is 3 percent on all transactions and nonpersonal deposits; and

---

[13] Actually, the Fed is involved to the extent that the excess reserves are on deposit at the Fed; thus, the transfer of funds from Bank A (a lender) to Bank B (a borrower) is handled electronically.

TABLE 16–1 Money Market Rates	Prime rate:	The basic rate charged by commercial banks for corporate loans. Many other loans (such as second mortgages) are based upon the prime rate. On April 7, 1989, the prime rate was 11.5 percent.
	Discount rate:	The rate charged commercial banks and other depository institutions on loans by the New York Federal Reserve Bank. The rate will vary slightly from one Federal Reserve bank to another. On April 7, 1989, the discount rate was 7 percent.
	Federal funds rate:	The rate charged for large (> $1 million) overnight loans among commercial banks. The federal funds rate is often viewed as a good barometer of excess reserves in commercial banks and thus serves as a guide for the conduct of monetary policy. On April 7, 1989, the rate varied between 9¾ percent and 9⅞ percent.
	Commercial paper:	The rate on high-grade unsecured promissory notes from major corporations and sold through dealers in multiples of $1,000. On April 7, 1989, the rate varied by maturity from 9.8 percent to 9.87 percent.
	Treasury bills:	The rate on short-term U.S. Treasury bill auctions on April 7, 1989, was 8.87 percent for securities maturing in 13 weeks and 8.84 percent for securities maturing in 26 weeks.
	Mortgage rates:	Conventional, fixed-rate, 30-year mortgages issued by commercial banks and other lenders averaged 11.01 percent on April 7, 1989.
	Certificates of deposit:	Depending upon maturity and denomination, rates ranged from 9.19 percent for one-month CDs to 10.3 percent for CDs with a maturity of one year in amounts greater than $1 million.

A reliable and handy source of current interest rates is published daily in *The Wall Street Journal.* Three money rates in particular are important indicators of general financial conditions: the prime rate, the federal funds rate, and the U.S. Treasury bill rate(s).

checkable deposits in excess of the benchmark carry a 12 percent reserve requirement. The Fed is empowered to change the transaction deposit requirements within a band of discretion ranging from 8 to 14 percent, and from 0 to 9 percent on nonpersonal time deposits. No changes have been made since the Monetary Control Act became law.

Changes in the reserve requirement have an immediate and significant effect on bank reserves. Increasing the *rr* essentially converts excess reserves to required reserves and results in decreased lending, tight credit, and higher interest rates. Decreasing the *rr* frees up existing required reserves and enables financial institutions to make loans. Because changes in the *rr* have such sweeping effects, the power to change the *rr* is often called a blunt instrument. Very small changes in the *rr* result in significant changes in required reserves. If the Fed were to increase the third level *rr* from 12 to 12.5 percent and checkable deposits totaled $600 billion, financial institutions would have to hold an additional $30 billion in required reserve. Needless to say, this would not delight many commercial bankers.

CURRENT MONETARY POLICY ISSUES

Does (or can) the Fed do a good job in controlling the money supply? Should it engage in fine-tuning, or should it adopt strict rules? Does the Fed exercise excessive power? Is the Fed really independent, or is it subservient to the political agenda of the current administration? Should it be independent, or should the Fed's monetary policy be controlled by the president? Should the Congress adopt specific monetary rules which the Fed would be forced to follow? Is the financial system in serious trouble because of excessive regulation? Too little regulation? These concerns surfaced soon after the passage of the Federal Reserve Act of 1913 and they have survived to this day.

Should the Fed Have Discretionary Policy?

This question is often raised by economists. Monetarists, in particular, see two main problems with active or discretionary monetary policy. First, they are opposed to all attempts to fine-tune the economy, be it fiscal or monetary. (As applied to monetary policy, fine-tuning means frequent discretionary actions to raise and lower system reserves.) Such actions, the monetarists contend, lead to chronic economic instability. Milton Friedman, the leading monetarist spokesman and Nobel Prize winning economist, likes to compare the Fed to an automobile racing through a tunnel, careening out of control, bouncing off one wall and then the other. Friedman and other monetarists also point out the time lags inherent in making monetary policy. In other words, it takes a long time between the Fed's policy decision and the time it takes for the policy effect to be translated into changes in employment, production, and prices. Furthermore, many critics of discretionary monetary policy cite the Fed's poor policy decisions in the Great Depression. Between 1929 and 1932, the Fed permitted, if not caused, the money supply to decline by nearly a third, greatly aggravating the economy's slump.

The second objection is that the Fed is too powerful. Critics of the Fed contend that Congress has bestowed too much power in the hands of unelected central bankers. In this view, the Fed is a contradiction of the U.S. democratic and free enterprise ideals. If we ask William Greider if the Fed has too much power, the answer is a resounding yes. In *Secrets of the Temple: How the Federal Reserve Runs the Country,* Greider argues that America's central bank operates unchecked—an undemocratic anomaly in a country that prides itself on government by the people. Greider contends that both the executive branch and the Congress could control the Fed more effectively, but they choose not to. Why? Each can act as irresponsibly as they wish regarding unemployment or inflation, taxes, or spending, safe in the knowledge that the Fed will come to the rescue and reduce inflation or stimulate job growth. In Greider's view, the Fed is the perfect scapegoat.

For most monetarists, the only sensible approach is to adopt a fixed money supply growth rule. As we noted earlier, most proponents of the fixed rule suggest that the money supply should grow by approximately 4 percent, year in and year out. Only this, they contend, will help to stabilize the economy and provide for regular economic growth.

Opponents of the fixed monetary rule believe that the monetarists have a weak case. First and foremost, proponents of discretionary monetary policy believe that a fixed rule is too inflexible. It runs the risk of permitting the economy to languish in protracted periods of recession, inflation, or both. They insist that the Fed must be empowered to exercise judgment and make decisions appropriate for changing economic conditions. For example, if a fixed rule were in force when the stock market crashed on October 19, 1987, the banking system would not have been able to provide sufficient reserves to stabilize the money markets.

Opponents of the monetary rule also ask what the rule would be. If an optimal growth rate of the money supply was identified, the Fed supporters argue that the Fed would be the first to adopt the policy. Finally, those opposing a rules approach point out that it is unreasonable to attack the Fed's current monetary policy based upon unsound decisions made more than fifty years ago. If discretionary monetary policies were ill advised in the past, that is a poor reason to disallow discretion in the future.

How Independent Is the Fed?

This is a tough question and obviously one that draws as much from political philosophy, constitutional theory, and practical politics as from economics. Given that the Fed governors are appointed and are formally required to report to Congress only twice a year, perhaps a more useful question is how independent should the Fed be?

Virtually every president has expressed a desire to have control over the Fed. Indeed, some proponents of this arrangement would like to see executive authority extended by providing the line-item veto over all appropriations bills. If this were to happen, say the supporters, much more integration of monetary and fiscal policy would be obtained.

In fact, the Congress has taken steps in recent years to reduce the Fed's independence. In the Federal Reserve Reform Act of 1977, Congress required that the appointment of the Fed chairman and vice chairman be confirmed by the Senate. Furthermore, the 1978 Humphrey-Hawkins amendment to the Employment Act requires the Fed to submit to Congress semiannual reports on economic trends, policy objectives, specific plans for the next 12 months, and how such plans relate to the economic objectives in the *Economic Report of the President*. Of course, some critics claim that this is political tinkering at its worst— "much ado about nothing" at least.

Some legal observers think that the Federal Reserve System is unconstitutional and that Congress has effectively created a fourth branch of government. By analogy, these critics ask if it would be constitutional for Congress to create a Department of War that is independent of the executive and legislative branches.[14]

Perhaps the best reply to such concerns about Fed independence comes from the late Arthur Burns, a former chairman of the Fed's Board of Governors, director of the National Bureau of Economic Research, and prolific writer. In a speech delivered at a college commencement, Burns said this:

> Under our scheme of governmental organization, the Federal Reserve can make the hard decisions that might be avoided by decision makers subject to the day-to-day pressures of political life. . . . I doubt that the American people would want to see the power to create money lodged in its presidency—which may mean that it would in fact be exercised by political aides in the White House.[15]

Is the Financial System in Trouble?

Issues of Fed power and independence aside, one issue of great concern in recent times is the health and vitality of U.S. financial institutions. In the face of increasing talk about further bank deregulation, many of the nation's banks and savings and loans (S&Ls) are in serious trouble. Indeed, post-Depression records of bank failures in 1987 and 1988 stand as grim reminders of imprudent bank lending practices and a look-the-other-way regulatory philosophy.

Nearly every day, we read of a bank failure or one S&L buying out another S&L that has gone bankrupt. With deposit insurance provided to commercial bank depositors by the Federal Deposit Insurance Corporation (FDIC) and to S&L depositors by the Savings Association Insurance Fund (SAIF, formerly the FSLIC), most observers think that there is sufficient security. But in recent years, even the insurance providers are in trouble. For example, the FSLIC was essentially bankrupt in 1986 when its liabilities exceeded its assets by $6.3 billion. Are prospects any better for the years ahead? Although the federal bailout of more than 350 insolvent S&Ls will help to stabilize financial markets,

---

[14] Tyrone Black and Donnie Daniel, *Money and Banking,* 3rd edition (Plano, Texas: Business Publications, Inc., 1988), p. 262.

[15] Ibid.

many observers worry that the survivors will remain in jeopardy for years to come. Indeed, several analysts think that federal deposit insurance actually leads to more reckless and imprudent loans and investments.

The FDIC is in similar financial straits. Traditionally a bulwark against commercial bank bankrupcies, the FDIC is rapidly depleting its insurance reserves. In 1984, it bailed out Continental Illinois and Trust to the tune of $4.5 billion. And in 1988, it extended a six-month $1 billion loan to the 73 banks owned by First RepublicBank Corporation of Dallas. Although the bank's assets totaled $30 billion, the bank's real estate and energy loans are highly questionable.

If you are left with a sour taste in your mouth after this discussion of current monetary issues, especially about the efficacy of monetary policy, the following CASE-IN-POINT may raise your spirits.

CASE
• IN •
POINT

How the Fed Avoided a Financial Disaster

On October 19, 1987, the stock market plummeted 508 points, losing nearly 23 percent of its value. With wild speculations of recession or worse, investors, market analysts, and government officials all waited with baited breath for a sign that this was not a harbinger of a widespread financial collapse. Within 24 hours, they had their answer.

The Fed took decisive and dramatic action. Knowing that liquidity would be a problem the next day and that lenders might panic and pull out their loans, the Fed pumped massive amounts of reserves into the banking system, especially into the New York and Chicago financial centers. The objective was to drive down interest rates, and down they went. The financial markets responded immediately, and within a month the federal funds rate, the rate of interest charged on overnight and other short-term loans between banks, came down by nearly a full percentage point. Moreover, the stock market had recovered more than a third of its loss by the end of the year. The Fed had intervened swiftly and successfully to avoid a potential disaster.

Fed Chairman Alan Greenspan had done his homework. Weeks before the crash, Greenspan secretly ordered several studies of how the Fed could respond to a number of potential disasters, including a stock market crash. Building a crisis-management team consisting of the Treasury secretary, the New York Fed's president and other Fed governors, Greenspan prepared for the worst. The team selected several trouble spots in the domestic and international economy and then discussed the optional strategies the Fed could follow to deal with each crisis. One section of the team's report dealt with ways to handle a stock market collapse.[16]

---

[16] See Alan Murray, "Passing a Test: Fed's New Chairman Wins a Lot of Praise on Handling the Crash," *The Wall Street Journal,* November 25, 1987, p. 1.

Questions to Consider

1. *What specific actions could Greenspan have taken to have such dramatic impact?*

2. *Do you think that the Fed should have this kind of power? Why or why not?*

After reviewing the issues of Fed power, independence, and effectiveness, it seems only appropriate to make a few closing remarks. The issue of independence, whether the Fed is, is not, or should be (more) independent is open to debate. However, it is useful to remember Arthur Burns' observation—that if the president were given the power to make monetary policy, not only would the process be politicized, but the control of the money supply would be in the hands of White House bureaucrats.

Issues of the Fed's power and effectiveness are really closely related. There is no doubt that the Fed is able to exercise great influence in the financial markets. Indeed, that is what makes it so powerful. Furthermore, unlike the critics who claim that the Fed blunders about forever correcting its mistakes, the Fed's record in recent years is remarkably clear of policy miscalculations.

If we compare the records of monetary policy and fiscal policy, using criteria such as timeliness, prompt decision making, and effectiveness (accomplishing stated objectives), monetary policy emerges the winner. Hardly perfect, monetary policy is more removed from political influence than any other form of economic policy. (It is considered good business to lobby members of Congress. Imagine the scandal if business tried to buy favors from the Fed's governors!) Precisely because the policymaking authority rests with a single Board of Governors, well reasoned decisions are made in a timely fashion. As we have identified, there are problems with monetary policy, but they pale in comparison to other kinds of economic policy.

IMPORTANT TERMS TO REMEMBER

borrowed reserves, p. 456
discount rate, p. 458
easy money, p. 446
equation of exchange, p. 449
federal funds, p. 459
monetarism, p. 451
nonborrowed reserves, p. 456
open market operations, p. 456

precautionary motive, p. 447
quantity theory of money, p. 451
reserve requirement, p. 459
speculative motive, p. 447
tight money, p. 446
transmission mechanism, p. 452
transactions motive, p. 446
velocity, p. 447

CHAPTER SUMMARY

1. There are two main views of how the money supply affects prices and output (nominal GNP).

   a. The equation of exchange, $MV \equiv PQ$, states that the money supply (M) times the Velocity (V) of money will always equal the nominal GNP. The nominal GNP is further broken down into its two elements, the price level (P) and the real GNP (Q).

      (1) The quantity theory of money was developed from this equation of exchange. The quantity theory states that the price level is determined by changes in the money supply. The quantity theorists assume that the velocity (or the number of times the money supply turns over each year) and the real GNP are reasonably fixed in the short run.

      (2) Quantity theorists are called monetarists. They believe that discretionary monetary policy should be abandoned in favor of a fixed growth rate of the money supply.

   b. The transmission mechanism. Keynesian economists argue that changes in the money supply will affect GNP (P and Q) only through changes in the interest rate. Symbolically, $\Delta M \rightarrow \Delta i \rightarrow \Delta C$ and $\Delta I \rightarrow \Delta GNP$.

2. Classical economists believed that money was not an important element in the economy. They emphasized savings and investment and how interest rates regulated these flows.

3. Keynes observed that people had three reasons for demanding (holding) money:

   a. The transaction motive—money used for routine expenses.

   b. The precautionary motive—money held for contingencies and emergencies, such as vacations and retirement; and

   c. The speculative motive—money held for investment. Keynes said that as bond prices fall and interest rates rise, the speculative demand for money would increase in anticipation of rising bond prices.

4. The supply of and demand for money together determine the market rate of interest.

5. Monetary policy is made by the Fed. There are three tools of monetary policy:

   a. The most important tool is open market operations.

      (1) When the Fed buys securities, it injects new reserves into the financial system and enables institutions to expand the money supply through lending excess reserves.

      (2) When the Fed sells securities, it withdraws reserves from the system and thereby reduces the money supply.

      (3) All open market operations are handled by the New York Federal Reserve Bank's Trading Desk.

   b. The discount rate. The discount rate is the interest rate charged by the Fed on loans (advances) made to depository institutions. A lower discount rate makes borrowed reserves cheaper and signals the Fed's interest in economic expansion.

   c. The reserve requirement(s). The legal reserve requirement (*rr*) is the percentage of deposits which all depository institutions must hold in noninterest bearing reserves. If the Fed lowers the *rr*, it creates more excess reserves and enables institutions to increase their loans.

6. Federal funds is the market for excess reserves held by depository institutions. Banks borrow from other banks, and the rate charged for these short-term reserve loans is called the federal funds rate. (Remember: It has little to do with the Fed or the federal government.)

7. Current monetary policy issues revolve around concerns that the Fed is too powerful, that it is (or is not) independent, and that discretionary monetary policy is ineffective.

DISCUSSION AND REVIEW QUESTIONS

1. The monetarists argue that changes in the money supply directly affect nominal GNP. Keynesian economists argue that interest rates must change in order for changes in the money supply to affect GNP. Can you reconcile these contrasting views? How can people obtain the money to spend if they do not borrow it?

2. If M = \$700 billion, P = 1.25, Q = \$3,080 billion, what is the velocity of money?

3. Discuss the pros and cons of the Federal Reserve as the monetary policy authority.

4. Diagram the supply of and demand for money. Illustrate and explain how changes in the money supply affect interest rates.

5. Monetary policy is sometimes likened to pulling on or pushing on a string; that is, monetary policy is regarded as a very effective instrument to tighten credit conditions and drive up interest rates, but it is considered much weaker in its ability to stimulate economic expansions via easy money policies. Explain why easy money policies may be less effective than tight money policies.

6. You have just been hired as the manager of the New York Fed's Trading Desk. You then receive the following directive from the FOMC.

> The Committee endorses its current general policy of moderating pressures in financial markets. Moreover, because of unusually large reserve losses associated with recent Treasury financing, and until the next meeting of the Committee, monetary policy should be conducted to replenish and then maintain reserves at desired levels.

Describe the open market operations necessary to comply with this directive.

7. The economy has just experienced three successive quarterly declines in real GNP, and the unemployment stands at 8.5 percent. What actions can the Fed take to halt the economic slump and produce an economic expansion? Describe how each policy works, and explain what problems, if any, may develop as a result of the policies.

A BRIEF LOOK AHEAD

The next chapter examines the important macroeconomic problems of unemployment and inflation. Because economic stabilization (a noninflationary and fully employed economy) is our chief macroeconomic objective, we must understand how inflation and unemployment are related. Is there a trade-off between unemployment and inflation? Can unemployment be reduced without building inflationary pressures? These and related questions will serve as our guide.

Unemployment and Inflation

Richard Sobol/ Stock, Boston

It is often said that *the* twin economic problems are inflation and unemployment. Although the United States has managed to avoid a prolonged hyperinflation, many countries are plagued by annual inflation rates exceeding 100 percent.

There is little doubt that hyperinflation is disruptive and creates a climate of uncertainty. However, unemployment is a problem that is potentially much more serious. While inflation erodes purchasing power and complicates economic planning, unemployment causes severe economic distress by depriving people of income and a sense of worth.

This chapter examines the types and causes of inflation and unemployment and attempts to unravel the complicated interrelationships between these twin problems.

After completion of this chapter, you should be able to do the following:

1. Identify, describe, and explain the types and causes of unemployment.
2. Diagram and explain the job search model of unemployment.
3. Identify and describe the types and causes of inflation.
4. Use the aggregate supply-demand price level model to illustrate demand-pull and cost-push inflation.
5. Diagram and explain the Phillips curve, and explain why there is no long-run trade-off between inflation and unemployment.

Displaced Workers: A Real Bombshell

The evidence can be found in nearly every midwestern city and town: a smokeless stack, a padlocked plant, an abandoned farm, a shuttered mine. The United States, most economists agree, is in the midst of a major economic restructuring—a shift that has put blue-collar workers and farmers either out of work or in jobs that once would have been foreign to them.

In 1987, more than 150,000 workers in Missouri and Illinois alone were dislocated or displaced—the government's terms for employees whose jobs have disappeared, probably permanently. Most of the displacements were the result of plant closings and layoffs as the economy lurched from a manufacturing to a service base.

For many employees, the change has meant an end to high wages and good benefits and perhaps a middle-class life-style. [While] the government has tried to help retrain those workers for the new economy and its new jobs, "the situation is a lot worse than the government says," warns Bennett Harrison of the Massachusetts Institute of Technology. "The rich are getting richer, and the poor are getting poorer, and middle-class blue-collar men are falling into the bottom," says Harrison, a professor of political economy and planning and the author of a new book entitled *The Great U-Turn: Corporate Restructuring and the Polarizing of America.*

A study of 1.2 million workers displaced from their jobs in the Great Lakes region from 1979 to 1983 showed that 51.4 percent had got new jobs at the end of the four-year period and that 33 percent were unemployed but looking for work. But 15 percent had left the labor force entirely.

"What we're seeing," said Harrison, "is a growing number of men 45–50 years old who are indeed disappearing—dropping out of the labor force and not looking for work. . . . [Others] drop into the service sector in part-time jobs or take substantial cuts in pay . . . or go into the underground economy." "This is bombshell stuff," added Ann Markusen, an economist and professor of social policy at Northwestern University.

Under the federal Job Training Partnership Act, nearly all states operate programs to reach out to displaced workers and help them land new jobs. [But] Helen Slesserev, associate director of the Illinois Unemployment and Job Training Project at the University of Chicago, observes that "there is a huge gap in the number of people dislocated and the number served. [Furthermore], much of the training taking place consists of resume-writing workshops and pep talks on how to get a job. While that may be adequate for skilled workers with long histories of working with the same employer, it cannot help workers with few skills find stable jobs. Nor are short six-to-eight-week vocational courses sufficient for training in any field except low-wage service employment."

Without more long-term training, once well-paid, stable workers will find themselves dislocated over and over again as they are forced to find employment in low-wage and unstable sectors of the economy. Minorities and women will be driven back into the service industries to which they were relegated for so long.[1]

Part of the dislocation problem in the first half of the eighties was the dollar. As the dollar appreciated against foreign currencies, due largely to the Treasury's huge deficit financing, imports became much cheaper and U.S. exports were priced out of international markets. Talk of the deindustrialization of the United States and the hollow corporation implied that many manufacturing jobs were permanently gone. Although this picture improved after 1985, the addiction to imports has remained strong, despite rising prices and a weaker dollar.

UNEMPLOYMENT: THE NATURE OF THE PROBLEM

Discouraged workers are people who have given up on any hope of finding work and dropped out of the labor force.

Perhaps nothing dramatizes more the economy in transition than the changing composition of the labor force. While there is a large segment of people who are classified as **discouraged workers,** people who have given up on any hope of finding work and dropped out of the labor force, the economy also shows a remarkable resilience in adapting and creating new jobs. For example, between 1980 and 1987, the economy generated more than 13 million jobs.

Thus, we have a perplexing problem. On the one hand, we find millions of people who no longer can effectively participate as active members of the labor force. Lacking skills, education, and experience, they fall further and further behind their better educated, well-trained and experienced counterparts. Even for those who do possess skills, technology is changing so rapidly that they can no longer compete in the labor market. Many of these people have been displaced as businesses adapt to the new capital requirements in order to remain efficient.

Contingent workers are those who work part-time or in temporary positions.

Another recent trend is a significant increase in the number of **contingent workers:** those who work part time or in temporary positions. Indeed, one fifth of the workforce is now employed part time, and over half of the new jobs created in the 1980s were filled with contingent workers. Although many earn high wages, these workers generally have no fringe benefits and no ladder of advancement in the organizations for which they work. Once the computer system is installed and the company's employees are trained, the "temps," as they are called, are back looking for new work. These are not your traditional sole proprietor-

---

[1] "New Jobs, Stability Elude Many Laid-Off Workers," *St. Louis Post-Dispatch,* January 3, 1988.

consulting operations that also do such work. Rather, they are a new breed of independent and temporary workers.

Underemployed *are people working at jobs in which they cannot fully utilize their skills, education, and experience.*

In addition to the discouraged and contingent workers, many people are considered to be **underemployed** if they are working at a job in which they cannot fully utilize their skills, education, and experience. Perhaps you know such individuals: the guy with a Ph.D. in romance languages who tends bar at a local pub or the gal who recently graduated with a degree in anthropology and is working as a sales clerk while working on her M.B.A. Although each is working and is thus classified as employed by the government, neither is doing what they were trained to do.

Of growing concern to business and government is the projection of serious worker and skill shortages in the 1990s. As the following CASE-IN-POINT indicates, it also may be a problem that is especially hard on minorities.

CASE
• IN •
POINT

Worker Scarcity in the 1990s

Workers are scarce in the Boston area—so hard to find that Boston University mailed out thousands of fliers to private homes advertising openings for clerical jobs. Some banks pay a $250 bonus to any employee who recruits a new worker. And fast-food workers in Norwich, Connecticut, earn $5 an hour or more while workers at fast-food restaurants in El Paso, Texas, earn the minimum wage of $3.35 an hour for the same work. Why the difference? The biggest reason for such regional wage differentials is the sharply contrasting unemployment rate, 3.4 percent in Norwich and 11.3 percent in El Paso, a reflection of labor market conditions.

This may be just the beginning. As the baby-bust generation reaches adulthood, a slower growing population is propelling the country into a period of labor scarcity that could last until the turn of the century, when the current baby boomlet will provide a fresh supply of new workers.

Nationally, the unemployment rate fell to 5.7 percent in March of 1988, a 10-year low. However encouraging, this figure disguises as much as it reveals. While unemployment for white men is 4.9 percent, 2.4 percent for managers and professionals, and 2.6 percent for executives and administrators, the rate remains in double digits for minorities and teenagers. Although most shortages are regional so far, unemployment has fallen below 4 percent in 31 major metropolitan areas in 19 states.

The problem is compounded by a widening mismatch between the skills workers have and the skills employers need. Many jobs in fast-growing service industries require more education than traditional jobs in shrinking blue-collar industries. But schools aren't keeping up with this change. Even worse, more than half a million students drop out of high school every year, and an additional 700,000 who graduate are barely able to read their own diplomas. As long as employers had a bountiful supply of baby boomers to draw on, the effect of these failures was muted. Now they're going to be very costly.

Workers who are qualified will do well in this environment. Older Americans will have the option of post-retirement careers. Women can look forward to better child care and maternity leave. College graduates will have more choices—including, for a change, jobs that fully utilize their educations.

The big question mark is the undereducated and the poor, who are disproportionately black and Hispanic. A new Labor Department study, *Workforce 2000,* warns that if these people don't become better prepared for work, companies will buy new technology or send jobs overseas. "Blacks are most likely to be put at risk if such strategies dominate," the report concludes. If that happens, the United States will miss a rare opportunity to deal with intractable joblessness.[2]

Questions to Consider

1. What factors may account for such dramatic regional differences in labor market conditions?

2. "Such projected labor shortages are not new to the U.S. economy. Every 10 years or so, the same thing happens in education, nursing, engineering, and many other occupations. As long as we have free markets, such shortages (and surpluses) will develop from time to time. If we're just patient and the let the market forces of supply and demand work, everything will work out." Do you agree or disagree with this statement? Why?

On the other hand, we can identify signs of encouragement and strength in the labor market. Aside from the general growth in jobs, one such indicator is the growing interest of women to participate in the labor force. As the Council of Economic Advisors observed, "The sharpest increases have been for wives with very young children. About 54 percent of wives with children under the age of six participate in the labor force. The rate for wives with infants is almost 50 percent, more than double the percentage in 1970."[3] The percent of the U.S. labor force that is female has increased from 18 percent in 1900 to 29 percent in 1950 to 44 percent in 1986.

Another encouraging sign is minority employment patterns. Although black and Hispanic unemployment rates in the fourth quarter of 1987 stood at 12.2 percent and 8.5 percent, respectively, each group accounted for a large share of the 3.1 million jobs created in 1987. For example, black workers, who comprised about 10 percent of the labor force in 1987, got 22 percent of 1987's new jobs. Hispanics, who made up only 7 percent of the labor market, filled 19 percent of the new po-

---

[2] "Help Wanted," *Business Week,* August 10, 1987, pp. 48–53.

[3] Council of Economic Advisors, *Economic Report of the President* (Washington, D.C.: Superintendent of Documents, 1987), p. 211.

sitions. Better still is the record posted by Cubans. In 1987 the Cuban unemployment rate was 5.2 percent, only negligibly higher than the 5 percent rate for whites.[4]

Before proceeding further with our analysis of the problems and prospects of the nation's changing labor force, it is important to define more carefully the types of unemployment and the composition of the unemployed.

Types of Unemployment

Because people are unemployed for different reasons, economists classify unemployment into three different categories: frictional, structural, and cyclical.[5]

Frictional Unemployment. When there is a *temporary* mismatch of jobs and job seekers, that is, when jobs exist and the unemployed either do not know of their availability or are not ready to accept employment, then there is **frictional unemployment.** In other words, frictional unemployment is largely unavoidable. One reason for this is the number of people who voluntarily quit their jobs before finding new work. Of all the unemployed in 1987, 13 percent were voluntarily unemployed. A second reason is geographic immobility. Jobs may be plentiful in Massachusetts, but unemployment may be near depression levels in Louisiana and West Virginia. College graduates who indicate in their job search a willingness to locate anywhere have a better chance of landing a job than the candidates who refuse to relocate.

Frictional unemployment *occurs when there is a temporary mismatch of jobs and job seekers.*

A third reason for frictional unemployment is related to the time the unemployed have spent looking for work. Many of the unemployed have only recently entered the labor force, either for the first time (high school and college graduates) or after a leave of absence. (The former group is called *new entrants;* the latter group is called *reentrants,* those who have left the labor force for varied reasons, such as illness, pregnancy, or because they were discouraged.) Indeed, 39 percent of the unemployed in 1987 were recent entrants into the labor market.

Structural Unemployment. Another more serious type of unemployment occurs when there is a mismatch of skills required on the job and the skills of the job seekers. Unlike frictional unemployment, which is

---

[4] "Economic Trends," *Business Week,* April 11, 1988, p. 27.

[5] Another way to classify the types of unemployment is to break the group of unemployed into two groups, the *voluntarily unemployed* and the *involuntarily unemployed.* The former group consists of those who quit their jobs before looking for new ones. The involuntarily unemployed are those who have lost their jobs because of layoffs and other staff reductions (often associated with plant closings), and reentrants and new entrants into the labor force.

primarily voluntary, structural unemployment is involuntary. When you have been dismissed because you do not possess the skills to do the job, or when you cannot find a job because the job requirements are beyond the scope of your ability and experience, **structural unemployment** occurs.

Structural unemployment *occurs when there is a mismatch of skills required on the job and the skills of the job seekers.*

Examples of structural unemployment are everywhere. In the 1970s and early 1980s, the smokestack industries furloughed thousands of workers in the face of mounting foreign competition. With the onset of the microcomputer revolution, stenographers who failed to learn word processing skills found themselves without jobs, and many firms systematically replaced clerks with automated systems. And when computerized numerical control systems were introduced in large manufacturing facilities, many machinist jobs were eliminated.[6] Steel workers, stenographers, clerks, and machinists are but four examples of the hundreds of skilled labor categories whose ranks have been depleted because of changing technology.

Natural unemployment *is the total of frictional unemployment and structural unemployment.*

Frictional unemployment and structural unemployment together constitute what economists call the rate of **natural unemployment.**[7] Workers will always quit their jobs to look for new ones. People who have never worked before will decide to enter the labor force for the first time. Others who have returned to school, will quit in order to raise a family, or those who have experienced a prolonged illness will decide to reenter the labor force. Still others, the structurally unemployed, discover that their skills are obsolete in relation to rapidly changing technological requirements. Together, these people represent so-called *natural unemployment*, the amount of joblessness associated with the economy in normal times. Unfortunately, in recent years the structural component has increased as evidenced by worker skill shortages in many areas.

THINKING IT THROUGH

What is "natural" about the natural rate of unemployment? Does the word *natural* suggest that little can be done to reduce it? What are some of the consequences that may be associated with very low unemployment?

---

[6] Numerical control systems are computer controlled and operated machines, equipment, and entire assembly lines.

[7] Another way to define this is "that rate of unemployment which persists in the absence of accelerating or decelerating inflation." We will discuss this in more detail in the section on inflation.

Cyclical Unemployment.   Unlike frictional or structural unemployment, **cyclical unemployment** occurs when aggregate demand is insufficient to sustain the number of jobs at the natural rate. As we have seen repeatedly in the last several chapters, as total spending decreases, businesses cut production and lay off workers. An especially severe example of this occurred in the 1981–82 recession. Unemployment jumped from 7.6 percent in 1981 to 10.7 percent in late 1982. For 1982 and 1983, the jobless rate averaged 9.7 percent and 9.6 percent, respectively. Using 6 percent as the natural rate of unemployment, the cyclical component of total unemployment averaged 3.5 percent. But, as the old adage says, what goes up must come down. With the stimulus of expansionary monetary and fiscal policies, the unemployment rate fell as rapidly as it had increased. By 1985, unemployment was 7.2 percent, and by December of 1987, it hit a 10-year low of 5.8 percent. Once the unemployment rate fell below the 6 percent threshold, and with the cyclical unemployment component erased, economists began wondering if the natural unemployment rate had declined, say to 5.5 or 5 percent. The jury is still out on this issue.

Cyclical unemployment *occurs when aggregate demand is insufficient to sustain the number of jobs at the natural rate.*

Job Losers, Job Leavers, and Entrants

It is important to observe that the ranks of the unemployed are constantly changing. Layoffs, voluntary quits, new entrants, and reentrants together are more like continuous flows than a homogeneous lump of unemployed workers. Table 17–1 illustrates the magnitude of these changes in the flows into and out of the civilian labor force for selected years.

Beginning with 1987, less than half of the unemployed lost their jobs because of employer decisions. However, as Table 17–1 shows, 35.3 percent of the unemployed were in the so-called *other job losers* category, a term which probably means such jobs are permanently gone. Another 12.7 percent of job losers were on layoff, generally a temporary situation, as occurs when auto plants retool for the next model year. (And auto workers and other unionized workers are eligible for supplemental unemployment benefits equal to 90 percent or more of their base pay for up to 26 weeks. Obviously, the pain of layoff is reduced dramatically with such benefits.)

The rest of the picture portrays a less ominous situation. First, the *Job leavers* category are those who have voluntarily quit their jobs. In 1987 they comprised 13 percent of the unemployed group, more than those who were laid off. Another category is the group of entrants, composed of reentrants and new entrants into the labor force. Together, they comprised 39 percent of the unemployed group. If we combine the 39 percent of reentrants and new entrants with the Job leavers (13 per-

TABLE 17–1   Reason for Unemployment, Selected Years

	1969		1983		1987	
	Percent of Unemployed	**Percent of Civilian Labor Force**	**Percent of Unemployed**	**Percent of Civilian Labor Force**	**Percent of Unemployed**	**Percent of Civilian Labor Force**
Job losers	35.9	1.3	58.4	5.6	48.0	3.0
Layoffs					[12.7]	
Other job losers					[35.3]	
Job leavers	15.4	0.5	7.7	0.7	13.0	0.8
Entrants	48.7	1.7	33.9	3.3	39.0	2.4
Reentrants	[34.1]	[1.2]	[22.5]	[2.2]	[26.6]	[1.6]
New entrants	[14.6]	[0.5]	[11.4]	[1.1]	[12.4]	[0.8]
Total	100.00	3.5	100.00	9.6	100.00	6.2

Reasons for unemployment are classified by the BLS into three main categories: losers, leavers, and entrants. Generally speaking, the stronger the economy, the lower is the percentage of job losers and the greater is the percentage of job leavers and both reentrants and new entrants.

SOURCE: *Economic Report of the President* (Washington, D.C., Superintendent of Documents, 1988), Table B-41, p. 294; and *Monthly Labor Review* (Washington, D.C., Superintendent of Documents, 1988), Table 9, p. 90.

cent), 52 percent of the unemployed in 1987 were people who did not lose their jobs.

Comparing other years is also instructive. For example, 1969 represents the lowest unemployment rate (3.5 percent) since the early fifties, and, in 1983, the economy was recovering from the worst recession since the 1930s. Looking over the data, we can detect fairly predictable flows among the various reasons for unemployment. Other things being equal, during prosperous times with tight labor markets, one would expect fewer job losers, more job leavers, and an increase in entrants. Conversely, during recessionary periods, we would expect to find an increase in job losers and fewer job leavers and entrants. This is precisely what the data show. For example, job losers comprised only about 36 percent of the unemployed in 1969, 48 percent in 1987, and nearly 60 percent in 1983. This is exactly what we would predict.

Duration of Unemployment

Duration of unemployment is the length of time without a job but seeking work.

Another important characteristic of the unemployed is the **duration of unemployment,** or the length of time without a job and seeking work. Even when the absolute number of unemployed remains unchanged, the jobless rate will rise if the average duration of unemployment increases. Table 17–2 compares selected years and summarizes the data for five different categories, including the mean and median duration.

In 1969, at the height of the Vietnam War, the unemployment rate averaged 3.5 percent, a rate reflected in the time spent unemployed. For

TABLE 17–2

Duration of
Unemployment,
Selected Years

Weeks of unemployment	PERCENT OF TOTAL UNEMPLOYED		
	1969	1983	1987
Less than 5 weeks	57.5	33.3	43.7
5 to 14 weeks	29.2	27.4	29.6
15 weeks and more	13.3	39.3	27.6
15 to 26 weeks	[8.6]	[15.4]	[12.7]
27 weeks and over	[4.7]	[23.9]	[14.0]
Mean duration	7.8	20.0	14.5
Median duration	4.4	10.1	6.5
Unemployment rate	3.5	9.6	6.2

The duration of unemployment is the length of time spent looking before securing a job. It is positively correlated with the unemployment rate and, conversely, as the time spent looking decreases, so does the unemployment rate. As with the previous table regarding the reasons for unemployment, when the economy is prosperous (such as 1969) unemployed workers find work much faster than during recessionary periods, such as 1983. In 1969, nearly 60 percent of the unemployed found work within a month. By comparison, only a third of the jobless in 1983 were able to find work in less than a month; 1987 represents a middle ground.

SOURCE: *Economic Report of the President* (Washington, D.C., Superintendent of Documents, 1988), Table B-41, p. 294; *Monthly Labor Review* (Washington, D.C., Superintendent of Documents, February 1988), Table 10, p. 90.

only 13.3 percent of the unemployed did it take more than 15 weeks to secure a job. The average job seeker found work in less than two months. In 1983, however, the year following a very deep recession, nearly 40 percent of the unemployed required 15 weeks or more to find work, and 24 percent needed more than 26 weeks. The average unemployed person in 1983 spent five months looking for work. The data for 1987 further corroborate our findings above; that is, 1987 represents a middle ground, when the unemployment rate averaged 6.2 percent. Nearly 3 out of every 4 unemployed found work within 15 weeks, and the average duration of unemployment was 14.5 weeks.[8]

As we have observed thus far, the unemployed are broken down into three classes: job losers, job leavers, and entrants. But to know that people are unemployed because they quit their jobs or that they are new entrants (or reentrants) into the labor force tells us little about why they are *still* unemployed. Although duration data help to some extent, we still do not know why people have trouble landing jobs. If we are to understand how and why people are unemployed, we need to look at the

---

[8] For statistical buffs, it is interesting to compare the mean and median duration periods. The median value is the number which splits the distribution in half; thus, for 1987, half the unemployed found work in 6.5 weeks, and half required more than 6.5 weeks. While the median and mean are both measures of central tendency, the median is not influenced by extreme values (e.g., very short or very long periods of unemployment). What do you think? Which measure is more meaningful—the mean or median duration of unemployment? Why?

job search process itself. Why do job seekers refuse an offer? What are the expectations of job seekers and prospective employers? How can the duration of unemployment be reduced?

The Job Search Process

Regardless of the perspective, employer or job seeker, the job search process is a match game. The employer wants productive, responsible, and dependable workers at the lowest possible wage or salary. The job seeker wants a good wage or salary, fringe benefits, desirable working conditions, and opportunity for advancement. When a candidate applies for a job, presents a resume and goes for an interview, how does the employer decide to hire or keep looking? Similarly, if an employer makes an offer to a job seeker, how does the person decide whether to take the job or continue the job search?[9]

Job search theory *states that the unemployed have a minimally acceptable (res-ervation) wage that must be met by a* wage offer *before employment is secured.*

Reservation wage *is the lowest acceptable wage, which, when offered, will induce the person to ac-cept employment.*

Figure 17–1 illustrates the **job search theory** as developed by econo-mists to describe how and when the search ends in a job. First, the average job seeker has some notion of a **reservation wage.** This is the lowest acceptable wage which, when offered, will induce the person to accept employment. As shown in Figure 17–1, the reservation wage (*RW*) starts high and decreases as the duration of unemployment in-creases.[10] The second element in the model is the wage offer. In the first few weeks, it is unlikely that the job seeker will receive the highest wage offer. As time passes, the wage offers generally will be slightly better on the average. However, after the candidate has spent months looking for work, the wage offers will probably be lower than those offered during the early weeks of job search. This pattern is represented as the wage offer curve (*WO*), rising slowly, peaking, and then declining gradually. When the reservation curve intersects the wage offer curve, shown at a wage of $6 per hour in the seventh week, the job search ends and em-ployment begins.

The job search process is thus little more than good old-fashioned common sense. That is, it is very obvious that most people expect (or

---

[9] It is well known that employers screen applicants using a wide variety of tests, job-related requirements, and personal preferences. Degrees, experience, and special skills are the most obvious and easiest ways to get a short list of most acceptable applicants. But then what? Age, sex, race, appearance, and other personal attributes enter the picture. Of course, using these latter criteria constitute job discrimination, so it is with extreme caution that employers reject candidates based solely upon such factors.

[10] Although we must generalize about such minima, reservation wages are different for each individual job seeker. Indeed, a neighbor of mine is a full-time high school student. Both parents have full-time jobs. She has worked only as a baby sitter and at odd jobs in her neighborhood. She wants a minimum of $5 per hour; she has not re-ceived any such offers. Her reservation wage is thus perfectly elastic (horizontal).

FIGURE 17–1

The Job Search Process

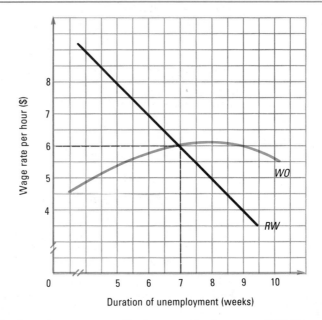

Those looking for work are represented by the reservation wage curve (*RW*). This curve depicts the minimum or lowest average wage the job seeker will accept for employment. The wage offer curve (*WO*) shows the average wages that the job seekers will be offered. This curve is based upon the assumption that wage offers will increase with time, but after some point such offers will then decline. When the *RW* is met by a wage offer, the search ends, and the person accepts the offer.

prefer) higher wages in the initial weeks of looking for work. However, as the job search process continues, as the bills pile up, the average job seeker tends to reduce reservation wage expectations and thus increases the probability of receiving an acceptable wage offer. The employer, on the other hand, generally does not change wage offers, unless market conditions are substantially different. The wage offer curve is thus viewed from the standpoint of the job seeker. In other words, in the first few weeks of the job search, the unemployed may receive wage offers substantially less than they want. As time passes, the probability is that patience will pay off, and higher wage offers will be forthcoming. However, after some threshold period (eight weeks in Figure 17–1), subsequent wage offers will begin to decline.

The job search process, as presented, is a static model; that is, it does not account for changes in demand, supply, inflation, and other variables. To convert our static model to one that is dynamic, we will consider the effects of inflation and inflationary expectations.

Inflationary Expectations and Unemployment.   If most people expect inflation to be the same as last year, what will happen to the job search process and unemployment? If inflation is fully anticipated, neither the reservation wage curve nor the wage offer curve will change. However, if the actual rate of inflation increases by more than what is expected, the wage offer curve will shift upward. Why? Businesses, which generally are more in tune with such changes, will realize that rising prices signify increased demand. Increased spending, in turn, means greater sales, production, and employment. Since business must hire more workers to meet increased demand, the most efficient way to communicate this desire is to increase wages. Higher wages are illustrated in Figure 17–2 as WO_2, intersecting RW at a lower duration of unemployment (six weeks) and a higher wage ($7.00). With people finding work at acceptable wages in a shorter time period, the unemployment rate declines.

A falsely expected inflation produces the opposite effect. In other words, if people expect higher inflation rates and they do occur, then job seekers will probably expect higher wage offers. Of course, since inflation has not accelerated, businesses are not making such offers. As shown in Figure 17–3, if job seekers falsely expect inflation, the reservation wage curve will shift upward, reflecting the expectation of higher wage offers following on the heels of more inflation. However, if those

FIGURE 17–2
Unexpected Inflation
Reduces Unemployment

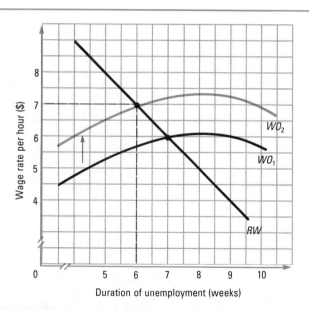

As aggregate demand increases, prices tend to rise along with output, and labor shortages occur in many markets. Businesses will raise wages in order to attract and maintain the supply of skilled labor. This is shown as an upward shift in the wage offer curve (from WO_1 to WO_2). The result is that wage offers will meet the reservation wage of job seekers earlier. Since the search time for jobs is less, the unemployment rate declines.

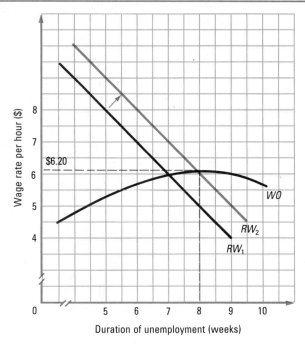

FIGURE 17–3
Falsely Expected
Inflation Raises
Unemployment

If job seekers expect inflation to increase, but the actual rate of inflation is less than what is expected, job seekers will wait for higher wage offers. This is depicted as a rightward shift of the reservation wage curve (from RW_1 to RW_2), resulting in a longer duration of unemployment and thus a higher unemployment rate.

higher wage offers are not made, that is, if the wage offer curve stays put, then people will remain unemployed for longer periods, and the unemployment rate will rise. Although we show wages increasing from $6.00 to $6.20 in Figure 17–3, the effect of increased reservation wages on the new wage rate will depend upon where the RW curve intersects the WO curve. Regardless of the new wage, however, the duration of unemployment and the unemployment rate clearly will rise.

The Employment Rate

Employment rate *is the percentage of the noninstitutional adult population that is working.*

When the Bureau of Labor Statistics releases the unemployment data each month, it is the unemployment rate that gets the headline.[11] Often overlooked in reports about the labor force, however, is the **employment rate,** the percentage of the noninstitutional adult population (or the working-age population) that is working. Many observers prefer to fol-

[11] Recall that the unemployment rate is computed by dividing the total number of unemployed by the total number of people in the labor force (employed plus the unemployed).

low the employment rate instead of the unemployment rate because they think that it is a better measure of the general health of the economy. Although this may appear to be a debate over whether the glass is half full or half empty, the difference is quite important. Let's see why.

First, the unemployment rate often rises even if the economy is generating more new jobs. In other words, the number of unemployed need not increase for the rate of unemployment to increase. If the percentage of entrants to the labor force that cannot find work is greater than the current unemployment rate, then the rate of unemployment will rise *even if the vast majority find new work*. Let's take a simple example. Assume that the working-age population is 160 million, the CLF is 100 million, employment is 96 million, and unemployment is 4 million. The unemployment rate is thus 4 percent. Now, if the CLF grows by 5 million people, and 4 million find jobs, the unemployment rate rises to 4.8 percent. Does this mean that the economy is in bad shape? Not necessarily, although we have all been trained to believe so. In fact, many of those joining the ranks of CLF as job seekers may have a primary breadwinner already working. Moreover, many may have just started their search as new entrants into the labor market, such as recent college graduates and housewives and househusbands (those formerly at home).

A second reason for tracking the employment rate is that it is not as volatile as the unemployment rate. Indeed, the growth of the noninstitutional adult population (NAP) is influenced by marriage and family decisions and other not strictly economic factors. In the period from 1980 to 1987, for example, employment grew by 9.4 percent while the NAP grew by 7.1 percent. (The NAP thus grew by only 75 percent of employed group.) Using the same numbers above and the assumption that the NAP grows by 75 percent of the additional employed, the NAP grows to 163.75, and the employment rate increases from 60 percent to 61 percent. This may seem like splitting hairs, but economists are always striving to improve upon measures of economic performance.

INFLATION

Besides unemployment, inflation occupies center stage as the most persistent economic problem. What causes inflation? Why is it so hard to control? And is there a trade-off between inflation and unemployment?

Demand-Pull Inflation

Demand-pull inflation *occurs when aggregate demand increases faster than the economy's ability to produce goods and services.*

Inflation is a rise in the general price level, as measured by the GNP deflator (or implicit price index; see Chapter 12). One type of inflation is **demand-pull inflation** (or excess demand). It occurs when, other

FIGURE 17–4

Demand-Pull Inflation

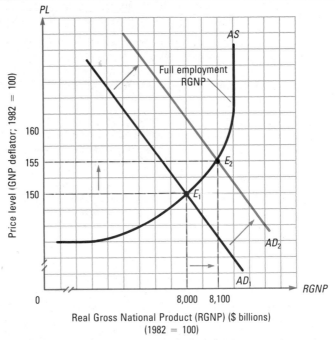

Demand-pull inflation occurs whenever aggregate demand increases faster than aggregate supply. As aggregate demand increases from AD_1 to AD_2, the equilibrium price level rises from E_1 to E_2 resulting in an increase in the rate of inflation and an increase in *real* GNP.

things being equal, aggregate demand increases faster than the economy's ability to produce goods and services. The upshot is that the price level rises. This is illustrated in Figure 17–4, a diagram that shows the relationship between the price level and real GNP.[12] As noted in our earlier discussions of this model, aggregate demand (*AD*) and aggregate supply (*AS*) are similar to the market supply and demand curves studied in microeconomics, except we focus here on the price level instead of the price of peaches or other individual products and on *all* goods and services in lieu of the quantity of peaches supplied and demanded. Let's begin our scenario in the year 2001 with a price level (or GNP deflator) of 150 and real GNP of $8,000 billion. This provides us with an equilibrium condition at E_1, since *AS* intersects AD_1 at the $8,000 billion level of output. Then things begin to change. Low interest rates on federal

---

[12] The *AS-AD* price level/real GNP diagram discussed here is identical to the model presented in Chapter 13. *A special word of warning is helpful, however*. Be careful not to confuse this graph with the Keynesian Cross (45-degree) graph. If you will remember, in that diagram, the price level was not part of the picture; expenditures were measured on the vertical axis and national income and product on the horizontal.

securities cause a decrease in demand for the dollar. The dollar thus begins to depreciate (fall in value) against several foreign currencies. Since a dollar depreciation makes it less expensive to buy U.S. goods, U.S. exports increase. The upshot is an increase in *AD,* shown as a shift of the curve from AD_1 to AD_2.

How does this lead to a rising price level? First, when *AD* increases, there will be inventory depletion. Then, as shortages become more apparent, businesses face the decision to increase production and employment, increase prices, or both. In our example, since the economy has room to grow, increased demand results in more real output and higher prices. The new equilibrium E_2 is reached when the excess demand (or aggregate shortage) is eliminated. At E_2 the price level is 155 and the real GNP is $8,100 billion. The economy has experienced demand-pull inflation. It is called demand-pull because the increased demand has pulled up prices.

Cost-Push Inflation

Although many inflations emanate from the demand side of the economy, once an inflation gets started, its momentum often is fueled by forces on the supply side. **Cost-push inflation** is the rise in the price level associated with higher labor and other resource costs. Normally, when unexpected inflation occurs, workers find that their real wages have declined. Anxious to catch up and protect themselves against further erosion of purchasing power, they negotiate for larger wage increases. If such wage and salary gains exceed productivity gains, management generally will raise prices (again) in order to protect profit margins. And, once the process begins, it often triggers a wage-price spiral. Let's see how it works.

Cost-push inflation *is the rise in the price level associated with higher labor and other resource costs.*

Assume that in year one inflation is 2 percent. Then demand-pull inflation leads to a higher inflation rate of 3.3 percent in year two. Wage gains have averaged 2 percent in each year, and productivity also is 2 percent per year.[13] Because workers have fallen behind, that is, because inflation exceeds the wage gains, they negotiate a 3.3 percent increase in wages—equal to the inflation rate. Management sees a red flag since wage gains now exceed productivity. In other words, management is now paying workers 3.3 percent more per hour to produce 2 percent more per hour. Management typically argues that this represents an increase in *unit labor costs,* or the labor cost per unit of output. Higher unit labor costs, especially for labor intensive operations in the service sector of the economy, will erode profits.

---

[13] Productivity is a measure of the change in the average worker's output per hour. For example, if a person produced 100 machine parts per hour last year and produces 102 parts per hour this year, productivity increases 2 percent.

The upshot is that businesses feel justified in raising prices by at least the difference between wage and productivity gains. Figure 17–5 illustrates how wage gains are translated into higher prices. As in the microeconomy, when costs of production rise, the supply curve shifts up and to the left (toward the vertical axis). This is shown as a shift from AS_1 to AS_2. The result is a higher price level and reduced real GNP. As the economy moves up the AD curve, real GNP (RGNP) declines to $8,000 billion, and the price level moves up to 161.25, producing an inflation rate of 4 percent.

Is the economy better off or worse off compared to its original position before demand-pull inflation? Table 17–3 helps us analyze the changes. (Recall that nominal GNP (NGNP) is computed by multiplying the price level times real GNP and dividing by 100.) With demand-pull inflation, both inflation and real GNP rose, 3.3 percent and 1.3 percent, respectively. With cost-push inflation, however, real GNP fell as the price level rose. Inflation after cost-push was 4 percent and real GNP declined by 1.2 percent. Although real GNP declined the nominal

FIGURE 17–5

Cost-Push Inflation

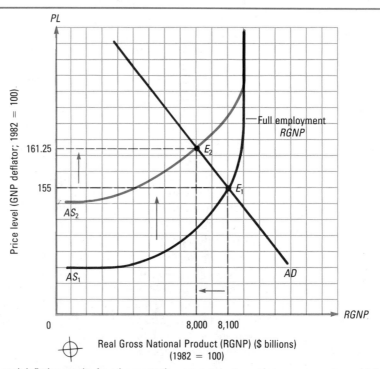

Cost-push inflation results from increases in resource costs, such as wages, rents, and interest rates. Cost-push generally follows demand-pull inflation as labor tries to recover its lost purchasing power. As wages rise, businesses pass through the costs in higher prices. This is depicted as a leftward shift of the aggregate supply curve, resulting in higher price level and lower real output.

TABLE 17–3
Effects of Demand-Pull
and Cost-Push Inflation

Demand-Pull Inflation:

        Cause: Increase in aggregate demand
        Effect: Inflation and increased RGNP

NGNP	RGNP	Percent Change in NGNP	Percent Change in RGNP	GNP Deflator	Inflation Percent Change in GNP Deflator
$12,000	$8,000			150.00	
		4.6	1.3		3.3
12,555	8,100			155.00	

Cost-Push Inflation:

        Cause: Decrease in aggregate supply
        Effect: Inflation and decreased RGNP

NGNP	RGNP	Percent Change in NGNP	Percent Change in RGNP	GNP Deflator	Inflation Percent Change in GNP Deflator
$12,555	$8,100			155.00	
		2.8	−1.2		4.0
12,900	8,000			161.25	

RGNP = Real Gross National Product
NGNP = Nominal Gross National Product

This table illustrates the main difference between demand-pull inflation and cost-push inflation. In the upper portion of the table, increased demand leads to a higher price level, as measured by the GNP deflator. The inflation rate is calculated by dividing the change in index numbers by the original value [(155 − 150)/150]. With demand-pull inflation, assuming that the economy has room to grow, production also increases, as shown by the percentage increase in RGNP. Adding the inflation rate (3.3 percent) and the change in RGNP (1.3 percent) gives us the percentage increase in nominal GNP, 4.6 percent.

In the lower portion of the table, a decrease in aggregate supply leads to inflation (4.0 percent) and a decrease in RGNP (−1.2 percent). As above, adding the inflation rate and the change in RGNP determines the change in NGNP (2.8 percent). Thus, under conditions of cost-push inflation, unlike demand-pull, real GNP declines.

GNP increased in each case, further evidence that focus on nominal GNP conceals the important separate effects of inflation and real GNP.

The wage-price spiral is in its infant stage in our example, but if history is any judge, workers will attempt to reclaim lost purchasing power caused by the increased inflation. This will set off another round of price and wage hikes. This process often ends in recession.

Unfortunately, this hypothetical scenario is played out in the real world all too often. Indeed, in the last 20 years there have been four recessions—1970, 1974 to 1975, 1980, and 1981 to 1982. In the first three episodes, both unemployment and inflation increased, what economists call *inflationary recessions* or, more simply, *stagflation*. Unlike the earlier slumps, the severity of the 1981 to 1982 recession actually reduced inflation. With unemployment reaching 10.7 percent in late 1982 and unemployment rates averaging 9.6 percent in both 1982 and 1983, and with real GNP down by 2.5 percent for 1982, inflation was literally wrung out of the economy. Although policymakers have been successful in com-

bating the single problem of inflation or of unemployment, economic policy has been unable to sustain long periods of full employment without
inflation during peacetime. Thus persists our most perplexing macroeconomic problem: how to fight the twin occurrence of inflation and
unemployment. In the next section, we turn our attention to a more
detailed discussion of this important issue.

INFLATION AND UNEMPLOYMENT—A TRADE-OFF

The decade of the 60s was marked by mixed blessings. It was a time
when society was bitterly divided over U.S. involvement in Vietnam and
torn by racial violence. But it was also a period of unparalleled economic expansion. More than 11 million new jobs were created, and unemployment averaged only 4.78 percent for the decade. Indeed,
unemployment in the last four years of the 1960s averaged about 3.6
percent. And then inflation reared its ugly head.

The Phillips Curve

Phillips curve *is a diagram
illustrating the relationship
between inflation and
unemployment.*

Our discussion thus far implies that as unemployment decreases, inflation increases, and vice versa. And this is precisely what policymakers
were led to believe in the 60s. Figure 17–6 illustrates this relationship, a
trade-off between inflation and unemployment known as the **Phillips
curve.**[14] The logic of the trade-off states that when unemployment is low
and there are skilled worker shortages, businesses will be forced to raise
wages to attract and maintain a qualified labor force. If productivity
does not increase, unit labor costs will rise and firms pass the costs on
in higher product prices.

The Phillips curve relationship for the 1960s seemed to offer a series
of alternative policy choices—a kind of economic policy menu. For example, if Washington, D.C., policymakers wanted to reduce unemployment, say from point *a* (6.7 percent) to point *b* (5.5 percent), increased
spending and/or tax cuts would move the economy up along the Phillips
curve. The cost of reduced joblessness was an increased rate of inflation, from 1.0 to 2.2 percent. Conversely, if policymakers thought that
inflation was excessive, they could deflate the economy with spending

---

[14] The curve is named after A.W. Phillips, a British economist who first observed
this relationship between wages and unemployment. Paul Samuelson, a Nobel-winning
economics professor at the Massachusetts Institute of Technology, converted the wage
variable to inflation by showing the close correspondence between percentage changes
in wages and inflation.

FIGURE 17–6
The Phillips Curve

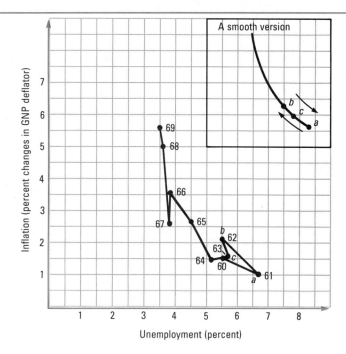

The Phillips curve depicts a trade-off between inflation and unemployment. The relationship for the 1960s seemed to promise a policy menu: more unemployment and less inflation, or less unemployment and more inflation. The small boxed-in diagram illustrates a smoothed-out version of the actual data.

cuts and/or tax hikes. The result is more unemployment, shown as a movement down the Phillips curve from point *b* to point *c*.[15]

What appeared to be a reasonably stable trade-off turned into a highly unstable, if not wholly unpredictable, relationship in the 1970s and 1980s. As Figure 17–7 shows, in only six years of the 1970 to 1988 period did a Phillips curve trade-off occur. Instead of the inverse relationship between unemployment and inflation, for most of this period, the economy experienced a direct relationship between joblessness and inflation.

What does this mean for the Phillips curve? As we have seen, there is no reliable pattern of short-run trade-offs between unemployment

---

[15] The relationship is even more stable if the CPI is used as the inflation measure. For example, while the GNP deflator marked a decline in inflation from 1963 to 1964 and from 1966 to 1967, the CPI increased from 1.2 to 1.3 percent for 1963 to 1964 and held steady at 2.9 percent for 1966 to 1967.

FIGURE 17-7

The Phillips Curve:
1970–1988 Where's the
Trade-off?

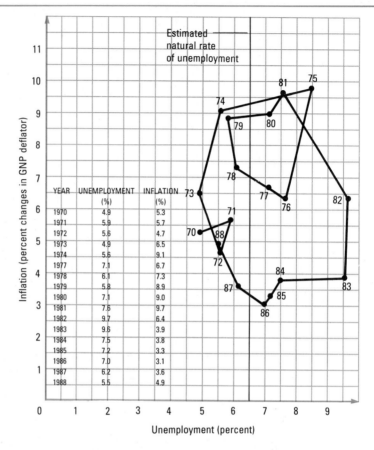

The data for the 1970 to 1988 period indicate that there was no stable trade-off between inflation and unemployment. Whenever unemployment was kept below the natural rate (arbitrarily
shown here as 6.5 percent), inflation accelerated. Conversely, when unemployment exceeded
the natural rate, inflation decelerated.

and inflation. Indeed, as shown in Figure 17–7, economists have identified a long-run vertical Phillips curve, roughly coincident with the
economy's natural rate of unemployment. The pattern of the inflation-
unemployment relationship for the 1970s and 1980s resembles a series of
clockwise loops, cycling to higher and higher rates until the early 80s.
Whenever unemployment was pushed below (and kept below) the natural rate (estimated to be roughly 6 percent during the 70s and early 80s),
inflation accelerated (1972 to 1974 and 1976 to 1979). The inflationary
momentum was broken in each period by recession (1974 to 1975, 1980,
and 1981 to 1982). Thus, a period of decelerating inflation occurred
whenever unemployment exceeded the natural rate.

Until the mid-1980s the Phillips curve appears to have shifted to the right, signifying more inflation for any given unemployment rate or more unemployment for any given inflation rate. Indeed, if we portray the relationship between inflation and unemployment by decade over the period from 1950 to 1988, the trade-off occurs only in the 1980s. Figure 17–8 illustrates the average unemployment and inflation rates by decade. We can observe that from 1950 to 1980, instead of a trade-off, the trend was more inflation and more unemployment. What happened? What went wrong?

Economic Turbulence: An Inflationary Era

The reasons for creeping inflation, higher unemployment, and stagflation are attributed to five main factors: a federal government propensity to spend beyond its means, especially in its commitment to expanding programs to help the poor and underprivileged; the occurrence of supply-side shocks to the economy; the growth of inflationary expectations; a changing composition of the labor force; and a burgeoning federal budget deficit.

FIGURE 17–8

Inflation-Unemployment Trend, 1950–1987

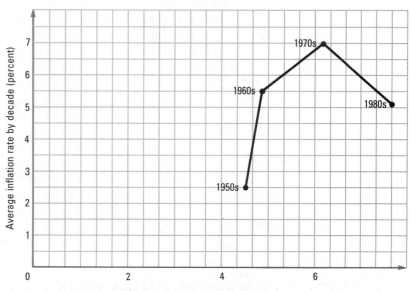

Using average inflation and unemployment rates for each decade, the long-run trend shows that both inflation and unemployment increased between 1950 and 1980. Average inflation rates declined in the 1980s, but only because average unemployment was significantly greater than the natural rate.

The early 1970s witnessed the winding down and end to the Vietnam War. It also marked the dark period of Watergate and the resignation of President Nixon. It was a time of escalating Middle East conflict and a growing incidence of international terrorism. As the Vietnam War came to an end, there was a striking decline in social protest and reform movements. Society seemed to turn inward in a desire to suppress the fact that the United States had lost the war in Vietnam and the war on poverty at home.

Vietnam and the Great Society—the Beginning. Although the inflationary virus did not really spread until the 1970s, the seeds of economic turbulence were planted in the 1960s. If there is one thing the study of economics conveys, it is, to coin a worn-out but appropriate phrase, "There is no such thing as a free lunch." Everything has its price, and the economic prosperity of the 60s is no exception. In retrospect, economists generally agree that President Johnson's unwillingness to raise taxes in order to pay for Vietnam and the Great Society programs ushered in an inflationary era.[16] It was a classic example of demand-pull inflation—excess spending financed by Treasury borrowing. It was only a short time before cost-push inflation added further inflationary pressure.

By late 1971, inflation seemed to be out of control. In response to increasing public pressure, President Nixon announced a *90-day freeze on wages and prices*. It would be no exaggeration to say that this was a total surprise. Although opposed to governmental interference in the marketplace, Nixon became convinced that even further decisive action was needed; thus, following the 90-day freeze, he instituted a period of *wage and price controls*. These tough measures seemed to do the job, as inflation edged downward in 1972. However, as a firm believer in the ability of the private marketplace to solve its own problems, Nixon removed the controls in 1973.

Supply-Side Shocks. When the very unpopular controls were lifted in 1973, two additional events caused inflationary havoc. First, OPEC (the infamous oil cartel) cut supplies and raised the price of oil fourfold. This had a profound ripple effect. Because oil was a basic resource in most manufacturing and a source of energy for millions of Americans, inflated oil prices translated into higher prices on a wide range of consumer

---

[16] The Great Society was a political label applied to the multitude of federal programs designed to reduce poverty, provide job training for the hard-core unemployed, provide more and better public housing, and so forth. It was in this era that the federal Food Stamps program was created, along with Jobs Corps, the Office of Economic Opportunity, a variety of housing subsidy programs, and miscellaneous income supplements.

goods. Second, the United States sold (dumped) millions of tons of surplus wheat to Russia, creating a severe shortage in the U.S. market. Taken by themselves, these two events provided *supply-side shocks* to the economy, a form of cost-push inflation.

But as the economic scenario unfolded, these were not isolated events. Applying wage and price controls in an economy experiencing inflationary pressure is much like putting a lid on the pressure cooker. To make matters worse, while the controls were in place during 1972, the Nixon administration increased spending.[17] The injection of increased expenditures exacerbated the inflation by turning up the heat beneath the pressure-cooker economy. When the controls were removed in 1973, all the conditions were ripe for an inflationary surge. And surge it did.

Inflationary Expectations. Fed by an inflationary psychology, inflation jumped from 3.4 percent in 1972 to 8.8 percent in 1973 (as measured by the CPI). At the end of 1973, consumers expressed their dismay and led the economy into its worst slump since the 1930s. Although unemployment averaged 8.5 percent in 1975, inflation actually increased to 9.8 percent (from 9.1 percent in 1974). Economists attributed the inflationary recession to cost-push factors fed by *inflationary expectations.* In other words, people assumed that prices would move higher and acted accordingly. Everyone from workers to bankers to landlords anticipated more inflation and thus built their expectations into higher wages, interest rates, and rents. Lagging productivity only compounded the problem, as businesses passed along these increased costs of doing business by raising prices.

The recession and high unemployment ultimately reduced some of the inflationary pressure. As Table 17–4 shows, inflation came down 3.4 percentage points from 1975 to 1976. However, the inflationary psychology was not broken, and inflation soon heated up again. By the end of President Carter's term of office, inflation reached 9 percent. Without any fiscal restraint from Capitol Hill, the Federal Reserve adopted tight monetary policies to combat inflation. Although these measures were perceived as too austere by President Reagan, most analysts pronounced that inflationary expectations were finally brought to an end. Once again a recession had vanquished inflation.

Changing Composition of the Labor Force. Another reason accounting for the worsening inflation-unemployment picture was the changing composition of the labor force. Beginning in the 1960s and accelerating in

---

[17] With the presidential election coming up, some observers saw this as a raw political maneuver to reduce unemployment and capture the favorable political fallout from an improved economic picture.

TABLE 17–4

Unemployment and
Inflation, 1970–1988

Year	Unemployment (percent)	Inflation (percent)
1970	4.9%	5.3%
1971	5.9	5.7
1972	5.6	4.7
1973	4.9	6.5
1974	5.6	9.1
1975	8.5	9.8
1976	7.7	6.4
1977	7.1	6.7
1978	6.1	7.3
1979	5.8	8.9
1980	7.1	9.0
1981	7.6	9.7
1982	9.7	6.4
1983	9.6	3.9
1984	7.5	3.8
1985	7.2	3.3
1986	7.0	3.1
1987	6.2	3.6
1988	5.5	4.9
Avg.	6.8	6.2

The data indicate the mixed and somewhat unpredictable relationship between unemployment and inflation. For example, although we observe a short-run Phillips curve type trade-off in some years (i.e., 1972–1973 and 1976–1979), there also are other periods in which inflation and unemployment either increased or decreased together (i.e., 1973–1975 [increasing] and 1982–1986 [decreasing]).

SOURCE: *Economic Report of the President* (Washington, D.C.: U.S. Government Printing Office, 1987), Table 31, pp. 280–81; *Monthly Labor Review* (Bureau of Labor Statistics, U.S. Department of Labor, Washington, D.C.), February 1989, Table 4, p. 88.

the 1970s, there was a dramatic increase in labor force participation of women and teenagers and a decline in labor force participation for men. (The *labor force participation rate (LFPR)* is calculated by dividing the civilian labor force by the noninstitutional population.) Because women and teenagers experienced significantly higher unemployment rates than the average, and because men traditionally had lower-than-average unemployment rates, greater female and teenage labor force participation translated into a higher rate of natural unemployment.[18]

---

[18] It is interesting to note that since 1980 the LFPR for women has continued its upward trend (56.0 in 1987), while the LFPR for teenagers has declined (to 54.7 percent in 1987). As the teenage labor pool shrinks moderately, this will tend to lower the natural rate of unemployment. As more women in the 1980s have elected careers in business, engineering, law, and medicine, compared to the career choices of social services, nursing, and teaching in earlier periods, pay disparities have diminished, and unemployment rates for men and women are roughly equal for the first time. This trend also implies a lower natural rate of unemployment.

TABLE 17-5
Average Deficits by
Decade, 1950–1988

Decade	Average Deficit ($ billions)
1950 to 1959	0.03
1960 to 1969	−2.02
1970 to 1979	−28.26
1980 to 1988	−133.48

Federal government deficits have increased each decade, from the 1950s to the 1980s. There were five surplus years in the 1950s, four surplus years in the 1960s, and no budget years of surplus in the 1970s or 1980s. The last year in which the federal government ran a surplus was 1969.

SOURCE: *Economic Report of the President* (Washington, D.C.: U.S. Government Printing Office, 1987), Table B-76, p. 335; *Survey of Current Business* (Bureau of Economic Analysis, U.S. Department of Commerce, Washington, D.C.), 69, no. 1 (January 1989), Table 3.2, p. 14.

The Growing Federal Deficit. As we have discussed before, not all deficits are bad. Indeed, during recessions, automatic stabilizers increase transfer payments, reduce tax revenues, and thus automatically increase the size of the deficit. This helps to cushion the economy against more severe fluctuations. However, in the last 20 years, Washington, D.C., policymakers have not taken the initiative to run surplus budgets during good times. The upshot is a deficit that keeps growing. Table 17-5 illustrates the average size of the deficit by decade. The table largely speaks for itself. From an average of $0.03 billion surplus in the 1950s, the red ink has swollen to an average of $133.48 billion in the 1980s.

To what extent are such deficits inflationary? The answer to this, as you may already suspect, is—it depends! Deficits are inflationary if, and only if, the economy is near or at full employment. In other words, it depends on the capacity of the economy to produce. The closer we move to potential GNP, the greater the inflationary consequences of deficit spending.

Before we move on to examine strategies to stabilize the economy, it is instructive to read the comments of expert witnesses concerning the inflation in recent decades.

CASE
▪ IN ▪
POINT

Views on Inflation

If one wants expert opinion, one should go to the experts. The following views on inflation are offered by some of the nation's most respected economists.

Inflation is the price paid for our becoming a more humane economy.
—*Paul Samuelson, Professor of Economics, MIT, Nobel Laureate in Economics*

The single most important reason for inflation is that we are a society that has tried to prevent deep recessions, to provide income security for people, and to help those who suffer. We no longer let big business go bankrupt or people go unemployed for a long time.

—*Robert Solow, Professor of Economics, MIT, Nobel Laureate in Economics*

Inflation results from the almost universal commitment to the objectives of full employment and the welfare state idea which holds that government ought to have a continuing active concern with the poor and the sick.

—*Milton Hudson, Senior Economist, Morgan Guaranty Trust*

And on inflationary expectations:

If as a manager of a household, you perceive a period of inflation as being limited, you save for this hurricane which has a beginning and an end. But if you perceive the weather system to be changing permanently, you start to advance large fixed purchases, and you come to think of buying now as saving. The result is a dangerous set of calculations that prompts spending, discourages saving, and fuels inflation.

—*Edwin Yeo, Chicago banker and former Under Secretary of the Treasury*

Questions to Consider

1. Is it a cop-out to attribute inflation to a nation's social agenda? Doesn't this imply that we must abandon the underprivileged if we want to keep a lid on inflation?

2. Assuming that these observations are correct, is there a consensus about the basic cause of inflation (e.g., demand–pull versus cost–push)?

IMPORTANT TERMS TO REMEMBER

contingent workers, p. 473	frictional unemployment, p. 476
cost-push inflation, p. 487	job search theory, p. 481
cyclical unemployment, p. 478	natural unemployment, p. 477
demand-pull inflation, p. 485	Phillips curve, p. 490
discouraged workers, p. 473	reservation wage, p. 481
duration of unemployment, p. 479	structural unemployment, p. 477
employment rate, p. 484	underemployment, p. 474

CHAPTER SUMMARY

1. Unemployment is broken down into three main types: (1) frictional—those who are temporarily between jobs, such as recent quits or entrants; (2) structural—those who cannot find work because the available jobs require skills which they do not possess; and (3) cyclical—those laid off or unable to find work because the economy is in recession.

2. The composition of the unemployed (or reasons for unemployment) consists of job losers, job leavers, and entrants (reentrants and new entrants).

3. The longer [shorter] the average duration of unemployment, the higher [lower] will be the unemployment rate.

4. The job search theory states that the unemployed have a minimally acceptable wage (the reservation wage) that must be met by a wage offer before employment is secured.

    a. Fully expected inflation will have no effect on the unemployment rate (although average wages will be higher).

    b. Unexpected inflation will result in a shorter duration of unemployment and a lower average wage rate.

    c. Falsely expected inflation will result in higher average wage levels and a longer duration (and rate) of unemployment.

5. Demand-pull inflation occurs as the *AD* for goods and services increases faster than *AS*. The upshot is a drawing down of inventories leading businesses to hire more workers, increase production, and raise prices.

6. Cost-push inflation originates on the supply-side of the economy. Higher wages and other resource costs, without a corresponding increase in productivity, will raise unit labor costs and give rise to higher product prices.

7. The Phillips curve describes a historical trade-off between inflation and unemployment: the lower the unemployment rate, the higher the inflation rate; the higher the unemployment rate, the lower the inflation rate. Although this was a reasonably stable short-term trend in the 1950s and 1960s, there appears to be no such consistent empirical relationship in the 1970s and 1980s.

8. Factors such as supply-side shocks (OPEC oil embargo), an inflationary psychology, and the changing composition of the labor force have combined to demolish any idea of a long-term Phillips curve trade-off (reminiscent of the 1960s).

DISCUSSION AND REVIEW QUESTIONS

1. Structural unemployment occurs primarily because technology has outpaced the skills possessed by people. Is it possible to reduce structural unemployment? Private businesses, colleges, and government agencies operate retraining programs to assist the displaced worker. Are these programs effective? Why or why not? How would you design a retraining program?

2. Why is the contingent worker share of the labor force increasing? What incentives do employers have to hire part-time workers and temps?

3. Evaluate this statement: "Because frictional unemployment is voluntary and largely unavoidable, it really doesn't represent an economic problem in the same sense that structural and cyclical unemployment do. To get a better picture of the real unemployment problem facing the country, the government should first substract all those in the frictional unemployment category before publishing the unemployment rate."

4. Answer the following concerning the Phillips curve:

    a. What is the logic behind the Phillips curve trade-off? Why would inflation increase as unemployment decreases (and vice-versa)?

    b. List three or more factors contributing to the breakdown of the Phillips curve trade-off in the 1970s and 1980s, and explain why the trade-off worsened.

5. Diagram, describe, and distinguish between demand-pull and cost-push inflation. How do expectations of more inflation (inflationary psychology) actually cause more inflation?

6. Natural unemployment is the total of frictional and structural unemployment, or the rate of unemployment which will persist in the absence of inflationary pressure. Explain why economists believed the natural rate rose to 6 or 6.5 percent in the 1970s and early 1980s, only to be revised downward again in the latter half of the 1980s.

7. The job search theory outlines the process by which the job seeker's reservation wage is matched by an employer's wage offer. Describe and explain the reservation wage curve in each of the diagrams below. Which of these situations best represents your preference for ending the job search?

FIGURE 17–9

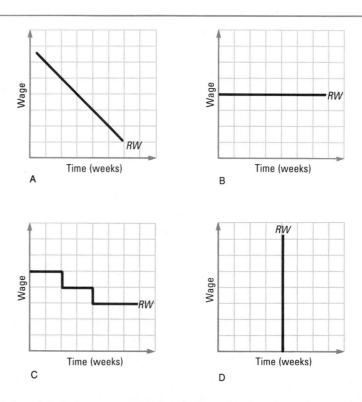

8. How will inflationary expectations affect the duration of unemployment and the wage at which a job is found?

A BRIEF LOOK AHEAD

We have covered a lot of ground in our chapters devoted to macroeconomics. The next chapter pulls much of this theory and practice together and examines various strategies of stabilization policy.

Economic Stabilization:
Prospects and Problems

Ron Sherman, Uniphoto

The purpose of this chapter is threefold: to survey some of the problems and prospects of maintaining maximum employment without inflation, to review and evaluate the current status of prevalent macroeconomic theories, and to present the chief policy prescriptions corresponding to each theory. Along the way, we will also study the important linkage between productivity, economic growth, unemployment, and inflation. In the conclusion, we will examine several unconventional and more controversial ideas that have been proposed to stabilize the economy.

After completion of this chapter, you should be able to do the following:

1. Compare and contrast the classical, Keynesian, monetarist, supply-side, and rational expectationist theories with regard to economic stabilization.
2. Describe and explain Okun's law.
3. Describe and explain tax-based incomes policies (TIPS).
4. Explain how the existence of unemployment benefits and welfare payments generally may keep unemployment rates high.
5. Compare and contrast mandatory workfare programs and Massachusetts's Employment and Training Choices (ETC) program.

"It's Starting to Turn Up!"

"It's starting to go up!"

As the cartoon so aptly conveys, economic observers get excited when the economy shows signs of improvement. But our cartoon characters, as gleeful as they appear to be, still suggest that there is a problem. Are they excited because economic policy has finally managed to end a recession or are they delighted because, *despite* specific policy initiatives, the economy has improved? However you interpret the ecstasy expressed by our cartoon characters, one fact remains: the economy often moves in directions unanticipated by even the most astute observers. No matter how sophisticated the economic model and regardless of the policy efforts to inflate or deflate the economy, policymakers, legislators, and presidents are routinely surprised by the economy's performance—especially as election time rolls around.

Following the October 19, 1987, stock market crash, a majority of economists thought a recession was imminent. They reasoned that the crash would deal a severe blow to consumer and investor confidence. With a slowdown in consumer and investment spending, the expansion would come to a swift halt. To everyone's surprise, the economy picked up steam at the end of 1987 and the first half of 1988. Indeed, the economy continued its record-setting pace of job formation, spending on plant and equipment increased, and the export picture improved substantially. Major stock market corrections and other fluctuations in the financial markets had little effect on consumption and production.

CONTEMPORARY MACROECONOMIC THEORIES

Economic stabilization refers to the policies and programs by which the government attempts to control inflation and unemployment.

Economic stabilization is a catchall term that refers to the policies and programs by which the government attempts to control inflation and unemployment, and the Employment Act stands as a symbol of U.S. commitment to economic stabilization. It formally recognized the acceptance of Keynesian economics and the importance of active demand management practices. But the landmark legislation also opened up a Pandora's box of competing views about how to go about fulfilling the objectives of the act. Increasingly, economists began to challenge the Keynesian approach as inherently inflationary and biased toward a larger role for the federal government.

Classical, Keynesian, monetarist, supply-side, and rational expectations theories offer different views of the macroeconomy and thus present different policy prescriptions to manage or provide for the health of the nation's economy. Indeed, these different views may be arrayed along a policy continuum, from activism to dogmatic nonintervention.

Policy activists believe in expansionary fiscal and monetary policies to combat recession and inflation.

Policy activists, generally of the Keynesian persuasion, believe in expansionary fiscal and monetary policies to combat recession, and, conversely, they advocate restrictive economic policies to reduce the adverse effects of inflation. Such actions are deemed to be the best approach to moderate what they see as the inherent instability of the business cycle.

Noninterventionists, or policy nonactivists, are an eclectic group of economists who argue that the Keynesian type of discretionary policymaking contributes to economic instability.

Noninterventionists, or policy nonactivists, are an eclectic group of economists, consisting of monetarists, supply-siders, and rational expectationists. As a group, they are often referred to as new classical economists because they derive much of their economic thinking from classical economics. They specifically reject the idea that the economy has built-in destabilizing forces. Indeed, they argue that the Keynesian type of discretionary policymaking contributes to economic instability. Instead of policy activism, the new classical economists advocate a more limited role of government and policy rules, such as a balanced budget and a fixed annual growth of the money supply.

Such ideas are not new. In fact, the changes in economic thought over the last 60 or 70 years have come full circle. What is the basis for the new classical economics? How is it different from its classical forerunner? Where do the other theories come in? In order to answer these and related questions, it is helpful to examine the evolution and salient features of these various economic schools of thought.

Classical Economics versus Keynesian Economics

It was Plato who said that necessity is the mother of invention, and no aphorism rings truer when applied to the development of economic theory. It took an economic holocaust like the Great Depression to dislodge classical economics and produce a more realistic explanation of the events and a solution to massive unemployment.

Classical economics states that full employment equilibrium is the natural economic state.

Classical economics was firmly rooted in microeconomic theory. In the classical model, markets were economic battlegrounds where the contestants were evenly matched. Buyers sought to maximize utility, and sellers opted to maximize profits. Surpluses and shortages in all markets would quickly be erased by fully flexible wages, prices, and interest rates. The result was a price that cleared the market. Left alone, the private markets and Adam Smith's invisible hand of competition would provide the optimum distribution of resources and incomes in society.

Extending the competitive micro model to the macroeconomy, the classical economists found an easy solution to recession and unemployment. If the economy went into a slump, surplus labor and output would cause wages and prices to fall. Responsive to such market incentives, businesses would hire workers, and consumers would increase spending. The upshot would be a return to full employment. Indeed, full employment equilibrium was considered to be the natural economic state.

Unfortunately, the actual behavior of businesses and consumers in the Great Depression was exactly the opposite of classical predictions. Although wages and prices did fall, business continued to lay off workers, and consumers showed no interest in buying more. Although an enigma to classical economists, Keynes offered a simple explanation. Classical economics was guilty of a logical fallacy. By transferring the logic of flexible wages and prices from individual markets to the entire economy, the classical economists were guilty of the fallacy of composition. In other words, they argued that what was true for the part (the micro market) was necessarily true for the whole (the macroeconomy). Therein lay the fallacy.

Where the classical economists emphasized the behavior of individual markets and extended the logic to the whole economy, Keynes focused on total spending, or aggregate demand. In other words, Keynes started with the macroeconomy. Since aggregate demand was determined by income, if wages (or income) fell, it was natural to expect a decline in spending. Decreases in consumption and investment spending set off, in turn, another decline in income and jobs. Thus, where the classical economists predicted more employment as wages (incomes) fell, Keynes showed why unemployment increased and income declined through the multiplier effect.

When the economy of the early 1930s showed no signs of improvement, the classical economists called for patience, arguing that more time was needed for falling wages and prices to provide the necessary incentives to hire and spend. Keynes, on the other hand, said that further declines in wages would only aggravate the job picture. Instead of returning to full employment, the economy could stall indefinitely at an equilibrium level of income with high unemployment. Unlike classical economists, who were content with a so-called *policy of watchful waiting*, Keynes promoted an active role for government—large increases in spending in order to counteract declining or inadequate private spending. Only via deficit spending, in which the federal government spent more than it taxed, would the economy recover from its prolonged slump.

The classical-Keynesian debate of the 1930s was waged primarily by academicians, for the principal policy idea of Keynesian economics, pump priming, was already being practiced by President Roosevelt and other nation's leaders.[1] But even Roosevelt's New Deal programs proved to be insufficient stimulus to shock the U.S. economy out of depression. Nonetheless, the Keynesian prescription still proved to be the proper medicine for the ailing economy. Unfortunately, it took a world war to trigger the amount of spending necessary to end the Depression and sustain a high level of employment.

The Keynesian Revolution

Keynesian economics is a label applied to economists and policymakers who believe in the essential logic of the income-expenditures model and the need for fine-tuning the economy.

The 20-odd years from the passage of the Employment Act of 1946 to the late 1960s was the era of **Keynesian economics.** Classical economics passed away under its own inertia, replaced by an activist Keynesian formula. With the postwar legislative mandate to pursue economic growth, full employment, and price stability, and armed with the policy tools to fine-tune the economy, the practices of Keynesian demand management reached their heyday in the Kennedy-Johnson years.

The label *Keynesian* is applied to economists and policymakers who believe in the essential logic of the income-expenditures model and the need for fine-tuning the economy. Their convictions that Keynesian economics provided the correct explanation of events was reinforced numerous times, by the failure of classical economics, and by the positive success of fine-tuning policies. But perhaps as important was a growing body of research that reinforced fine-tuning practices by showing the

---

[1] *Pump priming* was the term used during the Great Depression to describe the stimulus to the economy provided by increased government spending.

relationships between the critical macroeconomic variables—unemployment, inflation, and economic growth.

Still, a recurring and perplexing economic relationship is how unemployment varies with output and how each of these variables affects and is affected by inflation. As we saw in the previous chapter, the Phillips curve seemed to provide a trade-off between unemployment and inflation. Part of the logic behind this relationship is traced to the linkage between unemployment and real GNP, a subject about which much economic research has been devoted.

In the early 1960s Arthur Okun, a strong advocate of Keynesian economics and member of President Kennedy's Council of Economic Advisors, discovered an important and seemingly stable relationship between the nation's potential output, its actual real output, and the unemployment rate. Okun found that for every percentage point by which the growth of actual real ouput (real GNP) exceeded the potential growth rate (considered to be roughly 3 percent), the unemployment rate would fall by one third of a percent.[2] This relationship is called **Okun's law.** It means that if real GNP increased at a 6 percent rate, the unemployment rate would decline by one percentage point (e.g., from 7 percent to 6 percent). Conversely, if there was no change in real GNP, then unemployment would increase by one percentage point. (With real GNP growth equal to zero and the economy operating beneath its potential growth, firms would lay off workers, and new labor force entrants would find it harder to find jobs.)[3]

Okun's law *states that for every percentage point by which the growth of actual real output exceeded the potential growth rate, the unemployment rate would fall by one third of a percent.*

THINKING IT THROUGH

What would happen to the rate of unemployment if the real GNP growth equalled the potential GNP growth (3 percent)? Why?

Okun's law and the Phillips curve, together with improved statistical measurements and sophisticated computer models of the economy, combined to create a confidence in managing aggregate demand. And no

---

[2] The potential growth of the U.S. economy is calculated by multiplying the percentage increase in the labor force times a productivity index. The growth rate of potential GNP has averaged about 3 percent in the post-World War II period.

[3] It should be pointed out that Okun's law is probably a misnomer and more correctly might be called Okun's tendency. While the relationship between changes in unemployment and the difference between real and potential output is important, the relationship is not so precise as Okun originally observed. The relationship holds far better over extended time periods, such as 5 or 10 years, than it does from one year to the next.

economic policy better exemplifies Keynesian economics than the 1964 tax cut. As the following CASE-IN-POINT illustrates, all of the projections came true; everything conformed to the Keynesian model.

CASE
· IN ·
POINT

The Acid Test

The 1964 tax cut is an excellent example of Keynesian economics at work. Indeed, it has been called the *textbook tax cut*. Kennedy's economic advisors estimated the size of the GNP gap, identified the tax and expenditures multipliers, and proposed a combination of tax cuts and increased spending to close the gap. The tax cut was enacted in early 1964, and by mid-1965, the GNP gap was nearly closed.

Although considered a major success at economic stabilization, the tax cut also underscored the highly political nature of economic policy. Originally proposed in early 1963, President Kennedy did not live to see its passage. It took an orchestrated marketing effort, led by the chairman of the Council of Economic Advisors Walter Heller, to persuade prominent congressional leaders that a tax cut today would generate more revenue within a year or two. He explained that automatic stabilizers had generated the increased deficits, and a discretionary fiscal policy to increase the deficit further would only be temporary. In other words, Heller had to educate the Congress and the public to the multiplier process. By cutting taxes, Heller explained, households would receive additional income. According to Keynes' marginal propensity to consume, households would spend a large portion of their extra income. As more was spent on new goods and services, businesses would increase production, hire more workers, and increase investment in plant and equipment. Within a short time, the economy would be back to full employment, and the deficit would be erased. This also worked as planned.

Questions to Consider

1. *"A tax cut which reduces tax receipts today will increase tax revenue to-morrow." Explain this logic in detail.*

2. *Using a marginal propensity to consume of two thirds, and assuming that taxes were cut by $12 billion, illustrate the multiplier effect in a table or graph. (Hint: To keep things simple, use the lump-sum tax multiplier, that is, one less than the expenditures multiplier and negative.)*

Challenges to Keynesian Economics

As soon as the celebration ended, the critics took aim. On top of an economy moving rapidly toward full employment, the Johnson administration embarked upon an undeclared war in Vietnam. Government spending rose, and, within a brief 18 months, the specter of inflation appeared. Johnson, as the critics properly noted, was not following the Keynesian formula. In other words, once the economy had reached its full-employment potential, further (new) spending would only aggravate inflation and provide little if any gains in employment and private sector output. It was a classic case of demand-pull inflation.

Increasingly, economists of the Keynesian stripe came under fire from monetarists, supply-siders, and the new classical economists. Further attempts to fine-tune the economy had only marginal success at economic stabilization.[4] Indeed, as we discussed in the previous chapter, years of high-employment deficit spending produced an economy with a strong inflationary bias. The inflationary momentum lasted more than a decade, from the late 60s to the early 80s, and ended only after a recession engineered by the Fed produced post-Depression-high unemployment rates. In order to understand the failures of Keynesian economics, we need to examine the emerging macroeconomic theories challenging Keynesian theory.

Monetarism

If the fine-tuning Keynesian activists see the economy as a television set requiring regular adjustments, the monetarists envision the economy as a perpetual clock. Once set in motion, it needs no further adjustments. Closely akin to the classical economists, monetarists believe in the free market model. Assuming limited government intervention, the private market forces of supply and demand will provide for the optimum welfare of all parties.

Monetarism may be summarized in three basic propositions. First and foremost is the strong conviction that all inflations are caused by increases in the money supply in excess of the underlying real growth rate of the economy. Any monetary policy which stimulates the real growth of the economy beyond its natural rate (estimated at 3 to 4 percent) will be inflationary. Moreover, even if the *initial* effect of an expansionary monetary policy (e.g., buying bonds), is increased output, the ultimate result will be a higher price level and a return to the natural rate of unemployment.

This proposition, that inflation results from increases in *M1*, is derived from the equation of exchange ($MV \equiv PQ$). By assuming that the velocity of money is stable or constant and that the tendency of the economy is toward the natural rate of output at full employment, the monetarists effectively eliminate velocity and real GNP (V and Q) from

Monetarism is a body of economic thought consisting of three basic ideas: (1) all inflations are caused by increases in the money supply in excess of the underlying real growth rate of the economy; (2) activist discretionary fiscal and monetary policy is at best ineffective and likely to be destabilizing; and (3) monetary policy affects GNP directly.

---

[4] Examples include, among others, the 1968 surtax, the expansionary fiscal policy with wage and price controls still in place, the 1975 tax rebate, and federal-funds-rate-targeted monetary policies.

the equation; thus, any change in *M1* is automatically and fully reflected in the price level.

Milton Friedman, the father of modern monetarism, and several key research centers at the University of Chicago, the University of California at Los Angeles, and the Federal Reserve Banks of St. Louis and Los Angeles, have produced a significant amount of evidence showing the historical relationship between increases in the money supply and inflation. As Figure 18–1 illustrates, inflation rates generally have increased with increases in *M1*, albeit with a six- or nine-month lag.

In the mid-1980s, however, monetarists were surprised to see the relationship between the money supply and inflation evaporate. The rate of inflation declined in 1985 and 1986 despite significant increases in *M1* (12.5 percent and 16.5 percent, respectively). In spite of the monetarists' belief that excessive increases in the money supply *always* cause

FIGURE 18–1   Money and Inflation, 1960–1987

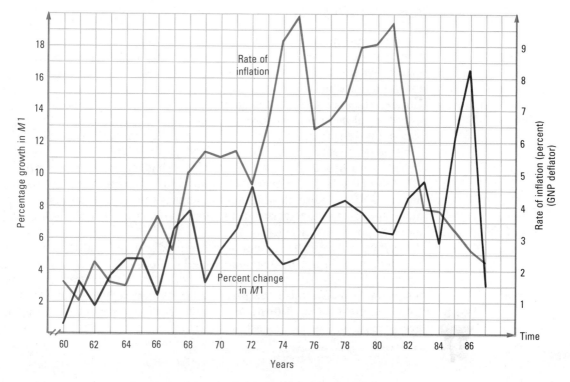

Although inflation and changes in the money supply generally exhibit a relatively stable direct relationship (with a six- to nine-month lag) in the 1960s and 1970s, the 1980s represent a serious break with the past. Despite large increases in *M1* in 1984 and 1985, for example, the rate of inflation continued to decline.

inflation, and that inflation is caused *only* by increases in the money supply, it appears that there is strong evidence to the contrary.

A second proposition is that activist discretionary fiscal and monetary policy is at best ineffective and likely to be destabilizing. As the monetarists see it, not only does economic policy act with long recognition, administrative, and impact lags, but policymakers have neither reliable data nor accurate forecasts upon which to base their policy decisions. The upshot is that the policy is often inappropriate, even harmful, by the time it takes effect. For example, shortly after the United States escalated its involvement in Vietnam, it became clear that inflationary pressure was mounting. In 1966, President Johnson's economic advisors urged him to increase taxes in order to reduce aggregate demand and sop up some of the inflationary purchasing power. After all, the Keynesian formula called for exactly this kind of contracyclical policy. But not until early 1967 did President Johnson finally decide to heed the advice, and it took another 12 months for the 1968 surtax bill to clear committee in the House of Representatives.

What happened along the way, from the president's proposal to Congress' disposal, vividly illustrates the monetarist criticism of fine-tuning. First was the bitter political infighting over the tax hike. Wilbur Mills, the powerful chairman of the House Ways and Means Committee, essentially locked up the bill in committee. Mills wanted cuts in spending to match the tax hike, dollar for dollar. The other criticism involves the inherent problem of policy lags. Desperately needed in 1967 (or even earlier), the need to reduce spending was even greater in 1968. However, as is typical in such legislative matters, the final bill contained the same surtax (in dollars) that the 1967 proposal called for. In other words, the 1968 surtax was too little, too late.

The third proposition of monetarism is that monetary policy affects GNP directly. Unlike Keynesians, who argue that the only way money affects GNP is indirectly through the impact of interest rates on investment spending, monetarists claim that if *M1* rises, people will spend more on goods and services.

Keynes believed that money was essentially a veil and that the only way increases in the money supply could affect GNP was through the financial markets. An expansionary monetary policy like buying bonds, for example, *might* raise the price of bonds and reduce interest rates. Lower interest rates, in turn, *may* lead to more investment spending (as firms responded to lower costs of borrowing money). More investment spending would give rise to a multiplied increase in GNP.[5]

---

[5] The use of modifiers here, such as *may* and *might,* are in keeping with Keynes' conviction that monetary policy was completely ineffective under conditions of severe unemployment. Keynes surmised that even if monetary policy brought about lower interest rates, such rates still might not induce more investment. He argued that sales

The monetarists assert that the money supply-interest rate-investment-GNP transmission linkage is too limited. Instead of focusing exclusively on the bond market, the monetarists argue that people hold a diverse portfolio of assets, such as stocks, real estate, collectibles, and a wide range of durable goods. An excess supply of money will thus cause people to increase spending on both financial and nonfinancial goods. More money in circulation will lead directly to increased nominal GNP because people have excess money balances.

Reservations.   If you are wondering how a larger *M1* will cause people to buy a refrigerator or a bicycle, you are in good company. Many economists have serious doubts about monetarism, especially how people obtain the funds to spend on real goods. In other words, the basic issue is how a bond purchase by the Fed will cause or enable you to increase spending without borrowing money.

One possible answer is that investors (in bonds and other financial assets) find that the expansionary monetary policy has increased their real wealth. That is, the value of their assets may increase as a direct result of the Fed's action. Simply stated, this **wealth effect** states that if you feel wealthier, you will spend more money. A concrete example may help. Assume that you purchased $10,000 worth of bonds last year (e.g., 10 bonds at $1,000 per bond). Then the Fed engages in open market purchases. This means that the demand for bonds increases relative to the supply, and bond prices rise. The price of the bond you bought last year is now $1,100. Your net worth is now $11,000, 10 percent more. With this increased wealth, you may feel wealthier and thus increase spending on real goods and services (e.g., a compact disc player or a long-postponed vacation). Of course, the monetarists would argue that the same phenomenon occurs in the stock market, in real estate, and so forth, in which investors are wealthier *on paper*. The irony of this explanation is that Keynes, the arch rival of the monetarists, placed primary emphasis on expectations—the very linchpin of the foregoing argument.

Wealth effect *states that if you feel wealthier, you will increase consumption.*

The Theory of Rational Expectations

An alternative explanation is offered by a group of economists known as **rational expectationists.** They argue that people make decisions based upon a continuous flow of information and derived expectations. Unlike their classical forefathers, the rational expectationists deny the existence of perfect information; thus, people must make decisions even

Rational expectationists *are economists who argue that consumers, businesses, and other economic decision makers make decisions based upon a continuous flow of information and derived expectations.*

and profits expectations were far more important as determinants of spending on capital goods and plant expansions. Investment, in other words, is likely to be very interest-inelastic in such circumstances; that is, it would take major changes in interest rates to coax even a small increase in investment.

if they lack good information. Indeed, imperfect information is a basic assumption of the theory. However, news that the money supply has increased at a 14 percent annual rate, for example, implies that inflation will increase, thus leading people to increase spending before prices rise again. Then, contrary to the Keynesian view of monetary policy, interest rates need not fall in order for a rise in the money stock to stimulate increased spending.

Developed in the early 1960s by James Muth, and refined by economists Robert Barro, Robert Lucas, and Thomas Sargent, the **theory of rational expectations** has grown in acceptance. Its chief proposition is that people are always thinking about the future. They form their expectations based not only upon past and present events, but upon a careful analysis of current policy and policy pronouncements made by influential governmental leaders. The theory does not require that such expectations are correct, only that people act in their self-interest by anticipating policy decisions. The theory does imply that people will not be fooled or surprised by anticipated governmental policy decisions. Let's see how this works.

For comparison purposes, let's assume that most people think that the rate of inflation next year will be the same as the inflation rate last year; that is, they form expectations for the future by adapting to their immediate past experiences. Thus, if inflation increases at a 4 percent rate this year, most people assume that inflation will continue at 4 percent next year. In this view, people will ignore or be unaware of public pronouncements regarding economic policy. Even if the Fed's chairman reports to Congress his intention to reduce inflationary pressure, as reported in the business press, most people will still assume inflation will continue at 4 percent. What are the consequences of this adaptive expectations process?

If the Fed adopts restrictive monetary policies in order to restrain inflation, interest rates will rise, and investment spending will decrease. As sales decline, business will lay off workers, close plants, and postpone major investment projects.[6] Those households expecting more inflation, however, continue to spend in anticipation of higher prices. Some may even take out home improvement loans. When the monetary crunch hits, some household members will receive layoff notices. If these same households have assumed loans and/or bought more goods, they will face tough times ahead. Without regular income and with less savings and greater debt, many households may even experience bankruptcy.

Theory of rational expectations *says that people are always thinking about the future and therefore form their expectations upon a careful analysis of current policy and policy pronouncements made by influential government leaders.*

---

[6] Note that this is a Keynesian interpretation. Although most economists subscribe to this transmission mechanism, monetarists would argue that the restrictive monetary policy will reduce *M1*, and, with less money balances available, people will reduce spending.

Rational expectationists paint a different picture. Businesses and consumers do not necessarily expect future inflation to be the same as last year's. Attentive to current policy initiatives, they would anticipate a business slump or major recession in response to a restrictive monetary policy. In turn, they would tighten their belts and, in a self-fulfilling prophecy, usher in the very economic downturn which they foresee. The only salvation is that they have not taken out loans or increased spending on consumer goods. The result may be the same (or worse), but households and businesses are less inclined to experience insolvency.

Supply-Side Economics

Supply-side economics *places primary emphasis on aggregate supply and the incentives necessary to increase saving, investment, and productivity.*

Closely akin to pre-Keynesian economics, **supply-side economics** places primary emphasis on aggregate supply and the incentives necessary to increase saving, investment, and productivity. In the spirit of "turnabout being fair play," just as Keynes repudiated much of classical economics, the new supply-side economists completely reject the central Keynesian idea that demand creates its own supply. Supply-side economics grew in popularity during the 1970s and 1980s as the traditional remedies of Keynesian economics failed to extricate the U.S. economy from its years of double-digit inflation, sluggish productivity, and low real economic growth.

Supply-siders argue that the Keynesian explanation of the Great Depression, inadequate aggregate demand, completely overlooked the obvious. Agreeing with the basic tenets of classical economists, the new supply-side economists insist that the alleged chronic instability of the economy and lack of aggregate demand were not the causes of the Depression. Rather, according to economic consultant Norman Ture, it was "an ill-conceived series of government actions [that] both precipitated the downturn and impeded the recovery: the tariff wars of the 1930s, a series of punitive tax hikes, a huge drop in the money supply, and antisupply measures such as the deliberate destruction of agricultural products."[7] Thus, instead of built-in forces producing business cycles, supply-side economists see governmental interference with private decision making as the chief source of economic instability. Remove the visible hand of government, so the supply-siders argue, and the economy will perform more efficiently and at a higher level of prosperity.

Supply-side economics consists of three main propositions. The first and most important prescription is that large and permanent cuts in personal and corporate taxes will stimulate increased saving and invest-

---

[7] From "A Guide to Supply-Side Economics," *Business Week*, December 22, 1980; quoted in Martin N. Baily and Arthur M. Okun, *The Battle against Unemployment and Inflation*, 3rd ed., (New York: W. W. Norton & Co., 1982), p. 204.

ment, greater work effort, and higher productivity. Second, it calls for a substantial reduction in the scope of government in the economy. Third, it endorses a balanced budget and a fixed monetary growth rule, and specifically rejects all forms of activist fine-tuning (discretionary fiscal and monetary policies). Let's look at each of these in turn.

The principal idea of supply-side economics is that high tax rates discourage work, saving, and investment, and thus impede the natural growth potential of the economy. Tax rates were so prohibitive in the 1960s and 1970s, say the supply-siders, that the growth of tax revenues was hampered and thus contributed to the large federal deficits. At the center of this proposition is an idea known as the **Laffer curve,** so named after Arthur Laffer, an economist at the University of Southern California. Convinced that marginal tax rates were excessive, Laffer advanced the simple truism that both zero and 100 percent tax rates would produce no tax revenue whatsoever. As Figure 18–2 shows, some marginal tax rate between these extremes would generate the optimum level of tax receipts. Believing that rates were excessive in 1979, Laffer said that by cutting taxes, the government would increase the incentive to work and save and create an environment conducive to increased business investment, production, and employment. A decline in tax rates would also increase federal tax receipts, illustrated in Figure 18–2 as a movement from point *a* to point *b*.[8]

Laffer curve *offers the simple truism that both zero and 100 percent tax rates would produce no tax revenue whatsoever, and therefore increased tax rates might erode work incentives and actually reduce tax revenue.*

If tax cuts are so beneficial, it is instructive to consider the opposite, that is, the economic effects of high or rising taxes. To supply-siders like University of Chicago economist Robert Mundell, rising taxes have such an inflationary impact that they have caused people to forgo consumption of goods and services in favor of performing the work themselves. Indeed, tax avoidance is so widespread that it is largely responsible for the growing underground economy. "Such activity," says Laffer, "not only reduces investment but, by failing to shoulder its share of the tax burden, results in higher taxes and lower incentives for the visible economy."[9]

Supply-side economics was adopted wholesale by President Reagan during his two terms of office. Strongly influenced by economists Robert Mundell, Arthur Laffer, and Paul Craig Roberts, and by Congressman Jack Kemp and Senator William Roth, the Reagan administration promoted supply-side economics at every opportunity. The capstone of

---

[8] The intuitive logic of the Laffer curve is quite appealing. However, the tax rate at which tax receipts are maximized is unknown. In other words, we have no idea if we have exceeded the rate that generates the greatest receipts.

[9] Baily & Okun, *The Battle against Unemployment and Inflation,* p. 205.

FIGURE 18–2
The Laffer Curve

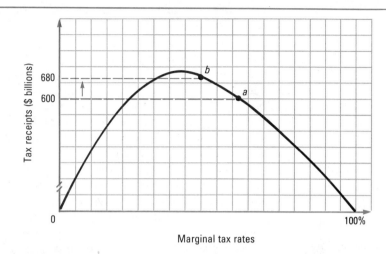

Laffer hypothesized that both zero and 100 percent marginal tax rates would yield no tax revenue. Assuming that tax rates were excessive at point *a*, he said that the government would increase tax receipts and stimulate savings, work, and investment by reducing tax rates to some level like point *b*.

The **1981 Tax Recovery Act (TRA)** *cut personal income tax rates by 25 percent over three years, introduced the Individual Retirement Account, and liberalized depreciation allowances on a wide range of capital investment.*

such efforts took shape in the 1981 Tax Recovery Act and, to a lesser extent, in the 1986 Tax Reform Act.

The **1981 Tax Recovery Act (TRA)** embodied most of the supply-side prescriptions. The TRA cut personal income tax rates by 25 percent over three years, introduced the Individual Retirement Account (IRA), a tax-deferred retirement savings plan, and liberalized depreciation allowances on a wide range of capital investment. Congress even went along with a $40 billion reduction in Carter's proposed 1980 budget. And the Federal Reserve continued its policy of monetary restraint under Paul Volcker.

A second element of supply-side economics is the primacy of free enterprise and a reaffirmation of the classical belief in the efficiency of the private market forces of supply and demand. As such, most of the supply-siders remain committed to reducing the scope of government, especially its regulatory activities in industries such as transportation, banking, and agriculture, and in general socioeconomic regulation of areas that cut across industry lines, such as consumer product safety, natural resources and environmental quality, and occupational health and safety. Supply-siders argue that such regulations unnecessarily raise costs of production and reduce productivity, thereby causing inflation, unemployment, and lower economic growth. Despite diminished competition after the flurry of mergers in the airline industry, the supply-siders like to cite the benefits derived from deregulation, such as improved operating efficiency, lower prices, and increased service.

The third proposition of supply-side economics is a wholesale rejection of all fine-tuning policies in favor of a balanced budget and a fixed money-supply growth rule. Supply-siders see all discretionary fiscal and monetary policies as destabilizing, essentially doing more harm than good. For example, tax cuts, increased spending, and expansionary monetary policies may produce increased employment and production in the short run, but along with these gains comes a higher rate of inflation. Policymakers then decide to step on the fiscal and monetary brakes in order to cool off the economy. This action succeeds in reducing inflation, to be sure, but only at the expense of reduced output and more unemployment. The government's actions are thus responsible for the excessive volatility of the business cycle, not any inherent tendencies of free market capitalism.

*The **1986 Tax Reform Act** made a base overhaul of the tax system, lowered tax rates, and collapsed the previous 14 tax brackets into 3 income brackets.*

The **1986 Tax Reform Act** made a basic overhaul of the tax system, most of which took full effect in 1988. Its chief supply-side feature was a dramatic restructuring of tax brackets. It lowered tax rates and collapsed the previous 14 tax brackets into 3 income brackets. (The new tax rates are 15 percent, 28 percent, and 33 percent.) It also raised the standard deduction, increased the personal exemption, and repealed the deduction for personal interest and state and local sales taxes.

Although this was claimed by the Reagan administration to be a major tax simplification as well as a total overhaul of the tax system, nearly all tax accountants were dumbfounded by the complexity of language, the proliferation of new forms, and the ambiguity of many provisions. The tax bill also purported to increase the fairness of the tax system by removing tax shelters, reducing tax rates, and taking low-income recipients off the tax rolls. However, since payroll taxes increased and most taxpayers wound up owing more state taxes, the average tax rate for many Americans actually increased.

Perhaps worse still is its inherent antisupply-side features. Because the tax reform repeals the IRA deduction for a large segment of households, eliminates the investment tax credit, now treats capital gains as regular income, and eliminates the dividend exclusion, many analysts think the effect will be to discourage saving, thwart investment, and hamper productivity growth. For the short term, foreign investment in the United States has compensated for the lack of domestic saving. But the willingness of foreigners to pump money into the U.S. economy is largely a function of a weak dollar and higher real (and relative) interest rates. Neither of these is desirable for sustained long-term growth.

Was the supply-side experiment successful? Did the Reagan revolution really perform the economic miracles claimed by the administration? As John Pisciotta argues in the following CASE-IN-POINT, Reaganomics worked, but not for the reasons supply-siders think.

CASE
• IN •
POINT

Reaganomics Worked—But Why?

Recovery from the [1981–1982] recession began in [late] 1982. The delayed demand-side effects of the 1981 tax cut, an easing of monetary policy, and improved expectations about the future combined to boost demand without rekindling inflation. By 1984 (the end of Reagan's first term), growth was robust, unemployment had started downward, nominal interest rates had fallen, and inflation remained in check. Only the deficit had failed to perform according to the Reagan script.

While growth slowed in the second term, continued increases in GNP meant that by the end of 1987 the economy had enjoyed 61 months of continuous expansion, the longest period of peacetime expansion since the 1920s. The unemployment rate [fell to] 5.7 percent [in February 1988], the lowest since 1979. The deficit, though, remains a serious problem.

Increased growth, lower unemployment, lower inflation—but a higher deficit. Three out of four ain't bad. Was the impressive performance of the 1980s a triumph of supply-side economics? My own view is that it was the demand-side of Reaganomics and Federal Reserve policy that prevailed.

Reaganomics worked. But it worked through its effects on aggregate income—not as a result of some supply-side miracle. [Indeed,] the experience of Reaganomics can be likened to a football team calling a pass to its wide receiver on the last play of the game. The pass is tossed, but tipped by the wide receiver into the hands of the team's tight end—who takes the ball in for the winning touchdown. Jubilant fans scream their approval. The play didn't work according to plan. But it worked nonetheless.[10]

Questions to Consider

1. Besides Reagan's campaign promise to reduce the scope of government in our lives, the main element of Reaganomics was a 25 percent cut in personal income taxes. Was this the main reason for the failure to balance the budget, one of his chief goals? Looking back to Figure 17–2, does this mean that the U.S. economy was really positioned somewhere on the rising portion of the Laffer curve? Why or why not?

2. Pisciotta plainly rejects any supply-side miracle in favor of the traditional Keynesian demand-side multiplier process. Which do you think is the better explanation? Why?

---

[10] Excerpted from a longer article: John Pisciotta, "Reaganomics Worked—But Why?" *The Margin* 3, no. 7 (The University of Colorado, March 1988), p. 18.

THE MODERN POLICY DEBATE

Fifty years ago, the economics profession was caught up in a debate between classical economists who argued that economic downturns would take care of themselves and upstart Keynesians who argued government was needed to fix them. Today, a new generation of economists is locked in a debate between Keynesians who are used to fixing things and upstart *new classical economists* who don't think there's anything to fix.[11]

New classical economics *is a loose confederation of monetarists, supply-siders, and rational expectationists that share a wholesale rejection of Keynesian economics.*

The **new classical economics** is a loose confederation of monetarists, supply-siders, and rational expectationists. Nearly all share a strong conviction that excessive governmental regulation is undesirable, if not because such actions raise costs of production and generally distort decision making, then because of a strong preference for free market economies. In addition to this laissez-faire common ground, these economic factions also favor balanced budgets, monetary rules (such as a 3 to 4 percent growth rate in *M1* per year), and a complete rejection of all discretionary economic policy. Although they part company on finer points, they all share a wholesale rejection of Keynesian economics. In order to get a better understanding of the differences in theory and policy between the Keynesians and new classical economists, we need to examine the the nature of the policy debate.

Keynesian Economics versus New Classical Economics

We may start by observing the obvious: Keynesians prefer discretionary policy (or fine-tuning), and the new classical economists believe in policy rules. But perhaps the best way to describe the differences between these competing macroeconomic perspectives is to understand how each group explains a business cycle downturn.

Stickiness *refers to the age-old issue of wage (and price) flexibility.*

The chief theoretical difference of opinion separating the two camps is over wage and price flexibility, an issue referred to as **stickiness.** Keynesians argue that wages and prices are highly rigid, especially downward, because of institutional rigidities such as large corporations that resist price-cutting and unions that fight against wage cuts. In the face of restrictive monetary policy, for example, Keynesians claim that a smaller money supply will mean higher interest rates, less investment spending, and reduced demand for labor. Union contracts prevent the natural market forces from decreasing wages, and oligopolies will resist price-cutting in favor of cost-cutting measures such as plant closings and

---

[11] Timothy Tregarthen, "Economic Ups and Downs: New Attempts to Explain an Age-Old Problem," *The Margin* 3, no. 6 (The University of Colorado, February 1988), p. 4.

layoffs. The upshot is that real wages will remain too high, and there will be a significant amount of involuntary unemployment.

Keynesians think that it is undesirable to wait for a so-called natural full-employment equilibrium to be restored, since undue hardship would be experienced as millions of additional people would become jobless before the economy turned around naturally. Unwilling to wait for the cycle to bottom out and turn upward, Keynesians advocate various fine-tuning policies to accelerate the recovery.

THINKING IT THROUGH

Situation: You are economic advisor to the president, and you are a dyed-in-the-wool Keynesian. What specific fiscal and monetary policies would you recommend to stimulate a recovery? What downside effects may occur?

The new classical economists see things in a different light. Instead of a demand-side origin to the slump, recessions always begin on the supply side. A slump or business downturn may begin, for example, with some change in technology that causes a decrease in productivity.[12] Any event that makes firms less productive will affect aggregate supply. For example, the oil embargo of the early 1970s reduced the quantity of oil available, causing firms to cut production and lay off workers. This decline in demand for labor reduces real wages and consumption and causes firms to scale back on their investment plans. As loan demand shrinks, and the volume of outstanding loans falls, the supply of money declines. As the money supply falls, prices and wages will decline (in time) far enough to keep the real money supply the same. The upshot is the economy will return automatically to its full employment equilibrium.[13]

New classical economists thus believe, as did their 19th- and early-20th-century intellectual mentors, that wages and prices are fully flexible. Moreover, they place primary emphasis on real economic variables,

---

[12] The impact of trade wars is an especially appropriate alternative scenario given the debate over protectionism in the 1988 presidential election campaign. A protectionist tariff, for example, is likely to cause retaliatory actions by other countries, leading to a reduction in exports and a decline in production.

[13] Another example of a supply shock occurred during the spring and summer of 1988, when the United States experienced a severe drought. Many analysts claimed that it was worse than the Dustbowl of the 1930s, and by some estimates it was the worst drought in 100 years. Fears of stunted crops and vastly reduced harvests sent commodity prices soaring. Soybean, corn, and wheat prices jumped by as much as 50 percent in a few months on the expectation that a severe shortage was imminent.

such as real wages and the real money supply (nominal values adjusted for price level changes). Because employers are likely to be very aware of changes in real values, they make hiring and firing decisions based upon real, not nominal, wages. Since real wages move in tandem with the business cycle, up during expansions and down during contractions, markets will always tend toward equilibrium.

To summarize the debate, we may say, "A Keynesian looks at unemployment and sees a problem that can be fixed with fiscal or monetary policy. A new classical economist looks at unemployment and yawns. Unemployed workers are simply choosing leisure."[14]

ALTERNATIVE STABILIZATION POLICIES

Even when conventional Keynesian or new classical economic policies are working according to plan, economists still seek innovative ways to improve upon stabilization policies. Because many ideas are political hot potatoes, they are not entertained seriously by legislative bodies. Many have received consideration, however, and it is these to which we now turn.

Reducing Inflation

If there is one lesson economists and policymakers have learned from inflation, it is that we should never let it get started in the first place. Knowing this is of little value, however, since economists do not make economic policy—thankfully, to some. Political pressures to reduce unemployment, as desirable as they may be, often have inflationary consequences. And despite successes of the new classical economics in the 1980s, policy activism appears to be the preferred political position for most lawmakers. Alternatives are clearly needed.

Tax-based incomes policies or TIPS *refer to the use of surtaxes and tax credits to penalize and reward compliance with a predetermined target of acceptable wage increases.*

Tax-Based Incomes Policies (TIPS). Perhaps the most talked-about proposal is a permanent program of **tax-based incomes policies (TIPS).** Instead of direct wage and price controls, TIPS would use surtaxes and tax credits to penalize and reward compliance with a predetermined target of acceptable wage increases.

The basis for TIPS is that most inflation is wage based. Since labor compensation consistently amounts to about 75 percent of national income, the underlying inflation rate (unit labor costs) cannot be reduced without moderating wage gains. Of course, productivity figures prominently in inflation as well, since unit labor costs are the difference be-

---

[14] Tregarthen, "Economic Ups and Downs: New Attempts to Explain an Age-Old Problem."

tween percentage changes in wages and productivity. For example, if the average wage gain is 5 percent and productivity gains average about 2 percent, then the average unit labor cost increase is 3 percent. If productivity gains rise to 3 percent, however, the wage-induced inflationary pressure is reduced. Productivity gains are thus important in the battle against inflation.

Although there are many variations, in its simplest form, TIPS would apply a surcharge on companies' tax liability if they grant wage increases in excess of the government target. Similarly, if firms hold wage gains below the target, companies would be eligible for a tax credit. Employee incentives would work in a similar way. If wage gains exceed the target, a surtax would be levied. If wage gains were less than the target, employees would receive a tax credit. During inflationary periods, such tax credits could even be put into a national trust fund. If a recession occurred and the economy needed the fiscal stimulus, such deferred compensation could be paid out to workers immediately via the withholding system.

The purpose of TIPS, much like a 55-MPH speed limit, is not to raise revenue. The idea is restraint and to keep people from hurting themselves. The advantage of TIPS is that it uses market forces instead of mandatory controls without any incentives. As with any such major economic policy, however, whether labor or management or Congress would ever approve of such a plan remains to be seen.

Balanced Budgets.   Many economists believe that fine-tuning efforts do more harm than good. They advocate instead balancing the federal budget annually in order to restrain inflation. Unlike less extreme proposals to have a cyclically balanced budget, the new classical economists feel that the only way to prevent undisciplined federal spending is through a constitutional amendment to balance the budget.

As desirable as this appears on the surface, there is a serious flaw in any mandate to balance the budget. What would happen, for example, as the economy slides into a recession? The automatic stabilizers would send the budget into deficit as tax receipts fall and transfer payments increase. To balance the budget would require that the government raise taxes and/or cut spending. Both of these pro-cyclical measures would greatly exacerbate the recession and possibly produce a depression. It thus remains a mystery why balanced budget advocates ignore these downside effects. Could it be a strong preference for limited government driving such ideas?

Lowering Unemployment

The most important agenda for many policy activists is to allocate resources to reduce structural and cyclical unemployment. Millions of Americans are chronically unemployed because they do not possess the education or the skills to compete in a rapidly changing labor force. Others are casualties of business reorganization, cost-cutting, efforts to improve productivity, and recessions. Although a wide variety of aid programs help to reduce the sting of unemployment, these forms of assistance are designed to provide only temporary relief. Aid to Families with Dependent Children (AFDC), food stamps, and housing subsidies notwithstanding, many observers believe that more permanent changes are needed.

Welfare versus Workfare.   Instead of supporting people to get training and jobs in order to get off welfare, most states have no systematic skill training programs connected to welfare. Indeed, most welfare programs simply distribute cash or in-kind benefits and thus actually foster dependency. This is what critics mean by the term *welfare state*.

More than 10 million people (3.7 million families with seven million children) in 1988 were supported by AFDC alone. Originally conceived in 1935 as a widow's benefit when women did not work outside the home, the program is now dominated by divorced and unwed mothers. This is indeed an anachronism in light of the fact that a majority of new mothers are at work within a year of having a child. No wonder that every president from Kennedy to Reagan has proclaimed the welfare system a national disaster.

Workfare *ties the welfare benefits received, such as AFDC, food stamps, and other assistance, to the participation in a job-training program, community service work, or a private sector job.*

Employment and Training Choices (ETC) *is a voluntary alternative to workfare.*

One viable alternative to welfare, but only for those actually capable of work, is an idea known as **workfare.** In general, workfare ties the benefits received, such as AFDC, food stamps, and other assistance, to the participation in a job-training program, community service work, or a private sector job. Although not a new idea, as practiced in Massachusetts, it holds a bright promise both for those on welfare and for the taxpayers who are funding the current welfare morass.

The workfare program in Massachusetts is called **Employment and Training Choices (ETC),** and *choices* is the key word. Unlike the other two dozen states that have a form of workfare, only the Massachusetts plan is completely voluntary. Started in 1983 under the tutelege of then-Governor Michael Dukakis, ETC's basic premise is that welfare mothers can be sold on work. The government invests heavily in an attractive array of no-dead-end job training and placement services, provides $2,500 for each participant to cover child care costs, and defrays health care and transportation costs—all designed to smooth the transition from welfare dependency to work.

ETC is also a real bargain. Although more expensive than any other workfare program (1987 costs averaged $6,300 per person placed in a job), it costs Massachusetts an average of $12,000 a year to support the typical welfare family. Such substantial savings reflect a strong job placement record. Over 45,000 welfare recipients have been placed in productive jobs with an average starting salary of $13,500 a year, about

40 percent above the poverty line. "The thing about ETC that's fascinating," says the Massachusetts Secretary for Human Services, "is that there's a waiting list of women who want [to join the program]. ETC by itself has demolished a lot of the mythology about welfare mothers—that they're lazy, shiftless, blah, blah, blah . . . We've learned that most people want to work, that they define themselves by what they do, and that if they're not doing anything, their problems . . . [are] exacerbated."[15] The ETC program in Massachusetts may not serve as a model for the nation, but it holds the real promise of helping thousands of families to become productive and independent.

Other Measures. Many other innovative proposals to lower unemployment have been offered. One idea advanced to reduce joblessness (especially the frictional variety) is a *national job bank.* Employers and job-seekers would register with the service, listing job requirements and worker characteristics. Its utter simplicity is very appealing, especially with the ability to match applicants against job openings with high speed computers. Implementation has been stalled for more than two decades, however, because of First Amendment freedom and privacy issues.

One especially troubling policy issue is the extent to which aid for the jobless actually creates more unemployment. For years, economists have argued that unemployment insurance enables the jobless to take more time searching for new jobs. Although such payroll-tax-financed assistance amounts to only one third to one half of a worker's gross pay, the benefits are tax exempt. The real benefits thus come close to fully replacing the workers' aftertax wages. Economist and former White House advisor Martin Feldstein has estimated that the current unemployment insurance system adds as much as 1.25 percentage points to the total unemployment rate. He proposes that some of the disincentive effect can be removed by taxing unemployment benefits as regular income. Canada currently does so, although benefits were raised sharply to offset the taxes.[16] Needless to say, this is an extremely controversial proposal, much like repealing minimum wage legislation.

More controversial still are proposals to reduce the workweek from 40 to 35 hours, modify social security laws to remove penalties for early retirement, reduce unnecessarily strict union apprenticeship programs, and increase years of compulsory education from 16 years to 17 years. Each of these carries obvious and hidden defects. For example, a man-

---

[15] "Workfare Program in Massachusetts Praised, Doubted." *St. Louis Post-Dispatch,* May 29, 1988.

[16] "Does Aid for the Jobless Create More Jobless?" *Business Week,* November 17, 1985, pp. 142–148; and *Doing Business in Canada* (New York: Price Waterhouse, Inc., 1985), p. 19.

datory reduction in the workweek to 35 hours has the inflationary effect of increasing wages by 14 percent. Moreover, would workers really be willing to take a 14 percent pay cut to spread the work around?

The important point to be made about these and other ideas to reduce unemployment is that continued search for aid to the jobless is both necessary and desirable. After all, the Employment Act and the Humphrey-Hawkins amendment have made full employment the centerpiece of national economic policy.

IMPORTANT TERMS TO REMEMBER

classical economics, p. 506
economic stabilization, p. 505
Employment and Training Choices (ETC), p. 524
Keynesian economics, p. 507
Laffer curve, p. 516
monetarism, p. 510
new classical economics, p. 520
noninterventionists, p. 505
Okun's law, p. 508
policy activists, p. 505

rational expectationists, p. 513
stickiness, p. 520
supply-side economics, p. 515
tax-based incomes policies (TIPS), p. 522
1981 Tax Recovery Act, p. 517
1986 Tax Reform Act, p. 518
theory of rational expectations, p. 514
wealth effect, p. 513
workfare, p. 524

CHAPTER SUMMARY

1. Economic stabilization refers to fiscal and monetary policies designed to smooth out or eliminate the fluctuations in the business cycle.

2. Classical economics, like its modern new classical counterpart, is based upon a belief in limited government and the primacy of the marketplace. Latter-day new classical economists believe that government intervention is destabilizing and harmful to the economy.

3. Keynesian economists believe in the need to use discretionary fiscal and monetary policies to address problems of inflation and recession: tax cuts and increased government spending to stimulate the economy, and tax increases and cuts in spending to halt inflationary momentum.

4. Okun's law states that for every percentage point by which actual real GNP differed from the potential real growth, the unemployment rate would change by one third of a percentage point.

5. Monetarism is the school of thought that advocates a fixed growth in the money supply to stabilize the economy. Monetarists believe that Keynesian fine-tuning is destabilizing.

6. Rational expectationists believe that fiscal and monetary policies may be completely ineffective if people anticipate those policies. They argue that people are rational decision makers and thus are informed about events which affect their lives.

7. Supply-side economics, often called *Reaganomics* because President Reagan was so receptive to its basic programs, rejects the Keynesian demand-side interpretation of business cycles. It emphasizes the impor-

tance of work, saving, and investment incentives in order to stimulate productivity and economic growth and to reduce inflation. All cyclical movements are traced to the supply side, caused by changes in business productivity.

8. The Laffer curve, a supply-side proposition, shows the relationship between tax rates and tax receipts and indicates that by reducing tax rates the government will increase tax revenue.

9. Tax-based incomes policies (TIPS) is an idea to control inflation. It consists of two parts: to tax corporations and wage-earners if wage gains are excessive and to grant tax credits if wage gains are beneath the target wage increases.

10. A constitutionally balanced budget is another idea to control inflation by restraining government spending. Its chief problem is that it is likely to be destabilizing.

11. Welfare, a Depression-born program designed to provide relief to widows, has become a national disgrace. Workfare, a variation of welfare, is currently practiced by nearly half the states. It is a mandatory program by which recipients of aid must either participate in job-training or do community service work. The Employment and Training Choices (ETC) program in Massachusetts is completely voluntary. It assumes that people want to work, but must be given the necessary support to make the transition from welfare dependency to work.

DISCUSSION AND REVIEW QUESTIONS

1. Evaluate the following statement. "Supply-side economics is little more than old wine in new bottles. It is merely a resurrection of classical economics, and Keynes permanently buried those arcane ideas."

2. Concerning policy activism, answer the following:
   a. What is the case for policy activism? Describe the specific policies by which Keynesian activists would promote economic stabilization.
   b. What is the case for nonintervention? What arguments are raised by monetarists, rational expectationists, and supply-siders against policy activism?

3. Did Reaganomics achieve economic stabilization? Evaluate the pros and cons of the 1981 Tax Recovery Act and the 1986 Tax Reform Act.

4. "A Keynesian looks at unemployment and sees a problem that can be fixed with fiscal or monetary policy. A new classical economist looks at unemployment and yawns." Explain the differences between these two schools of economics regarding economic stabilization.

5. "Rather than attacking Keynesian economics for its failure to contend satisfactorily with stagflation, we should be looking for the real culprit— the lawmakers who rarely have followed the basic Keynesian formula in a timely fashion. If legislators and presidents had the fortitude to restrict inflationary tendencies through tax hikes and spending cuts as readily as they have to stimulate the economy with tax cuts and increased spending, the monetarist, rational expectationist, and supply-side critics would be swiftly silenced." Please comment.

6. Following up on the previous question, is it reasonable to expect the federal government to make economic policy in a timely fashion? In other words, is it likely to reduce or eliminate the recognition and administrative policy lags? If not, does that strengthen the case for new classical economics? Why or why not?

7. The Employment and Training Choices (ETC) program in Massachusetts is seen by some as the national model in reforming the federal welfare system. However, many lawmakers object most strenuously to ETC's main premise—voluntarism. As one observer remarked recently, ETC is "a well-managed program that lacks the fundamental aspect of successful workfare programs: it's not mandatory. The evidence suggests [that] . . . it will probably not cause people to go to work who would not have done so already." What do you think?

8. As an alternative to conventional anti-inflationary policies, tax-based incomes policies (TIPS) is a much discussed solution. Would traditional Keynesians support TIPS? Would new classical economists support such a proposal? Do you think it would work? Why or why not?

A BRIEF LOOK AHEAD

Although the next chapter is the last one in this book, it is of vital importance. When the dollar weakened and the trade deficit soared in the 1980s, the United States awakened to the critical role of international trade. In the next chapter, we will explore the subjects of exchange rates, the balance of trade and payments, and the issue of protectionism versus free trade. Although we have discussed the international economy throughout the book, its growing importance deserves special consideration.

International Economics

Frank Siteman/ Stock, Boston

The deterioration of the U.S. balance of trade has been a disturbing feature of the 1980s. Indeed, by 1987, the United States ran a record $161 billion trade deficit and had become the world's largest debtor nation. What happened? Is there cause for alarm? Are federal budget deficits, anti-inflationary monetary policies, and high real interest rates responsible? Are protectionist trade policies and practices the culprit? These and other questions will guide us as we examine the patterns of U.S. exports and imports, foreign exchange markets, and trade policy.

After completion of this chapter, you should be able to do the following:

1. Describe and explain the law of comparative advantage, indicating why free international trade is beneficial to participating nations.

2. Identify and explain the effect of tariffs, quotas, subsidies, and product standard regulations on international trade, consumers, and producers.

3. Using supply and demand graphs, diagram and explain the effect of tariffs and quotas on production, employment, and prices.

4. List and explain the arguments for protectionist trade policies, and identify and explain the costs and benefits of protectionism.

5. Compare and contrast the fixed and fluctuating exchange rate systems.

6. Describe and explain the factors affecting exchange rates and dollar appreciation and depreciation.

7. Identify, describe, and explain the balance of payments.

8. Identify the term *competitiveness* and explain how a lack of competitiveness and currency appreciation may cause trade deficits.

FOCUS

A Petition from the Candlemakers

Steelmakers, auto assemblers, shoe and clothing makers are only a few of the industries impacted by vigorous and aggressive foreign competition. In the case of shoes, where the United States once enjoyed 80 percent of the world market, the shoe industry today holds a meager 2 percent foothold, if you will pardon the expression. In response to the invasion of European steel, Japanese automobiles, Italian shoes, and Taiwanese clothes, U.S. firms have lobbied the Congress for protection in the form of tariffs and quotas.

Protectionism is hardly new. In fact, as the following satire from the early 19th century so aptly conveys, many businesses are inclined to feel that any form of foreign competition is unfair.

PETITION OF THE MANUFACTURERS OF CANDLES, WAXLIGHTS, LAMPS, CANDLESTICKS, STREET LAMPS, SNUFFERS, EXTINGUISHERS, AND OF THE PRODUCERS OF OIL, TALLOW, RESIN, ALCOHOL, AND GENERALLY EVERYTHING CONNECTED WITH LIGHTING

To Messieurs The Members of the Chambers of Deputies

Gentlemen,

. . . We are suffering from the intolerable competition of a foreign rival, placed, it would seem, in a condition so far superior to our own for the production of light, that he absolutely *inundates* our national market with it at a price fabulously reduced. . . . This rival . . . is no other than the sun.

What we pray for, is, that it may please you to pass a law ordering the shutting up of all windows, skylights, dormer-windows, outside and inside shutters, curtains, blinds, bull's-eyes; in a word of all openings, holes, chinks, and fissures.

. . . If you shut up as much as possible all access to natural light and create a demand for artificial light, which of our French manufacturers will not benefit by it?[1]

---

[1] Robert L. Heilbroner, *The Worldly Philosophers*, 6th ed. (New York: Simon & Schuster, Inc., 1986), p. 181.

INTERNATIONAL TRADE

As we observed in Chapter 2, nations trade because they benefit from such transactions. The theory of comparative advantage tells us that even if the United States produces wheat and wine at a lower cost than France, both countries gain from trade if the United States specializes in wheat, the product with the least disadvantage, and trades wheat for wine. If each country produces both goods, the French and the Americans wind up with less of each good.[2]

Most of us nod our heads in agreement, but we hasten to add that the real world just does not work that way. Subsidies, tariffs, and quotas prevent the free market exchange of goods. Moreover, the bumper sticker that reads "Eat Your Import" is an unfriendly reminder of the Japanese automobile invasion over the last 20 years. After watching dozens of auto assembly plants close in the face of increasing foreign competition, we know that import competition costs U.S. jobs in many industries. "If our own government fails to protect U.S. jobs," ask the auto workers, "whom *can* we turn to?"

Most economists take a totally different perspective. As you can probably surmise by now, most western economists are prone to support market solutions to all problems. As such, they would argue that any form of government protectionism impedes the flow of resources, goods, and services; drives up prices; and reduces output and employment. The upshot is a decline in world trade. Given such dire consequences, most economists are adamantly opposed to the proliferation of trade restrictions.

One response is to beg the question. In other words, the United States is perhaps as involved in protectionist schemes as most of its trading partners. The 1983 *Tariff Schedules of the United States Annotated* amounts to a whopping 792 pages, plus a 78-page appendix. Over 200 tariff rates apply to watches and clocks alone. Because legal expertise is often required just to ascertain the appropriate tariff classification, for many businesses, the tariff serves as a substantial import deterrent. For example, identifying the correct duty on a piece of electronic equipment is extremely difficult because many types of materials are used. If it is more than 50 percent plastic, one duty is assessed; but if it is more than 50 percent metal, still another tariff classification is involved.

---

[2] Although the law of comparative advantage discussed in Chapter 2 dealt with two individuals within one country, this discussion is perfectly analogous to trade between nations. As you reread this section in Chapter 2, just substitute the United States and France for Mutt and Jeff and wheat and wine for photographs and tree trimming.

But we are putting the proverbial cart before the horse! In order to understand the issues involved, it will be helpful to define more carefully the various forms of protectionism. Then, once we are familiar with the terminology and arguments, we may proceed with the issues.

FORMS OF PROTECTIONISM

Protection of domestic industries from foreign competition may occur in three ways: (1) by increasing the domestic price of the foreign product or service, (2) by decreasing the costs of production at home, and (3) by restricting (or forbidding) the access of foreign producers to the home market. Regardless of the form of protection, the purpose is to improve the position of the domestic producer relative to the foreign producer.

Tariff *is a tax imposed upon imported goods, in order to raise the price and reduce the quantity of imports.*

Ad valorem tariff *increases as the value of imports increases.*

Specific tariff *is an absolute dollar value applied to the quantity per unit of imported goods.*

Tariffs. A **tariff** is simply a tax imposed upon imported goods. The purpose of the tariff is to raise the price and reduce the quantity of imports. There are two basic types of tariffs. An **ad valorem tariff** increases as the value of imports increases. For example, 256K computer chips may be duty free up to 50,000, but then subject to a sliding scale of duties from 1 to 20 percent. A **specific tariff,** on the other hand, is an absolute dollar value applied to the quantity per unit of imported goods. For example, imported Danish cheese might carry a 50 cent duty per pound. Tariffs are the most prevalent of all protectionist measures because they produce revenue that may be used either to finance government expenditures or to reduce taxes. They also give the illusion that the foreign seller is paying the duty.[3]

Figure 19–1 illustrates the effect of a tariff. In the absence of trade, the orange juice market is in equilibrium at a price of $1.50 with sales of 100 million cans sold (point E). When free trade begins, Mexican firms enter the U.S. market and undercut the former equilibrium price. The price of $1 is shown along the perfectly elastic supply curve (S_f), indicating the willingness of Mexican exporters to provide an unlimited quantity at a market-penetrating price. The upshot is that U.S. firms sell 60 million cans at $1 and thus lose 40 percent of their market share (distance Q_1 to Q_E), while the foreign firms acquire a share of 80 million cans, represented by the distance Q_2 to Q_1.

If domestic orange juice producers and workers win tariff protection, we can illustrate the effect of a tariff with an upward shift in the supply curve to S_t. At the higher price of $1.25, domestic producers gain an additional 20 million units in sales (Q_3 to Q_1) and Mexican exporters

---

[3] Much like a sales tax on a domestic good, to some extent the tariff is actually shifted forward to the buyer. If the demand is highly elastic, the seller will bear the brunt of the tariff in reduced sales. However, the more inelastic the demand, the greater will be burden on the buyer.

FIGURE 19–1

Effects of a Tariff

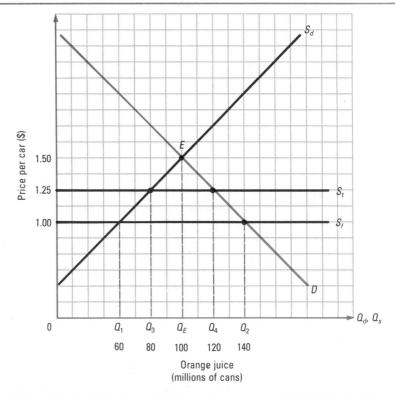

Equilibrium without trade in the orange juice market occurs at the $1.50 price-clearing output of 100 million cans. When free trade begins, Mexican firms adopt a market penetration strategy and sell all that they can at a price of $1.00, shown by the perfectly elastic supply curve S_f. U.S. firms lose 40 million cans ($Q_e - Q_1$) and Mexican firms acquire a market share of 80 million cans ($Q_2 - Q_1$). With tariff protection, the foreign supply curve shifts upward to S_t, at a price of $1.25. At this price U.S. producers gain an additional 20 million sales ($Q_3 - Q_1$) and Mexican producers lose 40 million [($Q_4 - Q_2$) + ($Q_3 - Q_1$)]. What are the effects of the tariff? Consumers pay higher prices, domestic producers and workers benefit from greater market share, and foreign producers lose market share.

lose 40 million cans (Q_4 to Q_2 plus Q_1 to Q_3). Consumers wind up paying higher prices and obtain less orange juice, and foreign producers lose market share. Domestic producers and workers benefit from increased sales. As we will see later, under the section on balance of payments, the net effect of protecting jobs and domestic production is estimated to cost $240,000 per job saved.

Tariffs can cause terrible economic disruption, such as that which occurred under the historic *Hawley-Smoot Tariff Act* of 1930. Although more than 1,000 prominent economists petitioned President Hoover to veto the legislation, he signed the bill into law and thereby raised the average duty to 41.6 percent. Arousing deep resentment abroad, 25 nations retaliated with high tariffs, hastening a further decline in trade and ushering in a worldwide depression.

Nontariff Regulatory Barriers.   Although tariffs are applied by all trading nations, nontariff regulatory barriers are equally pervasive and wide-ranging. A short list of such barriers includes *quotas* and *orderly marketing agreements* which limit imports, *administrative delays* in processing requests for import licenses and other intentional delays on import entry, *"buy-at-home" programs* which require governments to purchase from domestic suppliers, and a variety of *exchange controls*.

Quota *is a restriction on the quantity of an imported good.*

Quotas.   A **quota** is a restriction on the quantity of an imported good. Like a tariff, the purpose is to restrict entry in order to protect domestic producers. Unlike tariffs, quotas yield no revenue for the government.

The impact of quotas is nearly identical to tariffs, except that the policy acts on quantity instead of price. Using a different example, if the U.S. government wants to limit the amount of French wine imports to 9 million liters per year, we can easily illustrate the before and after conditions. Figure 19–2 shows the free trade—no quota equilibrium at point E_1, where Americans are importing 10 million liters of French wine at a price of $8 (48 French francs) per liter. (We assume that $1 = 6Fr, fixing the price per liter at $8 or 48 francs.) Note that we are dealing only with French supply, indicated by the supply curve S_f. When the U.S. government imposes the quota, French wineries may export no more than 9 million liters of wine to the United States. The supply curve becomes perfectly inelastic at the 9 million quota, forming an angular J-shaped curve. The result is a new equilibrium and quantity at E_2, 66 francs ($11) and 9 million liters of wine, respectively. With less French wine available, domestic vintners increase production and realize greater sales and profits. One side effect, however, is that domestic prices tend to be higher because there is less foreign competition.

Orderly marketing agreement *is a promise by the exporting nation to limit shipments of the product to the importing nation.*

A variation of the quota has been employed extensively in recent years. The **orderly marketing agreement** is a promise by the exporting nation to limit shipments of the product to the importing nation. The agreement is also called a voluntary export restriction, but this too is a misnomer since the decision by an exporting nation to restrict sales is rarely voluntary. Indeed, it usually transpires as a result of a threat by the importer nation to impose quotas if exports are not reduced. Such agreements generally are struck because the domestic government (the import-impacted industry) thinks that the foreign government has engaged in unfair trading practices, such as closing its markets, heavily subsidizing its exporters, dumping (selling below cost or well below world price), and other restrictive actions.

Negotiations between the domestic and foreign nations are central to voluntary export restrictions. For example, in the face of a growing def-

FIGURE 19–2
Effects of a Quota

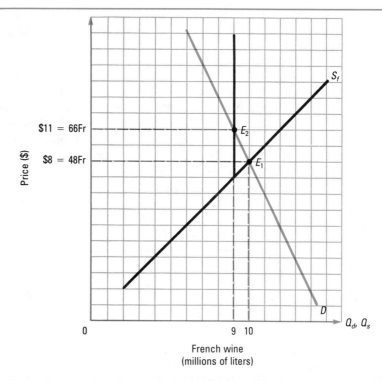

This diagram illustrates the effect of imposing a quota of 9 million liters of French wine. Before the quota, equilibrium price and quantity were $8.00 (or 48 fr) and 10 million liters, respectively. When a quota of 9 million liters is established, the supply curve becomes vertical at this quota. The quota leads to a new equilibrium at E_2: a higher price of $11 (or 66 fr) and 9 million liters.

icit with Japan in 1981, the U.S. Congress threatened to impose severe quotas. To forestall such extreme actions, Japan ultimately agreed to limit the export of televisions, automobiles, and semiconductors. Although such voluntary agreements to limit exports are similar to quotas, with Japan, they were basically an illusion. As Clyde Prestowitz reports in *Trading Places,* a book about how Japan has displaced the United States as the world's premier industrial nation, "We [the U.S.] had been handled. While we were debating whether to 'ensure' or 'seek to ensure' [voluntary limitations on their exports], Japan's industry continued its economic conquest. Nothing had changed."[4] In the case of automobiles, "a limitation by Japan was desirable both politically and . . . for the long term mobility of U.S. industry. Thus, how to obtain such a limitation without imposing it or asking for it became the question of the

---

[4] Clyde V. Prestowitz, Jr., *Trading Places: How We Allowed Japan to Take the Lead* (New York: Basic Books, 1988), p. 53.

hour."[5] Many observers believe these quasi-quotas are ineffective at best and, because they create a false sense of security, are more damaging than no agreement at all.

Product Standards.   Many nations impose regulatory barriers by requiring that imports meet specific criteria. These **product standards** generally require that imports pass certain domestic health and safety tests. The U.S. Food and Drug Administration (FDA), for example, has innumerable requirements and prohibitions on the importation of drugs and the use of certain medical practices. Thousands of cancer victims traveled to Mexico in a desperate search for relief with the drug laetrile because the FDA proclaimed the drug to be totally useless and a waste of money. Many Americans with disk-related lower back pain go to Canada to get enzyme injections, a procedure recently condemned by the FDA and the surgeon general as potentially fatal. And in Japan, the government forbids the importation of all frozen foods that contain any active ingredients, such as yeast. One U.S. company that has tried in vain to export freeze-dried bagels to Japan has met stiff resistance.

Product standards are regulatory barriers that generally require that imports pass certain domestic health and safety tests.

Although most product standards are in the food and health-related industries, many restrictions are imposed in machinery, consumer durables, and services that have little relationship to health and sanitation. For example, Argentina requires importers of automobiles to insure shipments with Argentinian firms, West Germany requires models for advertisements in West German magazines to be hired through a West German agency (even if the ad is made elsewhere); and Spain disallows dubbing of foreign films and thus forces people to read subtitles.[6]

Administrative Delays.   Intentional bureaucratic delays are difficult to prove, but complaints are widespread. For example, in order for the domestic firm to obtain an import license, many countries require the exporter to send samples in advance. In 1983, France required that all imported videotape recorders (VCRs) arrive through a small, understaffed customs entry office. The delays served to prevent Japanese VCRs from entering the market until France negotiated an orderly marketing agreement in which Japan limited its exports.[7]

"Buy-at-Home."   So-called *buy-at-home* legislation and programs are common in virtually all nations. Governments give preference to their own producers by requiring that they buy exclusively from domestic firms or by imposing local content laws. In the Japanese and U.S. telecommunications industries, for example, firms are required to buy most

---

[5] Ibid., p. 252.

[6] Laura Wallace, "The Rising Barriers," *The Wall Street Journal,* October 5, 1981, p. 1.

[7] "Japan to Curb VCR Exports," *New York Times,* November 21, 1983, p. D5.

or all of their supplies from home producers. Indeed, AT&T has been forced to use U.S. suppliers even though their prices have been as much as 30 percent higher than foreign bids.[8] *Local content legislation* compels domestic firms and foreign subsidiaries operating in the home market to use a minimum percentage of domestic parts in final products. Mexico requires that 50 percent of automobile components be made there, and Brazilian companies are mandated to buy computers made only in Brazil. Like all other forms of tariff and nontariff regulations, the buy-at-home and local content legislation protects domestic producers at the expense of foreign producers. This is one reason why such practices have been labeled *beggar-thy-neighbor* policies.

Exchange Controls. **Foreign exchange** is any financial instrument used to make payment from the currency of one nation to another. Bank drafts, which are similar to checks, are the most common form of international payment. Nations may reduce import activity by limiting access to foreign exchange. Such **exchange controls** limit the amount of currency or issuance of bank drafts to pay for imports. Conversely, a country may also promote exports by guaranteeing exporters a more favorable rate of exchange. For example, if the official exchange rate between U.S. dollars and British pounds is $1 = £.57 (or £1 = $1.75), and the U.S. government wishes to stimulate exports, it may offer the exporter an exchange of $1 = £.65 (or £1 = $1.54). This translates into increased profits for the exporter since each dollar buys more pounds (foreign exchange). Brazil, France, and many other countries also have limited the amount of a foreign currency that their citizens may purchase for trips abroad.

Export Subsidies. Although not technically an import barrier, export subsidies indirectly limit imports by reducing the costs associated with export activity. Thus, instead of limiting access to home markets via tariffs, quotas, and other nontariff laws and regulations, governments often subsidize domestic producers.

An **export subsidy** consists of government aid to businesses in the form of tax credits, loan programs, insurance, and direct cash payments. Examples of export subsidies are abundant. U.S. steel exporting firms are eligible for major tax breaks; the U.S. & Foreign Commercial Service, a division of the Department of Commerce, provides extensive assistance to exporters through trade shows and missions, market research, and help in obtaining agents and distributors (and customers) overseas; and the U.S. Export-Import Bank provides financial aid through direct loans, loan guarantees, and insurance. Wherever exports

Foreign exchange *is any financial instrument used to make payment from the currency of one nation to another.*

Exchange controls *are designed to reduce imports by imposing limits on the amount of currency or issuance of bank drafts to pay for imports.*

Export subsidy *consists of government aid to businesses in the form of tax credits, loan programs, insurance, and direct cash payments.*

[8] Edward Meadows, "Japan Runs into America Inc.," *Fortune,* 105, no. 6 (March 22, 1982), pp. 56–61.

are willing to turn out at the going market price. For example, the cost of building a ship in the United States is about twice what it would cost elsewhere. Were it not for the hefty subsidies and laws confining U.S. commercial shipping to U.S.-built and operated vessels, there would be little shipbuilding in the United States.[9]

Of course, export assistance and subsidies are widely practiced in many nations. For example, Canada gives cash grants to fishermen to buy trawlers and thus subsidizes exports of fish. Other countries, notably Japan, exempt all income of foreign subsidiaries from taxation. West Germany's value-added tax of 13 percent is not applied to exports.[10] And in most countries, including the United States, governments allow exporters to deduct their foreign losses from domestic income for income tax purposes.

THE HIGH COSTS OF PROTECTIONISM

Although protectionism is practiced by nearly all nations, economists generally agree that the costs of tariff and nontariff barriers far exceed the benefits. The beneficiaries of protectionism and export assistance are producers of the protected good and the government (when a tariff is involved). But protection also imposes costs upon domestic consumers and suppliers of firms in the protected industry. What are the specific costs and benefits, and how are they distributed?

Effects of Protectionism at Home.   As the quantity of foreign goods declines in response to higher import prices, domestic production and employment increases; thus, the domestic producer and to a lesser extent the firm's employees benefit from the protection. If the trade policy in question is a tariff, the government is also a beneficiary as it receives additional revenue from duties on the imported good.

Such gains in the protected industry, however, are generally at the expense of reduced output in other industries from which resources are attracted. Indeed, a recent study shows that protectionist legislation actually reduces overall employment.[11] Moreover, to the extent that pro-

---

[9] This is really as much a local or domestic content regulation as an export subsidy.

[10] Value-added taxes, levies which are placed upon all stages of production in the channel of distribution from raw materials to retail sales, are very prominent in Europe.

[11] A 1987 study estimated that 35,600 manufacturing jobs were eliminated as a result of the September 1984 voluntary export restrictions limiting steel imports. Although steel and supplier industry employment increased by 16,800, these gains were exceeded by the loss of 52,400 jobs in steel-using industries. Such losses caused by higher steel

tectionist trade policies result in higher prices, the consumer is a clear loser. Not only will they reduce consumption of the protected good, they will very likely spend less on goods in other industries as prices rise and output declines.

With the growing importance of and attention to international trade and talk of protectionism, economists have been busy doing research on the costs of protectionist trade policies. As the following CASE-IN-POINT shows, protectionism is more costly than most of us realize.

CASE
• IN •
POINT

Is Protection Worth the Cost?

In 1986, several economists did a rigorous study of 31 industries in which trade volumes exceeded $100 million and the United States imposed protectionist trade restrictions. The figures in Table 19–1 indicate that annual consumer losses exceed $100 million in all but six of the cases. The largest losses, $27 billion per year, come from protecting the textiles and apparel industry. There also are large consumer losses associated with protection in carbon steel ($6.8 billion), automobiles ($5.8 billion), and dairy products ($5.5 billion).

[Because] the purpose of protectionism is to protect jobs in specific industries, a useful approach to gain some perspective on consumer losses is to express these losses on a per-job-saved basis. In 18 of the 31 cases, the cost per-job-saved is $100,000 or more per year; the consumer losses per-job-saved in benzoid chemicals, carbon steel (two separate periods), specialty steel, and bolts, nuts, and screws exceeded $500,000 per year.

The table also reveals that domestic producers were the primary beneficiaries of protectionist policies; however, there are some noteworthy costs where foreign producers realized relatively large gains. For the U.S.-Japanese voluntary export agreement in automobiles, foreign producers gained 38 percent of what domestic producers lost, while a similar computation for the latest phase of protection for carbon steel was 29 percent.[12]

Questions to Consider

1. *Cost-benefit analysis is often required by the government in determining whether a project is desirable (e.g., damming up a river to make a reservoir for hydroelectric power). As a general rule of thumb, if the estimated total*

---

prices make steel-using firms less competitive in both domestic and foreign markets. [This information is detailed in a research study by Arthur T. Denzan, "How Import Restraints Reduce Employment," Formal Publication #80 (St. Louis: Washington University Center for the Study of American Business, June 1987).

[12] Cletus C. Coughlin, K. Alec Chrystal, and Geoffrey E. Wood, "Protectionist Trade Policies: A Survey of Theory, Evidence, and Rationale," *Review* 70, no. 1 (Federal Reserve Bank of St. Louis, January/February 1988), pp. 17–18.

TABLE 19–1

Distribution of Costs and
Benefits from Special
Protection

Case	CONSUMER LOSSES		PRODUCER GAINS	WELFARE COSTS OF RESTRAINTS	
	Totals (million dollars)	Per Job Saved (dollars)	Totals (million dollars)	Gain to Foreigners (million dollars)	Tariff Revenue (million dollars)
Manufacturing					
Book manufacturing	500	100,000	305	neg.	0
Benzoid chemicals	2,650	over 1 million	2,250	neg.	252
Glassware	200	200,000	130	neg.	54
Rubber footware	230	30,000	90	neg.	139
Ceramic articles	95	47,500	25	neg.	69
Ceramic tiles	116	135,000	62	neg.	55
Orange juice	525	240,000	390	neg.	128
Canned tuna	91	76,000	74	7	10
Textiles and apparel: Phase I	94,00	22,000	8,700	neg.	1,158
Textiles and apparel: Phase II	20,000	37,000	18,000	350	2,143
Textiles and apparel: Phase III	27,000	42,000	22,000	1,800	2,535
Carbon steel: Phase I	1,970	240,000	1,330	330	290
Carbon steel: Phase II	4,350	620,000	2,770	930	556
Carbon steel: Phase III	6,800	750,000	3,800	2,000	560
Ball bearings	45	90,000	21	neg.	18
Specialty steel	520	1,000,000	420	50	32
Nonrubber footwear	700	55,000	250	220	262
Color television	420	420,000	190	140	77
CB radios	55	93,000	14	neg.	32
Bolts, nuts, large screws	110	550,000	60	neg.	16
Prepared mushrooms	35	117,000	13	neg.	25
Automobiles	5,800	105,000	2,600	2,200	790
Motorcycles	104	150,000	67	neg.	21
Services					
Maritime industries	3,000	270,000	2,000	neg.	10
Agriculture and fisheries					
Sugar	930	60,000 690/acre	550	410	5
Dairy products	5,500	220,000 1,800/cow	5,000	250	34
Peanuts	170	1,000/acre	170	neg.	9
Meat	1,800	160,000 225/head	1,600	135	44
Fish	560	21,000	200	170	177
Mining					
Petroleum	6,900	160,000	4,800	2,000	11
Lead and zinc	67	30,000	46	4	

However measured, tariff and nontariff barriers are expensive. This study indicates that annual consumer losses exceed $100,000 in all but six cases. In 18 of the 31 industries studied, the cost-per-job-saved is $100,000 or more. And in the benzoid chemicals, carbon steel, specialty steel, and bolts, nuts, and screws industries, the cost-per-job-saved exceeded $500,000. (Note: The three phases for textiles and apparels and for carbon steel refer to three different time periods.)

SOURCE: Cletus C. Coughlin, K. Alec Chrystal, and Geoffrey E. Wood, "Protectionist Trade Policies: A Survey of Theory, Evidence and Rationale," *Review* 70, no. 1 (Federal Reserve Bank of St. Louis, January/February 1988), p. 18.

costs exceed the total benefits, the net benefits are negative, and the project is scrapped or redesigned.

According to the costs and benefits reported in the table above, what is the net benefit connected with protecting specialty steel?

2. *How can the government justify trade policies which cost as much as $1 million per job saved? Hint: Do you think that most consumers (voters) are aware of these costs? Even if they were, would they be able to exert any influence on Capitol Hill?*

Worldwide Effects of Protectionism. Several international organizations have produced research findings which show the adverse effects of protectionism. Two such organizations are the World Bank and the Organization of Economic Cooperation and Development (OECD).[13] One OECD study indicates that protectionist policies have generated costs far in excess of benefits. The study shows the following:

- That trade restrictions which result in reduced imports do not increase domestic employment.
- That restrictive trade practices will also reduce exports because the impacted nation has less income to spend.
- That the inflationary effect of protectionist legislation results in increased uncertainty, less investment, and lower economic growth.[14]

The OECD study also emphasizes the damage caused by protectionism on developing nations. Because Third World countries need a viable export sector to finance their debts, and because protectionist policies restrict access to export markets, developing nations find it difficult to pay their debts.[15]

Another study by the World Bank compares the effect of free trade versus protectionism on economic growth, measured by the average an-

---

[13] Efforts to promote economic growth, prosperity, and financial stability are the aims of numerous international organizations. The World Bank is one of the most active organizations. Its membership numbers over 140 countries. Financed by member nation subscriptions, its purpose is to lend money for capital projects such as dams and irrigation systems in order to enhance economic development. Another important thrust is provided by the Organization of Economic Cooperation and Development (OECD), a spin-off of the post-World War II European Recovery Plan—more popularly known as the Marshall Plan. Its members consist of the United States, Canada, and 18 European nations. Although made up primarily by industrial countries, its purpose is to promote the expansion of trade by assisting developing nations.

[14] Organization for Economic Cooperation and Development, *Costs and Benefits of Protection* (1985).

[15] This has been part of Mexico's problem in recent years. Confronted by stiff tariffs and quotas in several agricultural markets, Mexico was unable to earn enough foreign exchange to service its mounting international debts.

nual per capita growth in real GNP. Countries that imposed high tariffs and quotas uniformly had lower rates of economic growth than countries whose policies did not favor domestic production over exports. For the 1973 to 1985 period, growth rates for free trade and protectionist nations were 5.9 percent and −0.1 percent, respectively.[16]

THINKING IT THROUGH

Sometimes the time period selected badly biases the result of a study. But even for the previous 10-year period (1963–1973), the World Bank found that growth rates were 6.9 percent and 1.9 percent for free trade and protectionist nations, respectively. With such overwhelming evidence supporting freer trade, why do governments impose protectionist policies?

PROTECTIONIST ARGUMENTS

Although most economists are united in opposition to restrictive tariffs and quotas, many reasons have been offered to justify protectionist policies. Among the numerous arguments are the protection of infant industries, preserving national defense, protecting jobs, and correcting a trade imbalance. We will take these in turn, although not necessarily in the order of importance.

Infant industries argument is based upon the assumption that new firms or industries need temporary protection from foreign competitors.

Infant Industries. One of the oldest arguments is to protect industries which are newly formed and struggling to gain a foothold in a competitive world marketplace. The **infant industries argument** seeks protection from foreign competition until such time that it can realize economies of scale in production and, with lower costs of production, be more price-competitive with its foreign rivals. As workers and managers become more experienced and productive, so the argument goes, it will no longer be necessary to provide the tariff and quota protection.

Protection of infant industries has worked well in some instances. Automobile production in Brazil and Japan, for example, grew to be competitive because of government protection. However, as time passes, it has the adverse effect of enfeebling the domestic industry, creating a kind of corporate senility. Restrictive automobile trade policies in Argentina and Australia have done little to enhance competitiveness, and protection of the U.S. steel industry has driven prices so high as to cause U.S. businesses increasingly to buy from foreign steel firms. Un-

---

[16] World Bank, *World Development Report 1987* (Oxford University Press, 1987).

fortunately, once protection is given to an industry, the vested interests of owners, workers, and suppliers generally resist removal of protection.

National defense argument *for protection states that a nation should not depend upon potential enemies for products vital to national interest.*

National Defense.   The premise of the **national defense argument** is that wars (hot and cold) may cut off supplies of critical resources and goods essential to domestic production. The semiconductor industry is a recent and controversial example. Should the United States become dependent upon Japan to supply semiconductors for defense goods? Or should the United States impose major import barriers on semiconductors in order to preserve the capacity to produce its own semiconductors?[17] Footwear and clothing for the military, to cite other examples, are generally supplied by domestic firms unless the price advantage clearly favors the foreign producer.

The appeal for protection on national defense grounds should not be taken lightly. For example, the OPEC oil embargo raised serious doubts about the future ability of U.S. oil companies to supply sufficient quantities of petroleum and derivative products. On the other hand, the national defense argument ignores the possibility of storage and the purchase of desirable resources from friendly countries during emergencies.

Protecting jobs *is passing trade legislation that is designed to prevent imports from throwing people out of work.*

Protecting Jobs.   Perhaps the most politically sensitive argument is **protecting jobs**—passing trade legislation that is designed to prevent imports from throwing people out of work. "To men wearing work shirts and drinking beer in a neighborhood bar in Gary, Indiana, their lost jobs, misery, and suffering are caused by imports," said former U.S. Special Trade Representative Robert Strauss.[18] Politicians sensitive to the plight of steel workers and others displaced by imports will readily endorse protectionist policies to protect domestic jobs. But if it costs $1 million per job in specialty steel and $100,000 a year per U.S. auto worker, why do politicians supply restrictive trade legislation demanded by workers and businesses?

An exceptionally inviting answer to this important question is provided by a branch of economics called public choice. A recent review of trade policies by the St. Louis Federal Reserve Bank offers a poignant explanation.

The public choice literature views the politician as an individual who offers voters a bundle of governmentally supplied goods in order to win elections. Many argue that politicians gain by providing protectionist

---

[17] Semiconductors, often called *the rice of the electronic age* and *the crude oil of the 21st century,* are small silicon chips loaded with microscopic circuits capable of storing and processing immense amounts of information.

[18] John Hein, "A New Protectionism Rises," *Across the Board,* 20, no. 4, (April 1983), p. 3.

legislation. Even though the national economic costs exceed the benefits, the politician faces different costs and benefits.

Those harmed by a protectionist trade policy for a domestic industry, especially household consumers, will incur a small individual cost that is difficult to identify. For example, a consumer is unlikely to ponder how much extra a shirt costs because of protectionist legislation for the textiles and apparel industry. Even though the aggregate effect is large, the harm to each consumer may be small. This small cost, of which an individual may not even be aware, and the costs of organizing consumers deter the formation of a lobby against the legislation.

On the other hand, workers and other resource owners are very concerned about protectionist legislation for their industry. Their benefits tend to be large individually and easy to identify. Their voting campaign contributions assist politicians who support their positions and penalize those who do not. Thus, politicians are likely to respond to their demands for protectionist legislation.[19]

Correcting a trade imbalance *is a common argument for raising or lowering tariff and nontariff barriers.*

Correcting a Trade Imbalance. Policies and legislation made for the purpose of **correcting a trade imbalance**—raising or lowering tariff and nontariff barriers, are widely regarded as important to a nation's economic welfare.

Unfortunately, this argument is suspect on at least two grounds. First, a trade deficit is often caused by faster rates of economic growth at home than in other countries. Efforts to reduce the deficit would hurt exports and reduce real GNP. Second, attempts to reduce trade deficits through import limitation will tend to backfire because of retaliation by countries affected by the curbs on their exports.

International Finance and the Balance of Payments

In order for nations to trade with one another, it is necessary that currencies are readily convertible (e.g., that dollars are easily exchanged for yen). Since exporters want to be paid in their own currencies, it follows that there must be an efficient mechanism of conversion. Such is the purpose of foreign exchange markets.

Foreign exchange, however, is not always simple. Because governments attempt to regulate exchange values in order to improve their trade balances, it is often too expensive for one nation to do much business with another country. As we have already seen, although most nations espouse free trade, tariff and nontariff barriers remain serious impediments to open international economic activity. Indeed, even the

---

[19] Coughlin, et al., "Protectionist Trade Policies: A Survey of Theory, Evidence, and Rationale," p. 22.

type of exchange rate system used may be detrimental to world trade. These systems, ranging from fixed to freely fluctuating, is the subject of the next section.

FOREIGN EXCHANGE MARKETS

Exchange rate *is the ratio of one nation's currency expressed in terms of another country's currency.*

An **exchange rate** is the ratio of one nation's currency expressed in terms of another country's currency. More simply, an exchange rate is just the price of foreign money. For example, on July 12, 1988, the U.S. dollar was officially worth 132.5 yen, 6.19 French francs, 1.84 West German marks, and 2,270 Mexican pesos. These rates have fluctuated greatly over the last 20 years. For example, in 1968 the U.S. dollar exchanged for 360 yen, 4 marks, and 4.9 francs. What causes such fluctuations? What role do central bankers play? How are the exchange rates determined in the first place?

Fixed Exchange Rates. Most nations before World War I operated under a **gold standard** by which countries defined their currencies in terms of gold. For example, at one time the United States defined one dollar to be worth 1/20th of an ounce of gold. Britain, in turn, defined one pound as approximately 1/4th of an ounce of gold. With these values, one U.S. dollar was worth 1/5th of the British pound (£), and thus the exchange rate between the U.S. and Britain was fixed at £1 = $5 or $1 = £.20.

Gold standard *exists when countries define their currencies in terms of gold and promise to redeem claims in gold.*

Under a gold standard, the amount of money in circulation is a function of the gold supply. And, because gold backed a nation's money supply, nations on the gold standard pledged to convert their currencies to gold on demand. The amount of gold held by each nation thus affected its domestic money supply and, in turn, its domestic economic activity (production, employment, and prices). Using our U.S.-British exchange rate example, if the United States ran a trade deficit with Britain, gold would flow out of the U.S. Treasury into the British Treasury, the U.S. domestic money supply would fall (in proportion to the loss of gold), and prices would fall at home. As deflation occurs and domestic goods become cheaper, however, the dollar appreciates in value relative to the pound. (Lower U.S. prices at home make goods more attractive to British buyers.) This results in more exports and a return to the initial (or equilibrium) exchange rate. In other words, within the framework of fixed exchange rates under a gold standard, the forces of supply and demand are supposed to correct trade imbalances.

When World War I broke out, however, international trade was severely disrupted, and nations refused to redeem currencies for gold. Although most nations returned temporarily to the gold standard after World War I, the Great Depression dealt a death blow to the gold standard. As deflation and unemployment occurred on a worldwide scale, many nations tried to bolster their economies by **currency devaluation**— decreasing the value of the domestic currency in terms of gold or foreign exchange.[20] This proved to be essentially futile since one nation's devaluation was generally offset by devaluation by other countries.

Currency devaluation is a nation's formal policy of decreasing the value of the domestic currency in terms of gold or foreign exchange.

Near the end of World War II in Bretton Woods, New Hampshire, representatives from 44 nations met for the purpose of stabilizing the international monetary system. The outgrowth was the formation of the *International Monetary Fund (IMF)*. Now covering more than 140 non-communist-bloc nations, the IMF promotes exchange rate stability, combats exchange restrictions, and encourages multilateral systems of payment. Its principal function is to lend reserves to the member nations experiencing trade deficits.

The famous *Bretton Woods agreement* reestablished the principle of **fixed exchange rates** based upon the U.S. dollar convertibility to gold at $35 per ounce (for foreign governments and central banks only). In order to maintain the fixed exchange rates, central banks were supposed to buy and sell dollar assets (known as foreign exchange market intervention). Because the United States held more than 70 percent of official gold reserves after World War II, and because the U.S. dollar was especially strong during the 1940s and 1950s, most nations were content to buy and sell dollars in lieu of gold to settle international accounts. The dollar became the world's standard trading currency.

Fixed exchange rates establish currency convertibility to gold at some constant value.

The Bretton Woods system lasted a brief 26 years. From a world shortage of U.S. dollars in immediate post-World War II years, by 1971, European nations held a surplus of dollars. The U.S. gold supply had dwindled from $25 billion to $11 billion, and the United States was about to run its first trade deficit in nearly 100 years. What caused the turnabout?

This dramatic reversal may be attributed to four main factors. First and foremost, Europe had recovered from World War II, mainly because of major reconstruction grants and loans from the United States, but also because of domestic economic programs designed to stimulate growth. West Germany, for example, was no longer dependent upon

---

[20] Currency devaluation and currency depreciation accomplish virtually the same outcome, increased exports and reduced imports, but the process is totally different. Devaluation (or revaluation) occurs as the official policy of the government. Currency depreciation happens as a result of market forces; for example, the Japanese demand for U.S. dollars decreases, leading to a decline in the value of the dollar against the yen. (In other words, the dollar cannot buy as many yen after the depreciation.) Although devaluation does the same thing, the formal change in exchange rates may precipitate reciprocal devaluations by other nations.

other countries for raw materials and finished goods, and she transformed her deficit-ridden status of the 1950s into a trade surplus by the early 1960s. A second factor contributing to increased U.S. dollar holdings by foreign nations was U.S. government military spending overseas, both in Europe and in Asia. Building and maintaining NATO and military bases required enormous outlays, all of which contributed to the loss of dollars abroad. A third reason was increased overseas investment by U.S. multinational corporations. U.S. tourism abroad also contributed to the loss of U.S. dollars.

In response to a deteriorating trade position, domestic inflation, and sluggish economic growth, in August of 1971, President Nixon announced Phase I of his New Economic Policy. Along with a 90-day freeze on wages and prices, he declared that the United States would no longer redeem dollars for gold, effectively ending the Bretton Woods agreement. Not even two currency devaluations by the United States in 1972 and 1973 reversed the growing trade deficits. By 1973, the United States and its trading partners agreed to allow exchange rates to float.

The Current System: A Managed Float. By the mid-1980s a majority of the IMF countries still engaged in some type of fixed or pegged exchange rate system. For example, many South American nations peg their currencies to the U.S. dollar. Others either peg their currencies to IMF reserves or an index of several currencies. Still another example is the *European Economic Community (EEC),* more commonly known as a *common market.* A customs union that has abolished all internal tariffs and imposes a common external tariff, the EEC has recently developed a new trading currency known as the *European Currency Unit (ECU).* Indeed, there are only eight countries which purport to practice an independently floating exchange rate system, and even these occasionally engage in central bank intervention to stabilize exchange rates.[21]

Managed float system *of exchange rates is one in which central banks endeavor to prevent excessive (damaging) variation in currency value.*

A **managed float system** of exchange rates is one in which central banks endeavor to prevent excessive (damaging) variations in currency values. In order to stabilize free market fluctuations, the central banks will intervene to buy or sell domestic and foreign currencies. For example, if Japan thinks its trade surplus will generate currency appreciation and make its goods more expensive and imports more attractive, it will sell yen in the foreign exchange markets. Conversely, a U.S. trade deficit may be seen as undesirable because it is likely to cause currency depreciation, more expensive imports, and domestic inflation. To combat inflation, many countries have bought their own currencies in foreign exchange markets.

---

[21] These countries are Australia, Canada, Japan, Lebanon, South Africa, the United Kingdom, the United States, and Uruguay.

> ### THINKING IT THROUGH
>
> Why might a trade deficit cause currency depreciation? Why would a trade surplus likely cause currency appreciation?

Managed, fixed, or freely fluctuating, exchange rates are determined by a combination of market and political forces. Under the gold standard, supply and demand theoretically function to restore exchange rate equilibrium. Under the Bretton Woods system, there was an explicit understanding that nations were to intervene to stabilize their currency values. In either case, if market forces and foreign exchange intervention were ineffective, nations would make the political decision to devalue (or revalue) their currencies. Under the managed float system to which the United States and its trading partners have agreed, intervention by central banks is a common practice. Regardless of the system in place, however, if we can make one generalization it is that nations will always do that which is in their best interests. Call the system of exchange rates what you will, the more important question may be What's in a name?

THE BALANCE OF PAYMENTS

International transactions consist of exports and imports of merchandise and services, investment in foreign assets and government securities, and foreign travel. When a U.S. beverage distributor buys Heineken beer from Holland, when Exxon buys 10 percent of a Venezuelan oil company, or when you board the jet airliner Concorde bound for France, these transactions cause a drain of U.S. dollars to the respective countries. Conversely, exports of U.S. wheat to England, Japanese investments in Los Angeles real estate, and Canadian tourists visiting San Francisco all result in a U.S. dollar inflow.

Balance of payments (BOP) *is a record of a nation's transactions between its residents and the rest of the world.*

In order to keep track of such flows, each nation records all transactions between its residents and the rest of the world in an account called the **balance of payments (BOP).** Like the equality of the expenditures and income approaches in the GNP accounts, the BOP must balance by definition. Consisting of three major components, the current account, the capital account, and official reserves, the BOP is defined such that the total of these three items always equals zero (including, of course, a statistical discrepancy). Table 19–2 summarizes the 1987 U.S. balance of payments, and each item is discussed in detail in the following section.

TABLE 19–2	1. Balance on current account	−160.7
U.S. Balance of	2. Merchandise trade balance (deficit = −) −159.2	
Payments, 1987	3. Merchandise exports +250.8	
	4. Merchandise imports −410.0	
	5. Net invisibles (services) −1.5	
	6. Balance on capital account	+129.7
	7. Change in U.S. assets abroad	
	(increase = −) −72.9	
	8. Change in foreign assets	
	in United States (increase = +) +202.6	
	9. Change in U.S. official reserves	+9.2
	10. Statistical discrepancy	−21.8

Adding the balance on current account, the balance on capital account, and the change in U.S. official reserves—lines 1, 6, and 9, respectively, determines the statistical discrepancy. The latter item represents unaccounted outflows of dollars, chiefly in the form of assets changing hands. The total of items 1, 6, 9, and 10 is thus zero by definition. The Balance of Payments account always balances.

SOURCE: *Federal Reserve Bulletin* 74, no. 5 (Washington, D.C., Board of Governors of the Federal Reserve System, May 1988), Table 3.10, p. A 53.

The Current Account. The *current account* consists of merchandise exports and imports (tangible goods such as automobile parts, oil, and agricultural commodities) and so-called *invisibles*—a term that refers to a variety of intangible services, such as tourism, banking, insurance, transportation, and engineering. For 1987, the balance on current account was −$160.7 billion (line one, Table 19–2, the sum of lines two and five). A subdivision of the current account balance most often reported in the news media is the merchandise trade balance, the difference between exports and imports. In 1987, the United States had a *merchandise trade deficit* of −$159.2 billion.

The Capital Account. The *capital account* measures the change in net indebtedness between the domestic economy and the rest of the world. The account balance, shown in line six of Table 19–2, involves the flow of dividends, interest payments, stock and bond purchases, and related financial assets. For 1987, the United States incurred a net indebtedness of $129.7 billion, determined by the difference between the change in U.S. assets abroad (line seven) and the change in all foreign assets in the United States (line eight). U.S. investments abroad are negative items because dollars flow out of the circular flow; foreign investments in the United States are shown as positive (credits) because dollars flow into the economy. Although often confused with the export and import of capital goods, such as medical equipment and robotic technology, these physical goods are included in the merchandise trade account. The word *capital* is thus used to designate claims to financial assets, such as government securities.[22]

Official Reserves. The change in U.S. official reserves is the final item in the balance of payments (aside from the discrepancy). Official reserves consist mainly of foreign currencies, although reserves held by the International Monetary Fund, gold, and special drawing rights (SDRs) also are used to settle accounts.[23] In 1987, U.S. official reserves declined by $9.2 billion (see line nine in Table 19–2). Under a freely floating exchange rate system, the change in official reserves is always zero, and thus the current and capital account must total zero.

The total of lines one, six, and nine is − $21.8 billion, international economic activity for which there is no record. This *statistical discrepancy* indicates that some trade and/or capital flows are omitted. Although a fairly large omission, such errors are virtually inevitable given the difficulty of tracking and auditing the enormous numbers of transactions. Most analysts think that the bulk of the discrepancy originates in asset transfers which have escaped official records.

THINKING IT THROUGH

Some of the statistical discrepancy might be laundered money, for example, illegally earned income, or proceeds from illegal sales of assets deposited in numbered foreign bank accounts. What do you think?

To summarize thus far, the United States in 1987 purchased considerably more from abroad than it sold. With a current account deficit of − $160.7 billion, the United States financed its import binge by selling

---

[22] Of course, changes in assets also result from fluctuations in the market value of stocks and bonds. For example, shares of IBM owned by Canadian residents may increase in value, or U.S. Treasury bills held by Royal Dutch Shell may decrease in value (owing to an increase in U.S. interest rates). Such gains and losses, however, are not recorded in the capital account until there is a sale of assets. Only transactions are included.

[23] SDRs, often called *paper gold,* are a form of international reserves managed by the IMF for the settlement of balance of payments deficits. Much like the Federal Reserve System in the United States and the central banks of England and France, the IMF functions as a world central bank. Because all subscribing nations have domestic currencies on deposit with the IMF, if country A has a trade deficit with country B, the IMF can settle the debt by transferring SDRs from country A to country B. Created in 1970, SDRs are used only if a nation has insufficient foreign exchange to settle accounts.

assets to foreigners. These financial transactions represent a net increase in claims against the United States, a necessary outflow of dollars to settle the trade imbalance.

Although the capital and current accounts must balance, it is useful to consider what would happen if they were not equal. The following CASE-IN-POINT provides an interesting scenario, examines how floating exchange rates solve trade imbalances, and introduces the next section on the competitiveness issue.

CASE
▪ IN ▪
POINT

What If . . .?

Suppose, for example, that at current exchange rates a country is running a current account deficit, but its planned net capital flows are zero. [That is, it wants no change in its foreign indebtedness.] This means that the country is trying to spend more on imports than foreigners are willing to spend on its exports. This will produce an imbalance in its foreign exchange market. Attempted sales of domestic currency (for foreign exchange) will exceed attempted purchases. The market value of the currency will fall until the quantity of the currency demanded is equal to that supplied. At this point, either the current account has adjusted so that it is no longer in deficit, or the net export of assets is just equal to the current account deficit. Thus, the exchange rate will adjust to ensure that the current and capital accounts are exactly offsetting.

There is nothing magical about this outcome. The end result is the same for any individual. If you spend more than your income, you must borrow or sell the equivalent value of your assets to cover the difference; if you spend less than your income, you must inevitably acquire increased claims on someone else. Similarly, a nation that runs a current account deficit must either borrow from abroad or sell some of its assets, whether these assets are domestic or foreign.[24]

Questions to Consider

1. *Using the same logic, what happens when a nation runs a current account surplus?*

2. *How would you classify the economic thinking of this scenario: classical, Keynesian, or monetarist? Why?*

3. *Do you think that most governments have the patience to follow a free market solution to a trade imbalance? Why or why not?*

---

[24] K. Alec Chrystal and Geoffrey E. Wood, "Are Trade Deficits a Problem?" *Review* 70, no. 1, (Federal Reserve Bank of St. Louis, January/February 1988), p. 5.

THE ISSUE OF COMPETITIVENESS: CAN THE UNITED STATES COMPETE?

On the international scene, if not at home, this headline captured the attention of Americans in the 1980s. As the U.S. trade imbalance reached a historic high, the news media released one story after another about the deindustrialization of the United States, the hollow corporation, and declining U.S. competitiveness. A special commission appointed by President Reagan to study the problem reported the gloomy finding that the United States was losing its ability to compete.

Many analysts argue that the United States is losing its competitive foothold in world markets. Others claim that such concerns are ill-founded and that the real glitch is an overvalued dollar. In order to gain perspective on this issue, it is important to define our terms and examine causal relationships.

Competitiveness *means the degree to which a nation sustains its technological and commercial advantage and thereby supports increasing domestic production and employment.*

A nation's competitiveness is the ability "to produce goods and services that meet the test of international markets while simultaneously expanding the real incomes of its citizens."[25] **Competitiveness** thus requires steady technological and commercial progress so that the nation can realize increased production and expanded employment opportunities. Three measures of competitiveness are a steady rate of economic growth, rising living standards, and a favorable (surplus) balance of trade.

Rather than increased living standards, the recent record points the other way. According to one congressional study, real earnings of the average 30-year-old male in 1984 were 25 percent less than in 1973. Even two-earner families fared poorly. The average real income of two-parent families fell by 3 percent from 1973 to 1984.

The falling standard of living in turn is closely related to sluggish economic growth and lackluster productivity. Real growth rates declined from 4 percent in the 1950s and 1960s to 2.8 percent in the 1980s. Slumping economic growth and real incomes failed to halt consumer spending, however, especially for imports. In 1986, the United States spent nearly $150 billion more than it produced. To accomplish this feat, U.S. families and the federal government have plunged into the proverbial sea of red ink.[26]

But economists must look still further to get to the heart of the competitiveness issue. Economic growth, or the lack thereof, is linked to

---

[25] Stephen Cohen, David Teece, Laura D'Andrea Tyson, and John Zysman, "Competitiveness," *BRIE Working Paper #8* (Berkeley, California: Berkeley Roundtable on the International Economy, November 1984), p. 1.

[26] As a percent of personal income, consumer indebtedness exceeded 16 percent in 1986. Total U.S. debt to foreigners was more than $400 billion in 1987 and, if the pace continues, it could easily top $750 billion by 1990.

economic resources and their productive uses, generally called output per worker (productivity).[27] Since the early 1970s productivity has been growing at less than 1 percent per year, compared to a rate of more than 2 percent in the 1960s. If we had sustained the productivity gains of the 1960s, a typical worker's output would have doubled in about 30 years; at the slower and more recent rate, it would take more than 70 years to double output. If economic growth fails to quicken, the future generation will be saddled with increased poverty and a reduced standard of living.

The solution to the problem rests largely with U.S. industry, according to the Berkeley Roundtable on the International Economy (BRIE), a not-for-profit research institute at the University of California at Berkeley. "[W]e are not maintaining our manufacturing position or our comparative advantage in high technology. . . . At the core of the problem lies both a loss of manufacturing preeminance—and a declining technological advantage on which competitive position in R and D based sectors rests."[28] Instead of a nearsighted obsession with short-run profits, shuffling financial assets via mergers, and moving jobs, production, and technology overseas, U.S. companies will have to reorient their thinking from finance to manufacturing. A number of ideas are in the offing:

- Systems of flexible manufacturing that permit customizing and shifting to other product lines with the same equipment (the standard in Japan but resisted by mass production-oriented U.S. manufacturers).
- Just-in-time production systems that reduce inventory and increase efficiency.
- Quality control systems such as Statistical Process Control (SPC), which measures the performance of each step in manufacturing by monitoring changes in the item being produced.

Although the companies that have adopted such techniques have reaped the harvest of profits, most firms seem to be resistant to change.

While most economists agree that U.S. industry can benefit from flexible manufacturing and a greater emphasis on quality control, they also think that the competitiveness issue is a temporary foreign ex-

---

[27] The most important resource is people—the quality and skills of the labor force. However, the U.S. educational system is failing to produce the skilled labor force needed for the 21st century. For example, 8 percent of U.S. youths aged 14 to 21 test as functionally illiterate (unable to read or write at the 5th grade level); using the 8th grade as the standard, as much as 20 percent may be illiterate. By comparison, less than 1 percent of the Japanese labor force is functionally illiterate. (Source: Lester Thurow, "Creating a World-Class Team," *The Changing American Economy,* ed. David Obey and Paul Sabanes [New York: Basil Blackwell Inc., 1986], p. 173.)

[28] Ibid., p. 29.

change rate problem. According to Jeff Schott of the Institute for International Economics in Washington, D.C., "When people in this city talk about 'competitiveness,' they're really talking about the trade deficit."[29] If this is true, the important question is what caused the trade deficits?

Most economists argue that the trade deficit is caused by the increased price of the U.S. dollar which, in turn, is caused by high interest rates. And, as we have already seen earlier, high (real) interest rates are caused by Treasury borrowing to finance unusually large federal deficits. Although trade deficits could result from inflationary monetary policies, the Fed pursued a restrictive money policy during the years when the trade deficit rose.

Will dollar depreciation by itself ultimately restore a trade balance? In other words—using one of the favorite phrases of economists—is exchange rate readjustment a "necessary and sufficient" solution to the current payments deficit? Only time will tell.

IMPORTANT TERMS TO REMEMBER

ad valorem tariff,   p. 534
balance of payments,   p. 550
competitiveness,   p. 554
correcting trade imbalance
   argument,   p. 546
currency devaluation,   p. 548
exchange controls,   p. 539
exchange rate,   p. 547
export subsidy,   p. 539
fixed exchange rates,   p. 548
foreign exchange,   539

gold standard,   p. 547
infant industries argument,   p. 544
managed float system,   p. 549
national defense argument,   p. 545
orderly marketing agreement,
   p. 536
product standards,   p. 538
protecting jobs argument,   p. 545
quota,   p. 536
specific tariff,   p. 534
tariff,   p. 534

SUMMARY

1. International trade is based upon the theory of comparative advantage—the idea that nations should specialize in the production of goods that are relatively cheaper and trade for goods which are relatively more expensive.

2. Despite the infallible logic of the law of comparative advantage, nations adopt various protectionist (restrictive) policies, such as tariffs, quotas, orderly marketing agreements, product standards, buy-at-home programs, exchange controls, and export subsidies.

3. Tariffs, quotas, and other protectionist measures reduce foreign production and increase domestic production at the expense of higher consumer prices.

4. Protectionism carries a very high price tag, in terms of a lower rate of economic growth and the cost-per-job-saved.

---

[29] Timothy Tregarthen, "World Trade: Can the U.S. Compete?" *The Margin* 2, no. 4 (The University of Colorado, April, 1987), p. 1.

5. Despite the high cost, many arguments are advanced in favor of protectionism, such as infant industries, national defense, domestic jobs, and correcting a trade imbalance.

6. Foreign exchange markets enable nations to convert their domestic currencies into the currencies of other nations. The price of one currency in terms of another is called the *exchange rate*.

7. There are two basic kinds of exchange rate systems—fixed and floating, although all governments intervene to regulate currency values.

8. The balance of payments, the sum of the current account, the capital account, and official reserves, is the record of all transactions between one country and the rest of the world.

9. *Competitiveness* means the degree to which a nation sustains its technological and commercial advantage and thereby supports increasing domestic production and employment.

10. Economists and other observers disagree about the basic cause of the U.S. trade deficits. Economists generally agree that an overvalued currency caused by high interest rates (and fed by large federal deficits) is the culprit. Others think that U.S. industry has neglected to make the necessary investments in manufacturing and quality control to compete in our high-technology world.

DISCUSSION AND REVIEW QUESTIONS

1. Evaluate the following Senate debate between two old rivals:

   Senator Freemarket: "There's just no good substitute for supply and demand. Every time the government steps in to correct some trade problem its cure is 10 times worse than the disease. Why do we always have to be fixin' things that aren't broke?"

   Senator Fairtrade: "I couldn't agree more with my distinguished colleague, providing that supply and demand are still working. And that is the problem! Foreign governments have devastated our industries with export subsidies, high tariffs, unreasonable quotas, and absurd product standards. To compete effectively, we need a level playing field and that, ladies and gentlemen, requires stern countermeasures. Leave it up to supply and demand, and we are making the decision to throw millions of people out of work!"

2. If U.S. automobile companies develop an engine that gets 70 miles per gallon, what is likely to happen to the U.S. exchange rate? Why?

3. If the Japanese yen appreciates, are Americans likely to buy more or fewer Japanese cars? Why? What if the French franc depreciates? Will France export more or less wine? Why?

4. Is it possible for a nation to have a trade surplus, yet run a balance of payments deficit? Why or why not? (Hint: Check with any year's *Economic Report of the President* or past issue of *Survey of Current Business* if you want to get the actual data.)

5. For each of the following economic activities, indicate in which part of the balance of payments the transaction is recorded (current account,

capital account, or official reserves); also indicate whether the transaction is a payment or a receipt.

   a. Your next door neighbor spends her lottery winnings on a trip around the world.

   b. The Japanese firm Sony builds a television assembly plant in Chattanooga, Tennessee.

   c. A French citizen buys 1,000 shares of Sears stock.

   d. The U.S. government closes 10 military bases in Europe.

   e. Sri Lanka borrows money from the IMF to settle its deficit with West Germany.

   f. Nigeria buys 1,000 cash registers from the U.S. firm NCR.

6. What is the relationship between budget deficits and the balance of payments?

7. Explain how a balance of payments deficit may force the central bank to engage in restrictive monetary policy. What consequences will such action have?

8. True or false: "A country's large balance of payments surplus can cause or contribute to increased inflation, and a large payments deficit can cause unemployment." Explain.

9. What do most economists think is the basic cause of U.S. trade deficits? To what extent are the deficits attributed to a lack of competitiveness?

Glossary

A

Absolute measure of poverty Assuming that the poor spend one third of their budgets on food, the Department of Agriculture estimates the cost of a diet for a family of four (two adults and two children) and multiplies by three. The resulting number is used as the poverty level.

Accounting profit Total revenue less explicit costs.

Actual deficit The amount by which the government's budget outlays exceeds its receipts.

Administration lag The time required to formulate the economic policy, guide it through Congress, and obtain presidential approval.

Ad valorem tariff The tariff that increases as the value of imports increases.

Agency shop A contract provision whereby workers must pay dues even if they are not members of the union.

Aggregate demand (AD) An inverse relationship between the price level (as measured by the GNP deflator) and real GNP; graphically, it is a downward-sloping curve (line) with the price level measured on the vertical axis and real GNP on the horizontal axis.

Aggregate expenditures (AE) The *total* amount of planned spending on *all* domestic goods and services produced, consisting of consumption, planned investment, government, and net exports.

Aggregate production (AP) The total market value of goods and services produced.

Aggregate supply (AS) The total amount of goods and services that is supplied at various price levels.

Antitrust Any legislative or judicial action taken to arrest monopolistic behavior and the restraint of trade.

Artificial barriers Things such as patents, licenses, and franchises.

Automatic stabilizers Consist of federal, personal, and corporate income taxes; transfer payments (chiefly unemployment compensation and welfare); and certain expenditures. As national income declines, tax receipts decrease and transfer payments increase, thereby reducing leakages and increasing injections.

Autonomous consumption The term used to describe the amount of consumer spending that occurs when income is zero. In other words, it is that portion of consumption that does not depend upon income.

Average cost (AC) The cost per unit of output, calculated by dividing the total costs by the quantity of output. ($AC = TC \div Q$)

Average revenue (AR) The revenue per unit of output; AR is another term for price, calculated by dividing total revenue by the quantity of output.

$$AR = \frac{TR}{Q} = \frac{P \cdot Q}{Q} = P$$

B

Backward-bending supply curve of labor Shows that, after a certain number of hours of work at a specified wage, people will reduce the number of hours worked (or quantity of labor supplied) as wages rise.

Balanced budget multiplier *Always equal to 1,* and used whenever there are equal changes in expenditures and revenues. When taxes and expenditures change by the same amount, the final change in income will always be equal to the original change in expenditures (in the same direction, + or −).

Balance of payments (BOP) A record of a nation's transactions between its residents and the rest of the world.

Barter Instead of using money, goods are traded directly for other goods. Barter was used before money was readily accepted, but still is practiced in primitive societies or in industrial economies where there is an incentive to avoid records (e.g., to avoid taxation).

Base year Any year in the recent past that is representative of economic activity; used to compute real GNP, the GNP deflator, and the consumer price index.

Behaviorists Reject the structure-conduct-performance model, arguing that it is important to examine only the conduct of individual oligopolists and ask if the firm's actual behavior (decisions and activities) is detrimental and/or illegal.

Benefit-cost analysis A decision-making tool that estimates all costs and benefits associated with an economic activity.

Borrowed reserves Funds obtained when financial institutions borrow from the Fed or from depository institutions.

Breakeven The quantity of output at which total revenue equals total cost. It is also expressed in dollar terms: the total sales revenue that will cover a company's total costs.

Business cycle The recurring but irregular wave-like movement of the economy over a period of time.

C

Capital Physical assets used in production—machinery, equipment, buildings, inventory, and goods in various stages of completion. Examples of capital include things like computers, drill presses, copying machines, and company cars, but *not money.*

Cartels Formal (sometimes written) agreements to restrict output and increase prices. (They are illegal.)

Celler-Kefauver Act Plugged the asset loophole in the Clayton Act, making it illegal to acquire stock *or* the assets of another firm if the effect was to monopolize.

Change in demand A shift of the demand curve to a new position, caused by a change in one or more of the determinants of demand.

Change in quantity demanded Shown as a *movement along* the existing demand curve, from one point to another point; the change is caused by a change in product price.

Change in quantity supplied Represented as a *movement along* the existing supply curve and is caused by a change in the product price.

Change in supply A shift of the supply curve, caused by a change in one of the determinants of supply.

Checkable deposits *Demand deposits* or checking accounts at commercial banks, *share drafts* at credit unions, and *NOW accounts* at savings and loan associations (also known as *thrifts*). *NOW* means negotiated order of withdrawal, a checking account that earns interest.

Check clearing The process conducted by the Federal Reserve, the Federal Home Loan Bank, and other institutions, whereby reserves are transferred from one intermediary to another.

Civilian labor force (CLF) The total number of employed and unemployed.

Classical economics Holds that the private market forces of supply and demand will ensure full employment.

Clayton Act Prohibited corporations from acquiring the stock of another corporation engaged in interstate commerce where the effect would be to monopolize or reduce competition; it also prohibits interlocking directorates and certain types of price discrimination.

Closed shop   A contract clause requiring workers to join the union before they can be hired. This was declared illegal under the Taft-Hartley Act.

Collusion   A general term used to describe any agreement among business firms whose purpose is to limit competition (i.e., restrict output and raise prices).

Command economies   Characterized by highly centralized decision making, limited economic freedoms, and greatly restricted consumer choice. Government answers the *what, how,* and *for whom* questions.

Commercial banks   Share two essential functions: they receive deposits and they lend money.

Compensating wage differentials   Payments that adjust for the perceived unattractive quality of work.

Competition   When two or more sellers share the same market (prospective buyers), each vying for consumers' dollars. Also defined as the absence of market power; that is, competitive firms are unable to influence the price of their product(s) or service(s).

Competitiveness   The degree to which a nation sustains its technological and commercial advantage and thereby supports increasing domestic production and employment.

Composite index of 12 leading indicators   A series of business cycle signals that typically reach their cyclical peaks and troughs earlier than the corresponding turns of the business cycle.

Concentration ratio   Indicates the percentage of total industry assets or sales of the top four or eight firms in the industry.

Conglomerate merger   Occurs when two or more firms in different industries merge, such as AT&T and Godiva Chocolates.

Constant returns to scale   Occur if a firm's long-run average costs remain constant over a major range of output.

Consumer price index (CPI)   A measure of the average change in the prices paid by urban consumers for a fixed market basket of goods and services.

Consumer surplus   The extra (or surplus) satisfaction derived from buying a good or service. It is the difference between the market price and the demand price (the price we are willing to pay).

Contingent workers   Those who work part-time and in temporary positions; currently they make up about one fifth of the work force.

Contraction   A period of declining economic activity.

Correcting a trade imbalance   A common argument for raising or lowering tariff and nontariff barriers.

Cost-push inflation   The rise in the price level associated with higher labor and other resources costs.

Craft unions   Worker organizations in which all members share the same skill, such as the Pipefitters or Teamsters.

Credit unions (CUs)   Tax-exempt cooperative societies formed to serve individuals working for the same employer or members of the same union.

Crowding out   A decline in private investment because of the government's deficit financing.

Currency devaluation   A nation's formal policy of decreasing the value of the domestic currency in terms of gold or foreign exchange.

Cyclical unemployment   Occurs when aggregate demand is insufficient to sustain the number of jobs at the natural rate.

D

Deindustrialization   The long-term decline in domestic manufacturing, most notably in the areas of automobile production, textiles, and, more recently, even in the catchall category referred to as *high tech* (e.g., semiconductors and telecommunications).

Demand   The entire table or schedule of quantities bought at corresponding prices in some time period, other things being equal.

Demand-pull inflation Occurs when, other things being equal, aggregate demand increases faster than the economy's ability to produce goods and services. The result is a higher price level.

Deposit multiplier The reciprocal of the reserve ratio, expressed as $1/rr$.

Depression A period of prolonged and deep unemployment and decreasing real GNP.

Derived demand Means that the firm's demand for a resource (e.g., labor) is derived from the demand for its product or service.

Determinants of demand Grouped into five categories: (1) income, (2) tastes and preferences, (3) prices and availability of related goods or services [a. substitutes (coffee and tea; butter and margarine); b. complements (coffee and doughnuts; bread and butter)], (4) expectations about prices and income, and (5) number of consumers.

Determinants of elasticity of demand (1) The number and availability of substitutes, (2) total expenditures for the good, (3) whether the product or service is considered a luxury or a necessity, and (4) the time period.

Determinants of supply Grouped into five categories: (1) costs of production (wages, interest, rent, etc.), (2) technology, (3) expectations (about prices, sales and profits), (4) prices of related goods [a. substitutes, and b. complements], and (5) number of suppliers.

Direct relationship When both variables move in the same direction (e.g., as the temperature increases, attendance at a community pool also increases, and vice versa).

Discount rate The rate of interest charged for borrowed reserves (loans) from the Fed to financial institutions.

Discouraged workers People who have given up on any hope of finding work and dropped out of the labor force.

Discretionary fiscal policy Refers to *changes* in taxes, transfers, and governmental expenditures.

Discrimination Occurs when, given two or more groups of workers of equal productivity, employers hire or pay one group of workers more than another group.

Diseconomies of scale A special term that refers to increasing average costs.

Disequilibrium A state in which there is either a shortage or surplus.

Disposable income (DI) The total earnings of households after payment of personal income taxes.

Duration of unemployment The length of time a person is without a job but is seeking work.

E

Easy money A current money market condition or monetary policy in which the Fed increases reserves in order to drive down interest rates. This should create the economic climate conducive to more borrowing.

Economic efficiency Means that the economy's resources are allocated in such a way that it is impossible to improve the well-being of any one person without harming another. Also referred to as *allocative efficiency,* it means that no other mixture of resources, goods, and services will increase society's total satisfaction.

Economic equity A goal that refers to the normative economic issue of the fairness of resource, income, and product distribution.

Economic freedom The right to own resources and to use them in order to satisfy our wants. Included are the freedoms of occupational choice, property rights, and the freedom to purchase goods and services, subject, of course, to one's income.

Economic profit Calculated by subtracting from total revenues the total costs—implicit costs and explicit costs; the return above the owner's opportunity costs. (*Also see* Normal profit.)

Economic resources (or factors of production) An economy's land, labor, capital, and entrepreneurship.

Economics Studies how society allocates scarce resources to satisfy competing and unlimited wants.

Economic stabilization   A catchall term that refers to the policies and programs by which the government attempts to control inflation and unemployment.

Economic system   The organization of households, business firms, and government(s) to answer the basic questions of *what to produce, how to produce,* and *for whom to produce.*

Economies of scale   A term that means decreasing average costs of production.

Economizing problem   How to allocate scarce resources among competing and unlimited wants.

Elastic demand   Total revenue increases in response to a lower price or, total revenue decreases in response to a higher price.

Elasticity of supply   Measures the responsiveness of quantity supplied to changes in price.

Employed   Defined by the Bureau of Labor Statistics as being all people 16 years of age or older who have worked at least one hour for pay during the survey week or at least 15 hours without pay in a family business.

Employment Act of 1946   Made the federal government responsible for designing economic policies to pursue and maintain full employment and price stability.

Employment and Training Choices (ETC)   An alternative to workfare. This Massachusetts plan is completely voluntary. ETC's basic premise is that welfare mothers can be sold on work. The government invests heavily in an attractive array of no-dead-end job training and placement services, provides $2,500 for each participant to cover child-care costs, and defrays health care and transportation costs in order to smooth the transition from welfare dependency to work.

Employment rate   The percentage of the noninstitutional adult population (or the working-age population) that is working.

Entrepreneurship   The fourth factor of production—risk-taking, decision-making ventures that bring land, labor, and capital together in order to provide a good or service.

Equation of exchange   Establishes the relationship between the money supply, velocity, and nominal GNP. Briefly stated, it says that the amount of money spent equals the GNP. In equation form, this truism is expressed as $M \cdot V \equiv P \cdot Q$

Equilibrium   The intersection of the supply and demand curves; a market condition in which quantity supplied and quantity demanded are exactly equal at a unique price; also the intersection of aggregate supply and aggregate demand.

Excess reserves   The difference between total reserves and required reserves. (Excess reserves = total reserves − required reserves.)

Exchange controls   Designed to reduce imports by imposing limits on the amount of currency or issuance of bank drafts to pay for imports.

Exchange rate   The ratio of one nation's currency expressed in terms of another country's currency. Alternatively, an exchange rate is just the price of foreign money.

Expansion   A period of increasing economic activity.

Expansionary gap   Occurs when aggregate expenditures exceed aggregate production. The difference is the amount of unplanned inventory depletion, illustrated as the vertical distance between AP and the $C + I_p$ schedule at any income level less than equilibrium.

Explicit costs (or accounting costs)   Payments made to suppliers of resources that do not have a share in the ownership of the business. (These are often called out-of-pocket costs.)

Export subsidy   Government aid to businesses in the form of tax credits, loan programs, insurance, and direct cash payments.

External benefit (or positive externality)   Exists if the activity creates benefits to third parties.

External cost (or negative externality)   Exists if the activity imposes costs upon a third party.

Externality   The actions of a private business or household generate costs or benefits above the private costs and benefits associated with production or consumption (e.g., pollution).

F

Fallacy of composition error   Assuming that what is true for the part (the individual firm, for example) is also true for the whole (the entire economy).

Federal Deposit Insurance Corporation (FDIC) Established by the Congress in 1933 in order to restore confidence in the banking system, and to provide a federal role in bank regulation and economic stabilization. Today, the FDIC insures individual deposits to $100,000.

Federal funds   Very short-term loans of excess reserves from one financial institution to another.

The Federal Open Market Committee (FOMC) Created solely to buy and sell government securities (bonds) in order to provide further control over the money supply. Membership on the FOMC consists of the seven members of the BOG and five Federal Reserve Bank presidents.

Federal Reserve Bank (FRB)   A banker's bank, the FRB performs the same functions for the commercial bank that the financial institutions perform for its depositors.

Federal Reserve Board of Governors (BOG) The chief policymaking body of the system, the BOG has seven members appointed for 14-year terms by the president and confirmed by the Senate. The BOG is responsible for setting reserve requirements, discount rate, and determining open market operations policy.

Federal Reserve System (FRS)   The nation's central banker; it is the chief monetary authority in the United States and it bears the primary responsibility for maintaining the stability of U.S. financial markets.

Federal Trade Commission Act   Created the Federal Trade Commission (FTC); it classified as illegal any unfair or deceptive practices or methods of competition.

Financial intermediaries   Institutions that receive deposits from the public and lend these funds to consumers and businesses (commercial banks, savings and loans, credit unions, and savings banks).

Fine-tuning   An aggressive policy approach to regulate the economy. It is predicated upon a belief that the economy can be adjusted much like the resolution of a television set. Fiscal policy fine-tuning calls for reducing taxes and increasing expenditures during hard times.

Fiscal policy   The change in taxes, transfers, and expenditures designed to affect income and employment.

Fixed costs   Costs that do not change with output; they are constant. Examples of fixed costs are rent, insurance premiums, and depreciation.

Fixed exchange rates   Establish currency (e.g., the U.S. dollar) convertibility to gold at some constant value, such as $35 per ounce (for foreign governments and central banks only).

Flow   Measure of an activity or a process that occurs over a period of time, such as consumer saving during the month of July.

Foreign exchange   Any financial instrument used to make payment from the currency of one nation to another.

Free market economies   Economic systems in which most decisions are made by private businesses and households. The questions of *what, how,* and *for whom* are left to the market to answer.

Free rider problem   When people (try to) enjoy the benefits of consumption without sharing in the cost of providing the good.

Frictional unemployment   Occurs when there is a *temporary* mismatch of jobs and job seekers, that is, when jobs exist and the unemployed either do not know of their availability or are not ready to accept employment.

G

Gentlemen's agreement   An informal accord among industry firms to carve up the market and not to price compete against one another.

GNP deflator (or the implicit price index)   A ratio of prices in the current year to prices in the base year for all goods and services; the ratio of nominal GNP (NGNP) to real GNP (RGNP).

GNP gap The difference between the target (or full employment) level of income and the current or actual level of income.

Gold standard When countries define their currencies in terms of gold, such as one dollar is equal to 1/40th of an ounce of gold. If other nations do likewise, then one nation's currency is also defined in terms of all other currencies.

Graph Always illustrates a series of numbers, all linked together by some rule.

Gross national product (GNP) The total market value of all final domestic goods and services produced in one year.

H

High employment budget deficit or surplus Presents estimates of what expenditures and receipts would be *if* the economy were operating at full employment.

Horizontal merger The combination of two or more competing firms in the same industry, such as IBM and Digital Equipment Corporation.

Human capital Any investment in one's earnings capacity, such as education and health.

I

Impact lag The time required for the multiplier effect to change employment, income, and production.

Imperfect competition Means that firms possess market power, the ability to set prices without strict reliance upon supply and demand.

Implicit costs The costs to the business owners in using their labor and other resources in their business instead of in other activities.

Income effect Measures the change in consumption of a good attributed to a variation in real income caused by a change in price.

Induced consumption The amount of additional spending caused by increased income.

Industrial unions Organizations representing workers whose membership consists of all skill levels.

Inelastic demand Describes a condition in which buyers are not very sensitive to changes in price; reflected in a decline of total revenue to declining price or increasing total revenue in response to a higher price.

Infant industries argument Based upon the assumption that new firms or industries need protection from foreign competitors until such time that they can realize economies of scale in production and, with lower costs of production, be more price competitive with their foreign rivals.

Inflation *A rise in the general level of prices* on all goods and services or on a representative sample of goods.

Injections Inflows of dollars to the circular flow, consisting of investment spending, exports, and government purchases.

Inverse relationship When two variables move in opposite directions (e.g., as price decreases, the quantity demanded [sold] increases, and vice versa). *Indirect and negative* are two other terms which mean the same as inverse.

J

Job search theory States that the unemployed have a minimally acceptable wage (the *reservation wage*) that must be met by a *wage offer* before employment is secured.

K

Keynesian Cross model Relates aggregate expenditures to aggregate production, and shows that there are only three possible outcomes: a shortage (in which $AE > AP$), a surplus (in which $AP > AE$), and equilibrium (where $AE = AP$). For example, if a nation's planned expenditures exceed its output, the economy experiences inventory depletion. This sets the stage for an expansion of output and employment as businesses gear up to meet demand.

Keynesian economics A body of macroeconomic theory built on the premise that aggregate demand (expenditures) is the main determinant of income and employment. Keynesian economists and policymakers believe in the essential logic of the income-expenditures model and the need for fine-tuning the economy (using monetary and fiscal policies to pursue full employment and price stability).

L

Labor All forms of human exertion, physical and mental, applied to economic activity.

Laffer curve Named after Arthur Laffer, it offers the simple truism that both 0 and 100 percent tax rates would produce no tax revenue whatsoever, and therefore increased tax rates might erode work incentives and actually reduce tax revenue.

Land All natural resources, such as air, water, and forests.

Law of demand States that there is an inverse relationship between quantity demanded and price, other things being equal.

Law of diminishing marginal utility With each additional consumption of a good or service, the extra satisfaction (or marginal utility) declines.

Law of diminishing returns (or the law of diminishing marginal productivity) As additional units of a variable resource (such as labor) are added to fixed inputs, the extra output (marginal product) will eventually decrease.

Leakages Refer to income not spent (on foreign goods): income spent on goods produced in other countries (imports), income never received (taxes), and income not spent on goods at all (saving).

Long run A time period long enough to allow all inputs (or economic resources) to be changed, including the size and scale of operations.

M

M1 The basic definition of the money supply; it is composed of currency (coin and Federal Reserve notes) in circulation, all checkable deposits, and traveler's checks. It consists of the most liquid forms of money.

M2 Another definition of the money supply; M2 = M1 + time deposits less than $100,000, money market mutual funds, money market

deposit accounts, and other highly liquid assets.

Macroeconomics The study of the total economy and such performance measures as inflation, unemployment, gross national product, and related aggregates.

Managed float system of exchange rates One in which central banks endeavor to prevent excessive (damaging) variations in currency values. In order to stabilize free market fluctuations, the central banks will intervene to buy or sell domestic and foreign currencies.

Marginal benefit (much like marginal utility) The extra benefit received from an additional unit of consumption or production.

Marginal cost The extra cost associated with additional units of consumption or production. It is calculated by dividing the change in total cost by the change in output. ($MC = \Delta TC \div \Delta Q$.)

Marginal product The change in (or contribution to) total product per extra unit of resource. ($MP = \Delta TP \div \Delta L$, where $L = labor$.)

Marginal propensity to consume (MPC) The ratio of extra consumption to extra income, calculated by dividing the *change* in consumption by the *change* in disposable income. Expressed as a formula:

$$MPC = \frac{\text{Change in } C}{\text{Change in } Y_d} = \frac{\Delta C}{\Delta Y_d}$$

where Δ means "change in."

Marginal propensity to save (MPS) The ratio of extra saving to extra income, calculated by dividing the change in saving by the change in disposable income. (Note: $MPC + MPS = 1$, *always*.) Expressed as a formula:

$$MPS = \frac{\text{Change in } S}{\text{Change in } Y_d} = \frac{\Delta S}{\Delta Y_d}$$

Marginal resource (labor) cost (MRC) The extra cost of hiring the last worker; it is calculated by dividing the change in total labor costs by the change in quantity of labor hired.

$$MRC = \frac{\Delta TLC}{\Delta L},$$

where TLC = total labor cost
L = quantity of labor hired

Marginal revenue The extra revenue earned from selling one more unit of output.

$$MR = \frac{\Delta\,TR}{\Delta\,Q}$$

Marginal revenue product (MRP) A measure of a worker's contribution to total revenue and it represents the firm's demand curve for labor. It is computed by multiplying the worker's marginal physical product (units of output) times the marginal revenue from selling the last unit of output. Formula:

$$MRP = MPP_R \cdot MR_X, \text{ where } R = \text{resource}$$
$$X = \text{produce}$$

Marginal social benefits (MSB) The additional private and public benefits received from one additional unit of economic activity, such as cleaner air from pollution abatement programs.

Marginal social costs (MSC) The total opportunity costs involved in consumption or production of a product or service, such as what we give up to obtain a cleaner environment.

Marginal utility The change in total utility resulting from buying one additional unit of the item (change in total utility divided by the change in the number of items purchased).

Market An exchange mechanism through which buyers and sellers execute an economic transaction; a place where buyers and sellers meet for the purpose of exchange.

Market failure Occurs when too few or too many resources are allocated to production. There are three basic sources of market failure: (1) imperfect competition, (2) public goods, and (3) externalities.

Markup pricing Sets the price by adding a fixed percentage markup of product costs to the production and marketing costs.

Medium of exchange Perhaps the most important function of money. If money is to serve as a medium of exchange, it must be accepted as a means of payment and a measure of value.

Microeconomics The study of the individual units that make up the economy (business firms, labor unions, households, etc.).

Minimum wage An example of a price floor—a government-established minimum below which wages may not go for millions of workers.

Mixed capitalism An economic system in which private decision making is often regulated by government.

Monetarism A body of economic thought consisting of three basic ideas: (1) all inflations are caused by increases in the money supply in excess of the underlying real growth rate of the economy; (2) activist discretionary fiscal and monetary policy is at best ineffective and likely to be destabilizing; and (3) monetary policy affects GNP directly.

Monetarists believe that economic stabilization can be attained by adherence to a strict monetary rule, such as the growth of the money supply should approximate the average growth of real GNP.

Monetary Control Act or the **Depository Institutions Deregulation and Monetary Control Act of 1980** Major banking system reform that accomplished two major changes: (1) the Fed's jurisdiction in setting reserve requirements was extended to all depository institutions, and (2) Regulation Q was abolished. All interest rate ceilings were phased out (by April 1986).

Money Anything (even stone wheels) that is readily accepted as a medium of exchange.

Monopolistic competition A market structure consisting of thousands of firms producing a differentiated product or service with some degree of control over price; a market structure in which there are many sellers of differentiated goods and services and a considerable amount of non-price competition.

Multiple expansion of checkable deposits (or creation of money) The process by which loans from one bank become new deposits in other financial institutions and form the base for excess reserves and new loans. As this process continues, the money supply grows by a multiple of the original loan (excess reserves).

Multiplier The ratio of the final change in income to the original change in spending (aggregate expenditures or *AE*). It is also computed by taking the reciprocal of the *MPS*. The formula is:

$$m = \frac{1}{MPS}$$

Multiplier effect The process by which a change in spending results in a greater (magnified) change in income.

Mutual interdependence One of the foremost characteristics of oligopoly. Because there are relatively few firms, each company is very sensitive to the decisions made by its rivals, especially regarding price.

N

National defense argument (for protection) States that because wars (hot and cold) may cut off supplies of critical resources and goods essential to domestic production, a nation should not depend upon potential enemies for products vital to national interest.

National income The total wages, salaries, tips, commissions, dividends, rent, interest, and profits earned in producing goods and services.

National product The total market value of all goods and services produced, less depreciation.

Natural barriers to entry Consist of high capital requirements and raw material ownership which make it difficult for firms to enter an industry (especially oligopoly).

Natural monopoly A firm (and local industry) which experiences long-run economies of scale, such that it may produce at a lower average cost than if two or more firms shared the market.

Natural unemployment A term given to the total of frictional unemployment and structural unemployment.

Net exports The difference between exports and imports; there is a negative flow if imports exceed exports.

New classical economics A loose confederation of monetarists, supply-siders, and rational expectationists. They all share a wholesale rejection of Keynesian economics, and nearly all share a strong conviction that excessive governmental regulation is undesirable, and balanced budgets and monetary rules (such as a 3 to 4 percent growth rate in M1 per year) are necessary to improve economic stability.

Nominal GNP Current year output expressed in current year prices (e.g., 1989 production times 1989 prices).

Nonborrowed reserves The funds obtained by banks when new deposits are received or when the Fed engages in open market purchases.

Noninterventionists (or policy nonactivists) An eclectic group of economists who argue that the Keynesian type of discretionary policymaking contributes to economic instability. Instead of policy activism, the new classical economists, for example, advocate a more limited role of government and policy rules, such as a balanced budget and a fixed annual growth of the money supply.

Nonprice competition The means other than price reductions to increase sales, such as advertising and sales promotion activities.

Normal profit The minimum payment required to keep the business owner-entrepreneur in business.

Normative economics Opinions and statements which include value judgments.

O

Okun's law Named after Arthur Okun, it states that for every percentage point by which the growth of actual real output (real GNP) exceeds the potential growth rate (considered to be roughly 3 percent), the unemployment rate will fall by one third of a percent.

Oligopoly A market structure with only a few dominant firms, either a highly differentiated product (like autos) or a standardized product (like cement), and high barriers to entry. The barriers to entry may be natural (like economies of scale) or artificial (like patents and licenses). Product differentiation often is achieved through advertising and other forms of nonprice competition.

Opportunity cost The sacrifice of the best alternative; it is what you give up in order to get something else instead (e.g., each hour of study time is measured in terms of leisure time given up).

Orderly marketing agreement A promise by the exporting nation to limit shipments of the product to the importing nation. (Also called a *voluntary export restriction*.)

Origin The lower left-hand corner point at which the vertical and horizontal axes meet.

P

Peak (of a business cycle) A point where real GNP reaches a maximum. Business cycles are measured from peak to peak or from trough to trough.

Penetration pricing The strategy of charging a low enough price to attract the largest possible number of customers.

Per se violation A judicial decree that finds a merger or the agreement to merge by itself illegal; no evidence of monopolization is required.

Personal income (PI) The total income received by persons, excluding corporate flows.

Phillips curve A diagram illustrating the relationship between inflation and unemployment; originally thought to be a trade-off: more unemployment, less inflation; less unemployment, more inflation.

Policy activists Believe in expansionary fiscal and monetary policies to combat recession and, conversely, restrictive economic policies to reduce the adverse effects of inflation.

Positive economics Statements of fact, relationship among facts, and projections based upon facts.

Post hoc fallacy If event A precedes event B, then event A is the cause of event B.

Precautionary motive We hold money for special occasions, such as vacations, our children's education, retirement, weddings, and miscellaneous "rainy day" contingencies. (Also see *transactions motive*.)

Price discrimination The act of charging different prices to different customers without cost differentials accounting for the difference in prices.

Price elasticity of demand The responsiveness of consumers to changes in price, measured by changes in total revenue (price times quantity sold) and the percentage change in quantity demanded to a percentage change in price, other things equal.

Price fixing An agreement by firms to subdivide markets and charge those prices agreed to by the parties involved in the conspiracy.

Price index As a measurement of inflation, a price index is a ratio of prices in the current year to prices in the base year.

Price leadership A common behavior among oligopolists in which the biggest or most assertive firm announces changes in price and other firms merely follow suit.

Price searchers Firms that set their own prices. Although supply and demand conditions are still operative, nonprice competition plays a big role.

Price skimming Charging the highest price the market will bear.

Price takers Firms that sell at the prices determined by the market forces of supply and demand.

Private goods *Divisible* goods that yield *private benefits*. In other words, private goods are packaged so that only those who pay enjoy the benefits from consumption.

Private unregulated monopoly Generally a local industry or firm that dominates the market (e.g., newspapers and cable television).

Production function Lists economic resources in measured proportion in order to produce a quantity of output.

Production-possibilities curve Illustrates a nation's capabilities to produce, assuming full employment of resources and fixed technology.

Product standards Regulatory barriers that generally require that imports pass certain domestic health and safety tests.

Profit-maximizing rule States that firms should produce that output where MR equals MC (or, under conditions of perfect competition where $P = MR$, a company should produce until $P = MC$).

Protecting jobs Often advanced as a protectionist argument, that is, passing trade legislation that is designed to prevent imports from throwing people out of work.

Public choice The economic analysis of political behavior, of voters, of officeholders, and of others who provide public goods.

Public goods and services *Indivisible* goods that yield *collective benefits,* and are not sold in the private marketplace.

Pure competition A market structure in which there is a very large number of firms, each producing a homogeneous product with few barriers to entry and little if any nonprice competition.

Pure monopoly A single seller of a product or service for which there are no close substitutes.

Q

Quantity demanded The term used to refer to a specific amount bought at a specific price, (e.g., 100 six-packs at a price of $2.00 per six-pack).

Quantity supplied The term used to refer to a specific amount offered at a specific price (e.g., 150 six-packs at a price of $2.50 per six-pack).

Quantity theory of money Holds that any change in the money supply would be translated immediately into a change in the price level, assuming that velocity and real GNP are stable.

Quota A restriction on the quantity of an imported good. Although it restricts imports, it yields no revenue.

R

Rational behavior (rationality) Means that people seek the greatest expected return from each decision. This means that we prefer more to less, and thus we try to maximize satisfaction, however measured.

Rational expectationists Economists who argue that consumers, businesses, and other economic decision makers make decisions based upon a continuous flow of information and derived expectations. For example, instead of spending more income in response to a tax cut, people may save most of the tax cut in the expectation that the government will have to raise taxes in the future to reduce the budget deficit.

Real GNP Current year output expressed in base year prices (e.g., 1989 production times 1982 prices).

Recession A period of declining real GNP over a period of at least six months, characterized by increasing unemployment, declining real GNP, and *usually* a slowing of inflation.

Recessionary gap A condition in which aggregate expenditures are less than aggregate production. The difference is the amount of unplanned inventory accumulation, measured graphically as the vertical distance between AP and $C + I_p$ at any income level greater than equilibrium.

Recognition lag The time it takes to identify and define the problem.

Recovery A stage of the business cycle during which there is economic growth and job formation.

Regulation Q A provision of the Banking Act of 1933, now defunct; it authorized the Federal Reserve to set the maximum interest rates that commercial banks were allowed to pay on passbook accounts and time deposits.

Rent ceilings Maximum rents above which property owners may not charge.

Required reserves (RR) The dollar amounts determined by multiplying the reserve requirement (a percentage figure, like 10 percent) times the deposits.

$$RR = rr \times D.$$

Reservation wage   The lowest acceptable wage which, when offered, will induce the person to accept employment.

Reserve requirement (*rr*)   The formal legal required percentage of deposits that institutions must hold in idle reserves, either in their own vaults or on deposit at the Fed.

Right-to-work laws   State statutes that bar the union shop.

Rule for hiring labor (or using other economic resources)   In order to maximize profits or minimize costs, a firm will hire labor (or any resource) until the *MRP* equals the *MRC*.

Rule of reason   The Supreme Court ruled that not all mergers were per se violations and that only in cases involving *unreasonable restraints* of trade would the proposed merger be prohibited.

S

Satisficing   The decision to select a satisfactory profit level instead of trying to maximize profits.

Savings and loans   Banklike financial intermediaries whose chief function is to receive deposits and make loans (mainly for homes).

Savings banks (also called mutual savings banks)   Structured as cooperatives or mutuals with their depositors owning the institution.

Say's law   General overproduction is impossible because the act of supplying goods creates its own demand.

Scarcity   An insufficient amount of resources to satisfy our seemingly unlimited wants.

Self-interest   The idea that we make decisions which benefit ourselves (or, alternatively, that the benefits of some action exceed the costs).

Sherman Antitrust Act   Enacted in 1890, this first national antitrust legislation made every contract or combination (merger) in restraint of trade illegal.

Shortage   Occurs when the quantity demanded exceeds the quantity supplied at the current market price. It may also be defined as *excess quantity demanded.*

Short run   A length of time so short that the scale of operations cannot be changed (e.g., no time to expand or build new production space).

Shut-down rule   States that in the short run if $P < AVC$, shut down; if $P > AVC$, continue to produce.

Specific tariff   An absolute dollar value applied to the quantity per unit of imported goods.

Speculative motive   Keynes argued that people hold money for investment purposes, specifically in bonds. People currently hold savings in very liquid money market mutual funds or deposit accounts until bond prices begin to rise. As prices of bonds rise and interest rates fall, people will use their speculative (money market account) balances to buy bonds.

Stickiness   Refers to the age-old issue of wage (and price) flexibility. Keynesians argue that wages and prices are highly rigid, especially downward, because of institutional rigidities such as large corporations that resist pricecutting and unions that fight against wage cuts. New classical economists, however, believe that wages and prices are fully flexible. They cite employer responsiveness to real wages, and they point out how unions have accepted wage cuts in recent years in response to import competition and other job-threatening conditions.

Stock   A measure of accumulation at a moment in time, such as the number of cars produced in 1989.

Store of value   Because money may be sayed, it performs the important function of being a way to accumulate unspent earnings.

Structuralists   Argue that the structure of an industry determines the behavior (or conduct) of industry firms and the overall performance of the industry in the economy.

Structural unemployment Occurs when there is a mismatch of skills required on the job and the skills of the job seekers.

Substitution effect The change in consumption caused solely by a change in the price of the good relative to the prices of other goods (substitutes and complements).

Supply All of the quantities supplied at all of the market prices in some time period, other things being equal.

Supply-side economics Places primary emphasis on aggregate supply and the incentives necessary to increase saving, investment, and productivity. Supply-side economics consists of three main ideas: (1) large and permanent cuts in personal and corporate taxes will stimulate increased saving and investment, greater work effort, and higher productivity; (2) a substantial reduction in the scope of government in the economy is necessary to reduce the deficit and increase productivity; and (3) the government should operate a balanced budget and avoid fine-tuning.

Surplus Occurs when the quantity supplied exceeds the quantity demanded at the current price. It is also called the *excess quantity supplied.*

T

Tariff A tax imposed upon imported goods, with the purpose to raise the price and reduce the quantity of imports.

Tax-based incomes policies (TIPS) In order to control inflation more effectively, especially the cost-push variety, some economists favor the use of surtaxes and tax credits to penalize and reward compliance with a predetermined target of acceptable wage increases.

Tax multiplier (M_t) May be defined as the regular expenditures multiplier minus one, and negative. Written as a formula,

$$M_t = -(m - 1).$$

The 1981 Tax Recovery Act (TRA) Embodied most of the supply-side prescriptions. The TRA cut personal income tax rates by 25 percent over three years, introduced the Individual Retirement Account (a tax-deferred retirement savings plan), and liberalized depreciation allowances on a wide range of capital investment.

The 1986 Tax Reform Act Made a basic overhaul of the tax system, lowered tax rates, and collapsed the previous fourteen tax brackets into three income brackets. It also raised the standard deduction, increased the personal exemption, and repealed the deduction for personal interest and state and local sales taxes.

Theory (model) Sets of propositions based upon assumptions. Propositions are statements which define and describe relationships between the variables involved.

Theory (or law) of comparative advantage A person (business or nation) should produce that good or service for which the costs of production are least, measured in terms of opportunity cost.

Theory of rational expectations People are always thinking about the future and form their expectations based not only upon past and present events but upon a careful analysis of current policy and policy pronouncements made by influential governmental leaders. If people think that inflation will increase next year, they may spend more now. The result is a self-fulfilling prophecy: acting on the assumption of more inflation, increased spending will actually usher in a higher rate of inflation.

Tight money A monetary policy of slowing the growth of the money supply by reducing bank reserves. This will gradually result in higher interest rates and thus make borrowing more expensive.

Total cost The sum of fixed costs and variable costs. ($TC = TFC + TVC$, where TC = total costs, TFC = total fixed costs, and TVC = total variable costs.)

Transactions motive People want money for transactions and thus hold money in checking accounts (in order to pay our utilities, mortgage or rent, food, and related monthly bills) and in cash (in order to handle daily transactions, such as soda in vending machines, birthday cards, or lunch).

Transfer payments   One-way flows of tax revenue from government to individuals, such as federal food stamps and Aid to Families with Dependent Children (AFDC). Transfer payments are not included in GNP.

Transmission mechanism   Describes how changes in money are transmitted throughout the economy. For example, increased money leads to lower interest rates, which in turn encourages more investment spending and, through the expenditures multiplier, leads to increased GNP.

Trough   The bottom of the business cycle contraction, where real GNP stops declining (reaches its lowest level) before turning upward in the next expansion.

Trusts   Combinations of competitors to fix prices and control the market (much like OPEC).

U

Underemployed   People working at jobs in which they cannot fully utilize their skills, education, and experience, such as an attorney who works as a hotel desk clerk.

Underground economy   Refers to the unreported income from both legal sources (such as moonlighting plumbers) and illegal sources (such as gambling, prostitution, and drug traffic).

Unemployed   Those who do not have a job, but are actively seeking work.

Unemployment rate   Determined by dividing the number of unemployed by the civilian or total labor force. (If the total labor force is used, then the resident armed forces are included, and the unemployment rate is usually one tenth of a percent lower.)

Union shop   A provision of a union contract whereby an employee must join the union within 30 days after being hired, unless the states passed laws to the contrary.

Unit elastic (demand)   When prices change, either increasing or decreasing, and total revenue remains unchanged. Or, in response to a given percentage change in price, there is an equal (and opposite) percentage change in quantity demanded.

Unit of account (or yardstick of value)   Another important function of money is that everything is expressed in U.S. dollars, a common currency unit, enabling us to compare relative worth.

Unplanned inventory   The unintended addition to or the depletion of the stock of goods produced. More simply, it is the difference between aggregate production and aggregate expenditures.

Utility   A term used by economists to define the psychological satisfaction and need-fulfillment from the consumption of a service or product.

Utility maximization   The ratios of marginal utility to price for all goods and services consumed are equal.

V

Value added   An approach for computing GNP. Instead of adding total expenditures only on final goods, this approach adds the value added to the product at each stage of production. The sum of the values added will equal the expenditures by the end users.

Variable costs   Expenses which change as output changes. Wages and salaries, fringe benefits, and supplies are some common examples.

Velocity   The average number of times the money supply is spent each year.

Vertical merger   The consolidation of a firm and its supplier or wholesale or retail outlet(s).

W

Wealth effect   States that if you feel wealthier, you will increase consumption. Graphically illustrated as a shift of the consumption schedule.

Workfare   Ties the welfare benefits received, such as AFDC, food stamps, and other assistance, to the participation in a job-training program, community service work, or a private sector job.

X

X axis (horizontal axis) A horizontal line for measuring distances in the horizontal or west-east dimension.

Y

Y axis (vertical axis) The vertical line forming a right angle with the horizontal axis. It is used to measure distances in the vertical or north-and-south dimension.

Index